The Great Depression

This bibliography was conceived and compiled by editors at ABC-Clio Information Services.

Lance Klass, project coordinator

Susan Kinnell
Robert de V. Brunkow
Jeffery B. Serena

Pamela R. Byrne
Gail Schlachter

ABC-CLIO RESEARCH GUIDES

The ABC-Clio Research Guides are a new generation of annotated bibliographies that provide comprehensive control of the recent journal literature on high-interest topics in history and related social sciences. These publications are created by editor/historians and other subject specialists who examine every article entry in ABC-Clio Information Services' vast history database and select abstracts of all citations published during the past decade that relate to the particular topic of study.

Each entry selected from this database—the largest history database in the world— has been reedited to ensure consistency in treatment and completeness of coverage. The extensive subject profile index (ABC-SPIndex) accompanying each volume has also been reassessed, specifically in terms of the particular subject presented, to allow precise and rapid access to the entries.

The titles in this series are prepared to save researchers, students, and librarians the considerable time and expense usually associated with accessing materials manually or through online searching. ABC-Clio's Research Guides offer unmatched access to significant scholarly articles on the topics of most current interest to historians and social scientists.

Library of Congress Cataloging in Publication Data
Main entry under title:

The Great Depression, a historical bibliography.

Includes index.
1. Depressions–1929–United States–Bibliography.
2. United States–Economic conditions–1918-1945–
Bibliography. 3. United States–Economic policy–
1933-1945–Bibliography. 4. United States–Social
conditions–1933-1945–Bibliography. I. ABC-Clio
Information Services.
Z7165.U5G73 1983 [HC106.3] 016.3385'42 83-12234
ISBN 0-87436-361-6

Copyright © 1984 by ABC-Clio, Inc.

ABC-Clio Information Services
2040 Alameda Padre Serra, Box 4397
Santa Barbara, California 93103

Clio Press Ltd.
55 St. Thomas Street
Oxford 0X1 1JG, England

Cover design and graphics by Lance Klass
Printed and bound in the United States of America

The Great Depression

a historical bibliography

ABC-Clio Information Services

Santa Barbara, California
Oxford, England

ABC-CLIO RESEARCH GUIDES

Gail Schlachter, Editor
Pamela R. Byrne, Executive Editor

1.
World War II from an American Perspective
1982 LC 82-22823 ISBN 0-87436-035-8

2.
The Jewish Experience in America
1982 LC 82-24480 ISBN 0-87436-034-x

3.
Nuclear America
1983 LC 83-12227 ISBN 0-87436-360-8

4.
The Great Depression
1983 LC 83-12234 ISBN 0-87436-361-6

5.
Corporate America
1983 LC 83-11232 ISBN 0-87436-362-4

6.
Crime and Punishment in America
1983 LC 83-12248 ISBN 0-87436-363-2

7.
The Democratic and Republican Parties
1983 LC 83-12230 ISBN 0-87436-364-0

8.
The American Electorate
1983 LC 83-12229 ISBN 0-87436-372-1

CONTENTS

LIST OF ABBREVIATIONS x

INTRODUCTION xi

1. THE CRASH OF '29 AND ITS ECONOMIC AFTERMATH 1

2. THE NEW DEMOCRATIC COALITION AND THE
   REPUBLICAN RESPONSE 26

3. RELIEF, REFORM, AND RECOVERY: THE NEW DEAL
   PROGRAM 55

4. SOCIAL CONDITIONS, PROTEST, AND REACTION 108

5. THE CULTURE OF THE DEPRESSION 158

   SUBJECT INDEX 189

   AUTHOR INDEX 256

LIST OF ABBREVIATIONS

A.	Author-prepared Abstract	*Illus.*	Illustrated, Illustration
Acad.	Academy, Academie, Academia	*Inst.*	Institute, Institut-.
Agric.	Agriculture, Agricultural	*Int.*	International, Internacional,
AIA	Abstracts in Anthropology		Internationaal, Internationaux,
Akad.	Akademie		Internazionale
Am.	America, American	*J.*	Journal, Journal-prepared Abstract
Ann.	Annals, Annales, Annual, Annali	*Lib.*	Library, Libraries
Anthrop.	Anthropology, Anthropological	*Mag.*	Magazine
Arch.	Archives	*Mus.*	Museum, Musee, Museo
Archaeol.	Archaeology, Archaeological	*Nac.*	Nacional
Art.	Article	*Natl.*	National, Nationale
Assoc.	Association, Associate	*Naz.*	Nazionale
Biblio.	Bibliography, Bibliographical	*Phil.*	Philosophy, Philosophical
Biog.	Biography, Biographical	*Photo.*	Photograph
Bol.	Boletim, Boletin	*Pol.*	Politics, Political, Politique, Politico
Bull.	Bulletin	*Pr.*	Press
c.	century (in index)	*Pres.*	President
ca.	circa	*Pro.*	Proceedings
Can.	Canada, Canadian, Canadien	*Publ.*	Publishing, Publication
Cent.	Century	*Q.*	Quarterly
Coll.	College	*Rev.*	Review, Revue, Revista, Revised
Com.	Committee	*Riv.*	Rivista
Comm.	Commission	*Res.*	Research
Comp.	Compiler	*RSA*	Romanian Scientific Abstracts
DAI	Dissertation Abstracts	*S.*	Staff-prepared Abstract
	International	*Sci.*	Science, Scientific
Dept.	Department	*Secy.*	Secretary
Dir.	Director, Direktor	*Soc.*	Society, Societe, Sociedad,
Econ.	Economy, Econom-.		Societa
Ed.	Editor, Edition	*Sociol.*	Sociology, Sociological
Educ.	Education, Educational	*Tr.*	Transactions
Geneal.	Genealogy, Genealogical,	*Transl.*	Translator, Translation
	Genealogique	*U.*	University, Universi-.
Grad.	Graduate	*US*	United States
Hist.	History, Hist-.	*Vol.*	Volume
IHE	Indice Historico Espanol	*Y.*	Yearbook

INTRODUCTION

The Great Depression was a critical turning point in American history. The stock market crash of October 1929 and the period of social and economic desperation it engendered called into question the very principles on which the nation was founded. "Men and women all over the world," wrote historian A. J. Toynbee, "were seriously contemplating and frankly discussing the possibility that the Western system of Society might break down and cease to work."

The threat of ultimate collapse brought a radical response. From the Depression's wreckage arose a fundamental restructuring of the relationships among the nation's basic institutions. In business and industry, government and politics, society and popular culture, the fabric of American life was permanently transformed.

These profound changes, which have directed the course of the nation's development to the present day, have given rise to an immensely rich body of modern scholarship seeking to document and explain the transformation of American society. This scholarship is endowed with a particular currency as political, economic, and social issues of the Depression and the New Deal—the relationship between government and the individual, the regulation of business, the efficacy of voluntarism—are once again the subjects of a great national debate.

The Great Depression: A Historical Bibliography is an instrument by which students of American history can gain immediate and thorough access to the vast modern scholarship on the Depression in the United States. The 959 abstracts of articles presented in this volume summarize Depression scholarship published from 1973 to 1982. The abstracts are drawn from the database of ABC-Clio Information Services, the largest history database in the world, whose coverage extends across more than 2,000 journals in 42 languages, published in 90 countries.

Access to the article abstracts in this volume is provided by ABC-SPIndex, one of the most advanced and comprehensive indexing systems in the world. ABC-SPIndex links together the key subject terms and the chronology of each abstract to form a composite index entry that provides a complete subject profile of the journal article. Each set of index terms is rotated so that the complete profile appears in the index under each of the subject terms. Thus, the number of access points is increased severalfold over conventional hierarchical indexes, and irrelevant materials can be eliminated early in the search process.

An additional avenue to the scholarly works summarized in this volume is provided by the internal division of the bibliography into five chapters. Each of these chapters focuses on a major area of Depression scholarship. Scholars concerned primarily with specific issues or topics, such as the structure of the Depression economy, the federal government's relief programs, or the daily life of the unemployed, can turn immediately to the relevant chapter to gain a broad insight into the scope, thrust, and basic issues of current scholarship on these subjects.

Chapter 1, "The Crash of '29 and Its Economic Aftermath," focuses on the causes and consequences of the Great Depression in the context of the national economy. The second chapter, "The New Democratic Coalition and the Republican Response," is concerned with the political events that abruptly ended the domination of national politics by the Republican Party and paved the way for the establishment of Roosevelt's New Deal. Chapter 3, "Relief, Reform, and Recovery: The New Deal Program," is devoted to scholarship on the Roosevelt administration's actions to end the Depression crisis, emphasizing the New Deal's social programs and the federal government's assumption of a greater role in regulating the economy. Chapter 4, "Social Conditions, Protest, and Reaction," covers works on social problems created or revealed by the Depression, such as racism and economic inequities, and summarizes scholarship on the radicalism, protest movements, and labor actions that developed in response. The final chapter, "The Culture of the Depression," focuses on the daily life and popular culture of the American people during the Depression years.

The article abstracts were selected by the editors, who examined every abstract in the database for 1973-82. This careful selection process has provided very thorough coverage of the modern periodical literature on the Depression. The result far exceeds in breadth of coverage what is obtainable through an online search of the database or even an extensive manual search using the database's subject index. Great care has been taken to ensure consistency and clarity in the index terms. In addition, cross-references have been added to the subject index to facilitate rapid and accurate searching. The final product is a bibliography that combines easy accessibility with thorough coverage of the modern scholarship on a crucial era in American history.

1

THE CRASH OF '29
AND ITS ECONOMIC AFTERMATH

1. Allen, William R. IRVING FISHER, F.D.R., AND THE GREAT DE-PRESSION. *Hist. of Pol. Econ. 1977 9(4): 560-587.* Presents Professor Fisher's (1867-1947) analysis of and prescriptions for the Great Depression. Perhaps "the country's greatest scientific economist," he favored monetary remedies for the depression: reflation and stabilization of the dollar. He proposed 100% reserves against demand deposits in commercial banks, thus enabling monetary authorities to control the volume of money. His efforts were seconded by other leading economists, but the imminence of World War II blocked possible completion. 114 notes.   J. Tull

2. Anderson, Barry L. and Butkiewicz, James L. MONEY, SPENDING, AND THE GREAT DEPRESSION. *Southern Econ. J. 1980 47(2): 388-403.* Summarizes and criticizes Peter Temin's *Did Monetary Forces Cause the Great Depression?* (New York: Norton, 1976), a critique of the monetary hypothesis (which asserts that monetary forces were the causal factors in the Great Depression); finds Temin's criticism, analysis, and biases less than compelling.

3. Anhalt, Walter C. and Smith, Glen H. HE SAVED THE FARM? GOV-ERNOR LANGER AND THE MORTGAGE MORATORIA. *North Dakota Q. 1976 44(4): 5-17.* Economic depression in farming states resulting from overextension of credit during the boom years of World War I led to extensive mortgages and eventually foreclosures on agricultural lands in North Dakota and to the formation of the North Dakota Farmers' Holiday Association (which declared a 'holiday' on the public sale of foreclosed property); discusses the measures taken during 1933 by North Dakota governor William Langer to enforce a moratorium on sale of foreclosed property which aided farmers until passage of the federal legislation in 1934, the Emergency Farm Mortgage Act.

4. Auerbach, Jerold S. and Bardach, Eugene. "BORN TO AN ERA OF INSECURITY": CAREER PATTERNS OF LAW REVIEW EDITORS, 1918-1941. *Am. J. of Legal Hist. 1973 17(1): 3-26.* The 1929 Depression and the New Deal led many young lawyers to work for large law firms.

5. Barber, Clarence L. ON THE ORIGINS OF THE GREAT DEPRESSION. *Southern Econ. J. 1978 44(3): 432-456.* Examines interpretations of the causes of the Great Depression, focusing on the economic and social structure,

1900-31; proposes an alternative hypothesis based on a "spending" rather than "money" origin; presents a model for economic prediction and speculates on the possibility of a similar depression in the near future.

6.   Barro, Robert J.   SECOND THOUGHTS ON KEYNESIAN ECONOM-ICS.   *Am. Econ. Rev. 1979 69(2): 54-59.* Questions the positive influence of increasing the money stock in response to a recession. The key factor is the historical interpretation of the Great Depression by the policy activists (some flavor of Keynesianism) and nonactivists (anti-Keynesianism). The former argue that the Great Depression was the product of an inherently unstable private sector; the latter stress that inept monetary policy by the Federal Reserve Board, augmented by the New Deal's intervention and price regulation, retarded the economy. Favors the latter interpretation, but believes that final judgment can only come from empirical analysis.   D. K. Pickens

7.   Bauman, John F. and Coode, Thomas H.   DEPRESSION REPORT: A NEW DEALER TOURS EASTERN PENNSYLVANIA.   *Pennsylvania Mag. of Hist. and Biog. 1980 104(1): 96-109.* Reproduces journalist Lorena Hickok's 6 August 1933 report to Harry Hopkins. Based on the Hickok Papers, FDR Library, Hyde Park; 13 notes.   T. H. Wendel

8.   Beddow, James B.   DEPRESSION AND NEW DEAL: LETTERS FROM THE PLAINS.   *Kansas Hist. Q. 1977 43(2): 140-153.* Statistics show the impact of the depression and New Deal on farmers of the Great Plains, but they do not capture the emotional trauma and attitudinal change effected by hard times. Few farmers bothered to write national and state legislators during the booming 1920's, but during the 1930's files bulge with letters from rural constituents explaining the causes of the depression, expounding on the discrimination that broke small farmers and enriched speculators and corporate farmers, and aiming shafts at the New Deal's reliance on nonagricultural theorists and the regimenta-tion of the AAA. Archival material in Washington, D.C., Minnesota, South Dakota, North Dakota, and Kansas; 52 notes.   W. F. Zornow

9.   Bennett, Sheila Kishler and Elder, Glen H., Jr.   WOMEN'S WORK IN THE FAMILY ECONOMY: A STUDY OF DEPRESSION HARDSHIP IN WOMEN'S LIVES.   *J. of Family Hist. 1979 4(2): 153-176.* Drawing on the Berkeley Guidance Study that covers a group of families from 1928-29 to the present (the most recent panel wave was 1969-71). Examines the impact of the Great Depression on the lives on mothers and daughters. They find that the Great Depression had perhaps as much impact on increased female employment as World War II did. They show that Depression-caused changes in the employment status of mothers influenced the employment pattern of their daughters. 5 tables, 3 fig., 9 notes, biblio.   T. W. Smith

10.   Blackwelder, Julia Kirk.   LETTERS FROM THE GREAT DEPRES-SION: A TOUR THROUGH A COLLECTION OF LETTERS TO AN AT-LANTA NEWSPAPERWOMAN.   *Southern Exposure 1978 6(3): 73-77.* Mildred Seydell, a columnist for the Atlanta *Georgian* during the 1920's and 1930's, received a great number of letters from predominantly white southern men and women during the Depression graphically revealing their plight in the face of economic adversity. Several correspondents were so effective in the expres-

sion of their conditions that the columnist took steps to aid them through personal loans. Excerpts from the correspondence include expressions of self-blame on the part of some writers, while others called for the establishment of a dictatorship to change conditions. Young married women revealed their adverse condition caused by early marriage and by being forced to work long hours at low pay in textile mills.   N. Lederer

11.   Bolin, Winifred D. Wandersee.   THE ECONOMICS OF MIDDLE-INCOME FAMILY LIFE: WORKING WOMEN DURING THE GREAT DEPRESSION.   *J. of Am. Hist. 1978 65(1): 60-74.* Despite the traditionally conservative attitude among whites regarding working wives, the depression decade witnessed an increase in both the number and the proportion of married women in the labor force. With many families this was necessary just for survival. But with middle-income families, those earning at least $1,000 a year, this increase is attributable not to absolute economic need, but to a change in values. Wives from middle-income families entered the labor force not to procure necessities like food and clothing for their families, but to purchase items such as refrigeration, modern plumbing, and lighting. They worked to enable their families to pursue a higher standard of living, a value acquired during the late 1920's. 5 tables, 21 notes.   T. P. Linkfield

12.   Bornemann, Alfred H.   THE KEYNESIAN PARADIGM AND ECO-NOMIC POLICY.   *Am. J. of Econ. and Sociol. 1976 35(2): 125-136.* Keynesian marcoeconomic theory and the new theory of the hitherto neglected branch of political science, public administration, which were both independently introduced at about the same time in the New Deal period of the 1930's, complemented each other. Keynesian theory, emphasizing government fiscal policy and deficit spending as counter-depression, full-employment, and economic growth measures, became the generally accepted paradigm in economics and public finance. Public administration theory held that government agencies, motivated primarily by their own bureaucratic expansionary self-interest, would bring about an equilibrium of national interest. This provided the justification for agency initiative in stimulating and supporting the demands of interest and pressure groups whose regulation required increased agency activity. The theories and their outcome reflected the continuing decline of classical liberalism. Although of different origin, Keynesian theory and new concepts of public administration which emerged during the 1930's complemented each other and became increasingly significant in succeeding decades as government spending, undertaken as an aspect of Keynesian fiscal policy, supported the rising government structure associated with the theory and practice of public administration. Reflective of the growing influence of the social sciences generally, sociology was applied in efforts to induce social change, psychology in behavior modification, and social and economic control in expanding administrative and judicial authority. The present paper is primarily concerned with the effects of these developments on national economic policy. A future paper, "The Keynesian Paradigm and Public Administration," will deal with the political science aspects of this historical process.
                                                                                                    J

13.   Bow, James.   THE *TIMES'S* FINANCIAL MARKETS COLUMN IN THE PERIOD AROUND THE 1929 CRASH.   *Journalism Q. 1980 57(3): 447-450, 497.* The financial markets column in the *New York Times* from 13

October 1929 through 13 November 1929 was judged to be either neutral or optimistic more often than pessimistic regarding the stock market crash and its effects. The column's view that the crash could have some salutary effect on the market and the economy possibly partly explains the absence of a great deal of pessimism. Table, 9 notes. J. S. Coleman

14. Cahan, Cathy and Cahan, Richard. THE LOST CITY OF THE DE-PRESSION. *Chicago Hist. 1976-77 5(4): 233-242.* Discusses the building of the City of Progress, a building on Chicago's lakefront in celebration of Chicago's growth and economic development, whose construction was subject to extended lapses due to the lack of money during the Depression, 1933-34.

15. Caliguire, Joseph A., Jr. UNION TOWNSHIP SCHOOLS AND THE DEPRESSION, 1929-1938. *New Jersey Hist. 1975 93(3-4): 115-127.* Schools in Union Township progressed from the Civil War to the 1930's in relation to increased student population and community wealth. The economic strain of the Depression, however, resulted in smaller budgets, staff cutbacks, and fewer course offerings. The Board of Education was forced to postpone building and curriculum expansion. The Union Township Taxpayers Association was instrumental in effecting reductions. Concludes that despite retrenchments students did not suffer undue hardships. Based on primary and secondary sources; 2 illus., table, 21 notes. E. R. McKinstry

16. Chan, Loren B. CALIFORNIA DURING THE EARLY 1930S: THE ADMINISTRATION OF GOVERNOR JAMES ROLPH, JR., 1931-1934. *Southern California Q. 1981 63(3): 262-282.* Assesses the administration of California Governor James Rolph, Jr. Historians have rated Rolph as a do-nothing governor, but he deserves credit for his efforts to combat the economic depression. He was aware of the depression's impact on California's economy and employment. Rolph approved creation of state labor camps for work on highways and forestry, a model for the federal government's Civilian Conservation Corps. He used state surplus funds to meet expenses, and he applied for Reconstruction Finance Corporation loans for construction of the Oakland Bay Bridge and for emergency relief measures. But he also approved a state sales tax on retail items. By 1934 he was in poor health, and he died on 2 June. Although his record of achievement was spotty, Rolph served the state conscientiously and with some tangible accomplishments against a serious economic crisis. 94 notes. A. Hoffman

17. Chandler, Lester V. THE BANKING CRISIS OF 1933. *Rev. in Am. Hist. 1974 2(4): 558-563.* Review article prompted by Susan Estabrook Kennedy's *The Banking Crisis of 1933* (Lexington: U. Pr. of Kentucky, 1973) which outlines the book's contents, shows the significance of the February-March bank crisis, and assesses Kennedy's explication of the crisis.

18. Christiansen, John B. THE SPLIT LABOR MARKET THEORY AND FILIPINO EXCLUSION: 1927-1934. *Phylon 1979 40(1): 66-74.* Uses a theory presented by Edna Bonacich in "A Theory of Ethnic Antagonism: The Split Labor Market," *American Sociological Review* 1972 37(5): 547-559, to discuss economic conditions contributing to the exclusion of Filipino immigrants by the United States. Secondary sources; 30 notes. G. R. Schroeder

19. Coode, Thomas H. and Bauman, John F. "DEAR MR. HOPKINS": A NEW DEALER REPORTS FROM EASTERN KENTUCKY. *Register of the Kentucky Hist. Soc. 1980 78(1): 55-63.* Lorena Hickok, a journalist and a friend of Eleanor Roosevelt, was sent by Federal Emergency Relief Administration (FERA) head Harry Hopkins to inform the agency on relief needs and local conditions. This article contains one of her reports on her trip through eastern Kentucky in August-September 1933. Her report contains vivid details of deep poverty. Illus., 10 notes. J. F. Paul

20. Crouse, Joan M. PRECEDENTS FROM THE PAST: THE EVOLUTION OF LAWS AND ATTITUDES PERTINENT TO THE "WELCOME" ACCORDED TO THE INDIGENT TRANSIENT DURING THE GREAT DEPRESSION. Plesur, Milton, ed. *An American Historian: Essays to Honor Selig Adler* (Buffalo: State U. of N.Y., 1980): 191-203. History of the negative attitudes toward the transient poor in the United States during the Depression, derived from attitudes toward the wandering poor of medieval England, particularly the Statute of Labourers of the 14th century (in effect, a vagrancy law) and the Elizabethan Poor Law of 1572.

21. Currie, Lauchlin B. CAUSES OF THE RECESSION. *Hist. of Polit. Econ. 1980 12(3): 316-335.* Reprint of a 1938 article by Lauchlin Currie analyzing the causes of the 1937 recession in light of the general course of economic recovery during the preceding five years.

22. Curry, Robert P. FROM INSTABILITY TO STABILITY: THE COURTER HEINHOLD INFLUENCE. *Cincinnati Hist. Soc. Bull. 1981 39(3): 158-174.* Discusses "the problems precipitated by the depression" that were successfully faced by Dr. Claude V. Courter, Superintendent of Schools in Cincinnati, Ohio, 1937-59, and Dr. Fred W. Heinhold, President of the Board of Education during 1941-59, as an example to administrators facing economic problems in the 1970's.

23. Darby, Michael R. THREE-AND-A-HALF MILLION U.S. EMPLOYEES HAVE BEEN MISLAID: OR, AN EXPLANATION OF UNEMPLOYMENT, 1934-1941. *J. of Pol. Econ. 1976 84(1): 1-16.* A major conceptual error in the standard BLS and Lebergott unemployment estimates for 1930-43 is reported. Emergency workers (employees of government contracyclical programs such as WPA) were counted as unemployed on a normal-jobs-to-be-created instead of job-seekers unemployment definition. For 1933-41, the corrected unemployment levels are reduced by 2-3.5 million people and the rates by 4-7 percentage points. The corrected data show strong movement toward the natural unemployment rate after 1933 and are very well explained by an anticipations-search model using annual full-time earnings. J

24. Davis, Steve. THE SOUTH AS "THE NATION'S NO. 1 ECONOMIC PROBLEM": THE NEC REPORT OF 1938. *Georgia Hist. Q. 1978 62(2): 119-132.* The National Emergency Council *Report on the Economic Conditions of the South,* principally drafted by Clark Howell Foreman, caused much discussion in 1938. Many people approved of pointing out southern economic weaknesses as a means of correcting them, but others opposed President Franklin D. Roosevelt's attempt to use the report to unseat political opponents. The influence

of the report in improving southern economic conditions is undetermined. Primary sources; 26 notes.
                                                                    G. R. Schroeder

25. Donahue, Jim. DRAINAGE DISTRICTS AND THE GREAT DEPRESSION. *Ann. of Wyoming 1981 53(2): 12-21.* Wyoming's efforts at reclamation of arid lands began in 1888, when territorial engineer Elwood Mead began to devise a plan for state control of all water resources. Wyoming Senator Francis E. Warren and Congressman Frank E. Mondell campaigned for passage of the 1902 Newlands Acts, which greatly benefited the West with reclamation projects. Nine years later the Wyoming legislature created a system of drainage districts to conserve water. The 1920's and 1930's saw a downturn in prices of farm commodities, and farmers were unable to pay their assessments for indebtedness of the drainage districts. The state Farm Loan Board finally stabilized the situation by lowering the assessed value on each individual. Based on Wyoming state documents; 4 photos, 74 notes.
                                                                    M. L. Tate

26. Engerman, Stanley L. ON AVOIDING THE INTERNATIONAL ECONOMIC COLLAPSE OF THE 1930'S. *R. in Am. Hist. 1974 2(3): 425-429.* The economic policy of the United States in the 1930's and the origins and spread of the Depression are the subjects of Charles P. Kindleberger's *The World in Depression, 1929-1939* (Berkeley: U. of California Pr., 1974) and Herman van der Wee, ed., *The Great Depression Revisited: Essays on the Economics of the Thirties* (The Hague: Martinus Nijhoff, 1972).

27. Fausold, Martin L. PRESIDENT HOOVER'S FARM POLICIES 1929-1933. *Agric. Hist. 1977 51(2): 362-377.* The relationship between Herbert C. Hoover's concept of corporatism and its political implementation explains to a large degree the failures in farm policymaking during his presidency. Compares Hoover's farm program attempts with the speeches and actions of his Democratic political rival Franklin D. Roosevelt. Primary and secondary sources; 65 notes.
                                                                    R. T. Fulton

28. Fisher, Gideon L. FARMING IN THE DEPRESSION YEARS. *Pennsylvania Folklife 1979 29(1): 35-45.* Describes effects of the Great Depression on American agriculture, with some examples from Lancaster County, Pennsylvania, and includes discussions of crops grown, harvests, prices, and effects of Roosevelt's New Deal and compares them with agricultural statistics of the 1970's.

29. Fleisig, Heywood. WAR-RELATED DEBTS AND THE GREAT DEPRESSION. *Am. Econ. Rev. 1976 66(2): 52-58.* Because history is an uncontrolled experiment, it is questionable what would have happened to the war-related debts without the Depression. In any event, default was "destined" to occur.
                                                                    D. K. Pickens

30. Fossey, W. Richard. THE RED RIVER BRIDGE CONFLICT: A MINOR SKIRMISH IN THE WAR AGAINST DEPRESSION. *Red River Valley Hist. R. 1974 1(3): 233-247.* A legal dispute between Texas and Oklahoma led to a military confrontation between the Oklahoma National Guard and the Texas Rangers when the Red River Bridge Company lost income on its toll bridge due to the opening of the Denison-Durant free bridge.   S

31. Fossey, W. Richard. "TALKIN' DUST BOWL BLUES": A STUDY OF OKLAHOMA'S CULTURAL IDENTITY DURING THE GREAT DEPRESSION. *Chronicles of Oklahoma 1977 55(1): 12-33.* Oklahoma grew from a frontier heritage and adopted a "go-getter," "can-do" self-image. But the optimistic theme of progress and accomplishment received a severe setback during the Depression. As Oklahoma saw its lands dry up and its economy collapse, a new image of destitute "Okies" filing out of the state replaced the picture of a "Land of Opportunity." State officials failed to deal realistically with the desperate situation; they embraced the self-made man image of Will Rogers while bitterly resisting the images created by Woodie Guthrie's music and John Steinbeck's *The Grapes of Wrath.* Based on primary and secondary sources; 5 photos, 81 notes.   M. L. Tate

32. Fulton, Dan. FAILURE ON THE PLAINS. *Agric. Hist. 1977 51(1): 51-62.* Both ranchers and homesteaders had failed on the Montana Plains by 1930. Not appreciating the dry climate of the Plains, government officials promoted crops and laws better suited to the humid East. Most homesteaders had to give up because of the climate. High taxes on grazing land also made it difficult for ranchers to succeed. When farmers and ranchers failed so did much of the business community. 23 notes.   D. E. Bowers

33. Gandolfi, Arthur E. and Lothian, James R. THE DEMAND FOR MONEY FROM THE GREAT DEPRESSION TO THE PRESENT. *Am. Econ. Rev. 1976 66(2): 46-51.* Monetary policy is effective in counteracting substantial cyclical declines because if the money supply had not shrunk between 1929-33, income decline would have been mild and limited in scope. The Federal Reserve System failed to act in a proper manner. Tables, notes.

D. K. Pickens

34. Gandolfi, Arthur E. STABILITY OF THE DEMAND FOR MONEY DURING THE GREAT CONTRACTION—1929-1933. *J. of Pol. Econ. 1974 82(5): 969-983.* "This paper uses cross-sectional state data to test the stability of the demand for money (total bank deposits) during the Great Contraction. The demand for deposits is defined as a function of state permanent income, the rate of interest paid on deposits, and the rate of state bank failures. Separate yearly demand functions are estimated for each year of the period, and these results strongly suggest that the demand for deposits was stable over this period and that the contraction had a negligible effect on the size and significance of the income and interest-rate elasticities."   J

35. Garraty, John A. UNEMPLOYMENT DURING THE GREAT DEPRESSION. *Labor Hist. 1976 17(2): 133-159.* Comparing the impact of unemployment in western Europe and the United States, the effects were almost identical. Interests of workers and the unemployed were separated, political pressure on governments to solve unemployment increased, and the psychological impact of prolonged joblessness resulted in apathy and despair rather than revolutionary action. Based on published sources and governmental reports; 40 notes.

L. L. Athey

36. Glad, Paul W.   HAIL TO THE CHIEF!   *R. in Am. Hist. 1975 3(4): 477-482.* Discusses the historiography on Herbert Hoover in this review of Martin L. Fausold and George T. Mazuzan, eds. *The Hoover Presidency: A Reappraisal* (Albany: State U. of New York Pr., 1974), a collection of papers from a symposium at the State University of New York at Geneseo; and Joan Hoff Wilson's *Herbert Hoover: Forgotten Progressive* (Boston: Little, Brown, 1975), a biography.

37. Grant, H. Roger and Purcell, L. Edward.   A YEAR OF STRUGGLE: EXCERPTS FROM A FARMER'S DIARY, 1936.   *Palimpsest 1976 57(1): 14-29.* Provides excerpts from the diary of Elmer G. Powers, who from 1931 until his death in 1942 maintained a daily record and observance of activity on his 160-acre farm in Boone County, Iowa. Extracted from *Years of Struggle: The Farm Diary of Elmer G. Powers, 1931-1936*, edited by H. Roger Grant and L. Edward Purcell.   D. W. Johnson

38. Graves, Gregory R.   EXODUS FROM INDIAN TERRITORY: THE EVOLUTION OF COTTON CULTURE IN EASTERN OKLAHOMA. *Chronicles of Oklahoma 1982 60(2): 186-209.* During 1930-40, the population of Oklahoma's leading cotton-producing counties declined by more than 10%. Contrary to prevailing beliefs, this was not due to drought and dust bowl conditions, but rather to the long term change in the cotton culture. Farm tenancy has been declining since the mid-1920's, as had the need for cotton pickers who were being replaced by mechanization. Decreased demand for cotton and crop reduction programs of the Agricultural Adjustment Act further exacerbated the problems of farm tenants and sharecroppers who soon became the mobile "Okies" seeking jobs elsewhere.   Based on government reports, newspapers, and secondary sources; 6 photos, 82 notes.   M. L. Tate

39. Greene, Lorenzo J.   ECONOMIC CONDITIONS AMONG NEGROES IN THE SOUTH, 1930, AS SEEN BY AN ASSOCIATE OF DR. CARTER G. WOODSON.   *J. of Negro Hist. 1979 64(3): 265-273.* Relates, in a condensed version, what Carter G. Woodson and his companions witnessed and heard during their book-selling campaign throughout most of the South in the summer of 1930. Based upon a personal recollection; note.   N. G. Sapper

40. Griffith, Robert K., Jr.   QUALITY NOT QUANTITY: THE VOLUNTEER ARMY DURING THE DEPRESSION.   *Military Affairs 1979 43(4): 171-177.* Enlisted manpower procurement for the US Army during the Great Depression demonstrated the impact of economic conditions on the decision to enlist or reenlist. Recruiters enjoyed the luxury of waiting lists from 1930 to mid-1933. But in the long run, New Deal emphasis elsewhere pushed military considerations far from the mind of the President and Congress. Focus was on pay cuts, relief measures, and the Civilian Conservation Corps. Then in 1940, because of the grave threat, the volunteer system was scrapped for the draft. Based on US Army records and other primary sources; 56 notes.
                                                                                        A. M. Osur

41. Guttenberg, Albert Z.   THE LAND UTILIZATION MOVEMENT OF THE 1920'S.   *Agric. Hist. 1976 50(3): 477-490.* Ideas of limited agricultural production gained wide currency during the 1920's and challenged the traditional

American commitment to unlimited growth. Important farm leaders such as M. L. Wilson and Henry C. Taylor felt that some sort of rational planning was needed to sustain and control growth in the agricultural sector. With the general price collapse in the Great Depression, the same leaders turned to the New Deal. Based on primary and secondary sources; 44 notes.   R. T. Fulton

42. Hamilton, David E.   HERBERT HOOVER AND THE GREAT DROUGHT OF 1930. *J. of Am. Hist. 1982 68(4): 850-875.* Although the Great Drought of 1930 provided Herbert C. Hoover with an excellent opportunity to improve his image, Hoover's handling of the disaster was one of the sadder episodes of his public career and presidency. Because of Hoover's stubbornness and inflexibility regarding the proper role of the federal government in disaster relief, he pursued a policy that blinded him to the suffering of thousands of Americans. Hoover's handling of the disaster helped establish the image of him as a callous ultraconservative. Based on many primary sources including diaries, letters, and the Hoover Papers; 81 notes.   T. P. Linkfield

43. Haslam, Gerald. WHAT ABOUT THE OKIES? *Am. Hist. Illus. 1977 12(1): 28-39.* Discusses the migration, due to the ravages of the Oklahoma Dust Bowl, of Okies throughout the South and far west working as truck farmers and migrant laborers in the 1930's.

44. Hearst, James. WE ALL WORKED TOGETHER: A MEMORY OF DROUGHT AND DEPRESSION. *Palimpsest 1978 59(3): 66-76.* Personal history of the impact of the Great Depression (1929-39). The author's parents owned a farm in Black Hawk County, Iowa. During the 1930's they weathered drought, insects, personal illness, and the economic crisis. The author remembers the dust and despair of the era and his family's reaction to the rise of the Farmer's Holiday Movement. 6 photos.   T. M. Heskin

45. Holmes, Michael S.   FROM EUPHORIA TO CATACLYSM: GEORGIA CONFRONTS THE GREAT DEPRESSION. *Georgia Hist. Q. 1974 58(3): 313-330.* Georgia enjoyed renewed prosperity during the 1910's as a result of its cotton industry, but the depression of the 1920's had a great impact on its agricultural industry. Non-agricultural business was less affected until 1927, and by 1929 the whole state felt the full effects. Georgia was still in economic difficulty in 1932 when Roosevelt was elected President. Primary and secondary sources; 44 notes.   M. R. Gillam

46. Hurt, R. Douglas. DUST BOWL: DROUGHT, EROSION, AND DE-SPAIR ON THE SOUTHERN GREAT PLAINS. *Am. West 1977 14(4): 22-27, 56-57.* Drought, prairie fires, and overgrazing destroyed native grasses on the southern Great Plains causing the dust storms of the 19th century. Exposure of cultivated lands to wind and drought brought dust storms in the 20th century. The storms of the 1930's were more severe and frequent than ever before. The experience of the 1930's made the Dust Bowl farmers receptive to the Soil Conservation Service and its programs. Although drought and wind erosion are still recurrent problems, the black blizzards of the 1930's have not recurred. 7 illus., notes, biblio.   D. L. Smith

47. Hurt, R. Douglas. IRRIGATION IN THE KANSAS PLAINS SINCE 1930. *Red River Valley Hist. Rev. 1979 4(3): 64-72.* Spurred by the severe drought of the 1930's, irrigation in the Kansas plains has increased annually and, tempered by strict regulation to prevent ground water depletion and careful choice of seed crops, has increased agricultural output; 1930's-70's.

48. Hurt, R. Douglas. LETTERS FROM THE DUST BOWL. *Panhandle-Plains Hist. Rev. 1979 52: 1-13.* Reprints 12 letters from Dust Bowl farmers to the regional office of the Farm Security Administration (FSA) at Amarillo, Texas. The unsolicited letters came in response to Acting Regional Director Wilson Cowen's efforts to keep people on their farms during the Depression and to avoid the greater misery of migrating to California. Though most letter writers agreed with Cowen that California offered no more opportunity than the southern Plains, virtually all pointed to their desperate situation and the need for greater FSA help. 8 notes.　　　　　M. L. Tate

49. Johnson, H. Thomas. POSTWAR OPTIMISM AND THE RURAL FINANCIAL CRISIS OF THE 1920'S. *Explorations in Econ. Hist. 1973/74 11(2): 173-192.* Shows that bank failures and mortgage foreclosures were mainly the result of credit overextension during the war and postwar boom. When commodity prices and land values fell, hundreds of small banks encountered serious difficulties. Based on published documents and statistics, files of the Bureau of Agricultural Economics in the National Archives and the Federal Deposit Insurance Company, and secondary accounts.　　　　　P. J. Coleman

50. Johnson, James P. THE APPLE SELLERS OF THE GREAT DEPRESSION. *Am. Hist. Illus. 1980 14(9): 22-24.* Covers 1929-30.

51. Jones, Byrd L. LAUCHLIN CURRIE AND THE CAUSES OF THE 1937 RECESSION. *Hist. of Pol. Econ. 1980 12(3): 303-315.* Discusses the works and impact of Keynesian economist Lauchlin Currie on the economic policies of the New Deal; 1935-46.

52. Kaufman, Burton I. FINANCE AND AMERICAN FOREIGN POLICY IN THE 1930S. *Rev. in Am. Hist. 1977 5(2): 281-285.* Review article prompted by Frederick C. Adams's *Economic Diplomacy: The Export-Import Bank and American Foreign Policy, 1934-1939* (Columbia: U. of Missouri Pr., 1976).

53. Keller, Robert R. MONOPOLY CAPITAL AND THE GREAT DEPRESSION: TESTING BARAN AND SWEEZY'S HYPOTHESIS. *R. of Radical Pol. Econ. 1975 7(4): 65-75.* Examines income distribution, monopoly capitalism, and underconsumption in the Great Depression, and Paul Baran's and Paul Sweezy's *Monopoly Capital: An Essay on the American Economic and Social Order* (New York: Monthly Review Pr., 1966).

54. Kennedy, Susan Estabrook. THE MICHIGAN BANKING CRISIS OF 1933. *Michigan Hist. 1973 57(3): 237-264.* Weeks before the national banking moratorium in 1933, Michigan's banking structure collapsed. Needing substantial loans to survive the collapse of the economy, the two large holding companies that dominated the state's financial scene were unable to qualify for aid from the Reconstruction Finance Corporation because they lacked sufficient liquid assets. Michigan's crisis soon merged with the national collapse. 3 illus., 96 notes.　　　　　D. L. Smith

55. Kesselman, Jonathan R. and Savin, N. E.   THREE-AND-A-HALF MIL-
LION WORKERS NEVER WERE LOST. *Econ. Inquiry 1978 16(2): 205-225.*
The 3.5 million people working on US emergency relief projects should be
counted as employed during 1934-41; including this population seriously under-
mines earlier theories of employment during the depression.

56. Kimberly, Charles M.   THE DEPRESSION IN MARYLAND: THE
FAILURE OF VOLUNTARYISM. *Maryland Hist. Mag. 1975 70(2): 189-202.*
Baltimore business associations tried to maintain an optimistic outlook after the
onset of the Great Depression but by early 1931 unemployment stood at 19.2%.
Governor Albert C. Ritchie was a stalwart opponent of federal intervention in
local affairs, and continued to urge programs sponsored by the business community itself. Social welfare agencies based on state support expanded services as
much as possible, but beyond pushing ahead with "all feasible public works
projects" the state did little. Baltimore established a Commission on Employment
Stabilization but found work for only one-fifth of the job-seekers. Baltimore relief
agencies were soon overwhelmed and the election of Mayor Howard W. Jackson,
although bringing about municipal loans to the Citizens' Emergency Relief Committee, showed that local aid was simply inadequate. Ritchie agreed to issue state
bonds to aid Baltimore, but would not borrow from the new Reconstruction
Finance Corporation until mid-1933, and his luxury tax program met stiff opposition from county representatives opposed to new tobacco taxes. Originally
planned for $8 million, the Baltimore bond issue had to be $12 million as the state
economy floundered. Only reluctantly was federal assistance finally accepted.
Primary and secondary works; 63 notes.   G. J. Bobango

57. Kiser, George and Silverman, David.   MEXICAN REPATRIATION
DURING THE GREAT DEPRESSION. *J. of Mexican Am. Hist. 1973 3(1):
139-164.* Presents background to the repatriation of US resident Mexicans during
the Great Depression. Discusses interests supporting and opposing repatriation
in Mexico and the United States, and the role of the Hoover administration.
Describes the departure of Mexicans from Los Angeles and Detroit, and the fate
of the repatriates. Primary and secondary sources; 85 notes.   R. T. Fulton

58. Komatsu, Satoshi.   AMERIKA NO SEN-KYŪHYAKU-NIJŪ-
KYŪNEN KYŌKŌ [The American panic of 1929]. *Matsuyama Shōdai
Ronshū [Japan] 1967 18(3): 1-54.*

59. Koppes, Clayton R.   DUSTY VOLUMES: ENVIRONMENTAL DISAS-
TER AND ECONOMIC COLLAPSE IN THE 1930S. *Rev. in Am. Hist. 1980
8(4): 535-540.* Review essay of Paul Bonnifield's *The Dust Bowl: Men, Dirt, and
Depression* (Albuquerque: U. of New Mexico Pr., 1979) and Donald Worster's
Dust Bowl: The Southern Plains in the 1930s (New York: Oxford U. Pr., 1979);
1900's-30's.

60. Koprowski-Kraut, Gayle.   THE DEPRESSION'S EFFECTS ON A MIL-
WAUKEE FAMILY. *Milwaukee Hist. 1980 3(3): 84-92.* Based on the author's
interview with her great-aunt (name not provided), discusses the period from
1929 to 1941 and the effects of the Depression on one family in Milwaukee.

61.   Lambert, C. Roger.   HOOVER, THE RED CROSS AND FOOD FOR THE HUNGRY. *Ann. of Iowa 1979 44(7): 530-540.* By 1932 the question of food for hungry Americans had become one of the most controversial issues of the presidency of Herbert C. Hoover. Hoover believed that food relief was the responsibility of local charity organizations aided and supported by local government. This put great pressure upon the American Red Cross. Initially, national leaders of the Red Cross were reluctant to accept responsibility for Depression victims, but public opinion and congressional action eventually forced the organization to assume the broader relief role exemplied by its distribution of surplus wheat in 1932. Hoover's half-hearted acceptance of the surplus wheat distribution damaged his reputation as a humanitarian and helped to "destroy" the Hoover presidency. Primary and secondary sources; 2 photos, 28 notes.

P. L. Petersen

62.   Láng, Imre.   ATTEMPTS TO RESTORE ECONOMIC AND FINANCIAL RELATIONS BETWEEN CAPITALIST STATES, 1934-1938. *Études Hist. Hongroises [Hungary] 1980 (2): 411-440.* Reviews the world economic situation, then relates US efforts to improve its economic position and overcome the effects of the Depression by devaluing its currency, going off the gold standard, and following an aggressive policy of exporting goods and capital. Tariffs, monetary blocs, trade restrictions, and currency policies among the capitalist countries were major factors in the development of economic relations that led, before the outbreak of World War II, to huge influxes of wealth, mostly gold, to the United States. 60 notes. Russian summary.   S

63.   Láng, Imre.   KEYNES ÉS A NEW DEAL   [Keynes and the New Deal]. *Történelmi Szemle [Hungary] 1978 21(1): 33-69.* In developing his theoretical system John Maynard Keynes was considering British problems, yet his thinking covered the international economy. Thus, he had to take into account world economic consequences of the American economic potential. The ebb and flow of American economy played an important part throughout the evolution process of his theory. Prior to 1929 he was looking for theoretical answers, for economic policy purposes, to questions posed by the economic predominance of the United States, living then under the conditions of prosperity. Between 1929 and 1933 his analysis was concentrated on possibilities of withstanding the pressure of the depression emanating from America. After 1933 he was examining the alternatives of world economic interdependence. The paper follows the formation of Keynesian theory, as reflected by works published in the twenties and thirties. It presents Keynesian views on the alternatives of war debts, reparations, the 1925 stabilization of sterling, economic recovery and consolidation, free trade and protectionism, monetary versus commercial policy approach, gold standard and managed currency, international cooperation and national self-sufficiency. Keynes was in sympathy with the New Deal whose efforts seemed to bear resemblance to his views. At the same time, he criticized the controversial American measures, for lack of proper theoretical foundation. As from the end of 1933, Keynes' reservations were growing. He was dissatisfied with the progress of recovery, found public works insufficient, blamed the experiments for causing uncertainty, considered reform endeavors as premature, condemned the dollar policy. His mind was moving in two directions toward the middle of the thirties. He was looking for ways and means of economic freedom of action for the

capitalist state. On the other hand, he was pondering on the chances of international harmonization of national economic measures. In fact, he was examining two inseparable sides of his concept. The paper compares monetary, trade, and investment implications of Keynesian theory with the New Deal. It states that several elements of Keynes' views may be found in New Deal measures, so that their student is inclined to consider the New Deal as a derivative of Keynesian theory. In fact, the relation between the New Deal and the theory of Keynes should be considered as a fabric of accord and difference. Under the pressure of given situations Washington had to resort to compromises, yet fragments of theoretical considerations played a role in the decisions, too. Theory was hardly determining the course of the New Deal, it was rather generalizing and synthetizing the lessons drawn from American practice. No unequivocal causality may be detected between economic thought and the New Deal.   J

64. Lansky, Lewis. BUFFALO AND THE GREAT DEPRESSION, 1929-1933. Plesur, Milton, ed. *An American Historian: Essays to Honor Selig Adler* (Buffalo: State U. of N.Y., 1980): 204-213. Discusses the industrial city of Buffalo, New York, and the impact there of the stock market crash of October 1929 and the presidency of Herbert C. Hoover, who believed that economic relief should be a local concern; mentions efforts, private and, later, municipal, to cope with unemployment and the economic slump.

65. Legueu, F. F. D'UNE CRISE A UNE AUTRE [From one crisis to another]. *Écrits de Paris [France] 1978 (379): 5-11.* Discusses the causes, government responses to, and end of the economic crisis of the 1930's in the United States and Europe.

66. Levering, Patricia W. and Levering, Ralph B. WOMEN IN RELIEF: THE CARROLL COUNTY CHILDREN'S AID SOCIETY IN THE GREAT DEPRESSION. *Maryland Hist. Mag. 1977 72(4): 534-546.* Supports the hypothesis that in general local self-help efforts during 1929-33, before federal relief programs, failed first in large cities, then in smaller urban centers, and lasted longest in rural areas such as Carroll County, Maryland, where the unemployed could be provided with at least seed and land for growing their own food. Documents the organization and work of the Carroll County branch of the Maryland Children's Aid Society under Mrs. Frank T. Myers and the noted social worker Bonnie M. Custenborder. Helping children was the Society's primary function, but much was done toward finding employment for fathers. As community response to the Society's zealous efforts grew, it became the vehicle for most of the relief work in the county. Even given the Society's outstanding achievements, the severity of the Depression showed that relief no longer could be left entirely to voluntary organizations. Based on Society reports, minutes, personal interviews, and the *Democratic Advocate;* 52 notes.

G. J. Bobango

67. Lind, Leo. TALES OF A LOGGING RAILROAD BRAKEMAN. *J. of Forest Hist. 1977 21(4): 218-227.* Reminiscences by the author, a brakeman on the Markham and Callow Railroad in 1929. Discusses daily life, economic conditions during the Great Depression, and industrial accidents in the logging country near the Oregon coast.   S

68. Mayer, Thomas.   CONSUMPTION IN THE GREAT DEPRESSION. *J. of Pol. Econ. 1978 86(1): 139-145.* This paper criticizes [Peter] Temin's hypothesis that the Great Depression was caused by an exogenous decline in consumption in 1930. Using Temin's own consumption function, as well as two other ones on the levels of the data, there is little support for Temin's hypothesis. First difference regressions support Temin's hypothesis if one uses a dummy variable for 1930. But if one looks instead at the residuals from the regressions, then the data provide only very limited support for it.   J

69. Mayer, Thomas.   MONEY AND THE GREAT DEPRESSION: A CRITIQUE OF PROFESSOR TEMIN'S THESIS.   *Explorations in Econ. Hist. 1978 15(2): 127-145.* Milton Friedman and Anna Schwartz published a monetarist, anti-Keynesian interpretation of the Great Depression in their book *A Monetary History of the United States* (1963). Peter Temin's Keynesian rejoinder, *Did Monetary Forces Cause the Great Depression?* (1976) has fostered an academic debate. Summarizes the chief issues and indicates that Temin's work, while it does not discredit monetarist views, nevertheless shows that the Friedman-Schwartz explanation requires additional work. Based on published statistics and secondary accounts; table, 25 notes, biblio.   P. J. Coleman

70. McCloud, Emma Gudger.   "SO I SUNG TO MYSELF."   *Southern Exposure 1979 7(1): 18-26.* Gives Emma Gugder McCloud's impressions of her life as a member of a poor white sharecropping family living in the South during the Depression; she had been portrayed in James Agee and Walker Evans's *Let Us Now Praise Famous Men* (1934).

71. McCorkle, James L., Jr.   PROBLEMS OF A SOUTHERN AGRARIAN INDUSTRY: COOPERATION AND SELF-INTEREST.   *Southern Studies 1978 17(3): 241-254.* During 1925-40 Mississippi and Texas commercial tomato and cabbage growers were unable to maintain satisfactory prices by voluntary controls through regional cooperative markets. Individual self-interest overrode general prosperity. Appeals were made to the federal government for tariff agreements with Mexico and Canada, and the Federal Surplus Commodities Corporation bought excess production to maintain price stability. Only a regulated economy preserved these agricultural industries. Based on newspaper accounts; 51 notes.   J. Buschen

72. McDean, Harry C.   THE 'OKIE' MIGRATION AS A SOCIO-ECONOMIC NECESSITY IN OKLAHOMA.   *Red River Valley Hist. Rev. 1978 3(1): 77-92.* Serious soil depletion in Oklahoma, 1921-30's, made it economically and agriculturally necessary for farmers to move.

73. McGregor, Alexander C.   INDUSTRY ON THE FARM: MCGREGOR LAND AND LIVESTOCK AND THE TRANFORMATION OF THE COLUMBIA PLATEAU WHEAT BELT SINCE 1930.   *Pacific Northwest Q. 1982 73(1): 31-38.* Livestock and grain prices collapsed throughout Washington's Columbia Plateau during the early 1930's because of overproduction. The road to recovery was symbolized by highly efficient operations such as the McGregor Land and Livestock Company which by experimentation and diversification rebounded from the depression. It pioneered in the use of mechanized equipment, chemical fertilizers, insecticides, and cattle feed lots. Sheep production remained

more tenuous for the company and it sold the last herds in 1979. Based on government documents and interviews; 4 photos, 30 notes.   M. L. Tate

74. Mishkin, Frederick S. THE HOUSEHOLD BALANCE SHEET AND THE GREAT DEPRESSION. *J. of Econ. Hist. 1978 38(4): 918-937.* This paper focuses on changes in household balance sheets during the Great Depression as transmission mechanisms which were important in the decline of aggregate demand. Theories of consumer expenditure postulate a link between balance-sheet movements and aggregate demand, and applications of these theories indicate that balance-sheet effects can help explain the severity of this economic contraction. In analyzing the business cycle movements of this period, this paper's approach is Keynesian in character in that it emphasizes demand shifts in particular sectors of the economy; yet it has much in common with the monetarist approach in that it views events in financial markets as critical to our understanding of the Great Depression.   J

75. Mullins, William H. SELF-HELP IN SEATTLE, 1931-1932: HERBERT HOOVER'S CONCEPT OF COOPERATIVE INDIVIDUALISM AND THE UNEMPLOYED CITIZENS' LEAGUE. *Pacific Northwest Q. 1981 72(1): 11-19.* The Unemployed Citizens' League (UCL) of Seattle, Washington, created in 1931, closely paralleled President Herbert C. Hoover's call for voluntary, self-helf programs to solve the problems of the Depression. Mayor Robert Harlin agreed with the program and appointed I. F. Dix to coordinate public and private relief efforts. Initial UCL success in creating jobs was shortlived, however, as internal strife, local politics, loss of funding sources, and the leftward turn of UCL leaders undermined its efforts. By the end of 1932 the organization had lost its popular following and its power. Primary sources; 3 photos, 39 notes.
                                                                        M. L. Tate

76. Nall, Garry L. DUST BOWL DAYS: PANHANDLE FARMING IN THE 1930'S. *Panhandle-Plains Hist. Rev. 1975 48: 42-63.* The twin disasters of depression and drought descended over the Southern Plains during the 1930's and destroyed the agricultural economy. The situation steadily deteriorated until the advent of Franklin Roosevelt's New Deal legislation which provided direct relief and a production limitation program to stabilize falling prices. The various policies, ranging from the Agricultural Adjustment Act of 1933 to the Bankhead Cotton Control Act of 1935, received wide support from Texas Panhandle farmers but only divided sympathy from independent-minded cattlemen. The expansion of federal roles into irrigation projects, shelterbelt programs, and soil conservation efforts helped make the Panhandle more receptive to modern agricultural techniques and laid the foundation for modern agribusiness. Based on primary and secondary sources; 81 notes.   M. L. Tate

77. Noble, Richard A. PATERSON'S RESPONSE TO THE GREAT DEPRESSION. *New Jersey Hist. 1978 96(3-4): 87-98.* An already serious economic situation in Paterson, New Jersey, brought on by the exodus of its textile industry during the 1920's, was heightened by the Great Depression. By 1932, the city government finally had confronted the fiscal crisis by reducing the wages of its own employees, by not hiring new personnel, by cutting municipal improvements, and by appropriating fewer dollars for recreation. Relief programs included the use of state funds as well as private resources. While not fulfilling all

the hopes of the unemployed, Paterson's record of public assistance on the eve of the New Deal was relatively good. Based on annual messages of the mayors of Paterson, census records, newspaper sources and secondary sources; 4 illus., 37 notes.   E. R. McKinstry

78. Nye, Ronald L. THE CHALLENGE TO PHILANTHROPY: UNEM-PLOYMENT RELIEF IN SANTA BARBARA, 1930-1932. *California Hist. Q. 1977-78 56(4): 310-327.* Santa Barbara met the challenge of unemployment relief during the first two years of the Great Depression. Led by philanthropist Max Fleischmann, the community attempted to provide work relief, create jobs, and solicit private funds to subsidize public works projects. These goals were implemented through citizens' committees, especially the Emergency Unemployment Fund Committee, created in December 1930. Wealthy residents were urged to contribute. With conditions worsening by fall 1931, a second campaign raised almost $115,000. Santa Barbarans endorsed job creation, work relief, and priority aid to the city's jobless residents, including singles and Mexican Americans. Transients were encouraged to move on, and Mexican noncitizens were advised to return to Mexico. By mid-1932 the magnitude of the problem was recognized, and funding shifted to public agencies. Primary sources and secondary studies; illus., 59 notes.   A. Hoffman

79. O'Hara, Maureen and Easley, David. THE POSTAL SAVINGS SYS-TEM IN THE DEPRESSION. *J. of Econ. Hist. 1979 39(3): 741-753.* Examines the behavior of the postal savings system in the Depression. It is shown that because the system was created with an inflexible structure it was unable to carry out its prescribed function when economic conditions changed in the Depression. Instead, the system evolved from a small-scale government program designed for the low-income saver into a financial force capable of causing problems for the savings and loan industry, the housing market, and even the banking system. 2 tables, fig., 24 notes.   J

80. Olson, James S. THE BOISE BANK PANIC OF 1932. *Idaho Yester-days 1974/75 18(4): 25-28.*

81. Olson, James S. THE DEPTHS OF THE GREAT DEPRESSION: ECO-NOMIC COLLAPSE IN WEST VIRGINIA, 1932-1933. *West Virginia Hist. 1977 38(3): 214-225.* West Virginia was among the hardest-hit states during the Great Depression. Reconstruction Finance Corporation studies showed in 1932-33 that nearly half the state's families were destitute. Poverty was worst in the coal-mining northeast and the industrial north; the south-cental and eastern counties suffered least. Altogether, the RFC lent $9 million to West Virginia. Primary sources; 6 tables, 8 notes.   J. H. Broussard

82. Olson, James S. and Byford, Liz. OASIS IN EAST TEXAS: CONROE AND THE DEPRESSION, 1929-1933. *Texana 1974 12(2): 141-148.* The De-pression of 1929 was felt but shortlived in Conroe. After the community battled the economic crisis for two years, oil was discovered and it became a boomtown. The economy prospered and the town grew as never before. The same problems developed as in other boomtowns in Texas, and the town leaders were not able to cope successfully with them. Primary and secondary sources; 24 notes.
                                          B. D. Ledbetter

83.   Olson, James S.   REHEARSAL FOR DISASTER: HOOVER, THE R.F.C., AND THE BANKING CRISIS IN NEVADA, 1932-1933.   *Western Hist. Q. 1975 6(2): 149-161.* Despite the pump priming of millions of dollars by the Reconstruction Finance Corporation into the ailing Nevada banking institutions in the 1932-33 crisis, the bottom fell out of the state's banking structure and its liquid assets were quickly depleted. A state banking holiday failed to relieve the situation and Nevada was in serious difficulty. Nevada's experience was a rehearsal for the national banking crisis at the time of transition from the Herbert C. Hoover to the Franklin D. Roosevelt presidency. It generated some policy change by the Hoover administration, and reinforced the idea that the federal government would have to pour fresh capital into troubled banks. 27 notes.

D. L. Smith

84.   Ortquist, Richard T.   UNEMPLOYMENT AND RELIEF: MICHIGAN'S RESPONSE TO THE DEPRESSION DURING THE HOOVER YEARS.   *Michigan Hist. 1973 57(3): 209-236.* During the Depression, Michigan had the largest proportion of unemployment of industrial workers in the United States. Governor Wilber M. Brucker held traditional attitudes toward unemployment and believed that local and private resources were sufficient to alleviate the crisis. On the other hand, Mayor Frank Murphy of Detroit became one of the nation's leading advocates of federal aid. The Lansing-Detroit conflict continued even after Brucker was defeated for reelection. 4 illus., 48 notes.

D. L. Smith

85.   Patinkin, Don.   KEYNES AND CHICAGO.   *J. of Law and Econ. 1979 22(2): 213-232.* Discusses the reactions of Chicago school economists, in particular Henry C. Simons, to the views presented by John Maynard Keynes during his visit to Chicago in 1931 and after publication of Keynes's *General Theory* in 1936.

86.   Peppers, Larry C.   FULL-EMPLOYMENT SURPLUS ANALYSIS AND STRUCTURAL CHANGE: THE 1930S.   *Explorations in Econ. Hist. 1973 10(2): 197-210.* Evaluates the methodology and conclusions used by E. Cary Brown in appraising the role of fiscal policy (*American Economic Review* 1956 46: 857-879) and offers an alternate approach leading to different conclusions. More meaningful results will be forthcoming when an acceptable system of weighting full-employment surplus is devised.

P. J. Coleman

87.   Pessen, Edward.   THOSE MARVELOUS DEPRESSION YEARS: REMINISCENCES OF THE BIG APPLE.   *New York Hist. 1981 62(2): 188-200.* A historian reminisces about his youth in New York City during the late 1920's and the 1930's. 3 illus.

R. N. Lokken

88.   Pew, Thomas W., Jr.   ROUTE 66: GHOST ROAD OF THE OKIES.   *Am. Heritage 1977 28(5): 24-33.* Provides a brief history and some reminiscenses of Highway 66, the route of those fleeing from the Oklahoma dust bowl. 5 illus.

J. F. Paul

89.   Powell, Charles Stewart.   DEPRESSION DAYS IN TOBAR.   *Northeastern Nevada Hist. Soc. Q. 1978 7(4): 126-140.* Author recounts his daily life with his wife and daughter in the tiny town of Tobar, Nevada during the 1930's.

90.   Purdy, Virginia C., ed.   "DUST TO EAT": A DOCUMENT FROM THE DUST BOWL. *Chronicles of Oklahoma 1980-81 58(4): 440-454.* An article written in 1935 by farm wife Caroline Agnes Boa Henderson describing the bleak conditions of the Dust Bowl in western Oklahoma. Mrs. Henderson describes the erosion, constant windstorms and poor farming techniques which helped increase the devastation. New Deal programs which aided the farmers and provided employment receive special praise as Mrs. Henderson refutes the arguments of critics that the programs are financially wasteful and harmful to America's rugged individualism. 5 photos, 16 notes.   M. L. Tate

91.   Rees, Garonowy.   "JOIA NEAGRĂ" DE LA NEW YORK   ["Black Thursday" in New York]. *Magazin Istoric [Romania] 1975 9(12): 41-43.* Extracts translated into Romanian from *Capitalism in Crisis 1923-1933* (London: Weidenfeld and Nicholson), describing the Wall St. stock market crash of 19-29 October 1929.

92.   Remele, Larry.   THE NORTH DAKOTA FARM STRIKE OF 1932. *North Dakota Hist. 1974 41(4): 4-19.* Discusses farmers' strike for higher prices through the withholding of crops and livestock in North Dakota in 1932.

93.   Roberts, Dick.   THE GHOST OF 1929: THE LAST GREAT DEPRESSION AND THE COMING CRISIS.   *Internat. Socialist R. 1974 35(9): 18-23, 34-38.* Compares the present economic crisis with the 1929 Depression.   S

94.   Ryant, Carl G.   THE SOUTH AND THE MOVEMENT AGAINST CHAIN STORES.   *J. of Southern Hist. 1973 39(2): 207-222.* The movement against chain stores began in the southern states because of a fear of absentee control, and a desire to keep a state's money within the state. The Great Depression caused a suspicion of big business and the movement became national. Discriminatory state taxes were passed. Efforts to establish a national anti-chain store tax aroused opposition. Unions, farmers, and consumer groups fought the tax. The measure failed to get out of committee, and World War II finally finished the movement. 27 notes.   V. L. Human

95.   Schmidt, William T., ed.   LETTERS TO THEIR PRESIDENT: MISSISSIPPIANS TO FRANKLIN D. ROOSEVELT, 1932-1933.   *J. of Mississippi Hist. 1978 40(3): 231-252.* These letters, written to Franklin D. Roosevelt as he sought the presidency and first entered office, are representative of the plight of many Mississippians during the Depression. Of paramount concern was agriculture, particularly cotton, and the writers were not averse to placing blame on agencies such as the Federal Land Bank and the Federal Farm Board which many believed were aggravating the problem. They were quick to offer solutions to the farmers' plight and gave Roosevelt unsolicited counsel on individuals who could best help him carry the fight. Concludes that it is doubtful that those Mississippians who experienced the prolonged unemployment, the trauma of losing their farms, or the stigma of welfare, ever recovered from the psychological wounds.
                                                                      M. S. Legan

96.   Schroeder, Fred E. H.   RADIO'S HOME FOLKS, *VIC AND SADE:* A STUDY IN AURAL ARTISTRY.   *J. of Popular Culture 1978 12(2): 253-264.* Studies *Vic and Sade,* a popular radio program broadcast 1932-46, as an artifact of folklore history and a reflection of traditional values of home, family, and attitudes toward women.

97. Scriabine, Christine Brendel. THE FRAYED WHITE COLLAR: PRO-
FESSIONAL UNEMPLOYMENT IN THE EARLY DEPRESSION. *Pennsylvania Hist. 1982 49(1): 3-24.* Among the unemployed and underemployed
professionals discussed are architects, engineers, physicians, professors, teachers,
and lawyers. Their numbers increased during the 1930's. Based on government
documents, other primary sources, and a variety of secondary materials; 83 notes.
D. C. Swift

98. Seretan, L. Glen. THE "NEW" WORKING CLASS AND SOCIAL
BANDITRY IN DEPRESSION AMERICA. *Mid-America 1981 63(2): 107-
117.* The US working class did not suffer the depression without engaging in
criminal activity. Admiration for and cooperation with bank robbers, kidnappers,
and shooters of public officials, encouraged by the mass media, was a form of
striking at an oppressive society. The phenomenon withered with New Deal era
reforms of federal police operations, and with the attack on those social problems
that had led to identification with Robin Hood-like criminals. 21 notes.
P. J. Woehrmann

99. Shaver, James H. DROUTH, DUST, & THE GOOD TIMES. *Kansas
Q. 1980 12(2): 17-22.* The author reminisces about hazards and rewards of
country life in Sherman County, Kansas, during the 1920's-30's.

100. Simon, Daniel T. MEXICAN REPATRIATION IN EAST
CHICAGO, INDIANA. *J. of Ethnic Studies 1974 2(2): 11-23.* By the late
1920's East Chicago, Indiana, had a 10% Mexican minority, and Inland Steel in
that city was "the largest single employer of Mexican labor" in the United States.
White residents resented the Mexicans, who occupied the lowest socioeconomic
positions. At least a third of the city's population was on relief by 1932, including
half of the Mexicans. Relief agencies began programs of repatriation which
involved a degree of coercion. Since Mexicans were the newest and least established immigrant group and had a poor record of seeking citizenship, they were
most vulnerable. The local American Legion Post 266 took the leading role in
removal, under Russell F. Robinson and Paul E. Kelly. Conditions were created
to make it easier for Mexicans to accept repatriation than get relief funds. Spe-
cially scheduled nonstop trains took 1,032 Mexicans to Laredo, Texas, from East
Chicago. While the people were well-treated generally, the whole movement
illustrates the appeal of the simplistic solution for the Depression, the mistake
that it could be solved at the local level, and the increased ethnic tensions brought
by the 1930's. Based on primary and secondary works; 43 notes.
G. J. Bobango

101. Sirkin, Gerald. THE STOCK MARKET OF 1929 REVISITED: A
NOTE. *Business Hist. R. 1975 49(2): 223-231.* Disputes the view that stock
prices in 1929 were high as a result of overspeculation. Using quantitative analysis, argues that the median price-earnings ratio of stocks at the market peak was
in line with realistic profit expectation, and over-valuation was confined to only
20% of the stocks surveyed. Based on secondary sources; 2 tables, 11 notes.
C. J. Pusateri

102. Skaggs, Richard H. DROUGHT IN THE UNITED STATES, 1931-40. *Ann. of the Assoc. of Am. Geographers 1975 65(3): 391-402.* A climatological analysis of the widespread drought in the United States during the 1930's shows that the most intense drought occurred in the northern Rocky Mountains, the northern Plains, and the central Plains. S

103. Skocpol, Theda. POLITICAL RESPONSE TO CAPITALIST CRISIS: NEO-MARXIST THEORIES OF THE STATE AND THE CASE OF THE NEW DEAL. *Pol. & Soc. 1980 10(2): 155-201.* Examines three neo-Marxist theories, using the history of the New Deal, to assess their usefulness in understanding state intervention and political conflicts in advanced capitalism. All three, the instrumentalist based on the idea of corporate liberalism, the political-functionalist based on the work of Nicos Poulantzas, and the class struggle theory based on the work of Fred Block, are judged inadequate because they fail to afford sufficient attention to party organization and the structure of the state. Fig., 97 notes. D. G. Nielson

104. Sletten, Harvey, comp. and ed. "HAVING THE TIME OF MY LIFE": LETTERS FROM A WANDERER, 1930-1932. *North Dakota Hist. 1979 46(2): 14-21.* Letters sent to his family during the Depression years of 1930 to 1932 by Myron Sletten indicate that his lot was not unlike that of many other jobless rural and small-town youth of the period. Drifting from one area to another in search of casual, temporary work, Sletten maintained a relatively cheerful outlook on life and exhibited considerable curiosity about his surroundings. Sletten traveled by freight train and by hitchhiking throughout the West, usually with a companion. His letters provide information on prices of commodities and services in western towns, descriptions of jobs held, and physical descriptions of western locales. N. Lederer

105. Smith, Mark C. ROBERT LYND AND CONSUMERISM IN THE 1930'S. *J. of the Hist. of Sociol. 1979-80 2(1): 99-119.* Discusses Robert S. Lynd's little-studied research on American consumerism during the 1930's.

106. Snyder, J. Richard. HOOVER AND THE HAWLEY-SMOOT TARIFF: A VIEW OF EXECUTIVE LEADERSHIP. *Ann. of Iowa 1973 41(7): 1173-1189.* Evaluates Herbert Hoover's executive leadership during consideration of the Hawley-Smoot Tariff of 1930. S

107. Snyder, Robert E. THE COTTON HOLIDAY MOVEMENT IN MISSISSIPPI, 1931. *J. of Mississippi Hist. 1978 40(1): 1-32.* In 1931, the prospects of a glutted cotton market and a consequent price drop to about five cents per pound encouraged schemes to ameliorate over-production and price dislocation. Theodore G. Bilbo, then governor of Mississippi, suggested leaving every third row in the field. A similar proposal was advanced by the Federal Farm Board. When these programs were rejected by several southern states, the search resumed for workable alternatives which would have declared a holiday on cotton production for a year, and the Texas plan whereby farmers had to reduce their 1931 cotton acreage by 30% in both 1932 and 1933. Details the actions and reactions of Mississippi politicians, the farmers, and the press to these stringent alternatives. M. S. Legan

108. Snyder, Robert E. HUEY LONG AND THE COTTON-HOLIDAY OF 1931. *Louisiana Hist. 1977 18(2): 135-160.* Overproduction of cotton had become a major problem by 1931, but proposals to destroy part of the crop were rejected by southerners. Louisiana's Huey P. Long took the lead in proposing the cotton-holiday plan which would have solved the problem by prohibiting all cotton production in 1932. Following heated debate all over the South, the New Orleans Cotton Conference, in August 1931, endorsed Long's plan and the Louisiana legislature quickly became the first to enact a law prohibiting cotton production in the state in 1932. Most of the other cotton producing states appeared willing to follow Louisiana's lead, but waited to see what Texas would do. Texas Governor Ross Sterling strongly opposed Long's plan, the Texas legislature refused to enact it, and the cotton-holiday plan collapsed. A major defeat for Huey Long, it nevertheless represented the first step toward "scarcity of production" as a cure for the depression. Primary sources; 79 notes.

R. L. Woodward, Jr.

109. Sonnichsen, C. L. HARD TIMES IN TUCSON. *J. of Arizona Hist. 1981 22(1): 23-62.* Relates the highlights of Tucson history from 1929 to 1939, concentrating on the impact of the Depression on all segments of Tucson's population. Based on local records and reminiscences; 11 photos, 75 notes.

G. O. Gagnon

110. Sprunk, Larry J. AL J. VOHS—WILLISTON. *North Dakota Hist. 1977 44(4): 41-44.* Interviews Al J. Vohs. Techniques of butchering meat for sale by a Williston, North Dakota, meat market were primitive, but effective. Meat would be butchered at night for sale early the next morning. The Williston area was initially settled by large numbers of Germans followed by equally large numbers of Norwegians. During the 1930's, Vohs, as a member of the City Commission, founded a municipal soup kitchen based on donations of food and city funds which fed many individuals and families for some years. The relief enterprise was a successful venture of its type and attracted considerable attention from outside the community.

N. Lederer

111. Sprunk, Larry J. CHARLIE JUMA, SR.—STANLEY. *North Dakota Hist. 1977 44(4): 66-67.* Interviews a second-generation Syrian American, Charlie Juma. During the early 1900's, Syrian immigrants entered North Dakota, primarily to engage in house-to-house peddling. Some Syrians obtained homesteads and farmed near Ross, North Dakota. Religious services for the Syrians were conducted by lay persons in private homes until the erection of a church in 1929. Many Syrians left the area during the Depression and never returned.

N. Lederer

112. Sprunk, Larry J. GILBERT AND PEARL WICK—ROBINSON. *North Dakota Hist. 1977 44(4): 59-65.* Interviews Gilbert and Pearl Wick. Teaching in rural schools in the early 20th century in Kidder County, North Dakota, was a trying experience because of primitive heating facilities and the need to provide lunches to hungry school children. In the household, meat preservation was often accomplished through canning or, in the case of pork, through frying the meat and then storing it in large crocks sealed with animal fat. The arrival of the oil well near Robinson, under the sponsorship of Arthur H. Townley, was a big event. However, the well proved to be relatively unproduc-

tive, and many investors lost their money. The Depression in Jamestown, North Dakota, was severe. Many men were out of work, farmers were unable to realize prices over the cost of production, and many tramps begged for food from door to door.   N. Lederer

113. Sprunk, Larry J. HUGH O'CONNOR—NEW ROCKFORD. *North Dakota Hist. 1977 44(4): 46-50.* Interviews retired farmer Hugh O'Connor. During the early 1900's, it was still possible to pick up large quantities of buffalo bones on the North Dakota prairie. Farm life was very difficult for women, who often had large numbers of children, were isolated, and lived in primitive physical conditions. There was a definite technique and skill of handling oxen, which were common draft animals during the period. During the 1930's farmers existed by becoming as self-sufficient as possible. For most of the period, members of the Industrial Workers of the World worked as members of threshing teams for North Dakota farmers and presented few labor difficulties.   N. Lederer

114. Sprunk, Larry J. RUEBEN P. TARALSETH—METIGOSHE. *North Dakota Hist. 1977 44(4): 55-57.* Interviews Rueben P. Taralseth. Enterprising farmers erected power windmills, purchased feed grinders, and established blacksmith shops in order to accommodate their needs and those of their neighbors in the area near Landa, North Dakota, in the early 1900's. Social life included dances at the township hall. Many farmers lost their land during the Depression but were able to regain their property through the implementation of New Deal legislation. People during the 1930's were more gregarious and in better spirits than today despite the adverse conditions. The flu epidemic of 1918 had a severe effect on the area around Landa with virtually every family falling victim to the disease.   N. Lederer

115. Stein, Walter J. THE "OKIE" AS FARM LABORER. *Agric. Hist. 1975 49(1): 202-215.* During the 1930's, more than 300,000 white Protestant Americans from Oklahoma, Missouri, Texas, and Arkansas moved to California, where they displaced Mexican and Oriental agricultural laborers. Union officials thought that these people would provide the catalyst necessary for the complete unionization of farm workers, but this was unsuccessful. Suggests that as former tenant farmers "Okies" were accustomed to low wages and hard stoop labor and thus resisted unionization. Based on primary and secondary sources; 41 notes.
                                                                    R. T. Fulton

116. Sternsher, Bernard. VICTIMS OF THE GREAT DEPRESSION: SELF-BLAME/NON-SELF BLAME, RADICALISM, AND THE PRE-1929 EXPERIENCE. *Social Sci. Hist. 1977 1(2): 137-177.* There was little political radicalism during the Great Depression in America despite the existence of what some might consider ideal conditions. A review of several thousand welfare cases from the 1920's to the 1950's indicates that though many complained about the relief system, most felt the government had not let them starve. There were two groups of unemployed workers, the lower of which resembled the culture of poverty described in Michael Harrington's *The Other America.* They were used to poverty and became non-self blamers. Behavioralist theories help explain the upper culture. Based on welfare records and primary studies of Depression workers; 2 tables, fig., 107 notes.   T. L. Savitt

117. Strotzka, Heinz. DIE AMERIKANISCHE WIRTSCHAFTSKRISE 1929-1933 IN DIDAKTISCH-METHODISCHERSICHT [Didactic and methodological remarks upon the depression in the USA 1929-1933]. *Zeitgeschichte [Austria] 1974 1(6): 146-152.* Offers suggestions for effective teaching of the history of the Depression 1929-33. Warns of difficulties in studying economics in history classes due to the technicalities involved, and outlines a method for handling fundamental concepts. Sketches the main phases of the economic crisis and its social consequences, and recommends specific appropriate teaching goals. Based on secondary works; 4 tables, 25 notes.   J. B. Street

118. Swanson, Joseph A. ECONOMETRIC MODELS AND HISTORICAL EXPLANATION: THE GREAT CONTRACTION REVISITED. *Rev. in Am. Hist. 1977 5(2): 275-280.* Review article prompted by Peter Temin's *Did Monetary Forces Cause the Great Depression?* (New York: W. W. Norton, 1976).

119. Temin, Peter. LESSONS FOR THE PRESENT FROM THE GREAT DEPRESSION. *Am. Econ. Rev. 1976 66(2): 40-45.* The present recession is not nearly as severe as the depression during the 1930's. Despite economists' and politicians' knowledge and wisdom, structural changes in the economy have created benefits in holding off depressions. Notes.   D. K. Pickens

120. Towey, Martin G. HOOVERVILLE: ST. LOUIS HAD THE LARGEST. *Gateway Heritage 1980 1(2): 2-11.* Victims of the Great Depression of the 1930's formed a Hooverville at St. Louis in 1930. The community, reputedly the largest Hooverville in America, consisted of four distinct sectors. St. Louis's racially integrated Hooverville depended upon private philanthropy, had an unofficial mayor, created its own churches and other social institutions, and remained a viable community until 1936, when the federal Works Progress Administration allocated slum clearance funds for the area. Based on oral history and newspaper sources; 14 photos, 25 notes.   H. T. Lovin

121. Trescott, Paul B. FEDERAL RESERVE POLICY IN THE GREAT CONTRACTION: A COUNTERFACTUAL ASSESSMENT. *Explorations in Econ. Hist. 1982 19(3): 211-220.* During 1924-29 the Federal Reserve System pursued an economically logical monetary policy. However, beginning in December 1929, the reserve policy became deflationary, a significant deviation from its former pattern. This allows the magnitude of the reserve's contribution to contraction to be measured. Based on published statistics and documents and on secondary accounts; table, 12 notes, ref.   P. J. Coleman

122. Trout, Charles H. RECONSTRUCTING BOSTON IN THE 1930S: THE HISTORIAN AND THE CITY. *Massachusetts Hist. Soc. Pro. 1978 90: 58-74.* Urban history, to be both accurate and rich, needs to combine the old, elite-oriented styles of urban history with the new, quantitative methods of today's scholar. This wedding of old and new methodology was attempted by the author in his book, *Boston, the Great Depression, and the New Deal,* published in 1977. Based on the author's book, primary sources, and other secondary sources; 35 notes.   G. W. R. Ward

123. Vindex, Charles. SURVIVAL ON THE HIGH PLAINS, 1929-1934. *Montana 1978 28(4): 2-11.* Discusses problems on a small homestead near Plentywood, Montana, during the early years of the Great Depression. Drought, insects, and poor agricultural markets reduced farming to subsistence levels. Only individual ingenuity and perseverance made it possible for families to survive. Nothing was wasted. Recounts male and female family duties. Hard work and intelligent adjustment to experience improved the family situation, gradually removing hardships and supplying needs. The experience taught people to get the most out of everything, including inner resources. Based on author's experiences; 2 illus.   R. C. Myers

124. Walker, Forrest A. AMERICANISM VERSUS SOVIETISM: A STUDY OF THE REACTION TO THE COMMITTEE ON THE COSTS OF MEDICAL CARE. *Bull. of the Hist. of Medicine 1979 53(4): 489-504.* Beginning with debate at the 1926 convention of the American Medical Association, the movement began to investigate the economics of health care. At a meeting during the 1927 AMA convention, the Committee on the Cost of Medical Care was formed, with Ray Lyman Wilbur, former president of the AMA, as chairman. By 1931, a final report was developed, and in 1932 it was published, entitled *Medical Care for the American People.* It pointed out that Americans did not receive adequate medical care, due to lack of facilities, shortage of physicians, and inabiliy of the poor to pay for the cost of major illness. Yet, at the same time many physicians suffered from insufficient income. The report recommended group practice in hospitals, extension of all basic public health services, group payment for health care either financed by government or by private means, coordination of local and state services, and improved education. The AMA opposed the report, but it did stimulate discussion and some action on the federal level. 76 notes.   M. Kaufman

125. Webb, Bernice Larson. I REMEMBER SAPPA VALLEY. *Kansas Q. 1980 12(2): 25-34.* Recalls family life in rural Decatur County, Kansas, in the 1930's.

126. Webb, Pamela. BUSINESS AS USUAL: THE BANK HOLIDAY IN ARKANSAS. *Arkansas Hist. Q. 1980 39(3): 247-261.* Describes the situation in Arkansas immediately before and during the Depression bank holiday declared by President Franklin D. Roosevelt for 6-15 March 1933. Gives many examples of how businesses and citizens coped with the lack of ready money caused by the bank closure. Based mainly on newspapers, interviews, and correspondence; 35 notes.   G. R. Schroeder

127. Whisenhunt, Donald W. HUEY LONG AND THE TEXAS COTTON ACREAGE CONTROL LAW OF 1931. *Louisiana Studies 1974 13(2): 142-153.* Studies the reaction to Governor Huey P. Long's proposal that all cotton-producing states forbid the planting of cotton in 1932 as a means of bolstering the sagging price of cotton. Getting Texas' approval and cooperation was crucial to its success; hence great pressure, not only from Long but also from other states. Texas finally passed its own less stringent regulatory bill, but that law was declared unconstitutional. The debate, however, did have value for the future in preparing the thinking of southern agriculture for the later New Deal crop limitation measures. 69 notes.   R. V. Ritter

128. Whisenhunt, Donald W. THE TEXAN AS A RADICAL, 1929-1933. *Social Sci. J. 1977 14(3): 61-72.* Discusses the political reaction of Texans in the initial stages of the Depression, 1929-33, concentrating on radical reactions, demands for government action and general feelings of malaise for the capitalistic system and American traditions.

129. Whisenhunt, Donald W. THERE IS NO DEPRESSION. *Red River Valley Hist. Rev. 1980 5(4): 4-16.* Surveys the attitudes of Texans toward the depression between 1929 and 1933 and discovers that most people disbelieved that a depression was underway and avoided despair by looking for signs of improvement; that attitude served them ill in the long run because it prevented serious efforts to bring about economic recovery and prolonged human suffering longer than necessary.

130. Whisenhunt, Donald W. THE TRANSIENT IN THE DEPRESSION. *Red River Valley Hist. R. 1974 1(1): 7-20.*

131. Whisenhunt, Donald W. WEST TEXAS AND THE STOCK MAR-KET CRASH OF 1929. *West Texas Hist. Assoc. Year Book 1979 55: 59-69.* Discusses the local responses and theories regarding the origins and impact of the 1929 Stock Market Crash and the ensuing depression.

132. Wicker, Elmus. A RECONSIDERATION OF THE CAUSES OF THE BANKING PANIC OF 1930. *J. of Econ. Hist. 1980 40(3): 571-583.* The banking panic of 1930 has special significance for assessing the causal role of money during the Great Depression. A detailed examination of the panic-induced bank closings in November reveals that poor loans and investments in the 1920's were the principal factor contributing to the accelerated rate of bank suspensions. These findings are consistent with the Friedman-Schwartz interpretation of the 1930 banking panic as a purely autonomous disturbance largely unrelated to the decline in economic activity. They are inconsistent with Peter Temin's conjecture that declining prices of lower-grade corporate bonds and the agricultural situation played an important causal role.   J

133. Worster, Donald. GRASS TO DUST: THE GREAT PLAINS IN THE 1930'S. *Environmental Rev. 1977 3: 2-13.* Relates the history of the great dust storms of the 1930's and discusses how these disasters advanced the application of ecological concepts in agricultural development.

134. Wright, George C. THE FAITH PLAN: A BLACK INSTITUTION GROWS DURING THE DEPRESSION. *Filson Club. Hist. Q. 1977 51(4): 336-349.* Describes the successful efforts of J. Mansir Tydings and Whitney M. Young to keep Lincoln Institute in Kentucky from being closed during the depression of the 1930's. The two men saved the black school by encouraging outside donations, upgrading the school farm, and attracting new students. By 1937 faculty salaries were increased, library holdings were enlarged, and student activities were broadened. Based on interviews with Tydings and Young and school records; 71 notes.   G. B. McKinney

2

THE NEW DEMOCRATIC COALITION
AND THE REPUBLICAN RESPONSE

135. Adams, J. W. GOVERNOR GORDON BROWNING, CAM-
PAIGNER EXTRAORDINARY—THE 1936 ELECTION FOR GOVER-
NOR. *West Tennessee Hist. Soc. Papers 1976 (30): 5-23.* Depicts the 1936
gubernatorial primary campaign of Gordon Browning in Tennessee. Portrays
Browning's method of hard-hitting stumping, the 1936 campaign being a classic
of this type of campaign strategy. He won the Democratic primary by a two to
one margin over his opponent and was swept into office in the general election
which followed. While Boss Crump of Memphis supported him in the campaign,
he and Browning split over appointments after the latter assumed office. In 1938
the loss of Crump's support cost Browning his reelection, even though he had
given Tennessee a splendid reform administration. Browning was later reelected
Governor in 1949 and 1951. Based largely on files of Nashville newspapers in the
Gordon Browning Memorial Library, McKenzie, Tennessee; illus., 39 notes.
H. M. Parker, Jr.

136. Allen, Howard W. and Austin, Erik W. FROM THE POPULIST ERA
TO THE NEW DEAL: A STUDY OF PARTISAN REALIGNMENT IN
WASHINGTON STATE, 1889-1950. *Social Sci. Hist. 1979 3(2): 115-143.* This
quantitative study tests various recent theories of voting behavior (critical elections; maintaining, developing, and realigning elections; socioeconomic versus
ethnic and religious factors), using Washington during 1889-1950 as a case study.
Socioeconomic factors are more important than ethnic and cultural ones. There
was a major "critical realignment" during the New Deal years. Based on Inter-
university Consortium for Political and Social Research election data, census
reports, and other primary materials; 7 tables, 2 graphs, 17 notes, 2 appendixes.
L. K. Blaser

137. Alsop, Joseph. ROOSEVELT REMEMBERED. *Smithsonian 1982
12(10): 38-49.* A memoir on the life and presidency of Franklin D. Roosevelt to
commemorate his birth in 1882.

138. Antognini, Richard. THE ROLE OF A. P. GIANNINI IN THE 1934
CALIFORNIA GUBERNATORIAL ELECTION. *Southern California Q.
1975 57(1): 53-86.* Analyzes how A. P. Giannini, founder and head of the Bank
of America, switched from traditional support of the Republican Party to en-

dorsement of the Roosevelt candidacy in 1932, and eventual backing of the Republican gubernatorial candidate in 1934. Giannini came into conflict with the Federal Reserve Board, the head of San Francisco's Federal Reserve Bank, and the Reconstruction Finance Corporation. Unhappy with the Hoover Administration, Giannini endorsed Franklin D. Roosevelt in 1932; and in return Roosevelt promised to support policies friendly to Giannini's needs. After Upton Sinclair captured the 1934 Democratic gubernatorial nomination, the Giannini forces and Republican candidate Frank Merriam reached an agreement which permitted support of Merriam without damaging relations with the Roosevelt Administration. Primary and secondary sources, including the Bank of America Archives; 86 notes.   A. Hoffman

139. Barone, Louis A. THE FIGHTING LUMBERJACK: BERTRAND H. SNELL OF NEW YORK AND THE NEW DEAL, 1933-1939. Plesur, Milton, ed. *An American Historian: Essays to Honor Selig Adler* (Buffalo: State U. of N.Y., 1980): 159-166. New York lumberjack Bertrand H. Snell's political career from 1914 was that of a conservative Republican who exemplified the traditional values of those nurtured during the industrial revolution; focuses on his attempts to salvage the Republican Party when Franklin D. Roosevelt was elected in 1933, until the Republicans' comeback in 1939.

140. Best, Gary Dean. AN EVANGELIST AMONG SKEPTICS: HOOVER'S BID FOR THE LEADERSHIP OF THE GOP, 1937-1938. *Pro. of the Am. Phil. Soc. 1979 123(1): 1-14.* Immediately after the smashing defeat which the Republican Party suffered in 1936, Herbert C. Hoover laid plans for a conference of Republican leaders for early 1938 to revitalize the party and to establish a basic philosophy true to the party's historical position which would be an affirmative alternate to the coercion of the New Deal. Alfred M. Landon opposed this effort, viewing it as a ploy of Hoover to gain the nomination in 1940. Delineates the moves and countermoves of these two party leaders. Ultimately Hoover was forced to compromise, both from the timing of the conference as well as in establishing a basic Republican philosophy. The Republicans were highly successful in the 1938 elections, and both men took the credit. Based on the correspondence found in the Hoover Papers (Hoover Presidential Library) and the Landon Papers (Kansas State Historical Society) and contemporary newspaper accounts; 112 notes.   H. M. Parker, Jr.

141. Best, Gary Dean. HERBERT HOOVER AS TITULAR LEADER OF THE GOP, 1933-35. *Mid-America 1979 61(2): 81-97.* After the 1932 election Herbert C. Hoover was the discredited leader of the Republican Party. Between March 1933 and March 1935 he kept a self-imposed public silence on political affairs. In March 1935 he issued an off-the-cuff statement to a Tucson newspaper on the Roosevelt administration's abandonment of the gold standard. Later the same month he issued a letter to the California Republican Assembly attacking the New Deal. This ended his two-year silence, yet Hoover remained discredited. 86 notes.   J. M. Lee

142. Blayney, Michael Stewart. HONOR AMONG GENTLEMEN: HERBERT PELL, FRANKLIN ROOSEVELT, AND THE CAMPAIGN OF 1936. *Rhode Island Hist. 1980 39(3): 95-102.* Herbert Pell, a Knickerbocker patrician, was linked to Franklin D. Roosevelt by ties of class, liberalism, antibusiness

sentiment, a Hudson River estate near Roosevelt's, and an association dating back to their student days at Harvard. In the 1936 presidential campaign Pell served as a defender of Roosevelt against the charges that he was an enemy to his class. Based on papers in public repositories and private hands, interviews, and published documents; 4 illus., 40 notes.   P. J. Coleman

143. Braeman, John. THE MAKING OF THE ROOSEVELT COALI-TION: SOME RECONSIDERATIONS. *Can. Rev. of Am. Studies [Canada]* *1980 11(2): 233-253.* Six recent publications attempt anew to assess Franklin D. Roosevelt's New Deal of the 1930's: Kristi Andersen's *The Creation of a Democratic Majority, 1928-1936* (Chicago, 1979), Barbara Blumberg's *The New Deal and the Unemployed: The View from New York City* (Lewisburg, Pa., 1979), Sidney Fine's *Frank Murphy: The Detroit Years* (Ann Arbor, 1975) and *Frank Murphy: The New Deal Years* (Chicago, 1979), John W. Jeffries's *Testing the Roosevelt Coalition: Connecticut Society and Politics in the Era of World War II* (Knoxville, Tenn., 1979), and Martha H. Swain's *Pat Harrison: The New Deal Years* (Jackson, Miss., 1978). 37 notes.   H. T. Lovin

144. Chalmers, Leonard. THE CRUCIAL TEST OF LA GUARDIA'S FIRST HUNDRED DAYS: THE EMERGENCY ECONOMY BILL. *New-York Hist. Soc. Q. 1973 57(3): 237-253.* The Emergency Economy Bill served as a test for Mayor Fiorello La Guardia (1882-1947) when he took office in January 1934. New York City was on the verge of bankruptcy, with 1,000,000 people on some form of welfare. The measure called for stringent economy because no federal aid would be forthcoming until the budget was balanced. When the bill was passed by the state legislature, it was a personal triumph for the mayor and attested to his great political skill. Based on newspapers and secondary sources; 6 illus., 16 notes.   C. L. Grant

145. Cobb, James C. THE BIG BOY HAS SCARED THE LARD OUT OF THEM. *Res. Studies 1975 43(2): 123-125.* Examines Franklin D. Roosevelt's unsuccessful attempt in 1938 to purge the Democratic Party of conservative congressmen, particularly Walter F. George of Georgia.   S

146. Cobb, James C. NOT GONE, BUT FORGOTTEN: EUGENE TAL-MADGE AND THE 1938 PURGE CAMPAIGN. *Georgia Hist. Q. 1975* *59(2): 197-209.* Discusses the political career of Georgia Democratic governor Eugene Talmadge, 1926-38, emphasizing President Franklin D. Roosevelt's 1938 intervention to remove him from power due to attacks on the New Deal.

147. Conkin, Paul K. HONEYMOON FOR A SOPHOMORE. *R. in Am. Hist. 1974 2(3): 429-436.* The fourth volume of Frank Freidel's biography *Frank-lin D. Roosevelt: Launching the New Deal* (Boston: Little, Brown and Co., 1973) focuses on Roosevelt's political leadership and economic policy during the New Deal.

148. Coode, Thomas H. TENNESSEE CONGRESSMEN AND THE NEW DEAL, 1933-1938. *West Tennessee Hist. Soc. Papers 1977 31: 132-158.* Exam-ines the biographies, political attitudes, and voting records of US Senators and Representatives from Tennessee during the first six years of the New Deal. While there was some opposition to Franklin D. Roosevelt's initial programs, as the years passed the Tennessee delegation, with the exception of the two Republican

representatives, became enamored of the Administration. The Tennessee Valley Authority (TVA) legislation of 1933 was supported unanimously; however, opposition to packing the Supreme Court was very strong. By 1940 only two of the 1933 Tennessee congressional delegation remained in office, death having claimed several. Based on personal papers and the *Congressional Record;* 7 illus., 62 notes.   H. M. Parker, Jr.

149. Coode, Thomas H. WALTER CHANDLER AS CONGRESSMAN. *West Tennessee Hist. Soc. Papers 1975 29: 25-37.* Upon retiring from Congress in 1934, Congressman Edward Hull Crump of Memphis picked Walter Chandler, a veteran in the Crump organization, to succeed him. Chandler became a very effective congressman—rated by the *New York Times* in 1939 as one of the 10 ablest men in the House. Seldom speaking on the floor, Chandler was better noted for the legislation he developed, particularly as a member of the House Judiciary Committee, where he wrote up bankruptcy legislation which culminated in the Chandler Act of 1937. He remained loyal to the New Deal even when other Democrats were leaving it in 1938. He remained in Congress until 1940. After Crump was elected Mayor of Memphis in 1939, he took the oath of office on 1 January 1940, and resigned, and the city commission named Chandler the mayor. Thus ended a brief but brilliant and promising career in Congress. Based on secondary sources; photo, 27 notes.   H. M. Parker, Jr.

150. Daniels, Roger. DEPRESSION MAYOR. *Rev. in Am. Hist. 1976 4(1): 110-114.* Review article prompted by Sidney Fine's *Frank Murphy: The Detroit Years* (Ann Arbor: U. of Illinois Pr., 1975) which discusses Murphy's mayoral term in Detroit, 1930-33, emphasizing economic conditions in the city (as representative of many urban areas) and attempts to cope with the psychological effects of the depression.

151. Daniels, Roger. NEW DEAL PROCONSUL AND GOVERNOR. *Rev. in Am. Hist. 1980 8(1): 104-108.* Review essay of Sidney Fine's *Frank Murphy: The New Deal Years* (Chicago: U. of Chicago Pr., 1979); 1936-42.

152. Davis, Kenneth S. INCIDENT IN MIAMI. *Am. Heritage 1980 32(1): 86-95.* An account of the attempted assassination of Franklin D. Roosevelt by Giuseppe Zangara in Miami, Florida, on 15 February 1933. Zangara wounded several persons, including Chicago's Mayor Anton Cermak who died on 6 March. Zangara was tried and executed. Roosevelt refused to let the incident unnerve him. 12 illus.   J. F. Paul

153. Davis, Polly. COURT REFORM AND ALBEN W. BARKLEY'S ELECTION AS MAJORITY LEADER. *Southern Q. 1976 15(1): 15-31.* Examines 1937 judiciary reform and the contest for majority leadership in the US Senate which involved Byron P. Harrison and Alben W. Barkley. President Franklin D. Roosevelt's court pack fight receives primary consideration. The results of both struggles are evaluated. Concludes that the situations helped factionalize the Democratic Party. 53 notes.   R. W. Dubay

154. Dawson, Nelson L. LOUIS D. BRANDEIS, FELIX FRANKFURTER, AND FRANKLIN D. ROOSEVELT: THE ORIGINS OF A NEW DEAL RELATIONSHIP. *Am. Jewish Hist. 1978 68(1): 32-42.* The Brandeis-Frankfurter partnership influencing national political events began in 1917 (re the

appointment of an economic "czar"). By the 1920's the extensive correspondence between them included politics, law, and Zionism. By 1933, Frankfurter acted as the intermediary between Brandeis and Roosevelt. The intellectual relation of these three men demonstrates the importance of personal contact as a source of political influence and the truth of their philosophy's central thesis: that the richest sources of a democracy are the individuals in public service.

F. Rosenthal

155. Dorsett, Lyle W. FRANK HAGUE, FRANKLIN ROOSEVELT AND THE POLITICS OF THE NEW DEAL. *New Jersey Hist. 1976 94(1): 23-35.* Frank Hague was not pro-Roosevelt at the 1932 convention, but he enthusiastically supported him in the general election and helped deliver New Jersey's electoral votes to the Democratic ticket. Hague's political power was again demonstrated in his control of the New Deal's WPA and FERA programs in New Jersey. Abuses of the programs soon became common and the President's personal distaste for the Jersey City mayor grew. Roosevelt supported Charles Edison for governor in 1940, hoping to circumvent Hague with a friend in Trenton. As time passed it became evident that Hague could be embarrassed but not destroyed. Based on primary and secondary sources; 4 illus., 27 notes.

E. R. McKinstry

156. Dubay, Robert W. PYRRHIC VICTORY: THE ELECTION OF 1936. *Georgia Hist. Q. 1982 66(1): 69-72.* W. Fred Scott, J. Ellis Pope and DeLacey Allen ran for Lieutenant Governor of Georgia in 1936 in a mudslinging campaign overshadowed by the contests for Governor and Senator. Though Allen was elected, he was unable to serve because Proposition 2, which created the office of Lieutenant Governor, did not pass. 15 notes.

G. R. Schroeder

157. Ebner, Michael H. "WINNING . . . IT'S THE ONLY THING": FDR VERSUS BOSTON. *Rev. in Am. Hist. 1978 6(1): 120-125.* Review article prompted by Charles H. Trout's *Boston, the Great Depression, and the New Deal* (New York: Oxford U. Pr., 1977).

158. Ellis, William E. PATRICK HENRY CALLAHAN: A KENTUCKY DEMOCRAT IN NATIONAL POLITICS. *Filson Club Hist. Q. 1977 51(1): 17-30.* Patrick Henry Callahan of Louisville, Kentucky, was an innovative businessman and a major spokesman for Catholics in the national Democratic Party. Callahan achieved fame by introducing a highly successful profit sharing plan in his Louisville Varnish Company. His strong commitment to prohibition was strengthened by his friendship with William Jennings Bryan and led Callahan to oppose Al Smith's presidential nomination in 1928. Callahan was an early supporter of Franklin D. Roosevelt and the New Deal. He defended the Roosevelt administration against attacks on its Mexican policy and from the challenge of Father Charles Coughlin. Based on the Callahan Papers at Catholic University and the Roosevelt, Bryan, and Woodrow Wilson Papers; 50 notes.

G. B. McKinney

159. Erikson, Robert S. and Tedin, Kent L. THE 1928-1936 PARTISAN REALIGNMENT: THE CASE FOR THE CONVERSION HYPOTHESIS. *Am. Pol. Sci. Rev. 1981 75(4): 951-962.* Examines the extent to which the Democratic surge in the vote resulted from either the conversion of former

Republicans or the mobilization of newly active voters. Analyzing survey data from the *Literary Digest* straw polls and from early Gallup polls, the authors find evidence supporting the conversion hypothesis. New voters in 1928, 1932 and 1936 were only slightly more Democratic in their voting behavior than were established voters. Between 1924 and 1936, the vote among established voters was extremely volatile, largely accounting for the Democratic gains. After 1936, however, vote shifts became minimal and party identification had become highly consistent with presidential voting, suggesting a crystallization of the New Deal realignment by the late 1930's rather than a gradual evolution due to generational replacement.   J

160. Errico, Charles J.   THE NEW DEAL, INTERNATIONALISM AND THE NEW AMERICAN CONSENSUS, 1938-1940. *Maryland Hist. 1978 9(1): 17-31.* Contrasts Republican victories in the 1938 elections with the Democratic victories of 1940. Franklin D. Roosevelt, prompted by James Farley and Henry Wallace, emphasized the need for national unity in a time of international crisis even while continuing the unpopular domestic policies which had caused defeat in 1938. Based on correspondence and secondary sources; illus., 43 notes.
                                                                                    G. O. Gagnon

161. Feinman, Ronald L.   THE PROGRESSIVE REPUBLICAN SENATE BLOC AND THE PRESIDENTIAL ELECTION OF 1932. *Mid-America 1977 59(2): 73-91.* During the early 1930's the progressive Republican Senate bloc consisted of 12 senators from Midwestern and Western states. Most of them opposed Herbert Hoover's policies and sought options which would further progressivism. A third party alternative was rejected. Several considered opposing Hoover in the 1932 primaries, but this failed to materialize. Only two of the 12, Charles McNary of Oregon and Arthur Capper of Kansas, actively supported Hoover during the Presidential campaign. The others remained neutral or supported Roosevelt as the most progressive candidate. Based on archival material; 43 notes.   J. M. Lee

162. Fink, Gary M.   NORTHERN GREAT PLAINS SENATORS IN THE NEW DEAL ERA. *Capitol Stuides 1975 3(1): 129-147.* Discusses the rural liberalism of US senators from Great Plains states in the New Deal.

163. Fink, Gary M. and Hilty, James W.   PROLOGUE: THE SENATE VOTING RECORD OF HARRY S. TRUMAN. *J. of Interdisciplinary Hist. 1973 4(2): 207-235.* Reviews the Senate voting record of Harry S. Truman, using cluster analysis and Guttman scaling. His voting pattern suggests that he assumed an ideological position at the center of the party structure. As his power increased, so did the percentage of roll calls on which he failed to respond. It is significant that the change in his voting behavior started well before his 1940 campaign for reelection. 15 figs., 77 notes.   R. Howell

164. Finkelstein, Leo, Jr.   THE CALENDRICAL RITE OF THE ASCENSION TO POWER. *Western J. of Speech Communication 1981 45(1): 51-59.* President Franklin D. Roosevelt's first inaugural address in 1933 marked a change in both the style and substance of inaugural addresses: because agreement occurs more easily at higher levels of abstraction, addresses have become more abstract so as to appeal to an increasingly pluralistic society; and to cope with

crises such as the Great Depression of 1929 and with threats of armed conflict and Cold War, speeches have placed less emphasis on America's greatness than on the faith necessary to preserve that greatness.

165. Fischhoff, Baruch. INTUITIVE USE OF FORMAL MODELS: A COMMENT ON MORRISON'S "QUANTITATIVE MODELS IN HISTORY." *Hist. and Theory 1978 17(2): 207-210.* Responds to an article by Rodney J. Morrison, "Franklin D. Roosevelt and the Supreme Court: An Example of the Use of Probability Theory in Political History" (see abstract 216), correcting Morrison's flaw in statistical reasoning whereby he assumed that probability has a memory. 7 notes.   D. A. Yanchisin

166. Frank, Carrolyle M. WHO GOVERNED MIDDLETOWN? COMMUNITY POWER IN MUNCIE, INDIANA, IN THE 1930S. *Indiana Mag. of Hist. 1979 75(4): 320-343.* Three test cases fail to support the sociological theories of community power propounded by Helen Merrell Lynd and Robert S. Lynd in their *Middletown* treatises. Detailed analysis of the municipal airport affair and the controversies over the Civil Works Administration (New Deal) and sewage construction, major issues in Muncie, Indiana, in the 1930's, suggests that Mayor George R. Dale thwarted the efforts of the wealthy Ball family to control Muncie. Theories of elitism, pluralism and federalism do not explain the political situation of Muncie in the 1930's. Based on Muncie Council Records, City Hall Records, Court Records, newspapers, and interviews; 2 photos, 89 notes.
                    P. M. Cohen

167. Freund, Paul A. JUSTICE BRANDEIS: A LAW CLERK'S REMEMBRANCE. *Am. Jewish Hist. 1978 68(1): 7-18.* The author who served as Supreme Court justice Louis D. Brandeis's law clerk in 1932-33, calls him a working justice, incisive moralist, observant host, and ardent Zionist. Brandeis' power derived from a harmonious fusion of biblical moral responsibility, classical restraint and proportion, and the common law tradition of rubbing against the hard face of experience.   F. Rosenthal

168. Garcia, George F. BLACK DISAFFECTION FROM THE REPUBLICAN PARTY DURING THE PRESIDENCY OF HERBERT HOOVER, 1928-1932. *Ann. of Iowa 1980 45(6): 462-497.* During the presidency of Herbert Hoover, several factors contributed to growing black defections from the ranks of the Republican Party: Hoover's efforts to strengthen the southern wing of his party by purging black Republicans from leadership positions; his nomination of John J. Parker, a North Carolina judge with a racist past, to the Supreme Court; the president's failure to condemn the segregation of Gold Star mothers during a War Department sponsored trip to American cemeteries in France; and the reduction of black military units. By 1932 much of the black press was portraying Hoover as a racist and a shift of black allegiance from the Republicans to the Democrats was underway even before Franklin D. Roosevelt took office. Based on the Colored Question file, Presidential Papers, Herbert Hoover Presidential Library, West Branch, Iowa, and other primary sources; 40 notes.
                    P. L. Petersen

169. Gatrell, A. Steven. HERMAN GUY KUMP AND THE WEST VIR-
GINIA FISCAL CRISIS OF 1933. *West Virginia Hist. 1981 42(3-4): 249-284.*
Herman Guy Kump, a Democrat, became Governor in 1933 after 40 years of
Republican rule and immediately had to deal with an almost bankrupt state that
because of the Tax Limitation Amendment would lose 40% of its revenue. Based
on official state papers and the Kump Papers.   J. D. Neville

170. Giffin, William. BLACK INSURGENCY IN THE REPUBLICAN
PARTY OF OHIO, 1920-1932. *Ohio Hist. 1973 82(1/2): 25-45.* Complaints of
lack of patronage and the dissociation of white Republicans from black candidates led to fission in the Republican Party of Ohio. In Cincinnati, Columbus,
and Cleveland (where black efforts were most successful) blacks ran for city
council as independents, having failed to win Republican primary elections. The
lack of an anti-KKK stand by the Republicans in the presidential election of 1924
led to some disenchantment with the party of Lincoln. The net results of blacks'
frustrations with the Republican Party during the 1920's was alienation that
prepared the way for the mass desertion of blacks to the Democratic Party in the
1930's. Based particularly on newspapers; 2 illus., 73 notes.   S. S. Sprague

171. Goode, Thomas H. and Riggs, Agnew M. THE PRIVATE PAPERS OF
WEST VIRGINIA'S "BOY SENATOR," RUSH DEW HOLT. *West Virginia
Hist. 1974 35(4): 296-318.* The private papers of Rush Dew Holt (1905-1955)
include over 400 boxes of correspondence and other chiefly political material.
Holt was a Democratic state legislator and US Senator from West Virginia,
1935-41. An anti-New Dealer, Holt became a Republican in 1950 and ran unsuccessfully for several offices thereafter. The Senate papers are the bulk of the
collection, dealing with the Works Progress Administration, the "court-packing"
plan of 1937, the neutrality issue, and the growth of presidential power. Based
on the Holt papers; 73 notes.   J. H. Broussard

172. Grant, Philip A. THE PRESIDENTIAL ELECTION OF 1932 IN
IOWA. *Ann. of Iowa 1979 44(7): 541-550.* Franklin D. Roosevelt's resounding
defeat of Herbert C. Hoover in the 1932 presidential election in traditionally
Republican Iowa was the result of profound discontent over the precarious state
of Iowa's economy. Roosevelt's victory was extremely helpful to many Democratic Party candidates for state, congressional, and legislative offices. The presidential election of 1932 marks the beginning of a genuine two-party system in
Iowa. Primary and secondary sources; photo, 39 notes.   P. L. Petersen

173. Grant, Philip A., Jr. APPALACHIAN CONGRESSMEN DURING
THE NEW DEAL ERA. *Appalachian J. 1974 2(1): 72-77.*

174. Grant, Philip A., Jr. EDITORIAL REACTION TO THE HARRISON-
BARKLEY SENATE LEADERSHIP CONTEST, 1937. *J. of Mississippi Hist.
1974 36(2): 127-141.* A regional analysis of editorial reaction by major daily
newspapers to the election on 21 July 1937 by Senate Democrats of Kentucky's
Alben W. Barkley as their new floor leader (38-37) over Mississippi's Pat Harrison. 55 notes.   J. W. Hillje

175. Grant, Philip A., Jr. THE ELECTION OF HARRY S TRUMAN TO
THE UNITED STATES SENATE. *Missouri Hist. Soc. Bull. 1980 36(2, pt. 1):
103-109.* Of the three Missouri Democrats seeking their party's US senatorial

nomination in 1934, only Harry S. Truman (1884-1972) had no prior congressional service, but all were liberals sympathetic to Franklin D. Roosevelt's New
Deal. After prevailing in the primary election, Truman ignored opposition attacks
on his ties with the Pendergast political machine, reasserted his fealty to the New
Deal, and thundered against the rich whose interests Republicans assertedly
served. Truman captured 59.9% of the votes in the general elections. Based on
government documents and newspaper sources; 35 notes.   H. T. Lovin

176. Grant, Philip A., Jr. ESTABLISHING A TWO-PARTY SYSTEM:
THE 1932 PRESIDENTIAL ELECTION IN SOUTH DAKOTA. *Presiden-
tial Studies Q. 1980 10(1): 73-79.* Among the foremost farm states involved in
the presidential election of 1932 was South Dakota. With four electoral votes, it
became somewhat of a barometer of midwestern, even national, political sentiment. Franklin D. Roosevelt's candidacy in the 1932 election unquestionably
benefited from the discontent prevailing in South Dakota over the state's economic conditions. South Dakotans cast their votes against Herbert C. Hoover,
favoring a change in national leadership. This is how the genuine two-party
system began in the state. 47 notes.   G. E. Pergl

177. Grant, Philip A., Jr. THE PRESIDENTIAL ELECTION OF 1932 IN
MISSOURI. *Missouri Hist. Soc. Bull. 1979 35(3): 164-170.* During 1918-30, the
Missouri electorate consistently chose Republican candidates for most national
and state offices. But, in the 1932 elections, Democratic nominees prevailed
because Missouri voters were angry with the Herbert C. Hoover administration
failures to cope with the Great Depression. Showing their displeasure, electors
voted more against Hoover than for Franklin D. Roosevelt. Based on governmental publications and newspaper sources; table, 43 notes.   H. T. Lovin

178. Grant, Philip A., Jr. THE PRESIDENTIAL ELECTION OF 1932 IN
WESTERN MASSACHUSETTS. *Hist. J. of Western Massachusetts 1980 8(1):
3-13.* Franklin D. Roosevelt's success in western Massachusetts in the 1932
presidential election was related to widespread discontent with the regional economy, gains by the Democratic Party in the 1928 Al Smith campaign, and the
unity and strength of that party in the region. Based on newspapers, convention
proceedings, and secondary sources; 37 notes.   W. H. Mulligan, Jr.

179. Grant, Philip A., Jr. TEN MISSISSIPPIANS WHO SERVED IN CON-
GRESS, 1931-1937. *J. of Mississippi Hist. 1977 39(3): 205-212.* Briefly describes the two US Senators and eight Congressmen from Mississippi who were
sworn into office on 7 December 1931; during the next six years they "were
closely associated with the passage" of many major laws. Based on published
sources; 54 notes.   J. W. Hillje

180. Greenbaum, Fred. HIRAM JOHNSON AND THE NEW DEAL.
Pacific Historian 1974 18(3): 20-35. Discusses Republican senator from California Hiram Johnson's endorsement of Franklin D. Roosevelt for president in 1932,
his silence in 1936, and his opposition to Roosevelt's third term in 1940. Reviews
Johnson's support of New Deal domestic and foreign policy matters. 4 photos,
74 notes.   C. W. Olson

181. Greenberg, Irwin F. PHILADELPHIA DEMOCRATS GET A NEW DEAL: THE ELECTION OF 1933. *Pennsylvania Mag. of Hist. and Biog. 1973 97(2): 210-232.* In the 1920's Philadelphia "boss" William S. Vare, the local Republican leader, controlled the city's political affairs by dispensing patronage favors to his friend John O'Donnell, leader of Philadelphia's Democrats. In return O'Donnell did nothing to offend his GOP patrons. Reform-minded Democrats revolted against O'Donnell's leadership. Fielding its own candidates, the Independent Democratic Campaign Committee easily defeated O'Donnell's slate in the 1932 primary election. In the 1933 election the IDCC rode on the coattails of Franklin D. Roosevelt and the New Deal and defeated Vare and the Republicans. The election of 1933 signified the return of two-party politics to Philadelphia. Based on primary and secondary sources; 69 notes. E. W. Carp

182. Greer, Edward. SHOULD THE LEFT TRY TO "CAPTURE" THE DEMOCRATIC PARTY? *Monthly Rev. 1980 31(10): 58-62.* Review essay on Kristi Andersen's *The Creation of a Democratic Majority, 1928-1936* (Chicago: U. of Chicago Pr., 1979).

183. Hall, Alvin L. POLITICS AND PATRONAGE: VIRGINIA'S SENATORS AND THE ROOSEVELT PURGES OF 1938. *Virginia Mag. of Hist. and Biog. 1974 82(3): 331-350.* Examines President Franklin D. Roosevelt's attempt in 1938 to strip Virginia Senators Harry F. Byrd and Carter Glass of federal patronage and give it to anti-Byrd Democrats in Virginia. Byrd and Flood countered with the issue of "Senatorial Courtesy," and the overwhelming support they received in the senate dealt a serious blow to the already diminished prestige of the president. Based on primary and secondary sources; cartoon, 71 notes. R. F. Oaks

184. Hand, Samuel B. and Sanford, D. Gregory. CARRYING WATER ON BOTH SHOULDERS: GEORGE D. AIKEN'S 1936 GUBERNATORIAL CAMPAIGN IN VERMONT. *Vermont Hist. 1975 43(4): 292-306.* Aiken started his campaign for governor in 1933 by winning the speakership at 41 and publishing *Pioneering with Wildflowers*. As Lieutenant Governor, 1934-36, he was ready to succeed Gov. Charles M. Smith of Rutland, 78, who was expected to want a second term like his two predecessors, but had little but patronage in his favor, and never did announce his withdrawal. Aiken announced on 1 February while his rivals waited until May to see if Smith would run. His second horticultural book and reduced fees increased Aiken's instate wildflower slide show engagements where he could talk politics. He also cultivated Young Republicans, farm organizations, Democratic labor who could vote Republican in the open primary, and a thrifty, volunteer campaign organization. By avoiding any concrete platform, professing no patronage promises, and winning the support of Leonard Wing of Rutland, Aiken defeated H. Nelson Jackson by 4,500 votes in September. Jackson, Burlington publisher and American Legion leader, lacked legislative experience and had supported a Democrat in 1932. Speaker Ernest Moore, backed by Gov. Smith, ran a poor third. Aiken outran Landon in defeating his friend Democratic State Senator Heininger in November. Based on the Aiken Papers at the University of Vermont, and newspaper comment; 55 notes. T. D. S. Bassett

185.   Harrington, Jerry.   SENATOR GUY GILLETTE FOILS THE EXE-
CUTION COMMITTEE.   *Palimpsest 1981 62(6): 170-180.* Brief biography of
Iowa Congressman Guy M. Gillette, focusing on his election in 1932 on the
Democratic ticket, his two terms in office from 1933 to 1936, and his election to
the Senate in 1936; during the election, Franklin D. Roosevelt campaigned
against Gillette and other dissident Democrats who did not wholeheartedly accept the New Deal.

186.   Hass, Edward F.   DEPRESSION AND NEW DEAL IN URBAN
AMERICA.   *J. of Urban Hist. 1981 7(4): 507-514.* This review essay covers
Sidney Fine's *Frank Murphy: The Detroit Years;* Lyle W. Dorsett's *Franklin D.
Roosevelt and the City Bosses;* and Charles H. Trout's *Boston, the Great Depression, and the New Deal.* Political scientists have for some time described the
elections of 1928-36 as realigning elections which changed the country from being
Republican to Democratic. This basic and sustaining political shift was made
possible by the forging of the New Deal coalition of Southern Dixiecrats, unionists and other workers, liberal intellectuals, and Democratic politicians. These
works describe the forging of the urban link of the coalition. 6 notes.
                                                                     T. W. Smith

187.   Heinemann, Ronald L.   "HARRY BYRD FOR PRESIDENT": THE
1932 CAMPAIGN.   *Virginia Cavalcade 1975 25(1): 28-37.* Discusses the political campaign of Virginia governor Harry Flood Byrd for the presidential nomination of the Democratic Party convention in Chicago in 1932, emphasizing his
competition with Franklin D. Roosevelt.

188.   Henderson, F. P.   FDR AT WARM SPRINGS.   *Marine Corps Gazette
1982 66(7): 54-58.* Based on the author's experiences, describes President Franklin D. Roosevelt's frequent trips to the National Polio Foundation Center at
Warm Springs, Georgia, where he went for therapy accompanied by a detach-
ment of Marines from the base at Quantico, Virginia; focuses on an occasion when
the president invited a number of Marines to join him for cocktails.

189.   Henstell, Bruce.   WHEN THE LID BLEW OFF LOS ANGELES.
Westways 1977 69(11): 32-35, 68. In 1938 Clifford Clinton, a private detective,
and an organization known as CIVIC (Citizens' Independent Vice Investigating
Committee) succeeded in recalling Frank Shaw, the Mayor of Los Angeles and
leader of a generally corrupt administration.

190.   Herman, Alan.   DUST, DEPRESSION AND DEMAGOGUES: PO-
LITICAL RADICALS OF THE GREAT PLAINS, 1930-1936.   *J. of the West
1977 16(1): 57-62.* Biographical sketches of several Great Plains radical politi-
cians of the 1930's. Included are John Romulus Brinkley and "Alfalfa Bill"
Murray of Oklahoma, William Langer and William Lemke of North Dakota, and
Jim Ferguson and Miriam A. Ferguson of Texas.   R. Alvis

191.   Jakoubek, Robert E.   A JEFFERSONIAN'S DISSENT: JOHN W. DA-
VIS AND THE CAMPAIGN OF 1936.   *West Virginia Hist. 1974 35(2): 145-
153.* John W. Davis, the 1924 Democratic presidential nominee, believed in a
limited federal government. He supported Franklin D. Roosevelt in 1932 but
feared the liberalism of the first Hundred Days. He helped form the anti-New
Deal American Liberty League and as a constitutional lawyer argued many cases

against New Deal measures. Although Davis distrusted the Republican Party, he decided finally to openly oppose Roosevelt's re-election in 1936. Afterward, he stood apart from both parties. Based on Davis' private papers; 45 notes.

J. H. Broussard

192. Jensen, Richard. THE CITIES REELECT ROOSEVELT: ETH-NICITY, RELIGION, AND CLASS IN 1940. *Ethnicity 1981 8(2): 189-195.* Analyzing poll results, the author argues that Franklin D. Roosevelt's urban coalition was based largely on ethnic groups. While class and union support played a role, ethnicity was the key factor. 7 tables, 7 notes.   T. W. Smith

193. Jones, Gene Delon. THE ORIGIN OF THE ALLIANCE BETWEEN THE NEW DEAL AND THE CHICAGO MACHINE. *J. of the Illinois State Hist. Soc. 1974 67(3): 253-274.* In 1932, the Chicago political machine had tried to shout down Franklin D. Roosevelt's nomination, but by 1940, Mayor Edward J. Kelly could refer to him as "our beloved President." The "politics of relief" had allied Roosevelt with the bosses, to the dismay of reformers. Kelly's over-whelming mayoral victory in 1935 put him in excellent position to demand a large share of New Deal relief funds for Chicago. It also convinced Roosevelt that machine support was necessary to carry Illinois in 1936. Primary and secondary sources; 2 illus., 3 photos, 76 notes.   L. Woolfe

194. Kahn, Gilbert N. PRESIDENTIAL PASSIVITY ON A NONSALI-ENT ISSUE: PRESIDENT FRANKLIN D. ROOSEVELT AND THE 1935 WORLD COURT FIGHT. *Diplomatic Hist. 1980 4(2): 137-159.* In 1935, the US Senate seemed ready to approve American membership in the Permanent Court of International Justice (World Court). The issue was not a vital one, and President Franklin D. Roosevelt (1882-1945) had little to lose and much to gain by actively supporting the treaty of adherence. His failure to exercise decisive leadership in this, his first major foreign policy fight, allowed anti-World Court forces to prevail in the Senate. It further permitted the growth in the Senate of an isolationist sentiment which would cause him great problems on later foreign policy issues which were vital, and encouraged legislative independence of executive authority. 93 notes.   T. L. Powers

195. Klingman, Peter D. ERNEST GRAHAM AND THE HIALEAH CHARTER FIGHT OF 1937. *Tequesta 1974 (34): 37-43.* State Senator Ernest Graham of Dade County played an important part in Florida politics in 1937. He had a key role in abolishing the poll tax, and as a supporter of the New Deal attempted to challenge a political machine in Hialeah, a suburb of Miami. The Hialeah Charter Bill of 1937, sponsored by Graham, was passed by the legislature but was declared unconstitutional by the State Supreme Court. Conservative Floridians had successfully rebuffed Graham. Based primarily on newspaper articles and the Graham papers at the University of Florida, Gainesville; 31 notes.

H. S. Marks

196. Koeniger, A. Cash. THE NEW DEAL AND THE STATES: ROOSE-VELT VERSUS THE BYRD ORGANIZATION IN VIRGINIA. *J. of Am. Hist. 1982 68(4): 876-896.* Modifies two interpretations of President Roosevelt's patronage feud with the Byrd machine in Virginia during the middle and late 1930's: James T. Patterson's *The New Deal and the States: Federalism in Transi-*

tion (1969) and James MacGregor Burns's *Roosevelt: The Lion and the Fox* (1956). Senator Byrd's "organizaton" was even less secure than Patterson claimed it was, but the US Senate viewed Roosevelt's attempt to undermine Byrd's supremacy in Virginia's Democratic Party as an attack on its procedures. Had Roosevelt pressed his attack, as Burns claimed he should have, he might have damaged seriously his leadership ability in Congress. Based on the Harry F. Byrd Papers, the Carter Glass Papers, and the Franklin D. Roosevelt Papers; 74 notes.

T. P. Linkfield

197. Koeniger, A. Cash. THE POLITICS OF INDEPENDENCE: CARTER GLASS AND THE ELECTION OF 1936. *South Atlantic Q. 1981 80(1): 95-106.* In the 1936 presidential election, Carter Glass of Virginia ran considerably behind Franklin D. Roosevelt in vote-gathering. He essentially sat out the campaign because he could not support the New Deal. His role in the election marked the beginning of a hallmark in Virginia politics for the next three decades. Unable to reconcile his conservative convictions with the presidential candidate and national platform of his party, yet wedded to Democratic traditions, Glass took the only course that would enable him to maintain his integrity and remain a Democrat. His conduct met the approval of the Virginia electorate. It would be emulated and refined in the famed "golden silence" of Harry F. Byrd. Based on the Carter Glass Papers and the Harry F. Byrd Papers (both in the University of Virginia), the R. Walton Moore Papers (Franklin D. Roosevelt Library), and contemporary newspaper accounts; 27 notes.   H. M. Parker, Jr.

198. Kyvig, David E. RASKOB, ROOSEVELT, AND REPEAL. *Historian 1975 37(3): 469-487.* A prohibition repeal advocate, John J. Raskob exploited his chairmanship (1928-32) of the Democratic National Committee to secure repeal of the 18th Amendment. In so doing he collided with the presidential course of Franklin D. Roosevelt who mistakenly questioned the political wisdom of making any party commitment to repeal. However, Raskob was successful, first at the Democratic National Convention of 1932 with passage of a strong anti-prohibition plank to which Roosevelt gave opportunistic endorsement, and finally with the actual repeal on 5 December 1933. 83 notes.

199. Lear, Linda J. REMNANT WITHOUT A CAUSE. *Rev. in Am. Hist. 1981 9(4): 510-515.* Reviews Ronald L. Feinman's *Twilight of Progressivism: The Western Republican Senators and the New Deal* (1981), a study of the political activities and significance of twelve Republican senators from the West from the beginning of the Depression until 1941.

200. Lee, David D. THE TRIUMPH OF BOSS CRUMP: THE TENNESSEE GUBERNATORIAL ELECTION OF 1932. *Tennessee Hist. Q. 1976 35(4): 393-413.* After the death of Austin Peay in 1927 Edward Crump led an urban assault on Peay's successors who ran Tennessee politics until 1932. In a three-way primary campaign, Crump supported State Treasurer Hill McAlister in a campaign which witnessed rampant fraud and appeals to racism. McAlister won a narrow victory over Lewis Pope, the independent candidate who protested fraud, bolted the Democratic Party, and ran in the general election. Once again in a three-cornered campaign, Crump's candidate won. This began the 16-year domination of Tennessee politics by the Shelby County boss. Primary and secondary sources; 7 tables, 77 notes.   M. B. Lucas

201. Lee, David L. THE ATTEMPT TO IMPEACH GOVERNOR HOR-TON. *Tennessee Hist. Q. 1975 34(2): 188-201.* The close relationship between Governor Henry Horton and Rogers Caldwell led to an investigation of Caldwell's financial activities involving state funds upon the collapse of his empire in 1930. An investigation led by Horton's political opponent, E. H. Crump, soon implicated the Tennessee governor in negligent, if not fraudulent, handling of state money. In 1931, to avoid impeachment, Horton and his allies began making blatant political deals with Democrats and Republicans, a controversial policy which proved successful in the end. 37 notes. M. B. Lucas

202. Leupold, Robert J. THE KENTUCKY WPA: RELIEF AND POLI-TICS, MAY-NOVEMBER, 1935. *Filson Club Hist. Q. 1975 49(2): 152-168.* Destroys the myth that the Democrats purchased votes with Works Progress Administration funds during the 1935 Kentucky gubernatorial campaign. States that the rapid increase of personnel hired in the two weeks before election day was caused by administrative difficulties created by the demise of the Federal Emergency Relief Administration and the transfer of its functions to the WPA. Notes that less than half of those in the FERA work program in the spring of 1935 were receiving aid in November. Attributes the Democratic victory to the depression and the personality of Democratic candidate A. B. "Happy" Chandler. Based on newspapers; 100 notes. G. B. McKinney

203. Lovin, Hugh T. AGRARIAN RADICALISM AT EBB TIDE: THE MICHIGAN FARMER-LABOR PARTY, 1933-1937. *Old Northwest 1979 5(2): 149-166.* During Franklin Delano Roosevelt's first term as president (1933-37), agrarian rebel groups in Michigan, such as the Farmers' Educational and Cooperative Union, the Farmers' Holiday Association, and the Farmer-Laborites of Wisconsin Congressman Thomas Amlie, cooperated to form a Farmer-Labor Party to oppose New Deal programs. Party secretary D. D. Alderdyce, however, tried to sever ties with Amlie's national movement, and although his demotion and the support of the United Automobile Workers helped, Committee for Industrial Organization President John L. Lewis's support for Roosevelt hurt. The presidential candidacy of Union Party member William Lenke made party unity impossible. Based on the Thomas R. Amlie Papers, State Historical Society of Wisconsin, Madison, the Howard Y. Williams Papers, Minnesota Historical Society, St. Paul, and other primary sources; 41 notes. E. L. Keyser

204. Lovin, Hugh T. THE OHIO "FARMER-LABOR" MOVEMENT IN THE 1930'S. *Ohio Hist. 1978 87(4): 419-437.* Discusses Thomas Amlie and Herbert Hard's attempts to build a viable farmer-labor coalition as a third party to the left of the New Deal. Ohio Farmer-Labor Progressive Federation (1933-36) leaders viewed Ohio as a crucial state in their movement and hoped to draw on the well-organized movement of the unemployed and the rebellious union consciousness of the industrial worker to combat the conservative and intractable records of Governors White and Davey. The subsequent failure of the movement resulted not only from the personal popularity of FDR, the power of the CIO, the New Deal support of the AFL, Grange, and Farm Bureau, and the party schism created by the Communist-sponsored 1935 Popular Front, but from the leadership's inability to work with or appeal to the ethnic and urban laborites who dominated Ohio's work force. Based on the archives of Wayne State University, the Minnesota Historical Society, the State Historical Society of Wisconsin, and other primary sources; 44 notes. L. A. Russell

205.   Lovin, Hugh T.   THE PERSISTENCE OF THIRD PARTY DREAMS IN THE AMERICAN LABOR MOVEMENT, 1930-1938.   *Mid-America 1976 58(3): 141-157.* Reviews attempts of a faction of the American Federation of Labor (AFL) to form a labor- or farmer-labor-based third party in the 1930's. These attempts were discouraged by AFL leaders during the 1920's and 1930's, especially after Franklin D. Roosevelt's election and the ensuing New Deal. After 1934 a progressive faction began to promote the idea again, particularly in the garment unions, because the Democrats and Republicans were considered unreliable. There were too many obstacles to overcome, especially the opposition of union leaders. Based on contemporary news accounts, letters, and secondary sources; 70 notes.   J. M. Lee

206.   Lovin, Hugh T.   THOMAS R. AMLIE'S CRUSADE AND THE DISSONANT FARMERS: A NEW DEAL WINDFALL.   *North Dakota Q. 1981 49(1): 91-105.* Discusses Wisconsin Congressman Thomas Ryum Amlie's crusade to attract disgruntled farmers to the Farmer Labor Party, in the 1930's, which was a failure and resulted in a windfall for the New Deal administration which attracted Amlie's Farmer Laborites, farm conservatives, and North Dakota Congressman William Lemke's old Unionists.

207.   Lowitt, Richard.   "ONLY GOD CAN CHANGE THE SUPREME COURT."   *Capitol Studies 1977 5(1): 9-24.* Examines Franklin D. Roosevelt's attempts at reorganization of the judiciary in 1937 and the support, albeit lukewarm, lent by George W. Norris, to get the 75th Congress to yield to Roosevelt's wishes.

208.   Malone, Michael P.   MONTANA POLITICS AT THE CROSSROADS, 1932-1933.   *Pacific Northwest Q. 1978 69(1): 20-29.* Montana's 1932 election witnessed a landslide victory for Democratic candidates riding the coattails of Franklin D. Roosevelt. Never before and never again would one party so completely dominate the state and guarantee Montana a powerful position within national politics. The death of Senator Thomas J. Walsh in March 1933 created new tensions when Democratic Governor John E. Erickson maneuvered himself into the vacant Senate position, but efforts to unseat him were unsuccessful. Since then Montana Democrats have maintained their loyalty to Roosevelt's moderate liberalism. Primary and secondary sources; 2 illus., 41 notes.   M. L. Tate

209.   Manykin, A. S.   RESPUBLIKANSKAIA PARTIIA S.SH.A. V POISKAKH AL'TERNATIVY "NOVOMU KURSU" [The Republican Party of the U.S.A. and the search for an alternative to the "New Deal"].   *Vestnik Moskovskogo U., Seriia 8: Istoriia [USSR] 1978 (5): 44-59.* The Republicans developed a neoconservative view to oppose the New Deal. Hoover represented the faction opposing the New Deal while A. Landon opposed monopolies and accepted the principle of state regulation. After the 1936 election, J. Hamilton became head of the National Committee and fought to have Hoover end his active role. As a coalition of conservative Democrats and Republicans formed on the Supreme Court issue, the Republicans ended their policy of pure negation. They accepted some limited government regulation. The new conservative philosophy was expressed in a work of a commission which preceded the Republican convention of 1940. The new philosophy accepted social security under state authority and limited government regulation. The Republican Party was strengthened and the functioning of the two party system restored. 66 notes.   D. Balmuth

210. McCoy, Donald R.   SENATOR GEORGE S. MCGILL AND THE ELECTION OF 1938.   *Kansas Hist. 1981 4(1): 2-19.* George S. McGill was defeated for reelection in 1938. Many factors worked against him. He ran a dull campaign, many Democrats did not support him, the Department of Agriculture was slow in making loan payments, the Republicans ran an energetic campaign and many Kansans were aroused over judicial matters in Kansas and the president's court plan of 1937. Farm discontent predominated, but these other factors reinforced one another, helping to beat him at the polls. George McGill, Richard M. Long and Clifford R. Hope papers, Kansas State Historical Society; Randolph Carpenter papers, Wichita State University, interviews; illus., 52 notes.

W. F. Zornow

211. McFarland, Keith D.   SECRETARY OF WAR HARRY WOODRING: EARLY CAREER IN KANSAS.   *Kansas Hist. Q. 1973 39(2): 206-219.* Woodring moved quietly through several minor jobs to become a prominent banker. Then he became a leader of the American Legion. Finally, he appeared as a Democrat in a Republican state just when the voters were eager to elect him governor in 1930 and when he could ingratiate himself with Franklin D. Roosevelt by early advocacy of his election in 1932. Woodring first had to settle for an assistant secretaryship, but the way was open for him eventually to become Secretary of War. Based on newspapers, books, articles, and manuscripts in the National Archives, Library of Congress, and Kansas State Historical Society; 3 photos, 56 notes.

W. F. Zornow

212. McGuire, Jack B.   ANDREW HIGGINS PLAYS PRESIDENTIAL POLITICS.   *Louisiana Hist. 1974 15(3): 273-284.* Discusses the political work of Andrew J. Higgins, a Louisiana-born campaign worker for the Democratic Party, and his work in helping to elect Franklin D. Roosevelt and Harry S. Truman, 1944.

213. Mead, Howard N.   RUSSELL VS. TALMADGE: SOUTHERN POLITICS AND THE NEW DEAL.   *Georgia Hist. Q. 1981 65(1): 28-45.* The 1936 Georgia senatorial Democratic primary was a bitter race between incumbent Senator Richard B. Russell and Governor Eugene Talmadge. Russell, with his "patrician" view strongly supported Franklin D. Roosevelt and the then popular and successful New Deal programs and was elected, while Talmadge with his "nigger-baiting," demagogic, anti-New Deal views was defeated. Based on newspaper and secondary sources; 47 notes.

G. R. Schroeder

214. Miller, John E.   GOVERNOR PHILIP F. LA FOLLETTE'S SHIFTING PRIORITIES FROM REDISTRIBUTION TO EXPANSION.   *Mid-Am. 1976 58(2): 119-126.* Utilizing Frederick Jackson Turner's frontier thesis, Wisconsin Governor Philip F. LaFollette early subscribed to the mature-economy thesis propounded in Franklin D. Roosevelt's 1932 *Commonwealth Club Address.* LaFollette prescribed redistribution of purchasing power. By 1938, as the standard-bearer of the National Progressives of America, he had shifted to expansion because he opposed federal crop reduction policies, New Deal relief programs, and Huey P. Long's and Francis E. Townsend's redistribution plans, and because redistribution rhetoric hurt his national political ambitions. Based on LaFollette manuscripts, State Historical Society of Wisconsin, newspapers, and secondary sources; 21 notes.

T. H. Wendel

215. Morgan, Alfred L. THE SIGNIFICANCE OF PENNSYLVANIA'S 1938 GUBERNATORIAL ELECTION. *Pennsylvania Mag. of Hist. and Biog. 1978 102(2): 184-211.* The relatively noncontentious Republican primary explains the victory of their candidate, Arthur H. James. Internal dissension and charges of corruption disrupted the Democrats, who also bucked an anti-New Deal tide. The election reversed the trend of Democratic resurgence. Based on newspapers, officials records, and secondary works; 82 notes.   T. H. Wendel

216. Morrison, Rodney J. FRANKLIN D. ROOSEVELT AND THE SUPREME COURT: AN EXAMPLE OF THE USE OF PROBABILITY THEORY IN POLITICAL HISTORY. *Hist. and Theory 1977 16(2): 137-146.* Uses the historical problem of Roosevelt's attempt to pack the Supreme Court to support Fogel's arguments in favor of quantitative methods for more than economic history. Probability theory shows that Schlesinger's claim for the inevitability of Roosevelt's action was biased, subjective, and erroneous. 6 tables, 26 notes.   D. A. Yanchisin

217. Mulder, Ronald A. THE PROGRESSIVE INSURGENTS IN THE UNITED STATES SENATE, 1935-1936: WAS THERE A SECOND NEW DEAL? *Mid-America 1975 57(2): 106-125.* Though the bills fell short of their hopes, the insurgents voted 96.8% for the 1935 Public Utility Holding, Banking, and Wealth Tax Acts and the 1936 Revenue Act among others. Franklin D. Roosevelt, they believed, had discovered that big business and high finance were the enemy, yet they were uneasy with New Deal centralizing and they could not embrace the welfare state. Based on the Hiram Johnson, Roosevelt and Bronson Cutting papers, newspapers, published sources and secondary works; 47 notes.   T. H. Wendel

218. Mulder, Ronald A. RELUCTANT NEW DEALERS: THE PROGRESSIVE INSURGENTS IN THE UNITED STATES SENATE, 1933-1934. *Capitol Studies 1974 2(2): 5-22.* Details efforts of progressives in the Senate to revise presidential proposals and to retain traditional congressional prerogatives during the first years of the New Deal.   S

219. Nelsen, Clair E. HERBERT HOOVER, REPUBLICAN. *Centennial R. 1973 17(1): 41-63.* Herbert Clark Hoover's political collapse was due largely to his relationship with the Republican party. His failure to affiliate with the Republicans until 1920 and his liberal and internationalist stance affronted the "Old Guard," who opposed his selection as secretary of commerce in 1921. Although Hoover was head of the Republican party after winning the 1928 presidential nomination, he did not become part of it. As president, he often diverged from Republican policy and lost congressional support. Hoover's efforts at governmental intervention during the Depression made him a "transitional figure in American politics between the old and the new ideas of government." He had been elected to maintain the status quo and his failure was "the party's excuse for repudiating him in 1932." 40 notes.   A. R. Stoesen

220. Ninneman, Thomas R. WYOMING'S SENATOR JOSEPH C. O'-MAHONEY. *Ann. of Wyoming 1977 49(2): 193-222.* Following several unsuccessful campaigns for Wyoming public office, Joseph C. O'Mahoney was named First Assistant Postmaster General of the United States in 1933 because of his

crucial support for Franklin D. Roosevelt's presidential bid. At the end of the year he resigned the position to become Wyoming's Democratic Senator upon the death of John B. Kendrick. He remained in the Senate until 1960. O'Mahoney's opposition to Roosevelt's 1937 "Supreme Court-packing bill" produced a grudge by Roosevelt, who worked behind the scenes to undercut O'Mahoney's patronage power during the next seven years. Primary sources; photo, 66 notes.

M. L. Tate

221.   O'Brien, Patrick G.   A REEXAMINATION OF THE SENATE FARM BLOC, 1921-1933.   *Agric. Hist. 1973 47(3): 248-263.* The Senate farm bloc between 1921 and 1933 was not, as is generally believed, a tightly-knit group of rural senators supporting agricultural legislation, but rather a relatively unstable alliance whose voting cohesion changed from session to session. Cluster analysis of votes on agricultural issues makes it possible to divide each session's farm bloc into several groups, usually united by party and section. The bloc as a whole normally contained western and midwestern Republicans and southern and western Democrats. Historians have underestimated the influence of the Democrats. A list of senators with the most proagrarian voting behavior between 1921 and 1933 contains senators previously not thought to be agrarian sympathizers and omits such men as Charles Linza McNary and William Edgar Borah who were once closely identified with agricultural interests. Based on congressional roll calls and secondary sources; 7 tables, 18 notes.   D. E. Bowers

222.   Ortquist, Richard T.   TAX CRISIS AND POLITICS IN EARLY DE-PRESSION MICHIGAN.   *Michigan Hist. 1975 59(1-2): 91-119.* Republican Governor Wilber M. Brucker's outmoded ideas on taxation and fiscal policy, together with his weak executive leadership, spelled failure for his administration (1931-33) and an end to one-party governance in Michigan. Brucker's belief that rigid economy must precede tax reform brought about friction between himself and his administrative board. His administration dealt with pressing economic problems only on a temporary basis, and in 1932 Democrats swept the state including the governorship. Primary and secondary sources; 8 photos, 64 notes.

D. W. Johnson

223.   Parrish, E.   THE HUGHES COURT, THE GREAT DEPRESSION, AND THE HISTORIANS.   *Historian 1978 40(2): 286-308.* Analyzes several groups of historians who have concerned themselves with the Supreme Court under Chief Justice Charles Evans Hughes in the 1930's. One group, typified by Merlo Pusey and Samuel Hendel, was inclined to be generous with the Court, especially Hughes and Owen Roberts. They blamed the New Dealers for the constitutional difficulties. Another contingent, which included Edward Corwin, Robert Stern, Thomas Reed Powell, and others, were New Dealers who defended Roosevelt at the Court's expense. A later group, the revisionist historians of the 1960's, often failed to confront judicial issues, and consequently have ignored the significant civil rights and civil liberties stands of the 1930's Court. Evaluating the quantity and quality of the works on the Hughes Court, concludes that the body of literature is small and the works are of varying significance.

M. S. Legan

224.   Patenaude, Lionel V.   THE GARNER VOTE SWITCH TO ROOSE-VELT: 1932 DEMOCRATIC CONVENTION.   *Southwestern Hist. Q. 1975 79(2): 189-204.* Describes the complex political negotiations which led to the release of the delegates pledged to John Nance Garner and the nomination of Franklin D. Roosevelt on the fourth ballot at the Democratic Convention in Chicago, 1 July 1932. Sam Rayburn was the key man, aided by William Gibbs McAdoo head of the California delegation, and James A. Farley, Roosevelt's campaign manager. It was Roosevelt who made the decision to run with Garner; Garner accepted the vice-presidency "reluctantly and only as a party-saving gesture." 10 illus., 22 notes.   C. W. Olson

225.   Patenaude, Lionel.   VICE PRESIDENT JOHN NANCE GARNER: A STUDY IN THE USE OF INFLUENCE DURING THE NEW DEAL. *Texana 1973 11(2): 124-144.* Explores the impact which John Nance Garner, as vice president, had on New Deal policies; details relations between Garner and Franklin D. Roosevelt, 1933-38. 87 notes.

226.   Plesur, Milton.   THE REPUBLICAN CONGRESSIONAL COME-BACK OF 1938.   Plesur, Milton, ed. *An American Historian: Essays to Honor Selig Adler* (Buffalo: State U. of New York, 1980): 167-182. Causes of the Republican Party's comeback in the congressional elections of 1938 included that party's attempts to unify itself and to shed its reactionary image, dangerous setbacks to the economy starting in 1937, a purge in the Democratic Party, President Franklin D. Roosevelt's ill-fated attempt to remodel the Supreme Court, labor unrest, popular dissatisfaction with contradictions and complexities in the New Deal, and Roosevelt's foundering anti-isolationist foreign policy. The election of 1938 represented not a rejection of the New Deal, however, but a call to moderation in which the Democrats and Roosevelt suffered reverses even as the Republicans began to join them in a trend toward progressivism that would see the election of a Republican president 14 years later. 49 notes. Abridged from *Review of Politics* 1962 24(3): 525-562.   S

227.   Polenberg, Richard.   HISTORIANS AND THE LIBERAL PRESI-DENCY: RECENT APPRAISALS OF ROOSEVELT AND TRUMAN. *South Atlantic Q. 1976 75(1): 20-35.* Franklin D. Roosevelt and Harry S. Tru-man, usually praised by historians for their liberal achievements, have recently come under strong revisionist attacks. This revisionism is the combined result of access to previously classified manuscript materials, popularization of New Left attitudes, and disillusion with the presidency following Vietnam and Watergate. Revisionists find that neither president went far enough in reform attempts, especially in civil liberties. Methods used by Roosevelt and Truman to achieve policy goals severely compromised their success; for example, Truman is now seen as a defender of McCarthyism. Finally, their liberal goals are seen as sops to the masses while they shored up corporate capitalist elitism. While some concession to popularity is always due, some of these attacks amount to wishful thinking and hindsight. Based on secondary sources; 57 notes.
                                                      W. L. Olbrich

228.   Prindle, David F.   VOTER TURNOUT, CRITICAL ELECTIONS, AND THE NEW DEAL REALIGNMENT.   *Social Sci. Hist. 1979 3(2): 144-170.* Empirically tests "critical election" theory, using quantitative analysis of

material from Wisconsin, Pennsylvania, and the city of Pittsburgh, during the New Deal era. Democratic Party mobilization or increasing voter turnout was more important than party switching or voter realignment. No single election or sharply defined time period stands out as critical. Covers 1912-40. Based on local election returns, census data, voter registration lists, and other primary materials; 11 tables, 9 graphs. L. K. Blaser

229. Reiter, Howard L. THE PERILS OF PARTISAN RECALL. *Public Opinion Q. 1980 44(3): 385-388.* Questions the methodology in Kristi Andersen's "Generation, Partisan Shift, and Realignment: A Glance Back to the New Deal" in Norman H. Nie et al., *The Changing American Voter* (1976). Andersen's conclusion that there was no significant shift from Republican to Democratic affiliation in 1932 ignores the possibility that those whose affiliation changed may simply have forgotten that they were Republicans in the '20's. Illustrates this tendency using data—from Andersen's own source—on black and Jewish voters. Based on the University of Michigan's Survey Research Center surveys, 1952-72; 3 tables, note, 2 ref. L. Van Wyk

230. Ross, Hugh. JOHN L. LEWIS AND THE ELECTION OF 1940. *Labor Hist. 1976 17(2): 160-189.* The breach between John L. Lewis and Franklin D. Roosevelt in 1940 originated from domestic and foreign policy concerns. The struggle to organize the steel industry, and after 1938, business attempts to erode Walsh-Healy and the Fair Labor Standards Act provided the backdrop for the feud. But activities of Nazi agents, working through William Rhodes Davis, increased Lewis' suspicions of Roosevelt's foreign policy and were important in the decision to support Wendell Willkie. Based on correspondence, German foreign policy documents, and published sources; 63 notes. L. L. Athey

231. Ross, Irwin. FIFTEEN SECONDS OF TERROR. *Am. Hist. Illus. 1975 10(4): 10-13.* Discusses Giuseppi Zangara's attempted assassination of President-elect Franklin D. Roosevelt in Miami, Florida, in 1933.

232. Ruetten, Richard T. BURTON K. WHEELER AND THE MONTANA CONNECTION. *Montana 1977 27(3): 2-19.* Burton K. Wheeler (1882-1975) arrived in Butte, Montana, in 1905. His political views were a product of his Montana environment. He had a liberal bent and personally identified with the working man in opposition to the state's corporate influences, primarily the Anaconda Copper Company. Elected to the US Senate in 1922, Wheeler reflected his Montana experience. He opposed concentrated power, both public and private; worked to protect civil liberties; aided farmers and workers; and tried to help Indians. In 1930 Wheeler became an early supporter of Franklin D. Roosevelt for the Presidency, but he broke with Roosevelt over the Supreme Court issue in 1937, fearing concentrated power in the hands of the executive. Wheeler took a noninterventionist stance during 1939-41 and became more identified with conservatism. Always his own man, he did not represent his liberal constituents as much as he reflected them, their fears, and their aspirations. US involvement in World War II contributed to Wheeler's decline as a national political figure. He lost the Democratic primary in 1946 to liberal Leif Erickson and thus ironically preserved Montana's Democratic Party as a vehicle of the liberalism which he himself had constructed early in his career. Adapted from a 1976 lecture at Montana State University, Bozeman; 22 illus. R. C. Myers

233. Ryan, Halford Ross. ROOSEVELT'S FIRST INAUGURAL: A STUDY OF TECHNIQUE. *Q. J. of Speech 1979 65(2): 137-149.* In his first inaugural speech, Franklin D. Roosevelt (1882-1945) three times reworked a text by Raymond Moley. His changes tended to strengthen three major rhetorical devices: scapegoating, military metaphor, and a carrot-and-stick approach to Congress. His techniques parallel those of Hitler, but Roosevelt never sought the dictatorial power achieved by the German leader. Primary and secondary sources; 91 notes.   E. Bailey

234. Ryan, Thomas G. ETHNICITY IN THE 1940 PRESIDENTIAL ELECTION IN IOWA: A QUANTITATIVE APPROACH. *Ann. of Iowa 1977 43(8): 615-635.* After a statistical analysis of voting patterns in selected Iowa counties in 1936 and 1940, supports the traditional assumption of a large-scale defection of German American voters from Franklin D. Roosevelt. The data do not support, however, interpretations such as those of Robert E. Burke or Malcolm Moos which attribute Democratic losses between 1936 and 1940 to farm dissatisfaction, or the interpretations of Harold F. Gosnell or Warren Moscow which emphasize the general defection of Catholics from the Roosevelt coalition. Primary and secondary sources; 10 tables, 27 notes.   P. L. Petersen

235. Sanford, Dudley Gregory. YOU CAN'T GET THERE FROM HERE: THE PRESIDENTIAL BOOMLET FOR GOVERNOR GEORGE D. AIKEN, 1937-1939. *Vermont Hist. 1981 49(4): 197-208.* Six years after the Putney nurseryman entered politics, Aiken won national attention as a Republican who could be elected governor in the 1936 Democratic landslide. Aiken's "new Republicanism," formulated in *Speaking from Vermont* (1939), sought to win the votes of youth, labor, and small business by accepting more federal welfare without deficit spending and by fostering local "cooperation." The 1936 New England flood dramatized the need for regional flood control, and Aiken became the New England spokesman for one-purpose dams, leaving power and other rights to the states and private business. He campaigned outside Vermont, with the aid of Leo Casey, retiring publicity director of the Republican National Committee, less to win the 1940 presidential nomination than to rejuvenate the Republican Party as a bulwark against the New Deal flood control program. Based mainly on the Aiken Papers, University of Vermont; 30 notes.
                                                      T. D. S. Bassett

236. Sargent, James E. CLIFTON A. WOODRUM OF VIRGINIA: A SOUTHERN PROGRESSIVE IN CONGRESS, 1923-1945. *Virginia Mag. of Hist. and Biog. 1981 89(3): 341-364.* Chronicles the political career of independent Democrat from Roanoke, Clifton A. Woodrum, who came to public attention as a lawyer, popular singer and circuit judge. In 1922 he beat a lackluster incumbent congressman by means of a superior campaign organization and platform presence, and an appeal to upwardly mobile and younger men. Woodrum neither opposed nor embraced the Byrd organization. He supported Franklin D. Roosevelt in 1932, gained seniority, and by 1940 was an acknowledged expert on steering appropriation bills, particularly that for lend-lease. The later New Deal became too liberal and urbanized for Woodrum, and his influence declined. He was frustrated by Roosevelt's refusal to make him a federal judge, and by the long tenures of Carter Glass and Harry Byrd, which blocked advancement to the Senate. Woodrum retired in 1945. Based on Woodrum papers, *Congressional Record,* and interviews; 47 notes, illus.   P. J. Woehrmann

237. Schapsmeier, Edward L. and Schapsmeier, Frederick H. SCOTT W. LUCAS OF HAVANA: HIS RISE AND FALL AS MAJORITY LEADER IN THE UNITED STATES SENATE. *J. of the Illinois State Hist. Soc. 1977 70(4): 302-320.* Democrat Scott W. Lucas (1892-1968) used a homey style of politicking to win his first House seat in 1934 and Senate seat in 1938. His poor health and strong support of Truman's foreign policy made possible his defeat in 1950 by Everett M. Dirksen. Based on Lucas Papers; 18 illus., 67 notes. J

238. Schnell, J. Christopher. MISSOURI PROGRESSIVES AND THE NOMINATION OF F.D.R. *Missouri Hist. R. 1974 68(3): 269-279.* Reexamines the basis of support by Missouri Democratic delegates of Franklin D. Roosevelt for the presidential nomination in 1932. Many historians claim that the influence of Kansas City boss Thomas J. Pendergast swung Missouri support to Roosevelt. The support, however, was the result of efforts by a group of Wilsonian progressives, including many anti-Pendergast forces, led by Ewing Y. Mitchell, William Hirth, Judge Eldridge Dearing, and Louis Gualdoni. Pendergast had publicly supported the favorite son candidate, James A. Reed. The pro-Roosevelt group was well organized and had strong rural and "outstate" support. At the national convention the Missouri delegation increased its support of Roosevelt with each ballot, and all of the initial Missouri support came from these non-Pendergast forces. Based on contemporary newspaper reports, primary and secondary sources; 5 photos, 28 notes. N. J. Street

239. Schnell, J. Christopher. NEW DEAL SCANDALS: E. Y. MITCHELL AND F. D. R.'S COMMERCE DEPARTMENT. *Missouri Hist. R. 1975 69(4): 357-375.* Assistant Secretary of Commerce Ewing Young Mitchell worked to eliminate corruption and to streamline the four agencies under his direction to reduce waste and the number of political appointees. He ran afoul of the president when his investigations brought in some damning evidence against Boss Thomas J. Pendergast of Kansas City. Franklin D. Roosevelt was not a true Progressive. They had crusaded against big city machines, but FDR refused to support Mitchell's fight against one of his most productive allies. The same story was repeated in other cities where FDR sacrificed Progressive principles in favor of seeking aid from political machines. Based on primary and secondary sources; illus., 42 notes. W. F. Zornow

240. Shover, John L. THE EMERGENCE OF A TWO-PARTY SYSTEM IN REPUBLICAN PHILADELPHIA, 1924-1936. *J. of Am. Hist. 1974 60(4): 985-1002.* Samuel Lubell has popularized the thesis that Al Smith's ethnic appeal in the 1928 election foreshadowed the urban, ethnic, "New Deal coalition" that Franklin D. Roosevelt put together so effectively after 1932. The evidence for Philadelphia voting patterns demonstrates that 1928 was *not* a critical election. Some major ethnic groups did vote Democratic in that year, but Jews, blacks, and Germans were not a part of the coalition till much later, and the Irish and Italian vote, heavily Democratic for Smith in 1928, did not persist in 1930 or even 1932. Furthermore, there was no great surge of voter protest against the Depression in 1932. Casts doubt upon the concept of a "critical election," emphasizing rather the importance of a critical, fluctuating period when new voter patterns start to crystallize. 4 tables, 43 notes. K. B. West

241. Sinclair, Barbara Deckard. PARTY REALIGNMENT AND THE TRANSFORMATION OF THE POLITICAL AGENDA: THE HOUSE OF REPRESENTATIVES, 1925-1938. *Am. Pol. Sci. Rev. 1977 71(3): 940-953.* According to Walter Dean Burnham, party realignments "result in significant transformation in the general shape of policy." Through the analysis of House roll-call data, the New Deal realignment is examined to determine whether, in fact, a significant transformation took place and, if so, what its characteristics were. It was hypothesized that if a new political agenda emerged at that time, at least some of the stable policy dimensions which Aage Clausen finds as characterizing the modern Congress should have developed during the New Deal period. In terms of content and level of partisan voting evoked, the government management and the agricultural policy dimensions do take their modern form during the New Deal. A social welfare dimension developed but had not, by the late 1930s, taken its modern shape. It is argued that a major transformation of policy did take place and that, in the process, the ideological distance between the parties increased. This realignment, however, did not immediately change regional voting patterns within each party.   J

242. Singer, Donald L. UPTON SINCLAIR AND THE CALIFORNIA GUBERNATORIAL CAMPAIGN OF 1934. *Southern California Q. 1974 56(4): 375-406.* An account of the 1934 California gubernatorial campaign. Persuaded to change his affiliation from Socialist to Democrat, Upton Sinclair captured the party's nomination in a major primary victory. His End Poverty In California (EPIC) program, however, alarmed conservatives, although the Democrats modified and compromised it. Sinclair was smeared viciously; his only editorial support came from his own *EPIC News*, and almost all the state's newspapers denied him coverage. Not only Republicans but Communists feared his candidacy. He failed to receive endorsement from President Franklin Roosevelt, and his opponent, Governor Frank Merriam, let underlings carry on smear tactics. Having lost by some 250,000 votes, Sinclair attributed his defeat to defections by prominent Democrats, the smear campaign, and lack of newspaper coverage. Despite its defeat, the EPIC campaign indirectly helped turn the New Deal towards social welfare legislation, increased California's registration of Democrats, and gave budding Democratic leaders a boost in politics. Based on primary and secondary sources; 155 notes.   A. Hoffman

243. Skau, George H. FRANKLIN D. ROOSEVELT AND THE EXPANSION OF PRESIDENTIAL POWER. *Current Hist. 1974 66(394): 246-248, 274-275.* One of six articles in this issue on "The American Presidency."   S

244. Smith, Harold T. PITTMAN, CREEL, AND NEW DEAL POLITICS. *Nevada Hist. Soc. Q. 1979 22(4): 254-270.* Cecil Creel, a leading Nevada agricultural scientist, directed New Deal relief programs in Nevada until Frank Upman, Jr., replaced him in 1934. Although he was a competent administrator, Creel was ousted in response to demands of Nevada Senator Key Pittman (1872-1940). Pittman persuaded President Franklin Roosevelt and Harry Hopkins that Pittman's faction of Nevada Democrats should control New Deal relief work in the state. Based on primary materials in the National Archives and Franklin D. Roosevelt Library and newspaper sources; 50 notes.   H. T. Lovin

245. Snyder, Robert E. HUEY LONG AND THE PRESIDENTIAL ELEC-
TION OF 1936. *Louisiana Hist. 1975 16(2): 117-143.* The rise in popularity of
Huey Long's Share Our Wealth movement caused Franklin D. Roosevelt and his
supporters well-founded concern as the election of 1936 approached, not because
Long (1893-1935) had any chance of winning the presidency, but because his
candidacy could have given a strong Republican a better chance. Moreover,
Long's movement would have kept other pro-Roosevelt politicians from winning
office. Based on primary and secondary sources; 73 notes.   R. L. Woodward

246. Soapes, Thomas F. THE FRAGILITY OF THE ROOSEVELT COA-
LITION: THE CASE OF MISSOURI. *Missouri Hist. Rev. 1977 72(1): 38-58.*
Franklin D. Roosevelt's impressive electoral mandate in 1936 did not achieve
immediate permanence. In Missouri the Negroes, farmers, and workers were
weak links in the new Democratic alignment, as the Republican Party began to
revive during the 1940's. It was not until 1952 that the Democratic Party regained
most of the offices they lost in the 1940's. Republican leaders were only interested
in maintaining their power in the party, the party did not have a record to
compete with the Democrats, and the Republican areas of the state lost population. Roosevelt's fragile coalition had become a well-organized force by 1952.
Primary and secondary sources; illus., 45 notes.   W. F. Zornow

247. Spackman, S. G. F. ROOSEVELT. *Hist. Today [Great Britain] 1980
30 (June): 38-43.* Analyzes Franklin D. Roosevelt's policies from the 1920's to
his death in 1945 and concludes that he did much to create the modern presidency
and to make the diplomatic transition from the balance of power system to that
of the superpowers.

248. Spencer, Thomas T. "AS GOES MAINE, SO GOES VERMONT":
THE 1936 DEMOCRATIC CAMPAIGN IN VERMONT. *Vermont Hist.
1978 46(4): 234-243.* Republican control of Vermont relief programs, low Democratic Party campaign expenditures with little emphasis on FDR, a Republican
press, George D. Aiken's candidacy for governor, and a lively Republican campaign all resulted in a 19,000 plurality for Landon, compared to 23,000 for
Hoover in 1932. Based on Democratic National Committee correspondence and
on secondary sources; 35 notes.   T. D. S. Bassett

249. Spencer, Thomas T. AUXILIARY AND NON-PARTY POLITICS:
THE 1936 DEMOCRATIC PRESIDENTIAL CAMPAIGN IN OHIO.
Ohio Hist. 1981 90(2): 114-128. Discusses the 1936 presidential campaign in
Ohio, and the successful Democratic Party strategy of going outside the party to
attract voters by organizing auxiliary and nonparty committees. Especially important in appealing to labor, blacks, farmers, and women, Democratic auxiliary
committees such as the Non-Partisan Labor League, the Good Neighbor League,
and Roosevelt's All-Party Agricultural Committee helped to counter criticism of
the New Deal by attracting those voters with a vital stake in its success. Although
Democratic fears of losing the Midwestern states were exaggerated, the campaign
appeal of such organizations led to their becoming a "vital part of the Democratic
coalition in future elections." Based on the collections of the Franklin D. Roosevelt Library, Hyde Park, New York, the National Archives and Records Service,
the University of Iowa, and other primary sources; illus., 42 notes.
L. A. Russell

250.   Spencer, Thomas T.   BENNETT CHAMP CLARK AND THE 1936 PRESIDENTIAL CAMPAIGN.   *Missouri Hist. Rev. 1981 75(2): 197-213.* Clark won the Missouri senatorial election in 1932 without any help from the Democratic machine in Kansas City. His votes against New Deal bills often made him a thorn in President Franklin D. Roosevelt's side, but the president and party leaders recognized his ability and selected him for an important role in 1936. As chairman of the rules committee for the Democratic National Convention, Clark found his assignment to lead the fight against the two-thirds rule an easy one, since no strong support for the rule developed. His most challenging assignments were to deliver campaign speeches and to chair the Committee of One, an auxiliary organized to solicit support from individuals outside the regular party structure. Based on secondary sources, newspapers, James A. Farley Papers, Library of Congress, Frank Walker Papers, University of Notre Dame, Emil Hurja Papers and the Democratic National Committee Records, Franklin D. Roosevelt Library; illus., 37 notes.   W. F. Zornow

251.   Spencer, Thomas T.   THE GOOD NEIGHBOR LEAGUE COLORED COMMITTEE AND THE 1936 DEMOCRATIC PRESIDENTIAL CAMPAIGN.   *J. of Negro Hist. 1978 63(4): 307-316.* The Good Neighbor League Colored Committee, along with the Colored Voters Division of the Democratic Party, was a vital force in making Afro-Americans part of the Franklin D. Roosevelt coalition in 1936. Since 1936, blacks have continued to play an important part in Democratic campaigns. Based upon records in the Franklin D. Roosevelt Presidential Library; 32 notes.   N. G. Sapper

252.   Spencer, Thomas T.   "LABOR IS WITH ROOSEVELT": THE PENNSYLVANIA LABOR NON-PARTISAN LEAGUE AND THE ELECTION OF 1936.   *Pennsylvania Hist. 1979 46(1): 3-16.* In Pennsylvania, the Labor Non-Partisan League contributed much to Franklin D. Roosevelt's 1936 victory through its contributions, voter canvassing drives, and propaganda. Organized at the national level by John L. Lewis and Sidney Hillman, the league was comprised largely of C.I.O. unions and was intended to assure the president's reelection and function as a spokesman for liberalism. In 1943, it became the C.I.O.'s Political Action Committee. Based on the Pennsylvania Non-Partisan League Papers and other materials; 3 photos, 32 notes.   D. C. Swift

253.   Spencer, Thomas T.   THE NEW DEAL COMES TO THE "GRANITE STATE": THE 1936 DEMOCRATIC PRESIDENTIAL CAMPAIGN IN NEW HAMPSHIRE.   *Hist. New Hampshire 1980 35(2): 186-201.* Franklin D. Roosevelt surprised many political observers in defeating Alfred Landon in the 1936 presidential election in New Hampshire. Roosevelt's personal popularity and the success of New Deal relief and recovery programs probably account for the victory. The president carried only three of New Hampshire's 10 counties, but he carried populous Hillsborough County by more than 11,000 votes. Relief and recovery programs employed more than 9,000 workers in New Hampshire in the fall of 1936, mainly in urban areas. 34 notes.   D. F. Chard

254.   Spencer, Thomas T.   THE ROOSEVELT ALL-PARTY AGRICULTURAL COMMITTEE AND THE 1936 ELECTION.   *Ann. of Iowa 1979 45(1): 44-57.* Strategists for the Democratic Party in 1936 believed that the midwestern farm belt was crucial to Franklin D. Roosevelt's reelection bid. In

August 1936, the Franklin D. Roosevelt All-Party Agricultural Committee was formed. William Settle of Indiana was chairman. Other important members included Representative Marvin Jones of Texas, William Bradley of Iowa, and Paul Porter, chief of the Agricultural Adjustment Administration's press section. A study of the All-Party Agricultural Committee's activities in 1936 justifies several conclusions. First, Democratic leaders saw the farm vote as important and sought to bring farmers into the Roosevelt coalition. Second, the Committee was able to counter criticisms of New Deal agricultural policy. Finally, farmers were politically active in 1936 and many saw Roosevelt as their best hope for the future. 28 notes.   P. L. Petersen

255. Steele, Richard W. THE PULSE OF THE PEOPLE: FRANKLIN D. ROOSEVELT AND THE GAUGING OF AMERICAN PUBLIC OPINION. *J. of Contemporary Hist. [Great Britain] 1974 9(4): 195-216.* Franklin D. Roosevelt deliberately constructed and carefully maintained his channels to "those groups outside government whose attitudes at a given time might have a significant impact on his political plans." He monitored the press, used informants, encouraged the American people to write to him, and gathered intelligence from the Democratic National Committee and the State Directors of the Office of Government reports. He watched the opinion polls and studied analyses of them. He even established an Office of Facts and Figures for the sake of propaganda. All were utilized to great advantage during World War II. Primary sources; 37 notes.   M. P. Trauth

256. Stegh, Leslie J. A PARADOX OF PROHIBITION: ELECTION OF ROBERT J. BULKLEY AS SENATOR FROM OHIO, 1930. *Ohio Hist. 1974 83(3): 170-182.* Analyzes the impact of the repeal issue on the election of the "wet" Democrat Robert J. Bulkley to the US Senate from Ohio in 1930. Though repeal gained nationwide attention in the campaign, many other factors played a role in Bulkley's victory: the economy, the Hawley-Smoot tariff, agricultural relief, personalities, and other issues. Based on the Bulkley papers, newspapers, and journals; table, photo, 32 notes.   J. B. Street

257. Sternsher, Bernard. THE EMERGENCE OF THE NEW DEAL PARTY SYSTEM: A PROBLEM IN HISTORICAL ANALYSIS OF VOTER BEHAVIOR. *J. of Interdisciplinary Hist. 1975 6(1): 127-150.* Studies recent literature dealing with the transition from the "industrialized" political system of 1894-1932 to the "New Deal" political system from 1932 on. The concept of the 1928 election as a "critical" election is criticized both as a concept and with respect to the arguments used to support the concept. The "party-systems analytical framework" is open to several reservations. 4 graphs, 62 notes.
                                                                    R. Howell

258. Stevens, Susan. THE CONGRESSIONAL ELECTIONS OF 1930: POLITICS OF AVOIDANCE. Plesur, Milton, ed. *An American Historian: Essays to Honor Selig Adler* (Buffalo: State U. of N.Y., 1980): 149-158. Confusion over whether the Democrats or the Republicans would constitute the majority in the House of Representatives after the election of 1930 was compounded by a Republican insurgent faction, the prohibition problem, President Herbert C. Hoover, and the country's economic state, until 1931, when Democrat John Nance Garner was elected Speaker of the House.

259. Swain, Martha H.   THE LION AND THE FOX: THE RELATION-
SHIP OF PRESIDENT FRANKLIN D. ROOSEVELT AND SENATOR PAT
HARRISON.   *J. of Mississippi Hist. 1976 38(4): 333-359.* Describes the development (1928-37), cooling (1937-39), and renewal (1938-41) of the political
friendship of Franklin D. Roosevelt and Mississippi Democratic Senator Pat
Harrison, chairman of the powerful Committee on Finance. Harrison's problems
with Roosevelt stemmed partly from policy disagreements, especially on taxation,
and partly from the President's personality and methods. "In dealing with another master strategist . . . FDR often met his match." Based on primary sources,
especially newspapers and the papers of Harrison and Roosevelt; 67 notes.
                                                                  J. W. Hillje

260. Tarter, Brent.   A FLIER ON THE NATIONAL SCENE, HARRY F.
BYRD'S FAVORITE-SON PRESIDENTIAL CANDIDACY OF 1932.
Virginia Mag. of Hist. and Biog. 1974 82(3): 282-305. Former Virginia Governor
Harry F. Byrd ran as a favorite-son candidate for President in 1932, primarily
to consolidate his control over the Democratic political machinery in his state and
to prevent national issues, such as prohibition, from splitting his supporters.
Byrd's candidacy also reflected his suspicion of front runner Franklin D. Roose-
velt, and his participation in an anti-Roosevelt movement nearly succeeded.
Based on primary and secondary sources; cartoon, 44 notes.   R. F. Oaks

261. Valerina, A. F.   POLITICHESKAIA BOR'BA V SSHA V 1937G. VOK-
RUG PROEKTA REOFRMY VERKHOVNOGO SUDA   [The political
struggle in the United States in 1937 over the plan to reform the Supreme Court].
Vestnik Moskovskogo U., Seriia 8: Istoriia [USSR] 1978 (4): 36-54. President
Franklin D. Roosevelt's plan to reform the Supreme Court caused severe struggles in every stratum of American society and cast its shadow on the latter years
of the New Deal. The conservative majority in the Supreme Court, and the
conservatives in both parties in Congress, wished to prevent the federal government from interfering in state politics. Strengthened by an election victory in
1936, Roosevelt set about limiting the Court's powers. His proposals were not
unconstitutional, nor were they without precedent. Attacks on the reform were
based on conservative fears that it might just be the prelude to more radical
developments. Defeated, the President felt that he had won the war; however, a
neoconservatism was developing which was to have a great effect on American
politics after World War II. Based on the Congressional Record and on published
documents and secondary sources; 144 notes.   D. N. Collins

262. Waller, Robert A.   THE SELECTION OF HENRY T. RAINEY AS
SPEAKER OF THE HOUSE.   *Capitol Studies 1973 2(1): 37-47.*

263. Weiss, Stuart.   KENT KELLER, THE LIBERAL BLOC, AND THE
NEW DEAL.   *J. of the Illinois State Hist. Soc. 1975 68(2): 143-158.* Keller was
a stalwart member of the unofficial "liberal bloc" of Democrats, progressive
Republicans and independents in Congress during 1930-40. Representing
"Egypt," the 25th District in southern Illinois, he supported almost every item
of New Deal legislation that would benefit his coal-miner and small-farmer
constituents. Believing that public works projects would alleviate the mass unemployment in his area, he supported a scheme to provide cheap electric power for
his district through the construction by the federal government of a "little TVA"

on Crab Orchard Creek. By 1938 the liberal bloc had largely been dismantled in Congress and the defeat of Keller and other Congressmen in 1940 and 1942 marked the ascendancy of a conservative Congress hostile to the New Deal.

N. Lederer

264. Weiss, Stuart L. THOMAS AMLIE AND THE NEW DEAL. *Mid-Am. 1977 59(1): 19-38.* Sketches the political career of Thomas Amlie, US Representative from Wisconsin's First District. In 1931, Amlie began as a Republican; but he soon founded the Wisconsin Progressive Party and ended his career as a Democrat. During the 1930's he was an ardent New Dealer and proposed radical economic programs based on "production for use" and preserving "democratic values." His nomination to the Interstate Commerce Commission in 1939 was withdrawn at his own request because of conservative criticism from his home state. Amlie was a realistic liberal. Primary and secondary sources; 125 notes.

J. M. Lee

265. White, Mary. MARY WHITE: AUTOBIOGRAPHY OF AN OHIO FIRST LADY. *Ohio Hist. 1973 82(1/2): 63-87.* Widower George White became governor of Ohio in 1931 and his 24-year-old daughter Mary served as first lady. In 1958 she wrote a 58-page reminiscence about those years. The result was a personal view of the White administration. Mentions anecdotes about Coolidge and characterizations of Will Rogers, Eleanor Roosevelt, and other prominent figures. 9 illus.

S. S. Sprague

266. Winfield, Betty H. MRS. ROOSEVELT'S PRESS CONFERENCE ASSOCIATION: THE FIRST LADY SHINES A LIGHT. *Journalism Hist. 1981 8(2): 54-55, 63-70.* Discusses Eleanor Roosevelt's formation of the Press Conference Association and encouragement of women's press conferences, originally Associated Press reporter Lorena Hickok's idea, to help women reporters keep their jobs by writing about something besides society news during the Depression.

267. Winfield, Betty Houchin. F. D. R.'S PICTORIAL IMAGE, RULES AND BOUNDARIES. *Journalism Hist. 1978-79 5(4): 110-114.* Studies Franklin D. Roosevelt's photographic image during the 1930's, as it was controlled by certain rules and guidelines designed not to show his physical handicap.

268. Winfield, B. H. FRANKLIN D. ROOSEVELT'S EFFORTS TO INFLUENCE THE NEWS DURING HIS FIRST TERM PRESS CONFERENCES. *Presidential Studies Q. 1981 11(2): 189-199.* Examination of the record number of press conferences held during Franklin D. Roosevelt's first term as president, 1933-37, reveals specific tactics used to control information about himself and his administration. He used the press as a conduit for accurate information to the public and for making his assignment an important one. Roosevelt managed the flow of information by planting questions and also by his own personality. Even when the press became his adversary, he used it more than it abused him. This control shows one aspect of his great political skill. Primary sources; 115 notes.

A. Drysdale

269. Wolf, T. Phillip. BRONSON CUTTING AND FRANKLIN ROOSEVELT: FACTORS IN PRESIDENTIAL ENDORSEMENT. *New Mexico Hist. Rev. 1977 52(4): 317-334.* Roosevelt did not endorse the reelection of New Mexico's Bronson M. Cutting to the US Senate in 1934. Such liberal senators as

Hiram W. Johnson (California), George W. Norris (Nebraska), and Robert Marion La Follette, Jr. (Wisconsin), were endorsed by the President. Roosevelt did not endorse Cutting because Cutting did not endorse F. D. R. until two weeks before the election. Roosevelt and Cutting did not agree on veterans' benefits. The chief reason for Roosevelt's unwillingness to endorse Cutting was the weakness of the Democratic Party in New Mexico. 51 notes.   J. H. Krenkel

270. Wright, Gavin. THE POLITICAL ECONOMY OF NEW DEAL SPENDING: AN ECONOMETRIC ANALYSIS. *R. of Econ. and Statistics 1974 56(1): 30-38.* The allocation of money to the states by the federal government during the New Deal was often done to maximize electoral votes for the Democratic Party.   S

271. —. A FRANKLIN D. ROOSEVELT SYMPOSIUM: THREE PAPERS OBSERVING THE 100TH ANNIVERSARY OF HIS BIRTH. *Presidential Studies Q. 1982 12(1): 48-65.*
Roosevelt, James. STAFFING MY FATHER'S PRESIDENCY: A PERSONAL REMINISCENCE, *pp. 48-49.*
Helicher, Karl. THE EDUCATION OF FRANKLIN D. ROOSEVELT, *pp. 50-53.* Describes the formal education of Roosevelt, who viewed school as a means to an end and never an intense experience in itself. 17 notes.
Sheffer, Martin S. THE ATTORNEY GENERAL AND PRESIDENTIAL POWER: ROBERT H. JACKSON, FRANKLIN ROOSEVELT, AND THE PREROGATIVE PRESIDENCY, *pp. 54-65.* Franklin Roosevelt used Attorney General Robert H. Jackson to constitutionalize his presidential power. In three areas—the removal of members of the Tennessee Valley Authority, the acquisition of naval and air bases, and in the stressing of executive privilege—Jackson acted as a partisan advocate for the president. 83 notes.   D. H. Cline

3

RELIEF, REFORM, AND RECOVERY:
THE NEW DEAL PROGRAM

272. Amoruso, Vito. STATI UNITI: DIALETTICA DI UN'INTEGRAZ-IONE [The United States: The dialectic of an integration]. *Quaderni Storici [Italy] 1977 12(1): 173-195.* In *Dialectic of an Integration,* Vito Amoruso discusses the economic crisis of 1929. It has been a turning point for American society and the all capitalistic system. The New Deal mainly represents, with all its contradictions, a way of getting out of the crisis with capitalistic means, that is a planned economy, an integration of the workers within this capitalistic framework and planning. A deep change intervenes in the relationship between intellectual and American society. Many intellectuals with liberal, radical background became Marxists or faced the problems of socialism as an answer to the violent contradictions of a capitalistic society. But their critical attitude to the New Deal, even when it stands from a Marxist social analysis, is still deeply rooted in their progressive background with all its limits. Therefore their intellectual political role comes to an end exactly during the New Deal era.   J

273. Annunziata, Frank. THE PROGRESSIVE AS CONSERVATIVE: GEORGE CREEL'S QUARREL WITH NEW DEAL LIBERALISM. *Wisconsin Mag. of Hist. 1974 57(3): 220-233.* George Creel (1876-1953) was a progressive Democrat long before his appointment as chairman of the Committee on Public Information during World War I, and he remained an important progressive well into the New Deal. Although an early advocate of Roosevelt and the New Deal, (in his post as chairman of the National Advisory Board, Works Progress Administration), Creel turned passionately against both during the war years 1940-45. The causes of that change in attitude included his resentment of certain advisors close to Roosevelt, his failure to win an important administrative post during the war, and the death of his first wife. Ideologically, he felt that the New Deal, by moving to create a welfare state that accommodated demands of organized interest groups, had abandoned the major tenets "of the neutral regulatory progressive state." He then called unsuccessfully for a conservative coalition of southern Democrats and Republicans to reverse the trend, and he was disappointed with the policies of both Presidents Truman and Eisenhower. 3 photos, 61 notes.   N. C. Burckel

274.   Argersinger, Jo Ann E.   ASSISTING THE "LOAFERS": TRANSIENT
RELIEF IN BALTIMORE, 1933-1937.   *Labor Hist. 1982 23(2): 226-245.* The
sympathy of relief workers combined with the assumption of responsibility for
transient relief by the federal government in 1933 encouraged transients in Baltimore, Maryland, "to organize and bargain with local and national officials in an
attempt to receive better treatment, substantive work relief, and improved assistance." The Marine Workers' Industrial Union was especially active in trying to
secure improved relief for Baltimore's unemployed seamen. The return of transient relief programs to local officials in 1935 meant a return to inadequate and
indifferent assistance. Based on Federal Emergency Relief Administration, State
File records and other primary sources; 49 notes.   L. F. Velicer

275.   Armbrester, Margaret E.   JOHN TEMPLE GRAVES II: A SOUTH-
ERN LIBERAL VIEWS THE NEW DEAL.   *Alabama Rev. 1979 32(3): 203-
213.* John Temple Graves II (1892-1961), syndicated columnist with the Palm
Beach *Times,* warmly supported the New Deal until President Franklin D.
Roosevelt proposed Supreme Court reorganization and Congress passed the Fair
Labor Standards Act. Graves's support cooled thereafter, chiefly on grounds of
Wilsonian idealism, southern self-interest, and states' rights. Primary and second-
ary sources; 39 notes.   J. F. Vivian

276.   Avery, Inda.   SOME SOUTH DAKOTANS' OPINIONS ABOUT THE
NEW DEAL.   *South Dakota Hist. 1977 7(3): 309-324.* Traces South Dakota's
economy during the Great Depression, and discusses responses to a 14-point
questionnaire about the hardships and attitudes about New Deal relief policies.
South Dakotans share in a "western split personality:" they boast of individualis-
tic self-sufficiency and vote conservatively in local elections, yet they send liberals
to Congress and readily accept welfare from the national level. Notes reluctance
to admit accepting relief along with the admission that their friends do. 164
persons in 55 counties responded to 500 questionnaires. 3 photos, 8 notes, appendix.   A. J. Larson

277.   Babu, B. Ramesh.   UNEMPLOYMENT INSURANCE IN THE
UNITED STATES: AN ANALYSIS OF THE BEGINNING.   *J. of the U. of
Bombay [India] 1975-76 44-45(80-81): 139-172.* The Social Security Act (US,
1935), which provided for unemployment insurance, was part of Franklin D.
Roosevelt's second New Deal. Although intended to counter criticism from the
left, the Act was in fact a middle-of-the-road policy. It was preceded in 1934 by
two attempts at unemployment insurance which failed to secure Congressional
approval: the Wagner-Lewis Bill, intended to encourage the states to provide
benefits, and the Lundeen Bill, which proposed coverage for persons who had
been unable to secure employment for a minimum period. The Committee on
Economic Security, appointed in 1934 to advise Roosevelt on social security,
placed more emphasis on job creation than on unemployment insurance. They
recommended a federal-state system based on tax credits. The Social Security
Act, based on their recommendations but modified somewhat by the House of
Representatives and the Senate, became law on 14 August 1935. Although the
unemployment insurance provisions, criticized by the left and the right, were less
impressive than some of its others, the Act as a whole was a major development
in the evolution of the United States as a welfare state. Published government
documents, contemporary newspapers and journals and secondary works; 87
notes.   J. F. Hilliker

278. Banks, Ann. TOBACCO TALK. *Southern Exposure 1980 8(4): 34-45.* Describes the Federal Writers' Project, part of the New Deal's national work relief program, focusing on four brief accounts from the FWP tobacco study on tobacco farming during the 1930's.

279. Barnard, Harry V. and Best, John H. GROWING FEDERAL IN-VOLVEMENT IN AMERICAN EDUCATION, 1918-1945. *Current Hist. 1972 32(370): 290-292, 308.* Emphasizes economic policy and youth programs of the Roosevelt administrations.

280. Baskerville, Stephen W. FRANKFURTER, KEYNES AND THE FIGHT FOR PUBLIC WORKS, 1932-1935. *Maryland Hist. 1978 9(1): 1-16.* Summarizes the campaign led by Felix Frankfurter and assisted by John Maynard Keynes to influence New Deal decisions on public works and other policies. The ideas of Keynes were injected into policy because of the constant efforts of Frankfurter and Keynes's willingness to market them in the press and other public forums. Based on correspondence and secondary sources; photo, 58 notes.
G. O. Gagnon

281. Bauman, John F. BLACK SLUMS/BLACK PROJECTS: THE NEW DEAL AND NEGRO HOUSING IN PHILADELPHIA. *Pennsylvania Hist. 1974 41(3): 311-338.* The first two New Deal housing projects in Philadelphia were restricted to whites despite the fact that black housing conditions in the city were deplorable. The Philadelphia chapter of the National Negro Congress and the Tenants League led efforts to assure that future federal housing would be used to help Philadelphia Negroes. The fact that black votes had contributed to Democratic victories in Philadelphia was not lost upon New Deal policymakers, and federal funds made available through the Wagner-Steagall Act of 1938, built two housing projects for blacks. Notes that the projects were developed in such a way as to limit the expansion of black neighborhoods and reinforce segregation patterns. Based on Housing Division Records, Housing Association Papers, government reports and other materials; 2 illus., 31 notes.
D. C. Swift

282. Bauman, John F. SAFE AND SANITARY WITHOUT THE COSTLY FRILLS: THE EVOLUTION OF PUBLIC HOUSING IN PHILADELPHIA, 1929-1941. *Pennsylvania Mag. of Hist. and Biog. 1977 101(1): 114-128.* Traces the development of public housing in Philadelphia. The early impetus split between practical bureaucrats and persons who envisioned revivification of the community. The latter group weakened as money poured in from Washington, D.C. The bureaucrats had their way, constructed unimaginative structures, and were concerned only with minimum standards of health and sanitation. What finally developed was new slums inhabited by persons not really in need of them. Eliminating frills also eliminated pride and character. 37 notes. V. L. Human

283. Beasley, Maurine. LORENA A. HICKOK: WOMAN JOURNALIST. *Journalism Hist. 1980 7(3-4): 92-95, 113.* Journalist Lorena A. Hickok (1893-1968) investigated nationwide relief programs, then prepared reports for the Roosevelt administration, 1933-36.

284. Beasley, Maurine Hoffman. LORENA HICKOK TO HARRY HOP-KINS, 1933: A WOMAN REPORTER VIEWS PRAIRIE HARD TIMES. *Montana 1982 32(2): 58-66.* Reporter Lorena A. Hickok, the chief investigator

for the Federal Emergency Relief Administration (FERA), toured rural Minnesota, North and South Dakota, Nebraska, and Iowa during 1933. She wrote regularly to Eleanor Roosevelt and FERA chief, Harry Hopkins, on the agricultural, economic, social, and political situations she observed. Excerpts from the reports are reprinted along with biographical information on Hickok. Based on the Lorena Hickok and Harry Hopkins papers in the Franklin D. Roosevelt Library, Hyde Park, New York; 5 illus., 56 notes.   R. C. Myers

285.   Beezer, Bruce G.   ARTHURDALE: AN EXPERIMENT IN COMMUNITY EDUCATION.   *West Virginia Hist. 1974 36(1): 17-36.* The Arthurdale community was a New Deal experiment in rural homesteading which resettled 200 poor West Virginia coal mining families. Run by a succession of government agencies in the 1930's and with the heavy unofficial involvement of Eleanor Roosevelt, Arthurdale cost far more than expected and failed chiefly because there was no industry located there to provide permanent jobs. The Arthurdale school, run by Elsie Ripley Clapp, tried with some limited success to apply John Dewey's educational ideas about community-oriented schooling. Based on Clapp's own account and contemporary articles; 76 notes.   J. H. Broussard

286.   Benjamin, Jules R.   THE NEW DEAL, CUBA, AND THE RISE OF A GLOBAL FOREIGN ECONOMIC POLICY.   *Business Hist. Rev. 1977 51(1): 57-78.* Revises the conventional thesis that isolationism characterized early New Deal foreign policy. US involvement in Cuba increased during this period, and this helped to establish precedents for the global outlook of American policy in the 1940's and beyond. The new policy was especially visible in the use of the Reconstruction Finance Corporation and the Export-Import Bank to promote American interests. Based on State Department and other US governmental records; 39 notes.   C. J. Pusateri

287.   Benston, George J.   REQUIRED DISCLOSURE AND THE STOCK MARKET: AN EVALUATION OF THE SECURITIES EXCHANGE ACT OF 1934.   *Am. Econ. R. 1973 63(1): 132-155.* The Securities Exchange Act of 1934 "was one of the earliest, and, some believe, one of the most successful laws enacted by the New Deal." However, a statistical analysis and testing of the effects of the act on the stock market raises questions. Concludes: "The disclosure requirements had no measurable positive effect on the securities traded on the New York Stock Exchange. There appears to have been little basis for the legislation and no evidence that it was needed or desirable. Certainly there is doubt that more required disclosure is warranted." 5 tables, 3 figs., 27 notes, biblio.   R. V. Ritter

288.   Berens, John F.   THE FBI AND CIVIL LIBERTIES FROM FRANKLIN ROOSEVELT TO JIMMY CARTER: AN HISTORICAL OVERVIEW.   *Michigan Academician 1980 13(2): 131-144.* The history of the Federal Bureau of Investigation since the presidency of Franklin D. Roosevelt, whose mandates in 1936 and 1939 "opened the door to massive FBI surveillance of Americans who deviated from the established and normal politics of the day," has adequately shown the dangers to individual civil liberties of the FBI's programs.

289. Bernstein, Irving. PUBLIC POLICY AND THE AMERICAN WORKER, 1933-45. *Monthly Labor Rev. 1976 99(10): 11-17.* Focuses on the effect of the New Deal in guaranteeing workers the right of collective bargaining, thereby increasing membership in unions over the period 1933-45.

290. Billington, Monroe. THE ALABAMA CLERGY AND THE NEW DEAL. *Alabama Rev. 1979 32(3): 214-225.* Quantitative analysis of 327 Alabama clergy who responded to President Franklin D. Roosevelt's special query of September 1935. More than three-fourths supported the New Deal, notably for pragmatic rather than ideological reasons. Contradictions also were evident, chiefly between desired social services and disliked higher taxes. Primary and secondary sources; tables, 10 notes. J. F. Vivian

291. Billington, Monroe and Clark, Cal. THE MASSACHUSETTS CLERGY AND THE NEW DEAL. *Hist. J. of Massachusetts 1980 8(2): 12-29.* Analyzes the response of 363 Massachusetts clergymen to a letter from President Franklin D. Roosevelt in 1935 asking their advice on social problems. The clergymen were generally favorable to the New Deal, especially its relief programs. Manuscript letters in Franklin D. Roosevelt Library and secondary sources; 6 tables, 14 notes. W. H. Mulligan, Jr.

292. Birch, Eugenie Ladner. WOMAN-MADE AMERICA: THE CASE OF EARLY PUBLIC HOUSING POLICY. *J. of the Am. Inst. of Planners 1978 44(2): 130-144.* The 1937 Wagner-Steagall Act provided for the first permanent public housing program subsidized by the federal government. Although immediate economic conditions caused by the Depression provided the direct impetus for its passage, a painstakingly constructed intellectual background and grassroots political support created the climate for its acceptance. This atmosphere was the product of the work of many housing reformers. However, two women, Edith Elmer Wood and Catherine Bauer, stand out as leaders having the most significant impact on the formulation of the new policy. As women, they contributed two major facets to it: the recognition of the need for government construction of dwellings when the private sector did not build; the demand that publicly constructed homes be positively supportive of family life. J

293. Black, Wilfred W. AMERICA'S CONTRIBUTION OF STATE CAPITALISM. *Social Studies 1973 64(6): 266-270.* During the New Deal, the federal government, under Franklin D. Roosevelt, instituted welfare measures to help alleviate conditions produced by world depression. Such measures are America's contribution to "state capitalism." L. R. Raife

294. Blanchard, Margaret A. PRESS CRITICISM AND NATIONAL REFORM MOVEMENTS: THE PROGRESSIVE ERA AND THE NEW DEAL. *Journalism Hist. 1978 5(2): 33-37, 54-55.* Critics of the press supported the Progressive ideology of reform from within, 1890's-1920's, but during the New Deal belief that the press had subsumed journalistic ethics to economic gain led to reform moves sponsored by the federal government.

295. Blaynery, Michael S. "LIBRARIES FOR THE MILLIONS": ADULT PUBLIC LIBRARY SERVICES AND THE NEW DEAL. *J. of Lib. Hist. 1977 12(3): 235-249.* New Deal library programs created jobs for many white-collar workers and helped put culture back into the everyday life of the working

people. New Deal library projects were initiated through expanded public library services in adult education and rural extension. These changes had a lasting impact on the library profession. Based on primary and secondary sources; 37 notes.   A. C. Dewees

296. Braeman, John. THE HISTORIAN AS ACTIVIST: CHARLES A. BEARD AND THE NEW DEAL. *South Atlantic Q. 1980 79(4): 364-374.* American historian Charles A. Beard supported the first two administrations of Franklin D. Roosevelt, despite occasional trepidation. But when Roosevelt geared up for the 1940 campaign, Beard scathingly denounced the New Deal's failures. Long before Pearl Harbor he predicted that Roosevelt was determined to bring the United States into war with Hitler, either directly or by provoking a war with Japan. Beard's growing disillusionment with the New Deal roughly paralleled that of many liberal intellectuals. Even his commitment to isolationism was typical. What distinguished Beard was the depth and intensity of his bitterness. Based on the Beard File (microfilm), DePauw University Archives; the Roosevelt Papers, Franklin D. Roosevelt Library; Beard's letters and writings, and secondary materials; 26 notes.   H. M. Parker, Jr.

297. Branscome, James. THE TVA: IT AIN'T WHAT IT USED TO BE. *Am. Heritage 1977 28(2): 68-78.* Sketches the history of the Tennessee Valley Authority (TVA) from 1824, when John Calhoun first proposed it, to the present. Development of nitrate production facilities at Muscle Shoals, Alabama began in 1917. Attempts to dispose of this facility led to efforts by Senator George Norris and others to create the TVA in order to conserve natural resources and provide electric power. Success came in 1933, but the agency has been beset by critics ever since. Major contributions to the war effort in World War II helped silence many of them. Now critics question the agency's atomic plans, coal usage, and other aspects while the agency continues to serve a seven-state area in the South. 10 illus.   J. F. Paul

298. Bremer, William W. ALONG THE "AMERICAN WAY": THE NEW DEAL'S WORK RELIEF PROGRAMS FOR THE UNEMPLOYED. *J. of Am. Hist. 1975 62(3): 636-652.* Describes the ideal of a constructive and psychologically supportive work relief program formulated by New Deal administrators and social workers, including Harry Hopkins, William Matthews, and Homer Folks, and its partial and temporary implementation in the Civil Works Administration of 1933-34. Political and budgetary pressures soon ended the CWA experiment. Instead, more traditional relief practices were adopted which kept work relief less attractive than private employment and retained the animus of charity. New Dealers did not view work relief as a permanent policy which guaranteed a "right to work." Based on collected papers, journals, and secondary works; 70 notes.   J. B. Street

299. Brinkley, Alan. THE NEW DEAL: PRELUDE. *Wilson Q. 1982 6(2): 50-61.* Discusses reform traditions during 1900-33, which influenced Franklin D. Roosevelt's New Deal policies.

300. Bromert, Roger. THE SIOUX AND THE INDIAN-CCC. *South Dakota Hist. 1978 8(4): 340-356.* Studies measures taken to improve the condition of Indians, economically, educationally, and in health. The special Civilian Con-

servation Corps (Indian Divison) programs were very popular with the Sioux Indians, 1933-42. The projects significantly helped the reservations by way of road building, dams, reclamation projects, etc., in addition to the value to the Indians personally. The educational values incidental to carrying out the other projects were of major consequence. 7 photos, 38 notes.   R. V. Ritter

301.   Brown, D. Clayton.   HEN EGGS TO KILOWATTS: ARKANSAS RURAL ELECTRIFICATION. *Red River Valley Hist. Rev. 1978 3(1): 119-125.* Details cooperation between the Arkansas Light and Power Company and the Rural Electrification Administration, 1933-40.

302.   Brown, D. Clayton.   NORTH CAROLINA RURAL ELECTRIFICATION: PRECEDENT OF THE REA. *North Carolina Hist. Rev. 1982 59(2): 109-124.* During 1917-36, the North Carolina state government promoted rural electrification for agricultural residents. Among the leaders of this movement were Eugene C. Branson, professor of Rural Social Economics at the University of North Carolina, and Clarence H. Poe, editor of the popular journal, the *Progressive Farmer.* As the first state to attempt to initiate its own program, North Carolina set a precedent for, and effectively prodded the Roosevelt administration into, establishing the Rural Electrification Administration in 1935. Also, Branson's efforts publicized the necessity of electrification for modern farm life and politicized the issue. Based on REA documents, governors' and presidents' papers, and personal papers in the National and North Carolina State archives, newpapers and farm journal articles, and published government documents; 3 illus., 7 photos, 38 notes.   T. L. Savitt

303.   Brown, Lorraine.   FEDERAL THEATRE: MELODRAMA, SOCIAL PROTEST, AND GENIUS. *Q. J. of the Lib. of Congress 1979 36(1): 18-37.* Recounts the history of the Federal Theatre Project of the Works Progress Administration from its establishment in 1935 until its demise in 1939. Implemented by Harry L. Hopkins, director of the WPA, and directed by Hallie Flanagan, the Federal Theatre Project was begun to relieve unemployed theater people during the depression. Theatre centers nationwide produced a wide variety of plays independently and simultaneously, including works by Sinclair Lewis, George Bernard Shaw, and Eugene O'Neill. The Federal Theatre Project produced both regional and national projects and struggled against censorship and cuts in funds for four years before it was ended for political reasons. Based on the Federal Theatre Project Collection at the Library of Congress; 15 photos, 39 notes.   A. R. Souby

304.   Brown, Lorraine.   A STORY YET TO BE TOLD: THE FEDERAL THEATRE RESEARCH PROJECT. *Black Scholar 1979 10(10): 70-78.* Traces the history of early black theater in the United States since 1921, when the Charles Gilpin Players of Hartford were formed. Focuses on the Federal Theatre Project, a division of the Works Progress Administration established during the 1930's under the Roosevelt administration; briefly discusses the records of the Federal Theatre Project since World War II, particularly during the 1970's, when the records were rediscovered.

305. Brown, Richard C. MARK SULLIVAN VIEWS THE NEW DEAL FROM AVONDALE. *Pennsylvania Mag. of Hist. and Biog. 1975 99(3): 351-361.* Mark Sullivan, a widely read syndicated political columnist, felt that New Deal principles were a threat to the peaceful way of life epitomized by his farm at Avondale, Pennsylvania. An early supporter of Franklin D. Roosevelt, Sullivan became a cautious critic of the president's. By the end of Roosevelt's first term he felt there were "serious flaws in Roosevelt's character and performance." 39 notes.   C. W. Olson

306. Bryan, Frank M. and Bruno, Kenneth. BLACK-TOPPING THE GREEN MOUNTAINS: SOCIO-ECONOMIC AND POLITICAL CORRE-LATES OF ECOLOGICAL DECISION-MAKING. *Vermont Hist. 1973 41(4): 224-235.* The 1935 federal proposal for a Green Mountain Parkway, though defeated in the Vermont House, was approved for referendum; but it was defeated by a majority of 58 percent. Statistical manipulation of socioeconomic variables and both House votes and the referendum shows that Vermonters voted according to party affiliation. 3 tables, 18 notes.   T. D. S. Bassett

307. Buerki, Robert A. THE GEORGE-DEEN ACT OF 1936 AND THE "WISCONSIN PLAN." *Pharmacy in Hist. 1981 23(1): 17-34.* Discusses the George-Deen Act (US, 1936) which provided federal assistance to the states for the vocational education of distributive workers and sales personnel, including community pharmacists and their employees. The extensive Wisconsin Plan, developed by Wisconsin State Board of Pharmacy Secretary Sylvester H. Dretzka and member Edwin J. Boberg, served as the model of distributive education programs for practicing pharmacists after 1938. During the early 1940's, the major pharmaceutical associations stimulated the expansion of federally funded distributive pharmaceutical education. World War II adversely affected these programs, except for the flourishing Wisconsin Plan. The retrogressive George-Barden Act (US, 1946) which excluded practicing pharmacists from distributive pharmacy education, the withdrawal of pharmaceutical organizations' support, pharmacy schools' reluctance to use federal funds for continuing pharmaceutical education and their inability to provide qualified and challenging instructors, and the protracted controversy between pharmacists and educators over "the primacy of business or of professional motives," in pharmaceutical services delivery con-tributed to the demise of these distributive programs by 1949. Presented to AIHP, April, 1979. Photo, 63 notes.   S. C. Morrison

308. Bulkeley, Peter B. AGRARIAN CRISIS IN WESTERN NEW YORK: NEW DEAL REINFORCEMENT OF THE FARM DEPRESSION. *New York Hist. 1978 59(4): 391-407.* Examines the effect of New Deal farm policy on Allegany, Cattaraugus, and Chautauqua counties during 1934, and concludes that the policies of the Agricultural Adjustment Administration prolonged the agricultural depression in those counties. The problem in western New York was not a farm surplus but oligopoly in the field of distribution. The AAA's response to the problem was to stress urban consumption rather than restoration of the farmers' purchasing power. The AAA benefited the large commodity farms in the south and west rather than the small, diversified farms that prevailed in western New York. 5 tables, 7 illus., 54 notes.   R. N. Lokken

309. Burran, James A. THE WPA IN NASHVILLE, 1935-1943. *Tennessee Hist. Q. 1974 34(3): 293-306.* With the creation of the Works Progress Administration in Tennessee in 1935 Colonel Harry S. Berry was named administrator. First priority was given to construction, but service projects received considerable support. With the steady growth of projects, however, charges of misuse of money and power grew. Rumors of boondoggling led to a 1939 investigation which revealed numerous irregularities. Nevertheless, the WPA in Nashville no doubt did the best that might have been expected given the bureaucracy. Primary and secondary sources; 35 notes.   M. B. Lucas

310. Bystryn, Marcia N. VARIATION IN ARTISTIC CIRCLES. *Sociol. Q. 1981 22(1): 119-132.* Discusses the variation in artistic circles including what types of interests bring artists together, the types of structures they congregate around, and the types of linkages between different circles, based on data from the Works Progress Administration in the late 1930's and early 1940's, specifically the American Artists' Congress, the American Abstract Artists, and surrealism.

311. Carlisle, Rodney P. WILLIAM RANDOLPH HEARST: A FASCIST REPUTATION RECONSIDERED. *Journalism Q. 1973 50(1): 125-133.* There was little change in the Progressivism of William Randolph Hearst during the New Deal—his break with Roosevelt was a consequence of the 1935 Wealth Tax.
                                                                                  S

312. Carlson, Paul H. and Porter, Steve. SOUTH DAKOTA CONGRESSMEN AND THE HUNDRED DAYS OF THE NEW DEAL. *South Dakota Hist. 1978 8(4); 327-339.* The Congress convened in special session on 9 March 1933, on call of the newly elected president, Franklin D. Roosevelt, to face the problems of national depression. The Congress included four South Dakotans, the two senators, Peter Norbeck and William J. Bullow, and two first-term legislators, Fred Hildebrandt and Theodore B. Werner. They supported the president in most of his New Deal legislation, though with a few exceptions. Much of the legislation was of special value for South Dakota's severe problems. 4 photos, 40 notes.   R. V. Ritter

313. Carlson, Robert. O. LEONARD ORVEDAL—BISMARCK. *North Dakota Hist. 1977 44(4): 69-72.* Interviews educator, public servant, and FSA official O. Leonard Orvedal. The Resettlement Administraion of the Farm Security Administration in North Dakota during the 1930's dealt mainly with farm families and their rehabilitation and relief. At one time more than 46,000 grant checks were being delivered regularly to needy North Dakota farmers. The state was divided into districts which each had a committee who voted on the relief eligibility of their neighbors. The system worked well.   N. Lederer

314. Carroll, Eugene T. JOHN B. KENDRICK'S FIGHT FOR WESTERN WATER LEGISLATION, 1917-1933. *Ann. of Wyoming 1978 50(2): 319-333.* Wyoming governor and senator John B. Kendrick struggled for 23 years to establish a comprehensive water policy for his and surrounding states. His special concern was the North Platte River, whose waters were essential to agriculture, ranching, and urbanization on the central Plains. When President Franklin D. Roosevelt approved the Casper-Alcova project in 1935, it was the culmination of

Kendrick's career, but the project did not drastically expand Wyoming's economic growth. Based on Kendrick Papers at University of Wyoming; photo, 48 notes.   M. L. Tate

315.   Cassity, Michael J.   HUEY LONG: BAROMETER OF REFORM IN THE NEW DEAL.   *South Atlantic Q. 1973 72(2): 255-269.* "In his criticism of the New Deal, Long focused on what appeared to be a centralization of wealth and power." He assailed the establishment of regulatory commissions under the NRA as a reversal of the intent of the antitrust legislation. He contended that this sort of legislation removed public control, thus threatening democracy. In agriculture the New Deal did not respond to the needs of small farmers. Instead of the Civilian Conservation Corps he proposed giving young men an education. "Instead of widening the chasm between the very rich and the very poor he proposed to limit the depths to which a person could fall and to put a maximum on the profits he could accumulate." He was an eloquent spokesman for the progressive tradition of reform. 54 notes.   E. P. Stickney

316.   Christie, Jean.   NEW DEAL RESOURCES PLANNING: THE PROPOSALS OF MORRIS L. COOKE.   *Agric. Hist. 1979 53(3): 597-606.* Morris L. Cooke, independently wealthy former advisor to Pennsylvania Governor Gifford Pinchot, served as head of a number of New Deal agencies dealing with land and water conservation. Cooke's approach to conservation was a regional one. He believed in the watershed and river valley as the smallest division of a conservation unit. Cooke served with the Rural Electrification Administration and other government agencies until the era of conservation reform ended under President Harry S. Truman, who was preoccupied with the Korean War. Primary and secondary sources; 23 notes.   R. T. Fulton

317.   Clawson, Marion.   RESETTLEMENT EXPERIENCE ON NINE SELECTED RESETTLEMENT PROJECTS.   *Agric. Hist. 1978 52(1): 1-92.* A report by the author in 1943 on the progress of nine resettlement projects of the Farm Security Administration. Prepared for the Bureau of Agricultural Economics, US Department of Agriculture, the report was to have been used to help plan the Columbia Basin irrigation project but was never published. The nine projects studied included both irrigated and nonirrigated lands, and both individual and cooperative farms. Nearly all were failures. Resettled farmers improved their economic conditions somewhat, but their incomes and net worth remained below expectation. Average farm sizes were too small and supervision inadequate; settlers felt frustrated and many left. Includes recommendations for future resettlement projects. 10 tables, 6 notes.   D. E. Bowers

318.   Clayton, Ronnie W.   FEDERAL WRITERS' PROJECT FOR BLACKS IN LOUISIANA.   *Louisiana Hist. 1978 19(3): 327-335.* On the initiative of Lyle Saxon, the director of the Louisiana Federal Writers' Project, a black writers' project was formed at Dillard University in New Orleans for the purpose of writing a Negro history in Louisiana. The information they gathered was included in the publications of the Louisiana Writers' Project, guidebooks for Louisiana and New Orleans, and, more especially, in the folkloric *Gumbo Ya-Ya* (Boston, 1945). The Dillard group's projected Negro history, however, differed markedly from the interpretation of Louisiana's past as found in *Gumbo Ya-Ya,* but it was never published, despite Saxon's efforts. The records were deposited

at Dillard University, but they have since disappeared, only the outline and prospectus being preserved in the Saxon papers at Tulane University, on which this article is based. 34 notes. R. L. Woodward, Jr.

319. Collins, Robert M. POSITIVE BUSINESS RESPONSES TO THE NEW DEAL: THE ROOTS OF THE COMMITTEE FOR ECONOMIC DEVELOPMENT, 1933-1942. *Business Hist. Rev. 1978 52(3): 369-391.* Argues that previous scholars have not sufficiently noted the efforts of business elements that attempted to arrange a detente with the Roosevelt administration during the 1930's. One expression of this effort was the government's Business Advisory Council, a second was those businessmen who came to embrace the Keynesian solution of deficit spending, and a third spawned from academic-business dialogues initiated at the University of Chicago in 1936. All three of these sources played a role in the eventual formation of the Committee for Economic Development in 1942. The establishment of the CED was essentially the product of long-developing trend toward business-government collaboration begun years before. Based on private papers and published business periodicals; 90 notes. C. J. Pusateri

320. Coode, Thomas H. and Fabbri, Dennis E. THE NEW DEAL'S ARTHURDALE PROJECT IN WEST VIRGINIA. *West Virginia Hist. 1975 36(4): 291-308.* Arthurdale was the first self-help project funded under the National Industrial Recovery Act's Subsistence Homesteads Program to resettle unemployed miners on subsistence farms. Families were selected only after thorough investigation, and only native whites were allowed. From the beginning, Arthurdale suffered from mismanagement, delays, and cost overruns. Mrs. Eleanor Roosevelt and Louis Howe, though having no official connection with the project, intervened continually. Plans to attract industry never worked out, and cooperative farming failed also. Arthurdale was the most publicized project in the country and was extremely controversial. Finally, the goverment sold off the houses during World War II at a great loss. Based on Bushrod Grimes MSS and other primary sources; 49 notes. J. H. Broussard

321. Culbert, David H. THE INFINITE VARIETY OF MASS EXPERIENCE: THE GREAT DEPRESSION, W.P.A. INTERVIEWS, AND STUDENT FAMILY HISTORY PROJECTS. *Louisiana Hist. 1978 19(1): 43-63.* Both the Works Progress Administration life histories and the 240 family histories written by the author's Louisiana State University students are excellent sources for the history of the common people during the Depression. Analyzes these sources, comparing them on the basis of area of coverage, persons interviewed, interviewers, documentation, attitudes of interviewers, focus, language, and historical value. Concludes that the "life histories offer an extraordinary record of those who survived the 1930s outside, for the most part, conventional society," while "the family histories provide a rich account of entire families during the 1930s." 10 photos, 48 notes. R. L. Woodward

322. Culley, John J. and Petersen, Peter L. HARD TIMES ON THE HIGH PLAINS: FSA PHOTOGRAPHY DURING THE 1930S. *Panhandle-Plains Hist. Rev. 1979 52: 15-37.* Shortly after the creation of the Farm Security Administration (FSA) in 1937, a concentrated effort was launched to visually document the agency's efforts in behalf of rural America. Roy Emerson Stryker headed the

Historical Section within this federal agency and he enlisted the aid of gifted photographers such as Dorothea Lange and Ben Shahn to take the pictures. A bibliographical essay on the FSA and 17 FSA photographs from the Great Plains accompany the article.   M. L. Tate

323.   Daniel, Cletus E.   AGRICULTURAL UNIONISM AND THE EARLY NEW DEAL: THE CALIFORNIA EXPERIENCE.   *Southern California Q. 1977 59(2): 185-215.* Argues that the Franklin D. Roosevelt administraton, in the first phase of its New Deal policies, undercut the development of agricultural unionism in California. New Deal economic planners at first envisioned a harmonious relationship between employers and workers brought about through active federal mediation under the National Industrial Recovery Act (NIRA). Although New Deal labor policy dramatically changed after the end of the NIRA and the passage of the Wagner Act, California's agricultural labor movement suffered irreparably from the involvement of George Creel, self-styled NIRA mediator, in the San Joaquin cotton strike of October 1933. Creel effected a compromise which the Communist-led union accepted, and the chance to create an effective agricultural workers' union was lost. The Department of Labor sent Pelham Glassford to mediate labor disputes in the Imperial Valley. In 1934 he undercut the union by endorsing a company union, only to find that employers rejected both federal involvement and the company union. Thus the New Deal, remembered for its liberalism and reform, promoted the destruction of a vigorous effort to organize California agriculture. Primary and secondary sources; 68 notes.   A. Hoffman

324.   Daniel, Pete.   THE TRANSFORMATION OF THE RURAL SOUTH, 1930 TO THE PRESENT.   *Agric. Hist. 1981 55(3): 231-248.* A combination of government policies and mechanization has destroyed the traditional southern rural life based on tenant farming. New Deal agricultural subsidies encouraged landlords to get rid of sharecroppers. The Depression helped concentrate land ownership in the hands of insurance companies and cotton ginners who did not directly farm their land. The rice industry has been highly mechanized but neither rice nor tobacco was much affected by government programs. Cotton growing has been greatly changed by mechanization and has nearly disappeared from the Carolinas and Black Belt. Southern agriculture is now capital-intensive rather than labor-intensive. Based on National Archives records and other sources; 34 notes.   D. E. Bowers

325.   Davis, Kenneth S.   THE BIRTH OF SOCIAL SECURITY.   *Am. Heritage 1979 30(3): 38-51.* A history of the adoption of the Social Security Act (US, 1935). Essentially a conservative approach, the plan was limited in its scope by President Franklin D. Roosevelt and some of his closest advisors. Based on plans developed in Wisconsin and Ohio, and stimulated by the efforts of demagogues like Huey P. Long and Francis Townsend, the Roosevelt administration gradually realized the strong national support for such a proposal, but then made certain that it was limited in both cost and coverage. 19 illus.   J. F. Paul

326.   Dawson, Oliver B.   THE IRONWORK OF TIMBERLINE.   *Oregon Hist. Q. 1975 76(3): 258-268.* Timberline Lodge was built by the Art Project of the Works Progress Administration (WPA) and sponsored by the US Forest Project. The author, Oliver B. Dawson, a blacksmith, was appointed in 1935 to

be a project supervisor. Describes the pair of forged iron gates he designed, as well as andirons and other iron work, mostly with Indian design. The dedication by President and Mrs. Roosevelt was broadcast by radio. Illus.   E. P. Stickney

327.   Day, Greg and Delano, Jack.   FOLKLIFE AND PHOTOGRAPHY: BRINGING THE FSA HOME.   *Southern Exposure 1977 5(2-3): 122-133.* As a member of the photographic staff of the New Deal's Farm Security Administration, Jack Delano created a photographic essay on the effects of building a new lake on the lands of black and white farmers and tenants in the Santee-Cooper area of South Carolina in 1941. The photographs convey the heartrending anguish experienced by men and women forced to leave their native lands. Photos.
N. Lederer

328.   Dennis, James M.   GOVERNMENT ART: RELIEF, PROPANGANDA, OR PUBLIC BEAUTIFICATION?   *Rev. in Am. Hist. 1974 2(2): 275-282.* Review article prompted by Richard D. McKinzie's *The New Deal for Artists* (Princeton: Princeton U. Pr., 1973), an initial survey of New Deal patronage for the visual arts which focuses on the principal people and organizations dispensing aid. This "providential opportunity" was constantly hindered by problems of taste, tradition, and personality.   W. D. Piersen

329.   Duram, James C.   CONSTITUTIONAL CONSERVATISM: THE KANSAS PRESS AND THE NEW DEAL ERA AS A CASE STUDY. *Kansas Hist. Q. 1977 43(4): 432-447.* Analyzes the editorial treatment of constitutional law issues of the New Deal in 46 Kansas newspapers in 1934-35. The editorial response of the Kansas press to the New Deal was the product of the Republican backgrounds and probusiness attitudes of the editors. Many editorials excoriated the New Deal for excessive regulation of business, wild spending, socialistic concepts, dangerous experimentation, and hastily drawn legislation. Most of the Kansas papers welcomed the Supreme Court's decisions on legislation, and criticized some decisions for not being more conservative than they were. Primary sources; 2 tables, 46 notes.   A. W. Howell

330.   Duram, James C.   THE FARM JOURNALS AND THE CONSTITUTIONAL ISSUES OF THE NEW DEAL.   *Agric. Hist. 1973 47(4): 319-328.* Assesses the significance of the editorial response of nine major commercial agricultural and six major official farm organization publications to two crucial Supreme Court decisions, the invalidations of the National Industrial Recovery Act in May 1935 and the Agricultural Adjustment Act in January 1936. The constitutional positions of the farm journal editors were largely predetermined by their attitudes toward the New Deal. The position taken by the editors of the major farm organization journals was ambiguous, and thus Franklin Delano Roosevelt probably overestimated the support he would have received from farm organizations if a showdown with the Supreme Court could have been avoided. Based on farm journals; 30 notes.   R. T. Fulton

331.   Dwyer-Shick, Susan.   REVIEW ESSAY: FOLKLORE AND GOVERNMENT SUPPORT.   *J. of Am. Folklore 1976 89(354): 476-486.* Reviews William F. McDonald's *Federal Relief Administration and the Arts: The Origins and Administrative History of the Arts Projects of the Works Progress Administration* (Columbus: Ohio State U. Pr., 1969), and Jerre Mangione's *The Dream*

and the Deal: The Federal Writers' Project, 1935-1943 (New York: Avon, 1974) to examine federal funding and direction of folklore studies. 14 notes.

W. D. Piersen

332.   Ehrenhalt, Alan.   LAST HURRAHS FOR THE NEW DEAL.   *Washington Monthly 1976 7(11): 56-60* Discusses the National Democratic Issues Convention held at Louisville, Kentucky, in 1975 and the emerging skepticism about New Deal policies within the Democratic Party demonstrated there.

333.   Fairbanks, Robert B.   CINCINNATI AND GREENHILLS: THE RESPONSE TO A FEDERAL COMMUNITY, 1935-1939.   *Cincinnati Hist. Soc. Q. 1978 36(4): 223-242.* Rexford G. Tugwell's Greenbelt Towns during 1935-39 affected the establishment of Greenhills as a bedroom community outside Cincinnati which was to remove tenement and slum areas and replace them with city parks.

334.   Farran, Don.   THE HISTORICAL RECORDS SURVEY IN IOWA, 1936-1942.   *Ann. of Iowa 1975 42(8): 597-608.* The Historical Records Survey directed by Luther H. Evans, later Librarian of Congress, operated under the Works Progress Administration (WPA) and employed thousands who located and inventoried the public records of the United States: county records on births, marriages, and deaths, church and cemetery records, newspapers, schools, and memorabilia. Funds for the survey were discontinued with World War II, but its legacy is invaluable for the Bicentennial.   C. W. Olson

335.   Fickle, James E.   THE S.P.A. AND THE N.R.A.: A CASE STUDY OF THE BLUE EAGLE IN THE SOUTH.   *Southwestern Hist. Q. 1976 79(3): 253-278.* The Southern Pine Association, organized in 1914 to deal with industry problems, became the logical group to help formulate and oversee the NRA's lumber code in the 1930's. Although most small lumber mills remained outside the SPA, it set up an elaborate field structure to attempt enforcement of the Code. There were constant quarrels over production allotments, complaints of discrimination by the small non-SPA mills, and difficulties in maintaining wage, hour, and price levels. By the end of 1934 the Code had collapsed from lack of effective policing. Based on primary and secondary sources; 54 notes.

J. H. Broussard

336.   Finegold, Kenneth.   FROM AGRARIANISM TO ADJUSTMENT: THE POLITICAL ORIGINS OF NEW DEAL AGRICULTURAL POLICY. *Pol. & Soc. 1982 11(1): 1-27.* Examines the four major interrelated factors in the government's failure to intervene in the prolonged agricultural depression that followed World War I. Government intervention in the form of the Agricultural Adjustment Administration (AAA), brought into being early in 1933, was possible only after the shift in business opinion following the Great Crash, after the Democratic Party's victory in 1932, which in turn insured the effective use of the existing academic-governmental agricultural-economic complex, and after farm organizations provided the support necessary to win over acceptance of production controls by American farmers. 2 tables, 50 notes.   D. G. Nielson

337.   Freidel, Frank.   A YOUNG BRANDEIS FROM THE WEST.   *Rev. in Am. Hist. 1974 2(4): 553-557.* Review article prompted by William O. Douglas' *Go East, Young Man: The Early Years. The Autobiography of William O.*

Douglas (New York: Random House, 1974) which briefly surveys Douglas' public career, outlines the content of the autobiography, and focuses on the book's explication of Douglas' life, observations, and beliefs during the Roosevelt administration up to 1939.

338. Fulton, Tom. AGRICULTURAL LABOR LEGISLATION IN THE UNITED STATES: A REVIEW OF THE MAJOR NEW DEAL LEGISLATION, THE EMERGENCY FARM LABOR SUPPLY PROGRAM, AND THE AGRICULTURAL LABOR RELATIONS ACT OF CALIFORNIA. *J. of NAL Assoc. 1979 4(3-4): 49-58.* The above agricultural labor law shows that until recently farmworkers in the United States were not aided by government and did not enjoy a good relationship with American farmers; also gives a brief history of the rights and privileges of land ownership since 17th-century European settlement in North America.

339. Funigiello, Philip J. THE BONNEVILLE POWER ADMINISTRATION AND THE NEW DEAL. *Prologue 1973 5(2): 89-97.* Discusses the administration of the BPA from its establishment in 1937 to the interconnection of all electric utilities in the Pacific Northwest in 1942. Problems treated include the outworking of a federal power policy, the conflict between private and public power interests, and bureaucratic clashes with government officials and agencies. Based on primary sources; 31 notes.   D. G. Davis, Jr.

340. Garraty, John A. THE NEW DEAL, NATIONAL SOCIALISM, AND THE GREAT DEPRESSION. *Am. Hist. R. 1973 78(4): 907-944.* Compares government methods for coping with the Great Depression in Hitler's Germany and Roosevelt's United States. Nazi and New Deal antidepression policies displayed striking similarities and were distinct from those of other industrial nations. Focuses on the years 1933 to 1936. Of the two, the Nazis were the more successful; by 1936 the depression was substantially over in Germany, but far from finished in the United States. "However, neither regime solved the problem of maintaining prosperity without war." 6 figs., 71 notes.   R. V. Ritter

341. Ghosh, Partha Sarathy. PASSAGE OF THE SILVER PURCHASE ACT OF 1934: THE CHINA LOBBY AND THE ISSUE OF CHINA TRADE. *Indian J. of Am. Studies [India] 1976 6(1-2): 18-29.* Describes the activity of the congressional lobby in manipulating the passage of the Silver Purchase Act of 1934. Using the quite secondary issue of a depreciating China-US trade as its most handy weapon, the China lobby pushed through this act over the opposition of Franklin D. Roosevelt and Secretary of Treasury Henry Morgenthau. The silver purchase program enriched the act's promoters but it neither stabilized the Chinese currency nor revitalized the US-China trade. 54 notes.   L. V. Eid

342. Goldberg, Joseph P. FRANCES PERKINS, ISADOR LUBIN, AND THE BUREAU OF LABOR STATISTICS. *Monthly Labor Rev. 1980 103(4): 22-30.* Secretary of Labor Frances Perkins's influence on the Bureau of Labor Statistics was evidenced by her initiating a review of the Bureau's statistics and choosing Isador Lubin as Commissioner of Labor Statistics under Franklin Roosevelt's New Deal, both of which improved and modernized the Bureau; covers 1920's-40's.

343. Gower, Calvin W. CONSERVATISM, CENSORSHIP, AND CONTROVERSY IN THE CCC, 1930S. *Journalism Q. 1975 52(2): 277-284.* The Army and Robert Flechner administered the Civilian Conservation Corps camps. Their conservatism was illustrated by the exclusion of some reading material from the camps. The book *You and Machines* was the first publication of a project to provide special reading material for the camps. Its suppression in November 1934 raised considerable controversy. Army leaders ordered the Communistic newspaper *Champion of Youth* suppressed in the camps after it published a list of principles. Based on primary and secondary sources; 26 notes.   K. J. Puffer

344. Gower, Calvin W. THE STRUGGLE OF BLACKS FOR LEADERSHIP POSITIONS IN THE CIVILIAN CONSERVATION CORPS: 1933-1942. *J. of Negro Hist. 1976 61(2): 123-135.* The efforts of Negroes to gain equal opportunities through leadership positions in the Civilian Conservation Corps were not successful. This experience reflects the general failure of Afro-Americans to obtain significant improvement for themselves during the New Deal. Based on the records of the Civilian Conservation Corps; 24 notes.

N. G. Sapper

345. Grant, H. Roger and Purcell, L. Edward. IMPLEMENTING THE AAA'S CORN-HOG PROGRAM: AN IOWA FARMER'S ACCOUNT. *Ann. of Iowa 1976 43(6): 430-442.* Excerpts from the 1934 diary of Elmer Gilbert Powers (1886-1942), who farmed 160 acres in Boone County, Iowa. Powers was a township committeeman during the initial implementation of the Agricultural Adjustment Administrations "corn-hog" program in 1934. Although supportive of the policy of paying farmers to reduce their production of corn and hogs, Powers was often frustrated by the paper work associated with the scheme. A drought in 1934 curtailed corn production on Powers' farm even more than required by the government, and consequently he was forced to sell many of his hogs because he had no feed for them. Based on Powers' diary and on secondary sources; 3 photos, 7 notes.   P. L. Petersen

346. Guth, James L. THE NATIONAL COOPERATIVE COUNCIL AND FARM RELIEF, 1929-1942. *Agric. Hist. 1977 51(2): 441-458.* Envisioned by most of its founders as a trade-association spokesman for cooperative business interests, the National Cooperative Council was transformed under the impact of the Great Depression and the New Deal into a vehicle for broader agricultural policy concerns. Although somewhat limited by internal friction and competition from other farm groups, the Council was a vital instrument for molding the New Deal farm program to fit the needs and interests of farmer cooperatives. Eventually the Council was forced to abandon legislative activism because of proliferating internal splits, and it turned to another trade-association function, providing services to member groups. There it found a route to survival and growth once its political functions were rendered irrelevant by the very programs it had fostered. Primary and secondary sources; 43 notes.   R. T. Fulton

347. Guzda, Henry P. FRANCES PERKINS' INTEREST IN A NEW DEAL FOR BLACKS. *Monthly Labor Rev. 1980 103(4): 31-35.* Discusses Secretary of Labor Frances Perkins's commitment to making blacks' welfare a top priority of the Labor Department, 1933-45.

348. Hamilton, Virginia Van Der Veer. BARNSTORMING THE U.S. MAIL. *Am. Heritage 1974 25(5): 32-36, 86-88.* The short-lived efforts of the US Army Air Corps to provide air mail postal service.   S

349. Hargreaves, Mary W. M. LAND-USE PLANNING IN RESPONSE TO DROUGHT: THE EXPERIENCE OF THE THIRTIES. *Agricultural Hist. 1976 50(4): 561-582.* Drought on the Great Plains during the 1930's brought an interest in land-use planning. The federal government, cooperating with state and local planning agencies, set out to increase the number of irrigated acres and convert crop land to grazing land. The program proved difficult to implement due to difficulties in collecting data and frictions in local planning efforts. Better weather and the need for greater production during World War II removed inducements for land-use planning. 78 notes.   D. E. Bowers

350. Harrison, Lowell H. RECOLLECTIONS OF SOME TENNESSEE SLAVES. *Tennessee Hist. Q. 1974 33(2): 175-190.* Under the direction of the Federal Writers' Project in the 1930's, an effort was made to interview surviving ex-slaves in order to preserve the memories of slavery of those who had lived under the system. Though of uneven quality, some 2,000 interviews were completed, 26 of which were held in Tennessee. The interviews center around household activities, punishment, religion, and post-war developments. Primary and secondary sources; 3 notes.   M. B. Lucas

351. Hauptman, Laurence M. ALICE JAMISON: SENECA POLITICAL ACTIVIST, 1901-1964. *Indian Hist. 1979 12(2): 15-22, 60-62.* Alice Lee Jamison, a Seneca Indian, through the work of the American Indian Federation, was a major critic of the 1930's New Deal policy developed by John Collier, and of the Bureau of Indian Affairs, 1940's-50's.

352. Hauptman, Laurence M. THE IROQUOIS SCHOOL OF ART: ARTHUR C. PARKER AND THE SENECA ARTS PROJECT, 1935-1941. *New York Hist. 1979 60(3): 283-312.* The restoration and preservation of Iroquois art was undertaken by Arthur C. Parker at Tonawanda Reservation near Akron, New York, with financial assistance initially from the Temporary Emergency Relief Administration, a New York agency, and after 1935 from the Works Progress Administration. Indians played a major role in developing the Seneca Arts project, but Parker, who was not technically a Seneca but had roots deeply implanted in Iroquois history, was the key figure in the Iroquois School of Art. This New Deal experiment in reviving Seneca arts and crafts ended in 1941 when fire destroyed the old school building at Tonawanda where much material relating to Iroquois life and culture was housed. 10 illus., 57 notes.
R. N. Lokken

353. Heinemann, Ronald L. BLUE EAGLE OR BLACK BUZZARD? THE NATIONAL RECOVERY ADMINISTRATION IN VIRGINIA. *Virginia Mag. of Hist. and Biog. 1981 89(1): 90-100.* Interprets the rise and fall of the National Recovery Administration (NRA). Initial enthusiasm for this New Deal program in mid-1933 faded when resistance to enforcement of many of its codes developed, mostly over wage and hour violations. The NRA simultaneously fought the customary southern versus northern wage differential, cut hours and discharges instead of wage rates, a mixed reaction from business, and a generally

hostile press. In May 1935 the US Supreme Court declared the NRA unconstitutional. 29 notes.

P. J. Woehrmann

354. Hendrickson, Gordon O. THE WPA WRITERS' PROJECT IN WYOMING: HISTORY AND COLLECTIONS. *Ann. of Wyoming 1977 49(2): 175-192.* Surveys the problems and accomplishments of the Federal Writers' Project in Wyoming during the Depression. Henry G. Alsberg, first national director of the program, originally suggested that an American Guide Book should be assembled from the materials most relevant to each state's history. This launched a massive collecting process on a county level throughout the United States and ultimately produced not only a national guide but also one for each state. Under the direction of Mart Christensen and later Agnes Wright Spring, Wyoming assembled a state guide and several other publications, plus a Historical Records Survey pertinent to future historical studies. Based on WPA records; 3 photos, 53 notes.

M. L. Tate

355. Hendrickson, Kenneth E. THE NATIONAL YOUTH ADMINISTRATION IN SOUTH DAKOTA: YOUTH AND THE NEW DEAL, 1935-1943. *South Dakota Hist. 1979 9(2): 130-151.* The National Youth Administration (NYA), between its creation in 1935 and its demise in 1943, provided part-time employment for needy high school and college students and relief work for youth not in school. Although often caught up in political and bureaucratic difficulties, the NYA in South Dakota experienced its greatest success and popularity between 1937 and 1940 under Anna C. Struble as State Youth Director. The NYA program in South Dakota gave assistance and relief to thousands of youngsters and their families and demonstrated that the federal system can work effectively for the welfare of all the people. Primary sources; 6 photos, 35 notes.

P. L. McLaughlin

356. Hendrickson, Kenneth E., Jr. THE CIVILIAN CONSERVATION CORPS IN PENNSYLVANIA: A CASE STUDY OF A NEW DEAL RELIEF AGENCY IN OPERATION. *Pennsylvania Mag. of Hist. and Biog. 1976 100(1): 66-96.* Despite administrative interference by the Army, excessive allotment payments to dependents, declining enrollment, desertions, high injury rates, and complaints of poor food and hazing, Pennsylvania's Civilian Conservation Corps was a worthwhile, successful program. Most enrollees found the food good, camp life exhilarating, and the educational program an exceptional opportunity. The CCC's worth is evidenced by its reforestation projects, its road, bridge, and dam construction, and its fire-fighting. Based on primary and secondary sources; 80 notes.

E. W. Carp

357. Hendrickson, Kenneth E., Jr. THE CIVILIAN CONSERVATION CORPS IN SOUTH DAKOTA. *South Dakota Hist. 1980 11(1): 1-20.* Discusses the administration, organization, and achievements of the Civilian Conservation Corps (CCC) in South Dakota between 1933 and 1942. The CCC was one of the most effective federal relief programs in South Dakota. The program provided employment for more than 26,000 men and distributed over six million dollars to their families. The program also improved the South Dakota environment, particularly through soil conservation, timber stand improvement, and control of forest fires. Based on the records of the Civilian Conservation Corps-South Dakota in the National Archives, Washington, D.C., and other primary sources; 12 photos, 37 notes.

P. L. McLaughlin

358. Hendrickson, Kenneth E., Jr.   RELIEF FOR YOUTH: THE CIVILIAN CONSERVATION CORPS AND THE NATIONAL YOUTH ADMINIS-TRATION IN NORTH DAKOTA. *North Dakota Hist. 1981 48(4): 17-27.* The Civilian Conservation Corps and the National Youth Administration were both initially well received by officials and citizens of North Dakota. They provided work relief and assistance to needy families, performed conservation services, built recreation facilities, and provided practical training and education. World War II brought changes in purpose to both agencies, from need to aptitude and defense preparedness, and it reduced the number of applicants. Agencies functioned until funding was eliminated by Congress. Based on official records and published sources; 59 notes, 9 illus.   G. L. Olson

359. Hewins, Dana C.   REGULATION WITHOUT HISTORICAL JUS-TIFICATION: THE CASE OF HOUSEHOLD MOVING. *Res. in Econ. Hist. 1982 (Supplement 2): 71-92.* During the depression of the 1930's, the moving industry experienced intense competition, both among truckers, and with rail-roads. The Motor Carrier Act (US, 1935) was established in order to minimize that competition between the railroads and the interstate truckers and to promote financial responsibility and stability within the industry. The industry did not need to be regulated, however, and was simply the victim of an attempt by government to gather all motor carriers into a single industry. Primary sources; 13 notes, ref.   J. Powell

360. Hicks, Floyd W. and Lambert, C. Roger.   FOOD FOR THE HUNGRY: FEDERAL FOOD PROGRAMS IN ARKANSAS, 1933-42. *Arkansas Hist. Q. 1978 37(1): 23-43.* As a result of the Depression and several natural disasters, many Arkansas residents were lacking food. They benefited from Federal Surplus Relief Corporation (FSRC), Federal Emergency Relief Administration (FERA), and Works Progress Administration (WPA) programs which aimed to reduce farm surpluses by government purchase and then redistribution of food to the needy. Three methods of distribution were employed with varying success: direct distribution, food stamps, and school lunches. Primary and secondary sources; 43 notes.   G. R. Schroeder

361. Hirsch, Jerrold and Terrill, Tom E.   CONCEPTUALIZATION AND IMPLEMENTATION: SOME THOUGHTS ON READING THE FEDERAL WRITERS' PROJECT SOUTHERN LIFE HISTORIES. *Southern Studies 1979 18(3): 351-362.* The thousand life histories of southerners collected by the Federal Writers' Project (FWP) in the 1930's represent one of the earliest at-tempts to obtain an oral history of anonymous Americans. It includes ex-slave narratives, folklore and folksong, and biographies of ordinary people. Most of the interviewers were southern, middle class, white, nonprofessionals, who show decided biases. They combined amateur sociology and fictional techniques in creating the life histories. While the collection is a rich resource, historians must beware of these special problems in their use. Primary sources; 33 notes.
                                                            J. J. Buschen

362. Hodges, James A.   GEORGE FORT MILTON AND THE NEW DEAL. *Tennessee Hist. Q. 1977 36(3): 383-409.* Though he had been skeptical of Roosevelt during the 1932 campaign, George Fort Milton became an active New Dealer as a result of the Hundred Days. He used his editorial page to

vigorously support New Deal measures across the board, including racial liberalism, though moderately. He lived and wrote, however, in Tennessee, an area that was unfriendly to most of his liberalism. Primary and secondary sources; 118 notes.   M. B. Lucas

363. Hoffman, Abraham. STIMULUS TO REPATRIATION: THE 1931 FEDERAL DEPORTATION DRIVE AND THE LOS ANGELES MEXICAN COMMUNITY. *Pacific Hist. R. 1973 42(2): 205-219.* Studies the main thrust of Secretary of Labor James J. Davis' promise to reduce unemployment at the height of the depression—ousting aliens holding jobs, concentrating on illegal aliens, and curtailing legal entries. Although the campaign did not single out any one ethnic group, Mexicans were most affected. Of these most lived in Southern California, specifically in Los Angeles County. Analyzes the series of developments resulting from the activities of the federal agents which led to a mass exodus of 50,000 to 75,000 people. The fear tactics used by the federal agents had been designed to bring about that deportation and emigration. 43 notes.
                                                                                    R. V. Ritter

364. Holland, Reid. THE CIVILIAN CONSERVATION CORPS IN THE CITY: TULSA AND OKLAHOMA CITY IN THE 1930S. *Chronicles of Oklahoma 1975 53(3): 367-375.* Historians have generally treated the Civilian Conservation Corps as a rural-oriented project of the Depression years, but it also embraced urban programs. The construction of municipal parks occupied much of the CCC's attention, and many cities constructed or improved their parks only by this means. A majority of CCC activities were in the South, and Oklahoma contained a large percentage of these. Workers in the camps not only received a small salary, but also benefited from free room and board, medical care, clothing, and education in academic and vocational fields. Camps in Oklahoma City and Tulsa, which contained both white and black workers, were strictly segregated and equal benefits were not always extended to the blacks. Based on the *Camp Inspection Reports*; 3 photos, 11 notes.   M. L. Tate

365. Hornbein, Marjorie. JOSEPHINE ROCHE: SOCIAL WORKER AND COAL OPERATOR. *Colorado Mag. 1976 53(3): 243-260.* Sketches the life of Josephine Roche and emphasizes her labor reforms when she headed the Rocky Mountain Fuel Company. She was a classmate and friend of Frances Perkins, Denver's first policewoman, Franklin D. Roosevelt's Assistant Secretary of the Treasury and Administrator of the National Youth Administration, and a long-time United Mine Workers executive. Primary and secondary sources; 5 illus., 58 notes.   O. H. Zabel

366. Hunter, Robert F. THE AAA BETWEEN NEIGHBORS: VIRGINIA, NORTH CAROLINA, AND THE NEW DEAL FARM PROGRAM. *J. of Southern Hist. 1978 44(4): 537-570.* Although the South is still often considered a monolithic region, it has in fact many diverse political, economic, and social patterns. The complex and changing nature of the New Deal farm program produced varied, at times equivocating, hesitant responses from the senators of Virginia and North Carolina, Harry Byrd and Carter Glass from Virginia and Josiah W. Bailey, Robert R. Reynolds, and later, Lindsay Warren and John Hosea Kerr from North Carolina, particularly with regard to tobacco and cotton production. Manuscript and printed primary and secondary sources; 143 notes.   T. D. Schoonover

367. Ingalls, Robert P. NEW YORK AND THE MINIMUM-WAGE MOVEMENT, 1933-1937. *Labor Hist. 1974 15(2): 179-198.* Reviews the passage of the New York state Minimum-Wage Act covering women and children in 1933 and details the Tipaldo court case which resulted in the act being declared unconstitutional, a setback for Governor Herbert Lehman's "Little New Deal." After the Supreme Court reversed itself, New York again led the way in progress toward a national movement for a minimum wage. Based on the Mary W. Dewson Papers, the National Consumer's League Papers; and the Herbert H. Lehman Papers, 75 notes.   L. L. Athey

368. Ingram, Earl, ed. THE FEDERAL RELIEF ADMINISTRATION IN LOUISIANA. *Louisiana Hist. 1973 14(2): 194-201.* Describes and evaluates the more than 500 files of the Louisiana Emergency Relief Administration, 1933-35, located in the Louisiana State Archives. The files are valuable sources of data on relief administration in the state and are categorized under 10 major headings: Administrative (44 files); Individual correspondence (61 files); Correspondence between the central office in New Orleans and city, parish, and district offices (80 files); "Wages and wages committee" of the various parishes (70 files); Local, parish, state, and federal aid (17 files); Agriculture and various farm relief programs (43 files); Transient bureau and transients (29 files); Community cooperatives and self-help agencies (11 files); College student aid (5 files); and Miscellaneous reports.   R. L. Woodward, Jr.

369. Inouye, Arlene and Susskind, Charles. "TECHNOLOGICAL TRENDS AND NATIONAL POLICY," 1937: THE FIRST MODERN TECHNOLOGY ASSESSMENT. *Technology and Culture 1977 18(4): 593-621.* The 1937 report, begun in 1934 during Franklin D. Roosevelt's administration, was a continuation of efforts of the Herbert C. Hoover administration. "Its goal was to highlight new inventions that might affect living and working conditions in the United States during the following ten to 25 years." 98 notes.   C. O. Smith

370. Johnson, Charles. THE ARMY, THE NEGRO, AND THE CIVILIAN CONSERVATION CORPS: 1933-1942. *Military Affairs 1972 36(3): 82-88.* The problem of implementation of the nondiscrimination provisions of its organic act lasted throughout the life of the CCC. The Army, which operated the camps, followed no consistent policy on integration or segregation of individual companies. Because of local pressures, the recruiting of Negroes was limited after 1935 and the Army found it difficult to get local communities to accept the stationing of Negro companies in their midst. The Army believed that Negro troops performed best under white officers. In 1935 a limited number of Negro reserve medical officers and chaplains was authorized; but few would serve. In 1936 President Franklin Delano Roosevelt ordered the establishment of wholly Negro-operated camps, but only two were formed. Based on War Department records, memoirs, and monographs; 30 notes.   K. J. Bauer

371. Johnson, Dolores De Bower. ANNA DICKIE OLESEN, SENATE CANDIDATE. Stuhler, Barbara and Kreuter, Gretchen, ed. *Women in Minnesota: Selected Biographical Essays* (St. Paul: Minnesota Historical Society Press, 1977): 226-246. Born 3 July 1885, Anna Dickie grew up in rural Minnesota, loved school, practiced speaking, yearned for a larger world than that of the small town of Waterville, and developed an interest in politics. Her parents, who were Meth-

odists, Republicans, and teetotalers, encouraged reading and education. After finishing high school, Anna became a teacher. In 1905, she wed Peter Olesen, a Danish immigrant and bookseller who became a prominent educator. Anna Olesen became one of Minnesota's leading clubwomen, suffragists, and Democrats. Her speaking abilities became famous, and in 1918 she joined the Chautauqua circuit. In 1920, Anna was elected a delegate to the Democratic Party's national convention; and there was talk of her being a candidate for the vice-presidency. In 1922, she became the first woman to run for the US Senate as a major party candidate. Later she concerned herself with the problems of working women, the elderly, and day-care centers. Franklin D. Roosevelt appointed her state director of the National Emergency Council, an arduous job responsible for coordinating New Deal programs and agencies. In 1942, she retired to private life and moved to Georgia. She survived two husbands. In 1963 she returned to Northfield, Minnesota, where she died on 21 May 1971. Primary and secondary sources; photo, 53 notes.   A. E. Wiederrecht

372. Johnson, William R. RURAL REHABILITATION IN THE NEW DEAL: THE ROPESVILLE PROJECT. *Southwestern Hist. Q. 1976 79(3): 279-295.* Ropesville, near Lubbock, Texas, was a successful example of the New Deal's rural rehabilitation communities. During 1934-43, over 300 people (all local poor farm families) were settled on small farms in housing built by the federal Resettlement Administration. Under the close guidance of government managers, the project's residents improved their standard of living and developed good relations with the townspeople of Ropesville. The project ended in 1943 with the sale of the farms to the occupants. Based on primary sources; 49 notes.
                          J. H. Broussard

373. Kalin, Berkley. YOUNG ABE FORTAS. *West Tennessee Hist. Soc. Papers 1980 (34): 96-100+.* Abe Fortas (b. 1910) had a meteoric rise in the federal government. Ten letters to Hardwig Peres (Memphis attorney, author, and merchant) illustrate Fortas's intelligence, wit, gift of phrase, and varied interests. Peres had helped Fortas get into the Yale Law School in the early 1930's. One of Franklin D. Roosevelt's "bright young men," Fortas was appointed Undersecretary of the Interior in 1942, at age 32. This caused a small storm, and he resigned to enter the military, much against Roosevelt's desires, only to be discharged a month later for medical causes. Letters are from the Mississippi Valley Collection, Memphis State University, Tennessee.   H. M. Parker, Jr.

374. Kalmar, Karen L. SOUTHERN BLACK ELITES AND THE NEW DEAL: A CASE STUDY OF SAVANNAH, GEORGIA. *Georgia Hist. Q. 1981 65(4): 341-355.* Discrimination plagued lower-class blacks in Savannah during the New Deal programs of the 1930's. Any complaints made to the national Works Progress Administration (W.P.A.) were referred back to the state W.P.A. and were explained away rather than solved. Members of the black elite never supported other blacks in their attempts to gain justice. Based on Works Progress Administration papers; 38 notes.   G. R. Schroeder

375. Kelly, Lawrence C. ANTHROPOLOGY AND ANTHROPOLOGISTS IN THE INDIAN NEW DEAL. *J. of the Hist. of the Behavioral Sci. 1980 16(1): 6-24.* The use of anthropological techniques to analyze problems in American society was a product of the late 1920's and the New Deal era. A major

stimulus to the development of this "applied anthropology" was a series of projects initiated by John Collier in the Bureau of Indian Affairs beginning in 1935. Four of these experiments, the Applied Anthropology Unit, the Soil Conservation Service experiment on the Navajo reservation, the Technical Cooperation-Bureau of Indian Affairs soil conservation work on other Indian reservations, and the Indian Education, Personality, and Administration Research Project, are the subject of this article.   J

376. Kelly, Lawrence C. CHOOSING THE NEW DEAL INDIAN COMMISSIONER: ICKES VS. COLLIER. *New Mexico Hist. R. 1974 49(4): 269-284.* Many persons were surprised and some expressed dismay when President-elect Franklin D. Roosevelt in the spring of 1933 appointed two relative unknowns to high positions in the Interior Department. Harold Ickes, a Bull Moose Republican, was named Secretary and John Collier, who had consistently criticized federal Indian policy, was appointed Commissioner of Indian Affairs. The two men were not friends and were critical of each other. Notes.
J. H. Krenkel

377. Kelly, Lawrence C. THE INDIAN REORGANIZATION ACT: THE DREAM AND THE REALITY. *Pacific Hist. R. 1975 44(3): 291-312.* The Indian Reorganization Act (1934) fell short of the revolutionary changes in federal Indian policy attributed to it by John Collier, Commissioner of Indian Affairs 1933-45, and by historians who have accepted his interpretation. Collier aimed to completely reverse the previous assimilationist policy. Assimilated Indians successfully opposed extension of the Act to themselves. In referenda on the Act, less than half of the eligible Indians voted to establish tribal constitutions and even fewer voted to place themselves under the economic provisions of the Act. When Collier attempted to get around the limitations of the Act by administrative action, Congress refused to appropriate the necessary funds. Based on documents in the National Archives, on Congressional hearings and other published government documents, and on secondary sources; table, 32 notes.
W. K. Hobson

378. Koeniger, A. Cash. CARTER GLASS AND THE NATIONAL RECOVERY ADMINISTRATION. *South Atlantic Q. 1975 74(3): 349-364.* The usual view of New Deal liberals calmly carrying out the programs of earlier Progressives is not borne out in the example of Senator Carter Glass' struggle with the National Industrial Recovery Act and its administrative organization, the National Recovery Administration. Glass despised the program and fought it until the Supreme Court ruled it unconstitutional. Glass, like many Progressives, viewed the New Deal not as a reform program building evolutionarily on the past, but rather as a complete break with the past and the beginning of Fascist collectivism. This argument was at the heart of his objections. 38 notes.
V. L. Human

379. Kollmorgen, Walter M. KOLLMORGEN AS A BUREAUCRAT. *Ann. of the Assoc. of Am. Geographers 1979 69(1): 77-89.* As a staff geographer with the Agriculture Department, 1936-45, Walter M. Kollmorgen participated in project studies of the back-to-the-land movement, subsistence homesteads, farm population and rural life, and drainage and reclamation; from a special issue celebrating the 75th anniversary of the Association of American Geographers.

380. Koppes, Clayton R. FROM NEW DEAL TO TERMINATION: LIB-
ERALISM AND INDIAN POLICY, 1933-1953. *Pacific Hist. Rev. 1977 46(4):
543-566.* In Indian policies there was only a selective continuity of liberalism
from the New Deal to the Fair Deal. Roosevelt's commissioner of Indian affairs
(1933-45), John Collier, considered the loss of community the major problem of
modern society. His Indian policy was in the same spirit as other early New Deal
policies and programs which sought to foster cooperation and community rather
than competition and individualism. By World War II liberal support for such
programs had greatly eroded. The Truman administration allowed Indian policy
to return to its earlier emphasis on assimilation, in keeping with the Fair Deal's
own emphasis on economic prosperity and individual competition and on individual civil rights and freedom from group identity. Based on documents in the
National Archives, Yale University Library, Library of Congress, and Truman
Library, and on published primary and secondary sources; 39 notes.

W. K. Hobson

381. Kostiainen, Auvo. AMERIKANSUOMALAISTEN KUVA: TYÖT-
TÖMYYSTYÖNÄ Ą TALLENNETTUA MINNESOTAN SUOMALAIS-
TEN HISTORIAA [The portrait of Finnish Americans: Materials on the
Minnesota Finns collected by the WPA Writers' Project]. *Turun Hist. Arkisto
[Finland] 1976 31: 414-431.* In the state archives of the United States there are
preserved many kinds of materials on ethnic minorities collected in the 1930's.
The work was done by the employees of the Works Progress Administration
(WPA) Writers Project. They interviewed immigrants and their descendants,
collected clippings from newspapers, etc., and tried to compile histories on the
various states, counties and also ethnic minorities of the United States. Very few
of these histories, however, were completed. This article deals with the materials
on the Finns preserved at the Minnesota Historical Society, St. Paul, Minnesota
—first and foremost, the most valuable part of it, the interviews. Here an attempt
has been made to analyze the interviews, what kind of picture do they give on
the Minnesota Finn? The workers of the Writers Project interviewed 143 Finnish-
Americans, of whom 28 were second generation Finnish-Americans born in the
United States. The Finnish-Americans were asked their place and date of birth,
the time of arrival in America, the reasons for emigrating, their movements inside
the United States, occupation, education, social activities and so on. A few as yet
unstudied topics could be researched with the help of these interviews; namely
the mobility of Finnish-Americans and occupational changes of the immigrants
during these recent decades. The Minnesota Finns seem to be relatively mobile,
because half of them had been earlier living in other parts of the United States.
The occupational changes are also well described: many immigrants came to
work in the mines and lumbering industry, but when interviewed in the late
1930's only a few of them still worked in the mines. There occurred a great
diversification of occupations in benefit of services, business, and farming. The
information on the Minnesota Finns thus achieved was compared with the research results on Finnish-American history in general. Even if it seems that the
persons chosen for interviews in many cases were older immigrants, some of them
the children of the first Finns, who settled in Minnesota or persons belonging to
the so-called well-done-Finns, the information received through these interviews
for the most part agreed with the earlier findings. Accordingly, the work done
by the employees of the WPA Writers Project can be used in many different ways

when studying the history of ethnic minorities within the United States. These materials, however, have been taken advantage of only on relatively few occasions, and obviously research based on materials in all the States would be most fruitful, even if it requires a huge amount of work.   J

382. Krueger, Thomas A.   NEW DEAL HISTORIOGRAPHY AT FORTY. *R. in Am. Hist. 1975 3(4): 483-488.* The New Deal (Columbus: Ohio State U. Pr., 1975), edited by John Braeman, Robert H. Bremner, and David Brody, is a collection of essays on New Deal topics, volume 1 dealing with New Deal ideology, business, and a wide variety of labor policy, etc., on the national level; volume 2 covering the economic and political reform of the New Deal in state governments in the 1930's and 1940's.

383. Kruman, Marie W.   QUOTAS FOR BLACKS: THE PUBLIC WORKS ADMINISTRATION AND THE BLACK CONSTRUCTION WORKER. *Labor Hist. 1975 16(1): 37-51.* Harold Ickes instituted quotas for hiring skilled and unskilled blacks in construction financed through the Public Works Administration (PWA). Resistance from employers and unions was partially overcome by negotiations and implied sanctions. Although results were ambiguous, the plan helped provide blacks with employment, especially among unskilled workers. Based on files of the PWA in the National Archives; tables of compliance, 30 notes.   L. L. Athey

384. Lamoreaux, David and Eisenberg, Gerson.   BALTIMORE VIEWS THE GREAT DEPRESSION, 1929-1933.   *Maryland Hist. Mag. 1976 71(3): 428-442.* Evaluates trends and shifts in public opinion reflected in letters to the editor in the *Sunpapers* from the stock market crash to Roosevelt's inauguration. At first government was seen as innocent since business and its manipulation of the system were to blame. The Hawley-Smoot tariff and the mounting demand for repeal of Prohibition soon shifted attention to attacks on the extension of federal authority and the growth of permanent bureaucracies. While many came to conclude that only government could be the "broker" reconciling the demands of conflicting interest groups seeking relief, opinion remained ambivalent due to strong Jeffersonian notions of opposition to centralized power. Roosevelt's proposed program was successful apparently because it voiced the interests of farmer, worker, and small businessman without creating the impression of conflict. By 1933 people were increasingly suggesting solutions based on patterns of government intervention in the economy during the First World War, and this "provided a climate of opinion which Roosevelt was able to exploit on assuming the presidency," although the debate over political centralization continued. From the Baltimore *Sun* and *Evening Sun*, and secondary works; 43 notes.
                                                                        G. J. Bobango

385. Láng, I.   THE CONFLICT BETWEEN AMERICAN AND BRITISH COMMERCIAL POLICIES PRIOR TO WORLD WAR II.   *Acta Hist. [Hungary] 1979 25(3-4): 267-297.* Outlines the principles of US and British trade policies in the mid-1930's. The United States, in proposals submitted to the World Economic Conference in London in 1933, asked governments to refrain from increasing obstacles to international trade and to reduce existing barriers in order to rehabilitate the world economy after the Great Depression. In 1932, as outlined in Ottawa, the British government changed its commercial policy to one of

imperial protectionism, i.e., Great Britain and the Dominions formed a preferential trade group while at the same time attempting to prevent other groups from doing likewise. Washington claimed that Great Britain's partners were acting under duress in granting preferences and did so at the expense of the United States. This conflict between American free trade and British protectionism survived to post-World War II years. Primary sources; 50 notes. Russian summary.
                                                                    A. M. Pogany

386. Láng, Imre.   A ROOSEVELT-KORMÁNYZAT ELSŐ ÉVÉNEK GAZDASÁGPOLITIKAI DILEMMÁJA [The economic policy dilemma of the first year of the Roosevelt administration]. *Századok [Hungary] 1974 108(1): 136-185.* The Roosevelt administration considered the solution of the world economic crisis to lie in the regulation of the US economic policy, as an internal affair. He introduced the New Deal with the Agricultural Adjustment Act (US, 1933) and the National Industrial Recovery Act (US, 1933). In 1933, the gold standard was abandoned. All this led to economic isolationism. Yet this was an inevitable step to take. At the London Conference of 1933, the antagonism between the United States and the Gold Standard countries led by France was sharpened. This year was, however, an episode that pushed the Open Door policy temporarily into the background, but the latter was revived after 1934 as proposed by Foreign Secretary Cordell Hull. Primary sources; 135 notes.
                                                                    R. Hetzron

387. Lantz, Herman R.   FAMILY AND KIN AS REVEALED IN THE NARRATIVES OF EX-SLAVES. *Social Sci. Q. 1980 60(4): 667-675.* To assess the extent to which slavery in the United States created black family dismemberment, the author counts the number of ex-slaves and children of ex-slaves— interviewed as part of a Works Progress Administration (WPA) project during the 1930's—who could identify their parents, siblings, and kin. The results support the view that black families before the Civil War were more stable than had earlier been thought. Based on 1,735 WPA narratives of ex-slaves and 537 narratives of children of ex-slaves; 2 tables, 16 notes, biblio.   L. F. Velicer

388. Lear, Linda J.   HAROLD L. ICKES AND THE OIL CRISES OF THE FIRST HUNDRED DAYS. *Mid-America 1981 63(1): 3-17.* Harold L. Ickes, Secretary of the Interior, strove valiantly, but unsuccessfully, March through May 1933 to persuade President Roosevelt and Congress to approve far-reaching regulatory legislation to deal with the chaos within the oil industry. Ickes lobbied for the Marland-Caper Bill, which called for strict federal control, yet Roosevelt supported only the most general controls. These appeared as an amendment to an industrial recovery bill.   M. J. Wentworth

389. Lee, Bradford A.   THE NEW DEAL RECONSIDERED. *Wilson Q. 1982 6(2): 62-76.* Assesses the economic efficacy of Franklin D. Roosevelt's New Deal; during 1933-38 it had little effect, and in the end alienated business and the Farm Bureau.

390. Leiby, James.   STATE WELFARE ADMINISTRATION IN CALIFORNIA, 1930-1945. *Southern California Q. 1973 55(3): 303-318.* At the beginning of the Great Depression, public welfare administration in California was dominated by private agencies and a tradition of dealing with problems not

connected with the labor market—needy children, old people, and the disabled. The Depression created an unprecedented need to assist unemployed able-bodied workers, and when the Roosevelt administration launched its massive relief programs, incompetent officials controlled California's relief operation. By the end of World War II the state had clearly evolved to a new understanding of public responsibility, with morality judgments being less of a factor in determining aid. Problems still remained, especially in the area of employment in agriculture; the idea of a war on poverty not emerging until the 1960's. Based on interviews, unpublished sources, government documents and reports, and published studies; 46 notes. A. Hoffman

391. Leiter, William M. THE PRESIDENCY AND NON-FEDERAL GOVERNMENT: FDR AND THE PROMOTION OF STATE LEGISLATIVE ACTION. *Presidential Studies Q. 1979 9(2): 101-121.* Discusses the promotion of state legislative action on federal programs from 1933 to 1941 during the presidency of Franklin D. Roosevelt, and compares this to federal promotion of legislative action in a nonfederal sphere in the 1960's and 1970's.

392. Leiter, William M. THE PRESIDENCY AND NON-FEDERAL GOVERNMENT: THE BENEFACTOR-AVERSION HYPOTHESIS, THE CASE OF PUBLIC ASSISTANCE POLICIES IN THE NEW DEAL AND NIXON ADMINISTRATIONS. *Presidential Studies Q. 1980 10(4): 636-644.* Tests the benefactor-aversion hypothesis, where presidential administrations view state and local governments as responsible for governmental ills, for its validity during the Roosevelt and Nixon administrations. In both of these cases, the hypothesis holds true. Both administrations felt that the inferior governments were not living up to their responsibility and were the cause of the majority of problems. 30 notes. D. H. Cline

393. Lepawsky, Albert. THE PLANNING APPARATUS: A VIGNETTE OF THE NEW DEAL. *J. of the Am. Inst. of Planners 1976 42(1): 16-32.* Despite a lack of sophistication in the field of economic planning, the New Deal remains the high watermark of American planning thought and planning practice. This was most apparent in the realm of social and socioeconomic planning, including social security; in the planned use and development of natural resources and the related field of ecologic-environmental planning; in the correlation of national plans with local, state, regional, and international, including strategic, planning; and in the realm of political planning, that is, in the realization of progressive societal values through innovative public policy and adaptive planning technique. In search of a causative explanation for this unique American experience in the use of political intelligence and administrative expertise, the author offers this vignette of the New Deal and its planning apparatus. J

394. Leuchtenburg, William E. THE LEGACY OF FDR. *Wilson Q. 1982 6(2): 77-93.* Discusses the residual impact of Franklin D. Roosevelt's New Deal on three Democratic presidents: Harry S. Truman, John F. Kennedy, and Lyndon B. Johnson, with special attention to Johnson's Great Society legislation; 1933-68.

395. Longin, Thomas C. COAL, CONGRESS, AND THE COURTS: THE
BITUMINOUS COAL INDUSTRY AND THE NEW DEAL. *West Virginia
Hist. 1974 35(2): 101-130.* The depressed coal industry became a case study of
New Deal economic policy. The National Recovery Administration Bituminous
Coal Code temporarily boosted wages and prices. The Guffey Act (1935), supported by labor and small operators against the large companies, imposed wage
price controls and collective bargaining. Struck down by the Supreme Court, it
was replaced by a milder Coal Act (1937). Although these measures raised wages
and reduced hours, they never solved the basic long-term problem of over-
capacity; only World War II did that. Based on newspapers, congressional debates, and court cases; 47 notes.   J. H. Broussard

396. Louchheim, Katie. THE LITTLE RED HOUSE. *Virginia Q. Rev.
1980 56(1): 119-134.* This house in Washington, D.C., was where Thomas Gardiner Corcoran and Benjamin V. Cohen lived for three and a half years from June
1933. There they prepared and lobbied for many of the New Deal measures.
Provides short biographies of these men and sidelights on tactics, personalities,
and characteristics of many New Deal leaders.   O. H. Zabel

397. Lowitt, Richard. GEORGE W. NORRIS AND THE NEW DEAL IN
NEBRASKA. *Agric. Hist. 1977 51(2): 396-405.* Chronicles George W. Norris'
personal involvement in rectifying the damage done to farmers in Nebraska
during the Great Depression. As the senior senator from that state, Norris was
often in a position to intervene personally in existing federal programs to ensure
that Nebraskans received a full share of available relief funds. Primary and
secondary sources; 22 notes.   R. T. Fulton

398. Lowitt, Richard. HENRY A. WALLACE AND THE 1935 PURGE IN
THE DEPARTMENT OF AGRICULTURE. *Agric. Hist. 1979 53(3): 607-
621.* Newly published excerpts from Secretary of Agriculture Henry A. Wallace's
diary for January and February 1935 which show his position during the purge
of the Agricultural Adjustment Administration when Chester Dale fired Jerome
Frank and other liberal lawyers in the Office of the General Counsel. The liberals
wanted to force cotton planters to keep the same tenants on the land. Also
includes three related memoranda. 21 notes.   D. E. Bowers

399. Lowitt, Richard. THE NEW DEAL. *Pacific Northwest Q. 1977 68(1):
25-30.* Reviews the two-volume work *The New Deal,* edited by John Braeman,
et al. (Ohio State U. Pr., 1975) [see 13B:177]. Volume I contains 11 essays
covering the effects of New Deal policies on the national level, including impact
studies on agriculture, labor, corporate capitalism, fiction, blacks, and the legal
profession. Volume II offers 13 articles on New Deal programs at the state and
local levels. These assume a political orientation and clearly indicate that the
success and failure of Franklin D. Roosevelt's policies rested on the political
forces far below the national level. 4 photos.   M. L. Tate

400. Lowitt, Richard, ed. SHELTERBELTS IN NEBRASKA. *Nebraska
Hist. 1976 57(3): 405-422.* Two documents: one by George W. Norris, entitled
"Tree Planting In the Great Plains," originally published in the *Washington
Sunday Star,* 25 June 1939; the other, "A Plea For Great Plains Forestry,"
presented to the Congressional Joint Committee on Forestry on 19 December

1939 in Madison, Wisconsin. It was prepared by George E. Condra, director, Conservation and Survey Division, University of Nebraska; W. H. Brokaw, director, Agricultural Extension, University of Nebraska; and M. B. Jenkins, director, Forestry Research and Survey Division, University of Nebraska.   A

401. Lowry, Charles B. THE PWA IN TAMPA: A CASE STUDY. *Florida Hist. Q. 1974 52(4): 363-380.* Deals with the efforts of Ernest Kreher, founder of the Tampa Shipbuilding and Engineering Company, to secure a federal loan to build a dry dock in Tampa. Kreher first sought a loan in September 1932 from the Reconstruction Finance Corporation (RFC). By June 1933, with the RFC concerned only with the banking industry, Kreher shifted his attention to the Public Works Administration. Bureaucratic complications and political considerations produced a delay of more than two years before the loan contract was finally approved. The dry dock was almost completed by April 1937. Based on archival material from the University of Florida, newspapers, and secondary sources; 3 illus., 90 notes.   J. E. Findling

402. Lubove, Roy. THE NEW DEAL AND NATIONAL HEALTH. *Current Hist. 1977 72(427): 198-200, 224-226.* Examines health care provided by the New Deal, including the Federal Emergency Relief Administration, the Public Works Administration, the Farm Security Administration, and Social Security; discusses the move (via the Wagner bill) toward a national public health program funded by the federal government and the American Medical Association opposition to it on the basis of economic advantage and freedom and status of physicians, 1933-39.

403. Mal'kov, V. L. GARRI GOPKINS: STRANITSY POLITICHESKOI BIOGRAFII [Harry Hopkins: the pages of political biography]. *Novaia i Noevishaia Istoriia [USSR] 1979 (2): 124-144.* Discusses the life, activity, and ideas of Harry Hopkins, one of the closest advisors to President Franklin D. Roosevelt and the main proponent of the New Deal policies in the United States in the 1930's. Prior to his political career, Hopkins worked for charity organizations in New York and this enabled him to understand the limitations of the system of private monopoly capitalism. After Roosevelt's 1932 victory, he supervised the new administration's policies for alleviation of poverty and unemployment. Hopkins's influence grew but he realized that a mere tinkering with the system produced insignificant results incommensurable with the disastrous products of the great recession. Article to be continued. 82 notes.   V. Sobeslavsky

404. Marcello, Ronald E. THE SELECTION OF NORTH CAROLINA'S WPA CHIEF, 1935: A DISPUTE OVER POLITICAL PATRONAGE. *North Carolina Hist. R. 1975 52(1): 59-76.* State political issues were involved in Harry Hopkins's selection of a North Carolina Works Progress Administration chief. The Roosevelt administration owed favors to North Carolina's senators, Robert L. Doughton and Josiah Bailey. Doughton and Bailey favored conservative candidates, not wholly committed to the New Deal, and opposed certain liberal political rivals. At the last minute a compromise candidate, George W. Coan, Jr., appeared and was accepted by all factions. Based on interviews, personal papers, newspaper accounts, published government documents, and secondary sources; 6 illus., 61 notes.   T. L. Savitt

405. Mathews, Jane De Hart.   ARTS AND THE PEOPLE: THE NEW
DEAL QUEST FOR A CULTURAL DEMOCRACY.   *J. of Am. Hist. 1975
62(2): 316-339.* New Deal cultural projects of the 1930's sought to define and
implement a concept of cultural democracy. Federal projects in the visual and
performing arts and writing aimed at cultural accessibility for the public, social
and economic integration for the artists, and a new national art. The projects were
limited in their effectiveness by the economic distress of the era, bureaucratic
restrictions, and political opposition. The concept of a cultural democracy was
never clearly enunciated, and the effects of the projects are difficult to assess.
Based on project reports, contemporary journals, and secondary works; 2 illus.,
57 notes.   J. B. Street

406. May, Irvin, Jr.   MARVIN JONES: AGRARIAN AND POLITICIAN.
Agric. Hist. 1977 51(2): 421-440. A Texas panhandle Congressman during 1916-
40, Marvin Jones played a key role in the passage of such legislation as the
Agricultural Adjustment Act of 1933, the Jones-Connelly Farm Relief Act, the
Soil Conservation Act, the Domestic Allotment Act, the Bankhead-Jones Farm
Tenancy Act, and the Agricultural Adjustment Act of 1938. Primary and second-
ary sources; 49 notes.   R. T. Fulton

407. May, Irvin M., Jr.   SOUTHWESTERN AGRICULTURAL EXPERI-
MENT STATIONS DURING THE NEW DEAL.   *J. of the West 1979 18(4):
75-84.* Agricultural experiment stations in Texas, Oklahoma, New Mexico, and
Arizona had enjoyed a period of expansion before the states began to cut their
appropriations in 1931. Their few, but dedicated, scientists were forced to neglect
some areas of basic research in order to concentrate on the immediate problems
of farmers. Despite cutbacks in staff and funding, all of the stations reported some
progress, including the development of improved strains of crops, livestock disease control, soil and water conservation and other improvements in agricultural
science. Based on Department of Agriculture reports; 14 photos, 43 notes.
                                                                    B. S. Porter

408. McDean, Harry C.   FEDERAL FARM POLICY AND THE DUST
BOWL: THE HALF-RIGHT SOLUTION.   *North Dakota Hist. 1980 47(3):
21-31.* Despite extensive federal agricultural programs in the Great Plains by the
late 1930's, "the economy of the region has continued erratic, work opportunities
have remained limited, poverty is chronic to some areas, and out-migration has
stayed relatively constant." This is due primarily to a failure to understand the
complex history of the Plains and the need for nonagricultural employment
caused by the movement of unemployed industrial workers into some of the
region's poorest agricultural areas. Based on government documents and reports;
15 illus., 56 notes.   G. L. Olson

409. McHale, James M.   NATIONAL PLANNING AND RECIPROCAL
TRADE: THE NEW DEAL ORIGINS OF GOVERNMENT GUARANTEES
FOR PRIVATE EXPORTERS.   *Prologue 1974 6(3): 189-199.* An analysis of
the events which led the US government to underwrite export risks. The Great
Depression was perceived as being in large part a consequence of a decline in
international trade, as producers hesitated' to expand markets in a depression-
wracked world and foreign governments and currencies were unstable. An Import-Export Bank was established for the dual purposes of guaranteeing the

exporter a safe return on investments and for seeking out new markets, no matter how unsafe. 26 notes. V. L. Human

410. McLaughlin, Doris B. PUTTING MICHIGAN BACK TO WORK. *Michigan Hist. 1982 66(1): 30-37.* William Haber, professor emeritus, University of Michigan, was Michigan relief administrator, deputy Works Progress administrator and state National Youth administrator during the Depression. As a part of a larger oral history project, he gave his reflections of his work during the Depression. 19 pictures. L. E. Ziewacz

411. McQuaid, Kim. THE FRUSTRATION OF CORPORATE REVIVAL DURING THE EARLY NEW DEAL. *Historian 1979 41(4): 682-704.* Recent years have witnessed a shift in New Deal historiography, emphasizing continuities between the 1920's and 1930's. The concept of "corporate liberalism" has emerged from studies investigating the relationship between big business and the state. Examines two quasigovernmental agencies that enjoyed impressive measures of advisory influence during the early years of the New Deal—the Business Advisory Council of the Department of Commerce and the Industrial Advisory Board of the National Recovery Administration. Details the creation, early history, and membership of these agencies, and concludes that, while continuity between the New Era and the New Deal is overdrawn, corporate liberalism did weather the storm. Primary sources; 42 notes. R. S. Sliwoski

412. Meek, Edwin E. EUGENE OCTAVE SYKES, MEMBER AND CHAIRMAN OF FEDERAL COMMUNICATIONS COMMISSION AND FEDERAL RADIO COMMISSION, 1927-1939. *J. of Mississippi Hist. 1974 36(4): 377-386.* Describes the pioneer role in federal regulation of radio played by Eugene O. Sykes (1867-1945), a soft-spoken Mississippi lawyer and former member of the Mississippi Supreme Court, who was an original member of the Federal Radio Commission (1927-34), later chairman of it (1933-34), and first chairman of the Federal Communications Commission (1934-35), which replaced the FRC. Sykes served on the FCC until he resigned in 1939. Based on the *New York Times*; 38 notes. J. W. Hillje

413. Michelman, Irving S. A BANKER IN THE NEW DEAL: JAMES P. WARBURG. *Rev. Int. d'Hist. de la Banque [Italy] 1974 8: 35-59.* James P. Warburg, scion of one of the great German Jewish banking houses in the United States, was one of the few Wall Streeters to become part of the FDR administration. Drawn into the frantic preparations to reopen the banks in March 1933, Warburg became a delegate to the World Economic Conference in London, only to resign shortly after his appointment. Roosevelt made it clear that domestic monetary policy could not be compromised by international agreements. Roosevelt's decision to take the United States off the gold standard and to accept legislation which gave him far-reaching power to increase the money supply led Warburg to break with the administration. A successful polemicist and writer, Warburg became associated with the anti-New Deal faction and the Liberty League. Secondary sources; 24 notes. D. McGinnis

414. Miller, John E. PROGRESSIVISM AND THE NEW DEAL: THE WISCONSIN WORKS BILL OF 1935. *Wisconsin Mag. of Hist. 1978 62(1): 25-40.* Uses the controversy surrounding the unsuccessful Wisconsin Works Bill

as a means of studying the leadership of Governor Philip F. LaFollette; "the anomalous relationship between the Wisconsin progressives and the New Deal; the effectiveness of President Franklin Delano Roosevelt's strategy in co-opting potential left-wing opposition; and the declining influence of the states within the federal system." 10 illus., 43 notes.   N. C. Burckel

415. Miscamble, Wilson D. THURMAN ARNOLD GOES TO WASHINGTON: A LOOK AT ANTITRUST POLICY IN THE LATER NEW DEAL. *Business Hist. Rev. 1982 56(1): 1-15.* Thurman W. Arnold headed the Antitrust Division of the Justice Department during 1938-43. He was appointed by Franklin D. Roosevelt, who was not enthusiastic about a vigorous antitrust campaign and who did not expect Arnold to launch one. Roosevelt's attitude toward Arnold's campaign was ambivalent, merely permitting and not supporting it. When the demands of World War II production came into conflict with Arnold's activities, FDR offered, and Arnold accepted, a seat on the US Court of Appeals. FDR's failure to strongly support Arnold was a result of the New Deal's lack of a considered economic program and philosophy in its later years. Based on periodical material and published memoirs; illus., 60 notes.   C. J. Pusateri

416. Mitchell, Virgil L. THE LOUISIANA UNEMPLOYED AND THE CIVIL WORKS ADMINISTRATION. *Red River Valley Hist. Rev. 1980 5(3): 54-67.* Because federal relief programs instituted in 1932 in Louisiana to offset the effects of the Depression had failed to produce the desired results, President Roosevelt created the Civil Works Administration to aid the destitute through the winter of 1933-34 or until they could be absorbed by the Public Works Administration then being formed.

417. Moehring, Eugene P. PUBLIC WORKS AND THE NEW DEAL IN LAS VEGAS, 1933-1940. *Nevada Hist. Soc. Q. 1981 24(2): 107-129.* From 1933 to 1940, New Deal expenditures for public works programs in Nevada exceeded the federal government's per-capita spending in the rest of the states. Because Las Vegas city officials and the local Chamber of Commerce lobbied and waged particularly effective publicity campaigns, they secured ambitious public works projects that vastly improved the city and suburban enclaves, enhanced the city's acceptability to tourists, and stimulated the local economy sufficiently so that Las Vegas lost little momentum in its drive to achieve metropolitan standing. Based on newspapers and archival materials at the University of Nevada, Las Vegas; 2 photos, 2 maps, 64 notes.   H. T. Lovin

418. Monroe, Gerald M. THE 1930'S: ART, IDEOLOGY AND THE WPA. *Art in Am. 1975 63(6): 64-67.* Examines connections among artists working for the Works Progress Administration in the 1930's, art institutions, federal government art patronage, and the Communist Party.

419. Moore, James R. SOURCES OF NEW DEAL ECONOMIC POLICY: THE INTERNATIONAL DIMENSION. *J. of Am. Hist. 1974 61(3): 728-744.* In the earliest months of the New Deal, Franklin D. Roosevelt developed his pragmatic economic policies within an international dimension. He and his economic advisors advocated schemes for global public works programs backed by continued American loans, stabilization of currency exchange rates at devalued levels, a tariff "truce," and settlement of the thorny war debts issue. Pressed by

a Congress that advocated inflationary action and faced with an attitude of non-cooperation from France and Britain, Roosevelt turned to a frankly nationalistic economic policy. 50 notes.   K. B. West

420. Morgan, Thomas S., Jr.   A "FOLLY . . . MANIFEST TO EVERYONE": THE MOVEMENT TO ENACT UNEMPLOYMENT INSURANCE LEGISLATION IN NORTH CAROLINA, 1935-1936.   *North Carolina Hist. R. 1975 52(3): 283-302.* As part of Franklin D. Roosevelt's New Deal program, the Social Security Act (1935) provided unemployment insurance compensation to workers based on state compliance with certain stipulations by 1 January 1936. North Carolina was near the close of its biennial legislative session when Congress passed the law. For political and financial reasons, Governor J. C. B. Ehringhaus opposed calling a special session, but he was forced to in December 1937, only weeks before the regular session. Based on manuscript and printed public papers, newspaper accounts, and secondary sources; 5 illus., 70 notes.   T. L. Savitt

421. Myhra, David.   REXFORD GUY TUGWELL: INITIATOR OF AMERICA'S GREENBELT NEW TOWNS, 1935 TO 1936.   *J. of the Am. Inst. of Planners 1974 40(3): 176-188.* "Between 1935 and 1936, the United States Department of Agriculture (USDA) initiated a public housing program that resulted in the construction of planned new communities called Greenbelt Towns. The prime mover behind this effort was Rexford Tugwell. The significance of this idea was his advanced concept of resettling the rural poor in planned towns at the edge of urban areas. Tugwell recognized, earlier perhaps than many of his colleagues, the 'push-pull' tendencies emerging in American society in the 1930s. Arguing that urban growth was inevitable, Tugwell's Greenbelt concept was to demonstrate how housing could be surrounded with a more pleasing environment in order to accommodate the expanding rural to urban migration. In less than two years Tugwell's Resettlement Administration planned and constructed three new communities and litigated a fourth. By all standards, these accomplishments demonstrate an unprecedented speed record for action by a bureaucracy."   J

422. Myles, John.   THE TRILLION DOLLAR MISUNDERSTANDING.   *Working Papers Mag. 1981 8(4): 22-31.* Argues that the Reagan administration's rationale for saving the Social Security system by slashing benefits is untrue and unsound, and traces the history of the system that was a product of Franklin D. Roosevelt's New Deal in the 1930's in order to single out the logic behind the conservatives' attack on Social Security's soundness.

423. Nelson, Lawrence J.   NEW DEAL AND FREE MARKET: THE MEMPHIS MEETING OF THE SOUTHERN COMMISSIONERS OF AGRICULTURE, 1937.   *Tennessee Hist. Q. 1981 40(3): 225-238.* Following apparent recovery in 1936, cotton farmers in the South forgot about acreage reduction and expanded production in the following year. The result was predictable—prices fell. Southerners then looked to the Roosevelt administration for financial relief. In September, the Association of Southern Commissioners of Agriculture meeting in Memphis amidst considerable agitation found one of the leading cotton planters, Oscar G. Johnston of Mississippi, to be a persuasive advocate of federal policy based upon a combination of allotments and subsidies. The resulting controversy indicated that Southern opposition to New Deal farm policies was based more on a pragmatic approach to the economic programs than on opposi-

tion to the philosophy behind the New Deal. In a short time Southerners had begun to expect federal assistance. Mainly letters and newspapers; 54 notes.

C. L. Grant

424. Nelson, Lawrence J. OSCAR JOHNSTON, THE NEW DEAL, AND THE COTTON SUBSIDY PAYMENTS CONTROVERSY, 1936-1937. *J. of Southern Hist. 1974 40(3): 399-416.* Subsidies to corporate agribusiness enterprises have provoked controversy since the mid-1930's incidents involving Oscar Goodbar Johnston and the cotton industry. While retaining the presidency of the Delta & Pine Land Company, a large cotton producing corporation with majority British participation, Johnston also served the New Deal in the Agricultural Adjustment Administration, the Federal Cotton Producers' Pool, and the Commodity Credit Corporation. Republican Senator Arthur Vandenberg and the press raised the issues of conflict of interest and subsidies to foreign citizens by exposing the fact that while Johnston continued to administer cotton subsidies, one of the largest recipients of these funds was the Delta & Pine Land Company. Based on manuscripts and published primary and secondary sources; 75 notes.

T. D. Schoonover

425. Ober, Michael J. THE CCC EXPERIENCE IN GLACIER NATIONAL PARK. *Montana 1976 26(3): 30-39.* During its existence between 1933 and 1942, the Civilian Conservation Corps maintained camps in Glacier National Park and engaged in projects of construction and protection. The supervisors reported that the work was beneficial to the Park and to the members of the Corps. Based on official correspondence in the Park archives at the University of Montana, and on newspaper accounts. Illus.   S. R. Davison

426. Ohl, John Kennedy. TALES TOLD BY A NEW DEALER: GENERAL HUGH S. JOHNSON. *Montana 1975 25(4): 66-77.* Widely known as head of F. D. Roosevelt's National Recovery Administration, Hugh S. Johnson (1882-1942) had already combined careers as a military officer and as an author of short stories, published in *Harper's, Scribner's,* and other popular magazines. He earned a law degree in 1916, leading to administrative assignments with the Army in World War I, then retired to jobs in private industry, until the NRA interval. His last employment involved production of a syndicated newspaper column with an isolationist viewpoint. Illus.   S. R. Davison

427. Olson, James S. HARVEY C. COUCH AND THE RECONSTRUCTION FINANCE CORPORATION. *Arkansas Hist. Q. 1973 32(3): 217-225.*

428. O'Neill, Robert K. THE FEDERAL WRITERS' PROJECT FILES FOR INDIANA. *Indiana Mag. of Hist. 1980 76(2): 85-96.* The origins, development, and demise of the Federal Writers' Project in Indiana brought employment to idle authors and researchers and the publication of *Indiana: A Guide to the Hoosier State.* As the activities of the Federal Writers' Project ended early in World War II, so did this venture into local history. Based on the records of the Indiana Federal Writers' Project, secondary sources, and journal articles; 28 notes.   A. Erlebacher

429. Ostrower, Gary B. THE AMERICAN DECISION TO JOIN THE INTERNATIONAL LABOR ORGANIZATION. *Labor Hist. 1975 16(4): 495-504.* Support for American membership in the International Labor Orga-

nization arose from the Department of Labor under Frances Perkins. With the support of the Department of State and Franklin D. Roosevelt, opposition from isolationist sentiment and financial conservatives was overcome by 1934. Suggests that the New Deal may have been less isolationist than generally characterized. Based on archives of Departments of Labor and State; 23 notes.

L. L. Athey

430. Patenaude, Lionel. THE NEW DEAL: ITS EFFECT ON THE SO-CIAL FABRIC OF TEXAS SOCIETY, 1933-1939. *Social Sci. J. 1977 14(3): 51-60.* Discusses the condition of labor, the economy, and social issues in Texas during the New Deal; concludes that though Texans suffered during the Depression, relatively it was less drastic than for the remainder of the country.

431. Patterson, James T., ed. LIFE ON RELIEF IN RHODE ISLAND, 1934: A CONTEMPORARY VIEW FROM THE FIELD. *Rhode Island Hist. 1980 39(3): 79-91.* Reproduces, with editorial annotations, two letters to Harry L. Hopkins, head of the Federal Emergency Relief Administration, from Robert Washburn and Martha Gellhorn. Based on documents in the Roosevelt Library, Hyde Park, New York, and published documents and statistics; 11 illus., 9 notes.

P. J. Coleman

432. Pechatnov, Vladimir O. ZA KULISAMI VYRABOTKI "NOVOGO KURSA" (F. FRANKFURTER-U. LIPPMAN) [Behind the scenes of the New Deal (F. Frankfurter-W. Lippmann)]. *Voprosy Istorii [USSR] 1979 (7): 112-123.* Analyzes the debates and discussions among Franklin D. Roosevelt, Felix Frankfurter (1882-1965), Walter Lippmann (1889-1974), and others on the eve of the New Deal (1932). THe writings of Frankfurter released in 1945 show clearly that the New Deal temporarily quieted the economic crisis of the 1930's; the United States would remain a capitalist society. At the same time one cannot hide the fact that the outcome of the experiment continued to remain uncertain. Finally the economic success of the New Deal could not be proved because World War II completely changed the nature of the economic crisis of the 1930's. Based on correspondence between FDR and Frankfurter, the Walter Lippmann letters, and the Perkins Collection; 62 notes.

J. L. Evans

433. Pellanda, Anna. GLI ASPETTI MONETARI E CREDITIZI DEL NEW DEAL: RIFLESSI SULLA CONTEMPORANEA REALTÀ ITAL-IANA [Monetary and financial aspects of the New Deal: their relation to contemporary Italian reality]. *Econ. e Storia [Italy] 1977 24(4): 506-513.* Compares Franklin D. Roosevelt's monetary and financial policy with that of Benito Mussolini, 1922-36. The common aim was for monetary stability. The economist Irving Fisher visited Mussolini in 1927 and Roosevelt in 1933. The economic policies of these political leaders were antiquantitativist, or neo-Keynesian, because their intervention was not merely monetary. From 1925 to 1936 Mussolini made war on private banks. The contemporary American press praised the foundation of the Istituto Mobiliare Italiano (IMI) in 1931 and the Istituto per la Ricostruzione Industriale (IRI) in 1932, which were two instruments of control similar to Roosevelt's Reconstruction Finance Corporation. Secondary sources; 34 notes.

F. Busachi

434. Phillips, Waite and Trafzer, Clifford E.   VIEWS FROM THE RED RIVER VALLEY: A "LIBERAL" REPUBLICAN'S PHILOSOPHY.   *Red River Valley Hist. R. 1974 1(1): 70-77.* In two letters, Republican politician Waite Phillips expressed his political philosophy, his criticisms of the New Deal, and his assessment of the latter's impact on rugged individualism.   S

435. Pinkett, Harold T.   RECORDS OF A HISTORIC THRUST FOR CONSERVATION.   *Prologue 1976 8(2): 77-84.* Voluminous federal records detail the second momentous effort toward the conservation of natural resources during the New Deal. These records are scattered among the National Archives' holdings of many governmental agencies, including the Departments of Labor, Agriculture, War, Interior, National Park Service, Army Corps of Engineers, etc. Based on first-hand examination of holdings.   N. Lederer

436. Platschek, Hans.   ROOSEVELTS MALER   [Roosevelt's painters]. *Frankfurter Hefte [West Germany] 1975 30(7): 49-64.* During the New Deal, thousands of artists were given jobs painting public buildings; the style, which can still be seen on the walls of post offices and courthouses throughout the land, is a heroic, historical one, reminiscent of contemporary Russia's Socialist Realism.

437. Polenberg, Richard.   ROOSEVELT, CARTER, AND EXECUTIVE REORGANIZATION: LESSONS OF THE 1930'S.   *Presidential Studies Q. 1979 9(1): 35-46.* Lessons pertaining to scientific management, the nature of bureaucracy and the bureaucratic ethos, planning, congressional review, presidential power, and public opinion in executive reorganization learned by the Franklin D. Roosevelt administration during 1937-38 are of value to the Jimmy Carter administration, which seeks similar reforms.

438. Porter, David.   THE BATTLE OF THE TEXAS GIANTS: HATTON SUMNERS, SAM RAYBURN, AND THE LOGAN-WALTER BILL OF 1939.   *Texana 1974 12(4): 349-361.* The Logan-Walter Bill would have restricted the power of the executive agencies, thus limiting the power of President Roosevelt's New Deal. Two of the most influential members of the House of Representatives—both from Texas—took different sides in the heated debate on the bill; Hatton Sumners supported the bill and Sam Rayburn opposed the bill. Although the bill passed Congress, Roosevelt vetoed it, and his veto could not be overridden. Based on primary and secondary sources; 22 notes.
                                                        B. D. Ledbetter

439. Porter, David.   SENATOR CARL HATCH AND THE HATCH ACT OF 1939.   *New Mexico Hist. R. 1973 48(2): 151-164.* The Hatch Act of 1939 regulated the political activities of federal officials. Historians have written extensively about the act, but the sponsor of the bill has received little attention. Hatch was born in Kirwin, Kansas, November 1889. In 1912 he received a law degree from Cumberland University. When Hatch visited Clovis, New Mexico, he liked the area so well that he decided to settle there. Although Hatch supported most New Deal programs, he became concerned with the political activities of the WPA workers.   J. H. Krenkel

440. Porter, David L.   KEY PITTMAN AND THE MONETARY ACT OF 1939.   *Nevada Hist. Soc. Q. 1978 21(3): 205-213.* US Senator Key Pittman (1872-1940), long a crusader for laws increasing silver prices, at last scored

several victories for more costly silver early in the New Deal years. Finally, in 1939, he succeeded, by deft maneuvering with Republicans and conservative Democrats in the Senate, in orchestrating the passage of more favorable silver legislation. Based on US government documents and archival source materials; 30 notes. H. T. Lovin

441. Potter, Barrett G. THE CIVILIAN CONSERVATION CORPS AND NEW YORK'S "NEGRO QUESTION": A CASE STUDY IN FEDERAL-STATE RACE RELATIONS DURING THE GREAT DEPRESSION. *Afro-Am. in New York Life and Hist. 1977 1(2): 183-200.* Discusses employment discrimination against Negroes in the Civilian Conservation Corps in New York, 1933-42.

442. Pursell, Carroll W., Jr. GOVERNMENT AND TECHNOLOGY IN THE GREAT DEPRESSION. *Technology and Culture 1979 20(1): 162-174.* The New Deal, in the new agencies it set up and the reports they issued, began with doubts about the good effects of rapid technological change. But by 1940, as exemplified in the Tennessee Valley Authority and the Rural Electrification Administration, it encouraged most citizens to conform to the new technologies, offered some form of special welfare to those who were not benefitted, and "eschewed any serious attempt at national planning." 31 notes. C. O. Smith

443. Putnam, Carl M. THE CCC EXPERIENCE. *Military R. 1973 53(9): 49-62.* Surveys the US Army's participation in the Civilian Conservation Corps. After initially opposing its participation in CCC on grounds that it would interfere with the primary mission of defense preparedness, the Army became an enthusiastic participant as it realized the bonus the operation was paying in officer training, training in noncombat specialties, and favorable publicity. Primary and secondary sources; 7 illus., 70 notes. J. K. Ohl

444. Rader, Frank J. HARRY L. HOPKINS, THE AMBITIOUS CRUSADER: AN HISTORICAL ANALYSIS OF THE MAJOR INFLUENCES ON HIS CAREER, 1912-1940. *Ann. of Iowa 1977 44(2): 83-102.* Examines "leading conditioners" of New Dealer Harry Hopkins's (1890-1946) development from "an ambitious relief administrator into the selfless assistant president of the war years." Discusses Hopkins's family and his formal education at Grinnell College, his progressive views and social work career, the impact of his chronic poor health, his political ambitions, and "the emergency-charged ambiance of the New Deal years." Based on secondary and primary sources, including the Hopkins Papers at the Franklin D. Roosevelt Library; 3 photos, 59 notes.
P. L. Petersen

445. Rader, Frank J. WORK RELIEF AND NATIONAL DEFENSE: SOME NOTES ON WPA IN ALASKA. *Alaska J. 1976 6(1): 54-59.* Reviews Works Progress Administration's goals and objectives, and describes a WPA project at Palmer, Alaska. The project was primarily rural rehabilitation. 21 notes. E. E. Eminhizer

446. Rader, Frank J. THE WORKS PROGRESS ADMINISTRATION AND HAWAIIAN PREPAREDNESS, 1935-1940. *Military Affairs 1979 43(1): 12-17.* Early preparedness activities of the Works Progress Administration (WPA) in Hawaii and other territories proved to be an indication of a changing

US foreign policy. President Franklin D. Roosevelt took several surreptitious steps to strengthen the nation's outer defense network; one such move was the transfer of the Hawaiian WPA to War Department control in 1938. Thus, military projects would receive top priority in the allocation of relief funds and labor. Based on WPA records and secondary sources; 35 notes.   A. M. Osur

447.   Reading, Don C.   NEW DEAL ACTIVITY AND THE STATES, 1933 TO 1939.   *J. of Econ. Hist. 1973 33(4): 792-810.* New Deal per capita federal expenditures varied widely by state and region; western mountain states received the highest allocations. Percentage of decline in real income, rather than the absolute income of a region, corresponds with New Deal allocations. Regression analysis suggests that New Deal agencies distributed funds in a pattern contributing to relief, recovery, and improved use of natural resources, but not to effect reform by equalizing income. The South, which Roosevelt proclaimed the "Nation's Number One Economic Problem," received the lowest per capita allocations in nearly all programs. Raises questions about political motivations behind the varying allocations and their economic impact. Based on primary and secondary sources; 4 tables, 11 notes, biblio., appendix.   W. R. Hively

448.   Reeves, William D.   PWA AND COMPETITIVE ADMINISTRATION IN THE NEW DEAL.   *J. of Am. Hist. 1973 60(2): 357-372.* The competitive theory of administration developed by Franklin Delano Roosevelt has often been admired as producing efficiency. In the case of the Public Works Administration (PWA), however, the competition over the size of expenditure, the selection of the administrator, and the appointment of staff at the state level, led to delays and to the ultimate failure of PWA as a recovery instrument. As director of the budget, Lewis Douglas overrode the views of leading senators in reducing appropriations to $3,500,000,000 and in transferring much of that money to other agencies in lieu of their own specific appropriations. The cautious and penurious Harold Ickes won out over the more imaginative Hugh S. Johnson as chief of public works administration. Political competition between rival Democratic state organizations and between Democrats and Progressive Republicans led to delays in implementing PWA efforts on the local level. 60 notes.
                    K. B. West

449.   Reuss, Martin.   THE ARMY CORPS OF ENGINEERS AND FLOOD-CONTROL POLITICS ON THE LOWER MISSISSIPPI.   *Louisiana Hist. 1982 23(2): 131-148.* Contrasts the response to problems of flood control in two parts of the lower Mississippi watershed. In the Atchafalaya basin in south-central Louisiana, reasonable and theoretically valid engineering plans were developed in response to public and Congressional demands following the 1927 Mississippi flood. In the Yazoo basin in northwest Mississippi, seven reservoirs were built, despite analyses demonstrating a negative cost-benefit ratio for the projects, because of the persistence of the congressman from that district and because they fit the depression-induced demand for public works to help the unemployed. Based primarily on Mississippi River Commission papers and other government documents; 3 maps, 49 notes.   R. E. Noble

450.   Ring, Daniel F.   THE CLEVELAND PUBLIC LIBRARY AND THE WPA: A STUDY IN CREATIVE PARTNERSHIP.   *Ohio Hist. 1975 84(3): 158-164.* The desire of the New Deal to substitute work for relief was embodied

in several agencies, but it was the Works Progress Administration (WPA) that affected the Cleveland Public Library in two important categories: bibliographical service and fine arts. The Federal Writers' Project produced *The Annals of Cleveland*, the Union Catalogue, and the Historic Records Survey of Cuyahoga County. In the fine arts program, too, the main concern was to provide jobs for people, at the same time creating a cultural heritage for the community. 48 notes.

E. P. Stickney

451. Rison, David. FEDERAL AID TO ARKANSAS EDUCATION: 1933-1936. *Arkansas Hist. Q. 1977 36(2): 192-200.* The depression profoundly affected the Arkansas public schools. As the tax base withered, schools closed and teachers failed to receive salaries. The Federal Emergency Relief Administration (FERA) intervened with financial support to keep schools open. The Arkansas legislature did little to raise money within the state to support education, despite warnings from FERA administrator Harry Hopkins. Hopkins finally suspended relief funds until a state tax law was passed to raise school funds. Based on newspaper accounts and manuscript letters in the National Archives; 25 notes.

T. L. Savitt

452. Ritchie, Donald A. THE LEGISLATIVE IMPACT OF THE PECORA INVESTIGATION. *Capitol Studies 1977 5(2): 87-101.* Senator Ferdinand Pecora led the Senate Banking and Currency Committee's investigations into misdealings of Wall Street businessmen; the success of the Pecora investigations changed popular attitudes toward Senate investigations, resulted in reform legislation, and demonstrated the power of Congress, 1933.

453. Robbins, William G. THE GREAT EXPERIMENT IN INDUSTRIAL SELF-GOVERNMENT: THE LUMBER INDUSTRY AND THE NATIONAL RECOVERY ADMINISTRATION. *J. of Forest Hist. 1981 25(3): 128-143.* Unable to control competition in the rapidly contracting economy of the 1930's, lumber industry leaders experimented with industrial self-regulation under the auspices of the New Deal's National Recovery Administration. Minimum price regulations of the Lumber Code Authority were mainly the work of large operators. Despite industry receptiveness at the outset, the code proved disappointing. Regional rivalries, differences over the code's role in conserving forest resources, dissatisfaction among small operators, and the competitive nature of the industry plagued the relatively weak Lumber Code Authority. Non-compliance became critical in 1934, and the experiment had lost its credibility by April 1935. Based on records of various trade associations as well as personal papers, federal documents, and secondary sources; 7 photos, 58 notes.

R. W. Judd

454. Rosenstone, Robert A. THE FEDERAL (MOSTLY NON-) WRITERS' PROJECT. *Rev. in Am. Hist. 1978 6(3): 400-404.* Review article prompted by Monty Noam Penkower's *The Federal Writers' Project: A Study in Government Patronage of the Arts* (Urbana: U. of Illinois, 1977).

455. Ross, B. Joyce. MARY MCLEOD BETHUNE AND THE NATIONAL YOUTH ADMINISTRATION: A CASE STUDY OF POWER RELATIONSHIPS IN THE BLACK CABINET OF FRANKLIN D. ROOSEVELT. *J. of Negro Hist. 1975 60(1): 1-28.* Argues that the 1930's rather

than the 1960's should be termed the beginning of the "Second Reconstruction" because of the revival of federal support for racial equality. The existence of a so-called New Deal "Black Cabinet" was illustrated by the career of Mary McLeod Bethune with the National Youth Administration (NYA). As Director of the NYA's Division of Negro Affairs, Bethune was a symbol of black aspiration in the earliest years of the "Second Reconstruction." Based on primary sources in the records of the NYA in the National Archives; 39 notes.

N. G. Sapper

456.   Ross, Ronald.   THE ROLE OF BLACKS IN THE FEDERAL THE-ATRE, 1935-1939.   *J. of Negro Hist. 1974 59(1): 38-50.* The Federal Theatre Project (1935-39) was designed to make drama available to the masses for the first time. Within its program, the Federal Theatre established special ethnic projects which included black theater in several cities. By the project's conclusion, 22 U.S. cities had served as headquarters for black theater units. The success of the black writers, directors, stage designers, and actors proved that all these talented people needed was the opportunity. Secondary sources; 54 notes.   N. G. Sapper

457.   Saindon, Bob and Sullivan, Bunky.   TAMING THE MISSOURI AND TREATING THE DEPRESSION: FORT PECK DAM.   *Montana 1977 27(3): 34-57.* During 1933-43, the US Army Corps of Engineers constructed the largest earthen dam in the world across the Missouri River near the sight of an old fur trade post named Fort Peck. This dam and its reservoir provided flood control, irrigation water, (later) hydroelectric power, and employment for thousands. Constructed by hydraulic dredging, the dam began without congressional approval and was the product of midwest pressures for uniform water flows in the Missouri. It eventually employed 10,456 individuals and cost more than $160 million. The dam displaced many residents and inundated much productive land with little long- or short-range benefit for Montana, except employment. All aspects of Fort Peck Dam construction set records for size and haste. Downriver benefits for flood control, power generation, and navigation have outweighed costs. The dam stands today as an engineering wonder and a spectacular monument to the people who built it. Based on interviews, federal documents, and contemporary newspapers; 31 illus., map.   R. C. Myers

458.   Salamon, Lester M.   THE TIME DIMENSION IN POLICY EVALUATION: THE CASE OF THE NEW DEAL LAND REFORM EXPERIMENTS.   *Public Policy 1979 27(2): 129-185.* Long-term evaluation of resettlement programs which opened land ownership to black sharecroppers, indicates that though originally considered a failure in the 1930's-40's, the program was a success in the 1960's because it produced a permanent landed middle class which became the backbone of the civil rights movement.

459.   Saloutos, Theodore.   NEW DEAL AGRICULTURAL POLICY: AN EVALUATION.   *J. of Am. Hist. 1974 61(2): 394-416.* An analysis of the manifold aspects of New Deal farm policy demonstrates that efforts of the first Agricultural Adjustment Administration to raise prices to parity were not very successful, that acreage reduction was countered by expansion of yield per acre, that relatively few acres of crop land subject to erosion were in fact covered by plans of the Soil Conservation Service, and that the concept of the second AAA's "ever normal granary" did develop reserves and seemed to operate successfully.

In spite of the "agricultural establishment," more was done for tenant farmers, sharecroppers, and farm laborers than is commonly supposed. On the whole, the New Deal constituted "the greatest innovative epoch in the history of American agriculture." 72 notes.   K. B. West

460.   Sargent, James E.   F. D. R., FOREIGN POLICY, AND THE DOMES-TIC-FIRST PERSPECTIVE, 1933-1936: AN APPRAISAL.   *Peace and Change 1975 3(1): 24-29.* Evaluates the policies of Franklin Delano Roosevelt's first term as president.   S

461.   Sargent, James E.   FDR AND LEWIS W. DOUGLAS: BUDGET BAL-ANCING AND THE EARLY NEW DEAL.   *Prologue 1974 6(1): 33-43.* Ana-lyzes why the personal, political, and policymaking relationships of President Franklin D. Roosevelt and Lewis W. Douglas, director of the budget, changed and deteriorated during 1933-34. "In terms of their policy relationship, Douglas believed that the government must consistently adhere to orderly spending and economizing on the grounds that maintaining United States credit superseded and buttressed the entire recovery program. . . ." The president's "halfway com-mitments prevented him from determining whether he or Douglas was right about the federal government's capacity to spend America into prosperity during peacetime." Douglas' resignation was accepted on 30 August 1934.
                                                                                                                D. D. Cameron

462.   Sargent, James E.   ROOSEVELT'S ECONOMY ACT: FISCAL CON-SERVATISM AND THE EARLY NEW DEAL.   *Congressional Studies 1980 7(2): 33-51.* Analyzes the origins and decline of Franklin D. Roosevelt's fiscal conservatism as embodied in the Economy Act (US, 1933).

463.   Schön, Donald A.   PUBLIC SERVICE ORGANIZATIONS AND THE CAPACITY FOR PUBLIC LEARNING.   *Int. Social Sci. J. [France] 1979 31(4): 682-695.* Focusing on the Works Progress Administration (WPA), exam-ines how public service organizations implement and sometimes change the pub-lic policy they are designed to follow.

464.   Schuyler, Michael W.   DROUGHT AND POLITICS 1936: KANSAS AS A TEST CASE.   *Great Plains J. 1975 15(1): 2-27.* Analyzes the various drought relief and long-range agricultural programs of the New Deal in 1936 in Kansas. It is difficult to assess the influence of the drought on the presidential race between Franklin D. Roosevelt and Alfred M. Landon. However, the Roose-velt administration appears to have benefited in several ways. Primary and sec-ondary sources; 9 illus., 62 notes.   O. H. Zabel

465.   Schuyler, Michael W.   FEDERAL DROUGHT RELIEF ACTIVITIES IN KANSAS, 1934.   *Kansas Hist. Q. 1976 42(4): 403-424.* Snow and rain early in 1934 kept Kansans from feeling the full effect of the drought until the summer. By then the New Deal had formulated plans to buy surplus cattle, to provide feed for the reduced herds, to make seed loans, to purchase submarginal land, and to provide work projects for stricken areas that were concerned primarily with water conservation. Kansas farmers participated in all of these programs. Primary and secondary sources; 124 notes.   W. F. Zornow

466.   Schuyler, Michael W.   THE HAIR-SPLITTERS: RENO AND WAL-
LACE, 1932-1933.   *Ann. of Iowa 1976 43(6): 403-429.* During the agricultural
crisis of the early 1930's, Iowans Milo Reno and Henry Agard Wallace were often
pictured as "polar opposites by the press." Reno was the leader of the militant
Farmers' Holiday Association while Wallace, first as editor of *Wallaces' Farmer*
and then as Secretary of Agriculture, was thought to be more of a "defender of
the established order." Differences between the two men were real but "a careful
examination of their correspondence suggests many similarities in their approach
to the Depression of the 1930s." The bitter rivalry between the two men "can best
be understood as the result of differences in personality, style, circumstance, and
position, rather than disagreement on substantive ideological issues." Secondary
and primary sources, particularly correspondence in Reno and Wallace Papers;
2 photos, 90 notes.   P. L. Petersen

467.   Schwartz, Bonnie Fox.   NEW DEAL WORK RELIEF AND ORGA-
NIZED LABOR: THE CWA AND THE AFL BUILDING TRADES.
Labor Hist. 1976 17(1): 38-57. The Civil Works Administration, a first attempt
at work relief, faced immediate problems of hiring and wage practices in their
relationship to the American Federation of Labor's building trades. Under the
leadership of John Carmody federal regulations attempted to protect labor's right
to organize and uphold the prevailing wage rates, while mollifying the opposition
of local employers. The CWA provided a "first forum" to alleviate organized
labor's suspicions of work relief. Based on the CWA papers and the oral memoir
of John Carmody; 41 notes.   L. L. Athey

468.   Schwartz, Bonnie Fox.   SOCIAL WORKERS AND NEW DEAL POL-
ITICIANS IN CONFLICT: CALIFORNIA'S BRANION-WILLIAMS CASE,
1933-1934.   *Pacific Hist. R. 1973 42(1): 53-73.* The creation of the Federal Civil
Works Administration in 1933 set the stage in California for a major confrontation between social workers and the politicians of both parties who were eager
to control the funds and jobs of the federal project. Relief administrators Ray C.
Branion and Pierce Williams became Senator William G. McAdoo's target for
accusations of mismanagement of the California CWA and were eventually indicted. Social workers from coast to coast protested, organizing a prestigious
committee to raise funds and arouse public sentiment. The case was dismissed,
but it represented the most ambitious attempt of both McAdoo's machine and
California Republicans to use relief for patronage. 81 notes.   E. C. Hyslop

469.   Schwieder, Dorothy.   THE GRANGER HOMESTEAD PROJECT.
Palimpsest 1977 58(5): 149-161. In March 1934, Granger, Iowa, was chosen as
the site of a Federal Subsistence Homesteads Corporation project. Granger,
located in the heart of Iowa's depressed coal-mining region, was ideally suited for
the experiment because severe unemployment, substandard housing, and inadequate social and educational opportunities were chronic problems. Conceived
initially by Father Luigi Ligutti as a self-help project designed to promote cooperative rural living, the endeavor soon became a New Deal showplace. It did not
fulfill Father Ligutti's high expectations, but was very significant as a successful
social experiment. 3 photos, note on sources.   D. W. Johnson

470. Sears, James M. BLACK AMERICANS AND THE NEW DEAL. *Hist. Teacher 1976 10(1): 89-105.* A discussion of black support for Franklin D. Roosevelt and the New Deal. Blacks, disenchanted with the Hoover administration, anticipated inclusion in New Deal efforts to create jobs for the unemployed. Blacks benefitted from the New Deal in perhaps greater measure than they had anticipated. Without specifically committing himself, Roosevelt gave black Americans a stake in the governmental process. Black political and religious leaders, the black press and organizations, and Roosevelt's charisma helped place Negroes firmly in the Democratic party. Based on primary and secondary sources; 63 notes, biblio. P. W. Kennedy

471. Severson, Robert F., Jr. THE CIVILIAN CONSERVATION CORPS: A WORKFARE SOLUTION. *Res. in Econ. Hist. 1982 (Supplement 2): 121-126.* Income data for 1937-81 of former members of the Civilian Conservation Corps shows that the enrollees had higher income levels compared to the total working population. The Civilian Conservation Corps was a success in terms of the human investment value of giving young men jobs and skills. Primary sources; table, 7 notes. J. Powell

472. Sewall, Arthur F. KEY PITTMAN AND THE QUEST FOR THE CHINA MARKET, 1933-1940. *Pacific Hist. R. 1975 44(3): 351-371.* Although Nevada's Senator Key Pittman in the 1930's used the argument that overseas expansion of the American economic system comprised the best means of economic recovery, he did so as a tactical device to win additional support for programs devised to raise the domestic price of silver. He achieved this end in an agreement signed at the World Economic and Monetary Conference in 1933 and in the Silver Purchase Act of 1934. When the domestic price of silver reached 77 cents, Pittman ceased to emphasize the need to increase exports to China, despite the fact that they were on the decline. Based on the Pittman Papers (Library of Congress), the Senate Foreign Relations Committee Papers, the F. D. Roosevelt Papers, published government documents, other published primary sources, and secondary sources; 75 notes. W. K. Hobson

473. Shapiro, Edward S. CATHOLIC AGRARIAN THOUGHT AND THE NEW DEAL. *Catholic Hist. Rev. 1979 65(4): 583-599.* The American Catholic rural movement welcomed the election of Franklin D. Roosevelt in 1932. It believed the New Deal would embark upon an extensive program of rural rehabilitation, the restoration of the widespread ownership of productive property, and demographic decentralization. While initially favorably disposed toward the Agricultural Adjustment Act, the National Industrial Recovery Act, and other New Deal measures, Catholic ruralists had by the end of the 1930's concluded that the New Deal was a pragmatic response directed at propping up American capitalism rather than embarking upon a fundamental reconstruction of the economy along Catholic and Jeffersonian lines. A

474. Shapiro, Edward S. DONALD DAVIDSON AND THE TENNESSEE VALLEY AUTHORITY: THE RESPONSE OF A SOUTHERN CONSERVATIVE. *Tenn. Hist. Q. 1974 33(4): 436-451.* Though an early supporter of some of Franklin D. Roosevelt's programs, Donald Davidson soon became a vocal critic of the Tennessee Valley Authority (TVA). Unlike other agrarians, Davidson was suspicious that the TVA was a plot of northern business interests to

exploit and more completely dominate the South at the expense of southerners. He interpreted the TVA as an instrument of political collectivism, run by outsiders, designed to destroy the South's traditions. Primary and secondary sources; 28 notes.   M. B. Lucas

475. Shiner, John F. GENERAL BENJAMIN FOULOIS AND THE 1934 AIR MAIL DISASTER. *Aerospace Hist. 1978 25(4): 221-230.* Discusses the disastrous attempt by the Army Air Corps to fly the US mail and the part played by General Benjamin D. Foulois, Chief of the Air Corps. In February 1934, President Roosevelt decided that the government mail contracts with the commercial airlines were obtained by fraud and collusion. He therefore cancelled them and asked the Army Air Corps to fly. General Foulois was raised in the old school: when a superior wanted something done he should attempt it. Unfortunately the military pilots had not had the training nor the experience to fly in the winter weather situations and as a result suffered 12 deaths and 66 crashes while attempting to carry the mail. On the positive side, the adverse publicity generated public interest which acted to improve the capabilities of military aviation. It also led to improvements in Air Corps training. Foulois erred when he told the Administration that the Air Corps was capable of operating the mail system. The Air Corps operated the system for approximately three months. Based on official sources; 8 photos, 62 notes.   C. W. Ohrvall

476. Siegan, Bernard H. THE DECLINE AND FALL OF ECONOMIC FREEDOM. *Reason 1981 12(9): 48-51.* From 1897 until 1937, the US Supreme Court advocated economic due process and opposed social and economic regulation; three key decisions in the 1930's, however, marked the Court's change of direction: Judge Louis D. Brandeis's lengthy dissent in *New State Ice* v. *Liebmann* (US, 1932) foreshadowed the overthrow of due process, *Nebbia* v. *New York* (US, 1934) signaled its end, and *West Coast Hotel* v. *Parrish* (US, 1937) marked its formal termination.

477. Simmons, Dennis E. CONSERVATION, COOPERATION, AND CONTROVERSY: THE ESTABLISHMENT OF SHENANDOAH NATIONAL PARK, 1924-1936. *Virginia Mag. of Hist. and Biog. 1981 89(4): 387-404.* Discusses the political, social, legal, and financial problems that were overcome to establish the park, including the Skyline Drive. Conservationists, National Park Service leaders, and individuals desiring to restore and preserve scenic areas united with local and state business and political figures seeking profit and prestige and overcame opposition—federal, state, and local rivalries, uncertainty as to what the park should be, and resistance to removal from lands bought for the park. A private campaign raised money to buy the land. The Great Depression in effect cut down on the amount of land purchased, but New Deal work projects helped with construction. The early opening of one section of the park generated support for the completion of the park. By 1939, three years after the park opened, the facility had more visitors than any other in the National Park System. Drawn mainly from the author's 1978 PhD dissertation; 41 notes.
                                                                P. J. Woehrmann

478. Simmons, Jerold. DAWSON COUNTY RESPONDS TO THE NEW DEAL, 1933-1940. *Nebraska Hist. 1981 62(1): 47-72.* Reviews the response of central Nebraskans in Dawson County to the array of programs, agencies and

measures comprising the New Deal. Initially, the New Deal won widespread approval and attracted voters to the Democratic Party. But these voters refused to commit themselves permanently. By 1940 they had overwhelmingly returned to their traditionally Republican voting habits. Ethnic, economic and social reasons could explain the county's political response during the 1930's.

R. Lowitt

479. Sinclair, Barbara Deckard. THE POLICY CONSEQUENCES OF PARTY REALIGNMENT: SOCIAL WELFARE LEGISLATION IN THE HOUSE OF REPRESENTATIVES, 1933-1954. *Am. J. of Pol. Sci. 1978 22(1): 83-105.* Burnham's theory of the policy consequences of realignments is applied to social welfare legislation during the New Deal realignment and its aftermath. As predicted, social welfare legislation does emerge as a direct response to the depression. The most clearly nonincremental programs were passed during the height of the realigning era (1935-38) and little nonincremental legislation passed during the remaining years under study. Throughout the 1930s, the increased issue distance between the parties was reflected in highly partisan voting alignments on non-labor social welfare legislation. During the 1940s, centrifugal constituency related forces reasserted themselves. By the 80th Congress, a single dominant and highly stable social welfare dimension had developed. Southern Democrats, who had been highly supportive of social welfare legislation during the 1930s, were now the least supportive regional grouping within the Democratic party. Northeastern Republicans, once the most conservative segment of the Republican party, became the most supportive while west north central Republicans followed the opposite path.　　　　　J

480. Sivachev, N. V. "NOVYI KURS" F. RUZVEL'TA [The Roosevelt New Deal]. *Voprosy Istorii [USSR] 1981 (9): 45-63.* A survey of the main trends of American historiography on the New Deal that analyzes the economic, social, and political aspects of the New Deal policy as a process of the development of US monopoly capitalism into state-monopoly capitalism. The reforms in industry, agriculture, finance, labor relations, unemployment relief, and the introduction of the social security system are discussed. Reveals the role of the working class and democratic forces in winning social legislation, analyzes political struggle and the substantial changes in the two party system in the second half of the 1930's. Russian.　　　　　J

481. Skocpol, Theda and Finegold, Kenneth. STATE CAPACITY AND ECONOMIC INTERVENTION IN THE EARLY NEW DEAL. *Pol. Sci. Q. 1982 97(2): 255-278.* Discusses the failure of the National Recovery Administration and the relative success of the Agricultural Adjustment Administration (AAA) in the 1930's, to underline the greater capacity of the US government to intervene in the agricultural, rather than in the industrial, economy. Both administrations promised much during the early New Deal, but only the goals of the AAA were attainable. 75 notes.　　　　　J. Powell

482. Smathers, Mike. THE SEARCH FOR THE GARDEN. *Southern Exposure 1980 8(1): 57-63.* An in-depth comparison of the 250 homes built between 1934 and 1938 as part of the Cumberland Homesteads, a New Deal resettlement project on Tennessee's Cumberland Plateau, and the contemporary (1970 ff.) development of Fairfield Glade, a private undertaking in the same vicinity. Par-

ticularly important is the contrast in the entire sociology related to both projects. The Homesteaders represented a traditional genre of southerners; the Glade residents represent people from the Midwest with urban sympathies. 6 photos, map. H. M. Parker, Jr.

483. Smith, Elaine M. MARY MCLEOD BETHUNE AND THE NATIONAL YOUTH ADMINISTRATION. Deutrich, Mabel E. and Purdy, Virginia C., ed. *Clio Was a Woman: Studies in the History of American Women* (Washington, D.C.: Howard U. Pr., 1980): 149-177. The National Youth Administration existed during 1935-44 primarily to assist youth aged 16 to 24 in getting work. Mary McLeod Bethune persuaded the agency to recognize Negro leadership both by expanding the Office of Negro Affairs and by employing black administrative assistants in more than 25 states. Under her aegis, too, it addressed blacks' needs notably through the Special Graduate and Negro College Fund. She also promoted a policy which assured blacks the same defense training and placement opportunities as whites. A discussion summary follows. 107 notes.
J. Powell

484. Soapes, Thomas F. THE FEDERAL WRITERS' PROJECT SLAVE INTERVIEWS: USEFUL DATA OR MISLEADING SOURCE. *Oral Hist. Rev. 1977 (2): 33-38.* Reviews the methodologies used by the Federal Writers' Project in conducting the slave interviews of the 1930's, and their value as historical evidence, particularly as employed by Eugene D. Genovese and George P. Rawick. 15 notes. D. A. Yanchisin

485. Sobczak, John N. THE POLITICS OF RELIEF: PUBLIC AID IN TOLEDO, 1933-1937. *Northwest Ohio Q. 1976 48(4): 134-142.*

486. Sofar, Allan J. THE FOREST SHELTERBELT PROJECT, 1934-1944. *J. of the West 1975 14(3): 95-107.* Traces Franklin D. Roosevelt's Shelterbelt Project, a plan to plant a 1,300-mile long strip of trees from Texas to the Canadian border on the Great Plains, from its inception in 1934 until its completion in 1942; focuses on conservationist aims, initial displeasure among conservationists and congressmen, and the eventual acceptance and acknowledgement of success by the public. 36 notes.

487. Spencer, Thomas T. THE AIR MAIL CONTROVERSY OF 1934. *Mid-America 1980 62(3): 161-172.* The 1934 air and ocean mail contracts controversy involved the Hoover administration's award of contracts to private air carriers without competitive bids. A congressional resolution, passed before Franklin D. Roosevelt took office in March 1933, set up a special Senate investigation committee led by Hugo Black. The Black committee began public hearings in January 1934; and the Post Office Department began its own investigation leading to Postmaster General James A. Farley's decision to cancel the existing contracts in February 1934. The US Army Air Corps handled the mail amid much cricitism. By the end of March 1934 the administration had decided to return airmail to private contractors until Congress could write new legislation. Roosevelt failed to follow the cancellation order with reform proposals, yet his actions did point out the shift toward greater government regulation in the 1930's. Based on previously unused manuscript records such as the United States Senate, 74th Congress, Special Committee to Investigate Air Mail and Ocean Mail Contracts. M. J. Wentworth

488. Spencer, Thomas T. THE OCEAN MAIL CONTROVERSY OF 1934. *Am. Neptune 1981 41(2): 110-122.* A scandal arose when air and ocean mail contracts were awarded without competitive bidding. The ocean contracts were more complex than the air contracts since they were supposed to provide subsidies to build the merchant marine. The reaction to Franklin D. Roosevelt's quick canceling of the air contracts and his ordering of the army to fly the mails made him cautious in dealing with the ocean contracts. He made no suggestions to Congress, whose investigations lasted two years. The Merchant Marine Act of 1936 was passed to create the US Maritime Commission with powers to establish minimum wage and manning levels, set construction and operating subsidies (thus divorcing mail contracts from this function), and determine vital trade routes and services. Based on periodicals, documents in the National Archives and the Franklin D. Roosevelt Library, and secondary sources; 35 notes.

J. C. Bradford

489. Sternsher, Bernard. DEPRESSION AND NEW DEAL IN OHIO: LORENA A. HICKOK'S REPORTS TO HARRY HOPKINS, 1934-1936. *Ohio Hist. 1977 86(4): 258-277.* Lorena A. Hickok served as Harry Hopkins' Chief Field Investigator during his tenure as head of the Federal Emergency Relief Administration during 1933-35 and the Works Progress Administration (WPA) during 1935-38. Presents excerpts from three of her four reports to him on WPA activities, Franklin D. Roosevelt's prospects at the polls, and technological unemployment resulting from plant modernization in Ohio. Based on manuscripts, contemporary comments, and secondary sources; 2 illus., 30 notes.

N. Summers

490. Stetson, Frederick W. THE CIVILIAN CONSERVATION CORPS IN VERMONT. *Vermont Hist. 1978 46(1): 24-42.* Most Vermont politicians opposed New Deal programs, but "Vermonters found the C. C. C. both justifiable and popular." It provided steady jobs for disproportionately large numbers in Vermont, poured millions into the depressed Vermont economy, developed skills useful in World War II, and helped lay the foundations of Vermont's postwar recreation industry. 9 illus., table, 73 notes. T. D. S. Bassett

491. Strong, Elizabeth. SCIENCE AND THE EARLY NEW DEAL: 1933-1935. *Synthesis 1982 5(2): 44-63.* In the summer of 1933 President Roosevelt created a Science Advisory Board, made up of university and industrial scientists, with Karl Compton as chairman, to study technical problems of governmental agencies. The board responded to requests from several agencies. It also developed a proposal for a Recovery Program for Science, requesting funds to support research as a background for public works and to relieve unemployment among scientists. This proposal aroused sharp opposition, and the board was terminated in 1935. Its assigned duties were turned over to the National Academy of Science. Mainly secondary sources; 67 notes. M. M. Vance

492. Swain, Martha. PAT HARRISON AND THE SOCIAL SECURITY ACT OF 1935. *Southern Q. 1976 15(1): 1-14.* Examines Mississippi Senator Pat Harrison's efforts to secure the passage of the 1935 Social Security Act. His managerial abilities and role as chairman of the Senate Committee on Finance receive focus. Conflicting views concerning the measure are considered. Frances Perkins, Francis E. Townsend, and William Green are among the more notable personalities mentioned. 29 notes. R. W. Dubay

493. Swain, Martha H.   THE HARRISON EDUCATION BILLS, 1936-1941. *Mississippi Q. 1977-78 31(1): 119-132.* Though commonly held to be a staunch conservative, Mississippi senator Byron Patton Harrison was responsible for several federal aid to education bills during 1936-41.

494. Swanson, Merwin R.   THE NEW DEAL IN POCATELLO. *Idaho Yesterdays 1979 23(2): 53-57.* In Pocatello, Idaho, the 1930's were characterized by Democratic Party leadership in local politics and by a strong labor influence led by the Pocatello Central Labor Union. Its leader, August Rosqvist, did not always follow the national leadership of the AFL, particularly in its hostility toward the CIO. Visible results of the New Deal were the many public works projects which were built in Pocatello. Based on newspapers and unpublished letters; 3 illus., 18 notes.   B. J. Paul

495. Swanson, Merwin R.   POCATELLO'S BUSINESS COMMUNITY AND THE NEW DEAL. *Idaho Yesterdays 1977 21(3): 9-15.* The businessmen of Pocatello were in favor of New Deal programs which would provide economic relief to the community, once they realized the severity of the Depression. Nevertheless, they were suspicious of increased federal intervention in their businesses. Primary sources; 4 illus., 15 notes.   B. J. Paul

496. Swartout, Robert, Jr.   THE ROAD OVER NEAHKAHNIE MOUNTAIN, OREGON: A CASE STUDY IN PACIFIC NORTHWEST TRANSPORTATION HISTORY. *Pacific Hist. 1977 21(3): 300-308.* Attempts to build a route over or around Neahkahnie Mountain exemplify modernization in the West, especially the Oregon coast. In the 19th century, the area was connected by trails; in the early 20th century, interest turned toward Portland; and not until the increased automobile use and availability of public funds of the 1930's was interest and funding sufficient to build a road over the mountain along Oregon's coastline. Newspapers and government publications; 4 photos, 22 notes.
                                                                         G. L. Olson

497. Taylor, Graham D.   ANTHROPOLOGISTS, REFORMERS, AND THE INDIAN NEW DEAL. *Prologue 1975 7(3): 151-162.* Bureau of Indian Affairs Commissioner John Collier has been considered as one of the New Deal administrators who applied social sciences principles to the federal government for the first time. However, his analysis of Indian culture was prescriptive rather than descriptive. Collier was not completely successful in his reversal of previous policies aimed at assimilating Indians into white society. Anthropologists who shared his reformist commitment to preserve traditional cultures functioned effectively in the bureaucracy; those committed to professional academic standards and current methodology encountered hostility. The hypothesis of conflict between old-line administrators and young reformers is simplistic and inaccurate. Based on primary and secondary sources; 2 photos, 51 notes.   W. R. Hively

498. Taylor, Graham D.   THE TRIBAL ALTERNATIVE TO BUREAUCRACY: THE INDIAN'S NEW DEAL, 1933-1945. *J. of the West 1974 13(1): 128-156.* A critical analysis of the steps taken under the new Commissioner of Indian Affairs, John Collier, to change what had become "a frightening example of an arrogant, corrupt, and undirected bureaucracy" that left the Indians "mired in poverty and despair." Proponents of the New Deal saw the Indian tribes as

a convenient "laboratory" for experimenting with planned political and economic development. Although Collier attempted "a genuine and farsighted effort to bridge a cultural chasm and allow the Indians to build a new society on the foundations of traditional institutions," the reorganization foundered on the lack of understanding of Indian tribal and political patterns and the great variety represented. The result was "a revival of bureaucratic control and Congressional exploitation." 54 notes.   R. V. Ritter

499.   Terrill, Tom and Hirsch, Jerrold.   SUCH AS US.   *Southern Exposure 1978 6(1): 67-72.* Under the auspices of the New Deal Federal Writers' Project, more than 1,000 southern life stories were collected by researchers. The amassing of some of these biographies was supervised by W. T. Couch, regional director of the FWP in the Southeast and director of the University of North Carolina Press. He edited and published a number of these life stories in the volume *These Are Our Lives,* published in 1939. Some life stories still unpublished include recollections by a black tenant farmer in Johnston County, North Carolina, of the murder of his educated son by whites when the son refused to abide by southern racial mores. Another story concerns the vicissitudes of urban living for a poor white family in Knoxville, Tennessee, in the late 1930's.   N. Lederer

500.   Theoharis, Athan G.   THE FBI'S STRETCHING OF PRESIDENTIAL DIRECTIVES, 1936-1953.   *Pol. Sci. Q. 1976-77 91(4): 631-647.* Details the history of presidential directives issued between 1936 and 1953 bearing on the FBI's authority to investigate dissident political activities. He concludes that because presidential supervision of the FBI was inadequate, the FBI was able to self-define the scope of its authority.   J

501.   Tissot, Roland.   DE L'ARTISTE AU PRODUCTEUR D'ART: DEUX IMAGES DU *NEW DEAL*   [From artist to producer of art: two images of the New Deal]. *Rev. Française d'Études Américaines [France] 1979 4(7): 31-40.* The New Deal Art Project during 1933-41, which put artists, who were often in dire straits, to work painting murals and sculpting statues for public buildings or performing plays for factory workers, changed America's view of the artists: some saw it as good—the artist had come down from his garret and had become involved in mankind; others saw it in a negative light—the artist was no longer working for his individual vision of beauty or truth but for a wage; he had became a mere producer of art.

502.   Vacha, J. E.   THE CASE OF THE RUNAWAY OPERA: THE FEDERAL THEATRE AND MARC BLITZSTEIN'S *THE CRADLE WILL ROCK.*   *New York Hist. 1981 62(2): 133-152.* On 10 June 1937 the Works Progress Administration's (WPA) Federal Theatre Project locked out the cast of Marc Blitzstein's pro-union play, *The Cradle Will Rock,* on opening night at the Maxine Elliott Theatre in New York City. Blitzstein, John Houseman, and Orson Welles defied WPA rules by moving the cast and first night audience through the streets to the Venice at 59th Street and Seventh Avenue, where the play was performed with a piano on stage and the cast scattered in the audience. This defiance of WPA rules resulted in the demise of the New York theater project. Subsequently Welles and Houseman organized Mercury Theatre. Based on participants' replies to the author's questionnaire, John Houseman memoirs, and other primary sources; 8 illus., 30 notes.   R. N. Lokken

503.   Vlasich, James A.   TRANSITIONS IN PUEBLO AGRICULTURE, 1938-1948.   *New Mexico Hist. Rev. 1980 55(1): 25-46.* Agriculture has always been a vital concern to the existence of the Pueblo Indians. The Pueblos tradition-ally resist changes in their culture, but many of the New Deal agricultural programs instituted between 1938 and 1948 were gradually accepted without a decrease in Pueblo ceremonialism or religious character. The Pueblos today utilize some modern farming methods which were introduced during the depres-sion and war years, but they retain many of their traditional agricultural prac-tices. Primary sources; photo, 4 tables, 45 notes.   P. L. McLaughlin

504.   Wallis, John Joseph and Benjamin, Daniel K.   PUBLIC RELIEF AND PRIVATE EMPLOYMENT IN THE GREAT DEPRESSION.   *J. of Econ. Hist. 1981 41(1): 97-102.* The unemployment relief programs introduced by the federal government in the 1930's were the largest single factor in the growth of the federal budget over the decade. Cross-sectional data bearing on the operation of the Federal Emergency Relief Administration rejects the hypothesis that the federal relief programs reduced private employment. Individuals did respond to the incentives of relief benefits, but only by moving between relief and non-relief unemployment.   J

505.   Ware, James.   THE SOONER NRA: NEW DEAL RECOVERY IN OKLAHOMA.   *Chronicles of Oklahoma 1976 54(3): 339-351.* Examines mea-sures enacted by the National Recovery Administration to aid Dust Bowl Okla-homa, 1932-35.

506.   Warren-Findley, Jannelle.   MUSICIANS AND MOUNTAINEERS: THE RESETTLEMENT ADMINISTRATION'S MUSIC PROGRAM IN AP-PALACHIA, 1935-37.   *Appalachian J. 1979-80 7(1-2): 105-123.* Led by left-winger Charles Seeger of the Composers' Collective in New York City, the New Deal Resettlement Administration's music program in Appalachia intended "to integrate music, participation in the arts, and political education into a coherent whole which would enable resettled farmers, unemployed miners, impoverished lumbermen, and their families to take control of their own lives and situations."

507.   Watson, Thomas.   THE PWA COMES TO THE RED RIVER VAL-LEY: PHASE I, NON-FEDERAL PROJECTS IN TEXAS, JUNE 1933-FEB-RUARY 1934.   *Red River Valley Hist. R. 1974 31(2): 146-164.* The Public Works Administration did not create a boom in the Texas economy, but it did create many nonfederal jobs and projects.   S

508.   Weeks, Charles J.   THE EASTERN CHEROKEE AND THE NEW DEAL.   *North Carolina Hist. Rev. 1976 53(3): 303-319.* Though the Indian New Deal offered a program designed to reverse misguided policies of the previ-ous 50 years, it failed to have a significant impact on the social and economic condition of the Cherokees of western North Carolina. The influx of public money discouraged farming and handicraft work, thereby weakening the tribe's economic base. For personal, political, and economic reasons "white" Cherokees (mixed bloods who had adopted local white culture) resisted reforms offered by the New Deal. Based on manuscript archival records, published government documents, and secondary sources; 12 illus., 60 notes.   T. L. Savitt

509. Weisberger, Bernard A. READING, WRITING, AND HISTORY. *Am. Heritage 1974 25(2): 98-100.* Review essay of Jerre Mangione's *The Dream and the Deal: The Federal Writers' Project, 1935-1943* (Boston: Little, Brown, 1973). S

510. Weiss, Stuart. LEO T. CROWLEY: PRAGMATIC NEW DEALER. *Mid-America 1982 64(1): 33-52.* Recounts the public career of Leo T. Crowley, especially in Franklin D. Roosevelt's administration, 1934-45. Crowley came from a business, banking, and political advisory background in Wisconsin, loyally served Roosevelt as head of the Federal Deposit Insurance Corporation, as Alien Property Custodian, and as an expert on upper Midwest politics among other jobs. Roosevelt resisted, or ignored, persistent criticism of Crowley, centering on his private banking operations. When Roosevelt died, Crowley lost his political support, and President Truman allowed Crowley's positions either to expire or did not reappoint him. More sources are needed to write a definitive analysis of this New Dealer who sought historical obscurity. Based partly on the Crowley Papers and the Roosevelt Papers; 102 notes. P. J. Woehrmann

511. Welsch, Roger L. STRAIGHT FROM THE HORSE TRADER'S MOUTH. *Kansas Q. 1981 13(2): 17-26.* Identifies the general characteristics of horse trading stories collected during the late 1930's and early 1940's by Federal Writers Project fieldworkers in Nebraska, then reprints a typical story, told by Grant Dehart of Lincoln, Nebraska, when he was over 80.

512. Wigdor, David. LAW, REFORM, AND THE MODERN ADMINIS-TRATIVE STATE. *Rev. in Am. Hist. 1982 10(2): 234-240.* Review article on Donald A. Ritchie's *James M. Landis: Dean of the Regulators* (1980), a biography of the New Deal administrator, and Nelson L. Dawson's *Louis D. Brandeis, Felix Frankfurter, and the New Deal* (1980), about the intellectuals involved in the New Deal.

513. Williams, Bobby Joe. LET THERE BE LIGHT: TENNESSEE VAL-LEY AUTHORITY COMES TO MEMPHIS. *West Tennessee Hist. Soc. Papers 1976 (30): 43-66.* Traces the history of electric utilities in Memphis and the internecine struggles to bring Tennessee Valley Authority power from Muscle Shoals into Memphis in the 1930's. Traces the intricacies of the power struggle between a corporation owned utility as it is confronted by the prospects of a municipally owned utility which has access to inexpensive power created by a Federal agency. Based on the Watkins Overton Collection, Memphis State University, and contemporary newspapers; 2 illus., 88 notes.
H. M. Parker, Jr.

514. Winpenny, Thomas R. HENNING WEBB PRENTIS AND THE CHALLENGE OF THE NEW DEAL. *J. of the Lancaster County Hist. Soc. 1977 81(1): 1-24.* Discusses the conservative viewpoint of Henning Webb Prentis, Jr., president of Armstrong Cork Company in Lancaster, Pennsylvania, 1934-50, as representative of the economic and political leanings of big business during the New Deal.

515. Woodward, C. Vann. HISTORY FROM SLAVE SOURCES: A RE-VIEW ESSAY. *Am. Hist. R. 1974 79(2): 470-481.* A review of George P. Rawick, general editor, *The American Slave: A Composite Autobiography*

(Westport, Connecticut: Greenwood Publishing Co., 1972). This essay gives its main attention to the 17 volumes in which the Federal Writers Project interviews with ex-slaves are published. The interviews were taken 1936-38 and appear in these volumes without editorial change. Two additional volumes of interviews originating at Fisk University in 1929-30 are included. A short monograph by the editor, *From Sundown to Sunup: The Making of the Black Community* (volume 1 in the series), receives a brief notice. The main purpose of the review is to assess the ex-slave interviews as historical sources. They are found to have numerous faults and shortcomings, particularly the skewed sample interviewed and the ineptitude of the interviewers. These faults, however, are not considered to be too serious if sufficient precautions are taken. So used, the interviews can be an extremely valuable source of information on slavery as slaves saw and remembered it.   A

516.   Wright, Esmond.   HOW RELEVANT IS THE NEW DEAL?   *Encounter [Great Britain] 1982 58-59(6-1): 92-99.* Examines the development of the New Deal, focusing on the activities of presidents Herbert C. Hoover and Franklin D. Roosevelt, of John Maynard Keynes, and of others involved in this economic program; criticizes recent British suggestions that elements of the New Deal be applied to Britain's economic problems.

517.   Wrigley, Linda.   THE JEROME N. FRANK PAPERS.   *Yale U. Lib. Gazette 1974 48(3): 163-177.* Reviews the career of Jerome N. Frank (1889-1957), corporation lawyer, general counsel of the Agricultural Adjustment Administration, commissioner and chairman of the Securities and Exchange Commission, federal judge, legal theorist, author, and teacher. Frank was a respected scholar with catholic interests, and in the last 15 years of his life wrote 150 articles, reviews, and speeches. He published *Fate and Freedom* in 1945. The papers are now kept in Yale's Sterling Memorial Library.   D. A. Yanchisin

518.   Wyche, Billy H.   SOUTHERN NEWSPAPERS VIEW ORGANIZED LABOR IN THE NEW DEAL YEARS.   *South Atlantic Q. 1975 74(2): 178-196.* Southern newspapers presented a full spectrum of opinion on labor problems during the 1930's. Most of them broadly supported the New Deal in principle, but were sometimes less enthusiastic when its programs were put into practice. Strikes were almost unanimously abhorred, especially when violent, but violence against strikers was seldom condemned. The Congress of Industrial Organizations was generally disliked. The fulcrum of newspaper opinion moved more and more to an antilabor position as the decade advanced. 90 notes.

V. L. Human

519.   York, Hildreth.   THE NEW DEAL ART PROJECTS IN NEW JERSEY.   *New Jersey Hist. 1980 98(3-4): 132-174.* Describes the Public Works of Art Project—the Section of Painting and Sculpture of the Treasury Department later to become the Section of Fine Arts, the Treasury Relief Art Project, and the WPA art program. Considers the kinds of art work produced, the participants, locations of the work, and the administration of the programs. Included is a list of artists along with the type of work each did and a list of murals, reliefs, and public sculptures. Based on government records, material in the Archives of American Art, newspaper articles, and secondary sources; 10 illus., 19 notes, biblio.   E. R. McKinstry

520. Zeidel, Robert F. BEER RETURNS TO CREAM CITY. *Milwaukee Hist. 1981 4(1): 20-32.* Describes the citywide celebrations in Milwaukee that occurred when President Franklin D. Roosevelt signed the Cullen-Harrison Act (US, 1933), which repealed the Volstead Act of 1919 and legalized the brewing, distribution, and consumption of 3.2% beer as of 7 April 1933; focuses on the Volksfest attended by over 14,000 Milwaukeeans.

521. —. CIVILIAN CONSERVATION CORPS AND THE FARM IS-LAND CAUSEWAY. *South Dakota Hist. 1978 8(4): 312-326.* An annotated photographic documentary of the building of the rock causeway between the north bank of the Missouri River and Farm Island, South of Pierre, South Dakota, by CCC Company 796. The photographs were taken by Paul J. Hogan of New Rockford, North Dakota, one of the leaders of the company. 27 photos, map.   R. V. Ritter

522. —. THE CONTRIBUTIONS TO ECONOMICS AND ECONOMIC POLICY OF LAUCHLIN CURRIE IN THE 1930'S. *Hist. of Pol. Econ. 1978 10(4): 507-548.*
Jones, Byrd L. LAUCHLIN CURRIE, PUMP PRIMING, AND NEW DEAL FISCAL POLICY, 1934-1936, *pp. 509-524.* Traces the career of Lauchlin Currie, who joined the New Deal government. He understood Keynesianism and sought to convince the government that economic theory could be applied to improve society, 1920's-36.
Currie, Lauchlin. COMMENTS ON PUMP PRIMING, *pp. 525-533.* Memo-randum, ca. February-March 1935, on the benefits of government spending to rebuild the economy by stimulating production.
Currie, Lauchlin and Krost, Martin. FEDERAL INCOME-INCREASING EXPENDITURES, 1932-1935, *pp. 543-540.* Memorandum, ca. Novem-ber 1935, on determining the appropriate time during the business cycle to introduce deficit spending to increase personal income.
Currie, Lauchlin. COMMENTS AND OBSERVATIONS, *pp. 541-548.* The author describes how he became a Keynesian and his role in convincing New Dealers of the salutary effects of deficit spending, 1930's.

523. —. [THE FEDERAL WRITERS' PROJECT LIFE STORIES AS ORAL HISTORY].
Rapport, Leonard. HOW VALID ARE THE FEDERAL WRITERS' PROJECT LIFE STORIES: AN ICONOCLAST AMONG THE TRUE BELIEVERS. *Oral Hist. Rev. 1979: 6-17.* The historical validity of the Federal Writers' Project Life Stories housed in the Southern Historical Collection at the University of North Carolina and used by scholars is questionable. Many of the stories are fiction; 1935-79. 15 notes.
Terrill, Tom E. and Hirsch, Jerrold. REPLIES TO LEONARD RAPPORT'S "HOW VALID ARE THE FEDERAL WRITERS' PROJECT LIFE STO-RIES: AN ICONOCLAST AMONG THE TRUE BELIEVERS." *Oral Hist. Rev. 1980: 81-92.* Repudiates Leonard Rapport's criticism of the Fed-eral Writers' Project's southern life histories project as valid social documen-tation, which criticism casts doubt on the author's *Such As Us: Southern Voices of the Thirties* (Chapel Hill: 1978). Rapport's reiteration of his position follows. 6 notes.   D. A. Yanchisin

4

SOCIAL CONDITIONS,
PROTEST, AND REACTION

524. Abrahams, Edward. THE PAST FAILURE OF FASCISM IN THE U.S.A. *Patterns of Prejudice [Great Britain] 1974 8(2): 23-27.* Discusses fascist organizations and leaders in the United States in the 1930's, emphasizing anti-Semitism.

525. Accinelli, Robert D. MILITANT INTERNATIONALISTS: THE LEAGUE OF NATIONS ASSOCIATION, THE PEACE MOVEMENT, AND U.S. FOREIGN POLICY, 1934-38. *Diplomatic Hist. 1980 4(1): 19-38.* During the 1930's, as pacifists and isolationists worked to prevent political involvement abroad, a less publicized wing of the American peace movement was advocating international cooperation. The most dynamic group in this coalition, the League of Nations Association, played a significant, if ultimately ineffectual, role, by keeping the internationalist viewpoint before Congress, president, and public in a time of rising isolationism. 67 notes.   T. L. Power

526. Allen, John E. EUGENE TALMADGE AND THE GREAT TEXTILE STRIKE IN GEORGIA, SEPTEMBER 1934. Fink, Gary M. and Reed, Merl E., eds. *Essays in Southern Labor History: Selected Papers, Southern Labor History Conference, 1976.* (Westport, Conn.; London, England: Greenwood Pr., 1977): 224-243. Studies the history of the southern textile industry before and during the early years of the National Recovery Administration (NRA) as the setting for the strike of 1934, the course of the strike, and Governor Eugene Talmadge's role in getting the strike settled. That role was based philosophically in his staunchly conservative opposition to the whole NRA concept. The strike was an unmitigated disaster for Georgia's textile workers; no union men were rehired. Talmadge's duplicity regarding his intentions and "the brutality and flamboyance with which he suppressed the strike" was unprecedented. The workers were not fooled as to where his real loyalties lay, but the damage had been done. 74 notes.   R. V. Ritter

527. Ansley, Fran and Bell, Brenda. DAVIDSON-WILDER 1932: STRIKES IN THE COAL CAMP. *Southern Exposure 1974 1(3/4): 113-136.* After World War I, the coal mining companies in eastern Tennessee whittled away the gains won by the United Mine Workers. When the miners struck the companies retaliated with yellow dog contracts, injunctions, National Guard troops, black lists,

and deputized gunmen. Harrassment and violence were waged by both sides. The murder in 1933 of the local union president Barney Graham, along with the acquittal of his assailant, brought the turbulence to a climax. Leaderless, tired, and hungry, the miners went back to the mines without contracts. Based on oral interviews with participants and primary and secondary sources; 10 illus., 10 notes, biblio. G. A. Bolton

528. Asher, Robert. JEWISH UNIONS AND THE AMERICAN FEDER-ATION OF LABOR POWER STRUCTURE 1903-1935. *Am. Jewish Hist. Q. 1976 65(3): 215-227.* Jewish unions, i.e., those with a substantial number of Jewish members and led by Jewish officers, until the 1930's were largely in, but not of, the mainstream of the American labor movement. Recognizing their differences with the AFL, the Jewish unions cooperated with the AFL when they could, but went their own way politically in their attempt to build a welfare state through union institutions and trade agreements with employers. By the late 1920's the Jewish unions, especially the International Ladies' Garment Workers' Union, had drifted slowly to the right and the American Federation of Labor had moved toward the left, so that the Amalgamated Clothing Workers of America could be admitted into the AFL, and the ILGWU could be allowed into the AFL power structure (executive council and resolutions committee). The accomplishments of the New Deal Democratic Party accelerated this process. 23 notes. F. Rosenthal

529. August, Jack. THE ANTI-JAPANESE CRUSADE IN ARIZONA'S SALT RIVER VALLEY, 1934-35. *Arizona and the West 1979 21(2): 113-136.* The Japanese were highly successful and competitive farmers in Arizona's Salt River Valley. They circumvented state alien land laws through lease contracts and through their American-born children. The combination of their agricultural excellence and the depressed economic conditions of the 1930's evoked white militant reaction in 1934-35. Local white farmers organized to oust the Japanese farmers from the valley. Threats, terrorism, court and legal maneuvers, national press coverage, and political opportunism created a hostile anti-foreigner situation. The federal government applied pressure to quell the disturbance. The Salt River Valley anti-Japanese episode was not unique in western states. 4 illus., 52 notes. D. L. Smith

530. Barber, Henry E. THE ASSOCIATION OF SOUTHERN WOMEN FOR THE PREVENTION OF LYNCHING, 1930-1942. *Phylon 1973 34(4): 378-389.* Studies the effects of the Association of Southern Women for the Prevention of Lynching, 1930-42. S

531. Baughman, James L. CLASSES AND COMPANY TOWNS: LEG-ENDS OF THE 1937 LITTLE STEEL STRIKE. *Ohio Hist. 1978 87(2): 175-192.* Examines events in Canton, Youngstown, and Warren (Ohio) during the 1937 "Little Steel" strike, the first major strike since 1919. Discusses the relationship of the communities to the month-long labor-management conflict. After the strike of the Youngstown Sheet and Tube, Inland Steel, and Republic Steel, not solidarity but demoralization and internal division characterized the employees. The union never came close to victory—after four weeks the laborers began filing back into the mills and the managers had halted the impressive advance for CIO organization in the nation's basic industries. Through examination of the commu-

nities involved, discusses why the union lost. Based on primary and secondary sources; 3 illus., 48 notes.   N. Summers

532. Becker, William H. REINHOLD NIEBUHR: FROM MARX TO ROOSEVELT. *Historian 1973 35(4): 539-550.* In the early 1930's, theologian Reinhold Niebuhr considered himself to be a Christian Marxist, although 15 years later he believed a decent life could be attained within the framework of capitalism. S.udents of Niebuhr's thought explain this conversion in a variety of ways. Uses Niebuhr's editorials in *Radical Religion*, 1939-41, as the major source for the contention that increasing appreciation of the policies and programs of the Franklin D. Roosevelt administration was a major factor in the change in viewpoint. 44 notes.   N. M. Moen

533. Bellow, Saul. STARTING OUT IN CHICAGO. *Am. Scholar 1974/75 44(1): 71-77.* Analyzes the social and cultural environment in Chicago during the late 1930's and the efforts of immigrants and their children to be "American," and discusses the way "being American" has developed since then. Our biggest enemy is "the Great Noise," the terrible excitement and distraction generated by the crises of modern life. Based on a commencement address delivered at Brandeis University, Spring 1974.   R. V. Ritter

534. Bellush, Bernard and Bellush, Jewel. A RADICAL RESPONSE TO THE ROOSEVELT PRESIDENCY: THE COMMUNIST PARTY (1933-1945). *Presidential Studies Q. 1980 10(4): 645-661.* From the start of the New Deal to the first signs of the Cold War, the Communist Party of the United States of America continually shifted their rhetoric and policies. Four distinct and radical shifts occurred—all following shifts in the official USSR line. This fluctuation greatly reduced the CP-USA's credibility among the American left. 40 notes.
                                                    D. H. Cline

535. Bellush, Jewel. OLD AND NEW LEFT REAPPRAISALS OF THE NEW DEAL AND ROOSEVELT'S PRESIDENCY. *Presidential Studies Q. 1979 9(3): 243-266.* Briefly discusses the differences between the Old and the New Left, and focuses on both groups' opinion of Franklin D. Roosevelt's presidency and his New Deal.

536. Berman, Hyman. POLITICAL ANTISEMITISM IN MINNESOTA DURING THE GREAT DEPRESSION. *Jewish Social Studies 1976 38(3-4): 247-264.* Anti-Semitism was successfully used as a political weapon to unseat Minnesota Farmer-Labor Governor Elmer A. Benson in the campaign of 1938. Many of Benson's liberal political aides and associates were Jewish. They were libeled as radical Jewish elements seeking to import Marxism into the state by political opponents such as Hjalmar Petersen and Raymond Chase. Political anti-Semitism in Minnesota proved a valuable tool in the conservative effort to thwart further government intervention to assist the unemployed, the unions, and producer-cooperative farmer elements. Primary sources.   N. Lederer

537. Betten, Neil and Mohl, Raymond A. FROM DISCRIMINATION TO REPATRIATION: MEXICAN LIFE IN GARY, INDIANA, DURING THE GREAT DEPRESSION. *Pacific Hist. R. 1973 42(3): 370-388.* Relates the social, economic, and political discrimination faced by Mexican Americans in the 1920's-30's in Gary, Indiana, culminating in the forced exodus of a large segment

of the Mexican population during the early 1930's. The economic tensions generated by the Depression produced a new wave of nativism throughout the United States, and were fostered by antiethnic sentiments expressed in the *Saturday Evening Post* aimed particularly at Mexican Americans. "Undoubtedly the Mexican's darker skin, his Catholicism, and the usual problems and vices associated with the poor affected national opinion as well." From 1931 to May 1932 repatriation was voluntary, supported by most local institutions in Gary, including US Steel Co. and the International Institute, an immigrant-oriented welfare agency. However, "after May 1932, when the township trustee's office assumed direction of repatriation, repressive measures were used to force the return of reluctant voyagers." The organized efforts in Gary against Mexicans reflected the xenophobia present throughout American society during the early 1930's. 33 notes.

B. L. Fenske

538. Biebel, Charles D. PRIVATE FOUNDATIONS AND PUBLIC POLICY: THE CASE OF SECONDARY EDUCATION DURING THE GREAT DEPRESSION. *Hist. of Educ. Q. 1976 16(1): 3-34.* To bring about social change within secondary education during the 1930's, John D. Rockefeller's General Education Board used manipulation and control of established institutions and educational associations.

539. Blackwelder, Julia Kirk. QUIET SUFFERING: ATLANTA WOMEN IN THE 1930'S. *Georgia Hist. Q. 1977 61(2): 112-124.* During the Great Depression of the 1930's, women in Atlanta, Georgia, suffered from poverty and unemployment. A caste system based on a woman's race, age, and (sometimes) marital status determined the type of job she was likely to have. Statistics indicate that, generally, black women had greater difficulty in the job market and were employed as domestics, while white women held clerical positions. Primary sources; 20 notes.

G. R. Schroeder

540. Blackwelder, Julia Kirk. WOMEN IN THE WORK FORCE: ATLANTA, NEW ORLEANS, AND SAN ANTONIO, 1930 TO 1940. *J. of Urban Hist. 1978 4(3): 331-358.* By studying women in three ethnically distinct communities (Atlanta—white, New Orleans—black, and San Antonio—Hispanic), compares the work experiences and motivations of different cultural groups of women. Matriarchy does not appear to be the main explanation for black women entering the labor force, and was actually higher among the supposedly close-knit Hispanics. 12 tables, 20 notes.

T. W. Smith

541. Bolt, Ernest C., Jr. ISOLATION, EXPANSION, AND PEACE: AMERICAN FOREIGN POLICY BETWEEN THE WARS. Haines, Gerald K. and Walker, J. Samuel, ed. *American Foreign Relations: A Historiographical Review* (Westport, Conn.: Greenwood Pr., 1981): 133-157. American historians have remained fascinated by the roots, ideology, and significance of isolationism during the interwar years. This continued interest stems from the complex and sometimes contradictory nature of the isolationist position, the increasing availability of source materials, and changing American attitudes toward internationalism. Secondary sources; 58 notes.

J. Powell

542. Bonthius, Andrew. ORIGINS OF THE INTERNATIONAL LONG-SHOREMEN'S AND WAREHOUSEMEN'S UNION. *Southern California Q. 1977 59(4): 379-426.* Traces the organization of longshoremen and warehouse-men on the Pacific Coast from the founding of the International Longshoremen's Union in 1934 to the merger of their union and the warehousemen's union into the International Longshoremen's and Warehousemen's Union in 1937. Long-shoremen had been neglected by American Federation of Labor leadership for decades; they endured company unions, low wages, and wretched working condi-tions. Under radical and Communist leadership, the ILA made dramatic gains in the mid-1930's, eventually achieving affiliation with the Congress of Industrial Organizations. Finding duplication in their work, the ILA and the ware-housemen's union worked for common goals and eventual merger. Opposition came from the AFL hierarchy and the International Brotherhood of Teamsters. In an era filled with strikes, violence, and internecine labor struggles, the ILWU emerged as a powerful, militant union which successfully achieved a working relationship with the forces of capital. Primary and secondary sources; 131 notes.
                                                                A. Hoffman

543. Borisiuk, V. I. OT ZAKONA VAGNERA K ZAKONU TAFTA-KHARTLI: POVOROT K REAKTSII V TRUDOVOM ZAKONODA-TEL'STVE SSHA (1935-1947 GG.) [From the Wagner Act to the Taft-Hartley Act: the shift to reactionary labor legislation in the United States, 1935-47]. *Vestnik Moskovskogo U., Seriia 9: Istoriia [USSR] 1971 26(5): 15-31.* The Wag-ner Act (US, 1935), considered the most radical piece of labor legislation of the New Deal, generated sharp opposition from the right, manufacturers, and capital, and from their representatives in Congress. At first they sought to prove it unconstitutional; failing this they tried to amend it. They called the power of unions "un-American." During World War II there was a reactionary shift under the guise of protecting the war effort. After the war, with controls lifted, the number of strikes increased sharply. This set the stage for the victory of the right, the Taft-Hartley Act (US, 1947), which strictly regulated union activities. Based on published sources; 67 notes.   G. E. Munro

544. Boryczka, Ray. MILITANCY AND FACTIONALISM IN THE UNITED AUTO WORKERS UNION, 1937-1941. *Maryland Hist. 1977 8(2): 13-25.* Traces the impact of factionalism on United Automobile Workers of America efforts to generate consistent rank and file militancy. Concludes that pragmatic, self-serving factionalism prevented organized militancy. Based on oral and printed primary sources and secondary sources; illus., 33 notes.
                                                                G. O. Gagnon

545. Boryczka, Ray. SEASONS OF DISCONTENT: AUTO UNION FAC-TIONALISM AND THE MOTOR PRODUCTS STRIKE OF 1935-1936. *Michigan Hist. 1977 61(1): 3-32.* The Motor Products Corporation strike during 1935-36 illustrated conditions in automobile unionism between *Schechter* in 1935 and the major union upheavals of 1936. Factionalism, bred by conservatism within the United Auto Workers of America (UAW), produced a three-way contest between the corporation, the UAW, and the more militant independent unions. UAW president Francis Dillon vacillated constantly. Violence, scabbing, and employer belligerence further discouraged striking workers who became increasingly unwilling to support a seemingly futile endeavor. Although the

UAW won exclusive recognition and a contract from Motor Products in 1937, the overall impact of the strike was ambiguous. But factionalism was unquestionably the cause of defeat. Primary sources; illus., 7 photos, 98 notes.

D. W. Johnson

546. Brandes, Joseph. FROM SWEATSHOP TO STABILITY: JEWISH LABOR BETWEEN TWO WORLD WARS. *Yivo Ann. of Jewish Social Sci. 1976 (16): 1-149.* Traces the growth of the Jewish labor movement from its inception, with particular emphasis on the period between World War I and World War II. Stresses the uniqueness of the Jewish labor movement and puts particular emphasis on the growth of the Jewish labor movement within the garment industry. Describes the roles of such notable labor leaders as David Dubinsky and Sidney Hillquit. Particular stress is put on the International Ladies' Garment Workers' and the United Hebrew Trades' role in the development of Jewish labor in the 1920's-30's.

R. J. Wechman

547. Brax, Ralph S. WHEN STUDENTS FIRST ORGANIZED AGAINST WAR. *New-York Hist. Soc. Q. 1979 63(3): 228-255.* College student unrest was not new in the 20th century. However, before the 1930's it usually was directed against campus problems. During the Great Depression unrest increased, not, as one might have expected, against the economic system, but concentrating by the mid-1930's on opposition to war. Sparked at first by socialist and communist groups, three nationwide student strikes were held, the last in 1936 supposedly including half a million students, but probably no more than 350,000. The majority of the million college students took little or no active part. Yet, some success was attained even though the movement collapsed when the nation found itself in World War II. Primary sources; 4 illus., 56 notes.

C. L. Grant

548. Brinkley, Alan. HUEY LONG, THE SHARE OUR WEALTH MOVEMENT, AND THE LIMITS OF DEPRESSION DISSIDENCE. *Lousiana Hist. 1981 22(2): 117-134.* From his entrance into the US Senate in 1932 until his death in 1935, Huey P. Long of Louisiana was the head of a powerful national movement. At the center of this movement were the Share Our Wealth clubs. The Share Our Wealth plan called for high income taxes, estate taxes, and capital levies to limit fortunes. This money would be redistributed to the poor. The movement, however, was ideologically diverse and organizationally loose. Thus, though it enjoyed support, that support was not as focused as in many mass movements. Primary sources; 44 notes.

J. Powell

549. Brody, David. WORKING CLASS HISTORY IN THE GREAT DEPRESSION. *Rev. in Am. Hist. 1976 4(2): 262-267.* Review article prompted by Peter Friedlander's *The Emergence of a UAW Local, 1936-1939: A Study in Class and Culture* (Pittsburgh: U. of Pennsylvania Pr., 1975), which documents the growth of a Detroit local of the United Automobile Workers of America.

550. Brune, Lester H. "UNION HOLIDAY—CLOSED TILL FURTHER NOTICE": THE 1936 GENERAL STRIKE AT PEKIN, ILLINOIS. *J. of the Illinois State Hist. Soc. 1982 75(1): 29-38.* By February 1936, two years of antagonism at the American Distillery Company made Pekin the site of the fourth city-wide general strike in US history. In May 1934, American Federation of Labor organization efforts led to a strike at the distillery. The resulting one-

year contract ended in July 1935, and the company refused to renegotiate, took action against employees who testified before the National Labor Relations Board, and supported a rival Pekin Distillery Employees Association. Antiunion speeches by Mayor William E. Schurman and violent confrontations with police led the Pekin Trades and Labor Assembly to declare a labor holiday for 5 February. Violence was avoided as 1,500 workers participated in the two day demonstration, which effectively shut down the town and led the company to concede. 4 illus., 35 notes.   A. W. Novitsky

551. Bulkley, Peter B.   TOWNSENDISM AS AN EASTERN AND URBAN PHENOMENON: CHAUTAUQUA COUNTY, NEW YORK, AS A CASE STUDY. *New York Hist. 1974 55(2): 179-198.* Challenges the standard view that the Townsend Movement was primarily rural and Western, and supported by "Grant Wood type" native-born Americans. In New York's 43rd Congressional District (Chautauqua, Cattaraugus, and Allegany Counties), the Townsendites, in alliance with the minority Democratic party, came close to defeating the conservative Republican incumbent, Daniel A. Reed, in the 1936 elections. The pro-Townsend vote was strongest in Jamestown (the chief city of the district), which had a large immigrant population, and was weakest in the native American rural areas of the district. Townsendism, in this Eastern and highly industrialized region, had its greatest strength in urban areas with large immigrant populations. Based on primary and secondary works; 3 illus., map, table, 50 notes.
                                                                                    G. Kurland

552. Bulosan, Carlos.   AMERICA IS IN THE HEART, AN EXCERPT. *Amerasia J. 1975 3(1): 1-15.* Presents excerpts from the author's autobiography dealing with his attempts to organize Filipino Americans' labor unions in California 1934-38, including activities of leftist political factions.

553. Burgchardt, Carl R.   TWO FACES OF AMERICAN COMMUNISM: PAMPHLET RHETORIC OF THE THIRD PERIOD AND THE POPULAR FRONT. *Q. J. of Speech 1980 66(4): 375-391.* Before July 1935, pamphlets of the American Communist Party demanded the overthrow of capitalism in dogmatic and distorted language. Consequently, they were not adapted well to the non-Communist public. Pamphlets published after July 1935 attempted to overcome negative impressions of communism, but they were largely unsuccessful.
                                                                                    J

554. Cannistraro, Philip V.   FASCISM AND AMERICANS IN DETROIT, 1933-1935. *Internat. Migration R. 1975 9(1): 29-40.* Explores the impact of Italian Fascism on Italian Americans in Detroit during 1933-35, including the specific questions of Fascism and anti-Fascism within the community and the more general internal dynamics of the community's sociopolitical integration.

555. Capaldo, Charles.   HELL ON HIGH. *Mankind 1976 5(8): 24-28.* Eyewitness reports of the burning of the passenger dirigible *Hindenburg* at its mooring at the Naval Air Station at Lakehurst, New Jersey on 6 May 1937 graphically reveal the horror of the occasion. The 36 fatalities and the drama of the event brought the end of passenger dirigible transportation. Observers have never been completely satisfied with the various explanations advanced for the cause of the disaster.   N. Lederer

556. Carlisle, Rodney. THE FOREIGN POLICY VIEWS OF AN ISOLA-TIONIST PRESS LORD: W. R. HEARST & THE INTERNATIONAL CRISIS, 1936-41. *J. of Contemporary Hist. [Great Britain] 1974 9(3): 217-227.* William Randolph Hearst's press represented 12-14 percent of the total readership of daily newspapers in the United States during the mid-1930's. His isolationist opinion had the largest, single editorial influence of the time. Hearst believed the United States should establish a deterrent armed force, not threaten Germany, nor make moves on the European continent in support of the Versailles Treaty or the League of Nations, give no encouragement to Britain or France, and should watch Japan and the Soviet Union very carefully. He was at once a militant nationalist, anti-communist, and suspicious of the British, French, Japanese, and Russians. Primary sources; 24 notes.   M. P. Trauth

557. Carpenter, Gerald. PUBLIC OPINION IN THE NEW ORLEANS STREET RAILWAY STRIKE OF 1929-1930. Fink, Gary M. and Reed, Merl E., eds. *Essays in Southern Labor History: Selected Papers, Southern Labor History Conference, 1976.* (Westport, Conn.; London, England, Greenwood Pr., 1977): 191-207. Studies the New Orleans Street Railway Strike of 1929-30 as an illustration of the incorrectness of the usual stereotype of southern public opinion as united against trade unionism. This is seen both in company (New Orleans Public Service, Inc.) appeals which reflected the public's acceptance of unionism and in union (Street and Electric Railway Employees of America) appeals for support resting on "positive concern for the principles of organized labor and negative objections to outside control." The usual generalizations therefore must be examined more critically. 65 notes.   R. V. Ritter

558. Carpenter, Joel A. FUNDAMENTALIST INSTITUTIONS AND THE RISE OF EVANGELICAL PROTESTANTISM, 1929-1942. *Church Hist. 1980 49(1): 62-75.* "The revivalistic, millenarian movement that flourished in the urban centers of North America in the late nineteenth and early twentieth centuries continued under the banner of fundamentalism and left no break in the line of succession from Dwight L. Moody to Billy Graham. Fundamentalism bears all the marks of a popular religious movement which drew only part of its identity from opposition to liberal trends in the denominations. The movement had its own ideology and program to pursue." 57 notes.   M. D. Dibert

559. Cary, Lorin Lee. THE REORGANIZED UNITED MINE WORKERS OF AMERICA, 1930-1931. *J. of the Illinois State Hist. Soc. 1973 66(3): 244-270.* The Reorganized United Mine Workers of America was founded in 1930 by a coalition of traditionalists and radicals dissatisfied with the leadership of United Mine Workers of America president John L. Lewis. The reorganized union lasted for only one year, in which it illustrated the unusual problems of labor unions during the Depression. Inadequate funds, personality clashes, and membership distrust particularly hindered the establishment of a strong anti-Lewis union. 5 illus., 72 notes.   A. C. Aimone

560. Casey, Kareta G. WILEY H. POST'S AROUND THE WORLD SOLO FLIGHT. *Chronicles of Oklahoma 1977 55(3): 324-335.* As a self-taught pilot who barnstormed across Oklahoma during the 1920's, Wiley Post (1898-1935) gradually emerged as a seasoned flier. In 1931 he joined Harold Gatty to set a new speed record for an around-the-world flight. He surpassed that record two

years later on a solo flight by using a gyroscopic automatic pilot, radio homing machine, and new propeller construction. Based on newspapers and secondary accounts; 4 photos, map, 44 notes.   M. L. Tate

561.   Christy, Joe.   FREE SPIRIT IN A FREE BALLOON.   *Air Force Mag. 1974 57(9): 87-91.* Reproduces anecdotes about "Red" Carter, member of the Old 1st Balloon Squadron, Fort Sill, Oklahoma, 1930's.

562.   Cofer, Richard.   BOOTLEGGERS IN THE BACKWOODS: PROHIBITION AND THE DEPRESSION IN HERNANDO COUNTY.   *Tampa Bay Hist. 1979 1(1): 17-23.* Illegal manufacture of alcohol (moonshining) and rum-running were common in Hernando County, Florida, with the sanction of (or at least unchallenged by) local law enforcement because of the lucrative nature of the business; 1929-33.

563.   Condon, Richard H.   BAYONETS AT THE NORTH BRIDGE: THE LEWISTON-AUBURN SHOE STRIKE, 1937.   *Maine Hist. Soc. Q. 1981 21(2): 75-98.* Details the events of the Auburn and Lewiston, Maine, shoe workers' strike led by the United Shoe Workers of America (USWA), a Congress of Industrial Organizations affiliate. The USWA, attempting to gain union recognition and raise wages, organized a strike that lasted from 25 March to 28 June 1937. Although the USWA was generally successful in other locations, this strike essentially failed. This was due to the opposition of community leaders, including the French Roman Catholic priests, and to the fact that the leaders of the strike were outsiders, that local people had little militant labor experience, and that the strikers were quite poor. Based on local newspapers and interviews; 142 notes.
C. A. Watson

564.   Cooney, Terry A.   COSMOPOLITAN VALUES AND THE IDENTIFICATION OF REACTION: *PARTISAN REVIEW* IN THE 1930S. *J. of Am. Hist. 1981 68(3): 580-598.* Examines the shift in editorial emphasis in the *Partisan Review* from Communism to anti-Stalinism during the 1930's. The commitment by editors like William Phillips and Philip Rahv to cosmopolitan cultural values provided a basic continuity to the shift. First Communism and then anti-Stalinist socialism stood for cosmopolitan cultural values. 40 notes.
T. P. Linkfield

565.   Corbett, Katharine T.   ST. LOUIS WOMEN GARMENT WORKERS: PHOTOGRAPHS AND MEMORIES.   *Gateway Heritage 1981 2(1): 18-25.* Describes a project of the Women's Center at the University of Missouri, St. Louis. Using photohistory and oral history methods, researchers secured and interpreted the responses of female garment industry workers to strikes in the 1930's. Among the results have been an exhibit, "Dollar Dresses: St. Louis Women in the Garment Industry," comprised of 38 photographs and oral history comments solicited from seven retired garment workers. 17 photos, 9 notes.
H. T. Lovin

566.   Corn, Joseph J.   MAKING FLYING "THINKABLE": WOMEN PILOTS AND THE SELLING OF AVIATION, 1927-1940. *Am. Q. 1979 31(4): 556-571.* By the late 1920's, the aviation industry had succeeded in making the airplane a reliable means of transportation. But it was only the introduction of women as pilots that proved to a skeptical public that airplanes were safe and easy

to fly. Women were hired by corporations to race, tour, make special promotional flights, and handle airplane sales to the private sector. By 1940, with the public thoroughly convinced of airplane safety, the role of women as pilots was no longer encouraged. The number of women pilots declined rapidly thereafter. 36 notes.

D. K. Lambert

567.   Cowley, Malcolm.   1935: THE YEAR OF CONGRESSES.   *Southern Rev. 1979 15(2): 273-287.* Discusses the goals of the Communist International, the role of leftist American writers in the movement to destroy capitalism, and the meetings of the American Writers' Congress during 1935 which resulted in the formation of the League of American Writers in that same year.

568.   Coy, Harold and Coy, Mildred.   EXPERIMENTS IN HIGHER EDU-CATION: *EDUCATIONAL COMMUNE: THE STORY OF COMMON-WEALTH COLLEGE* BY RAYMOND AND CHARLOTTE KOCH. *Harvard Educ. R. 1973 43(2): 264-268.* Reviews the Koch's account (New York: Schocken Books, 1972) of Commonwealth College, which operated from 1923 to 1940 in Mena, Arkansas. It was founded by William E. Zeuch, an economist, to provide a general education for young disadvantaged working people. Headed by Lucien Koch after 1931, the faculty began training students for active participation in the labor movement. The college was fined into bankruptcy as a subversive institution in 1940. It also suffered from its remoteness from the industrial North and its inability to enroll black students. An illuminating account of the friction inherent in a communal venture which brought together people of diverse interests without the help of monetary incentives.

J. Herbst

569.   Damiani, Alessandro.   I COMMUNISTI E IL MOVIMENTO OP-ERAIO DENTRO LA CRISI: LA LIQUIDAZIONE DEI SINDICATI ROSSI, 1933-1935   [The communists and the workers' movement during the crisis: the liquidation of the red unions, 1933-1935]. *Movimento Operaio e Socialista [Italy] 1976 22(1-2): 87-110.* The year 1933 signaled the growth of worker agitation in the United States. The communist Trade Union Unity League (TUUL), which grew rapidly and proportionately more than the American Federation of Labor, was unable to keep in step with the increased radicalism of its members and the leadership necessary for a true revolutionary party of the masses. By late 1933 the Communist Party was vigorously supporting its old policy of "bore from within." The National Executive Committee of the TUUL proposed in October of 1934 to unify all unions, ultimately leading to the dissolution of the TUUL and many other independent unions. The entrance of large numbers of Communists into the AFL was undoubtedly an important cause of the breakup of the union movement and the eventual formation of the Committee for Industrial Organization, thus representing the first determining role ever played by the Communist Party in the workers' movement. Primary and secondary sources; 44 notes.

M. T. Wilson

570.   Daniel, Cletus E.   WOBBLIES ON THE FARM: THE IWW IN THE YAKIMA VALLEY. *Pacific Northwest Q. 1974 65(4): 166-175.* A study of the 1933 efforts of the reactivated Industrial Workers of the World ("Wobblies") to organize the fruit workers of the Yakima Valley. When picket lines were formed to enforce a strike the farmers organized into vigilante groups. The most notable and violent confrontation was at Congdon's Orchard, in the course of which a

large number of strikers were turned over to county authorities for arrest and trial. The farmers gained the sympathies of the area on "patriotic" grounds as a mask for their antiunionism, and the "Wobblies" were never again able to successfully revive their efforts. 51 notes.   R. V. Ritter

571.   Daniel, Walter C.   *THE CRISIS* AND *OPPORTUNITY* VS. WASHINGTON, D.C., BOARD OF EDUCATION.   *Crisis 1978 85(6): 205-207.* In the spring of 1936, *The Crisis* and *Opportunity* were banned from the approved reading list of the public schools in the District of Columbia. Members of the Board of Education believed that the magazines contained reading matter objectionable because it was militant propaganda. Antisubversive hysteria and the American reaction to the rise of fascism fostered this repressive climate. The Board also objected to the use of the word "nigger" in the magazines. The editors of both magazines failed to get the decision reversed for several years.
A. G. Belles

572.   Daniel, Walter C.   LANGSTON HUGHES' INTRODUCTION TO *ESQUIRE* MAGAZINE.   *J. of Popular Culture 1979 12(4): 620-623.* Describes the 1934 "plebiscite" conducted by Arnold Gingrich, editor of the then new men's magazine, *Esquire*, which asked whether or not a story by Langston Hughes (1902-67) should be published in the magazine. The incident illustrates the difficulty black artists experienced in placing their work before the public in commercial magazines. Illus., 11 notes.   D. G. Nielson

573.   Davidson, David.   THE STORY OF THE CENTURY.   *Am. Heritage 1976 27(2): 22-29, 93.* Bruno Hauptmann went on trial on 2 January 1935 in Flemington, New Jersey, for the kidnapping and murder of Charles and Anne Lindbergh's son. Although treated as a social event by some, and as a carnival by others, the trial did bring out concrete evidence which proved Hauptmann's guilt. 14 illus.   B. J. Paul

574.   Davin, Eric Leif and Lynd, Staughton.   PICKET LINE AND BALLOT BOX: THE FORGOTTEN LEGACY OF THE LOCAL LABOR PARTY MOVEMENT, 1932-1936.   *Radical Hist. Rev. 1979-80 (22): 43-63.* Using Berlin, New Hampshire, as a case study, discusses the widespread working-class participation in state and local politics through the formation of independent labor and farmer-labor parties during 1932-36, and the destruction of the movement in 1936 by the Congress of Industrial Organizations through the Non-Partisan League.

575.   De Marco, Joseph P.   THE RATIONALE AND FOUNDATION OF DU BOIS'S THEORY OF ECONOMIC CO-OPERATION.   *Phylon 1974 35(1): 5-15.* In 1940 W. E. B. DuBois evolved a careful, rational, and realistic plan for the economic betterment of a minority group during a severe depression. His plan called for a segregated racial economic cooperative. He rejected a communist solution. Cooperation was a primary aspect of African tribal life which carried over into slavery. He believed segregation could be overcome only if it was used to advantage through cooperation. "Partly through his examination of the effectiveness of boycotts he considered that the economic cycle began not with production, as most Americans assumed, but with consumption." A racial consumers' cooperative would be sound because it based production on consumer

needs. He failed to foresee the adoption of new economic policies by the government. 46 notes.   E. P. Stickney

576. Dewitt, Howard A. HIRAM JOHNSON AND EARLY NEW DEAL DIPLOMACY, 1933-1934. *California Hist. Q. 1974 53(4): 377-386.* Assesses Hiram Johnson's influence in directing American foreign policy toward isolationism in the 1930's. Although dismissed as self-seeking by some historians, Johnson sincerely worked to avoid war through a highly restrictive foreign policy. He sponsored legislation banning loans to nations that defaulted on their war debts and pressed for an arms embargo resolution that would apply impartially to all belligerents. President Roosevelt, concerned with the passage of domestic reforms in the early stages of the New Deal, acceded to Johnson's views in these areas. The Nye Committee thus had a major precedent in Johnson as a successful promoter of isolationist policies. Based on primary and secondary sources; illus., photos, 35 notes.   A. Hoffman

577. DeWitt, Howard A. THE WATSONVILLE ANTI-FILIPINO RIOT OF 1930: A CASE STUDY OF THE GREAT DEPRESSION AND ETHNIC CONFLICT IN CALIFORNIA. *Southern California Q. 1979 61(3): 291-302.* Examines the anti-Filipino riot in Watsonville, California, 19-23 January 1930. Hostility to Filipino Americans, most of whom lived in California, had been building for several years in the Watsonville area. Filipinos were victims of discrimination, exploitation, and stereotyping. Politicians and newspapers issued overtly racist statements concerning alleged Filipino threats in health, social relations, and vice. Following public anti-Filipino pronouncements by local political and business leaders, mobs of young men prowled Watsonville streets looking for Filipinos to beat up. One Filipino was shot dead. After five days the riots subsided as the public reacted negatively to the excessive violence. Police and sheriff's deputies acted impartially in protecting Filipinos but arrested few rioters. The California Filipino community failed to unite against the assault, its leaders divided on how to approach the problem. Onset of the Great Depression thus culminated years of anti-Filipino sentiment in the Watsonville riot. 33 notes.
                                                                    A. Hoffman

578. Diamond, Sander A. ZUR TYPOLOGIE DER AMERIKADEUTSCHEN NS-BEWEGUNG [On the typology of the German American National Socialist Movement]. *Vierteljahrshefte für Zeitgeschichte [West Germany] 1975 23(3): 271-296.* Analyzes four key German American Nazi organizations: "Teutonia" (1924-32), "Gau USA" (1931-36), adventurer Edmund Fürholzer's group around *Deutsche Zeitung* (1928-31), and the most notorious "Bund" ("Bund der Freunde des neuen Deutschland," later "Amerikadeutscher Volksbund," 1933-38). Composed largely of young, anti-Semitic, lower middle class, usually unemployed post-World War I immigrants, the groups eventually drew enough American mistrust upon themselves to be disowned even by their German Nazi supporters. Based on records primarily at the National Archives (Suitland); 68 notes.   D. Prowe

579. Dinwoodie, D. H. DEPORTATION: THE IMMIGRATION SERVICE AND THE CHICANO LABOR MOVEMENT IN THE 1930S. *New Mexico Hist. Rev. 1977 52(3): 193-206.* During the 1930's, Chicanos were the object of much investigation as to whether they had entered the United States

illegally. The investigations generally took place when the immigrants organized labor unions. In 1935, Julio Herrera was deported on charges that he had entered the United States illegally. The following year Jesus Pallares was deported, after subversion charges were brought against him. Actually he was deported as a result of his activities in organizing the *Liga Obrera de Habla Español.* Chicanos were encouraged to organize labor unions by the policies of the New Deal, although local authorities were opposed to these policies. 39 notes.

J. H. Krenkel

580.   Doenecke, Justus D.   THE ANTI-INTERVENTIONIST TRADITION: LEADERSHIP AND PERCEPTIONS.   *Literature of Liberty 1981 4(2): 7-67.* Presents a bibliographical essay on such leading anti-interventionists as Senator Robert A. Taft, Herbert C. Hoover, Charles A. Lindbergh, Jr., Anne Morrow Lindbergh, Senator William E. Borah, Senator Hiram Johnson, and Senator Gerald P. Nye, and presents a bibliography of anti-interventionist thought and activities; 1929-41.

581.   Doenecke, Justus D.   GENERAL ROBERT E. WOOD: THE EVOLU-TION OF A CONSERVATIVE.   *J. of the Illinois State Hist. Soc. 1978 71(3): 162-175.* Discusses Wood's (1879-1969) business leadership of Sears, Roebuck and Company (1928-54) and his association with several conservative organiza-tions, including America First, Americans for Constitutional Action, and the MacArthur-for-President movement. Progressive in his early support of fiscal and social programs of the New Deal, his administration of stock benefits for Sears employees, and his development of overseas markets, Wood was an isola-tionist in foreign policy. Based on Wood Papers and contemporary assessments; 4 illus., 60 notes.   J/S

582.   Doenecke, Justus D.   THE ISOLATIONISTS AND A USABLE PAST. *Peace and Change 1978 5(1): 67-73.* Review article prompted by James T. Patter-son's *Mr. Republican: A Biography of Robert A. Taft* (Boston: Houghton Mif-flin, 1972), Wayne S. Cole's *Charles A. Lindbergh and the Battle Against American Intervention in World War II* (New York: Harcourt Brace Jovano-vich, 1974), Ronald Radosh's *Prophets on the Right: Profiles of Conservative Criticism of American Globalism* (New York: Simon and Schuster, 1975), Mi-chele Flynn Stenehjem's *An American First: John T. Flynn and the America First Committee* (New Rochelle, New York: Arlington House, 1976), and Joan Hoff Wilson's *Herbert Hoover: Forgotten Progressive* (Boston: Little, Brown, 1975).

583.   Doenecke, Justus D.   ISOLATIONISTS OF THE 1930'S AND 1940'S: AN HISTORIOGRAPHICAL ESSAY.   *West Georgia Coll. Studies in the Social Sci. 1974 13: 5-39.*

584.   Doenecke, Justus D.   NON-INTERVENTION OF THE LEFT: THE KEEP AMERICA OUT OF THE WAR CONGRESS, 1938-41.   *J. of Contem-porary Hist. [Great Britain] 1977 12(2): 221-236.* After Norman Thomas visited Europe in 1937, he was ordered by the Socialist Party to form an antiwar coali-tion. Accordingly, the Keep America Out of War Congress was officially founded in New York on 6 March 1938, under the veteran pacifist reformer, Oswald Garrison Villard. The KAOWC was a makeshift coalition of left-wing pacifist

groups. Its ideological tenets were also a potpourri: jobs at home rather than abroad, anti-Asian involvement, neutrality, food not guns, etc. With the proximity of war, the movement dwindled. It died after Pearl Harbor. Based on materials in the Papers of the Socialist Party, Duke University; 51 notes.

M. P. Trauth

585. Douglas, William O. WHEN JUSTICE DOUGLAS TAUGHT AT YALE. *Yale Alumni Mag. 1974 38(1): 31-33.* Memoirs of Justice William O. Douglas' years on the Yale University Law School faculty (1928-34) describe colleagues, causes, and concepts in legal education. S

586. Dugger, Ronnie. NOBEL PRIZE WINNER PURGED AT THE UNIVERSITY OF TEXAS. *Southern Exposure 1974 2(1): 67-70.* Biologist Hermann J. Muller was dismissed from the staff of the University of Texas in 1936 for his Marxist opinions. S

587. Dunbaugh, Edwin L. THE NIGHTBOATS OF LONG ISLAND SOUND. *Sea Hist. 1981 (20): 9-14.* Describes the overnight steamers that sailed through Long Island Sound during the mid-1930's, based on the author's experiences as a boy watching the nightboats sail by.

588. Duram, James C. THE LABOR UNION JOURNALS AND THE CONSTITUTIONAL ISSUES OF THE NEW DEAL: THE CASE FOR COURT RESTRICTION. *Labor Hist. 1974 15(2): 216-238.* Assesses the editorial position of labor union periodicals on the constitutional issues posed by the New Deal between 1935 and 1937. A liberal interpretation of the constitution was demanded which would allow comprehensive economic and social legislation. The journals reacted to specific court decisions and carried general articles on judicial reform. During the court fight of 1937, labor union journals favored reorganization of the judiciary. The editorials reflect a relationship between the group's economic and constitutional positions and the fact that labor gave up its traditional independent approach to politics in the 1930's. 70 notes, appendix.

L. L. Athey

589. Duran, James C. ALGERNON LEE'S CORRESPONDENCE WITH KARL KAUTSKY: AN OLD GUARD PERSPECTIVE ON THE FAILURE OF AMERICAN SOCIALISM. *Labor Hist. 1979 20(3): 420-434.* Reprints five letters from Algernon Lee to Karl Kautsky which analyze the factionalism within the American Socialist Party from an "Old Guard" perspective. The letters are located in the International Institute of Social History in Amsterdam. Covers 1930-35. 25 notes.

L. L. Athey

590. Edward, C. NIGHTMARE AT SEA. *Am. Hist. Illus. 1979 14(3): 38-41.* Describes the tragedy of the burning of the *Morro Castle* in 1934 in which over 130 passengers of the ship died as a result of fire due to mysterious causes.

591. Emerson, Thomas I. SOUTHERN JUSTICE IN THE THIRTIES. *Civil Liberties Rev. 1977 4(1): 70-74.* Uses Charles H. Martin's *The Angelo Herndon Case and Southern Justice* (Baton Rouge: Louisiana State U. Pr., 1976) to chronicle the 1932 Atlanta, Georgia case against a young black Communist who organized a protest regarding depletion of county relief funds, was arrested and convicted under the Georgia Insurrection Law, was defended by the largely

Communist International Labor Defense of New York, and was freed from an 18-to-20-year sentence by the US Supreme Court in 1937.

592. Engelmann, Larry D. "WE WERE THE POOR PEOPLE": THE HOR-MEL STRIKE OF 1933. *Labor Hist. 1974 15(4): 483-510.* Narrates the formation of a union in the Hormel packinghouse in Austin, Minnesota, the conflict with the "benevolent dictatorship" of Hormel management and the violent strike of 1933. The union was sparked by an insurance proposal, issued as an edict, which would cost workers 20 cents per week. A strike ensued and peaked in November 1933 when workers seized the plant. The strike was successfully arbitrated after intervention by Governor Floyd B. Olson. Pay increases were granted, but union recognition was not achieved. The company shifted to a policy of "welfare capitalism." Based upon Austin, Minnesota, newspapers and personal interviews; 67 notes.   L. L. Athey

593. Feuer, Lewis S. THE PRAGMATIC WISDOM OF SIDNEY HOOK. *Encounter [Great Britain] 1975 45(4): 37-47.* Reviews the life and works of Sidney Hook, American philosopher and advocate of Marxist ideology, whose pragmatic writings during the 1930's included essays on ethical values, courage, and the need for general education in the university curriculum.

594. Filippelli, Ronald L. UE: THE FORMATIVE YEARS, 1933-1937. *Labor Hist. 1976 17(3): 351-371.* Study of the formation of the United Electrical and Radio Workers of America reveals its origins in the Philadelphia Philco strike of 1933, the early struggles over industrial vs. craft unionism, and three major groups for union activities among the U.E. All the elements for later internecine warfare were prevalent in the U.E. before 1937. Based on files of the U.E., oral interviews, and the Pennsylvania State University Labor Collection; 60 notes.   L. L. Athey

595. Fine, Sidney, ed. JOHN L. LEWIS DISCUSSES THE GENERAL MO-TORS SIT-DOWN STRIKE: A DOCUMENT. *Labor Hist. 1974 15(4): 563-570.* Presents a document about John L. Lewis discussing the General Motors sit-down strike of 1936-37. Lewis apparently hoped to place the problem in the lap of President Roosevelt. Document in the Heber Blankenhorn Papers in the Archives of Labor History and Urban Affairs of Wayne State University. 16 notes.   L. L. Athey

596. Finison, Lorenz J. AN ASPECT OF THE EARLY HISTORY OF THE SOCIETY FOR THE PSYCHOLOGICAL STUDY OF SOCIAL ISSUES: PSYCHOLOGISTS AND LABOR. *J. of the Hist. of the Behavioral Sci. 1979 15(1): 29-37.* This article traces briefly the roots of the Society for the Psychological Study of Social Issues in the movement to combat unemployment among psychologists during the mid-1930's. The principal topic is one aspect of the Society's history: the manner in which the Society responded to the issue of labor. There were two attempts to deal with this issue in the context of the Depression: the Society's Committee on Trade Union Affiliation and its Yearbook Committee on Industrial Conflict. These committees are described in the context of prolabor sympathies among academics during the period, and in the context of industrial conflict occurring at that time. The continuing conflict within the Society over its role as an "activist" organization versus its role as a research-supporting

organization is shown to have its roots in the very earliest efforts to organize the Society.   J

597.   Fisch, Dov.   THE LIBEL TRIAL OF ROBERT EDWARD EDMOND-SON: 1936-1938.   *Am. Jewish Hist. 1981 71(1): 79-102.* Covers events leading to, and Jewish reaction to, the 1936-38 libel trial of anti-Jew publisher Robert Edward Edmondson. Attacking high-ranking Jews in Franklin D. Roosevelt's administration as leading the nation to Communism, Edmondson even claimed that secretary of Labor Frances Perkins was a Russian Jew. Both conservative and liberal Jews hailed New York Mayor Fiorello La Guardia for instituting libel charges in 1936. But two years of delay altered Jewish opinion, and in 1938 three major Jewish organizations, seeking to prevent making a "martyr" of Edmondson, joined the American Civil Liberties Union in defending him. Edmondson claimed victory and resumed publishing, only to be indicted during World War II for sedition and conspiracy. Based on New York City Municipal Archives and other primary sources; 104 notes.   R. A. Keller

598.   Fox, Richard W.   REINHOLD NIEBUHR AND THE EMERGENCE OF THE LIBERAL REALIST FAITH, 1930-1945.   *R. of Pol. 1976 38(2): 244-265.* Reinhold Niebuhr attracted postwar liberals "not only because of his political analysis and theological achievement but because of his commitment to the realistic use of power." He symbolized for liberals, the intellectual dedicated not only to the pursuit of truth and knowledge, but also an advocate and practioner of democracy. Such activism and faith by Niebuhr almost succeeded in transforming "his own liberal realist faith into the kind of 'political religion' against which he had inveighed since 1930." 35 notes.   L. E. Ziewacz

599.   Fry, Joseph A.   RAYON, RIOT, AND REPRESSION: THE COVING-TON SIT-DOWN STRIKE OF 1937.   *Virginia Mag. of Hist. and Biog. 1976 84(1): 3-18.* The attempt by the Textile Workers Organizing Committee to orga-nize the Industrial Rayon Corporation's plant in Covington, Virginia, illustrates the problems which faced union leaders in the South. Though the movement did result in Virginia's first significant sit-down strike, the support of state officials and police for the management produced violence and ultimate failure. Based on the George C. Peery Papers, Virginia State Library, interviews with participants, newspapers, and additional primary sources; 55 notes.   R. F. Oakes

600.   Gall, Gilbert J.   HEBER BLANKENHORN, THE LAFOLLETTE COMMITTEE, AND THE IRONY OF INDUSTRIAL REPRESSION.   *Labor Hist. 1982 23(2): 246-253.* Presents a 1952 memorandum and postscript by Heber Blankenhorn, outlining his role in the origins of the Senate Investigation of Violations of Free Speech and Labor Rights, known as the LaFollette Commit-tee. Holding hearings from 1936-40, the committee exposed the anti-union prac-tices of employers in the 1920's and early 1930's; this helped to prevent a recurrence of such tactics in 1936 and 1937 and ameliorated public outrage at unions for their use of sit-down strikes. Based on the Heber Blankenhorn Collec-tion; 17 notes.   L. F. Velicer

601.   Galliher, John F. and Walker, Allyn.   THE PUZZLE OF THE SOCIAL ORIGINS OF THE MARIHUANA TAX ACT OF 1937.   *Social Problems 1977 (3): 367-376.* Neither pressure from the Federal Bureau of Narcotics nor

a real national marijuana crisis engendered the Marihuana Tax Act (US, 1937); the act was symbolic, inasmuch as the Bureau had promised that its passage would require no additional funding.

602. Genizi, Haim.   AMERICAN NON-SECTARIAN REFUGEE RELIEF ORGANIZATIONS (1933-1945).   *Yad Vashem Studies on the European Jewish Catastrophe and Resistance [Israel] 1976 11: 164-220.* Examines the activities and role of the American nonsectarian organizations in the general field of aid and relief to refugees from Nazi Germany. The creation of nonsectarian committees comprising Jews and Christians was designed to ensure the greatest possible public support for a task which also involved the fight against the rising wave of anti-Semitism in the United States. The establishment of nonsectarian committees also stemmed from the need to care for professional groups with specific problems. Based on archival and published sources; 185 notes.   J. P. Fox

603. Genizi, Haim.   EDMUND   WILSON   AND   *THE   MODERN MONTHLY,* 1934-5: A PHASE IN WILSON'S RADICALISM.   *J. of Am. Studies [Great Britain] 1973 7(3): 301-319.* Wilson (1895-1972), a distinguished intellectual, flirted with Communism but never joined the Communist Party. Hoping to Americanize Marxism, he joined the independent, radical, and anti-Stalinist magazine, *The Modern Monthly,* which V. F. Calverton (1900-40) founded. Wilson's experience left him disillusioned with the anti-Stalinist Marxists. Based on the Calverton Papers and on secondary sources; 86 notes.
                                                              H. T. Lovin

604.   Giebelhaus, August W.   FARMING FOR FUEL: THE ALCOHOL MOTOR FUEL MOVEMENT OF THE 1930S.   *Agric. Hist. 1980 54(1): 173-184.* A movement to use alcohol produced from food as a substitute for gasoline became important in the 1930's as a means of dealing with the problem of low farm prices and surplus crops. The petroleum industry defeated legislation to aid alcohol production but a privately sponsored plant at Atchison, Kansas, funded by the Chemical Foundation, went into production in 1936 and sold fuel at 2,000 service stations in the Midwest. The high cost of making alcohol led to its closing two years later. Many people objected to alcohol fuels because they clogged fuel lines, burned inefficiently, and tended to separate into their component parts. 41 notes.   D. E. Bowers

605.   Goodenow, Ronald K.   PARADOX IN PROGRESSIVE EDUCATIONAL REFORM: THE SOUTH AND THE EDUCATION OF BLACKS IN THE DEPRESSION YEARS.   *Phylon 1978 39(1): 49-65.* Progressive educational reforms in the South seemingly functioned to serve modernization, but paradoxically maintained racist patterns which were contradictory to progressive ideology. White educators emphasized occupational training for blacks at the expense of academic preparation and also advocated a biracial, segregated South. Black criticism of progressive education has called for testing the democratic ideology against the real conditions of oppression. Primary and secondary sources; 74 notes.   J. Moore

606.   Goodenow, Ronald K.   THE PROGRESSIVE EDUCATOR, RACE AND ETHNICITY IN THE DEPRESSION YEARS: AN OVERVIEW. *Hist. of Educ. Q. 1975 15(4): 365-394.* Focuses on the positions of progressive

educators regarding race and ethnicity in the United States during the Depression and their subsequent influence on education and society.

607. Gordon, Lawrence. A BRIEF LOOK AT BLACKS IN DEPRESSION MISSISSIPPI, 1929-1934: EYEWITNESS ACCOUNTS. *J. of Negro Hist. 1979 64(4): 377-390.* Six black Mississippians interviewed at a senior citizens' center in Jackson, Mississippi, recalled their lives between 1929 and 1934. All of the interviewees agreed that rural blacks faced less difficulty than blacks living in Jackson. Based on interview transcripts; 5 notes, appendix. N. G. Sapper

608. Gordon, Max. THE COMMUNISTS AND THE DRIVE TO ORGA-NIZE STEEL, 1936. *Labor Hist. 1982 23(2): 254-265.* Reproduces a report to John Stachel, the Communist Party's national trade union secretary by John Steuben, a Communist organizer in charge of the Steel Workers Organizing Committee's drive in Youngstown, Ohio. Steuben comments on the union drive in Youngstown, organizers and methods of organization, "partial struggles" resulting in some immediate worker victories, subversion of company unions, steel company policies, and the status of the local Communist Party. Based on the Nelson Frank papers; 19 notes. L. F. Velicer

609. Gottlieb, Peter. THE COMPLICATED EQUATION: WORKER RE-BELLION AND UNIONIZATION. *Appalachian J. 1979 6(4): 321-325.* Analyzes the growth of unions and workers' organizations in the United States during the 1930's despite the Depression and high unemployment; discusses John W. Hevener's *Which Side Are You On? The Harlan County Coal Miners, 1931-39* (Urbana: U. of Illinois Pr., 1978), an account of the Kentucky workers' struggle to organize.

610. Hargreaves, Mary W. M. DARKNESS BEFORE THE DAWN: THE STATUS OF WOMEN IN THE DEPRESSION YEARS. Deutrich, Mabel E. and Purdy, Virginia C., ed. *Clio Was a Woman: Studies in the History of American Women* (Washington, D.C.: Howard U. Pr., 1980): 178-188. Reviews two monographs, J. Stanley Lemon's *The Woman Citizen: Social Feminism in the 1920's* (Urbana: U. of Illinois Pr., 1973), and William H. Chafe's *The American Woman: Her Changing Social, Economic, and Political Roles, 1920-1970* (New York: Oxford U. Pr., 1972). The first delves into the depression decade to recount the collapse of women's leadership in social reform as their movement splintered on the issue of protective legislation. William Chafe points up the wealth of data in the working papers of the Women's Bureau deposited in the National Archives, questions whether women as workers had made significant advances during 1910-20 and views the intervening period to 1940 as a stalemate which culminated in the nadir of women's rights under the impact of depression. A discussion summary follows. 54 notes. J. Powell

611. Hastie, William H. TOWARD AN EQUALITARIAN LEGAL OR-DER: 1930-1950. *Ann. of the Am. Acad. of Pol. and Social Sci. 1973 (407): 18-31.* "Though the post-Civil War amendments to the Constitution promised black Americans that thereafter their rights and opportunities would not be demeaned because of race, the ensuing fifty years witnessed the comprehensive institutionalization of racial segregation and subordination by force of law. During the first quarter of this century the racist legal order was so firmly established,

with the support or acquiescence of most whites, that struggle against it seemed futile. But beginning about 1930, under the leadership of the National Association for the Advancement of Colored People, a nationwide legal campaign was planned and undertaken with an equalitarian legal order as its goal. Early lawsuits served to arouse public interest and support as well as to win significant peripheral changes in the segregated legal order. Social scientists and educators were persuaded to reexamine the segregated order critically. The federal government moved from a posture of neutrality to forthright assertion that laws requiring racial segregation could not be squared with the Constitution. Responding case by case, the Supreme Court progressively eroded antecedent constitutional doctrine that sanctioned American apartheid until, by 1950, the Court appeared ready to strike down all statutes and all other governmental action that imposed racial segregation or discrimination."   J

612.   Hauptman, Laurence M.   BIG DEAL?   *J. of Ethnic Studies 1981 9(2): 119-123.* Reviews Donald L. Parman's *The Navajos and the New Deal* (1976), Kenneth R. Philp's *John Collier's Crusade for Indian Reform, 1920-1954* (1977), and Graham D. Taylor's *The New Deal and American Indian Tribalism: The Administration of the Indian Reorganization Act, 1934-1945* (1980). Taken together, the works show that "historians have finally begun to take the sizeable Indian criticism of New Deal policies more seriously than in the past," and tend more to agree with those Native Americans who "have looked askance at the . . . legacy of the Collier years."   G. J. Bobango

613.   Hein, Virginia H. and Baylen, Joseph O.   AMERICAN INTELLECTU-ALS AND THE "RED DECADE."   *Studies in Hist. and Soc. 1977 2(1-2): 40-59.* The Depression drove many American authors to the Left and the radical Left during 1929-39, also called the "red decade." The appeal of communism grew, and many intellectuals praised the USSR and its supposed creation of a classless society. Discusses the literary output associated with the Communist Party, USA, the American section of the Communist Third International, which promoted the party line of Moscow. Factionalism characterized the literary output of left-wing intellectuals; however, the Popular Front Against Fascism grew in popularity, 1935-39. This united stand against Hitler and the fascist forces of the Spanish Civil War led to the American Writers' Congresses in 1935 and 1937. Discusses the activity of the League of American Writers, particularly when news of Stalinist purges began to divide intellectuals. The Nazi-Soviet pact of 1939 shattered the Popular Front Against Fascism program of the CPUSA; intellectuals' support of the Party collapsed. 94 notes.

614.   Helmer, William J.   THE DEPRESSION DESPERADOS: A STUDY IN MODERN MYTH-MAKING.   *Mankind 1975 5(2): 40-46.* Criminals such as John Dillinger spurred the Justice Department and the Federal Bureau of Investigation to modernize and coordinate the efforts of law enforcement agencies in 1933-34.

615.   Hendrick, Irving J.   CALIFORNIA'S RESPONSE TO THE "NEW EDUCATION" IN THE 1930's.   *California Hist. Q. 1974 53(1): 25-40.* During the 1930's California educators responded favorably to the idea of "progressive education." California became a leader in implementation of progressive education programs, encouraged by State Superintendent of Public Instruction Vierling

Kersey and Helen Heffernan, chief of the State Bureau of Elementary Education. Efforts were made to relieve school curricula from excessive rigidity in course content and methods of grading. The public accepted the movement, though educators themselves were cautious of favoring fads and frills over basic subjects. The overall effect of the "new" education was less impressive than the rhetoric about it, due to bureaucratic inertia and the control of a wide range of sanctioning bodies with various policy positions. Many current ideas regarding educational reform are similar to those of the 1930's, the chief difference being that in the 1930's educators were accepted as the makers of their own reforms. Based on government reports and published studies; illus., photo, 52 notes.

A. Hoffman

616. Herring, Neill and Thrasher, Sue. UAW SITDOWN STRIKE: AT-LANTA, 1936. *Southern Exposure 1974 1(3/4): 63-83.* Analysis of the labor strike at General Motor's Lakewood plant in Atlanta, one of a series of strikes that spread through the General Motors plants across the nation during 1935-37. Local conditions influenced the workers to strike while the United Auto Workers Executive Board played only a peripheral role. The workers and community cooperated to provide the necessities of life for the strikers. Job security resulted from the Atlanta strike. Based on oral interviews; 21 illus. G. A. Bolton

617. Hine, Darlene Clark. BLACKS AND THE DESTRUCTION OF THE DEMOCRATIC WHITE PRIMARY 1935-1944. *J. of Negro Hist. 1977 62(1): 43-59.* The adoption of the white primary by southern states in the 1890's became the most effective subterfuge to disenfranchise blacks. A 25-year legal struggle by the National Association for the Advancement of Colored People (NAACP) resulted in the victory of the Supreme Court decision in the case of *Smith* v. *Allwright* (US, 1944). 72 notes. P. J. Taylorson

618. Hine, Darlene Clark. THE N.A.A.C.P. AND THE SUPREME COURT: WALTER F. WHITE AND THE DEFEAT OF JUDGE JOHN J. PARKER, 1930. *Negro Hist. Bull. 1977 40(5): 753-757.* The NAACP and Walter F. White established themselves on the national scene as well as in North Carolina when they defeated the appointment of Judge John J. Parker to the Supreme Court. R. Jirran

619. Hoffman, Abraham. THE EL MONTE BERRY PICKERS' STRIKE, 1933: INTERNATIONAL INVOLVEMENT IN A LOCAL LABOR DIS-PUTE. *J. of the West 1973 12(1): 71-84.* A detailed account of the 1933 berry pickers' strike in El Monte, California, which involved "Mexican laborers, Communist agitators, Japanese employers, Los Angeles Chamber of Commerce and business representatives, and state and federal mediators . . . over issues of wages, hours, and working conditions. . . . The El Monte strike, however, claimed the distinction of direct involvement by the government of Mexico, in the form of diplomatic pressure, monetary assistance, and consular intervention. . . . In contrast to the active assistance of the Mexican consuls, the Japanese consul maintained a low profile, probably because of his awareness that excessive publicity would raise questions about Japanese leasing of property in a state that had already endorsed two alien land laws." 44 notes. D. D. Cameron

620. Hoffman, Abraham. THE FEDERAL BUREAUCRACY MEETS A SUPERIOR SPOKESMAN FOR ALIEN DEPORTATION. *J. of the West 1975 14(4): 91-106.* Discusses the correspondence between J. C. Brodie of Superior, Arizona and various federal public servants and the Bureau of Immigration about deportation of Mexicans who he believed took jobs away from American citizens, 1930-34.

621. Hoffman, Abraham. A NOTE ON THE FIELD RESEARCH INTERVIEWS OF PAUL S. TAYLOR. *Pacific Historian 1976 20(2): 123-131.* During 1927-30 Dr. Paul S. Taylor interviewed more than 1,000 people for the publication, *Mexican Labor in the United States*. Reports on the results of the National Endowment for the Humanities grant which funded the reorganization and editing of interviews. Based on primary sources; 8 notes.   G. L. Olson

622. Hofsommer, Donovan L. STEEL PLOWS AND IRON MEN: THE ILLINOIS CENTRAL RAILROAD AND IOWA'S WINTER OF 1936. *Ann. of Iowa 1976 43(4): 292-298.* The difficulties brought on by blizzards which struck Iowa during January and February 1936 are without parallel in the state's recorded history. Particularly hard hit were the railroads. Describes the struggles of one railroad—the Illinois Central—against the cold, wind, and snow of that ferocious winter. On one day, 23 January, 11 Illinois Central trains were snowbound at scattered locations across the state. Another day, the Illinois Central was forced to assign 22 locomotives to snow-clearing tasks in Iowa. Based on the "war report" of W. S. Williams, Superintendent, Iowa Division, Illinois Central Railroad, 25 March 1936; 3 photos, note.   P. L. Petersen

623. Homberger, Eric. PROLETARIAN LITERATURE AND THE JOHN REED CLUBS 1929-1935. *J. of Am. Studies [Great Britain] 1979 13(2): 221-244.* Prior to 1929, Communist leaders denounced Proletcult, expression of art and science ideas supposedly latent in the masses. American radicals such as Michael Gold persisted, and John Reed Clubs, organized to abet such expression, significantly influenced the American literary left during the 1920's. From 1930 to 1935, the clubs were subjected to Communist Party and Comintern pressures to conform to the ultrarevolutionary and then the contradictory Popular Front ideologies of those agencies. Based on memoirs, Proletcult writings and Communist journals, and secondary works; 52 notes.   H. T. Lovin

624. Homel, Michael W. THE LILYDALE SCHOOL CAMPAIGN OF 1936: DIRECT ACTION IN THE VERBAL PROTEST ERA. *J. of Negro Hist. 1974 59(3): 228-241.* During the 1960's black people marched, boycotted, sat-in, and took other forms of direct action to implement public school integration and to assure improved education for their children. Among earlier precedents for such direct action was an effort by black Chicagoans in 1936, at a time when most civil rights activity was verbal. Based on secondary sources; 33 notes.   N. G. Sapper

625. Hudson, James J. THE ROLE OF THE CALIFORNIA NATIONAL GUARD DURING THE SAN FRANCISCO GENERAL STRIKE OF 1934. *Military Affairs 1982 46(2): 76-83.* On 5 July 1934, the California National Guard was called upon in one of the most serious labor disputes of the 20th century, the San Francisco maritime and general strike of that year. This strike

was part of a larger one that affected the entire west coast of the United States. During its 3-week tour, the guard took control of the waterfront and established law and order, without trying to usurp the powers and duties of the civil authorities. Its performance was exemplary. Based on California National Guard and other primary sources; 55 notes.   A. M. Osur

626. Humphries, Jane. WOMEN: SCAPEGOATS AND SAFETY VALVES IN THE GREAT DEPRESSION. *Rev. of Radical Pol. Econ. 1976 8(1): 98-121.* Examines the role of women in the labor market and economic structure of the Depression; pressures from within the capitalist economy aggravate sex-linked relations of dominance and subordination, strengthen traditional ideas, and weaken women's drive for liberation.

627. Hurd, Rick. NEW DEAL LABOR POLICY AND THE CONTAINMENT OF RADICAL UNION ACTIVITY. *Rev. of Radical Pol. Econ. 1976 8(3): 32-43.* New Deal labor policies were designed to impart support for working class movements to discourage activism and militance on the part of labor radicals, 1930's.

628. Ingalls, Robert P. THE TAMPA FLOGGING CASE: URBAN VIGILANTISM. *Florida Hist. Q. 1977 56(1): 13-27.* In November 1935, three members of the Modern Democrats, a party opposed to municipal corruption, were kidnapped and flogged. One victim died. Although there was strong evidence of official complicity in the crime, the floggings and murder went unpunished. Discusses this case as an example of urban vigilantism, a violent, illegal means of preserving the status quo against any perceived threat. In this instance, the threat was political reform. Based on newspaper and manuscript sources; 54 notes.   P. A. Beaber

629. Jacklin, Thomas M. MISSION TO THE SHARECROPPERS: NEO-ORTHODOX RADICALISM AND THE DELTA FARM VENTURE, 1936-1940. *South Atlantic Q. 1979 78(3): 302-316.* The episode whereby northern neoorthodox theologians attempted to aid the southern sharecropper in the late 1930's provides a revealing commentary on the way in which the proponents of the new theology sought in a concrete manner to connect the Word with the world around them. In spite of purchasing two large farms in the Mississippi State delta area which were settled by both white and black tenant farmers, and in spite of the constant infusion of northern money into the operation to keep it solvent, the attempt of the theologians—who acted like absentee landlords—to provide a model whereby the plight of the sharecropper might be lifted up failed. They forgot that the way of righteousness can be as thorny as the way of sin, a truth which the neoorthodox critics labored long to impress on their liberal colleagues. Based largely on the Reinhold Niebuhr Papers (Manuscript Division), Library of Congress, and contemporary articles in the *Christian Century;* 40 notes.
                                              H. M. Parker, Jr.

630. Jeansonne, Glen. CHALLENGE TO THE NEW DEAL: HUEY P. LONG AND THE REDISTRIBUTION OF NATIONAL WEALTH. *Louisiana Hist. 1980 21(4): 331-339.* While earlier studies of Huey P. Long have emphasized positive results of his political career, the "long-range results of Longism" produced more corruption and insincerity in Louisiana politics than

improvement or reform. The real goal of Longism was power for Long in the national government to equal his control over Louisiana. Had Long lived, he would have divided the nation and created animosity without accomplishing anything. Rather than aiding the needy, Long's Share-Our-Wealth movement would have reduced the availability of capital needed for investment. Additionally, his program required a huge federal government resembling a police state. Based on Huey P. Long's *Every Man a King* and *My First Days in the White House;* 14 notes.   R. H. Tomlinson

631. Jeansonne, Glen.   GERALD L. K. SMITH AND THE SHARE OUR WEALTH MOVEMENT.   *Red River Valley Hist. Rev. 1978 3(3): 52-65.* Discusses the ecclesiastical-turned-political evangelist Gerald L. K. Smith of Louisiana and the Share-Our-Wealth movement which he inherited after the assassination of Huey P. Long in 1935.

632. Jeansonne, Glen.   PARTISAN PARSON: AN ORAL HISTORY AC-COUNT OF THE LOUISIANA YEARS OF GERALD L. K. SMITH. *Louisiana Hist. 1982 23(2): 149-158.* Gerald L. K. Smith was pastor of the Kings Highway Christian Church in Shreveport, Louisiana, 1929-33 and organizer of Huey Long's Share Our Wealth Society, 1933-35. His Louisiana years, and especially his association with Long whom he idolized, launched his national career as a spokesman for right-wing extremism. Interviews with Smith and those who knew him reveal a charismatic figure, highly emotional, engaged in frenzied activity, and addicted to a conspiratorial view of politics.   23 notes.
                                                                          R. E. Noble

633. Jeansonne, Glen.   PREACHER, POPULIST, PROPAGANDIST: THE EARLY CAREER OF GERALD L. K. SMITH.   *Biography 1979 2(4): 303-327.* Gerald L. K. Smith, born and reared in Wisconsin and educated in Indiana, served as a Christian minister before becoming Huey P. Long's Share Our Wealth Society organizer in 1934. Protestant Fundamentalism and political populism and progressivism prepared Smith for political activism. His evolution from radicalism to reaction is examined and the apparent disjunction explained.   J

634. Johnson, James P.   THEORIES OF LABOR UNION DEVELOP-MENT AND THE UNITED MINE WORKERS, 1932-1933.   *Register of the Kentucky Hist. Soc. 1975 73(2): 150-170.* Analyzes the resurgence of the United Mine Workers from October 1932 to mid-1933. General theories are examined, including strategic position, changing governmental attitudes, employer resistance, union leadership, dramatic discontent, and momentum, with examples from Alabama and Kentucky. Primary and secondary sources; 68 notes.
                                                                          J. F. Paul

635. Kahn, Lawrence M.   UNIONS AND INTERNAL LABOR MAR-KETS: THE CASE OF THE SAN FRANCISCO LONGSHOREMEN. *Labor Hist. 1980 21(3): 369-391.* West Coast longshoremen's unions transformed longshoring in San Francisco, California, in the 1930's from a secondary job characterized by low earnings and poor working conditions, to a primary job offering high relative earnings, job stability, and improved working conditions. The key to this transformation was the 1934 West Coast longshoremen's strike. Based on Bureau of Labor Statistics data, Works Progress Administration surveys, and other primary sources; 6 tables, 48 notes.   L. F. Velicer

636. Keeran, Roger R. THE COMMUNISTS AND UAW FACTIONAL-ISM, 1937-39. *Michigan Hist. 1976 60(2): 115-135.* Prevailing views distorted Communist responsibility for United Auto Workers' (UAW) factionalism in Michigan during the late 1930's. Throughout the period Communists worked to maintain unity within the UAW and with the Congress of Industrial Organizations. Only after UAW President Homer Martin thoroughly alienated rank and file unionists and their leaders did open, but reluctant, Communist opposition develop. Martin himself caused the factionalism, blamed the Communists, made them his unwilling adversaries, and brought about his own downfall. Primary and secondary sources; 2 photos, 36 notes. D. W. Johnson

637. Keeran, Roger R. HIS BROTHER'S KEEPER. *Rev. in Am. Hist. 1977 5(1): 100-105.* Review article prompted by Victor G. Reuther's *The Brothers Reuther and the Story of the UAW: A Memoir* (Boston: Houghton Mifflin Co., 1976), which discusses the brothers' involvement in organizing the United Automobile Workers of America (UAW) in the mid-30's.

638. Keller, Allan. "THE BABY IS FOUND ... DEAD!" *Am. Hist. Illus. 1975 10(2): 10-21.* Discusses the investigation of the kidnapping of Charles A. Lindbergh's son, Charles, Jr., in New Jersey in 1932 which led to the execution of Bruno Richard Hauptmann in 1936.

639. Kirby, John B. RALPH J. BUNCHE AND BLACK RADICAL THOUGHT IN THE 1930'S. *Phylon 1974 35(2): 129-141.* Reviews the political thought of Negro leader Ralph Bunche during the New Deal era. Bunche was decidedly further Left at the time. He considered the Negro's problems to be economic and social rather than racial; Bunche took a class position. He saw little hope in the labor unions or early New Deal policies. He created the National Negro Congress, but became disillusioned with its racial stress. Bunche's philosophy won few followers. As the decade drew to an end, he came more and more to support the New Deal program. 49 notes. V. L. Human

640. Kohler, Robert E., Jr. RUDOLF SCHOENHEIMER, ISOTOPIC TRACERS, AND BIOCHEMISTRY IN THE 1930'S. *Hist. Studies in the Physical Sci. 1977 8: 257-298.* The increased use of models and techniques drawn from the physical sciences helped transform biology into a modern discipline. In the 1930's fields such as biochemistry began to rise in status. Rudolf Schoenheimer's (1898-1941) application of isotopes to the study of intermediary metabolism from 1934 to 1941 illustrates both the use of physical science concepts and the rise in institutional status of these new scientists. Schoenheimer's research with isotopes led to the development of the tracer method. Based on the Rockefeller Foundation Archives and other primary sources; 194 notes. D. K. Lambert

641. Kostiainen, Auvo. AINO KUUSINEN KOMINTERNIN ASIAMIEHENÄ AMERIKASSA [Aino Kuusinen as a Comintern agent in America]. *Turun Hist. Arkisto [Finland] 1975 30: 234-256.* Aino Kuusinen, the second wife of the international Communist leader Otto Wille Kuusinen, spent the period from spring 1930 to summer 1933 in the United States. The reason for her coming to the United States appears to have been differences of opinion between the Communist Party of the United States and the Finnish-American

Communists, which had been going on for several years. In her capacity as a Comintern emissary, Aino Kuusinen-Morton soon took over a leading position in the communist Finnish Workers' Federation. Under the name of A. Morton, she began to write articles for the theoretical journal *Viesti*, and became its editor. It would appear that Aino Kuusinen-Morton was not a fully-authorized agent of the Comintern, but that she acquired considerable authority among the Finnish-American Communists. She gradually took over control of the Finnish Workers' Federation, and thus came into conflict with both Henry Puro and the American Communist leaders. These differences of opinion received considerable publicity in the press of the Finnish-American labor movement. Eventually the Finnish-American Communists and the Party leadership appealed to the Comintern to have Aino Kuusinen withdrawn, and she was soon afterwards ordered back to Moscow.   J

642. Kritzberg, Barry. AN UNFINISHED CHAPTER IN WHITE-COL-LAR UNIONISM: THE FORMATIVE YEARS OF THE CHICAGO NEWS-PAPER GUILD, LOCAL 71, AMERICAN NEWSPAPER GUILD, A.F.L.-C.I.O. *Labor Hist. 1973 14(3): 397-413.* The Chicago Newspaper Guild spearheaded the drive toward unionization in a strike against the Hearst newspapers, the *Examiner* and the *American.* The strike (November 1938-April 1940) was initially successful as a result of an N.L.R.B. decision, but the effect was to shift union leadership to the A.F.L. The A.F.L. had hotly contested the guild, which was affiliated with the C.I.O.; so although the American Newspaper Guild was strengthened nationally, it was sharply weakened in Chicago. Based on oral interviews, C.N.G. files, and Chicago newspapers; 78 notes, appendix.
L. L. Athey

643. Kuehl, Warren F. MIDWESTERN NEWSPAPERS AND ISOLA-TIONIST SENTIMENT. *Diplomatic Hist. 1979 3(3): 283-306.* A review of midwestern newspapers between the two world wars casts doubt upon the validity of the popular stereotype of the region at that time as a hot-bed of isolationism. "This region, if editorial views are representative of thought, endorsed internationalist policies more regularly than the opposite pole." Table, 52 notes.
T. L. Powers

644. Lanza, Aldo. TEATRO OPERAIO E "LABOR CHAUTAUQUAS" AL BROOKWOOD LABOR COLLEGE [Workers' theater and "Labor Chautauquas" at Brookwood Labor College]. *Movimento Operaio e Socialista [Italy] 1980 3(2-3): 199-220.* Brookwood Labor College, 40 miles north of New York City, was the first training school for union organizers. Its founders believed that labor unions should be more than instruments in an economic struggle and that its leaders should lay more stress on social thinking than on business psychology. In its curriculum was a course on labor dramatics to "quicken the spirit which animates tha labor movement." But lacking a basis of theoretical analysis and a political strategy the course did not contribute much to the task of transformation as distinguished from a stance of opposition to the status quo. In this sense the school shared in the failure of the Socialist Party and other third parties in the United States. 32 notes.   J. V. Countinho

645. Laslett, John H. M. GIVING SUPERMAN A HUMAN FACE: AMERICAN COMMUNISM AND THE AUTOMOBILE WORKERS IN THE 1930S. *Rev. in Am. Hist. 1981 9(1): 112-117.* Review essay of Roger Keeran's *The Communist Party and the Auto Workers Union* (1980).

646. Lauderbaugh, Richard A. BUSINESS, LABOR, AND FOREIGN POLICY: U.S. STEEL, THE INTERNATIONAL STEEL CARTEL, AND RECOGNITION OF THE STEEL WORKERS ORGANIZING COMMITTEE. *Pol. and Soc. 1976 6(4): 433-457.* "Private" foreign diplomacy led to the US Steel Corp.'s collective bargaining agreement with the Steel Workers Organizing Committee (SWOC) in early 1937. The agreement with the SWOC depended upon a verbal commitment to join the Entente Internationale de L'Acier (International Steel Cartel). In contravention of New Deal policies and US antitrust laws, the agreement included import restrictions, thereby controlling competition in the international steel market, and in turn protecting the US market. The agreement with SWOC served to camouflage the international aspects of the "invisible tariff" protecting the US steel market from the eyes of Roosevelt's New Dealers. 48 notes. D. G. Nielson

647. Leotta, Louis. ABRAHAM EPSTEIN AND THE MOVEMENT FOR OLD AGE SECURITY. *Labor Hist. 1975 16(3): 359-377.* Examines the activities of voluntary associations which promoted state old-age pension systems from 1920-35. Abraham Epstein, an important architect of old-age pension legislation, pressed for legislation through his positions with the Fraternal Order of the Eagles and then in the American Association for Old Age Security. The struggle kept the idea alive and provided part of the climate of opinion for its adoption in 1935. Based on records of the AAOAS, F.O.E. publications, and legislative records; 46 notes. L. L. Athey

648. Levenstein, Harvey. LENINISTS UNDONE BY LENINISM: COMMUNISM AND UNIONISM IN THE UNITED STATES AND MEXICO, 1935-1939. *Labor Hist. 1981 22(2): 237-261.* The Communist Party in the United States and Mexico during the Popular Front period (1935-39) encouraged its members to cooperate with other leftists and moderates in the organizing of workers in the two countries. The Communist Party's leadership, however, actively discouraged Communists from gaining and maintaining powerful positions in such US unions as the United Steelworkers and United Automobile Workers and in the *Confederación de Trabajadores Mexicanos* in Mexico. The restraint preached by its leadership weakened the Communist Party's position in union activities enough to facilitate a purge of all Communists from these unions in the 1940's. Based on the Earl Browder Papers and other primary sources; 44 notes. L. F. Velicer

649. Leverette, William E., Jr. and Shi, Daniel E. HERBERT AGAR AND *FREE AMERICA:* A JEFFERSONIAN ALTERNATIVE TO THE NEW DEAL. *J. of Am. Studies [Great Britain] 1982 16(2): 189-206.* Founded by Herbert Sebastian Agar, *Free America* began publication in 1937 and folded in 1947. From its inception the journal was committed to conservative criticism of the New Deal. It opposed welfare capitalism and countered with constructive proposals for decentralizing President Franklin D. Roosevelt's burgeoning federal establishment. Agar and his contributors also proposed schemes designed to

widen property-holding, revive individual self-sufficiency among Americans, restore farmers and small businessmen to primacy, and in other ways turn back the
clock to America's preindustrial age. Based on manuscripts, backfiles of *Free
America,* and other writings of the magazine's contributors and supporters; 41
notes.   H. T. Lovin

650.   Licht, Walter and Barron, Hal Seth.   LABOR'S MEN: A COLLECTIVE
BIOGRAPHY OF UNION OFFICIALDOM DURING THE NEW DEAL
YEARS.   *Labor Hist. 1978 19(4): 532-545.* Analyzes labor leadership during the
New Deal years from the 1940 edition of *Who's Who in Labor.* A sample of 400
officials reveals that labor leaders were predominantly male, white, and middle-
aged. Ideological factors were more important to the labor movement. 7 tables,
19 notes.   L. L. Athey

651.   Lichtenstein,   Nelson.   ANOTHER   TIME,   ANOTHER   PLACE:
BLACKS, RADICALS AND RANK AND FILE MILITANCY IN AUTO IN
THE 30S & 40S.   *Radical Am. 1982 6(1-2): 131-137.* Reviews three works with
slightly different political viewpoints but that share a focus on the secondary
leadership level of policymaking in the forming of the United Auto Workers:
Roger Keeran's *The Communist Party and the Auto Workers Unions* (1980),
Martin Glabermann's *The Struggle against the No-Strike Pledge during World
War II* (1980), August Meier and Elliot Rudwick's *Black Detroit and the Rise
of the UAW* (1979).   Note, 5 illus.   C. M. Hough

652.   Lovin, Hugh T.   THE AUTOMOBILE WORKERS UNIONS AND
THE FIGHT FOR LABOR PARTIES IN THE 1930S.   *Indiana Mag. of Hist.
1981 77(2): 123-149.* When the automobile workers began to organize unions in
the mid-1930's there were strong disputes about whether these industrial unions
should join one of the new labor-liberal parties or continue to reflect the nonpoliti-
cal bread and butter issues of the American Federation of Labor. After many
experiments and some indecision the United Automobile Workers of America in
Indiana and Ohio went along with the Democratic New Deal, but without much
enthusiasm. Based on official proceedings, monographs, manuscripts, and newspapers; 2 illus., 57 notes.   A. Erlebacher

653.   Lynd, Staughton.   THE UNITED FRONT IN AMERICA: A NOTE.
Radical America 1974 8(4): 29-37. Radicalism, labor organizing, and the New
Deal in the 1930's.   S

654.   Maddux, Thomas R.   RED FASCISM, BROWN BOLSHEVISM: THE
AMERICAN IMAGE OF TOTALITARIANISM IN THE 1930'S.   *Historian
1977 40(1): 85-103.* Reevaluates the origins of the idea of "Red Fascism" as
described by Les K. Adler and Thomas G. Paterson in 1970. Disputes their
contention that such an identification between the two regimes came primarily
during 1939-41, and argues instead that the American press had reached a
widespread consensus on the essential similarities between Stalinism and Nazism
long before the spring of 1939. The public expression of this Red Fascism analogy
in the press even influenced President Roosevelt's foreign policies before 1939.
Based on newspapers and periodicals of the 1930's.   M. S. Legan

655. Mal'kov, V. L. KOMMUNISTY, SOTSIALISTY I "NOVYI KURS" RUZVEL'TA: IZ ISTORII BOR'BY ZA EDINSTVO ANTIMONOPOLISTI- CHESKIKH SIL V SSHA [Communists, socialists and Roosevelt's "New Deal": From the history of the struggle for the unity of antimonopolist forces in the United States]. *Novaia i Noveishaia Istoriia [USSR] 1974 (5): 39-54.* The 7th Congress of Comintern in 1935 decreed that a united front of workers' and antifascist organizations was to be created. Aims to demonstrate the effect of this decree on the American Workers' movement in the 1930's. They attempted to establish a progressive antimonopolistic bloc in the decade before World War II. In November 1935 the Communist and Socialist parties in the United States cemented an alliance at a 20,000-strong meeting in New York. The two parties had hitherto been antagonistic: the Communists determined on revolution, the Socialists, permeated with evangelistic Christianity, were dedicated to a gradual- ist approach. The New Deal revealed their different approaches. The Communist Party stressed its negative features, the Socialist Party approved of its socialistic content. The Socialists, realizing the class character of the reforms, began to move toward the Communist position, especially in view of extreme right wing threats, they wavered. Discussions were held with the Communists about the creation of a united workers' and farmers' party. The Socialist Party's leadership eventually decided not to support the Communists, and the party membership fell drasti- cally. Based on the papers of N. Thomas, Chairman of the Socialist Party (New York Public Library) and on published sources; 60 notes. D. N. Collins

656. Marquart, Frank. FROM A LABOR JOURNAL: UNIONS & RADI- CALS IN THE DEPRESSION YEARS. *Dissent 1974 21(3): 421-430.* Dis- cusses the development of labor organizations in Detroit during the 1920's-30's. S

657. Marr, Warren. JUSTICE, AT LAST, FOR "SCOTTSBORO BOY?" *Crisis 1976 83(9): 310-312.* Clarence Norris is seeking a pardon for a crime that he insists the "Scottsboro Boys" never committed. On 18 October 1976, the NAACP joined Norris in asking George Wallace, governor of Alabama, to issue a pardon. In 1931 when Norris was 19, he and eight other black youths were accused of raping two white women on a freight train. Investigations have repeat- edly demonstrated that the boys were not guilty. He awaits the governor's action. A. G. Belles

658. Martin, Charles H. COMMUNISTS AND BLACKS: THE ILD AND THE ANGELO HERNDON CASE. *J. of Negro Hist. 1979 64(2): 131-141.* The International Labor Defense, a Communist-supported legal defense orga- nization, secured the freedom of Angelo Herndon, an Atlanta, Georgia, black arrested on that state's outmoded anti-insurrection laws, but failed to gain the continued support of Atlanta blacks due to contradictory actions in other similar cases, 1932-37.

659. Martin, Charles H. OKLAHOMA'S "SCOTTSBORO" AFFAIR: THE JESS HOLLINS RAPE CASE, 1931-1936. *South Atlantic Q. 1980 79(2): 175- 188.* The Jess Hollins rape case in Oklahoma, sometimes compared to Alabama's notorious Scottsboro rape case, attracted fleeting national interest. Although it never received the notoriety of Scottsboro, it did raise briefly a number of issues important in Afro-American, southern, and US history—the specters of black

rape and interracial sex, the fairness of the southern judicial system, the exclusion of blacks from juries, and the conflicting and competing tactics practiced by the National Association for the Advancement of Colored People (NAACP) and its archrival, the Communist-influenced International Labor Defense. Based largely on the NAACP Papers, Library of Congress, the *Oklahoma City Black Dispatch,* other newspaper accounts, and secondary sources; 30 notes.

H. M. Parker, Jr.

660. Martin, Charles H. WHITE SUPREMACY AND BLACK WORK- ERS: GEORGIA'S "BLACK SHIRTS" COMBAT THE GREAT DEPRES- SION. *Labor Hist. 1977 18(3): 366-381.* In Georgia during the 1930's the "Black Shirts," the American Order of Fascisti, tried to become a political force. Its major premise was white supremacy rather than a philosophy of fascism, and its main objective was employment for whites. Based on newspapers in Atlanta and Macon, Georgia; 41 notes.

L. L. Athey

661. Mathews, Allan. AGRARIAN RADICALS: THE UNITED FARM- ERS LEAGUE OF SOUTH DAKOTA. *South Dakota Hist. 1973 3(4): 408- 421.* Discusses farm protest against foreclosure and other economic and social ills during the Great Depression. The United Farmers League [before 1930 the United Farmers Educational League] gained the ascendency in northeastern South Dakota, attracting many farmer members with its relief programs as well as rhetoric, despite its Communist affiliation. Political organization, a protest march to the state capitol, physical violence, and an emotional trial all took place before the UFL's power and attractiveness faded. The league ran candidates in 1934, but its Communist affiliation plus the New Deal's farm programs combined to dissolve its support. Primary and secondary sources; 3 illus., 28 notes.

A. J. Larson

662. Maurer, D. W. LANGUAGE AND THE SEX REVOLUTION: WORLD WAR I THROUGH WORLD WAR II. *Am. Speech 1976 51(1-2): 5-24.* The dramatic change toward a freer attitude in respect to sexual mores from those of the Victorian Era coalesced in the United States at the end of World War I. The Jazz Age of the 1920's brought about looser attitudes reflected in even politely accepted language. The Great Depression broke down some of the final resistance in society between separate moral codes for males and females further advanced by wartime conditions.

D. A. Yanchisin

663. Mayer, Milton. THE RED ROOM. *Massachusetts R. 1975 16(3): 520- 550.* In the so-called Walgreen Affair in the 1930's, a futile attempt was made to rid the University of Chicago of certain faculty members who were accused unjustifiably of Communist associations and conspiracy. Leading the crusade were the Hearst newspapers and filing original charges was Charles R. Walgreen, founder of the drugstore chain. The case wound up with all those accused being exonerated and the university receiving $550,000 from Walgreen as a friendly gesture. Based on primary and secondary sources.

M. J. Barach

664. McBride, David and Little, Monroe H. THE AFRO-AMERICAN ELITE, 1930-1940: A HISTORICAL AND STATISTICAL PROFILE. *Phylon 1981 42(2): 105-119.* Afro-American leadership was diverse and dynamic during the 1930's. Eight characteristics permit comparison of the leaders with the

general population: sex, birthplace, residence, education, occupation, political affiliation, religion, and membership in voluntary organizations. This type of statistical, collective biography of Afro-American leaders reveals rich possibilities for further research.   A. G. Belles

665. McGinty, Brian. SHADOWS IN ST. JAMES PARK. *California History 1978-79 57(4): 290-307.* An account of mob violence in San Jose, California, in November 1933. Brooke Hart, son of a prominent local department store family, was kidnapped and brutally murdered on 9 November 1933. Within a week, Thomas Thurmond and John Holmes were taken into custody. When Hart's body was recovered from San Francisco Bay on 26 November many San Jose citizens urged the lynching of the suspects. That evening thousands of people surrounded the jail, broke down the door, took out the two suspects, and hanged them. Governor James Rolph aroused national controversy by endorsing the mob's action. Evidence against the suspects was persuasive but not conclusive, and a trial would have provided answers to important questions. The incident is remembered as "San Jose's shame" since law enforcement had been effective in capturing the suspects, the community was a prosperous middle-class one, and the violence seemed inexcusable. Primary and secondary sources; 7 photos, 102 notes.   A. Hoffman

666. McGoff, Kevin. THE BONUS ARMY. *Am. Hist. Illus. 1978 12(10): 28-37.* A 1924 Congressional Act awarded veterans' certificates based on World War I service. They were not to be paid until 1945, but Congressman Wright Patman introduced a bill in 1932 to pay them then. 20,000 veterans went to Washington to support Patman's bill. Troops under Douglas MacArthur used tear gas to disperse the veterans, and then burned their shanty towns. The officers included George Patton and Dwight Eisenhower. Press reaction to the action was mixed, but the American Legion, for the first time, endorsed Patman's bill. Congress voted to honor the certificates in 1936. Primary and secondary sources; 10 illus.   D. Dodd

667. McGovern, James R. HELEN HUNT WEST: FLORIDA'S PIONEER FOR ERA. *Florida Hist. Q. 1978 57(1): 39-53.* Helen Hunt West (1892-1964) in association with the National Women's Party, lectured and wrote on the need for an Equal Rights Amendment. Her major contribution to Florida politics was as a sponsor and supporter of a 1935 election law requiring equal participation by women at all levels of state party organization. A powerful lobbyist for the ERA in the US Congress during 1935-39, she eventually saw the endorsement of ERA by Republican and Democratic national conventions. Based mainly on the Helen Hunt West papers, Schlesinger Library; photo, 72 notes.
                                                                P. A. Beaber

668. McGovern, James R. and Howard, Walter T. PRIVATE JUSTICE AND NATIONAL CONCERN: THE LYNCHING OF CLAUDE NEAL. *Historian 1981 43(4): 546-559.* Although upstaged by the Scottsboro cases, the lynching of Claude Neal in Greenwood, Florida, 26 October 1934 significantly helped to eliminate public lynchings because it focused national attention on the odious practice. Recounts the history of lynchings of Negroes in Jackson County, Florida, the background and series of events leading to Neal's death, and the reaction to that lynching. The fear of exposure through the media, more critical

attitudes among Southerners, and the beginning of intervention by the federal government began to make lynching too costly. Primary sources; 63 notes.

R. S. Sliwoski

669.   McKinney, Fred.   FUNCTIONALISM AT CHICAGO—MEMORIES OF A GRADUATE STUDENT, 1929-1931.   *J. of the Hist. of the Behavioral Sci. 1978 14(2): 142-148.* The author recounts his memories of the personalities and activities of the faculty members, the courses, the students, and the intellectual climate in the Department of Psychology at the University of Chicago in the early 1930's. Functionalism at Chicago is described as a non-self-conscious eclectic movement, loosely systematic, empirical, and broad in scope. It is suggested that the functional tradition persists, and is manifested in current, widely adopted textbooks, in the structure of the APA, and in the wide range of interests found in present-day psychology departments.   J

670.   McQuaid, Kim.   COMPETITION, CARTELLIZATION AND THE CORPORATE ETHIC: GENERAL ELECTRIC'S LEADERSHIP DURING THE NEW DEAL ERA, 1933-1940.   *Am. J. of Econ. and Sociol. 1977 36(4): 417-428.* Relations between General Electric Co. leaders and New Deal economic advisors and agencies resulted in sincere attempts at humanizing the managerial-capitalist order, an ideal which did not last long within the corporate structure.

671.   Milkman, Ruth.   WOMEN'S WORK AND THE ECONOMIC CRISIS: SOME LESSONS FROM THE GREAT DEPRESSION.   *Rev. of Radical Pol. Econ. 1976 8(1): 73-97.* Investigates work roles of women, both paid and unpaid, during the 1930's; though women readily entered the labor force during economic expansion, sexual segregation of labor created an inflexibility which did not allow for expulsion during economic contraction.

672.   Miller, Kathleen Atkinson.   THE LADIES AND THE LYNCHERS: A LOOK AT THE ASSOCIATION OF SOUTHERN WOMEN FOR THE PREVENTION OF LYNCHING.   *Southern Studies 1978 17(3): 221-240.* In 1930 Jessie Daniel Ames (b. 1893), Director of Woman's Work for the Commission on Interracial Cooperation (CIC), helped found the Association of Southern Women for the Prevention of Lynching (ASWPL). Until 1942 this association of Southern white women, working through church and civic groups, attempted to curb lynchings by educating the public and officials and by eliciting and publicizing commitments against lynching by prominent citizens, public officials, and newspapers. The basic reasons for the increased lynchings during the Depression were economic rivalry and racial antipathy. Based on papers of ASWPL at Atlanta U., primary and secondary sources; 72 notes.   J. Buschen

673.   Monroy, Douglas.   LA COSTURA EN LOS ANGELES, 1933-1939: THE ILGWU AND THE POLITICS OF DOMINATION.   Mora, Magdalena and DelCastillo, Adelaida R., ed. *Mexican Women in the United States: Struggles Past and Present* (Los Angeles: U. of California Chicano Studies Res. Center, 1980): 171-178. Describes the situation which Mexicanas in Los Angeles confronted in la costura during the Depression, the enthusiastic union organization drives, and the ideology and political philosophy of the International Ladies' Garment Workers' Union as related to the Mexicana rank and file. From this can be seen some negative effects of successful union organizing. Often another layer

of authority, the union leadership, rarely Mexicano or female, burdened Mexicanas. In this case, while making crucial gains in wages and hours, the union did not significantly increase the power and control which rank and file women exercised over their work. Secondary sources; 33 notes. J. Powell

674. Montgomery, David and Schatz, Ronald. FACING LAYOFFS. *Radical Am. 1976 10(2): 15-27.* Examples of union activity in the 1930's-40's emphasize that the most significant moments of American working-class unity have been those when workers fought simultaneously for control of layoffs and for organization of the unemployed. Even during these struggles important differences of opinion remained between the workers still employed and their unemployed colleagues. It is only through some form of collective action that workers can prevent seniority from being used against them. Based on primary and secondary sources. N. Lederer

675. Morris, James K. OUTPOST OF THE COOPERATIVE COMMONWEALTH: THE HISTORY OF THE LLANO DEL RIO COLONY IN GILA, NEW MEXICO, 1932-1935. *New Mexico Hist. Rev. 1981 56(2): 177-195.* Discusses the attempt by practitioners of the cooperative ideal to establish a colony in Gila, New Mexico. The Llano del Rio colony was to be an outpost of support, especially for foodstuffs, for Newllano, a successful cooperative located in western Louisiana. Despite some success by the colonists from Newllano in growing crops, the experiment failed because of litigation over debts on the property and a split among the cooperative members whether the mother colony should support Llano del Rio. Primary sources; 2 illus., 2 photos, 41 notes. P. L. McLaughlin

676. Mugleston, William F. CORNPONE AND POTLIKKER: A MOMENT OF RELIEF IN THE GREAT DEPRESSION. *Louisiana Hist. 1975 16(3): 279-288.* The affair began with a dinner given in 1931 by Governor Huey P. Long of Louisiana for some bankers who the following day bought $15 million worth of state highway bonds. "Long credited the sale to the delectable potlikker and cornbread he had served." The *Atlantic Constitution* developed a debate as to whether cornbread should be dunked or crumbled. The episode was a delightful interlude to millions of Southerners struggling with the hard times of the Depression. Illus., 16 notes. E. P. Stickney

677. Myers, Constance Ashton. AMERICAN TROTSKYISTS: THE FIRST YEARS. *Studies in Comparative Communism 1977 10(1-2): 133-151.* Trotskyists were involved in the organization of the Workers' Party, a result of fusion with A. J. Muste's Conference for Progressive Labor Action. In 1935 the Trotskyists expelled those who opposed the "French turn" (coalition with the socialists). They moved to take over the Socialist Party but were expelled in 1937. Thereafter the Trotskyists split in 1940 on the issue of Soviet Russia and on organizational issues. The two groups were the unorthodox Schachtman wing and the Cannon unorthodox wing. Trotskyism influenced many writers in the 1930's. Cannon's Socialist Workers' Party played a role in opposing the Vietnam War. 44 notes. D. Balmuth

678.   Naison, Mark.   COMMUNISM AND HARLEM INTELLECTUALS IN THE POPULAR FRONT: ANTI-FASCISM AND THE POLITICS OF BLACK CULTURE.   *J. of Ethnic Studies 1981 9(1): 1-25.* Explores the Communist Party approach to the Harlem intelligentsia and middle class in the late depression years, through incorporating the black community into anti-Fascist alliances with white liberals and radicals. The most successful efforts resulted from abandoning the party line of class struggle and striving for a "Negro People's Front," through organizations such as the United Aid for Ethiopia and the new National Negro Congress, but the Party's greatest source of prestige came from its attempts to gain institutional support for the black arts, centered primarily on the WPA Artists and Writers' Project. Based on contemporary newspapers, secondary sources; 59 notes.   G. J. Bobango

679.   Naison, Mark.   HISTORICAL NOTES ON BLACKS AND AMERICAN COMMUNISM: THE HARLEM EXPERIENCE.   *Sci. and Soc. 1978 42(3): 324-343.* The actions of the Communist Party (CPUSA) in Harlem in support of black rights attracted favorable attention from the black community from the 1920's onward. The Communists were far more successful in attracting black support than were their Socialist predecessors. Such factors as Communist affirmation of Afro-American nationalism in accordance with perceived Soviet nationalities policy, internal eradication of "white chauvinism" in Party ranks, and involvement in virtually every issue involving blacks gained the allegiance and even the entry into Party ranks of many Harlem blacks. However, the growing awareness of the Party's subservience to Moscow and its rigid adherence to dogma regardless of American realities caused otherwise sympathetic blacks to fall away from engagement in Party activities. Based on primary research and oral interviews.   N. Lederer

680.   Naison, Mark.   LEFTIES AND RIGHTIES: THE COMMUNIST PARTY AND SPORTS DURING THE GREAT DEPRESSION.   *Radical Am. 1979 13(4): 47-59.* Under the aegis of the Communist Party, youth, fraternal, and trade union organizations during the period of the 1920's to the 1940's supported independent sports leagues in various cities, took part in the boycott of two Olympics, supported many track meets and benefit games for political prisoners, and took part in a vigorous campaign to open the ranks of major league baseball teams to blacks. The sports leagues, manned mainly by immigrants, were but a small shadow of their counterparts in Europe. In the 1930's Communist publications such as *Young Worker* and *Daily Worker* moved in their sports coverage to "Americanize" their approach, eschewing dogma in favor of relatively impartial coverage of sports. The Communists played an important role in bringing about the integration of major league baseball in the 1940's. Based mainly on printed primary sources.   N. Lederer

681.   Naison, Mark D.   COMMUNISM AND BLACK NATIONALISM IN THE DEPRESSION: THE CASE OF HARLEM.   *J. of Ethnic Studies 1974 2(2): 24-36.* "The political struggle between nationalists and communists in Harlem had its roots in the Twenties. Communists in the African Blood Brotherhood . . . waged a bitter ideological struggle with Marcus Garvey . . . over questions of race loyalty vs. class loyalty." The Garvey movement and its spinoffs were business-oriented, seeking to develop a Negro entrepreneur class. Its answer to massive black unemployment was the "Don't Buy Where You Can't Work"

campaign pushed by the Harlem Business Men's Club and the *Negro World.* By 1933 a picket campaign against stores was going on. The Party insisted on black-white working class solidarity, and along with the Young Liberators and the League of Struggle for Negro Rights maintained separate picketing operations. Meanwhile a Citizen's League under Harlem ministers and the *New York Age* sought to unite diverse organizations. The March 1935 riots brought the Party new acceptance as they helped in exposing social conditions in the community during the postriot investigations. From then to 1939 the Party played a role in every major coalition of protest, but its political "victory" over Negro nationalism "was never really secure." Contemporary and secondary sources; 46 notes.

G. J. Bobango

682. Nastri, Anthony D. AN ORDINARY JOE. *US Naval Inst. Pro. 1978 104(11): 71-77.* Joseph P. Verduci enlisted in the Marine Corps in June 1934. Fresh out of high school, Verduci served in a number of units during the next four years, his last being the Marine Barracks, New York Navy Yard. He served well and loyally, did all that was asked of him, and apparently thoroughly enjoyed his enlistment. He kept several scrapbooks, which he turned over to his son, Alexander, who now serves as a Marine Corps captain. The latter, in turn, has donated those books to the Marine Corps Historical Center. Joseph Verduci was never again on active military service but, because of people like him, the Marine Corps was a far more professional military unit in the 1930's than it might have been. 19 photos. A. N. Garland

683. Nelson, Daniel ORIGINS OF THE SIT-DOWN ERA: WORKER MILITANCY AND INNOVATION IN THE RUBBER INDUSTRY, 1934-38. *Labor Hist. 1982 23(2): 198-225.* Workers in the rubber industry of Akron, Ohio, pioneered the sit-down strike between mid-1934 and late 1936. The sit-down was not a creation of United Rubber Workers (URW) leaders, but an expression of rank and file militancy. While the early sit-down strikes yielded changes in factory operation, the sit-downs of 1937-38 were less effective, as management regained its initiative and URW officials diverted labor militancy to more "positive" ends. Based on National Labor Relations Board Files and newspaper accounts; 81 notes. L. F. Velicer

684. Nelson, H. Viscount. THE PHILADELPHIA NAACP: RACE VERSUS CLASS CONSCIOUSNESS DURING THE THIRTIES. *J. of Black Studies 1975 5(3): 255-276.* Correspondence of the Philadelphia chapter of the NAACP from the 1930's shows that its membership was made up of middle- and upper-class blacks who were almost totally unconcerned with the plight of poorer blacks. Their main concern was fund-raising and keeping on good terms with members of the white community. Though they took stands on blatantly racist issues they generally avoided taking positions which would jeopardize their social standing in the community. Notes, biblio. K. Butcher

685. Newbill, James G. YAKIMA AND THE WOBBLIES, 1910-1936. Conlin, Joseph R., ed. *At the Point of Production: The Local History of the I.W.W.* (Westport Conn.: Greenwood Pr., 1981): 167-190. Describes confrontations between the Industrial Workers of the World and ranchers and farmers in Yakima before 1933, the combination of depression economics and racism which led to mass meetings and eventual violence, fruit rancher-laborer difficulties in

July and August 1933, and the "Congdon orchards battle" of 24 August 1933, and its aftermath. The major confrontation at Congdon resulted from a distorted image the IWW held of their own strength, and the fear of the farming community of the union. The confrontation and legal actions against the union in 1933 resulted in the collapse of the union's power in the Yakima Valley. Based on newspaper, journal, and personal accounts; 53 notes.   J. Powell

686. Nyden, Linda. BLACK MINERS IN WESTERN PENNSYLVANIA, 1925-1931: THE NATIONAL MINERS UNION AND THE UNITED MINE WORKERS OF AMERICA. *Sci. and Soc. 1977 41(1): 69-101.* The National Miners Union kept the spirit of unionism in the coal fields alive during the late 1920's and early 1930's when open shop efforts by operators, coupled with poor and dispirited leadership of the United Mine Workers of America, threatened to drive collective bargaining from the region. The NMU was a class struggle trade union which organized the unorganized, fought wage cuts, and led mass picket lines. It successfully organized and elevated blacks to leadership positions in the union at a time when the UMW segregated them from a meaningful role in its ranks and operators employed huge numbers of blacks as strikebreakers. Without the efforts of the NMU, conditions for the miners would have been far worse and the situation would not have been readied for the later resurgence of the UMW.
                                                                                    N. Lederer

687. O'Brien, Larry D. THE OHIO NATIONAL GUARD IN THE COAL STRIKE OF 1932. *Ohio Hist. 1975 84(3): 127-144.* "The most interesting characteristic of the National Guard's participation in the 1932 strike was the balance which existed in the attitudes of the guard officers and the moderating influence they exercised." What gains the miners could claim were due to this moderating influence. Governor George White's decision to send in troop units reduced the level of violence during the strike. Illus., 73 notes.
                                                                                    E. P. Stickney

688. O'Farrell, M. Brigid and Kleiner, Lydia. ANNA SULLIVAN: TRADE UNION ORGANIZER. *Frontiers 1977 2(2): 29-36.* Anna Sullivan (b. 1904), who in 1936 began organizing the Massachusetts textile industry for the Textile Workers Union of America (TWUA), recalls her career in labor and politics; part of a special issue on women's oral history.

689. Oliver, Donald W. REFLECTIONS ON PETER CARBONE'S *THE SOCIAL AND EDUCATIONAL THOUGHT OF HAROLD RUGG.* *Social Educ. 1978 42(7): 593-602.* Review article prompted by Peter F. Carbone, Jr.'s *The Social and Educational Thought of Harold Rugg* (Durham, North Carolina: Duke U. Pr., 1977) discusses Rugg's belief in liberalism, his confidence in reform, and his desire to encourage the individual development of each student during the 1930's.

690. O'Rourke, James S. THE SAN FRANCISCO *CHRONICLE* AND THE AIR MAIL EMERGENCY OF 1934: THE HEISENBERG PRINCIPLE EXEMPLIFIED IN JOURNALISM. *Journalism Hist. 1979 6(1): 8-13.* After the US Post Office cancelled all private air carrier contracts during Hugo L. Black's investigation of possible illegality and impropriety in air and ocean mail contracts, the San Francisco *Chronicle* (along with other national newspapers)

used slanted viewpoint, extension of editorial opinion, and outright propaganda in their attempt to manipulate public opinion in their favor, 1934.

691.   Painter, Nell and Hudson, Hosea.   HOSEA HUDSON: A NEGRO COMMUNIST IN THE DEEP SOUTH.   *Radical Am. 1977 11(4): 7-23.* A worker in basic industry in Birmingham, Alabama in the 1920's, Hosea Hudson remained apolitical until drawn into politics through the agitation over the Scottsboro Boys trial in the early 1930's. He became involved in clandestine Communist Party work and has remained an active member of the party until the present. As a political radical, Hudson was involved in Deep South campaigns to organize the unemployed through welfare marches and demonstrations at social welfare offices. His politically extremist activities caused him to lose a succession of factory jobs once his involvement became known. Based on extensive oral interviews with Hudson.   N. Lederer

692.   Papachristou, Judith.   AN EXERCISE IN ANTI-IMPERIALISM: THE THIRTIES.   *Am. Studies 1974 15(1): 61-77.* Critics of Franklin D. Roosevelt's foreign policy in the 1930's were not really isolationists or pacifists, but anti-imperialists. They criticized American motives, methods, and goals, but were not opposed to internationalism per se. These men saw economic motives guiding foreign policy, especially toward the Pacific, and did not think investments worth the risk of war with Japan. Based on primary and secondary sources; 62 notes.
                                                                                                                                                                   J. Andrew

693.   Papanikolas, Helen Z.   UNIONISM, COMMUNISM, AND THE GREAT DEPRESSION: THE CARBON COUNTY COAL STRIKE OF 1933.   *Utah Hist. Q. 1973 41(3): 254-300.* In 1933 the United Mine Workers of America and the National Miners Union attempted to unionize the bituminous coal fields of Carbon County. Immigrant laborers were attracted to the NMU. A strike set for Labor Day spread unrest, protests, and violence throughout the county. Mine operators called for the National Guard, maintaining that strikers were anarchists and communists. Many strikers were arrested and placed in bullpens at a ball park. While the NMU was involved with the strike the UMWA negotiated with operators on a coal code, which was adopted in October. The NMU declined in importance thereafter. Significant gains for labor did occur in Carbon County in 1933. Map, illus., 147 notes.   H. S. Marks

694.   Parker, Robert V.   THE BONUS MARCH OF 1932: A UNIQUE EXPERIENCE IN NORTH CAROLINA POLITICAL AND SOCIAL LIFE.   *North Carolina Hist. R. 1974 51(1): 64-89.* The Bonus Army that marched on Washington, D.C., (1932) involved North Carolina veterans, American Legionnaires, and politicians. Henry L. Stevens, Jr. (1896-1971), a Carolinian and American Legion national commander, opposed a cash bonus for servicemen despite the lobbying of legionnaires and rising unemployment. Nearly 300 North Carolinians joined the Bonus Army and hundreds marched through the state on route to the capital. Primary sources; illus., 103 notes.   W. B. Bedford

695.   Peterson, Keith.   FRANK BRUCE ROBINSON AND PSYCHIANA.   *Idaho Yesterdays 1979 23(3): 9-15, 26-29.* Frank Bruce Robinson established the world's largest mail-order religion in the 1930's. Operating out of several buildings in Moscow (Idaho), Psychiana was a blend of ideas from the New Thought

movement, the beliefs of the power of positive thinking, and the possibility of material success and happiness. Psychiana had appeal to a great many people; they enrolled in correspondence courses to learn more of Robinson's teachings. Covers 1929-48. Based on materials in the University of Idaho library, and in the Latah County Historical Society; 6 illus., 44 notes.   B. J. Paul

696.   Peyton, Rupert.   REMINISCENCES OF HUEY LONG.   *North Louisiana Hist. Assoc. J. 1976 7(4): 161-164.* The author first met Huey P. Long in August 1917, and during the following years their paths crossed many times. The author was a newspaperman in Shreveport and covered Long during the latter's term as governor and his campaign for election to the United States Senate. In 1932, the author was elected as one of four state representatives from Caddo Parrish and fought against many of Long's attempts to have the state legislature "enact dictatorial laws, many of which were directed against the Roosevelt administration." He was still serving on 10 September 1935, when Long died. To the author, "Long was not without his good qualities, although he advocated a form of government that belonged to the Dark Ages."   A. H. Garland

697.   Pfaff, Daniel W.   THE PRESS AND THE SCOTTSBORO RAPE CASES, 1931-32.   *Journalism Hist. 1974 1(3): 72-76.* Studies newspaper reporting of trials involving the sentencing of eight Negro youths to death on rape charges in Scottsboro, Alabama, in 1931.

698.   Pietrusza, David A.   NEW DEAL NEMESIS.   *Reason 1978 9(9): 29-31.* The American Liberty League, 1934-36, disseminated materials on civil rights and against federal regulation, and was composed primarily of business executives.

699.   Prickett, James R.   COMMUNISTS AND THE AUTOMOBILE INDUSTRY IN DETROIT BEFORE 1935.   *Michigan Hist. 1973 57(3): 185-208.* Traces the trade union activities of the Communist Party USA in Detroit automobile unionism before the formation of the United Automobile Workers in 1935. Such Communist leaders as Philip Raymond and Anthony Gerlach dominated the Automobile Workers Union in the 1920's and early 1930's. The AWU was particularly active in the wave of strikes of 1933. Communist rhetoric was tempered by pragmatism. 4 illus., 86 notes.   D. L. Smith

700.   Radosh, Ronald.   THE SUCCESS OF SOCIALIST FAILURE.   *Rev. in Am. Hist. 1975 3(3): 371-375.* Review article prompted by Frank Warren's *An Alternative Vision: The Socialist Party in the 1930's* (Bloomington: Indiana U. Pr., 1974); places Warren's book within the historiography of American socialism and suggests the importance of the book to assessing the success of American socialists during the 1930's.

701.   Ribuffo, Leo.   FASCISTS, NAZIS AND AMERICAN MINDS: PERCEPTIONS AND PRECONCEPTIONS.   *Am. Q. 1974 26(4): 417-432.* Review essay of several monographs on the American reaction during the New Deal era to Italian Fascism, German Nazism and the German-American Bund, Father Charles Coughlin's home-grown brand of extremism, and the United States and countersubversives on the eve of World War II: John P. Diggins, *Mussolini and Fascism: The View from America* (Princeton: Princeton U. Press, 1972); Sander A. Diamond, *The Nazi Movement in the United States 1924-1941* (Ithaca, N.Y.:

Cornell U. Press, 1973); Leland V. Bell, *In Hitler's Shadow: The Anatomy of American Nazism* (Port Washington, N.Y.: Kennikat Press, 1973); Sheldon Marcus, *Father Coughlin: The Tumultuous Life of the Priest of the Little Flower* (Boston: Little, Brown, 1973); Geoffrey S. Smith, *To Save a Nation: American Countersubversives, the New Deal, and the Coming of World War II* (New York: Basic Books, 1972). 12 notes.   C. W. Olson

702. Rocha, Guy Louis. THE IWW AND THE BOULDER CANYON PROJECT: THE FINAL DEATH THROES OF AMERICAN SYNDICAL-ISM. *Nevada Hist. Soc. Q. 1978 21(1): 2-24.* Construction began in 1931 on the Boulder Canyon project (later, Hoover Dam) on the Colorado River, a project that Bureau of Reclamation officials speeded to create employment. Genuine grievances about living and working conditions developed among the workers. Industrial Workers of the World (IWW) organizers fanned the discontent and provoked repressive measures by Las Vegas townsmen and civil authorities. The workers went on strike 8-14 August 1931 and obtained redress of part of their grievances. Despite IWW aid and leadership of the strike, most workers never joined the IWW and (in 1933) ignored a second IWW strike call on the Boulder Canyon project. Newspaper and secondary sources; 4 photos, 59 notes.
                                                                          H. T. Lovin

703. Rocha, Guy Louis. THE I.W.W. AND THE BOULDER CANYON PROJECT: THE DEATH THROES OF AMERICAN SYNDICALISM. Conlin, Joseph R., ed. *At the Point of Production: The Local History of the I.W.W.* (Westport, Conn.: Greenwood Pr., 1981): 213-234. Nevada was the site of the birth and death of the Industrial Workers of the World. The first major organizational campaigns took place within the state, in 1905. On 16 August 1931, the final significant organizational activity of the IWW in the state terminated with an unsuccessful strike at the Boulder Canyon Project, one of the last important IWW activities in America. The working conditions at the Boulder Canyon Project, constructing Hoover Dam, were extremely hazardous. In 1930 President Herbert C. Hoover felt it necessary to 1) employ some of the vast number of jobless Americans on the project and 2) rush the project. The Six Companies, Inc., of San Francisco, exploited the workers, leading to the IWW-backed strike, 7-16 August. Based on newspaper and journal articles; 59 notes.
                                                                          J. Powell

704. Rosenof, Theodore. THE POLITICAL EDUCATION OF AN AMERICAN RADICAL: THOMAS R. AMLIE IN THE 1930'S. *Wisconsin Mag. of Hist. 1974 58(1): 19-30.* Wisconsin congressman Thomas R. Amlie served in the House of Representatives first as a La Follette Republican from 1931 to 1933 and then as a Progressive from 1935 to 1939. The author traces the intellectual evolution of Amlie's radicalism as he responded to the depression and the political philosophy of the New Deal. At first Amlie sought to alter society through the formation of a third party. He gradually abandoned that idea in hopes of transforming Franklin D. Roosevelt and the New Deal into a new radical force, but ended the decade disillusioned by 'the New Dealers' dogmatically limited solution." 5 illus., 36 notes.   N. C. Burckel

705. Rosenzweig, Roy. ORGANIZING THE UNEMPLOYED: THE EARLY YEARS OF THE GREAT DEPRESSION, 1929-1933. *Radical Am. 1976 10(4): 37-60.* The unemployed councils formed by the Communists, Socialists, and Musteites after 1929 failed to create a mass revolutionary movement of the unemployed. The movement was, however, a significant example of locally based, grassroots organization under radical leadership that worked creatively and militantly to meet the concrete, immediate needs of the unemployed. Based on oral and printed primary sources.   N. Lederer

706. Rosenzweig, Roy. RADICALS AND THE JOBLESS: THE MUST-EITES AND THE UNEMPLOYED LEAGUES, 1932-1936. *Labor Hist. 1975 16(1): 52-77.* The Unemployed Leagues (UL), formed under the direction of Abraham J. Muste, illustrate the dilemmas faced by radicals in efforts to build mass organizations of the jobless. Initial growth of the UL was fostered by the emphasis upon meeting local needs for jobs, relief, etc. When the radical leaders shifted to revolutionary tactics, the leagues split along ideological lines because the rank and file were not prepared for revolution. Besides organizational problems, the leagues demonstrate some limited successes of the radical movement in the 1930's. Based on papers and publications of the UL and Musteites, and on interviews; 45 notes.   L. L. Athey

707. Rosenzweig, Roy. "SOCIALISM IN OUR TIME": THE SOCIALIST PARTY AND THE UNEMPLOYED, 1929-1936. *Labor Hist. 1979 20(4): 485-509.* Socialists played an important role, especially after 1932, in organizing the unemployed. Led by young socialists, practical action for relief was important in Chicago, New York, Baltimore, and other cities. The practical focus, when combined with external events such as the rise of the Nazis, led socialists toward being absorbed into New Deal liberalism. Their Depression activism should not be forgotten. Based on the Norman Thomas manuscript, Socialist Party manuscript, and files in the Tamiment Library; 39 notes.   L. L. Athey

708. Rubenstein, Harry R. THE GREAT GALLUP COAL STRIKE OF 1933. *New Mexico Hist. Rev. 1977 52(3): 173-192.* As a result of the depression, union membership in New Mexico declined. AFL craft unions began to reorganize and the mine workers became the most active in regard to strikes. The Gallup mining community was involved in the most serious strikes. The coal miners were affected most by the depression. The National Guard was used against the strikers. The eastern mining districts had more serious strikes than those in New Mexico. The Gallup strike was not isolated, but a part of the turmoil of the 1930's. 65 notes.   J. H. Krenkel

709. Rupp, Leila J. A RAW DEAL FOR WOMEN. *Rev. in Am. Hist. 1980 8(4): 454-458.* Review essay of Lois Scharf's *To Work and to Wed: Female Employment, Feminism, and the Great Depression* (Westport, Conn.: Greenwood Pr., 1980).

710. Ryan, James Gilbert. THE MAKING OF A NATIVE MARXIST: THE EARLY CAREER OF EARL BROWDER. *Rev. of Pol. 1977 39(3): 332-362.* Earl Browder, an advocate of "Stalinist Orthodoxy," emerged as a darkhorse candidate for the general secretary of the American Communist Party in 1934. Ironically, he would be removed 11 years later because of his "evolution

toward an independent, unorthodox, Marxism" and because he replaced "revolutionary rhetoric and programs with those of domestic reform." 67 notes.

L. E. Ziewacz

711. Ryon, Roderick M.   AN AMBIGUOUS LEGACY: BALTIMORE BLACKS AND THE CIO, 1936-1941.   *J. of Negro Hist. 1980 65(1): 18-33.* Black people in Baltimore largely were left untouched by the Congress of Industrial Organizations (CIO) membership campaigns. Despite its shortcomings, the CIO was perceived as a friend of black workers by white workers who feared integrated unions. As World War II approached, the character of the CIO changed with beginning of the war boom. Large numbers of black migrants swelled the ranks of the CIO and were vital ingredients to its success. 49 notes.

N. G. Sapper

712. Sageser, A. Bower.   I REMEMBER WHEN THE STRATOSPHERE BALLOON WENT PFFT.   *Kansas Q. 1976 8(2): 55-58.* During the Great Depression new and stimulating ideas evolved, such as the growing interest in stratospheric balloon flights, leading to several failures, and the eventual success of Orvil A. Anderson and Albert W. Stevens' Explorer II flight on 11 November 1935.

713. Schacht, John N.   TOWARD INDUSTRIAL UNIONISM: BELL TELEPHONE WORKERS AND COMPANY UNIONS, 1919-1937.   *Labor Hist. 1975 16(1): 5-36.* Development of company unions in the Bell Telephone System helped prepare the way for the emergence of industrial unions after 1935. The structure of the company union helped erase distinctions between workers, and leadership and organizational skills were learned by workers. Success in converting the Bell Company union into an industrial union may help explain why other company unions failed to make the transformation. Based on oral history interviews, company publications, dissertations, and government reports; 43 notes.

L. L. Athey

714. Schlatter, Richard.   ON BEING A COMMUNIST AT HARVARD. *Partisan Rev. 1977 44(4): 605-615.* The author's experience as a member of the Communist Party at Harvard University in the 1930's was mainly a matter of style and intellectual sympathy. Explains how one was attracted from a comfortable middle class background to communism via intellectual choice and emotional commitment. His student experiences in England and Europe contributed to his ideological development; but the brutal facts of Soviet life and foreign policy brought his membership in the late 1930's to an end. He left the Party.

D. K. Pickens

715. Schnell, R. L.   EXPRESSIVE AND INSTRUMENTAL POLITICS IN THE AMERICAN STUDENT MOVEMENT: THE 1930S AS A CASE STUDY.   *Paedagogica Hist. [Belgium] 1977 17(2): 386-421.* Both Lewis Feuer and Seymour Martin Lipset characterized student activism of the 1930's as being instrumental and relatively disciplined by political affiliations. This observation is tested by examining the principal student organizations of the 1930's and 1940's to see how militant student groups operated in an environment of political affiliation and instrumental programs, how they responded to the demands of external political groups, and how their policies and programs related to social and political conditions. 70 notes.

J. M. McCarthy

716.   Scott, William R.   BLACK NATIONALISM AND THE ITALO-ETHIOPIAN CONFLICT, 1934-1936.   *J. of Negro Hist. 1978 63(2): 118-134.* Anger and indignation over Italy's unchallenged invasion of Ethiopia in 1935 spawned a wave of black nationalism in the United States which was manifest in pro-Ethiopian press from traditional black organizations, formation of associations to raise money for Ethiopia, and political activism leading to Pan-Africanism within the black community.

717.   Scott, William R.   RABBI ARNOLD FORD'S BACK-TO-ETHIOPIA MOVEMENT: A STUDY OF BLACK EMIGRATION, 1930-1935.   *Pan-African J. [Kenya] 1975 8(2): 191-202.* An account of the career of Rabbi Arnold Ford (1876-1935), early black Nationalist and leader of the back-to-Ethiopia movement. Accompanied by three other members of his congregation, Rabbi Ford arrived in Addis Ababa in 1930 in an attempt to obtain concessions for the rest of his group, who, it was hoped, would follow soon after. Records the difficulties encountered by those 60 members who made the journey to Addis Ababa during 1930-34. Twenty-five members returned shortly after their arrival and none remained after Ford's death in 1935 and the outbreak of the Italo-Ethiopian War. Primary and secondary sources; 52 notes.   M. Feingold

718.   Sears, Stephen W.   "SHUT THE GODDAM PLANT!"   *Am. Heritage 1982 33(3): 49-64.* The sit-down strike at the General Motors Corporation's Fisher Body plant in Flint, Michigan, began 30 December 1936. Other plants were also involved. For six weeks, the conflict continued. Tension led to violence and brought quick action from Governor Frank Murphy who sent National Guardsmen to Flint. The end came on 11 February with a negotiated settlement accepting the presence of the United Automobile Workers of America. 18 illus.
J. F. Paul

719.   Shankman, Arnold.   BLACK PRIDE AND PREJUDICE: THE AMOS 'N' ANDY CRUSADE.   *J. of Popular Culture 1978 12(2): 236-252.* Protest directed at the popular radio program, *Amos 'n' Andy,* by black groups made the public aware of the stereotypes used to portray blacks, taught blacks valuable lessons about economic boycotts of radio advertiser's products, and caused blacks to question demeaning stereotypes used in popular comic strips, 1930's.

720.   Shankman, Arnold.   THE FIVE-DAY PLAN AND THE DEPRESSION.   *Historian 1981 43(3): 393-409.* One panacea proposed to alleviate the Depression was the Five-Day Plan. Developed by Mary (1874-1966) and Mildred (1888-1960) Hicks, two Socialists living in Bainbridge, Georgia, the plan attracted only modest attention during the 1930's. Inspired by Charles and Mary Beard's *Rise of American Civilization,* which argued that shifting taxes could transfer wealth from one class to another, the Hicks Five-Day Plan of 1931 proposed a 100% tax on all income above $50,000 and a 100% tax on all bequests above $100,000. Dissatisfaction with the trends of Roosevelt's New Deal turned the Hickses toward Huey Long and his Share-Our-Wealth society. His death effectively signaled the end of the Hicks Plan. Primary sources; 63 notes.
R. S. Sliwoski

721.   Shapiro, Edward S.   THE CATHOLIC RURAL LIFE MOVEMENT
AND THE NEW DEAL FARM PROGRAM.   Am. Benedictine Rev. 1977
28(3): 307-332. Analyzes the Catholic agrarian movement of the 1930's and
compares its goals with New Deal farm programs. The New Deal did not alleviate
the problems noted by the Catholic agrarian movement. Based on original and
secondary sources; 35 notes.   J. H. Pragman

722.   Shiner, John F.   THE 1937 STEEL DISPUTE AND THE OHIO NA-
TIONAL GUARD.   Ohio Hist. 1975 84(4): 182-195. Governor Martin L.
Davey contemplated using the National Guard to curb the growing violence in
the strike area. Troops acted as a screen behind which it was easier to operate
a struck plant. Davey was not anti-labor, but wanted the National Guard merely
to restore order. Unintentionally, however, he employed the guard as a strike-
breaking force, and "the overwhelming majority of the people of the state supported him in that action." 72 notes.   E. P. Stickney

723.   Sholes, Elizabeth.   WOMEN IN THE MEDIA: A REPORT ON
FEMALE PROFESSIONALISM DURING THE AMERICAN DEPRES-
SION.   Modernist Studies [Canada] 1974-75 1(3): 27-38. Professional women in
journalism, radio, and film were able to improve their economic and personal
status during the depression because of their personal styles and because the
media was less affected by hard times in the 1930's.

724.   Sifuentes, Roberto.   APROXIMACIONES AL "CORRIDO DE LOS
HERMANOS HERNANDEZ EJECUTADOS EN LA CAMARA DE GAS
DE LA PENITENCIARIA DE FLORENCE, ARIZONA EL DIA 6 DE
JULIO DE 1934"   [Approaches to the "Corrido de los Hermanos Hernández
Ejecutados en la Cámara de Gas de la Penitenciaría de Florence, Arizona, el día
6 de Julio de 1934"].   Aztlán 1982 13(1-2): 95-109. Analyzes the content of the
ballad of the Hernández brothers by Epifanio Alonso, based on a true incident.
Federico and Manuel Hernández were convicted of murdering an old miner in
the Arizona desert in 1934. Originally sentenced to die by hanging, the brothers
were chosen to be the first to test the state's new gas chamber. The ballad places
the Hernández brothers and the state of Arizona in opposition, symbolizing the
conflict between the Mexican minority in the United States and Anglo dominance
of that minority. Ballad text and secondary sources; 3 notes. A. Hoffman Spanish.

725.   Simms, Adam.   A BATTLE IN THE AIR: DETROIT'S JEWS AN-
SWER FATHER COUGHLIN.   Michigan Jewish Hist. 1978 18(2): 7-13. A
memorandum written in 1939 by executive director William I. Boxerman outlines
the initial stages of the Jewish Community Council's radio campaign against
Charles Edward Coughlin's anti-Semitism.

726.   Snyder, Robert E.   THE CONCEPT OF DEMAGOGUERY: HUEY
LONG AND HIS LITERARY CRITICS.   Louisiana Studies 1976 15(1): 61-84.
Huey P. Long (1893-1935) of Louisiana, the most famous of southern dema-
gogues, aroused great criticism from politicians, novelists, and his own family.
Long saw himself as an enlightened populist reformer, but others found him
self-seeking, deceptive, and a threat to society. Hamilton Basso's novel Sun in
Capricorn (1942) is one of four major novels in the 1940's which used Long's life

to show the evils of demagoguery. The chief character, Gilgo Slade, uses sham, deceit, and blackmail to achieve power. Based on primary and secondary sources; 76 notes. J. Buschen

727. Spears, James E. WHERE HAVE ALL THE PEDDLERS GONE? *Kentucky Folklore Record 1975 21(3): 77-81.* Comments on the disappearance of peddlers in the 1930's due to the advent of the automobile in Kentucky.

728. Stephanson, Anders. THE CPUSA CONCEPTION OF THE ROOSEV-ELTIAN STATE, 1933-1939. *Radical Hist. Rev. 1980 (24): 160-176.* Discusses the Communist Party of the United States of America's (CPUSA) analysis of "the Rooseveltian State" in order "to demonstrate the *political effects* of the absence of theoretical work" and "to offer a critique, often between the lines, of Communist Marxism."

729. Strogovich, M. S. DELO IUNOSHEI V SCOTTSBORO [The Scotts-boro affair]. *Voprosy Istorii [USSR] 1974 (3): 137-142.* Considers the proceedings in Scottsboro, Alabama, in 1931, when eight Negro youths were condemned to death by a totally white jury (the sentence being subsequently commuted to lengthy imprisonment) for the alleged rape of two white girls on a train. The case is considered characteristic of US legal attitudes toward nonwhite races, particularly Negroes. Describes the accounts of the attack given by the Negro boys and the white boys and girls involved, and considers the court hearings and later accounts of other individuals, as reported in H. Patterson and E. Conrad's *Scottsboro Boy: The Story that America Wanted to Forget.* Based on the above work and other secondary works; 8 notes. L. Smith

730. Supina, Philip D. HERNDON J. EVANS AND THE HARLAN COUNTY COAL STRIKE. *Filson Club Hist. Q. 1982 56(3): 318-335.* Herndon J. Evans, editor of the Pineville *Sun,* tried to present a balanced account of the coal miners' strike in Harlan County, Kentucky, during 1931-32. Evans, a local booster, deeply resented the efforts of Theodore Dreiser, Waldo Frank, and John Dos Passos in portraying Harlan County as a violent area. His efforts won some national recognition, but they did little to alleviate the suffering of the local population or to restore civil rights to miners who tried to join labor unions. Based on the Evans collection at the University of Kentucky Library. G. B. McKinney

731. Swanson, Merwin R. STUDENT RADICALS AT THE "SOUTHERN BRANCH": CAMPUS PROTEST IN THE 1930'S. *Idaho Yesterdays 1976 20(3): 21-26.* In the 1930's, students at the University of Idaho Southern Branch at Pocatello protested Franklin D. Roosevelt's economic and foreign policies by bringing in Socialist speakers and by trying to seize control of the student newspaper. Primary sources; 2 illus., 18 notes. B. J. Paul

732. Symonds, Craig L. WILLIAM VEAZIE PRATT AS CNO: 17 SEP-TEMBER 1930-30 JUNE 1933. *Naval War Coll. Rev. 1980 33(2): 17-33.* The beginning of a severe economic depression, midway between two world wars, is hardly the period any officer aspiring to become Chief of Naval Operations would choose for his tenure. To be considered a heretic by his fellow officers, including his immediate predecessor, for his naval limitations views merely added complications to the challenges faced by Admiral William Pratt. This article is taken from

the forthcoming (June 1980) book to be published by the Naval Institute Press: *The Chiefs of Naval Operation,* edited by Robert W. Love, Jr. 46 notes.   J

733. Taylor, Paul F. LONDON: FOCAL POINT OF KENTUCKY TUR-BULENCE. *Filson Club Hist. Q. 1975 49(3): 256-265.* London was the site of the federal court for southeastern Kentucky, and the author concentrates on two important cases tried there in the 1930's. The first occurred in 1932 when the American Civil Liberties Union enjoined Bell County officials to let them enter the county. The ACLU lost the case. In 1938 mine owners and law enforcement officials were placed on trial for violating the civil rights of coal miners. The sensational trial made London the center of national attention and resulted in hung juries and the freeing of the defendants. Documentation from newspapers; 55 notes.   G. B. McKinney

734. Tedlow, Richard S. THE NATIONAL ASSOCIATION OF MANU-FACTURERS AND PUBLIC RELATIONS DURING THE NEW DEAL. *Business Hist. Rev. 1976 50(1): 25-45.* Traces the experience of the National Association of Manufacturers, in its public relations campaign of the 1930's. Describes it as an attempt to counter labor militancy and the public and political criticism the business community was receiving. The message of the campaign was that businessmen were the leaders of the nation and that they could be trusted with the public interest. As a result of the N.A.M. experience, the concept of public relations for business as a legitimate sphere of activity became a permanent part of the corporate scene. Based on N.A.M. records and publications and on governmental documents; 63 notes.   C. J. Pusateri

735. Thrasher, Sue. RADICAL EDUCATION IN THE THIRTIES. *Southern Exposure 1974 1(3/4): 204-210.* Reviews Martin Duberman's *Black Mountain, An Exploration in Community* (New York: E. P. Dutton and Co., 1972), Raymond and Charlotte Koch's Educational Commune, *The Story of Commonwealth College* (Schocken Books, 1972), and Frank Adams' and Myles Horton's *Unearthing Seeds of Fire, The Idea of Highlander* (John F. Blair, 1974). The three colleges grew out of the social and political climate of the 1930's creating "in the present a semblance of a society they envisioned for the future." Black Mountain was concerned with arts and education, Commonwealth trained leaders for the "revolution," and Highlander trained the common people to take control over their own lives. 4 illus.   G. A. Bolton

736. Thrasher, Sue and Wise, Leah. THE SOUTHERN TENANT FARM-ERS' UNION. *Southern Exposure 1974 1(3/4): 5-32.* During the Depression, black and white sharecroppers organized the Southern Tenant Farmers' Union which became a mass movement. Explores the plight of the tenants and the union's relationships with the Communist Party, American Federation of Labor, Congress of Industrial Organizations, and black and white sharecroppers. The Agricultural Adjustment Administration caused the eviction of thousands of sharecroppers who then sought work in industrial plants outside the South during World War II. Based on papers in Southern Historical Collection, University of North Carolina, and oral interviews; 12 illus., 3 notes, biblio.   G. A. Bolton

737.   Tomlins, Christopher L.   AFL UNIONS IN THE 1930S: THEIR PER-
FORMANCE IN HISTORICAL PERSPECTIVE.   *J. of Am. Hist. 1979 65(4):
1021-1042.* Challenges traditional interpretations and suggests a new analytic
framework to explain American Federation of Labor (AFL) successes. Histori-
cally, AFL unions had adapted to the changing industrial environment; this
tendency continued in the 1930's when the AFL faced Congress of Industrial
Organizations (CIO) competition. AFL unions made major contributions to the
growth of the organized labor movement in the 1930's, especially in transport,
communications, service trades, and retail trades. 4 tables, 50 notes.
                                                                        T. P Linkfield

738.   Toy, Eckard, V., Jr.   THE OXFORD GROUP AND THE STRIKE OF
THE SEATTLE LONGSHOREMEN IN 1934.   *Pacific Northwest Q. 1978
69(4): 174-184.* Traces the development of the Oxford Group from its founding
in 1921 as a Christian mediation group devoted to settling labor and international
problems. During the 1934 longshoremen's strike in Seattle, Oxford Group leaders George Light, James Clise, and Walter Horne worked themselves into a
mediating role which helped end the deadlock by June. Throughout the negotiations, they unabashedly supported management over labor which was consistent
with the entire Oxford Group movement. Primary and secondary sources; 2
photos, 41 notes.   M. L. Tate

739.   Trilling, Diana.   LIONEL TRILLING, A JEW AT COLUMBIA.
Commentary 1979 67(3): 40-46. Describes the difficulties Lionel Trilling had to
face as a Jew in the early 1930's establishing himself as an English professor at
Columbia University.

740.   Tselos, George.   SELF-HELP AND SAUERKRAUT: THE ORGA-
NIZED UNEMPLOYED, INC., OF MINNEAPOLIS.   *Minnesota Hist. 1977
45(8): 306-320.* The Reverend George H. Mecklenburg founded the Organized
Unemployed, Inc. in 1932. In this organization, individuals, through self-help,
could lift themselves out of economic adversity. Headquartered in an old girls'
high school in Minneapolis, the organization harvested, processed, and canned
produce, operated a cafeteria and stores, cut wood for fuel, made clothing, and
provided housing and employment services. It lasted until 1935 when superseded
by government efforts. Scrip money was used as a medium of exchange, awarded
in return for services to the organization. The organization's slogan, "Work Not
Dole," indicated that its efforts represented a backward attempt to alleviate
poverty through private endeavors rather than through organizing the poor to
exert pressure on the government to provide jobs and sustenance. Primary
sources.   N. Lederer

741.   Valerina, A. F.   ROL' BESPARTIINOI RABOCHEI LIGI VO VNU-
TRENNEI POLITICHESKOI BOR'BE S. SH. A. (1936-1938 GG.)   [The role
of the Labor Non-Partisan League in the internal political struggle in the US,
1936-38]. *Vestnik Moskovskogo U., Seriia 9: Istoriia [USSR] 1975 30(6): 38-57.*
Outlines the activities of the League, the most progressive labor organization in
the United States during the 1930's. It represented the true feelings of the workers, tried to provide them with independent political representation, and stimulated important legislation which improved working conditions in the country.
129 notes.   N. Dejevsky

742. VanWest, Carroll. PERPETUATING THE MYTH OF AMERICA: SCOTTSBORO AND ITS INTERPRETERS. *South Atlantic Q. 1981 80(1): 36-48.* In the telling of their Scottsboro stories, whether offered at the time or in retrospect, the guardians of the myth of America have said much more about the manner in which American society views itself and its relationship to the past than they have about the true meaning of that sad series of events in depression-ridden northeastern Alabama. Discusses the various myths which have arisen out of the 1931 Alabama incident. 26 notes.   H. M. Parker, Jr.

743. Verba, Sidney and Schlozman, Kay Lehman. UNEMPLOYMENT, CLASS CONSCIOUSNESS, AND RADICAL POLITICS: WHAT DIDN'T HAPPEN IN THE THIRTIES. *J. of Pol. 1977 39(2): 291-323.* The failure of socialism in the United States has been attributed to lack of class consciousness and alienation from political and economic institutions among workers. Even during the Depression of the 1930's, the working class supported the New Deal rather than more radical changes. Two national surveys conducted by Elmo Roper for *Fortune Magazine* in 1939 reveal working class attitudes. Although class consciousness and alienation increased from upper white collar, lower white collar, wage worker to unemployed, they remained fully developed in only a small minority. This seems to be attributable to the acceptance of the American Dream of rugged individualism and optimism. Based on primary and secondary sources; 14 tables, 24 notes.   A. W. Novitsky

744. Wald, Alan M. THE MENORAH GROUP MOVES LEFT. *Jewish Social Studies 1976 38(3-4): 289-320.* A group of Jewish intellectuals clustered around Elliott Ettleson Cohen and worked on *The Menorah Journal* in the 1920's. They generated the development of a Jewish humanism that led to a Jewish cultural renaissance. In the early 1930's, Cohen, Lionel Trilling, George Novack, Herbert Solow and others in the group gravitated toward the Communists and became especially prominent in the National Committee for the Defense of Political Prisoners. By the mid-1930's, most of these individuals broke from the Communists and supported Trotskyist and other radical organizations. Tess Slesinger's novel, *The Unpossessed,* provides a vivid portrait of the attitudes and personality traits of some members of the Menorah Group.   N. Lederer

745. Walker, William O., III. CONTROL ACROSS THE BORDER: THE UNITED STATES, MEXICO, AND NARCOTICS POLICY, 1936-1940. *Pacific Hist. Rev. 1978 47(1): 91-106.* Between 1936-40 US narcotic diplomacy transformed Mexican drug policy. The United States defined as illegal all non-medical and nonscientific use of narcotics and made little distinction between users and peddlers. Although Mexico formally agreed to these policies in agreements signed in 1930 and 1932, its enforcement efforts did not gain American approval. In 1938, Leopold Salazar Viniegra became head of Mexico's Federal Narcotics Service. He did not believe in a punitive drug control program; instead he favored channeling the flow of illegal drugs through government controlled distribution centers. American diplomatic pressure led to Salazar's removal in August 1939 and to a more vigorous Mexican law enforcement policy. Based on documents in National Archives, the Bureau of Narcotics Library, and Mexican newspapers; 51 notes.   W. K. Hobson

746. Weisbord, Vera Buch. GASTONIA 1929: STRIKE AT THE LORAY MILL. *Southern Exposure 1974 1(3/4): 185-203.* The author, a labor organizer, views the textile workers' strike in which she was harassed, jailed, and tried on charges stemming from her participation in the strike. The National Textile Workers Union organized the strike which also was supported by International Labor Defense and the Young Communist League. Tension between white and black workers was exploited, while the National Guard were used as strikebreakers. The mills had not been unionized by 1974. Based on unpublished autobiography and oral interviews; 8 illus.   G. A. Bolton

747. Weiss, Richard. ETHNICITY AND REFORM: MINORITIES AND THE AMBIENCE OF THE DEPRESSION YEARS. *J. of Am. Hist. 1979 66(3): 566-585.* Analyzes the changing attitudes of many Americans, especially intellectuals, regarding the relationship of ethnic groups to American culture during the 1930's. By the eve of World War II, many Americans had begun to view ethnic variety in American nationality not only as positive, but as essential. Racial and ethnic tolerance increased as a reaction to the racism of Nazi Germany. During the Depression years, immigrants and blacks were viewed as victims of the society, not as threats to it. 78 notes.   T. P. Linkfield

748. Whisenhunt, Donald W. THE CONTINENTAL CONGRESS OF WORKERS AND FARMERS, 1933. *Studies in Hist. and Soc. 1974-75 6(1): 1-14.* The 1933 congress, modelled after the 1776 Second Continental Congress, was organized by Clarence Senior, with support from leading Socialists including Norman Thomas. Planned in the aftermath of the 1932 presidential election, when Franklin D. Roosevelt appeared only slightly less conservative than Herbert Hoover, the Congress convened two months after Roosevelt took office—the period during which the New Deal was most active and least opposed. Unclear goals, exclusion of Communists, uncertainty over the best means of promoting Socialist politics, and poor timing with regard to the New Deal prevented permanent gains for the Socialist Party of America and allied groups. Based on primary sources; 98 notes.   G. H. Libbey

749. Whitaker, W. Richard. OUTLINE OF HITLER'S "FINAL SOLUTION" APPARENT BY 1933. *Journalism Q. 1981 58(2): 192-200, 247.* An analysis of the contents of the *New York Times* for 1933 shows that this newspaper was making clear the plight of German Jews under Hitler and was painting a forbidding picture of their future under Nazism. In all, over 300 articles that year dealt with anti-Semitism in Germany. An 11 September dispatch mentions the possibility of their extermination. Although there were some protests from the public, the Great Depression seems to have kept the attention of the public focused on economic concerns. Based on newspaper reports; 73 notes.
                                                                    J. S. Coleman

750. Williams, David. "THEY NEVER STOPPED WATCHING US": FBI POLITICAL SURVEILLANCE, 1924-1936. *UCLA Hist. J. 1981 2: 5-28.* Demonstrates that during 1924-36 Federal Bureau of Investigation Director J. Edgar Hoover violated a restriction on surveillance activities imposed by Attorney General Harlan Fiske Stone. Although Hoover officially declared that the FBI was not interested in political opinions protected by law, he continued to direct political surveillance activities until 1936, when President Franklin Roose-

velt approved an expansion of the FBI's function. Hoover justified surveillance in the name of national security. The American Civil Liberties Union, Trade Union Education League, and mass political demonstrations attracted Hoover's attention. Only a vigilant Congress can prevent such constitutional abuses, by adopting an FBI charter prohibiting such surveillance and holding the agency accountable for its actions. Primary and secondary sources; 53 notes.

A. Hoffman

751. Williams, Lillian S., ed. ATTICA PRISONERS SEEK AID FROM NAACP (1932). *Afro-Am. in New York Life and Hist. 1977 1(2): 211-212.* Reprints a letter by black inmates of New York's Attica State Prison in 1932 asking the NAACP to investigate prison conditions of blacks.

752. Williams, R. E. THE AIRCRAFT OF DONALD DOUGLAS. *Am. Aviation Hist. Soc. J. 1981 26(1): 72-79.* Pictorial essay of the achievements of Donald Douglas in the design and development of airplanes; 1932-38.

753. Zieger, Robert H. THE LIMITS OF MILITANCY: ORGANIZING PAPER WORKERS, 1933-1935. *J. of Am. Hist. 1976 63(3): 638-657.* Analyzes efforts to organize workers in the converted paper industry in the early years of the New Deal. The mid-1930's form a discrete segment of transitional trial-and-error organizational techniques in which grass roots militancy played a major role. This early militancy lacked staying power and represented a false start. The claims of militancy conflicted with those of permanent organization and erratic, ineffective local unions quarreled with the international organization, the International Brotherhood of Pulp, Sulphite, and Paper Mill Workers, AFL. Primary and secondary sources; 44 notes.

W. R. Hively

754. Zieger, Robert H. OLDTIMERS & NEWCOMERS: CHANGE AND CONTINUITY IN THE PULP, SULPHITE UNION IN THE 1930'S. *J. of Forest Hist. 1977 21(4): 188-201.* The International Brotherhood of Pulp, Sulphite, and Paper Mill Workers was organized in 1909, but it failed to expand as rapidly as did the paper industry. In the mid-1930's, however, it did expand rapidly to include urban workers, many of whom were European immigrants and women. When it expanded into the South, it had to establish separate charters for black and white workers at the paper mills. Its new locals in the Pacific Northwest "exhibited a remarkable degree of suspicion and even contempt for the international union." Based on the IBPSPMW Papers and on primary and secondary sources; 12 illus., 27 notes.

F. N. Egerton

755. Zimmerman, Tom. "HAM AND EGGS, EVERYBODY!" *Southern California Q. 1980 62(1): 77-96.* Traces the rise and decline of the California Life Payments Plan, popularly known as the Ham and Eggs movement, of the 1930's. It was to distribute pensions to unemployed people over age 50. The proposal, originally called $25 Every Monday Morning, was created by Robert Noble, a radio personality, in 1937. Noble was maneuvered out of the scheme by Willis and Laurence Allen, advertising agents and promoters who enlarged the proposal, changed its name to $30 Every Thursday, and attracted statewide attention. Twenty-five percent of the state's registered voters placed the proposal on the ballot as an initiative measure. It was barely defeated in November 1938. The Ham and Eggers renewed their efforts with a second initiative. Opponents, in-

cluding the state's newspapers and businessmen, cited the unworkability of the plan, the danger of inflation, and destruction of public services. California voters, unwilling to take so radical a step as to experiment with their state's basic economic structure, rejected the initiative in 1939. 66 notes.   A. Hoffman

756. Zolov, A. V. AMERIKANSKII IZOLIATSIONISM I PRINIATIE ZAKONA O NEITRALITETE 1935 GODA [American isolationism and the enactment of the Neutrality Act (1935)]. *Vestnik Moskovskogo U., Seriia 8: Istoriia [USSR] 1979 (1): 32-44.* Isolationists were divided into four groups. The liberal democratic group feared that war would end domestic reform. The left radical groups feared that war would impede socialism in America. The conservatives feared that war would bring social reform and wanted the United States to be an arbiter of a Europe weakened by war. Fascists such as Fr. Coughlin, Long, and Hearst constituted a fourth group. President Franklin D. Roosevelt saw that isolationist sentiment was strong and so acted cautiously in dealing with the Neutrality Act. Roosevelt did win a concession from Congress that the embargo on the shipment of military goods would last only six months. Many groups in America were happy at the passage of the bill. 81 notes.   D. Balmuth

757. Zucker, Bat-Ami. RADICAL JEWISH INTELLECTUALS AND THE NEW DEAL. Artzi, Pinhas, ed. *Bar-Ilan Studies in History* (Ramat-Gan, Israel: Bar-Ilan U. Pr., 1978): 275-283. American socialists, communists and liberals of the 1930's were predominantly non-Jewish, but they contained small pockets of Jewish radicals, who had originated in the 1900's. Argues that the second generation Jews in the 1930's faced an "alienation" crisis because of their transition from poverty to wealth; therefore, many became radicals. But Franklin D. Roosevelt's election campaign of 1932 promised Jews greater social and economic freedom. This made it much easier for Jewish radicals to accept the new Establishment, which they saw as more unified than the Left. Based on newspapers and secondary works; 34 notes.   A. Alcock

758. —. [THE COMMUNIST PARTY AND ELECTORAL POLITICS IN THE 1930'S]. *Radical Hist. Rev. 1980 (23): 104-135.*
Waltzer, Kenneth. THE PARTY AND THE POLLING PLACE: AMERICAN COMMUNISM AND AN AMERICAN LABOR PARTY IN THE 1930'S, *pp. 104-129.* The Communist Party tried to deal with electoral politics during the 1930's by forming a labor party made up of united front alliances and by adopting a low profile in the American Labor Party and elsewhere.
Gordon, Max. THE PARTY AND THE POLLING PLACE: A RESPONSE, *pp. 130-135.* Critique of Waltzer's article on the Communist Party and the American Labor Party during the 1930's, based on author Gordon's experience as a Communist Party organizer during the 1930's and as a Party journalist during the 1940's and 1950's; although the Popular Front lasted only four years, it nevertheless served as an example "for socialist tactics in a strongly capitalist society."

759. —. [SENATOR AUSTIN AND THE NEUTRALITY ACTS]. *Vermont Hist. 1974 42(3): 228-244.*
Porter, David L. SENATOR WARREN R, AUSTIN AND THE NEUTRALITY ACT OF 1939. *pp. 228-238.* Reviews the actions taken by Senator

Warren R. Austin of Vermont to repeal the provisions of the Neutrality Act of 1937 which had prevented the United States from aiding the Allies in the years prior to World War II. Austin had been an early supporter of the Neutrality Act of 1935, but events in Asia and Europe had altered his views. Working within the Senate and by radio to the public, he attacked the isolationists and their philosophy, and helped to assure removal of restrictive sections of the proposed Neutrality Act of 1939. 33 notes.

Mazuzan, George H.   THE FAILURE OF NEUTRALITY REVISION IN MID-SUMMER, 1939: WARREN R. AUSTIN'S MEMORANDUM OF THE WHITE HOUSE CONFERENCE OF JULY 18,   *pp. 239-244.* The conference, called by FDR, concerned the Senate's reluctance to revise or repeal the Neutrality Act of 1937. The issue was left temporarily unresolved.

V. L. Human

5

THE CULTURE
OF THE DEPRESSION

760. Ahlander, Leslie Judd. MEXICO'S MURALISTS AND THE NEW YORK SCHOOL. *Américas (Organization of Am. States) 1979 31(5): 18-25.* Describes the influence of the Mexican mural artists on the New York school beginning in the early 1930's at the height of the Depression.

761. Alexander, William. *THE MARCH OF TIME* AND *THE WORLD TODAY. Am. Q. 1977 29(2): 182-193.* The film documentaries produced under the auspices of *Time Magazine* and shown in 1930 movie theaters under the title *The March of Time* combined actual documentary film footage with reconstructed dramatic scenes to convey vivid accounts of events of the day in highly melodramatic fashion. Although supposedly objective, the documentaries actually presented a definite point of view which some left-wing critics described as fascistic. The left-wing New York city film group, Nykino, produced the documentary series, *The World Today,* presumably as a radical counterpart to the *Time* series. *The World Today* producers stressed the employment of the persons being filmed as participants in the film planning, the provision of complete background documentation for the event depicted, and the use of an authentic film style. Primary sources.   N. Lederer

762. Alley, Kenneth D. *HIGH SIERRA:* SWAN SONG FOR AN ERA. *J. of Popular Film 1976 5(3-4): 248-262.* Examines Humphrey Bogart's portrayal of the fictional character Roy Earle in the film *High Sierra* (1941) and examines gangster films of the 1930's.

763. Alter, Robert. THE TRAVELS OF MALCOLM COWLEY. *Commentary 1980 70(2): 33-40.* Sees a conflict between the literary calling of Malcolm Cowley and other New York City intellectuals and their infatuation with revolutionary Marxism during the 1930's, focusing on Cowley's recently published memoirs from the period, *The Dream of the Golden Mountains.*

764. Anders, Leslie. THE WATERSHED: FORREST HARDING'S *INFANTRY JOURNAL*, 1934-1938. *Military Affairs 1976 40(1): 12-16.* Discusses the role of Edwin Forrest Harding in improving the quality and expanding the scope of *The Infantry Journal*. With interesting and controversial articles, book reviews, and editorials, Harding maximized its instructional potential and demonstrated moral courage with a political awareness. The American *Journal*

received praises from writers of many nationalities and demonstrated that erudition and professional scholarship were not alien to the infantry. Primary and secondary sources; 16 notes. A. M. Osur

765. Ansley, Fran; Bell, Brenda; and Reece, Florence. "LITTLE DAVID BLUES": AN INTERVIEW WITH TOM LOWRY. *Southern Exposure 1974 1(3/4): 137-143.* The folk song "Little David Blues" was written by coal miner Tom Lowry during the 1932 Davidson-Wilder strike in Tennessee. The song tells of the miners' poor working and living conditions. Lowry relates how he came to compose the song. Based on oral interview; 4 illus. G. A. Bolton

766. Arthur, Thomas H. AN ACTOR IN POLITICS: MELVYN DOUGLAS AND THE NEW DEAL. *J. of Popular Culture 1980 14(2): 196-211.* Chronicle of the political activities of actor Melvyn Douglas during the Roosevelt New Deal era. Essentially apolitical before joining the Hollywood Anti-Nazi League in 1936, Douglas went on to become a liberal Democratic political activist, and gained substantial recognition at both the state and national levels prior to US entry into World War II. Subsequent to his service in the army during the war, however, Douglas did not play as active a role in politics, and in fact disagreed with many postwar Democratic Party policies. Based on interviews and Douglas's papers; 88 notes. D. G. Nielson

767. Baker, Howard. THE GYROSCOPE. *Southern Rev. 1981 17(4): 735-757. The Gyroscope: A Literary Magazine,* published quarterly between May 1929 and February 1930, served two main functions: 1) it was the vehicle which Yvor Winters used to enunciate his matured thinking and to demonstrate his decisive resolution of his own problem in writing poetry, and 2) it contained the earliest work of authors who are now among the most highly esteemed figures in mid-century American letters (Katherine Anne Porter, Carolyn Gordon, etc.).

768. Banks, Ann. A TEACHER'S GUIDE TO *FIRST-PERSON AMERICA: VOICES FROM THE THIRTIES. Social Educ. 1981 45(6): 443-450.* Presents tips for teachers on how to effectively present and discuss the series of six radio programs called *First-Person America: Voices from the Thirties,* based on oral history interviews collected by the Federal Writers' Project during the 1930's dealing with vaudeville and carnivals, immigrants, unions, managing economically during the Depression, industrial work, and urban blacks.

769. Banks, Dean. H. L. MENCKEN AND "HITLERISM," 1933-1941: A PATRICIAN LIBERTARIAN BESIEGED. *Maryland Hist. Mag. 1976 71(4): 498-515.* Charles Angoff's *H. L. Mencken: A Portrait from Memory* (1956) was a chief source of the charges of "Hitlerism" leveled at H. L. Mencken after 1933. The book "marshalled selected data" and stressed Mencken's insensitivity to anti-Semitism. In reality, Mencken had an attachment to liberty and freedom of speech which also carried with it the "right to refrain from expression, the right to judicious restraint or silence." Mencken's elitist distrust of public opinion and mass emotionalism restrained him from actively joining the anti-Hitler militants. While scorning political radicalism, he consistently championed the right of free speech for all American extremists. Mencken's growing anti-New Deal sentiments would have spurred much resentment among intellectuals after early 1933 anyway; but his consistent scorn for chauvinism and emotional group behavior

of all sorts, his basic belief that Nazism was most akin to Ku Klux Klanism, and the memory of his World War I attitude toward the "dangerous hysterias of democracy," made him equally oppose Jewish nationalism, 100 percent Americanism, and German racialism during the 1930's. Primary and secondary materials; 89 notes.   G. J. Bobango

770. Barra, Allen. THE SINGING BRAKEMAN. *Horizon 1979 22(9): 70-73.* Describes the career of country music singer and writer Jimmie Rodgers, whose greatest popularity lasted from 1927 to 1933, when he died at the age of 35 from tuberculosis.

771. Barshay, Robert. ETHNIC STEREOTYPES IN FLASH GORDON. *J. of Popular Film 1974 3(1): 15-30.*

772. Bauer, Harry C. MULLING OVER MENCKEN'S *MERCURY. Serials Librarian 1976 1(1): 13-22.* Examines the role played by H. L. Mencken during his stint with the *American Mercury*, 1920's-30's, as well as his other passions and publications during the period.

773. Benson, Jackson J. and Loftis, Anne. JOHN STEINBECK AND FARM LABOR UNIONIZATION: THE BACKGROUND OF *IN DUBIOUS BATTLE. Am. Literature 1980 52(2): 194-223.* Analyzes the degree of realism in Steinbeck's *In Dubious Battle,* which portrays agricultural strikes in southern California during the early 1930's. The novel's main characters, strike, and strike location were all composites of actual people, events, and locations in California in 1933. Steinbeck may have created realistic (true to life) human speech, situations, and events, but he did not realistically portray the human motives and feelings that accompanied the people and events he used as composites. *In Dubious Battle* is too brutal to be considered a realistic portrayal of an agricultural strike in California in 1933. Based on personal interviews and secondary sources; 77 notes.   T. P. Linkfield

774. Blanchard, Margaret A. FREEDOM OF THE PRESS AND THE NEWSPAPER CODE: JUNE 1933-FEBRUARY 1934. *Journalism Q. 1977 54(1): 40-49.* The American Newspaper Publishers Association (ANPA) saw code-or-licensing provisions of the National Industrial Recovery Act (1933) as a threat to newspapers; ANPA and the National Recovery Administration negotiated and finally settled on a voluntary Daily Newspaper Code in which the government insisted it had no intention of abridging the rights of the free press.

775. Bogardus, Ralph F. READING—AND RE-READING—THE THIRTIES: A REVIEW ESSAY. *Southern Humanities Rev. 1980 14(4): 351-360.* Review essay of Stephen Spender's *The Thirties and After* (New York: Random House, 1978), Bernard Bergonzi's *Reading the Thirties* (Pittsburgh, Pa.: U. of Pittsburgh Pr., 1979), and *Social Poetry of the 1930s: A Selection,* edited by Jack Salzman and Leo Zanderer (Burt Franklin and Co., 1978).

776. Bonner, Thomas, Jr. A BIBLIOGRAPHICAL INTRODUCTION TO THE AMERICAN LITERATURE OF THE 1930'S AND THE BACKGROUNDS. *Bull. of Biblio. and Mag. Notes 1974 31(2): 57-66, 70.*

777. Brady, Gabriel M. LOU GEHRIG: THE IRON MAN. *Manuscripts 1980 32(2): 84-89.* Henry Louis Gehrig, the "Pride of the Yankees," was an old-fashioned hero, whose name still is synonymous with strength of character and integrity. After 14 years of consecutive play in 2,130 baseball games with the New York Yankees, first baseman Gehrig dropped out of the lineup for the first time, 2 May 1939. On 17 September 1939, Gehrig, a victim of amyotrophic lateral sclerosis, wrote an encouraging letter to another person named "Lou" who was troubled by illness. Based on an original letter; 9 notes.   D. A. Yanchisin

778. Brauer, Ralph A. WHEN THE LIGHTS WENT OUT: HOLLYWOOD, THE DEPRESSION AND THE THIRTIES. *J. of Popular Film and Television 1981 8(4): 18-29.* The films of 1930-40 reflect various cinematic responses to both the Depression and the New Deal—responses ranging from the cynical anarchy of the Marx Brothers to the good-natured optimism of Frank Capra—a variety that reflects conflicting popular attitudes.

779. Brinckmann, Christine. ZITIERTE DOKUMENTARITÄT: ÜBERLEGUNGEN ZUR VERFILMUNG DES ROMANS *THE GRAPES OF WRATH* [Borrowed documentarism: Reflections on the adaptation for the screen of the novel *The Grapes of Wrath*]. *Amerikastudien/ American Studies [West Germany] 1974 19(1): 88-110.* The problems arising from the combination of the documentary and fictional mode of presentation in John Steinbeck's novel *The Grapes of Wrath* (1939) are compounded in its adaptation for the screen in the 1939-40 Twentieth Century Fox production. Most of Steinbeck's original documentary material, except for occasional photographic reminiscences, was eliminated, leaving indirect, borrowed documentarism as the only way of presenting themes of direct social and political relevance. Economic pressures on the film industry and its unrealistic, fictionalized, and star-dominated tradition prevented a more direct documentary approach. 8 photos, 53 notes.   G. Bassler

780. Brooks, Cleanth. ALLEN TATE AND THE NATURE OF MODERNISM. *Southern Rev. 1976 12(4): 685-697.* Examines the continuity in artistic and intellectual development as well as overall unity of thought of novelist and poet Allen Tate; touches on the historicity of his writing, especially his view of modern western life, 1929-30.

781. Carringer, Robert L. THE SCRIPTS OF *CITIZEN KANE*. *Critical Inquiry 1978 5(2): 369-400.* Using evidence in the archives of RKO General Pictures in Hollywood, traces the seven stages of the preparation of the *Citizen Kane* filmscript, and establishes that Orson Welles's contribution to the script, attributed by others to Herman J. Mankiewicz, was not only substantive but definitive.

782. Christian, Henry A. FROM TWO HOMELANDS TO ONE WORLD: LOUIS ADAMIC'S SEARCH FOR UNITY. *Papers in Slovene Studies 1975: 133-144.* Louis Adamic (b. 1898 in Blato, Slovenia) was an American writer who realized that to be Americanized was to suffer the loss of valuable traditions, but that to remain totally foreign meant isolation. In an attempt to make America one nation, he began to concentrate on what he called the unity in diversity. His quest for unity in diversity was implicit in *Grandsons* (1935), made up a portion of *My America* (1938), and was the basis of his Nation of Nations series: *From*

Many Lands (1940), *Two-Way Passage* (1941), *What's Your Name?* (1942), and *A Nation of Nations* (1945). 20 notes.   T. Hočevar

783.   Clark, William Bedford.   "EZ SEZ": POUND'S "PITHY PROMUL-GATIONS."   *Antioch Rev. 1979 37(4): 420-427.* Discusses the 17 articles published by Ezra Pound as "Pithy Promulgations" under the heading "Ez Sez" in the Santa Fe newspaper, the *New Mexican,* March-October 1935.

784.   Coburn, Mark D.   AMERICA'S GREAT BLACK HOPE.   *Am. Heritage 1978 29(6): 82-91.* Recalls the two fights between black American Joe Louis and Max Schmeling in 1936 and 1938. Notes the international and racial impact of the fight. 9 illus.   J. F. Paul

785.   Cole, Martin.   FROM MOSCOW TO A COW PASTURE IN AMERICA.   *Am. West 1975 12(1): 10-13.* Narrates the July 1937 flight of three Russians from Moscow to California. The trans-polar flight established a new nonstop distance record.   D. L. Smith

786.   Coppock, James.   A CONVERSATION WITH ARTHUR BERGER. *Partisan Rev. 1981 48(3): 366-379.* In this interview, Arthur Berger, a contemporary composer and music critic, discussed his musical and journalistic background. Berger's observations on the Works Progress Administration and the fine arts are of particular historical importance. He completes the interview with comments on the university and music.   D. K. Pickens

787.   Corn, Joseph J.   AN AIRPLANE IN EVERY GARAGE.   *Am. Heritage 1981 32(5): 48-55.* History suggests that the dream of an airplane in every garage was an escapist fantasy, but US enthusiasm for private flying is undiminished. Examines the role of the federal government during the 1930's and that of individual enthusiasts like Eugene L. Vidal. 9 illus.   J. F. Paul

788.   Cowley, Malcolm.   WHAT BOOKS SURVIVE FROM THE 1930'S? *J. of Am. Studies [Great Britain] 1973 7(3): 293-300.* Lists novels and memoirs published 1932-42 which "reward a second reading." The list excludes proletarian novels and omits criticism and poetry because little was written that captured the "spirit" of the era. Except for Ernest Hemingway's work, Cowley omitted works about the "struggle against fascism" and intellectuals disillusioned after the Hitler-Stalin pact.   H. T. Lovin

789.   Crepeau, Richard C.   URBAN AND RURAL IMAGES IN BASE-BALL.   *J. of Popular Culture 1975 9(2): 315-324.* Baseball during the 1920's-30's stressed its rural origins and bound itself to the agrarian myth in American culture. *The Sporting News* reiterated baseball's connection with rural life and values and expressed resentment of the city. The concern with rural-urban issues declined in the 1930's and even more so in the 1940's. 28 notes.   J. D. Falk

790.   Culbert, David H.   "CROAK" CARTER: RADIO'S VOICE OF DOOM.   *Pennsylvania Mag. of Hist. and Biog. 1973 97(3): 287-317.* During the period 1935-38 Boake Carter, radio news commentator, achieved enormous popularity and influence through his caustic and slightly irresponsible criticism of Franklin D. Roosevelt and the New Deal. One of the first news analyzers on commercial radio, Carter saw his popularity and power go into a sudden and mysterious eclipse after 1938. In the process of successfully attacking Roosevelt's

administration, Carter revealed for the first time the immense power of radio as a medium for political criticism. Primary and secondary sources; 91 notes.

E. W. Carp

791. Culbert, David H. RADIO'S RAYMOND GRAM SWING: "HE ISN'T THE KIND OF MAN YOU WOULD CALL RAY." *Historian 1973 35(4): 587-606.* Raymond Gram Swing's career as a radio news commentator does more than identify a sequence of foreign and domestic assignments; it also describes the emergence of a profession. Swing's moral approach to the news and his scholarly analysis suggests much about the social history of the United States during the 1930's. Drawn from articles, addresses, memoirs, and the Swing papers in the Library of Congress; 83 notes.

N. W. Moen

792. Curtis, James C. and Grannen, Sheila. LET US NOW APPRAISE FAMOUS PHOTOGRAPHS: WALKER EVANS AND DOCUMENTARY PHOTOGRAPHY. *Winterthur Portfolio 1980 15(1): 1-23.* Walker Evans won recognition as a photographer before the publication of *Let Us Now Praise Famous Men* (1941). An analysis of James Agee's word pictures and Evans's photographs reveals numerous discrepancies. Evans rearranged his subjects and households for the sake of beauty and art. He wanted to show that southern sharecroppers were not helpless. His photographs attempted to portray the sharecroppers' strengths and dignity, not their weaknesses. Tenant farmers may not have shared Evans's artistic vision. Based on the Evans photographs, Farm Security Administration Collection, Lib. of Congress and other primary sources; 16 photos, 44 notes.

N. A. Kuntz

793. Dent, Tom. OCTAVE LILLY, JR.: IN MEMORIAM. *Crisis 1976 83(7): 243-244.* Octave Lilly was a successful black insurance executive as well as a southern black writer and poet. He worked for the WPA Federal Writers Project in the late 1930's. His poems were published in *Opportunity* and the *Crisis*. He did not write again until the late 1960's, at the age of 60. He died while some of his work was being published. Through his poetry he fought for economic survival and artistic expression for Negroes.

A. G. Belles

794. de Vries, John A. BILL MCMAHON, THE MOONEY "FLIVVER" AND THE GRAY GOOSE. *Am. Aviation Hist. Soc. J. 1979 24(4): 288-290.* Bill McMahon, an airline electrician, combined forces with designers Al Mooney and his brother Art Mooney in Denver, Colorado, to produce a monoplane named the Mooney *Flivver* in 1930, and then he joined the Lewis-American Aircraft Co. in Denver to build the *Gray Goose* in 1933.

795. Dieterich, Herbert R. THE NEW DEAL CULTURAL PROJECTS IN WYOMING: A SURVEY AND APPRAISAL. *Ann. of Wyoming 1980 52(2): 30-44.* Despite Wyoming citizens' general skepticism toward New Deal programs, they did accept a number of federal relief programs to provide jobs for the white-collar unemployed and culture for the masses. The largest and best known was the Federal Art Project of the Works Progress Administration, which was divided into four components—music, theater, writers, and art. Additional programs operating under the Public Works of Art Project, Treasury Relief Art Project, and the Treasury Section of Painting and Sculpture, provided murals, art classes, and community art centers across the state. Though the writers' project

ran less smoothly than the art projects, it produced a satisfactory book, *Wyoming: A Guide to Its History, Highways, and People* (1941). Based on National Archives materials; 4 illus., 46 notes.   M. L. Tate

796. Douglas, Ann. *STUDS LONIGAN* AND THE FAILURE OF HISTORY IN MASS SOCIETY: A STUDY IN CLAUSTROPHOBIA. *Am. Q. 1977 29(5): 487-505.* A study of James T. Farrell's fiction trilogy *Studs Lonigan* (New York: Signet Books, 1965; originally 1933-35) and its implications for society's sense of history, or loss of such a sense. Studs loses all sense of content in the forms of life he has been socialized to define as society; the Church, the family, the gang, have no substance. "His physical self had provided his only metaphor for hope." We can die without having lived, and our society has developed the mechanisms for insuring that very thing.   R. V. Ritter

797. Downs, Alexis. GEORGE MILBURN: OZARK FOLKLORE IN OKLAHOMA FICTION. *Chronicles of Oklahoma 1977 5(3): 309-323.* George Milburn's collection of short stories in *Oklahoma Town* (1931) and *Hobo's Hornbook* (1930) ensured his reputation as an inventive regional writer. Drawing many of his stories from Ozark folklore, he analyzed human folly satirically. His writings are compared to similar works of the 1920's and 1930's. Primary and secondary sources; 2 photos, 60 notes.   M. L. Tate

798. Dunaway, David King. UNSUNG SONGS OF PROTEST: THE COMPOSERS COLLECTIVE OF NEW YORK. *New York Folklore 1979 5(1-2): 1-19.* Discusses the beginnings and ideology of the left-wing Composers Collective in New York City, which existed from 1931 to 1936, and its evolution from an outspoken antifolk song ideology to its later use of folk song materials.

799. Ebner, Michael H. STUDENTS AS ORAL HISTORIANS. *Hist. Teacher 1976 9(2): 196-201.* Discusses the course "Oral and Community History" taught at Lake Forest College. The course deals with the experiences of the residents of Lake Forest, Illinois, during the Great Depression. Each student is responsible for background reading and field research which culminates in an interview, and the student then prepares a paper placing the material in context. The course is recommended for advanced undergraduates. Primary and secondary sources; 12 notes.   P. W. Kennedy

800. Eckey, Lorelei F. PILGRIMS OF THE IMPOSSIBLE. *Palimpsest 1980 61(1): 26-32.* Founded in Cedar Rapids, Iowa, the Universal Production Company trained young women to organize amateur theatricals for civic and church groups throughout the United States and Canada during the Depression.

801. Edmonds, Anthony O. THE SECOND LOUIS-SCHMELING FIGHT: SPORT, SYMBOL, AND CULTURE. *J. of Popular Culture 1973 7(1): 42-50.* Discusses the 1938 boxing match between Joe Louis and Max Schmeling (the latter from Germany), the racial image which Louis cultivated for the American white community, and the anti-Nazi sentiments generated by Louis' victory.
                                                                                    S

802. Eyster, Warren. CONVERSATIONS WITH JAMES AGEE. *Southern Rev. 1981 17(2): 346-357.* Recounts conversations with James Agee during 1935-41, paying special attention to Agee's personal magnetism, his desire to

upgrade man through literature, and his fascination with film and conviction that it was "the greatest opportunity in history for the artist to communicate through the eye and the ear feelings too delicate and too intricate and too simultaneous for words."

803. Fang, Irving E.   BOAKE CARTER, RADIO COMMENTATOR. *J. of Popular Culture 1978 12(2): 341-346.* Harold Thomas "Boake" Carter, a radio commentator during 1931-38, earned a reputation as a huckster for all the commercial products sponsoring his shows and as a controversial news broadcaster who challenged authority, particularly that of the US military.

804. Faulkner, Jim.   [MEMORIES OF WILLIAM FAULKNER].
MEMORIES OF BROTHER WILL.   *Southern Rev. 1980 16(4): 907-920.* William Faulkner's (1897-1962) brother reminisces about growing up in the 1930's in Oxford in north-central Mississippi.
NO PISTOL ROCKET.   *Southern Rev. 1981 17(2): 358-365.* Recounts incidents in which William Faulkner figured prominently, especially brother Will's reaction to his younger sibling's accident with a blank gun.

805. Fellman, David.   A GAG ON A RAG.   *Rev. in Am. Hist. 1982 10(1): 120-122.* Reviews Fred W. Friendly's *Minnesota Rag: The Dramatic Story of the Landmark Supreme Court Case that Gave New Meaning to Freedom of the Press* (1981), an analysis of *Near* v. *Minnesota* (US, 1931).

806. Filene, Peter.   RECAPTURING THE THIRTIES: HISTORY AS THEATER.   *Change 1974 6(1): 40-44.* A history professor tours his state with a Depression documentary, and learns something about humanizing the humanities.   J

807. Fine, David M.   JAMES M. CAIN AND THE LOS ANGELES NOVEL.   *Am. Studies 1979 20(1): 25-34.* Surveys James M. Cain's Los Angeles novels of the 1930's and 1940's, which have now been revived amid the rediscovery of thirties Los Angeles in text and film. The gangster and the tough guy pervade these works, reflecting the fantasies and nightmares of the depression years. Cain presented us with the major metaphors for the literary identity of Los Angeles—the road, the landscape, and the commonplace. Primary and secondary sources; 11 notes.   J. A. Andrew

808. Fishbein, Leslie.   A LOST LEGACY OF LABOR FILMS.   *Film and Hist. 1979 9(2): 33-40.* Films were made of the Communist-led mass marches of the unemployed, battles of eviction, milk strikes, and workers fighting against police and company thugs during the Depression by the Workers' Film and Photo League, a section of Workers' International Relief, when commercial filmmakers were avoiding controversy.

809. Frisch, Michael.   ORAL HISTORY AND *HARD TIMES:* A REVIEW ESSAY.   *Oral Hist. Rev. 1979: 70-79.* Reviewers impressed by the hope and spirit described by Studs Terkel in *Hard Times: An Oral History of the Great Depression* have overlooked the deeper questions posed by the work. Oral history's methodological dependence on memory inevitably qualifies its value as a primary historical source. The question of relativity in producing contemporary history also arises. (Reprinted from *Red Buffalo: A Journal of American Studies* 1972 1(2-3): 217-231).   D. A. Yanchisin

810.   Garcia, Lois B.   H. BEDFORD JONES: KING OF THE WOOD-PULPS.   *Lib. Chronicle of the U. of Texas 1978 (10): 73-75.* Discusses the correspondence between Erle Stanley Gardner and H. Bedford-Jones, the acknowledged leader among "woodpulp" story and novel writers during the 1920's and 1930's.

811.   Garvey, Timothy J.   FROM "GOD OF PEACE" TO "ONYX JOHN": THE PUBLIC MONUMENT AND CULTURAL CHANGE.   *Upper Midwest Hist. 1981 1: 4-26.* Carl Milles's enormous onyx war memorial *God of Peace,* commissioned for the St. Paul City Hall and Ramsey County Court House in 1932, demonstrates how cultural change has a significant impact upon public opinion of monumental sculpture. Originally disliked and scorned as too costly, not done by a local artist, and too modern, it eventually became a popular tourist attraction nicknamed the "Indian" and "Onyx John," a symbol of the American Indian. Based on government documents; 64 notes, 12 illus.   G. L. Olson

812.   Gehring, Wes D.   FRANK CAPRA—IN THE TRADITION OF WILL ROGERS AND OTHER CRACKER-BARREL YANKEES.   *Indiana Social Studies Q. 1981 34(2): 49-56.* Discusses Frank Capra's *Mr. Deeds Goes to Town* (1936), *You Can't Take It with You* (1938), *Mr. Smith Goes to Washington* (1939), and *Meet John Doe* (1941), which were "in the tradition of American humor's capable crackerbarrel Yankee"; the films concerned politics.

813.   Gehring, Wes D.   MCCAREY VS. CAPRA: A GUIDE TO AMERICAN FILM COMEDY OF THE '30'S.   *J. of Popular Film and Television 1978 7(1): 67-84.* Discusses two popular forms of comedic heroes in films in the 1930's: the antihero created by Leo McCarey and the backwoods Yankee created by Frank Capra.

814.   Gelber, Steven M.   WORKING TO PROSPERITY: CALIFORNIA'S NEW DEAL MURALS.   *California History 1979 58(2): 98-127.* Analyzes the work of California artists during the Great Depression. More than 200 artists painted murals for libraries, schools, courthouses, post offices, and other public buildings. As part of New Deal work relief, the federal government established five overlapping programs to sponsor mural art, of which the Federal Art program of the WPA is best known. The artists generally subscribed to the American Scene school of art which preceded the 1930's. This style was influenced by the Mexican muralists, but in style rather than substance. It included two appraoches, Regionalism and Social Realism. California artists were overwhelmingly Regionalist. They rejected Social Realism's disenchantment with the economic system in favor of scenes depicting faith in America's people, places, and history. Murals depicted healthy blue-collar workers and farmers at work, glorifications of the Hispanic era, and tributes to American pioneers. Very few California murals aroused public controversy; this suggest that the artists' celebration of American ideals reflected their own faith in the system despite the calamities of economic depression. Illus., 92 notes.   A. Hoffman

815.   Genauer, Emily.   AN ART DECO MEMORY.   *Horizon 1980 23(2): 60-63.* The interior design of Radio City Music Hall in New York City was planned, directed, and in part executed by architect Donald Deskey during 1929-34; Deskey did it and the apartment of the author (1937) in the art deco style.

816. Gillette, Howard. FILM AS ARTIFACT: *THE CITY* (1939). *Am. Studies (Lawrence, KS) 1977 18(2): 71-85.* Argues for the intelligent use of films to explore patterns in American culture, focusing on the documentary tradition. *The City* was an effort to draw attention to America's urban crisis in the 1930's —for exposure at the 1939 New York World's Fair. The film emphasized the need for city planning, and sought to recreate a semipastoral environment in an urban setting—the garden city. Planners tried to recast existing congested urban forms to decentralized suburban sectors and into regional frameworks. Primary and secondary sources; 6 illus., 38 notes.   J. A. Andrew

817. Gomery, Douglas. RETHINKING U.S. FILM HISTORY: THE DE-PRESSION DECADE AND MONOPOLY CONTROL. *Film and Hist. 1980 10(2): 32-38.* Discusses the concept of finance capitalism which originated in Russia with Lenin's *Imperialism: The Highest State of Capitalism* (1916), and criticizes the common acceptance of the belief that financiers gained control of the American film industry in the 1930's, suggesting instead that monopolistic corporations, with the government's support, controlled the industry.

818. Gordon, Caroline. LIFE AT BENFOLLY, 1930-1931: LETTERS OF CAROLINE GORDON TO A NORTHERN FRIEND, SALLY WOOD. *Southern Rev. 1980 16(2): 301-336.* Reprints Caroline Gordon's letters written from Benfolly, near Nashville, Tennessee, a "gathering place for Southern writers" to Sally Wood in Rochester, New York.

819. Gossard, Wayne H., Jr. THREE RING CIRCUS: THE ZACK MILL-ER-TOM MIX LAWSUITS, 1929-1934. *Chronicles of Oklahoma 1980 58(1): 3-16.* In April 1929, cowboy film star Tom Mix allegedly entered into a verbal agreement with Zack Miller to join the latter's 101 Ranch Real Wild West Show. Miller initiated a breach of contract suit when Mix subsequently signed with the rival Sells-Floto Circus. Hounded by the complicated legal procedures, Mix settled out of court in December 1934, but the $9,500 came too late to save Miller's 101 Ranch and the Wild West Show from bankruptcy. Based on archives of Miller Brothers' 101 Ranch; 6 photos, 31 notes.   M. L. Tate

820. Gray, Ralph D. *GAS BUGGY* REVISITED: A "LOST" NOVEL OF KOKOMO, INDIANA. *Indiana Mag. of Hist. 1974 70(1): 24-43.* Examines Robert Patterson's 1933 novel *Gas Buggy,* which recreates with considerable accuracy the careers of Elwood Haynes and Elmer Apperson, two Indiana pioneers in the automobile industry. Compares the factual basis of the novel with the facts of the true story and points out divergences as well as similarities. How the author learned what he knew remains a mystery, and the book fails any stiff test of historical accuracy; yet the book offers valuable insights into the people and events discussed. Based on secondary sources; 9 illus., 39 notes.
                                                                N. E. Tutorow

821. Greene, Murray. THE ALASKAN FLIGHT OF 1934: A SPECTACU-LAR OFFICIAL FAILURE. *Aerospace Hist. 1977 24(1): 15-19.* Discusses the Alaskan flight by 10 B-10's in 1934 and the lack of official recognition which resulted in the "wounding" of the flight personnel involved. "Recognition of the Alaskan fliers was swallowed up in the Byzantine military politics of that era." The flight from the District of Columbia to Fairbanks, Alaska, was a huge

success. It was the first time such a feat had been accomplished and occurred when the US Army Air Corps was reeling from its disastrous attempt to carry the mail. General Douglas MacArthur, as Chief of Staff, reacted to the threat of another Billy Mitchell incident. The War Department General Staff was also examining the Baker Board report which denied that the Air Corps should be separated from the Army. The effect on the Alaskan flight personnel was that the recommended award of the Distinguished Flying Cross was first downgraded to a letter of recommendation from the Secretary of War and then further downgraded by General MacArthur to one letter to "Hap" Arnold, the flight leader, from the Adjantant General in the name of the Secretary of War. The actions of Arnold in this matter also come under indictment. 4 photos, map.

C. W. Ohrvall

822. Gustafson, Richard. THE VOGUE OF THE SCREEN BIOGRAPHY. *Film and Hist. 1977 7(3): 49-58.* Discusses films, 1929-49, which concentrated on serious biographies of famous and historical figures.

823. Harris, Neil. ARTISTS OF CAPITALISM. *Rev. in Am. Hist. 1981 9(1): 106-111.* Review essay of Jeffrey L. Meikle's *Twentieth Century Limited: Industrial Design in America, 1925-1939* (1979).

824. Havig, Alan R. CRITIC FROM WITHIN: FRED ALLEN VIEWS RADIO. *J. of Popular Culture 1978 12(2): 328-340.* Disdain for the incursion of commercialism and the bureaucratic structure of the radio broadcasting industry brought fame to Fred Allen, 1932-49. He was a humorist who criticized the radio industry during a period when little criticism was generated otherwise.

825. Hellerstein, Alice. THE 1936 OLYMPICS: A U.S. BOYCOTT THAT FAILED. *Potomac Rev. 1981 (21): 1-9.* Germany was awarded the 1936 Olympic Games shortly before the Nazis came to power in 1933. Soon after, a series of discriminatory laws against its Jewish citizens made it obvious that Nazi Germany would also attempt to exclude German Jews from competing in the 11th Olympiad. In response, a three-year debate took place in the United States between officials of several athletic associations about sending a team to Berlin. Beset by its own economic problems in the Depression, the United States could not muster the moral force to demonstrate by means of a boycott its opposition to a totalitarian regime that had repudiated the democratic ideals of the Olympic Games. Based primarily on original sources; 35 notes.   B. Reiner

826. Hemenway, Robert. FOLKLORE FIELD NOTES FROM ZORA NEALE HURSTON. *Black Scholar 1976 7(7): 39-46.* Zora Neale Hurston (1901-60) wrote four novels, two collections of folklore, numerous short stories and essays, and an autobiography. As a member of the Florida Federal Writers' Project, she began editing a book on Negroes in Florida but left the project in 1939, never completing the book. Included are some of the notes, never published before, on her projected volume. Primary and secondary sources; 11 notes.

B. D. Ledbetter

827. Hightower, Paul. A STUDY OF THE MESSAGES IN DEPRESSION-ERA PHOTOS. *Journalism Q. 1980 57(3): 495-497.* Compares the impressions photographer Russell Lee attaches to his Depression-era photographs with the impressions of selected subjects. 8 photos, table, 4 notes.   J. S. Coleman

828. Hirsch, Jerrold. READING AND COUNTING. *Rev. in Am. Hist. 1980 8(3): 312-317.* Review essay of Paul D. Escott's *Slavery Remembered: A Record of Twentieth-Century Slave Narratives* (Chapel Hill: U. of North Carolina Pr., 1979); the narratives were recorded by interviewers from the Federal Writer's Project during the New Deal.

829. Hodgkinson, Anthony W. *FORTY-SECOND STREET* NEW DEAL: SOME THOUGHTS ABOUT EARLY FILM MUSICALS. *J. of Popular Film 1975 4(1): 33-46.* Discusses musical films of the 1930's. S

830. Holman, C. Hugh. THOMAS WOLFE, *SCRIBNER'S MAGAZINE,* AND "THE BEST NOUVELLE". In James Woodress, ed., et al., *Essays Mostly on Periodical Publishing in America: A Collection in Honor of Clarence Gohdes. (Durham, N.C.: Duke U. Press, 1973), pp. 205-220.* Even Wolfe's "severest critics have recognized his ability to realize fully and intensely a dramatic scene or situation." His method of writing was to fit brief and self-contained units into larger structures. "Maxwell Perkins's insistence that *Look Homeward, Angel* should be followed by a 'big book' was injurious to Wolfe's career." The short novel was his best medium and fortunately for Wolfe, it was a form in which *Scribner's Magazine* was interested. Discusses many short novels published by *Scribner's* in the early 1930's, including a number by Wolfe. 60 notes.

E. P. Stickney

831. Honey, Maureen. IMAGES OF WOMEN IN *THE SATURDAY EVENING POST* 1931-1936. *J. of Popular Culture 1976 10(2): 352-358.* Women struggling to overcome the handicaps associated with being female in a masculine world were popular themes in *Post* fiction during the 1930's, but traditional she-devil and girl-next-door images conveyed the message of their "proper" role. Career and marriage were not to be mixed. Most positive images were exclusively of middle class whites; images of blacks and lower class whites were almost invariably negative. Primary and secondary sources; 2 notes. D. G. Nielson

832. Hook, Sidney. LETTERS FROM GEORGE SANTAYANA. *Am. Scholar 1976-77 46(1): 76-84.* Series of letters sent during 1929-38 from George Santayana to Sidney Hook. The letters reflect on books that Hook had sent to Santayana. They illustrate the fundamental difference between Santayana's sympathy with 20th-century totalitarianism and Hook's opposition to it.

F. F. Harling

833. Hoopes, James. MODERNIST CRITICISM AND TRANSCENDENTAL LITERATURE. *New England Q. 1979 52(4): 451-466.* Ivor Armstrong Richards's (b. 1893) language theory and his modernist literary criticism detrimentally influenced James Agee's (1909-55) *Let Us Now Praise Famous Men.* Agee was led to attempt to give an illusion of embodiment, rather than to address the subject itself. Discusses the style of Agee's prose. Based on Agee's writing; 29 notes. J. C. Bradford

834. Hundley, Patrick D. *PEOPLE OF THE CUMBERLAND* (1937): AN ATTEMPT AT SYNTHETIC DOCUMENTARY. *Film & Hist. 1976 6(3): 56-62.* Discusses *People of the Cumberland,* a 1937 documentary film about the Cumberland Mountains region of Tennessee; though not pictorially accurate, the film touches on historical events of the 1930's and realistically portrays the emotional and political atmosphere of the area and era. 21 notes.

835. Hux, Samuel. THE NECESSITY OF IRRELEVANT TRADITIONS. *Antioch Rev. 1980 38(1): 108-118.* Discusses Allen Tate's agrarianism of the 1930's, which espoused intellectual, cultural, and moral traditions as an antidote to the alienation imposed by modern industrial society.

836. Isenberg, Michael T. AN AMBIGUOUS PACIFISM: A RETROSPECTIVE ON WORLD WAR I FILMS, 1930-1938. *J. of Popular Film 1975 4(2): 98-115.* American films between the wars show a strain of pacifism but they do not question the conduct of war or the necessity of war in times of extreme crisis.
S

837. Jayne, Edward. ME, STEINBECK, AND ROSE OF SHARON'S BABY. *Amerikastudien/Am. Studies [West Germany] 1975 20(2): 281-305.* Like literary criticism, fiction involves a dialectic of blindness and insight, but its duplicity is compounded by distortive literary techniques suggestive of Gombrich's theory of artistic illusion. For example, Steinbeck's *The Grapes of Wrath,* supposedly realistic in its treatment of the plight of Okies, illustrates a number of distortive techniques, including its one-dimensional characterization, its exaggeration of dramatic confrontations, its combination of the archetypal wilderness quest with strike novel conventions popular during the thirties, and its use of "instantaneous description" to intensify the effect of thwarted expectations, bringing economic contradiction into style itself. But its most extraordinary deception is in the radical "truth" Steinbeck wanted to convey that Okies were being driven to the choice between destruction and revolutionary activism, since in fact they were soon provided with jobs by World War II and then kept employed by the Cold War, sustaining their collective faith in the American way of life. So Steinbeck used lies of technique in order to convey a bigger lie in his message, though of course history might once again bring us to such a catastrophe. For this reason the novel remains a remarkable document of depression, the nightmarish alternative to our current tottering prosperity.
J

838. Johnson, Abby Arthur and Johnson, Ronald W. REFORM AND REACTION: BLACK LITERARY MAGAZINES IN THE 1930'S. *North Dakota Q. 1978 46(1): 5-18. Challenge* magazine and Claude McKay's literary organization dramatize the conflicting ideologies and artistic concerns of black writers in the 1930's.

839. Johnson, Glen M. THE PASTNESS OF *ALL THE KING'S MEN. Am. Literature 1980 51(4): 553-557.* Robert Penn Warren's *All The King's Men* (1946) contains a rhetorical structure that involves the reader as a participant in history on two levels, fictional and factual. On one level, many events in the novel parallel actual events in the life of Huey P. Long. But on another level, the novel's structure suggests a parallel to 1930's antecedents of World War II. Willie Stark's state (Huey Long's Louisiana) is analogous to world events of the 1930's. 6 notes.
T. P. Linkfield

840. Jones, Alfred Haworth. *ULYSSES'* AMERICAN ODYSSEY. *Am. Hist. Illus. 1982 17(3): 10-17.* Account of *United States* v. *One Book Called "Ulysses"* (US, 1932), which was promoted by Random House publishing company owner, Bennett Cerf, and defended by civil liberties lawyer Morris Ernst in order to legalize the publication of an American edition of James Joyce's *Ulysses,* first published in 1922 in France.

841. Jones, James P. NANCY DREW, WASP SUPER GIRL OF THE 1930'S. *J. of Popular Culture 1973 6(4): 707-717.* Nancy Drew books, juvenile formula fiction, abounded in racial and national stereotypes and avoided direct political comment, but opposed New Deal welfare policies. Many titles have been rewritten in the 1960's-70's.   S

842. Josephson, Matthew. LEANE ZUGSMITH: THE SOCIAL NOVEL OF THE THIRTIES. *Southern Rev. 1975 11(3): 530-552.* Short biography incorporating the works of Leane Zugsmith, a woman writer of the 1930's whose work fell into the category of the social novel.

843. Kass, D. A. THE ISSUE OF RACISM AT THE 1936 OLYMPICS. *J. of Sport Hist. 1976 3(3): 223-235.* Evaluates the major arguments for or against the US-proposed boycott of the 1936 Olympic Games at Berlin. After the International Olympic Committee (IOC) decided on 7 June 1933 to keep the games in Germany, the arguments concerning discrimination against Jews were ineffective. The American controversy became an argument over the best way the United States could show the Nazis that their ideology was wrong. One viewpoint was to boycott the games, showing US disapproval of the Nazis. The opposing view was that America's participation could destroy the myth of Aryan superiority, and Jesse Owens did that when he won four gold medals. 43 notes.

M. Kaufman

844. Kehl, James A. DEFENDER OF THE FAITH: ORPHAN ANNIE AND THE CONSERVATIVE TRADITION. *South Atlantic Q. 1977 76(4): 454-465.* *Little Orphan Annie* began as an entertainment cartoon strip, but its creator, Harold Gray, soon converted it into editorials against the New Deal. Annie and "Daddy" Warbucks represented the traditional virtues of the 1920's "rugged individualism" and they continually fought the pseudocommunists, minions of labor unions, and federal government regulation. Annie usually took on the small-time cheats and grafters while "Daddy" was pitted against union officials and government bureaucrats. Gray's cartoons, although popular, garnered him lawsuits from local officials, parodies from the socialists, and cancellation from some newspapers during World War II for his attacks on wartime rationing and planning.

W. L. Olbrich

845. Kennedy, Richard S. THOMAS WOLFE'S LAST MANUSCRIPT. *Harvard Lib. Bull. 1975 23(2): 203-211.* Thomas Wolfe did plan the scheme for the novel which appears as his last manuscript, and his secretary did type the title pages. Refutes published allegations to the contrary. Based on the MS. in Harvard University's Houghton Library; 4 illus., 26 notes.

L. Smith

846. Klug, Michael A. JAMES AGEE AND THE FURIOUS ANGEL. *Can. Rev. of Am. Studies [Canada] 1980 11(3): 313-326.* In the 20th century, American novelists have adopted objectivity as an ideal, although it forces them to capture and accept the reality of common people's lives as would a camera. But that course provokes stresses for writers who face contradictory imperatives of their art and the reality of ordinary life. A writer particularly torn by such conflict, James Agee (1909-55) wrestled with the problem in *Let Us Now Praise Famous Men* (New York, 1941). Based on Agee's writings and secondary sources; 5 photos, 5 notes.

H. T. Lovin

847. Kobal, John. HOLLYWOOD PORTRAITS. *Society 1981 18(3): 77-81.* Describes the work of Hollywood studio photographers as it helped extol and glorify the star system of the 1930's in America.

848. Koolhaas, Rem. THE FUTURE'S PAST. *Wilson Q. 1979 3(1): 135-140.* Examines several actual and proposed examples of architecture designed by Ivan Leonidov and Konstantin Melnikov which aimed at creating self-contained, therapeutic environments for work, research, and recreation; covers 1929-31.

849. Kowalke, Kim H. DER LINDBERGHFLUG: KURT WEILL'S MUSICAL TRIBUTE TO LINDBERGH. *Missouri Hist. Soc. Bull. 1977 33(3): 193-196.* Analyzes *Der Lindberghflug* and describes radio broadcast performances of it in Europe and America in 1929, 1930, and 1931. The composition, a cantata, is one of the major writings of Kurt Weill (1900-50) and Bertolt Brecht (1898-1956). In 1950 the cantata was retitled, *Der Ozeanflug* in accord with Brecht's wishes. Secondary sources; 12 notes. H. T. Lovin

850. Kramer, Victor A. AGEE'S SKEPTICISM ABOUT ART AND AUDIENCE. *Southern Rev. 1981 17(2): 320-331.* James Agee's frequently expressed skepticism about the possibilities of language (especially within a society where materialism remained the core of activities) interacted with his life and creative work and the combination generated a significant body of writing which judged language, culture, and contemporary civilization in often critical terms.

851. Kruger, Arnd. "FAIR PLAY FOR AMERICAN ATHLETES": A STUDY IN ANTI-SEMITISM. *Can. J. of Hist. of Sport and Physical Educ. [Canada] 1978 9(1): 42-57.* In his 1935 pamphlet "Fair Play for American Athletes" and elsewhere, American Olympic Committee President Avery Brundage, in opposing the proposed boycott of the 1936 Olympic Games to be held in Berlin, indulged in anti-Semitism.

852. Kusenda, Mike. THE KEITH RIDER R-6: BEHIND THE EIGHT BALL. *Am. Aviation Hist. Soc. J. 1981 26(1): 15-25.* Discusses racing plane designer Keith Rider's desire to build the fastest plane in the world during the 1930's, and describes Rider's specifications and design of the plane, which was built during 1936-37.

853. Lal, Malashri. THE SPANISH CIVIL WAR AND ERNEST HEMINGWAY: FROM REPORTAGE TO NOVEL. *Indian J. of Am. Studies [India] 1980 10(1): 65-77.* Distinguishes Ernest Hemingway's journalistic accounts of the Spanish Civil War (1936-39) from his novel *For Whom the Bell Tolls* (1940). The nonfictional accounts are propagandistic, but his novel reflects his commitment to the code of good fiction writing. Hemingway's novel emerges from his propagandist journalism but transcends the genre. 47 notes. L. V. Eid

854. Landon, Brooks. "NOT SOLVE IT BUT BE IN IT": GERTRUDE STEIN'S DETECTIVE STORIES AND THE MYSTERY OF CREATIVITY. *Am. Literature 1981 53(3): 487-498.* *Blood On the Dining-Room Floor* (1933), the result of Gertrude Stein's long interest in detective stories, marked the beginning of an important phase in her literary career. She was attempting to reconcile the conflict in her writing between human nature and the human mind. Stein was

then struggling to adjust to her new-found literary success and to redefine her role as a writer. 28 notes. T. P. Linkfield

855. Leab, Daniel J. WRITING HISTORY WITH FILM: TWO VIEWS OF THE 1937 STRIKE AGAINST GENERAL MOTORS BY THE UAW. *Labor Hist. 1980 21(1): 102-112.* Reviews two films: *The Great Sitdown* (1976) by British filmmaker Stephen Peet and *With Babies and Banners* (1978) by Lorraine Gray and Lynn Goldfarb. The films rewrite history from the United Automobile Workers of America (UAW) strikers' and women's perspectives. 20 notes. L. L. Athey

856. Lichty, Lawrence W. and Bohn, Thomas W. RADIO'S *MARCH OF TIME*: DRAMATIZED NEWS. *Journalism Q. 1974 51(3): 458-462.* Fred Smith's early programs as director of radio station WLW in Cincinnati led to national dramatization of news on *March of Time* and further experimental news and documentary coverage on radio in the 1930's. S

857. Lundén, Rolf. THEODORE DREISER AND THE NOBEL PRIZE. *Am. Literature 1978 50(2): 216-229.* In posterity's judgment, the Nobel selection committee in 1930 robbed Theodore Dreiser of the Nobel Prize for Literature which rightfully belonged to him, not Sinclair Lewis. Each author coveted the prize, and each had his backers in Europe. Lewis's books, however, sold much better in Europe than did Dreiser's, and Lewis was more proficient at cultivating the Swedish public. The Nobel committee chose Lewis over Dreiser in 1930 because Lewis's caricatures conformed to Swedish preconceptions of Americans. Although Dreiser's *An American Tragedy* was deeper and closer to the truth, Dreiser was less popular in Europe as a writer. The Nobel Prize in 1930 rewarded the clever satirist, not the plodding pathfinder. 41 notes. T. P. Linkfield

858. Lynn, Kenneth S. ONLY YESTERDAY. *Am. Scholar 1980 49(4): 513-518.* Traces the motivations and prejudices of journalist Frederick Lewis Allen's best-selling book of 1931, *Only Yesterday.* Allen's view of history derived from his Puritan heritage, professional training, and political liberalism. F. F. Harling

859. Macmillan, Robert. HOLLYWOOD IN THE 1930'S: A DISCUSSION OF PAULINE KAEL. *Hist. J. of Film, Radio and Television [Great Britain] 1981 1(2): 151-159.* Reviews Pauline Kael's *Raising Kane,* which discusses the writing and making of films in Hollywood in the 1930's using *Citizen Kane* as a model.

860. Magnusson, Tor. FATS WALLER WITH GENE AUSTIN ON THE RECORD. *J. of Jazz Studies 1976 4(1): 75-83.* Discusses the musical collaboration of singer-composer Gene Austin and jazz pianist (Thomas) "Fats" Waller, 1929-39.

861. Maland, Charles. *MR. DEEDS* AND THE AMERICAN CONSENSUS. *Film and Hist. 1978 8(1): 10-15.* Frank Capra in his 1936 film *Mr. Deeds Goes to Town* reflects the changing social order in America and portrays capitalism as evil, but with the potential of benefiting the masses.

862. Marcus, Steven. DASHIELL HAMMETT AND THE CONTINEN-
TAL OP. *Partisan R. 1974 41(3): 362-377.* Explores the central tension of
Hammett's career during the 1930's between his Marxist politics and the demands of being a pulp writer. Because his writing approached the status of
literature, Hammett never solved the conflict between means and ends. His hero,
the Continental OP (or Sam Spade), parallels the moral tensions in Hammett's
own life.   D. K. Pickens

863. Marvin, Carolyn. AVERY BRUNDAGE AND AMERICAN PAR-
TICIPATION IN THE 1936 OLYMPIC GAMES. *J. of Am. Studies [Great
Britain] 1982 16(1): 81-105.* President of the American Olympic Committee from
1929 to 1953, Avery Brundage claimed that sports remained healthy by nurturing
excellence and individualism; hence, sports must remain apart from politics. In
1936, controversy brewed over the proposal that the US Olympic team boycott
Olympic events at Berlin to protest Nazi Germany's treatment of Jews. Brundage
blocked a withdrawal of the American team, insisting on American participation
for political reasons. He accused Eastern liberals and Jewish interest groups of
promoting the boycott, and Brundage believed that democracy gained advantages
over Communism if the Berlin Olympics were staged successfully. Based on the
Avery Brundage Papers at the University of Illinois; 85 notes.

864. Massu, Claude. BROADACRE CITY DE FRANK LLOYD
WRIGHT: L'UTOPIE D'UNE AMÉRIQUE AGRAIRE ET ANTI-
URBAINE [Frank Lloyd Wright's Broadacre City: America's agrarian and
antiurban utopia]. *Rev. Française d'Études Américaines [France] 1981 6(11):
55-65.* Frank Lloyd Wright's 1935 Broadacre City project and prototype in
Bartlesville, Oklahoma, was not only a means to alleviate the economic crisis but
a new instance in the current trend toward decentralization that goes back to the
very origins of the American nation.

865. Maurer, Joyce C. FEDERAL THEATRE IN CINCINNATI. *Cincin-
nati Hist. Soc. Bull. 1974 32(1-2): 29-45.* Discusses plays staged by the Federal
Theatre Project in conjunction with the Works Progress Administration in Cincinnati 1935-39, including the employment of actors.

866. McGinty, Brian. A PINKERTON MAN IN SPADES. *Westways 1977
69(3): 28-31.* Discusses the career of Dashiell Hammett, a detective writer whose
main character, Sam Spade, and whose locale, San Francisco, became archetypes
for detective novels of the 1930's.

867. Medhurst, Martin J. and Benson, Thomas W. *THE CITY:* THE RHET-
ORIC OF RHYTHM. *Communication Monographs 1981 48(1): 54-72.* Discusses Ralph Steiner and Willard van Dyke's 1939 documentary of the problems
confronting urban planners, *The City,* an appeal to an idealistic garden city of
a type envisioned by President Franklin D. Roosevelt and one of several documentary films of the 1930's concerned with both a critique and an idealization
of the United States.

868. Meehan, James. BOJANGLES OF RICHMOND: "HIS DANCING
FEET BROUGHT JOY TO THE WORLD." *Virginia Cavalcade 1978 27(3):
100-113.* Discusses the career in film, radio, and on Broadway of black dancing
star Bill "Bojangles" Robinson, 1930's-49.

869. Meehan, James. SEED OF DESTRUCTION: THE DEATH OF THOMAS WOLFE. *South Atlantic Q. 1974 73(2): 173-183.* Thomas Wolfe's death in 1938 was due to an illness diagnosed as an incurable "military tuberculosis of the brain." A new theory has recently developed: that he died of a fungus disease, coccidioidomycosis, also known as desert or valley fungus, on which little research was done until after World War II. 6 notes.   E. P. Stickney

870. Meikle, Jeffrey L. NORMAN BEL GEDDES AND THE POPULARIZATION OF STREAMLINING. *Lib. Chronicle of the U. of Texas 1980 (13): 91-110.* Reviews the life of the industrial designer Norman Bel Geddes, focusing on the 1930's, when he emerged as the main popularizer of streamlining with novelties such as the teardrop auto and the General Motor's Futurama at the Chicago World's Fair in 1939.

871. Menig, Harry. WOODY GUTHRIE: THE OKLAHOMA YEARS, 1912-1929. *Chronicles of Oklahoma 1975 53(2): 239-265.* Popular folksinger and journalist Woody Guthrie grew up in Okemah, Oklahoma, an oil boom town which had a lasting effect upon his life and music. A close attachment to his parents made him a life-long advocate of strong family ties, and his small town upbringing made him conscious of the rights of the common man. From Okemah's black community he also developed an appreciation of the blues which became an integral part of his ballad style. Deeply affected by the calamitous Dust Bowl and Great Depression, Guthrie represented a national voice for the dispossessed and their search for self-respect. Based on primary sources; interviews, 3 photos, 53 notes.   M. L. Tate

872. Menig, Harry. WOODY GUTHRIE—*THE COLUMBIA* AND THE B.P.A. DOCUMENTARY: *HYDRO. Film and Hist. 1975 5(2): 1-10.* Describes Woody Guthrie's musical contributions (1939-1949) to the Bonneville Power Administration's documentary *The Columbia* (1949).   S

873. Michelet, Jean. THOMAS WOLFE, OU L'AUTOBIOGRAPHE MALGRE LUI [Thomas Wolfe, or the reluctant autobiographer]. *Rev. Française d'Etudes Américaines [France] 1982 7(14): 225-236.* Describes the autobiographical content in the works of novelist Thomas Wolfe, especially *Look Homeward, Angel,* and discusses Wolfe's place in the American literary scene of the 1920's-30's. French.

874. Miller, Jeanne-Marie A. SUCCESSFUL FEDERAL THEATRE DRAMAS BY BLACK PLAYWRIGHTS. *Black Scholar 1970 10(10): 79-85.* Examines the plays produced by the Federal Theatre Project, established by the Works Progress Administration in 1935, such as Frank Wilson's *Brother Mose,* Hughes Allison's *The Trial of Dr. Beck,* and Theodore Ward's *Big White Fog.*

875. Morrison, David E. KULTUR AND CULTURE: THE CASE OF THEODOR W. ADORNO AND PAUL F. LAZARSFELD. *Social Res. 1978 45(2): 331-355.* Different ideas of the meaning of culture and cultural improvement and specifically about the place of culture in American social organization of the 1930's between Theodor W. Adorno (hired by Paul F. Lazarsfeld to supervise a study of music in American culture) within the Rockefeller-funded Princeton Radio Research Project led in 1939 to the demise of Adorno's project, as did Adorno's difficult personality and research methods.

876.   Morson, Gary Saul.   THE WAR OF THE WELL(E)S.   *J. of Communication 1979 29(3): 10-20.* Examines Orson Welles's radio dramatization of H. G. Wells's *The War of the Worlds* of 1938, noting his use of metafictional devices and his awareness of the power of mass media on public behavior.

877.   Morton, Marian J.   "MY DEAR, I DON'T GIVE A DAMN": SCARLETT O'HARA AND THE GREAT DEPRESSION.   *Frontiers 1980 5(3): 52-56.* Margaret Mitchell's Scarlett O'Hara had relevance for women during the Depression, particularly in their concern with mere survival, and in choosing "between new and old roles, between earning money and maintaining custom."

878.   Myers, Carol Fairbanks.   SUPPLEMENT TO "A BIBLIOGRAPHICAL INTRODUCTION TO THE AMERICAN LITERATURE OF THE 1930'S AND THE BACKGROUNDS": BLACK AMERICAN LITERATURE.   *Bull. of Biblio. and Mag. Notes 1977 34(2): 68-72.* Prompted by an earlier article (see abstract 12A:5737). Includes anthologies, poetry, drama, novels, short stories, detective fiction, autobiography, criticism of history, poetry, drama, fiction, and periodicals during the 1930's, dealing with black authors and critics.

879.   Naison, Mark.   RICHARD WRIGHT & THE COMMUNIST PARTY.   *Radical Am. 1979 13(1): 60-63.* In *American Hunger,* completed in 1944 as the last third of his autobiographical novel, *Black Boy,* Richard Wright discussed his experiences during the Depression in Chicago and detailed his "effort to function as a creative intellectual within the [Communist] Party during his Chicago years."

880.   Narber, Gregg R. and DeLong, Lea Rosson.   THE NEW DEAL MURALS IN IOWA.   *Palimpsest 1982 63(3): 86-96.* Reproduces some of the 50 public murals, painted in Iowa as part of the New Deal's efforts to put people to work through agencies such as the Works Progress Administration, the Public Works of Art Project, and the Treasury Relief Art Project.

881.   Nelson, Joyce.   *MR. SMITH GOES TO WASHINGTON:* CAPRA, POPULISM, AND COMIC-STRIP ART.   *J. of Popular Film 1974 3(3): 245-255.* Discusses the images of American politics set forth in Frank Capra's *Mr. Smith Goes To Washington.*   S

882.   Nochlin, Linda.   FLORINE STETTHEIMER: ROCOCO SUBVERSIVE.   *Art in Am. 1980 68(7): 64-83.* The work of American rococo artist Florine Stettheimer is a combination of social consciousness and camp; focuses on the interest in black culture portrayed in her paintings and the sets and costumes she designed for the original 1934 production of Gertrude Stein and Virgil Thomson's *Four Saints in Three Acts* with an all-black cast, and her four *Cathedrals* series celebrating American life as exemplified by New York City, on which she worked from 1929 until her death in 1944.

883.   Nye, Russel B.   THE THIRTIES: THE FRAMEWORK OF BELIEF.   *Centennial R. 1975 19(2): 37-58.* Four major intellectual trends characterize the 1930's: "the discovery of culture; the rediscovery of sin; the acceptance of relativism; the promise of plenty." After publication of Ruth Benedict's *Patterns of Culture* (1934), the concept of culture came to mean "the relationship between

each human being, who had his own specific hereditary environment and particular life history, and the culture in which he lived." The relativism advocated by Benedict was reinforced by Carl Becker in the *Heavenly City of the Eighteenth Century Philosophers* (1932), in which he called for recognition of facts and truth as relative, "changing entities, the character and significance of which can be fully grasped only by regarding them in an endless process of differentiation, of unfolding, of waste and repair." Sin came to hold a new meaning in Reinhold Niebuhr's *Moral Man and Immoral Society* (1932), which directed theology toward the concern of man with God and away from a man-centered faith. A new definition of wealth evolved from John M. Keynes's *The General Theory of Employment, Interest, and Money* (1936), which "shifted the focus of economic theory from prices and costs to income and investment, or from the machinery of the marketplace to the distribution of income and the use people made of it." The long-run effect of these ideas on American intellectual life is as profound as the impact of the New Deal on politics and the function of government. 15 notes.

A. R. Stoesen

884.   O'Connor, John.   "KING COTTON": THE FEDERAL THEATRE PROJECT.   *Southern Exposure 1978 6(1): 74-81.* Discusses the presentations of plays by the Federal Theatre Project during the New Deal. Dealing with contemporary southern themes, the plays were almost always portrayed in northern locales. Only occasionally did southern FTP units produce plays concerning their own region and history. Exceptions were the New Orleans unit's production of *African Vineyard* dealing with race relations in a South African setting, and the Birmingham, Alabama, unit's presentations of *Great Day* dealing with blacks on chain gangs and of *Swamp Mud* covering the panorama of black history. The "living newspaper" plays, incorporating contemporary factual subject matter within a dramatic structure, included *King Cotton,* written by Betty Smith, Robert Finch, William Perry and Clemon White. The play, never produced by the FTP, dealt with the subject of poor white and black farmers and textile workers in the South oppressed and exploited by the cotton economy.

N. Lederer

885.   Orlin, Lena Cowen.   *NIGHT OVER TAOS:* MAXWELL ANDERSON'S SOURCES AND ARTISTRY.   *North Dakota Q. 1980 48(3): 12-25.* Discusses the plot and style of Maxwell Anderson's 1932 play, *Night Over Taos,* based on two of six articles in *American Mercury* (May-October 1931), entitled "Rio Grande," about the civilization of Spanish New Mexico, 18th and 19th centuries.

886.   Orvell, Miles.   LETTING THE FACTS SPEAK FOR THEMSELVES: THIRTIES AMERICA.   *Am. Scholar 1974 43(4): 671-678.* Reviews three works on the cultural history and rediscovery of the 1930's through documentary expression (photography, radio, film, reportage), and the Writers' Project of the Works Progress Administration: F. Jack Hurley's *Portrait of a Decade: Roy Stryker and the Development of Documentary Photography in the Thirties* (Baton Rouge: Louisiana State U. Press, 1972); Jerre Mangione's *The Dream and the Deal: The Federal Writers' Project, 1935-1943* (Boston: Little, Brown, 1972); and William Stott's *Documentary Expression and Thirties America* (New York: Oxford U. Press, 1973).

C. W. Olson

887. Osgood, Richard. THE BIRTH OF THE LONE RANGER. *Horizon 1981 24(3): 52-55.* Discusses the beginnings of radio's most popular show, the *Lone Ranger,* first written by Fran Striker, after George Trendle, one of the three owners of radio station WXYZ in Detroit, came up with the idea of producing a Western show to raise the station out of debt in 1933; focuses on the show's early popularity with its first star, George Seaton, and second star, Jack Deeds.

888. Otto, John Solomon. HARD TIMES BLUES (1929-40): DOWNHOME BLUES RECORDINGS AS ORAL DOCUMENTATION. *Oral Hist. Rev. 1980: 73-80.* The themes of the down-home blues recordings issued between 1924 and 1941 expressed the concerns of the great mass of black laborers. Because the blues reflect attitudes and problems articulated nowhere else, these recordings constitute important sources of social history. 22 notes.   D. A. Yanchisin

889. Otto, Solomon and Otto, John Solomon. I PLAYED AGAINST "SATCHEL" FOR THREE SEASONS: BLACKS AND WHITES IN THE "TWILIGHT" LEAGUES. *J. of Popular Culture 1974 7(4): 797-803.* Reminiscences of Solomon Otto about Negroes and whites in the semiprofessional baseball leagues in the upper Midwest. Otto played for the Dickinson (North Dakota) Cowboys, 1929-31.   S

890. Pauly, Thomas H. *GONE WITH THE WIND* AND *THE GRAPES OF WRATH* AS HOLLYWOOD HISTORIES OF THE DEPRESSION. *J. of Popular Film 1974 3(3): 202-222.*

891. Peck, David. SALVAGING THE ART AND LITERATURE OF THE 1930'S: A BIBLIOGRAPHICAL ESSAY. *Centennial R. 1976 20(2): 128-141.* The arts and literature of the thirties have been ignored and feared. They were ignored by those who considered the work of the era frivolous and forced, and feared by those who thought it was pervaded by Marxist ideology. Careful reexamination of the era reveals that its literary and artistic production was both significant and in the American mainstream. Compared to the work of the thirties, the work of the succeeding two decades was "sterile," largely because of attacks from Congress which caused intellectuals to be "frightened silly." The arts and letters of the thirties have the potential of making the past a source of strength and love because they "gave us social and sympathetic portraits of Americans as they were." Note.   A. R. Stoesen

892. Perry, Thelma D. MELVIN J. CHISUM, PIONEER NEWSMAN. *Negro Hist. Bull. 1973 36(8): 176-180.* Discusses Chisum, his newspaper, the *Tribune,* and his efforts to aid in the election of Franklin Delano Roosevelt.
                                                                                    S

893. Pfaff, Daniel W. JOSEPH PULITZER II AND ADVERTISING CENSORSHIP, 1929-1939. *Journalism Monographs 1982 (77): 1-38.* Discusses the role of American publisher Joseph Pulitzer, II, in establishing and maintaining, without outside pressure, a program to curtail deceptive advertising in the St. Louis *Post-Dispatch.*

894. Phillips, A. H. THE HOLLYWOOD THAT WAS. *Blackwood's Mag. [Great Britain] 1978 324 (1958): 505-511.* Relates anecdotes about the author's experiences as a writer in the Hollywood film industry during the 1930's.

895. Phillips, William. HOW PARTISAN REVIEW BEGAN. *Commentary 1976 62(6): 42-46.* *Partisan Review* began as a monthly in the early 1930's. It was an organ of the leftist-oriented John Reed Writers Club. It lasted for two years and nine issues and, in 1937, was revived with a new goal. The new *Partisan Review* attempted to serve as an independent radical literary journal. Its early issues included contributions by Wallace Stevens, James Agee, Sidney Hook, and Lionel Trilling. Commercial publications did not offer fees to serious writers, and the *Partisan Review* provided a center during a period when literature and politics could coexist. Based on personal recollections.   S. R. Herstein

896. Pintó, Alfonso. WHEN HOLLYWOOD SPOKE SPANISH. *Américas 1980 32(10): 3-8.* Discusses Hollywood's Spanish-language films made during the 1930's for Spanish and Latin American audiences; mentions Mexican, Latin American, Portuguese, and Spanish stars who appeared in them.

897. Pommer, Richard. THE ARCHITECTURE OF URBAN HOUSING IN THE UNITED STATES DURING THE EARLY 1930'S. *J. of the Soc. of Architectural Hist. 1978 37(4): 235-264.* Political considerations combined with the failure of US architects and critics of the 1930's to understand European modernism's principle of the inseparability of housing, planning, and architecture. The result produced the dreary urban housing developed between the late 1930's and early 1960's. During 1932-34, under the Reconstruction Finance Corporation and the Public Works Administration, there was a brief but decisive period of developmental freedom. After that, standardization killed the architectural quality of urban housing. Focuses on Philadelphia, Cleveland, and New York. Compares the US Garden City planning, Beaux-Arts design, and the European Modern Movement, particularly as seen in the Zeilenbau system and the City of Three Million by Le Corbusier. Concludes that only in the early 1960's were the European and US approaches successfully combined. Henry Wright was particularly important in bringing about the fusion.   R. J. Jirran

898. Powers, Richard Gid. THE ATTORNEY GENERAL AND THE G-MAN: HOLLYWOOD'S ROLE IN HOOVER'S RISE TO POWER. *Southwest Rev. 1977 62(4): 329-346.* Examines the effects of Hollywood films, especially *G-Men* (1935), on J. Edgar Hoover's rise to prominence, and Attorney General Homer Cummings's eclipse; Cummings, not Hoover, had been primarily responsible for the government's success against crime.

899. Pratt, Linda Ray. IMAGINING EXISTENCE: FORM AND HISTORY IN STEINBECK AND AGEE. *Southern R. 1975 11(1): 84-98.* One of six essays in this issue "On Self and Society."   S

900. Prouty, L. Fletcher. JIMMY DOOLITTLE AND THE GEE BEE. *Air Force Mag. 1973 56(2): 77-81.* Describes Jimmy Doolittle's sudden engagement in 1930 to pilot the Gee Bee racing plane in which he soon set a world landplane speed record.

901. Redding, Mary Edrich. CALL IT MYTH: HENRY ROTH AND *THE GOLDEN BOUGH*. *Centennial R. 1974 18(2): 180-195.* Describes Henry Roth's use of symbol and myth in his novel *Call It Sleep* (New York: Cooper Square, 1934) as influenced by James G. Frazer's *The Golden Bough* (1890) and T. S. Eliot's *The Wasteland* (1922). In a story which emphasizes time, family,

and history, symbolism is used to develop a "sense of seasonal cycles, disintegration, and rebirth." In dealing with the developing awareness of a child, Roth's achievement rests on the generation of "spiritual electricity" combined with "archetypal poetry and existential encounter." 31 notes.   A. R. Stoesen

902. Remley, David A.   UPTON SINCLAIR AND H. L. MENCKEN IN CORRESPONDENCE: "AN ILLUSTRATION OF HOW NOT TO AGREE." *Southern California Q. 1974 56(4): 337-358.* Although their philosophies were poles apart, Upton Sinclair and H. L. Mencken found common cause as critics of American life and politics, including religion, education, and journalism. With Sinclair the perpetual reformer and Mencken the caustic anti-reformer, their letters were controversial and lively; their admiration for each other remained distinct from their philosophical disagreements. As a newspaper columnist and magazine editor Mencken reviewed many of Sinclair's books. The most significant period of their correspondence was during 1918-34; after a harsh exchange of letters in *American Mercury* over the End Poverty in California (EPIC) campaign the correspondence cooled, though it continued until Mencken's death in 1951. Based on the Sinclair-Mencken correspondence and secondary sources; 53 notes.   A. Hoffman

903. Reverby, Susan.   *WITH BABIES AND BANNERS:* A REVIEW. *Radical Am. 1979 13(5): 63-69.* Discusses the award-winning political documentary film made by the Women's Labor History Film Project, which details the key role of women in the 1937 United Auto Workers of America victory in Flint, Michigan.

904. Riggio, Thomas P.   DREISER ON SOCIETY AND LITERATURE: THE SAN FRANCISCO EXPOSITION INTERVIEW.   *Am. Literary Realism 1870-1910 1978 11(2): 284-294.* An interview of Theodore Dreiser during the 1939 Golden Gate International Exposition provides a glimpse of Dreiser's reflections on American society.

905. Rollins, Peter and Elder, Harris J.   ENVIRONMENTAL HISTORY IN TWO NEW DEAL DOCUMENTARIES.   *Film and Hist. 1973 3(3): 1-7.* Two documentary films by Pare Lorentz, *The Plow That Broke the Plains* (1936) and *The River* (1937), were not only environmental histories of the west and westward movement, but aided in the establishment of the US Film Service under the New Deal.

906. Rollins, Peter C.   IDEOLOGY AND FILM RHETORIC: THREE DOCUMENTARIES OF THE NEW DEAL ERA.   *J. of Popular Film 1976 5(2): 126-145.* Discusses three films of the 1930's which were historical documentaries, *The March of Time* (1935-51), *The River* (1937), and *Native Land* (1942).

907. Rosengarten, Theodore.   READING THE HOPS: RECOLLECTIONS OF LORENZO PIPER DAVIS AND THE NEGRO BASEBALL LEAGUE. *Southern Exposure 1977 5(2-3): 62-79.* Interviews Lorenzo Piper Davis. It was impossible for the majority of players in the Negro Leagues to earn their livings entirely through their sport, even during the heyday of black baseball in the 1930's-40's. Many such as Lorenzo Piper Davis supplemented their income with factory jobs where they played on company teams. Many of the black baseball players were equal in ability to contemporary white major leaguers, but did not

receive an opportunity to play on integrated teams, or were past their prime when their chance finally came. Traveling on the road with black baseball teams such as the Birmingham Barons meant staying at "Jim Crow" hotels or private homes, eating in segregated restaurants, and relying on the instinct and knowhow of their bus drivers to avoid racial problems. Black baseball players were thoroughly professional in their approach to the game, in spite of their reputation among whites as being "clowns." N. Lederer

908. Rubin, Louis D., Jr. TROUBLE ON THE LAND: SOUTHERN LIT-ERATURE AND THE GREAT DEPRESSION. *Can. Rev. of Am. Studies [Canada] 1979 10(2): 153-174.* During the South's literary renaissance of the 1930's, its leading authors generally wrote little about the Great Depression. They commented even less frequently on the immediate social and economic consequences of that crisis upon their region. Even Erskine Caldwell, James Agee, and Thomas Wolfe, all of whom wrote about the South in the depression era, stressed instead the underlying forces and process producing urbanization and industrialization at the expense of the older, traditionally rural South. 5 photos. H. T. Lovin

909. Salo, Mauno. AMELIA EARHART: A SHORT BIOGRAPHY. *Am. Aviation Hist. Soc. J. 1977 22(2): 82-86.* Short biography of Amelia Earhart, 1897-1937, including her interest in aviation and her preparation for a round-the-world airplane flight; discusses her training for the attempt.

910. Salzman, Jack. CONROY, MENCKEN, AND *THE AMERICAN MERCURY. J. of Popular Culture 1973 7(3): 524-528.* H. L. Mencken's *American Mercury*, supposedly in decline, published six pieces by Jack Conroy 1930-33 which were the base for Conroy's *The Disinherited*, one of the "few essential testaments of the 1930's." S

911. Scheurer, Timothy E. REVIEW ESSAY. *J. of Popular Film and Television 1981 9(2): 95-97.* Reviews Bruce F. Kawin, ed., *To Have and Have Not* (1980) and Arthur Hove, ed., *Gold Diggers of 1933* (1980); praises Kawin's book, which provides the text of the screenplay and all the changes Howard Hawks made in the course of filming and criticizes Hove's attempt for his pathetic discussion of the music of the *Gold Diggers of 1933* as well as his confusion over the concept of integration in musical films.

912. Scott, Robert L. DIEGO RIVERA AT ROCKEFELLER CENTER: FRESCO PAINTING AND RHETORIC. *Western J. of Speech Communication 1977 41(2): 70-82.* Frescos of America as a country of energy and democratic promise by Mexican muralist Diego Rivera at Rockefeller Center, New York City, were misinterpreted as a reflection of his Communist sympathies, 1933.

913. Shapiro, Edward S. AMERICAN CONSERVATIVE INTELLECTU-ALS, THE 1930'S, AND THE CRISIS OF IDEOLOGY. *Modern Age 1979 23(4): 370-380.* New Deal policies compelled American conservatives to attempt an ideological definition. An initial response was the founding of Seward Collins's *American Review* in 1933. Herbert Agar and Allen Tate, proponents of Distributist and Agrarian conservatism respectively, contributed to this journal until Collins's fascist and monarchist sentiments received national attention in a published interview. Agar and Tate reacted by founding *Free America* in 1937. Most

conservatives found agreement in endorsing political decentralization, but economic decentralization, specifically economic levelling, continues as a source of contention. Based on the papers of Herbert Agar, Seward Collins, Donald Davidson, and Allen Tate, and other primary sources; 43 notes.   C. D'Aniello

914.   Shepardson, D. E.   IN THE PRIME OF HIS TIME: H. L. MENCKEN. *Am. Hist. Illus. 1975 9(9): 10-19.* Reviews the life and works of H. L. Mencken (1880-1956), an enormously prominent literary figure of the 1920's. Mencken's antidemocratism and faith in irrationality fitted well the cynical posture of the age. Mencken used biting satire to push his opinions. The Great Depression proved to be his downfall, as the mood of the nation changed while he did not. His refusal to denounce the Nazi and Fascist regimes in Europe finished his productive career entirely. 7 Photos.   V. L. Human

915.   Shils, Edward.   SOME ACADEMICS, MAINLY IN CHICAGO. *Am. Scholar 1981 50(2): 179-196.* The author recounts his study of sociology at the University of Chicago during 1932-36. His favorite teachers, Frank Knight, Louis Wirth, Robert Park, Talcott Parsons, and Harold Lasswell, each made a personal and unique contribution to him. The University of Chicago is still intellectually alive and flourishing, even though these teachers have long since departed.   F. F. Harling

916.   Short, John D., Jr.   JOHN STEINBECK: A 1930'S PHOTO-RECOLLECTION.   *San Jose Studies 1976 2(2): 75-81.* The author recollects his acquaintance with novelist John Steinbeck during the 1930's with the assistance of photographs collected by his mother, Marie Hathaway Short.

917.   Shout, John D.   THE FILM MUSICAL AND THE LEGACY OF SHOW BUSINESS.   *J. of Popular Film and Television 1982 10(1): 23-26.* Discusses *Show Boat* and *San Francisco,* both released in 1936, in the context of the use of popular art forms for didactic purposes by film musicals.

918.   Skefos, Catherine Hetos.   THE SUPREME COURT GETS A HOME. *Supreme Court Hist. Soc. Y. 1976: 25-36.* Traces the construction of the present Supreme Court building in Washington, D.C., during 1929-35; it was built as a result of the persistence of Chief Justice William Howard Taft and gave the court its first permanent meeting place.

919.   Snyder, Stephen.   FROM WORDS TO IMAGES: FIVE NOVELISTS IN HOLLYWOOD.   *Can. Rev. of Am. Studies [Canada] 1977 8(2): 206-213.* In *Some Time in the Sun* (New York: Charles Scribner's Sons, 1976), Tom Dardis refuted charges that major writers wasted their creative talents by accepting Hollywood writing assignments. He demonstrated that F. Scott Fitzgerald, William Faulkner, Aldous Huxley, Nathanael West, and James Agee wrote movie scripts during the 1930's and 1940's and all benefited creatively. The challenges of movie scriptwriting stimulated their "creative powers." 14 notes.
                                                                  H. T. Lovin

920.   Sobchack, Vivian C.   *THE GRAPES OF WRATH* (1940): THEMATIC EMPHASIS THROUGH VISUAL STYLE.   *Am. Q. 1979 31(5): 596-615.* Discusses the visual style of John Ford's cinematic adaptation of John Steinbeck's novel *The Grapes of Wrath.* Usually the movie is examined in terms of its literary

roots or its social protest. But the imagery of the film reveals the important theme of the Joad family's coherence. The movie shows the family in closeups, cramped in small spaces on a cluttered screen, isolated from the land and their surroundings. Dim lighting helps abstract the Joad family from the reality of Dust Bowl migrants. The film's emotional and aesthetic power comes from its generalized quality attained through this visual style. 4 photos, 31 notes.   S

921. Soderbergh, Peter A. MOONLIGHT AND SHADOWS: THE BIG BANDS, 1934-1974. *Midwest Q. 1974 16(1): 85-96.* The Swing Era was born in 1934, but its heyday was over by 1945. During this period big bands led the swing movement. Many reasons are given for the demise of swing, but perhaps the major reason was the waning fervor of the swing aficionado, who was young but grew up and turned to other interests. Based on secondary sources.
                                                                                        H. S. Marks

922. Stepanek, Robert H. THE RIDER R-3 AT THE BRADLEY AIR MUSEUM. *Am. Aviation Hist. Soc. J. 1979 24(2): 122-124.* Describes the racing airplane, the Rider R-3, which flew during the 1930's, and is now part of the aviation collection at the Bradley Air Museum in Connecticut.

923. Stewart, Garrett. MODERN HARD TIMES: CHAPLIN AND THE CINEMA OF SELF-REFLECTION. *Critical Inquiry 1976 3(2): 295-314.* Studies, in the light of Charles Dickens's *Hard Times* (1854), Charlie Chaplin's 1936 industrial polemic, *Modern Times,* and discusses his social outlook as expressed in this film.

924. Synott, Marcia G. THE "BIG THREE" AND THE HARVARD-PRINCETON FOOTBALL BREAK, 1926-1934. *J. of Sport Hist. 1976 3(2): 188-202.* In 1926 Harvard entered into an agreement to play football against the University of Michigan instead of Princeton, and that agreement threatened to destroy the "Big Three" relationship of the time. Harvard's actions were based on the fact that games with Princeton had been marred by fights and roughness. During the 1930's, the "Big Three" was restored, and in 1939 it was enlarged to the Ivy League. 28 notes.   M. Kaufman

925. Tamony, Peter. BESSIE: VOCUMENTARY. *JEMF Q. 1980 16(60): 196-198.* Reprinted from *Jazz 4,* Fall 1959, this provides a sociocultural definition of some of the terms and phrases in Bessie Smith's recording of "Gimme a Pigfoot" in 1933 at her last recording session.

926. Tamony, Peter. BOP, THE WORD. *JEMF Q. 1980 16(59): 147-151.* Reprints the article which originally appeared in the Spring 1959 issue of *JEMF Quarterly,* defining the word "bop," derived from "bebop" which was coined by Dizzy Gillespie to describe the music he played, although the word can be heard in a number of recordings from 1928 to the early 1940's; also includes a number of references added after 1959.

927. Tamony, Peter. SWING, THE BIG WORD. *JEMF Q. 1980 16(59): 152-154.* Reprints this article from the Winter 1960 issue of *JEMF Quarterly,* on the coinage of the word "swing" to "describe a dynamic of American jazz" which emerged in the early 1930's and by 1936 "was almost solely employed to characterize a suddenly-appreciated style that was getting daily, nationwide publicity as the new sound," although the word appeared in song titles as early as 1908.

928. Taylor, Joshua C. A POIGNANT, RELEVANT BACKWARD LOOK AT ARTISTS OF THE GREAT DEPRESSION. *Smithsonian 1979 10(7): 44-55.* With the Depression, private patronage of the arts declined; with federal sponsorship, contemporary art emerged from its cultural cocoon and entered public consciousness, 1930's.

929. Teichroew, Allan. AS FAR AS THE EYE CAN SEE: SOME DEPRESSION PHOTOGRAPHS OF MENNONITE FARMERS. *Mennonite Life 1978 33(3): 4-15.* During the 1930's Depression and Dust Bowl, the Farm Security Administration intended to provide welfare services to displaced farmers and to furnish loans for those still working the land. A side effect of the investigation into farm conditions was the accumulation of thousands of striking photographs of rural poverty. In 1937 Russell Lee photographed the 15-member John Harshenberger family of Montana, Mennonites who lived in grim deprivation yet maintained a strong integrity. Dorthea Lange photographed the more prosperous 5-member John Unruf (Unruh) family of Boundary County, Idaho in 1939, pioneers determined to build a new farm. From the Farm Security Administration collection, Library of Congress; 12 photos, 8 notes.   B. Burnett

930. Telotte, J. P. DANCING THE DEPRESSION: NARRATIVE STRATEGY IN THE ASTAIRE-ROGERS FILMS. *J. of Popular Film and Television 1980 8(3): 15-24.* Employs a structuralist perspective to analyze the mythos of the Fred Astaire-Ginger Rogers films of 1930-39, especially as they gave expression to the subtle conflicts and contradictions within the depression era of American society.

931. Thomas, Donald W. AMELIA EARHART'S FATAL DECISION. *Am. Aviation Hist. Soc. J. 1977 22(2): 87-90.* Discusses Amelia Earhart's attempted round-the-world airplane flight of 1937, examining much of the speculation surrounding her mysterious crash; lack of proper radio equipment may have caused her crash.

932. Thomas, James W. LYLE SAXON'S STRUGGLE WITH *CHILDREN OF STRANGERS*. *Southern Studies 1977 16(1): 27-40.* Lyle Saxon was an established reporter for the New Orleans *Times-Picayune.* He wrote four nonfictional works on regional Louisiana history during 1927-30, but his great desire was to write a novel about plantation life. An opportunity to reside at Melrose plantation provided him with the time and atmosphere, but the novel took seven years to complete *Children of Strangers* (1937). A distinguished regional novel, it was the only significant work Saxon published. A combination of alcoholism, procrastination, involvement with the Works Progress Administration, laziness, and excessive socializing contributed to his failure to achieve more. Based on Saxon letters at Northwestern State University of Louisiana, other primary and secondary sources; 44 notes.   J. Buschen

933. Thorp, Gregory. ITS GLORY VANISHED, VAST CINCINNATI TERMINAL BOWS OUT. *Smithsonian 1974 5(3): 64-69.* The Cincinnati Union Terminal, a multimillion-dollar showplace completed in 1933, "has all come down except its mighty rotunda building, which may be purchased by the city of Cincinnati and used as a multipurpose transportation center or for governmental offices. The destruction of the station symbolizes the end of railroading's

golden age—just at a time, ironically, when wistful thoughts of a resurrection of the rails are in everyone's mind. . . . A spirited fund-raising effort, led by Alfred Moore, saved the rotunda structure, along with the concourse mosaics (for reinstallation in the expanding airport). . . . The problem facing Cincinnati symbolizes one of the illnesses that disrupts our present society." 3 photos, 4 illus.

D. D. Cameron

934. Tibbetts, John. THE WISDOM OF THE SERPENT: FRAUDS AND MIRACLES IN FRANK CAPRA'S "THE MIRACLE WOMAN." *J. of Popular Film and Television 1979 7(3): 293-309.* Frank Capra's film, *The Miracle Woman* (1931), is about the career of evangelist Sister Florence Fallon, played by Barbara Stanwyck; notes the significance of the political, military, and spiritual issues which are questioned in this film in light of the Depression.

935. Twining, Mary. HARVESTING AND HERITAGE: A COMPARISON OF AFRO-AMERICAN AND AFRICAN BASKETRY. *Southern Folklore Q. 1978 42(2-3): 159-174.* Discusses the revival of basketmaking techniques among Afro-Americans in the 1930's as a result of a project undertaken by the Works Progress Administration, comparing the tools and techniques of Afro-Americans to Africans, an example "of the continuity of traditional material culture between West Coast Africa and the United States"; 1930's-78.

936. Underhill, Irving S. A DOG'S TALE. *Am. Book Coll. 1975 25(4): 17-19.* Author describes his efforts to obtain all issued pamphlets of a Mark Twain short story and the unauthorized issuance of a second edition, 1930-31.

937. Unsigned. R. D. GINTHER, WORKINGMAN ARTIST AND HISTORIAN OF SKID ROW. *California Hist. Q. 1975 54(3): 263-271.* A profile of Ronald Debs Ginther (1906-1969), self-taught artist and labor radical. His 85 water-color drawings of labor unrest are owned by the Washington State Historical Society and are currently on exhibit in the San Francisco area. Ginther's work deals with the Great Depression and Skid Row, including scenes of Hoovervilles, labor-police confrontations, breadlines, and jail holding tanks. 13 illus.

A. Hoffman

938. Vitz, Robert C. CLUBS, CONGRESSES, AND UNIONS: AMERICAN ARTISTS CONFRONT THE THIRTIES. *New York Hist. 1973 54(4): 425-447.* The Great Depression made artists acutely aware of how peripheral they were to American life. American artists made organized efforts to raise their economic status and increase their political importance in American society. Among the organizations studied are the John Reed Clubs, the American Contemporary Art Gallery, the Artists Committee for Action, the Unemployed Artists Group, and the American Artists Union. All were radical in their political persuasion, and some were adjuncts of the American Communist Party. All championed "socialist realism" and social relevancy, and all were short-lived organizations accomplishing little. Based on primary and secondary works; 3 illus., 59 notes. G. Kurland

939. Vitz, Robert C. STRUGGLE AND RESPONSE: AMERICAN ARTISTS AND THE GREAT DEPRESSION. *New York Hist. 1976 57(1): 81-98.* The artists' struggle to preserve their identity resulted in a growing sense of community, new artistic perceptions, and "a profusion of creative talent in the 1940's and 1950's." 4 illus., 85 notes. R. N. Lokken

940.	Wald, Alan.	EDMUND WILSON'S ENCOUNTER WITH MARX-ISM.	*Internat. Socialist R. 1974 35(8): 32-39.* Discusses Edmund Wilson (1895-1972), one of America's foremost literary critics, and his political transition in the 1930's.					S

941.	Wald, Alan.	MIKE GOLD AND THE RADICAL LITERARY MOVEMENT OF THE 1930'S.	*Internat. Socialist R. 1973 34(3): 34-37.* Review essay on Michael Folsom's *Mike Gold: A Literary Anthology* (New York: International Publishers, 1972).					S

942.	Webb, Max.	FORD MADOX FORD AND THE BATON ROUGE WRITERS' CONFERENCE.	*Southern R. 1974 10(4): 892-903.* Discusses Ford Madox Ford's participation in the Writers' Conference on Literature and Reading in the South and Southwest as a way "to examine his relationship with the major literary movement of the South, the Fugitives-turned-Agrarians."					S

943.	Weinrott, Lester A.	CHICAGO RADIO: THE GLORY DAYS.	*Chicago Hist. 1974 3(1): 14-22.* Recounts the "Glory Days" of Chicago radio, 1930-40.					S

944.	Welty, Eudora.	LOOKING BACK AT THE FIRST STORY.	*Georgia Rev. 1979 33(4): 741-755.* In writing her first published story, "Death of a Traveling Salesman," the author (b. 1909) was inspired by the tales and traveling life of a neighbor in Jackson, Mississippi, in the 1930's. Like all of her stories, its generative force came from real life and was influenced by the fairy tales and myths that she read as a child.					J. N. McArthur

945.	Wertheim, Arthur Frank.	RELIEVING SOCIAL TENSIONS: RADIO COMEDY AND THE GREAT DEPRESSION.	*J. of Popular Culture 1976 10(3): 501-519.* The radio comedy *Amos 'n Andy* relieved social tension by poking fun at economic crisis, reaffirming American values, creating a sense of common participation in suffering, and promoting audience identification with the program characters.

946.	Wheelock, Alan S.	DARK MOUNTAIN: H. P. LOVECRAFT AND THE "VERMONT HORROR."	*Vermont Hist. 1977 45(4): 221-228.* H. P. Lovecraft's 26,000-word science fiction story, "The Whisperer in the Darkness" *(Weird Tales Magazine,* August 1931), grew out of his visit to Windham County, Vermont.					T. D. S. Bassett

947.	Whitaker, Rosemary.	VIOLENCE IN OLD JULES AND SLOGUM HOUSE.	*Western Am. Literature 1981 16(3): 217-224.* Mari Sandoz won the Atlantic nonfiction prize in 1935 for her first book, a biography of her father. Although it was praised by many critics for its vigorous style, some reviewers felt that the portrayal of Old Jules was insensitive and sometimes brutal. *Slogum House* was published in 1937. Reviewers again praised Sandoz's powerful style, but emphasized that brutality and violence were present. In both books the action focuses on the individual who wishes to dominate, and will pursue that end by the use of violence. However, it should not be forgotten that Sandoz also portrayed her characters as possessing a "staying power" and a means to survive.					M. Genung

948. Whitehead, James L. JOHN ALBOK'S RECORD OF THE PEOPLE OF NEW YORK: 1933-45. *Prologue 1974 6(2): 100-117*. Portfolio of Depression-era photographs by John Albok, Hungarian immigrant. Albok discovered success and happiness in America, but the Great Depression shocked him. A tailor by trade, he set out to record the people of New York through photography. 16 photos.   V. L. Human

949. Wiles, Timothy J. TAMMANYITE, PROGRESSIVE, AND ANARCHIST: POLITICAL COMMUNITIES IN *THE ICEMAN COMETH*. *Clio 1980 9(2): 179-196*. Analyzes the social theme of Eugene O'Neill's *The Iceman Cometh* (1939) by demonstrating how the play creates three distinct political communities: the community of illusions, the community of progressive reform, and the community of radical revolution. The community of illusions, represented by Harry Hope's Bedrock Bar and its regular customers, triumphs at the end of the play. 14 notes.   T. P. Linkfield

950. Wilkinson, Dave. "WRONG WAY" CORRIGAN. *Am. Hist. Illus. 1978 12(9): 24-33*. On 16 July 1938, Douglas Corrigan flew out of New York City's Floyd Bennett Field in "Sunshine," a Curtis Robin with a 165 hp engine, apparently on a transcontinental flight to California. Supposedly he got turned around while passing through a cloud and flew 26 hours the wrong way, eventually landing in Dublin, Ireland. Government inspectors repeatedly had denied Corrigan's requests for a trans-Atlantic flight, so a hoax was suspected, but Corrigan stuck to his story. His autobiography, *That's My Story,* was made into a movie, *The Flying Irishman,* and he grossed $75,000 before his national fame faded. Primary and secondary sources; 6 illus.   D. Dodd

951. Wolfe, G. Joseph. "WAR OF THE WORLDS" AND THE EDITORS. *Journalism Q. 1980 57(1): 39-44*. National newspaper editorial reaction to Orson Welles's 1938 radio broadcast of *War of the Worlds* generally followed three themes: 1) an indictment of listeners for lack of intelligence, 2) a theory that the unsettled state of world affairs, particularly in Europe, and a genuine fear of air attack had helped create a sense of paranoia that had acted to intensify the effects of the broadcast, and 3) a lambasting of the radio industry for failing to regulate itself enough to prevent a hoax being passed off as a news bulletin. Based on newspaper editorials; 33 notes.   J. S. Coleman

952. Wolfenstein, Judith. OKAY OKIE. *Westways 1979 71(7): 33-35*. Notes the life of American songwriter and balladeer Woody Guthrie from 1937, when he first visited Los Angeles, until his death in 1967, followed by reprints of two short articles he wrote for *The Hollywood Tribune* in 1939 on being a newcomer to California from the Dust Bowl.

953. Woodward, Robert H. JOHN STEINBECK, EDITH MCGILLICUDDY AND *TORTILLA FLAT:* A PROBLEM IN MANUSCRIPT DATING. *San José Studies 1977 3(3): 70-73*. Traces the manuscript dating of a John Steinbeck short story, "How Mrs. McGillicuddy Met R. L. Stevenson," to 1934 through references in *Tortilla Flat* and Steinbeck's journals.

954. Wright, Richard. WITH BLACK RADICALS IN CHICAGO. *Dissent 1977 24(2): 156-161*. Excerpts a chapter of the author's unpublished autobiographical work, *American Hunger;* mentions his difficulties in the Communist Party in Chicago during the 1930's.

955. Young, William H. THAT INDOMITABLE REDHEAD: LITTLE ORPHAN ANNIE. *J. of Popular Culture 1974 8(2): 309-319.* Examines Harold Gray's famous comic strip "Little Orphan Annie" and the right-wing philosophy it editorialized throughout the Depression and World War II. Annie generally admires the very rich and helps poor people get financially ahead without resorting to handouts. "Daddy" Warbucks, a wealthy war profiteer, symbolizes the Carnegie brand of capitalism. Most of Annie's friends are industrialists or small shopkeepers and farmers whose poverty stems from personal rather than economic causes. Gray used the strip to rage against Roosevelt and the New Deal, implying that stability and traditions were being undermined by liberal ideas. During World War II Gray became engrossed with spies and internal subversion, and during 1941-44 Annie turned to shooting Nazis and blowing up submarines. Always self-reliant, Annie represents the social conservatism of the middle class. 12 notes.   K. McElroy

956. Zimmerman, Paul. L. A.'S XTH OLYMPIAD. *Westways 1976 68(8): 54-57, 78.* Recounts events of the 1932 Olympics held in Los Angeles.

957. —. [BONNIE AND CLYDE].
Rich, Carroll Y. CLYDE BARROW'S LAST FORD. *J. of Popular Culture 1973 6(4): 631-641.* Describes the fortunes of the Ford automobile in which Bonnie Parker and Clyde Barrow were killed, from its purchase by Jesse Warren in 1934 to the Bonnie and Clyde revival of 1967.
Wollheim, Peter. THE CASE OF BONNIE AND CLYDE. *J. of Popular Culture 1973 7(3): 602-605.* Criticizes Rich's article for its lack of penetration of the psychological level of the fascination with Barrow's Ford automobile, and begins an analysis of the gangster myth in American culture.
                                                                                         S

958. —. REGINALD MARSH: ARTIST OF THE DEPRESSION YEARS. *Am. Hist. Illus. 1982 16(9): 25-29.* Reginald Marsh, first an illustrator for "slick magazines," later observed and painted New York City life; reflecting America's disillusionment, he remained sympathetic to the human condition.

959. —. [STORY AND DISCOGRAPHY OF THE BEVERLY HILL BILLIES]. *JEMF Q. 1980 16(57): 2-17.*
Griffis, Ken. THE BEVERLY HILL BILLIES, *pp. 2-14.*
Griffis, Ken. BEVERLY HILL BILLIES DISCOGRAPHY, *pp. 15-17.* History of the music and members of the Beverly Hill Billies, the first country music group on the radio in the Los Angeles area; it was widely popular from 1930 to 1932, when the group split up; lists all the group's recordings.

SUBJECT INDEX

Subject Profile Index (ABC-SPIndex) carries both generic and specific index terms. Begin a search at the general term but also look under more specific or related terms.

Each string of index descriptors is intended to present a profile of a given article; however, no particular relationship between any two terms in the profile is implied. Terms within the profile are listed alphabetically after the leading term. The variety of punctuation and capitalization reflects production methods and has no intrinsic meaning; e.g., there is no difference in meaning between "History, study of" and "History (study of)."

Cities, towns, and counties are listed following their respective states or provinces; e.g., "Ohio (Columbus)." Terms beginning with an arabic numeral are listed after the letter Z. The chronology of the bibliographic entry follows the subject index descriptors. In the chronology, "c" stands for "century"; e.g., "19c" means "19th century."

Note that "United States" is not used as a leading index term; if no country is mentioned, the index entry refers to the United States alone. When an entry refers to both Canada and the United States, both "Canada" and "USA" appear in the string of index descriptors, but "USA" is not a leading term. When an entry refers to any other country and the United States, only the other country is indexed.

The last number in the index string, in italics, refers to the bibliographic entry number.

A

Academic Freedom. Marxist opinions. Muller, Hermann J. (dismissal). Texas, University of. 1936. *586*

Accidents. Daily Life. Faulkner, Jim. Faulkner, William. Mississippi (Oxford). Personal narratives. Youth. 1930-39. *804*

Acculturation. Bellow, Saul. Illinois (Chicago). Immigrants. ca 1937-74. *533*

Actors and Actresses. Douglas, Melvyn. Political Activism. 1936-42. *766*

Actors, employment of. Drama. Federal Theatre Project. Ohio (Cincinnati). Works Progress Administration. 1935-39. *865*

Adamic, Louis (writings). Immigrants. Unity in diversity (theme). 1935-45. *782*

Adams, Frederick C. (review article). Credit. Export-Import Bank. Foreign policy. International Trade. 1934-39. 1976. *52*

Adorno, Theodor W. Culture. Lazarsfeld, Paul F. Music. Princeton Radio Research Project. Social organization. 1930's. *875*

Advertising. Allen, Laurence. Allen, Willis. California Life Payments Plan. Economic structure. Noble, Robert. Pensions. Referendum. 1937-39. *755*

—. Carter, Boake. Military. News. Political Commentary. Radio. 1931-38. *803*

—. Censorship. Missouri. Newspapers. Pulitzer, Joseph, II. St. Louis *Post Dispatch*. 1929-39. *893*

Aeronautics. California. Trans-polar flight (nonstop). USSR (Moscow). 1937. *785*

—. Circumnavigation, attempted. Earhart, Amelia. 1897-1937. *909*

—. Circumnavigation, attempted. Earhart, Amelia. Radio equipment. 1937. *931*

—. Circumnavigation (solo). Oklahoma. Post, Wiley. 1920's-35. *560*

—. Rider, Keith. R-6 (aircraft). 1936-37. *852*

Africa, West. Basketmaking. Negroes. Works Progress Administration. 1935-78. *935*

Agar, Herbert. Collins, Seward. Conservatism. Decentralization. Ideology. Intellectuals. Tate, Allen. 1933-50. *913*

—. Conservatism. *Free America* (periodical). New Deal. 1937-47. *649*

Agee, James. Eyster, Warren. Films. Literature. Personal narratives. 1935-41. *802*

—. Journalism. Literature. Steinbeck, John. 1935-39. *899*

—. Language. Literature. Social criticism. 1930-40. *850*

Agee, James (*Let Us Now Praise Famous Men*). Daily Life. Evans, Walker. Photography, documentary. Sharecroppers. South. 1930-1941. *792*

—. Daily Life. Literature. Realism. 1930-41. *846*

—. Language. Literary criticism. Richards, Ivor Armstrong. 1930-40. *833*

Agrarianism. Alienation. Industrialization. Tate, Allen. 1930's. *835*

—. Broadacre City. City Planning. Decentralization. Oklahoma (Bartlesville). Wright, Frank Lloyd. 1935. *864*

Agricultural Adjustment Administration. Agricultural policy. Attitudes. New Deal. 1920-33. *336*

—. Agriculture and Government. "Corn-hog" program. Farmers. Iowa (Boone County). Powers, Elmer G. (diary). 1934. *345*

—. Farmers. Federal Policy. New Deal. New York, western. 1934. *308*

—. Federal Government. National Recovery Administration. 1933-39. *481*

—. Labor Unions and Organizations. Sharecroppers. Southern Tenant Farmers' Union. ca 1930's. *736*

—. New Deal. North Carolina. Senate. Virginia. 1933-39. *366*

—. New Deal. Soil Conservation Service. 1933-41. *459*

Agricultural Adjustment Administration (Office of the General Counsel). Dale, Chester. Frank, Jerome. Wallace, Henry A. 1935. *398*

Agricultural experiment stations. Arizona. New Deal. New Mexico. Oklahoma. Texas. 1926-39. *407*

Agricultural Industry. Economic Regulations. Federal government. Mississippi. Prices. Texas. Voluntarism. 1925-40. *71*
—. Georgia. 1910-32. *45*
Agricultural Labor. California. Labor Unions and Organizations. National Industrial Recovery Act (1933). 1933-34. *323*
—. California, southern. Steinbeck, John *(In Dubious Battle)*. Strikes. 1933. *773*
—. Farmers. Industrial Workers of the World. Labor Disputes. Ranchers. Washington (Yakima Valley). 1910-36. *685*
Agricultural Labor Relations Act (1975). California. Emergency Farm Labor Supply Program. Labor law. New Deal. ca 1930-79. *338*
Agricultural laborers. California. Labor Unions and Organizations. Migration, Internal. "Okies". 1930's. *115*
Agricultural policy. Agricultural Adjustment Administration. Attitudes. New Deal. 1920-33. *336*
—. Association of Southern Commissioners of Agriculture. Cotton. New Deal. South. Tennessee (Memphis). 1936-37. *423*
—. Corporatism, concept of. Hoover, Herbert C. Politics. Roosevelt, Franklin D. 1929-33. *27*
—. Dust Bowl. Federal Government. Great Plains. Unemployment. ca 1930-80. *408*
—. Dust Bowl. New Deal. Texas Panhandle. 1930's. *76*
—. Great Plains. Roosevelt, Franklin D. Shelterbelts. Trees. 1934-44. *486*
—. Jones, Marvin. Legislation. New Deal. Political Leadership. 1916-40. *406*
—. National Cooperative Council. New Deal. Trade associations. 1929-42. *346*
Agricultural Production. Irrigation. Kansas. 1930's-70's. *47*
Agricultural production, limited. Farm leaders. Land utilization movement. 1920's. *41*
Agricultural programs. Droughts. Kansas. New Deal. Political Campaigns (presidential). 1936. *464*
Agricultural Reform. Catholic Church. New Deal. Roosevelt, Franklin D. (administration). Social Theory. 1933-39. *473*
—. Clawson, Marion (report). Economic conditions. Farm Security Administration. Resettlement projects. 1935-43. *317*
Agriculture *See also* Farmers, Rural development.
—. Alcohol. Business. Fuel. Motors. Prices. Surpluses. 1930's. *604*
—. Cotton. Oklahoma, eastern. Sharecroppers. 1920-40. *38*
—. Dust storms. Ecology. Great Plains. 1930's. *133*
—. Letters. Mississippi. Roosevelt, Franklin D. 1932-33. *95*
—. Pennsylvania (Lancaster County). 1928-36. 1970's. *28*
—. Politics. Reno, Milo. Wallace, Henry A. 1932-33. *466*
—. Rural Development. South. 1930-80. *324*
Agriculture and Government. Agricultural Adjustment Administration. "Corn-hog" program. Farmers. Iowa (Boone County). Powers, Elmer G. (diary). 1934. *345*
—. Constitutional issues. Farm journals. New Deal. 1935-36. *330*
—. Indian-White Relations. New Deal. New Mexico. Pueblo Indians. 1938-48. *503*
—. Land. Langer, William. Mortgage moratoria. North Dakota. 1930's. *3*
Agriculture Department. Geography. Kollmorgen, Walter M. 1936-45. *379*
Agriculture (legislation). Sectionalism. Senate farm bloc. 1921-33. *221*

Aiken, George D. Flood control. Governors. Political Campaigns (presidential). Republican Party. Vermont. 1937-39. *235*
—. Political Campaigns (gubernatorial). Republican Party. Vermont. 1933-36. *184*
Air Mail Service. Army Air Corps. Foulois, Benjamin D. 1934. *475*
—. Army Air Corps. Foulois, Benjamin D. Postal service. 1933-34. *348*
—. Black, Hugo. Contracts. Farley, James A. Hoover, Herbert C. (administration). Legislative Investigations. 1933-34. *487*
—. Contracts. Merchant Marine. Ocean mail service. Roosevelt, Franklin D. 1933-37. *488*
Air Mail Service (private). Contracts. Editorials. San Francisco *Chronicle* (newspaper). 1934. *690*
Air races. Bradley Air Museum. Connecticut. Rider R-3 (aircraft). 1930's-70's. *922*
Airplane flights. Alaska (Fairbanks). Army Air Corps. B-10 (aircraft). District of Columbia. Politics. 1934. *821*
Airplane flights, transatlantic. Corrigan, Douglas. Ireland (Dublin). New York City. 1938-50. *950*
Airplane Industry and Trade. Pilots. Public Relations. Safety. Women. 1927-40. *566*
Airplanes. Douglas, Donald. Photographs. 1932-38. *752*
—. Federal government. 1903-80. *787*
Alabama. Clergy. New Deal. Roosevelt, Franklin D. 1935-36. *290*
—. Kentucky. Labor Unions and Organizations (development). United Mine Workers of America. 1932-33. *634*
—. NAACP. Norris, Clarence. Pardon request. Scottsboro Case. 1931-76. *657*
—. Race Relations. Rape, alleged. Scottsboro case. Trials. 1931-49. *729*
Alabama (Birmingham). Communist Party. Hudson, Hosea. Negroes. South. 1920's-70's. *691*
Alabama (Muscle Shoals). Electric Power. Public Utilities. Tennessee (Memphis). Tennessee Valley Authority. 1880-1940. *513*
Alabama (Scottsboro). Historiography. Myths and Symbols. Racism. Trials. 1931-80. *742*
Alaska (Fairbanks). Airplane flights. Army Air Corps. B-10 (aircraft). District of Columbia. Politics. 1934. *821*
Alaska (Palmer). Defense. Rural rehabilitation. Works Progress Administration. 1935-40. *445*
Albok, John. New York. Photographs. 1933-45. *948*
Alcohol. Agriculture. Business. Fuel. Motors. Prices. Surpluses. 1930's. *604*
Alien Property Custodian. Banking. Crowley, Leo T. Federal Deposit Insurance Corporation. Politics. Roosevelt, Franklin D. (administration). 1934-45. *510*
Alienation. Agrarianism. Industrialization. Tate, Allen. 1930's. *835*
—. Intellectuals. Jews. Leftism. New Deal. Roosevelt, Franklin D. 1930's. *757*
Allen, DeLacey. Elections (state). Georgia. Lieutenant governors. Pope, J. Ellis. Proposition 2. Scott, W. Fred. 1936. *156*
Allen, Fred. Bureaucracies. Commercialism. Criticism. Humor. Radio. 1932-49. *824*
Allen, Frederick Lewis *(Only Yesterday)*. Historiography. Journalism. Liberalism. Puritanism. 1931. *858*
Allen, Laurence. Advertising. Allen, Willis. California Life Payments Plan. Economic structure. Noble, Robert. Pensions. Referendum. 1937-39. *755*

Allen, Willis. Advertising. Allen, Laurence. California Life Payments Plan. Economic structure. Noble, Robert. Pensions. Referendum. 1937-39. *755*

Allison, Hughes. Drama. Federal Theatre Project. Negroes. Ward, Theodore. Wilson, Frank. 1930's. *874*

All-Party Agricultural Committee. Farmers. Great Plains. North Central States. Political Campaigns (presidential). Roosevelt, Franklin D. 1936. *254*

American Abstract Artists. American Artists' Congress. Artists. Social Organization. Surrealism. 1935-45. *310*

American Artists' Congress. American Abstract Artists. Artists. Social Organization. Surrealism. 1935-45. *310*

American Civil Liberties Union. Civil rights. Kentucky (Bell County, London). Miners. Trials. 1932-38. *733*

—. Demonstrations. Federal Bureau of Investigation. Hoover, J. Edgar. Political surveillance. Trade Union Education League. 1924-36. *750*

American Distillery Company. American Federation of Labor. General strikes. Illinois (Pekin). 1934-36. *550*

American Federation of Labor. 1930's. *737*

—. American Distillery Company. General strikes. Illinois (Pekin). 1934-36. *550*

—. Carmody, John. Civil Works Administration. New Deal. Work relief. 1933-34. *467*

—. Chicago Newspaper Guild. Illinois. Labor Unions and Organizations (white-collar). 1933-40. *642*

—. Coal Mines and Mining. New Mexico (Gallup). Strikes. 1933. *708*

—. Communist Party. Labor Unions and Organizations. Radicals and Radicalism. Trade Union Unity League. 1933-35. *569*

—. International Brotherhood of Pulp, Sulphite, and Paper Mill Workers. Labor Unions and Organizations. Militancy. Paper industry. 1933-35. *753*

—. International Ladies' Garment Workers' Union. Jews. Labor Unions and Organizations. 1930's. *528*

—. New Deal. Third parties (suggested). 1920's-30's. *205*

American Indian Federation. Bureau of Indian Affairs. Collier, John. Indians. Jamison, Alice Lee. New Deal. Political activism. 1930's-50's. *351*

American Labor Party. Communist Party. Gordon, Max (account). Politics. Popular Front. ca 1930-39. *758*

American Legion. Bonus Army. District of Columbia. North Carolina. Political Protest. Stevens, Henry L., Jr. Veterans (benefits). 1932. *694*

American Liberty League. Business. Civil rights. Federal Regulation. Government, Resistance to. New Deal. 1934-36. *698*

—. Davis, John W. New Deal (opposition to). Political Campaigns. 1932-36. *191*

American Medical Association (Committee on the Cost of Medical Care). Attitudes. Medical Care (costs). *Medical Care for the American People* (report). 1926-31. *124*

American Mercury (periodical). Anderson, Maxwell *(Night Over Taos)*. New Mexico. 18c-19c. 1932. *885*

—. Conroy, Jack. Mencken, H. L. Publishers and Publishing. 1930-33. *910*

—. Mencken, H. L. 1920's-30's. *772*

American Newspaper Publishers Association. Daily Newspaper Code. Freedom of the press. National Industrial Recovery Act (1933). National Recovery Administration. Politics and Media. 1933-34. *774*

American Olympic Committee. Anti-Semitism. Boycotts, proposed. Brundage, Avery. "Fair Play for American Athletes" (pamphlet). Germany (Berlin). Olympic Games. 1935-36. *851*

American Order of Fascisti. Employment. Georgia. Negroes. White supremacy. 1930-33. *660*

American Writers' Congress. Capitalism. Comintern. League of American Writers. 1935. *567*

Ames, Jessie Daniel. Association of Southern Women for the Prevention of Lynching. Lynching. South. Women. 1928-42. *672*

Amlie, Thomas R. Economic programs. Liberals. New Deal. Politics. Wisconsin. 1931-39. *264*

—. Farmer-labor movement. Hard, Herbert. New Deal. Ohio Farmer-Labor Progressive Federation. Third Parties. 1930-40. *204*

—. Farmer-Labor Party. New Deal. Wisconsin. 1930-38. *206*

Amlie, Thomas R. (political career). New Deal. Radicals and Radicalism. Roosevelt, Franklin D. Wisconsin. 1930-39. *704*

Amos 'n Andy (program). Boycotts. Comic strips. Negroes. Radio. Stereotypes. 1930's. *719*

—. Humor. Radio. Social Problems. 1929-30's. *945*

Amyotrophic lateral sclerosis. Baseball. Character. Gehrig, Lou. Letters. New York Yankees (team). 1939. *777*

Andersen, Kristi. Blumberg, Barbara. Fine, Sidney. Jeffries, John W. New Deal (review article). Roosevelt, Franklin D. Swain, Martha H. 1933-39. *143*

—. Democratic Party. Partisanship. Republican Party. Voting and Voting Behavior. 1920-32. *229*

Andersen, Kristi (review article). Democratic Party. Leftism. 1928-36. 1979. *182*

Anderson, Maxwell *(Night Over Taos)*. *American Mercury* (periodical). New Mexico. 18c-19c. 1932. *885*

Anderson, Orvil A. Balloon flights, stratospheric. Stevens, Albert W. 1920's-35. *712*

Anthropology. Bureau of Indian Affairs. Collier, John. Federal Programs. Indians. New Deal. 1930's. *375*

Antidemocratism. Cynicism. Journalism. Mencken, H. L. Satire. 1920's-56. *914*

Anti-Imperialism. Foreign Policy (critics). Pacific Area. Roosevelt, Franklin D. World War II (antecedents). 1930's. *692*

Anti-Nazi sentiments. Boxing. Louis, Joe. Racism. Schmeling, Max. 1930's. *801*

Anti-Semitism. American Olympic Committee. Boycotts, proposed. Brundage, Avery. "Fair Play for American Athletes" (pamphlet). Germany (Berlin). Olympic Games. 1935-36. *851*

—. Benson, Elmer A. Minnesota. Political Campaigns (gubernatorial). 1930's. *536*

—. Boxerman, William I. Coughlin, Charles. Jewish Community Council. Michigan (Detroit). Radio. 1939. *725*

—. Columbia University. Trilling, Lionel. 1930's. *739*

—. Edmondson, Robert Edward. Libel. Trials. 1934-44. *597*

—. Elites. Freedom of speech. Mencken, H. L. Public opinion. 1917-41. *769*

—. Fascism. 1930's. *524*

—. Germany. Nazism. *New York Times.* Reporters and Reporting. 1932-33. *749*
Antitrust. Appellate Courts. Arnold, Thurman W. Justice Department. Roosevelt, Franklin D. (administration). 1935-43. *415*
Antiwar sentiment. Colleges and Universities. Leftism. Political Protest. 1920-36. *547*
—. Keep America Out of War Congress. Socialist Party. Thomas, Norman. Villard, Oswald Garrison. World War II (antecedents). 1938-41. *584*
Appalachia. Congressmen. New Deal. 1933-39. *173*
—. Leftism. Mountaineers. Music. Resettlement Administration (music program). Seeger, Charles. Social Organization. 1935-37. *506*
Appellate Courts. Antitrust. Arnold, Thurman W. Justice Department. Roosevelt, Franklin D. (administration). 1935-43. *415*
Apple sellers. 1929-30. *50*
Architecture. City planning. Europe. Housing. Modernism. New Deal. 1932-60. *897*
—. Design (review article). Industry. Meikle, Jeffrey L. 1925-39. 1979. *823*
—. Leonidov, Ivan. Melnikov, Konstantin. 1929-31. *848*
Archives, National. Conservation of natural resources. New Deal. 1930's. 1976. *435*
Arizona. Agricultural experiment stations. New Deal. New Mexico. Oklahoma. Texas. 1926-39. *407*
—. Ballads. Capital Punishment. "Corrido de los Hermanos" (ballad). Hernández, Federico. Hernández, Manuel. 1934. *724*
Arizona (Salt River Valley). Farmers. Japanese Americans. Race Relations. 1934-35. *529*
Arizona (Superior). Brodie, J. C. (correspondence). Bureau of Immigration. Deportation. Mexicans. 1930-34. *620*
Arizona (Tucson). Daily Life. 1929-39. *109*
Arkansas. Bank holiday. Business. Roosevelt, Franklin D. 1933. *126*
—. Disasters. Federal Programs. Food Supply. 1933-42. *360*
—. Federal Aid to Education. Federal Emergency Relief Administration. Hopkins, Harry. Public schools. 1933-36. *451*
Arkansas Light and Power Company. Electrification, rural. Rural Electrification Administration. 1933-40. *301*
Arkansas (Mena). Colleges and Universities. Commonwealth College. 1923-40. *568*
Armaments. Embargoes. Isolationism. Neutrality Act (US, 1935). 1935. *756*
Armies. Censorship. Civilian Conservation Corps. Communism. Conservatism. Flechner, Robert. 1934-42. *343*
—. Civilian Conservation Corps. New Deal. 1933-42. *443*
Armstrong Cork Company. Business. New Deal. Pennsylvania (Lancaster). Prentis, Henning Webb, Jr. 1934-40. *514*
Army. Civilian Conservation Corps. Military Organization. Negroes. 1933-42. *370*
Army Air Corps. Air Mail Service. Foulois, Benjamin D. 1934. *475*
—. Air mail service. Foulois, Benjamin D. Postal service. 1933-34. *348*
—. Airplane flights. Alaska (Fairbanks). B-10 (aircraft). District of Columbia. Politics. 1934. *821*
Army Corps of Engineers. Employment. Fort Peck Dam. Missouri River. Montana. 1932-61. *457*
—. Flood control. Mississippi River (lower). Politics. 1927-41. *449*

Arnold, Thurman W. Antitrust. Appellate Courts. Justice Department. Roosevelt, Franklin D. (administration). 1935-43. *415*
Art. Indians. Iroquois School of Art. New Deal. New York (Akron). Parker, Arthur C. Seneca Arts project. Tonawanda Indian Reservation. 1935-41. *352*
—. Literature. 1930's. *891*
—. Mexico. Murals. New York school. 1930's. *760*
Art and Society. Negroes. New York City. Painting. Stage Setting and Scenery. Stettheimer, Florine. 1929-44. *882*
Art and State. New Deal. New Jersey. Public Works of Art Project. 1932-40. *519*
Art deco. Deskey, Donald. Genauer, Emily (account). Interior decorating. New York City. Radio City Music Hall. 1929-37. *815*
Artists. 1930's-50's. *939*
—. American Abstract Artists. American Artists' Congress. Social Organization. Surrealism. 1935-45. *310*
—. Buildings, public. Federal Programs. New Deal. 1930's. *436*
—. City life. Marsh, Reginald. New York City. 1930's. *958*
—. Communist Party. Federal funding. Works Progress Administration. 1930's. *418*
—. Ginther, Ronald Debs. Labor unrest. Skid row. ca 1920-69. *937*
—. New Deal. 1930's. *928*
—. New Deal. 1933-41. *501*
—. Organizations. Radicals and Radicalism. 1930's. *938*
Arts. Berger, Arthur. Criticism. Music. Personal narratives. Works Progress Administration. 1930-80. *786*
—. Cultural democracy. New Deal. 1933-42. *405*
Arts, visual. McKinzie, Richard D. (review article). New Deal. Subsidies. 1933-40. *328*
Assassination. Cermak, Anton. Florida (Miami). Roosevelt, Franklin D. Zangara, Giuseppi. 1933. *152*
Assassination, attempted. Florida (Miami). Roosevelt, Franklin D. Zangara, Giuseppi. 1933. *231*
Assimilation (opposition to). Collier, John. Federal Policy. Indian Reorganization Act (1934). 1933-45. *377*
Association of Southern Commissioners of Agriculture. Agricultural Policy. Cotton. New Deal. South. Tennessee (Memphis). 1936-37. *423*
Association of Southern Women for the Prevention of Lynching. Ames, Jessie Daniel. Lynching. South. Women. 1928-42. *672*
—. Lynching. Negroes. South. Women. 1930-42. *530*
Astaire, Fred. Films. Popular Culture. Rogers, Ginger. 1930-39. *930*
Atlanta *Georgian* (newspaper). Economic Conditions. Georgia. Letters. Seydell, Mildred. 1930's. *10*
Attica State Prison. NAACP. Negroes. New York. Prison conditions. 1932. *751*
Attitudes *See also* Values.
—. Agricultural Adjustment Administration. Agricultural policy. New Deal. 1920-33. *336*
—. American Medical Association (Committee on the Cost of Medical Care). Medical Care (costs). *Medical Care for the American People* (report). 1926-31. *124*
—. Blitzstein, Marc *(Cradle Will Rock)*. Censorship. Federal Theatre Project. Labor. New York City. Works Progress Administration. 1937. *502*

—. Chicago, University of. Economic Theory.
Keynes, John Maynard. Simons, Henry. 1930's.
85
—. Daily Life. Lee, Russell. Photographs.
1932-40. *827*
—. Federal Policy. New Deal. Technology.
1927-40. *442*
—. Films. New Deal. 1930-40. *778*
—. Great Britain. Law. Poor. Vagrancy.
14c-1939. *20*
—. Morality. Sex. 1918-55. *662*
—. New Deal. Roper, Elmo. Socialism, failure of.
Working class. 1939. *743*
—. Stock Market Crash. Texas (western). 1929-33.
131
—. Texas. 1929-33. *129*
Attorney General. Cummings, Homer Stillé.
Federal Bureau of Investigation. Films. *G-Men*
(film). Hoover, J. Edgar. 1933-35. *898*
Austin, Gene. Music (jazz). Waller, Fats. 1929-39.
860
Austin, Warren R. Foreign Policy. Neutrality Act,
1939 (proposed). Roosevelt, Franklin D. Senate.
1935-39. *759*
Authors. Dardis, Tom. Films. Hollywood.
Scriptwriting. 1936-45. 1976. *919*
—. End Poverty in California program. Mencken,
H. L. (letters). Sinclair, Upton (letters). Social
Reform. ca 1918-51. *902*
—. Industrialization. Social Conditions. South.
Urbanization. 1930's. *908*
—. Johnson, Hugh S. (career). Military officers.
National Recovery Administration. ca 1903-42.
426
Authors (southern). Gordon, Caroline. Letters.
New York (Rochester). Tennessee (Benfolly).
Wood, Sally. 1930-31. *818*
Autobiography. Douglas, William O. (review
article). Judges. Roosevelt, Franklin D.
(administration). 1933-39. 1974. *337*
—. Federal Writers' Project. Oral history. South.
1930-39. *361*
—. Novels. Wolfe, Thomas. 1924-38. *873*
Automobile, advent of. Kentucky. Peddlers,
disappearance of. 1930's. *727*
Automobile Industry and Trade. Communist Party
(review article). Keeran, Roger. Labor Unions
and Organizations. 1930-39. 1980. *645*
—. Dillon, Francis. Michigan. Motor Products
Corporation. Strikes. United Automobile
Workers of America. 1933-39. *545*
—. Indiana. Labor parties. New Deal. Ohio.
United Automobile Workers of America.
1935-40. *652*
—. Indiana (Kokomo). Patterson, Robert *(Gas
Buggy)*. 1933. *820*
Automobile Workers Union. Communist Party.
Labor Unions and Organizations. Michigan
(Detroit). 1920's-1935. *699*
Automobiles. Geddes, Norman Bel. Industrial
design. Streamlining. 1930-39. *870*

B

Balance sheets, household. Consumers. Demand,
aggregate. Economic Theory. 1929-38. *74*
Ballads. Arizona. Capital Punishment. "Corrido de
los Hermanos" (ballad). Hernández, Federico.
Hernández, Manuel. 1934. *724*
Balloon flights, stratospheric. Anderson, Orvil A.
Stevens, Albert W. 1920's-35. *712*
Balloons. Carter, "Red". First Balloon Squadron.
Fort Sill. Oklahoma. 1930's. *561*
Baltimore *Sun*, *Evening Sun* (newspapers).
Government intervention. Letters-to-the-editor.
Maryland. Roosevelt, Franklin D. 1929-33.
384

Bands. Music. Swing Era. 1934-45. *921*
Bank deposits. Economic Conditions. Great
Contraction. Money (demand). 1929-33. *34*
Bank failures. Credit overextension. Economic
Conditions. Rural financial crisis. 1920's.
49
Bank holiday. Arkansas. Business. Roosevelt,
Franklin D. 1933. *126*
Bank of America. California. Elections
(gubernatorial). Giannini, Amadeo P. Merriam,
Frank. Roosevelt, Franklin D. Sinclair, Upton.
ca 1923-34. *138*
Banking. Alien Property Custodian. Crowley, Leo
T. Federal Deposit Insurance Corporation.
Politics. Roosevelt, Franklin D. (administration).
1934-45. *510*
—. Federal government. Hoover, Herbert C.
Nevada. Reconstruction Finance Corporation.
1932-33. *83*
—. Idaho (Boise). Reconstruction Finance
Corporation. 1932. *80*
—. Monetary policy. New Deal. Roosevelt,
Franklin D. (administration). Warburg, James P.
1932-41. *413*
—. Money. Panic of 1930. 1920-30. *132*
Banking crisis. Kennedy, Susan Estabrook (review
article). 1933. 1973. *17*
—. Michigan. Reconstruction Finance Corporation.
1933. *54*
Baran, Paul. Capitalism (review article). Sweezy,
Paul. 1930's. 1966. *53*
Barkley, Alben W. Democratic Party. Harrison,
Byron Patton (Pat). Newspapers. Senate
(majority leader). 1937. *174*
—. Democratic Party. Roosevelt, Franklin D.
Senate (majority leader). Supreme Court (issue).
1937. *153*
Barrow, Clyde. Ford automobile. Gangster myth.
Parker, Bonnie. Rich, Carroll Y. Warren, Jesse.
1934-67. *957*
Baseball. Amyotrophic lateral sclerosis. Character.
Gehrig, Lou. Letters. New York Yankees
(team). 1939. *777*
—. Davis, Lorenzo Piper (interview). Negro
Leagues. 1930's-40's. *907*
—. Rural-urban issues. *Sporting News* (newspaper).
1920's-30's. *789*
Baseball, semiprofessional. Negroes. North Dakota
(Dickinson). Otto, Solomon (reminiscences).
Race Relations. 1929-31. *889*
Basketmaking. Africa, West. Negroes. Works
Progress Administration. 1935-78. *935*
Basso, Hamilton. Demagoguery, concept of. Long,
Huey P. Louisiana. Novels. 1920-76. *726*
Bauer, Catherine. Federal Policy. Public housing.
Reform. Wagner-Steagall Act (US, 1937).
Wood, Edith Elmer. 1890's-1940's. *292*
Beard, Charles A. Historians. Intellectuals.
Isolationism. Liberalism. New Deal. Roosevelt,
Franklin D. 1932-48. *296*
Bedford-Jones, H. Gardner, Erle Stanley. Novels
(pulp). 1920's-30's. *810*
Beer. Cullen-Harrison Act (US, 1933). Festivals.
Wisconsin (Milwaukee). 1933. *520*
Behavior. Radio. Welles, Orson. Wells, H. G. *(War
of the Worlds)*. 1938. *876*
Bell Telephone System. Company unions. Labor
Unions and Organizations. 1919-37. *713*
Bellow, Saul. Acculturation. Illinois (Chicago).
Immigrants. ca 1937-74. *533*
Benefactor-aversion hypothesis. Local government.
Nixon, Richard M. (administration). Roosevelt,
Franklin D. (administration). State Government.
1933-45. 1969-74. *392*
Benson, Elmer A. Anti-Semitism. Minnesota.
Political Campaigns (gubernatorial). 1930's.
536

Berger, Arthur. Arts. Criticism. Music. Personal narratives. Works Progress Administration. 1930-80. *786*

Bergonzi, Bernard. Literature (review article). Salzman, Jack. Spender, Stephen. Zanderer, Leo. ca 1930-39. 1978-79. *775*

Berkeley Guidance Study. California. Employment. Family. Women. 1930-70. *9*

Berry, Harry S. Political Corruption. Tennessee (Nashville). Works Progress Administration. 1935-43. *309*

Berry pickers. California (El Monte). Foreign Relations. Japan. Mexico. Strikes. 1933. *619*

Bethune, Mary McLeod. Black Cabinet. National Youth Administration. Negroes. New Deal. 1930-40. *455*

—. Equal opportunity. National Youth Administration. Negroes. Public Policy. Youth. 1935-44. *483*

Beverly Hill Billies (group). California (Los Angeles). Country music. Discographies. 1930-32. *959*

Bibliographies. Intervention. Leadership. Political Attitudes. 1929-41. *580*

—. Literature. 1930's. *776*

—. Literature. Negroes. 1930's. *878*

"Big Three" relationship. Football. Harvard University. Ivy League. Princeton University. 1926-39. *924*

Biochemistry. Isotopes. Research. Schoenheimer, Rudolf. 1934-41. *640*

Biography. Couch, W. T. Federal Writers' Project. New Deal. South. 1938-39. *499*

—. Family history. Interviews. Louisiana State University. Students. Works Progress Administration. 1930's. 1978. *321*

—. Films. 1929-49. *822*

Black Cabinet. Bethune, Mary McLeod. National Youth Administration. Negroes. New Deal. 1930-40. *455*

Black, Hugo. Air mail service. Contracts. Farley, James A. Hoover, Herbert C. (administration). Legislative Investigations. 1933-34. *487*

Black nationalism. Communism. Garvey, Marcus. New York City (Harlem). 1931-39. *681*

—. Ethiopia. Invasions. Italy. Negroes. Pan-Africanism. 1934-36. *716*

Blankenhorn, Heber. Industrial Relations. LaFollette Committee. Legislative Investigations. Strikes, sit-down. 1935-40. *600*

Blitzstein, Marc *(Cradle Will Rock)*. Attitudes. Censorship. Federal Theatre Project. Labor. New York City. Works Progress Administration. 1937. *502*

Blizzards. Illinois Central Railroad. Iowa. 1936. *622*

Blumberg, Barbara. Andersen, Kristi. Fine, Sidney. Jeffries, John W. New Deal (review article). Roosevelt, Franklin D. Swain, Martha H. 1933-39. *143*

Bogart, Humphrey. Films, gangster. *High Sierra* (film). Roy Earle, fictional character. 1930's-41. *762*

Bonneville Power Administration. Electric utilities. New Deal. Pacific Northwest. Public Utilities. 1937-42. *339*

—. Films. Folk Songs. Guthrie, Woody. 1939-49. *872*

Bonnifield, Paul. Dust Bowl (review article). Great Plains (southern). Worster, Donald. ca 1900-39. 1979. *59*

Bonus Army. American Legion. District of Columbia. North Carolina. Political Protest. Stevens, Henry L., Jr. Veterans (benefits). 1932. *694*

—. District of Columbia. Legislation (proposed). Patman, Wright. Veterans' certificates. 1932. *666*

Book Collecting. Twain, Mark (short story). 1930-31. *936*

Boomtowns. Oil Industry and Trade. Texas (Conroe). 1929-33. *82*

Bootlegging. Florida (Hernando County). Law enforcement. Liquor. Prohibition. 1929-33. *562*

Bop (term). Gillespie, Dizzy. Music. 1928-40's. *926*

Boulder Canyon project. Colorado River. Hoover Dam. Industrial Workers of the World. Nevada. Strikes. 1931. *702*

—. Hoover Dam. Industrial Workers of the World. Nevada. Six Companies, Inc. Strikes. 1931. *703*

Boxerman, William I. Anti-Semitism. Coughlin, Charles. Jewish Community Council. Michigan (Detroit). Radio. 1939. *725*

Boxing. Anti-Nazi sentiments. Louis, Joe. Racism. Schmeling, Max. 1930's. *801*

—. Germany. Louis, Joe. Nazism. Negroes. Schmeling, Max. 1936-38. *784*

Boycotts. *Amos 'n Andy* (program). Comic strips. Negroes. Radio. Stereotypes. 1930's. *719*

—. Brundage, Avery. Olympic Games. 1936. *863*

—. Germany. Olympic Games. 1932-36. *825*

Boycotts, proposed. American Olympic Committee. Anti-Semitism. Brundage, Avery. "Fair Play for American Athletes" (pamphlet). Germany (Berlin). Olympic Games. 1935-36. *851*

—. Germany (Berlin). Olympic Games. Racism, issue of. 1933-36. *843*

Bradley Air Museum. Air races. Connecticut. Rider R-3 (aircraft). 1930's-70's. *922*

Braeman, John (review article). Historiography. New Deal. Reform. State government. 1930's-40's. *382*

—. New Deal (policies, programs). Politics. Roosevelt, Franklin D. 1930's. *399*

Brandeis, Louis D. Dawson, Nelson L. Frankfurter, Felix. Landis, James M. Law. New Deal (review article). Ritchie, Donald A. 1930's. *512*

—. Due process. Economic Regulations. *Nebbia v. New York* (US, 1934). *New State Ice v. Liebmann* (US, 1932). Supreme Court. *West Coast Hotel v. Parrish* (US, 1937). 1897-1937. *476*

—. Frankfurter, Felix. New Deal. Politics. Roosevelt, Franklin D. World War I. 1917-33. *154*

—. Freund, Paul A. (reminiscences). Law. Supreme Court. 1932-33. *167*

Branion-Williams case (California). California. Federal Civil Works Administration. McAdoo, William G. Patronage. Social workers. 1933-34. *468*

Branson, Eugene C. Electric Power. North Carolina. Poe, Clarence H. Rural Electrification Administration. State Government. 1917-36. *302*

Breach of contract. Lawsuits. Miller, Zack. Mix, Tom. Sells-Floto Circus. Verbal agreements. 101 Ranch Real Wild West Show. 1929-34. *819*

Brecht, Bertolt. Lindbergh, Charles A. (tribute). Music. Radio broadcasts. Weill, Kurt. 1929-31. *849*

Bridges (toll, free). Interstate relations. Oklahoma National Guard. Red River Bridge Company. Texas Rangers. 1931. *30*

Broadacre City. Agrarianism. City Planning. Decentralization. Oklahoma (Bartlesville). Wright, Frank Lloyd. 1935. *864*

Brodie, J. C. (correspondence). Arizona (Superior). Bureau of Immigration. Deportation. Mexicans. 1930-34. *620*

Brookwood Labor College. Labor Unions and Organizations. New York. 1926-36. *644*

Browder, Earl. Communist Party. 1934-45. *710*

Brown, E. Cary. Employment. Fiscal policy, role of. Full-employment surplus analysis. 1930's. 1956. 1973. *86*

Browning, Gordon. Elections (gubernatorial). Political machines. Tennessee. 1936. *135*

Brucker, Wilber M. Michigan. Murphy, Frank. Unemployment. 1929-33. *84*

—. Michigan. Politics. Tax reform. 1929-33. *222*

Brundage, Avery. American Olympic Committee. Anti-Semitism. Boycotts, proposed. "Fair Play for American Athletes" (pamphlet). Germany (Berlin). Olympic Games. 1935-36. *851*

—. Boycotts. Olympic Games. 1936. *863*

Budgets (state allocations). Democratic Party. New Deal. Political Campaigns. 1932-40. *270*

Buildings. Cincinnati Union Terminal. Moore, Alfred. Ohio. Railroads. 1933-73. *933*

—. Supreme Court. 1789-1935. *918*

Buildings, public. Artists. Federal Programs. New Deal. 1930's. *436*

—. California. Murals. National Self-image. New Deal. 1933-46. *814*

Bulkley, Robert J. Elections. Ohio. Prohibition. Senate. 1918-30. *256*

Bulosan, Carlos (autobiography). California. Filipino Americans. Labor Unions and Organizations. Leftism. 1934-38. *552*

Bunche, Ralph. National Negro Congress. Negroes. New Deal. Political Attitudes. 1930-39. *639*

Bureau of Immigration. Arizona (Superior). Brodie, J. C. (correspondence). Deportation. Mexicans. 1930-34. *620*

Bureau of Indian Affairs. American Indian Federation. Collier, John. Indians. Jamison, Alice Lee. New Deal. Political activism. 1930's-50's. *351*

—. Anthropology. Collier, John. Federal Programs. Indians. New Deal. 1930's. *375*

—. Collier, John. Ickes, Harold. Interior Department. Presidential appointments. Roosevelt, Franklin D. 1933. *376*

—. Collier, John. Indians (government relations). New Deal. 1933-45. *498*

—. Collier, John. New Deal. Public Administration. Social sciences principles. 1933-45. *497*

Bureau of Labor Statistics. Lubin, Isador. New Deal. Perkins, Frances. Statistics. Unemployment. 1920-49. *342*

Bureau of Narcotics. Marihuana Tax Act (US, 1937). 1937. *601*

Bureaucracies. Allen, Fred. Commercialism. Criticism. Humor. Radio. 1932-49. *824*

Bureaucrats. Pennsylvania (Philadelphia). Public housing. 1929-41. *282*

Business. Agriculture. Alcohol. Fuel. Motors. Prices. Surpluses. 1930's. *604*

—. American Liberty League. Civil rights. Federal Regulation. Government, Resistance to. New Deal. 1934-36. *698*

—. Arkansas. Bank holiday. Roosevelt, Franklin D. 1933. *126*

—. Armstrong Cork Company. New Deal. Pennsylvania (Lancaster). Prentis, Henning Webb, Jr. 1934-40. *514*

—. Conservatism. Isolationism. New Deal. Sears, Roebuck and Company. Wood, Robert E. 1928-50's. *581*

—. Idaho (Pocatello). New Deal. 1930's. *495*

—. Labor Unions and Organizations. New Deal. Taft-Hartley Act (US, 1947). Wagner Act (US, 1935). World War II. 1935-47. *543*

—. National Association of Manufacturers. New Deal. Public relations. 1930's. *734*

Butchering. North Dakota (Williston). Soup kitchen. Vohs, Al J. (interview). 1900's-30's. *110*

Byrd, Harry F. Democratic Party. Elections (presidential). Roosevelt, Franklin D. State Politics. Virginia. 1932. *260*

—. Democratic Party. Glass, Carter. Roosevelt, Franklin D. Senate. Virginia. 1938. *183*

—. Democratic Party. Patronage. Senate. Virginia. 1935-39. *196*

—. Democratic Party (convention). Political Campaigns. Presidential nomination. Roosevelt, Franklin D. 1932. *187*

B-10 (aircraft). Airplane flights. Alaska (Fairbanks). Army Air Corps. District of Columbia. Politics. 1934. *821*

C

Cain, James M. California (Los Angeles). Novels. 1925-45. *807*

California. Aeronautics. Trans-polar flight (nonstop). USSR (Moscow). 1937. *785*

—. Agricultural Labor. Labor Unions and Organizations. National Industrial Recovery Act (1933). 1933-34. *323*

—. Agricultural Labor Relations Act (1975). Emergency Farm Labor Supply Program. Labor law. New Deal. ca 1930-79. *338*

—. Agricultural laborers. Labor Unions and Organizations. Migration, Internal. "Okies". 1930's. *115*

—. Bank of America. Elections (gubernatorial). Giannini, Amadeo P. Merriam, Frank. Roosevelt, Franklin D. Sinclair, Upton. ca 1923-34. *138*

—. Berkeley Guidance Study. Employment. Family. Women. 1930-70. *9*

—. Branion-Williams case (California). Federal Civil Works Administration. McAdoo, William G. Patronage. Social workers. 1933-34. *468*

—. Buildings, public. Murals. National Self-image. New Deal. 1933-46. *814*

—. Bulosan, Carlos (autobiography). Filipino Americans. Labor Unions and Organizations. Leftism. 1934-38. *552*

—. Democratic Party. End Poverty In California program. Political Campaigns (gubernatorial). Sinclair, Upton. ca 1933-34. *242*

—. Governors. Public Welfare. Ralph, James, Jr. 1931-34. *16*

—. Guthrie, Woody. Migration, Internal. 1937-67. *952*

—. Labor. Public welfare administration. ca 1930-45. *390*

—. Progressive education. ca 1930-40. *615*

California (El Monte). Berry pickers. Foreign Relations. Japan. Mexico. Strikes. 1933. *619*

California (Hollywood). *Citizen Kane* (film). Films. Kael, Pauline (review article). 1930-39. *859*

—. Films. Hispanic Americans. Spanish language. 1930-39. *896*

—. Films. Photography. Popular Culture. Publicity. 1930-39. *847*

California Life Payments Plan. Advertising. Allen, Laurence. Allen, Willis. Economic structure. Noble, Robert. Pensions. Referendum. 1937-39. *755*

California (Los Angeles). Beverly Hill Billies (group). Country music. Discographies. 1930-32. *959*

—. Cain, James M. Novels. 1925-45. *807*
—. City Government. Clinton, Clifford. Recall. Shaw, Frank. 1938. *189*
—. International Ladies' Garment Workers' Union. Mexican Americans. Women. Working Conditions. 1933-39. *673*
—. Olympic Games. 1932. *956*
California (Los Angeles County). Davis, James J. Deportation. Mexicans. Unemployment. 1931. *363*
California (San Francisco). Dreiser, Theodore (interview). Literature. Social Conditions. 1939. *904*
—. General strikes. National Guard. Waterfronts. 1934. *625*
—. Hammett, Dashiell. Novels, detective. Sam Spade (fictional character). 1920-30's. *866*
—. Labor markets. Longshoremen. Strikes. 1934-39. *635*
California (San Jose; St. James Park). Hart, Brooke (murder). Holmes, John. Kidnapping. Lynching. Thurmond, Thomas. 1933. *665*
California (Santa Barbara). Fleischmann, Max. Philanthropy. Relief work. Unemployment. 1930-32. *78*
California, southern. Agricultural Labor. Steinbeck, John *(In Dubious Battle)*. Strikes. 1933. *773*
California (Watsonville). Filipino Americans. Racism. Riots. Violence. 1926-30. *577*
Callahan, Patrick Henry. Catholic Church. Democratic Party. Kentucky (Louisville). 1866-1940. *158*
Capital Punishment. Arizona. Ballads. "Corrido de los Hermanos" (ballad). Hernández, Federico. Hernández, Manuel. 1934. *724*
—. Negroes. Newspapers. Rape. Reporters and Reporting. Scottsboro Case. Trials. 1931-32. *697*
Capitalism. American Writers' Congress. Comintern. League of American Writers. 1935. *567*
—. Capra, Frank. Films. *Mr. Deeds Goes to Town* (film). Social Organization. 1936. *861*
—. Government. Marxism. New Deal. Political Theory. 1933-39. 1980. *103*
—. Marxism. Niebuhr, Reinhold. *Radical Religion* (periodical). Roosevelt, Franklin D. (administration). 1930-43. *532*
—. Political Attitudes. Radicals and Radicalism. Texas. 1929-33. *128*
Capitalism (review article). Baran, Paul. Sweezy, Paul. 1930's. 1966. *53*
Capitalist countries. Economic relations. 1934-38. *62*
Capra, Frank. Capitalism. Films. *Mr. Deeds Goes to Town* (film). Social Organization. 1936. *861*
—. Films. Humor. McCarey, Leo. 1930's. *813*
—. Films. *Mr. Smith Goes To Washington* (film). Politics. Populism. 1939. *881*
—. Films. Politics. Yankee (character). 1936-41. *812*
—. *Miracle Woman* (film). Values. 1930's. *934*
Carbon County Coal Strike (1933). National Miners Union. Strikes. United Mine Workers of America. Utah. 1900-39. *693*
Carbone, Peter F., Jr. (review article). Liberalism. Public Schools. Reform. Rugg, Harold. 1930's. *689*
Career patterns. Lawyers. New Deal. 1918-41. *4*
Carmody, John. American Federation of Labor. Civil Works Administration. New Deal. Work relief. 1933-34. *467*
Carter, Boake. Advertising. Military. News. Political Commentary. Radio. 1931-38. *803*

—. New Deal. News commentator. Political criticism. Radio. Roosevelt, Franklin D. 1935-38. *790*
Carter, Jimmy (administration). Executive reorganization. Roosevelt, Franklin D. (administration). 1937-38. 1977-78. *437*
Carter, "Red". Balloons. First Balloon Squadron. Fort Sill. Oklahoma. 1930's. *561*
Cartoonists. Gray, Harold. *Little Orphan Annie* (comic strip). Social conservatism. World War II. 1930's-40's. *955*
Catholic Church. Agricultural Reform. New Deal. Roosevelt, Franklin D. (administration). Social Theory. 1933-39. *473*
—. Callahan, Patrick Henry. Democratic Party. Kentucky (Louisville). 1866-1940. *158*
—. Farm programs. New Deal. Rural life movement. 1930's. *721*
Causeways. Civilian Conservation Corps (co. 796). Missouri River. South Dakota (Farm Island). 1934. *521*
Censorship. Advertising. Missouri. Newspapers. Pulitzer, Joseph, II. St. Louis *Post Dispatch*. 1929-39. *893*
—. Armies. Civilian Conservation Corps. Communism. Conservatism. Flechner, Robert. 1934-42. *343*
—. Attitudes. Blitzstein, Marc *(Cradle Will Rock)*. Federal Theatre Project. Labor. New York City. Works Progress Administration. 1937. *502*
—. Cerf, Bennett. Ernst, Morris. Joyce, James *(Ulysses)*. United States v. *One Book Called "Ulysses"* (US, 1932). 1922-32. *840*
—. *Crisis* (periodical). District of Columbia. *Opportunity* (periodical). Public schools. School Boards. 1936. *571*
Cerf, Bennett. Censorship. Ernst, Morris. Joyce, James *(Ulysses)*. United States v. *One Book Called "Ulysses"* (US, 1932). 1922-32. *840*
Cermak, Anton. Assassination. Florida (Miami). Roosevelt, Franklin D. Zangara, Giuseppi. 1933. *152*
Chafe, William H. Lemon, J. Stanley. Politics. Women's movement (review article). 1920-70. *610*
Chain stores. South. Taxes. ca 1925-40. *94*
Challenge (periodical). Literature. McKay, Claude. Negroes. 1930's. *838*
Chandler, A. B. ("Happy"). Elections (gubernatorial). Federal Emergency Relief Administration. Kentucky. Works Progress Administration. 1935. *202*
Chandler, Walter. Crump, Edward. Democratic Party. House of Representatives. Tennessee. 1933-40. *149*
Chaplin, Charlie. Dickens, Charles *(Hard Times)*. Films. Great Britain. *Modern Times* (film). 1854. 1936. *923*
Character. Amyotrophic lateral sclerosis. Baseball. Gehrig, Lou. Letters. New York Yankees (team). 1939. *777*
Charities. Children's Aid Society. Maryland (Carroll County). Rural areas. 1928-35. *66*
Cherokee Indians. Indian policy. New Deal. North Carolina, western. 1930's. *508*
Chicago Newspaper Guild. American Federation of Labor. Illinois. Labor Unions and Organizations (white-collar). 1933-40. *642*
Chicago, University of. Attitudes. Economic Theory. Keynes, John Maynard. Simons, Henry. 1930's. *85*
—. Communist sympathizers, alleged. Illinois. Newspapers. Walgreen, Charles R. 1930's. *663*
—. Educators. Personal Narratives. Shils, Edward. Sociology. 1932-36. *915*

Chicago, University of (Psychology Department). Functionalism. McKinney, Fred (reminiscences). Psychology. 1929-31. *669*

Chief of Naval Operations. Navies. Pratt, William Veazie. 1930-33. *732*

Children's Aid Society. Charities. Maryland (Carroll County). Rural areas. 1928-35. *66*

China. Congress. International Trade. Lobbying. Roosevelt, Franklin D. (administration). Silver Purchase Act (1934). 1934. *341*

—. International Trade. Pittman, Key. Senate. Silver Purchase Act (1934). 1933-40. *472*

Chisum, Melvin J. Journalism. Negroes. Roosevelt, Franklin D. (election). *Tribune* (newspaper). ca 1932. *892*

Christensen, Mart. Federal Writers' Project. Spring, Agnes Wright. Works Progress Administration. Wyoming. 1935-41. *354*

Christianity. Longshoremen. Oxford Group movement. Strikes. Washington (Seattle). 1921-34. *738*

Cincinnati Union Terminal. Buildings. Moore, Alfred. Ohio. Railroads. 1933-73. *933*

Circumnavigation, attempted. Aeronautics. Earhart, Amelia. 1897-1937. *909*

—. Aeronautics. Earhart, Amelia. Radio equipment. 1937. *931*

Circumnavigation (solo). Aeronautics. Oklahoma. Post, Wiley. 1920's-35. *560*

Cities (review article). Democratic Party. Dorsett, Lyle W. Fine, Sidney. Trout, Charles H. 1930-40. *186*

Citizen Kane (film). California (Hollywood). Films. Kael, Pauline (review article). 1930-39. *859*

Citizen Kane (filmscript). Welles, Orson. 1940. *781*

City (film). City planning. Films. 1939. *816*

—. City Planning. Social criticism. Steiner, Ralph. VanDyke, Willard. 1932-39. *867*

City Government. California (Los Angeles). Clinton, Clifford. Recall. Shaw, Frank. 1938. *189*

—. Fine, Sidney (review article). Michigan (Detroit). Murphy, Frank. 1930-33. 1975. *150*

—. Fiscal Policy. New Jersey (Paterson). Public Welfare. Textile industry. 1920-32. *77*

—. Flogging case. Florida (Tampa). Political Corruption. Vigilantism. 1935-38. *628*

City Government (relations with state government). Emergency Economy Bill (New York, 1934). La Guardia, Fiorello Henry. New York City. 1934. *144*

City life. Artists. Marsh, Reginald. New York City. 1930's. *958*

—. New York City. Personal Narratives. Pessen, Edward. 1929-39. *87*

City of Progress. Construction. Economic development. Illinois (Chicago). 1933-34. *14*

City Planning. Agrarianism. Broadacre City. Decentralization. Oklahoma (Bartlesville). Wright, Frank Lloyd. 1935. *864*

—. Architecture. Europe. Housing. Modernism. New Deal. 1932-60. *897*

—. *City* (film). Films. 1939. *816*

—. *City* (film). Social criticism. Steiner, Ralph. VanDyke, Willard. 1932-39. *867*

City Politics. Massachusetts (Boston). New Deal. Roosevelt, Franklin D. (administration). Trout, Charles H. (review article). 1929-39. 1977. *157*

Civil rights. American Civil Liberties Union. Kentucky (Bell County, London). Miners. Trials. 1932-38. *733*

—. American Liberty League. Business. Federal Regulation. Government, Resistance to. New Deal. 1934-36. *698*

—. Constitutional History. Legal order, equalitarian. 1930-50. *611*

—. Federal Bureau of Investigation. Roosevelt, Franklin D. 1936-80. *288*

Civil rights activity. Illinois (Chicago). Negroes. School integration. 1936. *624*

Civil War. Fiction. Hemingway, Ernest *(For Whom the Bell Tolls).* Propaganda. Reporters and Reporting. Spain. 1936-40. *853*

Civil Works Administration. American Federation of Labor. Carmody, John. New Deal. Work relief. 1933-34. *467*

—. Louisiana. 1932-34. *416*

—. New Deal. Work relief. 1933-39. *298*

Civilian Conservation Corps. Armies. Censorship. Communism. Conservatism. Flechner, Robert. 1934-42. *343*

—. Armies. New Deal. 1933-42. *443*

—. Army. Military Organization. Negroes. 1933-42. *370*

—. Discrimination, employment. Negroes. New York. 1933-42. *441*

—. Economic Conditions. New Deal. Vermont. 1933-42. *490*

—. Employment. Environment. South Dakota. 1933-42. *357*

—. Equal opportunity (failure). Negroes. New Deal. 1933-42. *344*

—. Glacier National Park. Montana. 1933-42. *425*

—. Income. 1937-81. *471*

—. National Youth Administration. North Dakota. 1930-45. *358*

—. New Deal. Pennsylvania. 1933-40. *356*

—. Oklahoma (Tulsa, Oklahoma City). Segregation. Urban programs. 1930's. *364*

Civilian Conservation Corps (co. 796). Causeways. Missouri River. South Dakota (Farm Island). 1934. *521*

Civilian Conservation Corps (Indian Division). Indians (reservations). Sioux Indians. South Dakota. 1933-42. *300*

Clapp, Elsie Ripley. Education, community. Homesteading and Homesteaders. New Deal. Roosevelt, Eleanor. West Virginia (Arthurdale). 1933-44. *285*

Clark, Bennett Champ. Committee of One. Democratic Party. Missouri. Political Campaigns (presidential). 1936. *250*

Class consciousness. NAACP. Negroes. Pennsylvania (Philadelphia). Race. 1930's. *684*

Clawson, Marion (report). Agricultural Reform. Economic conditions. Farm Security Administration. Resettlement projects. 1935-43. *317*

Clergy. Alabama. New Deal. Roosevelt, Franklin D. 1935-36. *290*

—. Massachusetts. New Deal. Roosevelt, Franklin D. Social problems. 1933-36. *291*

Cleveland Public Library. Federal Writers' Project. Ohio. Works Progress Administration. 1933-39. *450*

Climatological analysis. Droughts. Great Plains. Western States. 1931-40. *102*

Clinton, Clifford. California (Los Angeles). City Government. Recall. Shaw, Frank. 1938. *189*

Coal industry. Congress. New Deal. Supreme Court. 1932-40. *395*

Coal Mines and Mining. American Federation of Labor. New Deal. New Mexico (Gallup). Strikes. 1933. *708*

—. Colorado. Labor reform. Roche, Josephine. Roosevelt, Franklin D. (administration). Social work. 1886-1976. *365*

—. Davidson-Wilder Strike of 1932. Graham, Barney. Strikes. Tennessee, eastern. United Mine Workers of America. 1932-33. *527*

—. Editors and Editing. Evans, Herndon J. Kentucky (Harlan County). Pineville *Sun* (newspaper). Strikes. 1929-32. *730*

—. Folk songs. Lowry, Tom (interview). Tennessee. 1932. *765*

—. Hevener, John W. Kentucky (Harlan County). Labor Unions and Organizations. 1930's. *609*

—. National Guard. Ohio. Strikes. White, George. 1932. *687*

Coan, George W., Jr. Hopkins, Harry. North Carolina. Patronage. Works Progress Administration. 1935. *404*

Cohen, Benjamin V. Corcoran, Thomas Gardiner. Democratic Party. District of Columbia. New Deal. 1933-37. *396*

Collective bargaining. Labor Unions and Organizations (membership). New Deal. Public policy. 1933-45. *289*

Collectivism (objections to). Glass, Carter. Liberals. National Recovery Administration. New Deal. 1933-35. *378*

Colleges and Universities. Antiwar sentiment. Leftism. Political Protest. 1920-36. *547*

—. Arkansas (Mena). Commonwealth College. 1923-40. *568*

—. Education, Experimental Methods (review article). Radicals and Radicalism. 1930's. *735*

—. Feuer, Lewis. Lipset, Seymour Martin. Politics. Student activism. 1930's-40's. *715*

Collier, John. American Indian Federation. Bureau of Indian Affairs. Indians. Jamison, Alice Lee. New Deal. Political activism. 1930's-50's. *351*

—. Anthropology. Bureau of Indian Affairs. Federal Programs. Indians. New Deal. 1930's. *375*

—. Assimilation (opposition to). Federal Policy. Indian Reorganization Act (1934). 1933-45. *377*

—. Bureau of Indian Affairs. Ickes, Harold. Interior Department. Presidential appointments. Roosevelt, Franklin D. 1933. *376*

—. Bureau of Indian Affairs. Indians (government relations). New Deal. 1933-45. *498*

—. Bureau of Indian Affairs. New Deal. Public Administration. Social sciences principles. 1933-45. *497*

—. Federal Government. Indians. Liberalism. Roosevelt, Franklin D. (administration). Truman, Harry S. (administration). 1933-53. *380*

Collins, Seward. Agar, Herbert. Conservatism. Decentralization. Ideology. Intellectuals. Tate, Allen. 1933-50. *913*

Colorado. Coal Mines and Mining. Labor reform. Roche, Josephine. Roosevelt, Franklin D. (administration). Social work. 1886-1976. *365*

Colorado (Denver). Design. *Flivver* (aircraft). *Gray Goose* (aircraft). Lewis-American Aircraft Co. McMahon, Bill. Mooney brothers. 1930-33. *794*

Colorado River. Boulder Canyon project. Hoover Dam. Industrial Workers of the World. Nevada. Strikes. 1931. *702*

Columbia University. Anti-Semitism. Trilling, Lionel. 1930's. *739*

Comic strips. *Amos 'n Andy* (program). Boycotts. Negroes. Radio. Stereotypes. 1930's. *719*

—. Conservatism. Gray, Harold. *Little Orphan Annie* (comic strip). New Deal. World War II. 1920's-40's. *844*

Comintern. American Writers' Congress. Capitalism. League of American Writers. 1935. *567*

—. Communist Party. Finnish Workers' Federation. Kuusinen, Aino (pseud. A. Morton). 1930-33. *641*

Comintern (7th Congress). Communist Party. New Deal. Socialist Party. 1935-39. *655*

Commerce Department. Mitchell, Ewing Young. Pendergast, Thomas J. Political machines. Progressivism. Roosevelt, Franklin D. 1933-36. *239*

Commerce Department (Business Advisory Council). Committee for Economic Development. Keynesianism. New Deal. Roosevelt, Franklin D. (administration). Scholars. 1933-42. *319*

—. Corporate liberalism (concept). Historiography. National Recovery Administration (Industrial Advisory Board). New Deal. 1933-35. 1970's. *411*

Commercialism. Allen, Fred. Bureaucracies. Criticism. Humor. Radio. 1932-49. *824*

Committee for Economic Development. Commerce Department (Business Advisory Council). Keynesianism. New Deal. Roosevelt, Franklin D. (administration). Scholars. 1933-42. *319*

Committee of One. Clark, Bennett Champ. Democratic Party. Missouri. Political Campaigns (presidential). 1936. *250*

Commonwealth College. Arkansas (Mena). Colleges and Universities. 1923-40. *568*

Communes. Llano del Rio colony. New Mexico (Gila). 1932-35. *675*

Communism. Armies. Censorship. Civilian Conservation Corps. Conservatism. Flechner, Robert. 1934-42. *343*

—. Black nationalism. Garvey, Marcus. New York City (Harlem). 1931-39. *681*

—. Demonstrations. Georgia Insurrection Law. *Herndon v. Lowry* (US, 1937). International Labor Defense. Martin, Charles H. (review article). 1932-37. *591*

—. Farm protest. South Dakota. United Farmers League. 1923-34. *661*

—. Films. Labor Disputes. Propaganda. Workers' Film and Photo League. 1930-38. *808*

—. Folsom, Michael. Gold, Mike. Literature. Radical literary movement. 1914-37. *941*

—. Intellectuals. Jews. Menorah Group. 1930's. *744*

—. *Modern Monthly* (periodical). Wilson, Edmund. 1934-35. *603*

—. Nazism. Press. Red Fascism analogy. Totalitarianism. 1930's. 1970's. *654*

Communist Party. Alabama (Birmingham). Hudson, Hosea. Negroes. South. 1920's-70's. *691*

— American Federation of Labor. Labor Unions and Organizations. Radicals and Radicalism. Trade Union Unity League. 1933-35. *569*

—. American Labor Party. Gordon, Max (account). Politics. Popular Front. ca 1930-39. *758*

—. Artists. Federal funding. Works Progress Administration. 1930's. *418*

—. Automobile Workers Union. Labor Unions and Organizations. Michigan (Detroit). 1920's-1935. *699*

—. Browder, Earl. 1934-45. *710*

—. Comintern. Finnish Workers' Federation. Kuusinen, Aino (pseud. A. Morton). 1930-33. *641*

—. Comintern (7th Congress). New Deal. Socialist Party. 1935-39. *655*

—. Culture. Intellectuals. Negroes. New York City (Harlem). Popular Front. 1935-39. *678*

—. Georgia (Atlanta). Herndon, Angelo. International Labor Defense. Negroes. 1932-37. *658*

—. Glabermann, Martin. Keeran, Roger. Labor Unions and Organizations. Meier, August. Negroes. Rudwick, Elliot. United Automobile Workers of America (review article). 1930's-40's. *651*

—. Harvard University. Schlatter, Richard (account). 1930's. *714*

—. Illinois (Chicago). Intellectuals. Negroes. Wright, Richard *(American Hunger)*. ca 1930-44. *879*

—. Illinois (Chicago). Negroes. Wright, Richard (personal account). 1930's. *954*

—. Intellectuals. Literature. Popular Front Against Fascism. 1929-39. *613*

—. John Reed Clubs. Literature, proletarian. Proletcult. 1929-35. *623*

—. Labor Unions and Organizations. Mexico. 1935-39. *648*

—. Labor Unions and Organizations. Ohio (Youngstown). Steel Workers Organizing Committee. Steuben, John. 1936. *608*

—. Negroes. New York City (Harlem). 1928-36. *679*

—. Pamphlets. Rhetoric. 1929-39. *553*

—. Policymaking. Roosevelt, Franklin D. (administration). 1933-45. *534*

—. Roosevelt, Franklin D. (administration). 1933-39. *728*

—. Sports. 1920's-40's. *680*

Communist Party (review article). Automobile Industry and Trade. Keeran, Roger. Labor Unions and Organizations. 1930-39. 1980. *645*

Communist sympathizers, alleged. Chicago, University of. Illinois. Newspapers. Walgreen, Charles R. 1930's. *663*

Communists. Factionalism. Martin, Homer. Michigan. United Automobile Workers of America. 1937-39. *636*

Company towns. Ohio. Social Classes. Steel Industry. Strikes. 1937. *531*

Company unions. Bell Telephone System. Labor Unions and Organizations. 1919-37. *713*

Composers Collective. Folk Songs. Leftism. New York City. 1931-36. *798*

Congress. China. International Trade. Lobbying. Roosevelt, Franklin D. (administration). Silver Purchase Act (1934). 1934. *341*

—. Coal industry. New Deal. Supreme Court. 1932-40. *395*

—. Federal Regulation. Ickes, Harold. Oil Industry and Trade. Roosevelt, Franklin D. 1933. *388*

—. Illinois. Keller, Kent. Liberalism. New Deal. 1930-42. *263*

—. Mississippi. Political Leadership. 1931-37. *179*

—. New Deal. Political attitudes. Roosevelt, Franklin D. Tennessee. 1933-40. *148*

—. New Deal. Roosevelt, Franklin D. Social Security Act (US, 1935). Unemployment insurance. 1934-35. *277*

—. New Deal. Roosevelt, Franklin D. South Dakota. 1933. *312*

—. Norris, George W. Roosevelt, Franklin D. Supreme Court (issue). 1937. *207*

Congress of Industrial Organizations. Elections (presidential). Labor Non-Partisan League. Pennsylvania. Roosevelt, Franklin D. 1936. *252*

—. Labor. New Hampshire (Berlin). Nonpartisan League. Political Parties. 1932-36. *574*

—. Labor Disputes. New Deal. Newspapers. South. 1930-39. *518*

—. Maryland (Baltimore). Negroes. 1930-41. *711*

Congressmen. Appalachia. New Deal. 1933-39. *173*

—. New Deal. Politics. Roosevelt, Franklin D. Virginia. Woodrum, Clifton A. 1922-45. *236*

Congressmen, conservative. Democratic Party. George, Walter F. Political Change. Roosevelt, Franklin D. 1938. *145*

Connecticut. Air races. Bradley Air Museum. Rider R-3 (aircraft). 1930's-70's. *922*

—. Long Island Sound. New York. Ships. 1930-35. *587*

Conroy, Jack. *American Mercury* (periodical). Mencken, H. L. Publishers and Publishing. 1930-33. *910*

Conservation of natural resources. Archives, National. New Deal. 1930's. 1976. *435*

—. Cooke, Morris L. New Deal. Rural Electrification Administration. 1933-51. *316*

—. Electric power. South. Tennessee Valley Authority. 1917-70's. *297*

Conservatism. Agar, Herbert. Collins, Seward. Decentralization. Ideology. Intellectuals. Tate, Allen. 1933-50. *913*

—. Agar, Herbert. *Free America* (periodical). New Deal. 1937-47. *649*

—. Armies. Censorship. Civilian Conservation Corps. Communism. Flechner, Robert. 1934-42. *343*

—. Business. Isolationism. New Deal. Sears, Roebuck and Company. Wood, Robert E. 1928-50's. *581*

—. Comic Strips. Gray, Harold. *Little Orphan Annie* (comic strip). New Deal. World War II. 1920's-40's. *844*

—. Constitutional law. Kansas. New Deal. Newspapers. Supreme Court. 1934-35. *329*

—. Creel, George. New Deal. Progressivism. Works Progress Administration. 1900-53. *273*

—. Davidson, Donald. Roosevelt, Franklin D. (programs). South. Tennessee Valley Authority. 1930's. *474*

—. Economy Act (US, 1933). Fiscal Policy. New Deal. Roosevelt, Franklin D. 1932-36. *462*

—. Long, Huey P. Louisiana. Share Our Wealth movement. Smith, Gerald L. K. Speeches and addresses. 1929-35. *632*

—. New Deal. New York. Republican Party. Snell, Bertrand H. 1933-39. *139*

Constitutional Amendments (18th and 21st). Democratic Party (convention). Prohibition repeal. Raskob, John J. Roosevelt, Franklin D. 1928-33. *198*

Constitutional History. Civil Rights. Legal order, equalitarian. 1930-50. *611*

Constitutional issues. Agriculture and Government. Farm journals. New Deal. 1935-36. *330*

—. Editorials. Labor union journals. New Deal. Supreme Court. 1935-37. *588*

Constitutional law. Conservatism. Kansas. New Deal. Newspapers. Supreme Court. 1934-35. *329*

Construction. City of Progress. Economic development. Illinois (Chicago). 1933-34. *14*

—. Employment. Ickes, Harold. Negroes. Public Works Administration. Quotas. 1933-40. *383*

Consumerism. Lynd, Robert S. Research. Sociology. 1930's. *105*

Consumers. Balance sheets, household. Demand, aggregate. Economic Theory. 1929-38. *74*

Consumption, decline in. Temin, Peter (theory). 1930-41. *68*

Continental Congress of Workers and Farmers. Senior, Clarence. Socialist Party. 1933. *748*

Contracts. Air mail service. Black, Hugo. Farley, James A. Hoover, Herbert C. (administration). Legislative Investigations. 1933-34. *487*

—. Air Mail Service. Merchant Marine. Ocean mail service. Roosevelt, Franklin D. 1933-37. *488*

—. Air Mail Service (private). Editorials. San Francisco *Chronicle* (newspaper). 1934. *690*

Cooke, Morris L. Conservation of Natural Resources. New Deal. Rural Electrification Administration. 1933-51. *316*

Cooperatives (proposed). DuBois, W. E. B. Economic Theory. Negroes. 1940. *575*

Corcoran, Thomas Gardiner. Cohen, Benjamin V. Democratic Party. District of Columbia. New Deal. 1933-37. *396*

"Corn-hog" program. Agricultural Adjustment Administration. Agriculture and Government. Farmers. Iowa (Boone County). Powers, Elmer G. (diary). 1934. *345*

Corporate liberalism (concept). Commerce Department (Business Advisory Council). Historiography. National Recovery Administration (Industrial Advisory Board). New Deal. 1933-35. 1970's. *411*

Corporate structure. General Electric Co. New Deal. 1933-40. *670*

Corporatism, concept of. Agricultural Policy. Hoover, Herbert C. Politics. Roosevelt, Franklin D. 1929-33. *27*

Correspondence courses. Idaho (Moscow). Psychiana (religion). Robinson, Frank Bruce. 1929-48. *695*

"Corrido de los Hermanos" (ballad). Arizona. Ballads. Capital Punishment. Hernández, Federico. Hernández, Manuel. 1934. *724*

Corrigan, Douglas. Airplane flights, transatlantic. Ireland (Dublin). New York City. 1938-50. *950*

Cotton. Agricultural Policy. Association of Southern Commissioners of Agriculture. New Deal. South. Tennessee (Memphis). 1936-37. *423*

—. Agriculture. Oklahoma, eastern. Sharecroppers. 1920-40. *38*

Cotton Acreage Control Law (Texas, 1931). Crop limitation. Long, Huey P. New Deal. South. 1931-33. *127*

Cotton holiday movement. Mississippi. Prices. 1931. *107*

Cotton industry. Delta & Pine Land Company. Economic Regulations. Federal Government. Johnston, Oscar Goodbar. Subsidies. 1933-37. *424*

Cotton production. Long, Huey P. Louisiana. South. Texas. 1931. *108*

Couch, Harvey C. Reconstruction Finance Corporation. 1932-34. *427*

Couch, W. T. Biography. Federal Writers' Project. New Deal. South. 1938-39. *499*

Coughlin, Charles. Anti-Semitism. Boxerman, William I. Jewish Community Council. Michigan (Detroit). Radio. 1939. *725*

—. Countersubversives. Fascism (review article). German-American Bund. Nazism, American (review article). 1924-41. *701*

Countersubversives. Coughlin, Charles. Fascism (review article). German-American Bund. Nazism, American (review article). 1924-41. *701*

Country life. Delano, Jack. Farm Security Administration. New Deal. Photography. South Carolina (Santee-Cooper). 1941. *327*

—. Documents. Federal Emergency Relief Administration. Great Plains. Hickok, Lorena A. Hopkins, Harry. Iowa. Minnesota. 1933. *284*

—. Droughts. Kansas (Sherman County). Shaver, James H. (reminiscences). 1923-35. *99*

—. Family. Kansas (Decatur County). Webb, Bernice Larson (reminiscences). 1930's. *125*

—. Farm Security Administration. Mennonites. Photographs. Western States. 1930's. *929*

Country music. Beverly Hill Billies (group). California (Los Angeles). Discographies. 1930-32. *959*

Courter, Claude V. Education, Finance. Heinhold, Fred W. Ohio (Cincinnati). 1937-59. *22*

Cowen, Wilson. Dust Bowl. Farm Security Administration. Letters. Migration, Internal. Texas (Amarillo). 1940. *48*

Cowley, Malcolm. Intellectuals. Literature. Marxism. New York City. 1932-40. *763*

Credit. Adams, Frederick C. (review article). Export-Import Bank. Foreign policy. International Trade. 1934-39. 1976. *52*

Credit overextension. Bank failures. Economic Conditions. Rural financial crisis. 1920's. *49*

Creel, Cecil. Democratic Party. Nevada. New Deal. Pittman, Key. Political Factions. Public Welfare. 1933-34. *244*

Creel, George. Conservatism. New Deal. Progressivism. Works Progress Administration. 1900-53. *273*

Crime and Criminals. Federal Bureau of Investigation. Justice Department. Law enforcement. 1933-34. *614*

—. New Deal. Working class. 1929-39. *98*

Criminal investigations. Hauptmann, Bruno. Kidnapping. Lindbergh, Charles A. New Jersey. 1932-36. *638*

Crisis (periodical). Censorship. District of Columbia. *Opportunity* (periodical). Public schools. School Boards. 1936. *571*

Criticism. Allen, Fred. Bureaucracies. Commercialism. Humor. Radio. 1932-49. *824*

—. Arts. Berger, Arthur. Music. Personal narratives. Works Progress Administration. 1930-80. *786*

Crop limitation. Cotton Acreage Control Law (Texas, 1931). Long, Huey P. New Deal. South. 1931-33. *127*

Crowley, Leo T. Alien Property Custodian. Banking. Federal Deposit Insurance Corporation. Politics. Roosevelt, Franklin D. (administration). 1934-45. *510*

Crump, Edward. Chandler, Walter. Democratic Party. House of Representatives. Tennessee. 1933-40. *149*

—. Democratic Party. Elections (gubernatorial). Politics. Tennessee (Shelby County). 1932. *200*

Cuba. Economic policy. Foreign policy. 1933-34. *286*

Cullen-Harrison Act (US, 1933). Beer. Festivals. Wisconsin (Milwaukee). 1933. *520*

Cultural democracy. Arts. New Deal. 1933-42. *405*

Cultural identity. Oklahoma. State Government. 1930's. *31*

Culture. Adorno, Theodor W. Lazarsfeld, Paul F. Music. Princeton Radio Research Project. Social organization. 1930's. *875*

—. Communist Party. Intellectuals. Negroes. New York City (Harlem). Popular Front. 1935-39. *678*

—. Federal Art Project. New Deal. Wyoming. 1933-41. *795*

Culture, concept of. Economic theory. Intellectual trends. Relativism. Theology. 1930's. *883*

Cumberland Homesteads. Fairfield Glade. Housing. New Deal. Resettlement. Tennessee. 1934-80. *482*

Cumberland Mountains. Films (documentary). Historical accuracy. *People of the Cumberland* (film). Tennessee. 1930's. *834*

Cummings, Homer Stillé. Attorney General. Federal Bureau of Investigation. Films. *G-Men* (film). Hoover, J. Edgar. 1933-35. *898*
Currie, Lauchlin. Economic Policy. New Deal. 1935-46. *51*
—. Economic Theory. Recessions. 1932-38. *21*
—. Fiscal policy. Income. Keynesianism. New Deal. 1920's-30's. *522*
Cutting, Bronson M. Democratic Party. New Mexico. Political Campaigns. Roosevelt, Franklin D. Senate. 1934. *269*
Cynicism. Antidemocratism. Journalism. Mencken, H. L. Satire. 1920's-56. *914*

D

Daily Life. Accidents. Faulkner, Jim. Faulkner, William. Mississippi (Oxford). Personal narratives. Youth. 1930-39. *804*
—. Agee, James *(Let Us Now Praise Famous Men)*. Evans, Walker. Photography, documentary. Sharecroppers. South. 1930-1941. *792*
—. Agee, James *(Let Us Now Praise Famous Men)*. Literature. Realism. 1930-41. *846*
—. Arizona (Tucson). 1929-39. *109*
—. Attitudes. Lee, Russell. Photographs. 1932-40. *827*
—. Dust Bowl. Farmers. Henderson, Caroline Agnes Boa. New Deal. Oklahoma, western. 1935. *90*
—. Economic conditions. Lind, Leo (reminiscences). Markham and Callow Railroad. Oregon. 1929-38. *67*
—. Family. Wisconsin (Milwaukee). 1929-41. *60*
—. Fiction. Mississippi (Jackson). Welty, Eudora ("Death of a Traveling Salesman"). 1936-79. *944*
—. Homesteading and Homesteaders. Montana (Plentywood). Vindex, Charles (reminiscences). 1929-34. *123*
—. Nevada (Tobar). 1930's. *89*
Daily Newspaper Code. American Newspaper Publishers Association. Freedom of the press. National Industrial Recovery Act (1933). National Recovery Administration. Politics and Media. 1933-34. *774*
Dale, Chester. Agricultural Adjustment Administration (Office of the General Counsel). Frank, Jerome. Wallace, Henry A. 1935. *398*
Dale, George R. Elites. Indiana (Muncie). Local Politics. Lynd, Helen Merrell. Lynd, Robert S. 1930-40. *166*
Dance. Entertainers. Negroes. Robinson, Bill "Bojangles". 1930's-49. *868*
Dardis, Tom. Authors. Films. Hollywood. Scriptwriting. 1936-45. 1976. *919*
Davey, Martin L. National Guard. Ohio. Steel Industry. Strikes. 1937. *722*
Davidson, Donald. Conservatism. Roosevelt, Franklin D. (programs). South. Tennessee Valley Authority. 1930's. *474*
Davidson-Wilder Strike of 1932. Coal Mines and Mining. Graham, Barney. Strikes. Tennessee, eastern. United Mine Workers of America. 1932-33. *527*
Davis, James J. California (Los Angeles County). Deportation. Mexicans. Unemployment. 1931. *363*
Davis, John W. American Liberty League. New Deal (opposition to). Political Campaigns. 1932-36. *191*
Davis, Lorenzo Piper (interview). Baseball. Negro Leagues. 1930's-40's. *907*

Dawson, Nelson L. Brandeis, Louis D. Frankfurter, Felix. Landis, James M. Law. New Deal (review article). Ritchie, Donald A. 1930's. *512*
Dawson, Oliver B. (reminiscences). Ironwork. Oregon. Timberline Lodge. Works Progress Administration. 1935-37. *326*
Decentralization. Agar, Herbert. Collins, Seward. Conservatism. Ideology. Intellectuals. Tate, Allen. 1933-50. *913*
—. Agrarianism. Broadacre City. City Planning. Oklahoma (Bartlesville). Wright, Frank Lloyd. 1935. *864*
Defense. Alaska (Palmer). Rural rehabilitation. Works Progress Administration. 1935-40. *445*
Dehart, Grant. Federal Writers' Project. Folklore. Horse trading. Nebraska. ca 1938-43. *511*
Delano, Jack. Country life. Farm Security Administration. New Deal. Photography. South Carolina (Santee-Cooper). 1941. *327*
Delta & Pine Land Company. Cotton industry. Economic Regulations. Federal Government. Johnston, Oscar Goodbar. Subsidies. 1933-37. *424*
Demagoguery, concept of. Basso, Hamilton. Long, Huey P. Louisiana. Novels. 1920-76. *726*
Demand, aggregate. Balance sheets, household. Consumers. Economic Theory. 1929-38. *74*
Democracy. Inaugural addresses. Political Speeches. Roosevelt, Franklin D. Values. 1901-77. *164*
—. Liberals. Niebuhr, Reinhold. Religion. 1930-45. *598*
Democratic Party. Andersen, Kristi. Partisanship. Republican Party. Voting and Voting Behavior. 1920-32. *229*
—. Andersen, Kristi (review article). Leftism. 1928-36. 1979. *182*
—. Barkley, Alben W. Harrison, Byron Patton (Pat). Newspapers. Senate (majority leader). 1937. *174*
—. Barkley, Alben W. Roosevelt, Franklin D. Senate (majority leader). Supreme Court (issue). 1937. *153*
—. Budgets (state allocations). New Deal. Political Campaigns. 1932-40. *270*
—. Byrd, Harry F. Elections (presidential). Roosevelt, Franklin D. State Politics. Virginia. 1932. *260*
—. Byrd, Harry F. Glass, Carter. Roosevelt, Franklin D. Senate. Virginia. 1938. *183*
—. Byrd, Harry F. Patronage. Senate. Virginia. 1935-39. *196*
—. California. End Poverty In California program. Political Campaigns (gubernatorial). Sinclair, Upton. ca 1933-34. *242*
—. Callahan, Patrick Henry. Catholic Church. Kentucky (Louisville). 1866-1940. *158*
—. Chandler, Walter. Crump, Edward. House of Representatives. Tennessee. 1933-40. *149*
—. Cities (review article). Dorsett, Lyle W. Fine, Sidney. Trout, Charles H. 1930-40. *186*
—. Clark, Bennett Champ. Committee of One. Missouri. Political Campaigns (presidential). 1936. *250*
—. Cohen, Benjamin V. Corcoran, Thomas Gardiner. District of Columbia. New Deal. 1933-37. *396*
—. Congressmen, conservative. George, Walter F. Political Change. Roosevelt, Franklin D. 1938. *145*
—. Creel, Cecil. Nevada. New Deal. Pittman, Key. Political Factions. Public Welfare. 1933-34. *244*
—. Crump, Edward. Elections (gubernatorial). Politics. Tennessee (Shelby County). 1932. *200*

—. Cutting, Bronson M. New Mexico. Political Campaigns. Roosevelt, Franklin D. Senate. 1934. *269*
—. Domestic Policy. Internationalism. New Deal. Political Campaigns. Roosevelt, Franklin D. 1938-40. *160*
—. Elections, congressional. Garner, John Nance. Hoover, Herbert C. House of Representatives. Republican Party. 1930-31. *258*
—. Elections (critical, concept). Ethnic groups. Pennsylvania (Philadelphia). 1924-36. *240*
—. Elections (presidential). Iowa. Roosevelt, Franklin D. 1932. *172*
—. Elections (presidential). Massachusetts. Roosevelt, Franklin D. Smith, Al. 1928-32. *178*
—. Elections (senatorial). Missouri. New Deal. Primaries. Truman, Harry S. 1934. *175*
—. Erickson, John E. Montana. State Politics. Walsh, Thomas J. 1932-33. *208*
—. Georgia. New Deal. Roosevelt, Franklin D. Talmadge, Eugene. 1926-38. *146*
—. Gillette, Guy M. House of Representatives. Iowa. Political Campaigns. Roosevelt, Franklin D. 1932-48. *185*
—. Hague, Frank. New Deal. New Jersey. Roosevelt, Franklin D. 1932-40. *155*
—. Higgins, Andrew J. Political Campaigns (presidential). Roosevelt, Franklin D. 1944. *212*
—. Idaho. New Deal. Pocatello Central Labor Union. Rosqvist, August. 1930-36. *494*
—. Illinois. Lucas, Scott W. Senate (majority leader). 1938-50. *237*
—. Kentucky (Louisville). National Democratic Issues Convention. New Deal policies. 1975. *332*
—. Minnesota. Oleson, Anna Dickie. Politics. Women. 1905-71. *371*
—. Missouri. Pendergast, Thomas J. Political Conventions. Roosevelt, Franklin D. State Politics. 1932. *238*
—. Missouri. Political coalitions. Republican Party. Roosevelt, Franklin D. 1936-52. *246*
—. NAACP. Negro Suffrage. Primaries. *Smith* v. *Allwright* (US, 1944). South. Supreme Court. 1890's-1944. *617*
—. New Deal. Ohio. Political Campaigns (presidential). 1936. *249*
—. New Deal. Pennsylvania (Pittsburgh). Political Theory. Quantitative Methods. Voting and Voting Behavior. Wisconsin. 1912-40. *228*
—. New Deal. Primaries (senatorial). Russell, Richard B. Talmadge, Eugene. 1936. *213*
—. O'Mahoney, Joseph C. Patronage. Postal Service. Roosevelt, Franklin D. Senate. Wyoming. 1916-45. *220*
—. Political Campaigns (presidential). Republican Party. 1936. *248*
—. Voting and Voting Behavior. 1928-36. *159*
Democratic Party (Colored Voters Division). Good Neighbor League Colored Committee. Negroes. Political Campaigns (presidential). Roosevelt, Franklin D. 1936. *251*
Democratic Party (convention). Byrd, Harry F. Political Campaigns. Presidential nomination. Roosevelt, Franklin D. 1932. *187*
—. Constitutional Amendments (18th and 21st). Prohibition repeal. Raskob, John J. Roosevelt, Franklin D. 1928-33. *198*
—. Garner, John Nance. Rayburn, Sam. Roosevelt, Franklin D. 1932. *224*
Democratic Party (reformist). Elections (city). Pennsylvania (Philadelphia). 1933. *181*
Demonstrations. American Civil Liberties Union. Federal Bureau of Investigation. Hoover, J. Edgar. Political surveillance. Trade Union Education League. 1924-36. *750*

—. Communism. Georgia Insurrection Law. *Herndon* v. *Lowry* (US, 1937). International Labor Defense. Martin, Charles H. (review article). 1932-37. *591*
Deportation. Arizona (Superior). Brodie, J. C. (correspondence). Bureau of Immigration. Mexicans. 1930-34. *620*
—. California (Los Angeles County). Davis, James J. Mexicans. Unemployment. 1931. *363*
—. Immigrants. Labor Unions and Organizations. Mexican Americans. New Deal. 1930's. *579*
Depressions (causes). Economic Conditions. Social Conditions. 1900-33. *5*
—. Economic History. Models. Monetary Systems. Temin, Peter (review article). 1920's. 1976. *118*
Depressions (review article). Economic policy. Kindleberger, Charles P. VanderWee, Herman. 1930's. *26*
Desert fungus. Wolfe, Thomas (death). 1938. *869*
Design. Colorado (Denver). *Flivver* (aircraft). *Gray Goose* (aircraft). Lewis-American Aircraft Co. McMahon, Bill. Mooney brothers. 1930-33. *794*
Design (review article). Architecture. Industry. Meikle, Jeffrey L. 1925-39. 1979. *823*
Deskey, Donald. Art deco. Genauer, Emily (account). Interior decorating. New York City. Radio City Music Hall. 1929-37. *815*
Dickens, Charles *(Hard Times)*. Chaplin, Charlie. Films. Great Britain. *Modern Times* (film). 1854. 1936. *923*
Dillard University. Federal Writers' Project. Folklore. *Gumbo Ya-Ya* (publication). Louisiana. Negroes. Saxon, Lyle. 1930's. *318*
Dillon, Francis. Automobile Industry and Trade. Michigan. Motor Products Corporation. Strikes. United Automobile Workers of America. 1933-39. *545*
Diplomacy. Drug Abuse. Law enforcement. Mexico. Salazar Viniegra, Leopold. 1936-40. *745*
Disaster Relief. Droughts. Farmers. Federal Government. Kansas. New Deal. 1934. *465*
Disasters. Arkansas. Federal Programs. Food Supply. 1933-42. *360*
—. Germany. *Hindenburg* (dirigible). New Jersey (Lakehurst). 1937. *555*
Discographies. Beverly Hill Billies (group). California (Los Angeles). Country music. 1930-32. *959*
Discrimination. Elites. Georgia (Savannah). Negroes. New Deal. Works Progress Administration. ca 1930-39. *374*
—. Indiana (Gary). Mexican Americans. Nativism. Repatriation. 1920's-30's. *537*
Discrimination, employment. Civilian Conservation Corps. Negroes. New York. 1933-42. *441*
—. Georgia (Atlanta). Labor. Racism. Women. 1930's. *539*
District of Columbia. Airplane flights. Alaska (Fairbanks). Army Air Corps. B-10 (aircraft). Politics. 1934. *821*
—. American Legion. Bonus Army. North Carolina. Political Protest. Stevens, Henry L., Jr. Veterans (benefits). 1932. *694*
—. Bonus Army. Legislation (proposed). Patman, Wright. Veterans' certificates. 1932. *666*
—. Censorship. *Crisis* (periodical). *Opportunity* (periodical). Public schools. School Boards. 1936. *571*
—. Cohen, Benjamin V. Corcoran, Thomas Gardiner. Democratic Party. New Deal. 1933-37. *396*

Dix, I. F. Hoover, Herbert C. Local politics. Self-help. Unemployed Citizens' League. Washington (Seattle). 1931-32. *75*
Documentaries, historical. Films. Ideology. Rhetoric. 1930's. *906*
Documentarism. Film industry. Novels. Steinbeck, John *(The Grapes of Wrath)*. 1939-40. *779*
Documentary expression (review article). Federal Writers' Project. New Deal. Works Progress Administration. 1930's. *886*
Documents. Country Life. Federal Emergency Relief Administration. Great Plains. Hickok, Lorena A. Hopkins, Harry. Iowa. Minnesota. 1933. *284*
Domestic Policy. Democratic Party. Internationalism. New Deal. Political Campaigns. Roosevelt, Franklin D. 1938-40. *160*
—. Elections (presidential). Foreign policy. Lewis, John L. Roosevelt, Franklin D. 1936-40. *230*
—. Foreign Policy. Roosevelt, Franklin D. 1920-79. *247*
—. Foreign policy. Roosevelt, Franklin D. 1933-36. *460*
Doolittle, Jimmy. Gee Bee (aircraft). Pilots. 1930-32. *900*
Dorsett, Lyle W. Cities (review article). Democratic Party. Fine, Sidney. Trout, Charles H. 1930-40. *186*
Douglas, Donald. Airplanes. Photographs. 1932-38. *752*
Douglas, Lewis. Economic Policy. New Deal. Roosevelt, Franklin D. 1933-34. *461*
—. Ickes, Harold. Public Administration. Public Works Administration. 1933. *448*
Douglas, Melvyn. Actors and Actresses. Political Activism. 1936-42. *766*
Douglas, William O. (memoirs). Legal education. Yale University Law School. 1928-34. *585*
Douglas, William O. (review article). Autobiography. Judges. Roosevelt, Franklin D. (administration). 1933-39. 1974. *337*
Drainage districts. Reclamation of Land. Wyoming. 1888-1939. *25*
Drama. Actors, employment of. Federal Theatre Project. Ohio (Cincinnati). Works Progress Administration. 1935-39. *865*
—. Allison, Hughes. Federal Theatre Project. Negroes. Ward, Theodore. Wilson, Frank. 1930's. *874*
—. Federal Theatre Project. New Deal. South. 1930's. *884*
—. O'Neill, Eugene *(The Iceman Cometh)*. Political communities. 1939. *949*
Dramatists. Films. Hollywood. Phillips, A. H. (reminiscences). 1930's. *894*
Dreiser, Theodore. Lewis, Sinclair. Literature. Nobel Prizes. Public Opinion. Sweden. 1920's-30. *857*
Dreiser, Theodore (interview). California (San Francisco). Literature. Social Conditions. 1939. *904*
Droughts. Agricultural programs. Kansas. New Deal. Political Campaigns (presidential). 1936. *464*
—. Climatological analysis. Great Plains. Western States. 1931-40. *102*
—. Country life. Kansas (Sherman County). Shaver, James H. (reminiscences). 1923-35. *99*
—. Disaster Relief. Farmers. Federal Government. Kansas. New Deal. 1934. *465*
—. Farms. Hearst, James (reminiscences). Iowa (Black Hawk County). 1934-41. *44*
—. Federal government. Great Plains. Land-use planning. 1930's. *349*
—. Hoover, Herbert C. 1930. *42*

Drug Abuse. Diplomacy. Law enforcement. Mexico. Salazar Viniegra, Leopold. 1936-40. *745*
DuBois, W. E. B. Cooperatives (proposed). Economic Theory. Negroes. 1940. *575*
Due process. Brandeis, Louis D. Economic Regulations. *Nebbia* v. *New York* (US, 1934). *New State Ice* v. *Liebmann* (US, 1932). Supreme Court. *West Coast Hotel* v. *Parrish* (US, 1937). 1897-1937. *476*
Dust Bowl. Agricultural Policy. Federal Government. Great Plains. Unemployment. ca 1930-80. *408*
—. Agricultural Policy. New Deal. Texas Panhandle. 1930's. *76*
—. Cowen, Wilson. Farm Security Administration. Letters. Migration, Internal. Texas (Amarillo). 1940. *48*
—. Daily Life. Farmers. Henderson, Caroline Agnes Boa. New Deal. Oklahoma, western. 1935. *90*
—. Farmers. Migration, Internal (necessity). Oklahoma. Soil depletion. 1921-30's. *72*
—. Farmers, truck. Migrant Labor. Migration, Internal. Oklahoma. 1930's. *43*
—. Films. Ford, John. *Grapes of Wrath* (film). 1940. *920*
—. Migration, Internal. Oklahoma. Route 66. Southwest. 1930's. *88*
—. National Recovery Administration. New Deal. Oklahoma. Public Welfare. 1932-35. *505*
Dust Bowl (review article). Bonnifield, Paul. Great Plains (southern). Worster, Donald. ca 1900-39. 1979. *59*
Dust storms. Agriculture. Ecology. Great Plains. 1930's. *133*
—. Great Plains. 1930's. *46*

E

Earhart, Amelia. Aeronautics. Circumnavigation, attempted. 1897-1937. *909*
—. Aeronautics. Circumnavigation, attempted. Radio equipment. 1937. *931*
Ecological decision-making. Green Mountain Parkway. Vermont. Voting and Voting Behavior. 1935-36. *306*
Ecology. Agriculture. Dust storms. Great Plains. 1930's. *133*
Economic conditions. Agricultural Reform. Clawson, Marion (report). Farm Security Administration. Resettlement projects. 1935-43. *317*
—. Atlanta *Georgian* (newspaper). Georgia. Letters. Seydell, Mildred. 1930's. *10*
—. Bank deposits. Great Contraction. Money (demand). 1929-33. *34*
—. Bank failures. Credit overextension. Rural financial crisis. 1920's. *49*
—. Civilian Conservation Corps. New Deal. Vermont. 1933-42. *490*
—. Daily Life. Lind, Leo (reminiscences). Markham and Callow Railroad. Oregon. 1929-38. *67*
—. Depressions (causes). Social Conditions. 1900-33. *5*
—. Elections (presidential). Hoover, Herbert C. Political Parties. Roosevelt, Franklin D. South Dakota. 1932. *176*
—. Exclusion policy. Filipinos. Immigration. Split labor market theory. 1927-34. *18*
—. Foreman, Clark Howell. National Emergency Council (report). Politics. Roosevelt, Franklin D. South. 1938. *24*
—. Labor. New Deal. Texas. 1929-39. *430*
—. National Recovery Administration. New Deal. Supreme Court. Virginia. 1933-35. *353*

—. Negroes. South. Woodson, Carter G. 1930. *39*

—. New Deal. 1933-38. *389*

—. Unemployment. 1929. 1974. *93*

Economic development. City of Progress. Construction. Illinois (Chicago). 1933-34. *14*

—. Employment. Public Works Administration. Texas. 1933-34. *507*

Economic History. 1929. *58*

—. Depressions (causes). Models. Monetary Systems. Temin, Peter (review article). 1920's. 1976. *118*

—. Friedman, Milton. Schwartz, Anna. Temin, Peter. 1894-1938. 1963-76. *69*

Economic planning. New Deal. Public policy. 1932-41. *393*

Economic policy. Cuba. Foreign policy. 1933-34. *286*

—. Currie, Lauchlin. New Deal. 1935-46. *51*

—. Depressions (review article). Kindleberger, Charles P. VanderWee, Herman. 1930's. *26*

—. Douglas, Lewis. New Deal. Roosevelt, Franklin D. 1933-34. *461*

—. Federal Government. Public Schools. Roosevelt, Franklin D. Youth. 1918-45. *279*

—. Federal Reserve System. Money (demand). 1929-76. *33*

—. Fiscal policy. Keynesian Economics. Public administration. 1930's. *12*

—. Foreign Policy. New Deal. Public works programs, global. Roosevelt, Franklin D. 1933. *419*

—. Foreign Relations. Roosevelt, Franklin D. (administration). 1933-34. *386*

—. Freidel, Frank (review article). New Deal. Political leadership. Roosevelt, Franklin D. 1930's. *147*

—. Great Britain. New Deal. 1930's. 1980's. *516*

—. Import-Export Bank. International trade. New Deal. 1934-74. *409*

Economic Policy (similarities). Germany. Nazism. New Deal. ca 1933-36. *340*

Economic programs. Amlie, Thomas R. Liberals. New Deal. Politics. Wisconsin. 1931-39. *264*

Economic Reform. Fisher, Irving. Roosevelt, Franklin D. 1930's. *1*

—. Five-Day Plan. Hicks, Mary. Hicks, Mildred. 1931-40. *720*

—. Long, Huey P. Share Our Wealth movement. 1932-35. *548*

Economic Regulations. Agricultural Industry. Federal government. Mississippi. Prices. Texas. Voluntarism. 1925-40. *71*

—. Brandeis, Louis D. Due process. *Nebbia* v. *New York* (US, 1934). *New State Ice* v. *Liebmann* (US, 1932). Supreme Court. *West Coast Hotel* v. *Parrish* (US, 1937). 1897-1937. *476*

—. Cotton industry. Delta & Pine Land Company. Federal Government. Johnston, Oscar Goodbar. Subsidies. 1933-37. *424*

—. New Deal. Securities Exchange Act of 1934. Stock market. 1934. *287*

Economic relations. Capitalist countries. 1934-38. *62*

Economic speculation. Stocks and Bonds (median price-earnings ratio). 1929. *101*

Economic structure. Advertising. Allen, Laurence. Allen, Willis. California Life Payments Plan. Noble, Robert. Pensions. Referendum. 1937-39. *755*

—. Labor markets. Sex roles. Women. 1930's. *626*

Economic Theory. Attitudes. Chicago, University of. Keynes, John Maynard. Simons, Henry. 1930's. *85*

—. Balance sheets, household. Consumers. Demand, aggregate. 1929-38. *74*

—. Cooperatives (proposed). DuBois, W. E. B. Negroes. 1940. *575*

—. Culture, concept of. Intellectual trends. Relativism. Theology. 1930's. *883*

—. Currie, Lauchlin. Recessions. 1932-38. *21*

—. Keynes, John Maynard. New Deal. 1920's-30's. *63*

Economy Act (US, 1933). Conservatism. Fiscal Policy. New Deal. Roosevelt, Franklin D. 1932-36. *462*

Editorials. Air Mail Service (private). Contracts. San Francisco *Chronicle* (newspaper). 1934. *690*

—. Constitutional issues. Labor union journals. New Deal. Supreme Court. 1935-37. *588*

—. Great Plains. Internationalism. Isolationism. Newspapers. North Central States. 1918-35. *643*

—. Newspapers. Radio. *War of the Worlds* (broadcast). Welles, Orson. 1938. *951*

Editors and Editing. Coal Mines and Mining. Evans, Herndon J. Kentucky (Harlan County). Pineville *Sun* (newspaper). Strikes. 1929-32. *730*

—. Liberalism. Milton, George Fort. New Deal. Tennessee. 1930's. *362*

—. *Partisan Review* (periodical). Socialism. Stalinism. 1930's. *564*

Edmondson, Robert Edward. Anti-Semitism. Libel. Trials. 1934-44. *597*

Education. Jackson, Robert H. Presidency. Roosevelt, Franklin D. 1933-45. *271*

Education, community. Clapp, Elsie Ripley. Homesteading and Homesteaders. New Deal. Roosevelt, Eleanor. West Virginia (Arthurdale). 1933-44. *285*

Education, Experimental Methods (review article). Colleges and Universities. Radicals and Radicalism. 1930's. *735*

Education, Finance. Courter, Claude V. Heinhold, Fred W. Ohio (Cincinnati). 1937-59. *22*

Educators. Chicago, University of. Personal Narratives. Shils, Edward. Sociology. 1932-36. *915*

Ehringhaus, J. C. B. Legislation. North Carolina. Social Security Act (US, 1935). Unemployment insurance. 1935-37. *420*

Elections. Bulkley, Robert J. Ohio. Prohibition. Senate. 1918-30. *256*

—. New York (43rd Congressional District). Townsend Movement. 1936. *551*

Elections (city). Democratic Party (reformist). Pennsylvania (Philadelphia). 1933. *181*

Elections, congressional. Democratic Party. Garner, John Nance. Hoover, Herbert C. House of Representatives. Republican Party. 1930-31. *258*

—. New Deal. Republican Party. Roosevelt, Franklin D. 1937-38. *226*

Elections (critical, concept). Democratic Party. Ethnic groups. Pennsylvania (Philadelphia). 1924-36. *240*

Elections (gubernatorial). Bank of America. California. Giannini, Amadeo P. Merriam, Frank. Roosevelt, Franklin D. Sinclair, Upton. ca 1923-34. *138*

—. Browning, Gordon. Political machines. Tennessee. 1936. *135*

—. Chandler, A. B. ("Happy"). Federal Emergency Relief Administration. Kentucky. Works Progress Administration. 1935. *202*

—. Crump, Edward. Democratic Party. Politics. Tennessee (Shelby County). 1932. *200*

—. James, Arthur H. Pennsylvania. 1938. *215*
Elections (presidential). Byrd, Harry F. Democratic Party. Roosevelt, Franklin D. State Politics. Virginia. 1932. *260*
—. Congress of Industrial Organizations. Labor Non-Partisan League. Pennsylvania. Roosevelt, Franklin D. 1936. *252*
—. Democratic Party. Iowa. Roosevelt, Franklin D. 1932. *172*
—. Democratic Party. Massachusetts. Roosevelt, Franklin D. Smith, Al. 1928-32. *178*
—. Domestic Policy. Foreign policy. Lewis, John L. Roosevelt, Franklin D. 1936-40. *230*
—. Economic conditions. Hoover, Herbert C. Political Parties. Roosevelt, Franklin D. South Dakota. 1932. *176*
—. Ethnic groups. Religion. Roosevelt, Franklin D. Social Classes. 1940. *192*
—. German Americans. Iowa. Roosevelt, Franklin D. 1936-40. *234*
—. Hoover, Herbert C. Missouri. Roosevelt, Franklin D. 1932. *177*
—. Hoover, Herbert C. Progressivism. Republican Party. Senate. 1930-32. *161*
—. Long, Huey P. Roosevelt, Franklin D. Share Our Wealth movement. 1932-36. *245*
Elections (senatorial). Democratic Party. Missouri. New Deal. Primaries. Truman, Harry S. 1934. *175*
—. Kansas. McGill, George S. 1938. *210*
Elections (state). Allen, DeLacey. Georgia. Lieutenant governors. Pope, J. Ellis. Proposition 2. Scott, W. Fred. 1936. *156*
Electric Power. Alabama (Muscle Shoals). Public Utilities. Tennessee (Memphis). Tennessee Valley Authority. 1880-1940. *513*
—. Branson, Eugene C. North Carolina. Poe, Clarence H. Rural Electrification Administration. State Government. 1917-36. *302*
—. Conservation of Natural Resources. South. Tennessee Valley Authority. 1917-70's. *297*
Electric utilities. Bonneville Power Administration. New Deal. Pacific Northwest. Public Utilities. 1937-42. *339*
Electrification, rural. Arkansas Light and Power Company. Rural Electrification Administration. 1933-40. *301*
Elites. Anti-Semitism. Freedom of speech. Mencken, H. L. Public opinion. 1917-41. *769*
—. Dale, George R. Indiana (Muncie). Local Politics. Lynd, Helen Merrell. Lynd, Robert S. 1930-40. *166*
—. Discrimination. Georgia (Savannah). Negroes. New Deal. Works Progress Administration. ca 1930-39. *374*
—. Negroes. 1930-40. *664*
Embargoes. Armaments. Isolationism. Neutrality Act (US, 1935). 1935. *756*
Emergency Economy Bill (New York, 1934). City Government (relations with state government). La Guardia, Fiorello Henry. New York City. 1934. *144*
Emergency Farm Labor Supply Program. Agricultural Labor Relations Act (1975). California. Labor law. New Deal. ca 1930-79. *338*
Emigration. Ethiopia (Addis Ababa). Ford, Arnold. Negroes. 1930-35. *717*
Employment *See also* Unemployment.
—. American Order of Fascisti. Georgia. Negroes. White supremacy. 1930-33. *660*
—. Army Corps of Engineers. Fort Peck Dam. Missouri River. Montana. 1932-61. *457*
—. Berkeley Guidance Study. California. Family. Women. 1930-70. *9*

—. Brown, E. Cary. Fiscal policy, role of. Full-employment surplus analysis. 1930's. 1956. 1973. *86*
—. Civilian Conservation Corps. Environment. South Dakota. 1933-42. *357*
—. Construction. Ickes, Harold. Negroes. Public Works Administration. Quotas. 1933-40. *383*
—. Economic Development. Public Works Administration. Texas. 1933-34. *507*
—. Federal Emergency Relief Administration. 1933-40. *504*
—. Federal Programs. 1934-41. *55*
—. Feminism. Scharf, Lois (review article). Women. 1929-39. *709*
—. Minorities in Politics. Negroes. New Deal. Roosevelt, Franklin D. 1930-42. *470*
Employment, part-time. National Youth Administration. New Deal. South Dakota. Struble, Anna C. Youth. 1935-43. *355*
End Poverty in California program. Authors. Mencken, H. L. (letters). Sinclair, Upton (letters). Social Reform. ca 1918-51. *902*
—. California. Democratic Party. Political Campaigns (gubernatorial). Sinclair, Upton. ca 1933-34. *242*
Entertainers. Dance. Negroes. Robinson, Bill "Bojangles". 1930's-49. *868*
Environment. Civilian Conservation Corps. Employment. South Dakota. 1933-42. *357*
—. Films. Lorentz, Pare. New Deal. Roosevelt, Franklin D. (administration). Westward movement. 1936-40. *905*
Epstein, Abraham. Legislation. Old age security. Pension systems. Voluntary associations. 1920-35. *647*
Equal opportunity. Bethune, Mary McLeod. National Youth Administration. Negroes. Public Policy. Youth. 1935-44. *483*
Equal opportunity (failure). Civilian Conservation Corps. Negroes. New Deal. 1933-42. *344*
Equal Rights Amendment (proposed). Florida. National Women's Party. Politics. West, Helen Hunt. Women. 1917-52. *667*
Erickson, John E. Democratic Party. Montana. State Politics. Walsh, Thomas J. 1932-33. *208*
Ernst, Morris. Censorship. Cerf, Bennett. Joyce, James *(Ulysses)*. *United States* v. *One Book Called "Ulysses"* (US, 1932). 1922-32. *840*
Escott, Paul D. (review article). Federal Writers' Project. New Deal. Slave narratives. 1935-39. 1979. *828*
Esquire (periodical). Gingrich, Arnold. Hughes, Langston. Negroes. Public Opinion. Publishers and Publishing. 1934. *572*
Ethiopia. Black nationalism. Invasions. Italy. Negroes. Pan-Africanism. 1934-36. *716*
Ethiopia (Addis Ababa). Emigration. Ford, Arnold. Negroes. 1930-35. *717*
Ethnic groups. Democratic Party. Elections (critical, concept). Pennsylvania (Philadelphia). 1924-36. *240*
—. Elections (presidential). Religion. Roosevelt, Franklin D. Social Classes. 1940. *192*
—. Films. *Flash Gordon* (film). Stereotypes. 1936-38. *771*
—. Georgia (Atlanta). Labor. Louisiana (New Orleans). Texas (San Antonio). Women. 1930-40. *540*
Ethnicity. Intellectuals. National Characteristics. Public Opinion. 1930's. *747*
—. Progressive education. Race. 1929-45. *606*
Europe. Architecture. City planning. Housing. Modernism. New Deal. 1932-60. *897*
—. Government. 1930's. *65*
Europe, western. Unemployment. 1929-41. *35*
Evangelism. Fundamentalism. 1929-42. *558*

Evans, Herndon J. Coal Mines and Mining. Editors and Editing. Kentucky (Harlan County). Pineville *Sun* (newspaper). Strikes. 1929-32. *730*

Evans, Luther H. Historical Records Survey. Iowa. Public records. Works Progress Administration. 1936-42. *334*

Evans, Walker. Agee, James *(Let Us Now Praise Famous Men)*. Daily Life. Photography, documentary. Sharecroppers. South. 1930-1941. *792*

Exclusion policy. Economic conditions. Filipinos. Immigration. Split labor market theory. 1927-34. *18*

Executive leadership. Hawley-Smoot Tariff Act (1930). Hoover, Herbert C. 1922-32. *106*

Executive Power (expansion). Roosevelt, Franklin D. 1933-45. *243*

Executive Power (restrictions). House of Representatives. Logan-Walter Bill (vetoed, 1939). Rayburn, Sam. Sumners, Hatton. Texas. 1939. *438*

Executive reorganization. Carter, Jimmy (administration). Roosevelt, Franklin D. (administration). 1937-38. 1977-78. *437*

Export-Import Bank. Adams, Frederick C. (review article). Credit. Foreign policy. International Trade. 1934-39. 1976. *52*

Ex-slaves, interviews with. Historical sources. Rawick, George P. (review essay). Slavery. 19c. 1930's. *515*

Eyster, Warren. Agee, James. Films. Literature. Personal narratives. 1935-41. *802*

F

Factionalism. Communists. Martin, Homer. Michigan. United Automobile Workers of America. 1937-39. *636*

—. Kautsky, Karl. Lee, Algernon. Letters. Socialist Party. 1930-35. *589*

—. Militancy. United Automobile Workers of America. 1937-41. *544*

"Fair Play for American Athletes" (pamphlet). American Olympic Committee. Anti-Semitism. Boycotts, proposed. Brundage, Avery. Germany (Berlin). Olympic Games. 1935-36. *851*

Fairfield Glade. Cumberland Homesteads. Housing. New Deal. Resettlement. Tennessee. 1934-80. *482*

Family. Berkeley Guidance Study. California. Employment. Women. 1930-70. *9*

—. Country Life. Kansas (Decatur County). Webb, Bernice Larson (reminiscences). 1930's. *125*

—. Daily Life. Wisconsin (Milwaukee). 1929-41. *60*

—. Folklore. Radio. Values. *Vic and Sade* (program). Women. 1932-46. *96*

—. Interviews. Slavery. South. Works Progress Administration. 1850's-60's. 1930's. *387*

Family history. Biography. Interviews. Louisiana State University. Students. Works Progress Administration. 1930's. 1978. *321*

Far Western States. International Longshoremen's and Warehousemen's Union. Labor Unions and Organizations. 1934-37. *542*

Farley, James A. Air mail service. Black, Hugo. Contracts. Hoover, Herbert C. (administration). Legislative Investigations. 1933-34. *487*

Farm journals. Agriculture and Government. Constitutional issues. New Deal. 1935-36. *330*

Farm leaders. Agricultural production, limited. Land utilization movement. 1920's. *41*

Farm programs. Catholic Church. New Deal. Rural life movement. 1930's. *721*

Farm protest. Communism. South Dakota. United Farmers League. 1923-34. *661*

Farm Security Administration. Agricultural Reform. Clawson, Marion (report). Economic conditions. Resettlement projects. 1935-43. *317*

—. Country life. Delano, Jack. New Deal. Photography. South Carolina (Santee-Cooper). 1941. *327*

—. Country Life. Mennonites. Photographs. Western States. 1930's. *929*

—. Cowen, Wilson. Dust Bowl. Letters. Migration, Internal. Texas (Amarillo). 1940. *48*

—. Great Plains. Photography. Stryker, Roy Emerson. 1937-39. *322*

Farm Security Administration (Resettlement Administration). North Dakota. Orvedal, O. Leonard (interview). 1930's. *313*

Farm tenancy. Mississippi. Protestant Churches. Theologians, neoorthodox. 1936-40. *629*

Farmer-labor movement. Amlie, Thomas R. Hard, Herbert. New Deal. Ohio Farmer-Labor Progressive Federation. Third Parties. 1930-40. *204*

Farmer-Labor Party. Amlie, Thomas R. New Deal. Wisconsin. 1930-38. *206*

—. Michigan. New Deal. State Politics. 1933-37. *203*

Farmers *See also* Agriculture, Rural development.

—. Agricultural Adjustment Administration. Agriculture and Government. "Corn-hog" program. Iowa (Boone County). Powers, Elmer G. (diary). 1934. *345*

—. Agricultural Adjustment Administration. Federal Policy. New Deal. New York, western. 1934. *308*

—. Agricultural Labor. Industrial Workers of the World. Labor Disputes. Ranchers. Washington (Yakima Valley). 1910-36. *685*

—. All-Party Agricultural Committee. Great Plains. North Central States. Political Campaigns (presidential). Roosevelt, Franklin D. 1936. *254*

—. Arizona (Salt River Valley). Japanese Americans. Race Relations. 1934-35. *529*

—. Daily Life. Dust Bowl. Henderson, Caroline Agnes Boa. New Deal. Oklahoma, western. 1935. *90*

—. Disaster Relief. Droughts. Federal Government. Kansas. New Deal. 1934. *465*

—. Dust Bowl. Migration, Internal (necessity). Oklahoma. Soil depletion. 1921-30's. *72*

—. Government. Great Plains. Letters. New Deal. 1930-40. *8*

—. Industrial Workers of the World. North Dakota. O'Connor, Hugh (interview). Women. 1900's-30's. *113*

—. Iowa (Boone County). Powers, Elmer G. (diary). 1936. *37*

—. Legislation. New Deal. North Dakota (Landa). Taralseth, Rueben P. (interview). 1900's-30's. *114*

—. Meat preservation. North Dakota (Kidder County). Oil Industry and Trade. Schools, rural. Wick family (interview). 1900's-30's. *112*

—. Nebraska. New Deal. Norris, George W. Relief funds. 1933-36. *397*

—. North Dakota. Prices. Strikes. 1932. *92*

Farmers, truck. Dust Bowl. Migrant Labor. Migration, Internal. Oklahoma. 1930's. *43*

Farms. Droughts. Hearst, James (reminiscences). Iowa (Black Hawk County). 1934-41. *44*

Farrell, James T. *(Studs Lonigan)*. History. Institutions. Social Organization. 1933-35. *796*

Fascism. Anti-Semitism. 1930's. *524*

—. Italian Americans. Michigan (Detroit). Sociopolitical integration. 1933-35. *554*
—. Italy. Monetary policy. Mussolini, Benito. New Deal. Roosevelt, Franklin D. 1922-36. *433*
Fascism (review article). Coughlin, Charles. Countersubversives. German-American Bund. Nazism, American (review article). 1924-41. *701*
Faulkner, Jim. Accidents. Daily Life. Faulkner, William. Mississippi (Oxford). Personal narratives. Youth. 1930-39. *804*
Faulkner, William. Accidents. Daily Life. Faulkner, Jim. Mississippi (Oxford). Personal narratives. Youth. 1930-39. *804*
Federal Aid to Education. Arkansas. Federal Emergency Relief Administration. Hopkins, Harry. Public schools. 1933-36. *451*
—. George-Barden Act (US, 1946). George-Deen Act (US, 1936). Pharmacy. Vocational education. Wisconsin Plan. 1936-49. *307*
—. Harrison, Byron Patton (Pat). Legislation. Mississippi. 1936-41. *493*
Federal Art Project. Culture. New Deal. Wyoming. 1933-41. *795*
Federal assistance (opposition to). Maryland (Baltimore). Ritchie, Albert C. State Government. 1929-33. *56*
Federal Bureau of Investigation. American Civil Liberties Union. Demonstrations. Hoover, J. Edgar. Political surveillance. Trade Union Education League. 1924-36. *750*
—. Attorney General. Cummings, Homer Stillé. Films. *G-Men* (film). Hoover, J. Edgar. 1933-35. *898*
—. Civil Rights. Roosevelt, Franklin D. 1936-80. *288*
—. Crime and Criminals. Justice Department. Law enforcement. 1933-34. *614*
—. Political activities, dissident. Presidential directives. 1936-53. *500*
Federal Civil Works Administration. Branion-Williams case (California). California. McAdoo, William G. Patronage. Social workers. 1933-34. *468*
Federal Communications Commission. Federal Radio Commission. Radio. Sykes, Eugene O. 1927-39. *412*
Federal Deposit Insurance Corporation. Alien Property Custodian. Banking. Crowley, Leo T. Politics. Roosevelt, Franklin D. (administration). 1934-45. *510*
Federal Emergency Relief Administration. Arkansas. Federal Aid to Education. Hopkins, Harry. Public schools. 1933-36. *451*
—. Chandler, A. B. ("Happy"). Elections (gubernatorial). Kentucky. Works Progress Administration. 1935. *202*
—. Country Life. Documents. Great Plains. Hickok, Lorena A. Hopkins, Harry. Iowa. Minnesota. 1933. *284*
—. Employment. 1933-40. *504*
—. Hickok, Lorena A. Hopkins, Harry. Kentucky, eastern. Poverty. 1933. *19*
—. Hopkins, Harry. Letters. Public Welfare. Rhode Island. 1934. *431*
Federal expenditures. New Deal. States. 1933-39. *447*
Federal funding. Artists. Communist Party. Works Progress Administration. 1930's. *418*
—. Folklore (review article). Mangione, Jerre. McDonald, William F. 1935-43. *331*
Federal Government *See also* names of individual agencies, bureaus, and departments, e.g. Bureau of Indian Affairs, etc.
—. Agricultural Adjustment Administration. National Recovery Administration. 1933-39. *481*

—. Agricultural Industry. Economic Regulations. Mississippi. Prices. Texas. Voluntarism. 1925-40. *71*
—. Agricultural Policy. Dust Bowl. Great Plains. Unemployment. ca 1930-80. *408*
—. Airplanes. 1903-80. *787*
—. Banking. Hoover, Herbert C. Nevada. Reconstruction Finance Corporation. 1932-33. *83*
—. Collier, John. Indians. Liberalism. Roosevelt, Franklin D. (administration). Truman, Harry S. (administration). 1933-53. *380*
—. Cotton industry. Delta & Pine Land Company. Economic Regulations. Johnston, Oscar Goodbar. Subsidies. 1933-37. *424*
—. Disaster Relief. Droughts. Farmers. Kansas. New Deal. 1934. *465*
—. Droughts. Great Plains. Land-use planning. 1930's. *349*
—. Economic policy. Public Schools. Roosevelt, Franklin D. Youth. 1918-45. *279*
—. Homesteading and Homesteaders (failure of). Montana. Ranchers. 1900-30. *32*
—. New Deal. Press. Progressivism. Reform. 1890's-1930's. *294*
—. New Deal. Public health. 1933-39. *402*
Federal loan. Florida (Tampa). Kreher, Ernest. Public Works Administration. Tampa Shipbuilding and Engineering Company. 1932-37. *401*
Federal officials. Hatch Act (1939). Hatch, Carl. 1939. *439*
Federal Policy. Agricultural Adjustment Administration. Farmers. New Deal. New York, western. 1934. *308*
—. Assimilation (opposition to). Collier, John. Indian Reorganization Act (1934). 1933-45. *377*
—. Attitudes. New Deal. Technology. 1927-40. *442*
—. Bauer, Catherine. Public housing. Reform. Wagner-Steagall Act (US, 1937). Wood, Edith Elmer. 1890's-1940's. *292*
—. Hopkins, Harry. New Deal. Poverty. Roosevelt, Franklin D. Unemployment. 1910's-38. *403*
—. Indians (review articles). New Deal. Parman, Donald L. Philp, Kenneth R. Taylor, Graham D. 1934-74. *612*
Federal Programs. Anthropology. Bureau of Indian Affairs. Collier, John. Indians. New Deal. 1930's. *375*
—. Arkansas. Disasters. Food Supply. 1933-42. *360*
—. Artists. Buildings, public. New Deal. 1930's. *436*
—. Employment. 1934-41. *55*
—. Marine Workers' Industrial Union. Maryland (Baltimore). Unemployment. 1933-37. *274*
—. Roosevelt, Franklin D. State Legislatures. 1933-70's. *391*
Federal Radio Commission. Federal Communications Commission. Radio. Sykes, Eugene O. 1927-39. *412*
Federal Regulation. American Liberty League. Business. Civil rights. Government, Resistance to. New Deal. 1934-36. *698*
—. Congress. Ickes, Harold. Oil Industry and Trade. Roosevelt, Franklin D. 1933. *388*
Federal Reserve Board. Keynesianism. Monetary policy. New Deal. Private sector. 1929-79. *6*
Federal Reserve System. Economic Policy. Money (demand). 1929-76. *33*
—. Monetary Systems. 1924-33. *121*
Federal Subsistence Homesteads Corporation. Iowa (Granger). Ligutti, Luigi. New Deal. Social experiments. 1934-51. *469*

Federal Theatre Project. Actors, employment of. Drama. Ohio (Cincinnati). Works Progress Administration. 1935-39. *865*
—. Allison, Hughes. Drama. Negroes. Ward, Theodore. Wilson, Frank. 1930's. *874*
—. Attitudes. Blitzstein, Marc *(Cradle Will Rock)*. Censorship. Labor. New York City. Works Progress Administration. 1937. *502*
—. Drama. New Deal. South. 1930's. *884*
—. Flanagan, Hallie. Hopkins, Harry. Politics. Theater. Works Progress Administration. 1935-39. *303*
—. Negroes. Public Records. Theater, black. 1930's-70's. *304*
—. Negroes. Theater. 1935-39. *456*
Federal Writers' Project. Autobiography. Oral history. South. 1930-39. *361*
—. Biography. Couch, W. T. New Deal. South. 1938-39. *499*
—. Christensen, Mart. Spring, Agnes Wright. Works Progress Administration. Wyoming. 1935-41. *354*
—. Cleveland Public Library. Ohio. Works Progress Administration. 1933-39. *450*
—. Dehart, Grant. Folklore. Horse trading. Nebraska. ca 1938-43. *511*
—. Dillard University. Folklore. *Gumbo Ya-Ya* (publication). Louisiana. Negroes. Saxon, Lyle. 1930's. *318*
—. Documentary expression (review article). New Deal. Works Progress Administration. 1930's. *886*
—. Escott, Paul D. (review article). New Deal. Slave narratives. 1935-39. 1979. *828*
—. Finnish Americans. Interviews. Minnesota. 1930's. *381*
—. Florida. Folklore. Hurston, Zora Neale. Negroes. 1901-60. *826*
—. Genovese, Eugene D. Interviews. Methodology. Rawick, George P. Slavery. 1930's. 1970's. *484*
—. Indiana. Local history. 1936-43. *428*
—. Literature. New Deal. Penkower, Monty Noam (review article). 1930's. 1977. *454*
—. Mangione, Jerre (review article). New Deal. 1935-43. *509*
—. Negroes. Slavery, memories of. Tennessee. 1930's. *350*
—. North Carolina, University of (Southern Historical Collection). Oral History. 1935-80. *523*
—. Tobacco. 1933-39. *278*
Feinman, Ronald L. (review article). New Deal. Progressivism. Republican Party. Senate. Western States. 1929-41. *199*
Feminism. Employment. Scharf, Lois (review article). Women. 1929-39. *709*
Festivals. Beer. Cullen-Harrison Act (US, 1933). Wisconsin (Milwaukee). 1933. *520*
Feuer, Lewis. Colleges and Universities. Lipset, Seymour Martin. Politics. Student activism. 1930's-40's. *715*
Fiction. Civil War. Hemingway, Ernest *(For Whom the Bell Tolls)*. Propaganda. Reporters and Reporting. Spain. 1936-40. *853*
—. Daily Life. Mississippi (Jackson). Welty, Eudora ("Death of a Traveling Salesman"). 1936-79. *944*
—. Folklore. Milburn, George. Oklahoma. Ozark Mountains. 1930's. *797*
—. History. Long, Huey P. Warren, Robert Penn *(All The King's Men)*. World War II (antecedents). 1930's-40's. *839*
—. Manuscript dating. Steinbeck, John. 1934. *953*
—. *Saturday Evening Post* (periodical). Stereotypes. Women. 1931-36. *831*
Fiction (detective). Stein, Gertrude. Women. 1933-36. *854*
Fiction, formula. Nancy Drew books. New Deal. Stereotypes. 1930's. 1960's-70's. *841*
Field research interviews. *Mexican Labor in the United States* (study). National Endowment for the Humanities. Taylor, Paul S. 1927-30. *621*
Filipino Americans. Bulosan, Carlos (autobiography). California. Labor Unions and Organizations. Leftism. 1934-38. *552*
—. California (Watsonville). Racism. Riots. Violence. 1926-30. *577*
Filipinos. Economic conditions. Exclusion policy. Immigration. Split labor market theory. 1927-34. *18*
Film industry. Documentarism. Novels. Steinbeck, John *(The Grapes of Wrath)*. 1939-40. *779*
—. Finance capitalism (concept). Lenin, V. I. *(Imperialism: The Highest Stage of Capitalism)*. Monopolies. 1916-39. *817*
Films. Agee, James. Eyster, Warren. Literature. Personal narratives. 1935-41. *802*
—. Astaire, Fred. Popular Culture. Rogers, Ginger. 1930-39. *930*
—. Attitudes. New Deal. 1930-40. *778*
—. Attorney General. Cummings, Homer Stillé. Federal Bureau of Investigation. *G-Men* (film). Hoover, J. Edgar. 1933-35. *898*
—. Authors. Dardis, Tom. Hollywood. Scriptwriting. 1936-45. 1976. *919*
—. Biography. 1929-49. *822*
—. Bonneville Power Administration. Folk Songs. Guthrie, Woody. 1939-49. *872*
—. California (Hollywood). *Citizen Kane* (film). Kael, Pauline (review article). 1930-39. *859*
—. California (Hollywood). Hispanic Americans. Spanish language. 1930-39. *896*
—. California (Hollywood). Photography. Popular Culture. Publicity. 1930-39. *847*
—. Capitalism. Capra, Frank. *Mr. Deeds Goes to Town* (film). Social Organization. 1936. *861*
—. Capra, Frank. Humor. McCarey, Leo. 1930's. *813*
—. Capra, Frank. *Mr. Smith Goes To Washington* (film). Politics. Populism. 1939. *881*
—. Capra, Frank. Politics. Yankee (character). 1936-41. *812*
—. Chaplin, Charlie. Dickens, Charles *(Hard Times)*. Great Britain. *Modern Times* (film). 1854. 1936. *923*
—. *City* (film). City planning. 1939. *816*
—. Communism. Labor Disputes. Propaganda. Workers' Film and Photo League. 1930-38. *808*
—. Documentaries, historical. Ideology. Rhetoric. 1930's. *906*
—. Dramatists. Hollywood. Phillips, A. H. (reminiscences). 1930's. *894*
—. Dust Bowl. Ford, John. *Grapes of Wrath* (film). 1940. *920*
—. Environment. Lorentz, Pare. New Deal. Roosevelt, Franklin D. (administration). Westward movement. 1936-40. *905*
—. Ethnic Groups. *Flash Gordon* (film). Stereotypes. 1936-38. *771*
—. History Teaching. North Carolina. 1930's-74. *806*
—. Pacifism. War. World War I. 1930-39. *836*
Films (as history). *Gone With The Wind* (film). *Grapes of Wrath* (film). 1929-39. *890*
Films (documentary). Cumberland Mountains. Historical accuracy. *People of the Cumberland* (film). Tennessee. 1930's. *834*
—. *March of Time* (series). Political Attitudes. *The World Today* (series). 1930's. *761*

—. Michigan (Flint). Strikes. United Automobile Workers of America. *With Babies and Banners* (film). Women. 1937. *903*

Films, gangster. Bogart, Humphrey. *High Sierra* (film). Roy Earle, fictional character. 1930's-41. *762*

Films (musicals). 1930's. *829*

—. San Francisco (film). *Show Boat* (film). 1936. *917*

Films (review article). *Gold Diggers of 1933* (film). Hove, Arthur. Kawin, Bruce F. Screenplays. *To Have and Have Not* (film). 1930's-44. *911*

Finance. *New York Times.* Newspaper columns. Stock Exchange. 1929. *13*

Finance capitalism (concept). Film industry. Lenin, V. I. *(Imperialism: The Highest Stage of Capitalism).* Monopolies. 1916-39. *817*

Fine, Sidney. Andersen, Kristi. Blumberg, Barbara. Jeffries, John W. New Deal (review article). Roosevelt, Franklin D. Swain, Martha H. 1933-39. *143*

—. Cities (review article). Democratic Party. Dorsett, Lyle W. Trout, Charles H. 1930-40. *186*

Fine, Sidney (review article). City Government. Michigan (Detroit). Murphy, Frank. 1930-33. 1975. *150*

—. Murphy, Frank. New Deal. 1936-42. *151*

Finnish Americans. Federal Writers' Project. Interviews. Minnesota. 1930's. *381*

Finnish Workers' Federation. Comintern. Communist Party. Kuusinen, Aino (pseud. A. Morton). 1930-33. *641*

Fire. *Morro Castle* (vessel). 1934. *590*

First Balloon Squadron. Balloons. Carter, "Red". Fort Sill. Oklahoma. 1930's. *561*

First ladies (state). Ohio. State Government. White, George. White, Mary (reminiscences). 1931-35. *265*

First-Person America: Voices from the Thirties (program). History Teaching. Personal narratives. 1930's. 1980. *768*

Fiscal policy *See also* Monetary policy.

—. City government. New Jersey (Paterson). Public Welfare. Textile industry. 1920-32. *77*

—. Conservatism. Economy Act (US, 1933). New Deal. Roosevelt, Franklin D. 1932-36. *462*

—. Currie, Lauchlin. Income. Keynesianism. New Deal. 1920's-30's. *522*

—. Economic Policy. Keynesian Economics. Public administration. 1930's. *12*

—. Governors. Kump, Herman Guy. State Government. West Virginia. 1930's. *169*

Fiscal policy, role of. Brown, E. Cary. Employment. Full-employment surplus analysis. 1930's. 1956. 1973. *86*

Fisher, Irving. Economic Reform. Roosevelt, Franklin D. 1930's. *1*

Five-Day Plan. Economic Reform. Hicks, Mary. Hicks, Mildred. 1931-40. *720*

Flanagan, Hallie. Federal Theatre Project. Hopkins, Harry. Politics. Theater. Works Progress Administration. 1935-39. *303*

Flash Gordon (film). Ethnic Groups. Films. Stereotypes. 1936-38. *771*

Flechner, Robert. Armies. Censorship. Civilian Conservation Corps. Communism. Conservatism. 1934-42. *343*

Fleischmann, Max. California (Santa Barbara). Philanthropy. Relief work. Unemployment. 1930-32. *78*

Flivver (aircraft). Colorado (Denver). Design. *Gray Goose* (aircraft). Lewis-American Aircraft Co. McMahon, Bill. Mooney brothers. 1930-33. *794*

Flogging case. City Government. Florida (Tampa). Political Corruption. Vigilantism. 1935-38. *628*

Flood control. Aiken, George D. Governors. Political Campaigns (presidential). Republican Party. Vermont. 1937-39. *235*

—. Army Corps of Engineers. Mississippi River (lower). Politics. 1927-41. *449*

Florida. Equal Rights Amendment (proposed). National Women's Party. Politics. West, Helen Hunt. Women. 1917-52. *667*

—. Federal Writers' Project. Folklore. Hurston, Zora Neale. Negroes. 1901-60. *826*

—. Graham, Ernest. Hialeah Charter Bill. Poll tax. 1931-38. *195*

Florida (Greenwood). Lynching. Neal, Claude. Negroes. 1930-40. *668*

Florida (Hernando County). Bootlegging. Law enforcement. Liquor. Prohibition. 1929-33. *562*

Florida (Miami). Assassination. Cermak, Anton. Roosevelt, Franklin D. Zangara, Giuseppi. 1933. *152*

—. Assassination, attempted. Roosevelt, Franklin D. Zangara, Giuseppi. 1933. *231*

Florida (Tampa). City Government. Flogging case. Political Corruption. Vigilantism. 1935-38. *628*

—. Federal loan. Kreher, Ernest. Public Works Administration. Tampa Shipbuilding and Engineering Company. 1932-37. *401*

Folk Songs. Bonneville Power Administration. Films. Guthrie, Woody. 1939-49. *872*

—. Coal Mines and Mining. Lowry, Tom (interview). Tennessee. 1932. *765*

—. Composers Collective. Leftism. New York City. 1931-36. *798*

—. Guthrie, Woody. Oklahoma (Okemah). 1912-29. *871*

Folklore. Dehart, Grant. Federal Writers' Project. Horse trading. Nebraska. ca 1938-43. *511*

—. Dillard University. Federal Writers' Project. *Gumbo Ya-Ya* (publication). Louisiana. Negroes. Saxon, Lyle. 1930's. *318*

—. Family. Radio. Values. *Vic and Sade* (program). Women. 1932-46. *96*

—. Federal Writers' Project. Florida. Hurston, Zora Neale. Negroes. 1901-60. *826*

—. Fiction. Milburn, George. Oklahoma. Ozark Mountains. 1930's. *797*

Folklore (review article). Federal funding. Mangione, Jerre. McDonald, William F. 1935-43. *331*

Folsom, Michael. Communism. Gold, Mike. Literature. Radical literary movement. 1914-37. *941*

Food relief. Hoover, Herbert C. Red Cross. Wheat, surplus. 1932-33. *61*

Food Supply. Arkansas. Disasters. Federal Programs. 1933-42. *360*

Football. "Big Three" relationship. Harvard University. Ivy League. Princeton University. 1926-39. *924*

Ford, Arnold. Emigration. Ethiopia (Addis Ababa). Negroes. 1930-35. *717*

Ford automobile. Barrow, Clyde. Gangster myth. Parker, Bonnie. Rich, Carroll Y. Warren, Jesse. 1934-67. *957*

Ford, Ford Madox. Literature. Louisiana (Baton Rouge). South. Writers' Conference on Literature and Reading in the South and Southwest. 1935. *942*

Ford, John. Dust Bowl. Films. *Grapes of Wrath* (film). 1940. *920*

Foreign policy. Adams, Frederick C. (review article). Credit. Export-Import Bank. International Trade. 1934-39. 1976. *52*

—. Austin, Warren R. Neutrality Act, 1939 (proposed). Roosevelt, Franklin D. Senate. 1935-39. *759*

—. Cuba. Economic policy. 1933-34. *286*

—. Domestic Policy. Elections (presidential). Lewis, John L. Roosevelt, Franklin D. 1936-40. *230*

—. Domestic Policy. Roosevelt, Franklin D. 1920-79. *247*

—. Domestic Policy. Roosevelt, Franklin D. 1933-36. *460*

—. Economic policy. New Deal. Public works programs, global. Roosevelt, Franklin D. 1933. *419*

—. Great Britain. International trade. 1932-38. *385*

—. Hawaii. Preparedness. Roosevelt, Franklin D. Works Progress Administration. 1935-40. *446*

—. Hearst, William Randolph. Isolationism. Newspapers. 1936-41. *556*

—. Historiography. Isolationism. 1919-39. *541*

—. Import restrictions. International Steel Cartel. Labor. Steel Workers Organizing Committee. US Steel Corporation. 1937. *646*

—. International cooperation. Isolationism. League of Nations Association. Peace. 1934-38. *525*

—. International Labor Organization. Isolationism. New Deal. Perkins, Frances. Roosevelt, Franklin D. 1921-34. *429*

—. Isolationism. Johnson, Hiram. Nye Committee. Roosevelt, Franklin D. (administration). ca 1933-34. *576*

—. Isolationism. Political Leadership. Roosevelt, Franklin D. Senate. World Court. 1935. *194*

Foreign Policy (critics). Anti-Imperialism. Pacific Area. Roosevelt, Franklin D. World War II (antecedents). 1930's. *692*

Foreign Relations. Berry pickers. California (El Monte). Japan. Mexico. Strikes. 1933. *619*

—. Economic policy. Roosevelt, Franklin D. (administration). 1933-34. *386*

Foreman, Clark Howell. Economic conditions. National Emergency Council (report). Politics. Roosevelt, Franklin D. South. 1938. *24*

Fort Peck Dam. Army Corps of Engineers. Employment. Missouri River. Montana. 1932-61. *457*

Fort Sill. Balloons. Carter, "Red". First Balloon Squadron. Oklahoma. 1930's. *561*

Fortas, Abe. Interior Department. Lawyers. Letters. Peres, Hardwig. Roosevelt, Franklin D. 1930-44. *373*

Foulois, Benjamin D. Air Mail Service. Army Air Corps. 1934. *475*

—. Air mail service. Army Air Corps. Postal service. 1933-34. *348*

Frank, Jerome. Agricultural Adjustment Administration (Office of the General Counsel). Dale, Chester. Wallace, Henry A. 1935. *398*

Frank, Jerome (papers). Lawyers. 1916-57. *517*

Frankfurter, Felix. Brandeis, Louis D. Dawson, Nelson L. Landis, James M. Law. New Deal (review article). Ritchie, Donald A. 1930's. *512*

—. Brandeis, Louis D. New Deal. Politics. Roosevelt, Franklin D. World War I. 1917-33. *154*

—. Keynes, John Maynard. New Deal. Public works. 1932-35. *280*

—. Lippmann, Walter. New Deal. Roosevelt, Franklin D. World War II. 1932-45. *432*

Free America (periodical). Agar, Herbert. Conservatism. New Deal. 1937-47. *649*

Freedom of speech. Anti-Semitism. Elites. Mencken, H. L. Public opinion. 1917-41. *769*

Freedom of the press. American Newspaper Publishers Association. Daily Newspaper Code. National Industrial Recovery Act (1933). National Recovery Administration. Politics and Media. 1933-34. *774*

—. Friendly, Fred W. (review article). *Near v. Minnesota* (US, 1931). 1931. *805*

Freidel, Frank (review article). Economic policy. New Deal. Political leadership. Roosevelt, Franklin D. 1930's. *147*

Freund, Paul A. (reminiscences). Brandeis, Louis D. Law. Supreme Court. 1932-33. *167*

Friedlander, Peter (review article). Michigan (Detroit). United Automobile Workers of America. Working Class. 1936-39. 1975. *549*

Friedman, Milton. Economic History. Schwartz, Anna. Temin, Peter. 1894-1938. 1963-76. *69*

Friendly, Fred W. (review article). Freedom of the Press. *Near v. Minnesota* (US, 1931). 1931. *805*

Fuel. Agriculture. Alcohol. Business. Motors. Prices. Surpluses. 1930's. *604*

Full-employment surplus analysis. Brown, E. Cary. Employment. Fiscal policy, role of. 1930's. 1956. 1973. *86*

Functionalism. Chicago, University of (Psychology Department). McKinney, Fred (reminiscences). Psychology. 1929-31. *669*

Fundamentalism. Evangelism. 1929-42. *558*

—. Long, Huey P. North Central States. Populism. Progressivism. Smith, Gerald L. K. 1934-48. *633*

G

Gangster myth. Barrow, Clyde. Ford automobile. Parker, Bonnie. Rich, Carroll Y. Warren, Jesse. 1934-67. *957*

Gardner, Erle Stanley. Bedford-Jones, H. Novels (pulp). 1920's-30's. *810*

Garment industry. Jews. Labor movement. 1920's-30's. *546*

—. Missouri (St. Louis). Personal narratives. Photographic essays. Strikes. Women. ca 1930-39. *565*

Garner, John Nance. Democratic Party. Elections, congressional. Hoover, Herbert C. House of Representatives. Republican Party. 1930-31. *258*

—. Democratic Party (convention). Rayburn, Sam. Roosevelt, Franklin D. 1932. *224*

—. New Deal policies. Roosevelt, Franklin D. 1933-38. *225*

Garvey, Marcus. Black nationalism. Communism. New York City (Harlem). 1931-39. *681*

Geddes, Norman Bel. Automobiles. Industrial design. Streamlining. 1930-39. *870*

Gee Bee (aircraft). Doolittle, Jimmy. Pilots. 1930-32. *900*

Gehrig, Lou. Amyotrophic lateral sclerosis. Baseball. Character. Letters. New York Yankees (team). 1939. *777*

Genauer, Emily (account). Art deco. Deskey, Donald. Interior decorating. New York City. Radio City Music Hall. 1929-37. *815*

General Education Board. Public policy. Rockefeller, John D. Secondary education. Social change. 1930's. *538*

General Electric Co. Corporate structure. New Deal. 1933-40. *670*

General Motors Corporation. Georgia (Atlanta). Strikes. United Automobile Workers of America. 1936. *616*

—. *Great Sitdown* (film). Historiography. Strikes. United Automobile Workers of America. *With Babies and Banners* (film). 1937. 1976-79. *855*

—. Lewis, John L. Strikes, sit-down. 1936-37. *595*

—. Michigan (Flint). Strikes. United Automobile Workers of America. 1936-37. *718*

General strikes. American Distillery Company. American Federation of Labor. Illinois (Pekin). 1934-36. *550*

—. California (San Francisco). National Guard. Waterfronts. 1934. *625*

Genovese, Eugene D. Federal Writers' Project. Interviews. Methodology. Rawick, George P. Slavery. 1930's. 1970's. *484*

Geography. Agriculture Department. Kollmorgen, Walter M. 1936-45. *379*

George, Walter F. Congressmen, conservative. Democratic Party. Political Change. Roosevelt, Franklin D. 1938. *145*

George-Barden Act (US, 1946). Federal Aid to Education. George-Deen Act (US, 1936). Pharmacy. Vocational education. Wisconsin Plan. 1936-49. *307*

George-Deen Act (US, 1936). Federal Aid to Education. George-Barden Act (US, 1946). Pharmacy. Vocational education. Wisconsin Plan. 1936-49. *307*

Georgia. Agricultural industry. 1910-32. *45*

—. Allen, DeLacey. Elections (state). Lieutenant governors. Pope, J. Ellis. Proposition 2. Scott, W. Fred. 1936. *156*

—. American Order of Fascisti. Employment. Negroes. White supremacy. 1930-33. *660*

—. Atlanta *Georgian* (newspaper). Economic Conditions. Letters. Seydell, Mildred. 1930's. *10*

—. Democratic Party. New Deal. Roosevelt, Franklin D. Talmadge, Eugene. 1926-38. *146*

—. National Recovery Administration. State Government. Strikes. Talmadge, Eugene. Textile industry. 1934. *526*

Georgia (Atlanta). Communist Party. Herndon, Angelo. International Labor Defense. Negroes. 1932-37. *658*

—. Discrimination, Employment. Labor. Racism. Women. 1930's. *539*

—. Ethnic Groups. Labor. Louisiana (New Orleans). Texas (San Antonio). Women. 1930-40. *540*

—. General Motors Corporation. Strikes. United Automobile Workers of America. 1936. *616*

Georgia Insurrection Law. Communism. Demonstrations. *Herndon* v. *Lowry* (US, 1937). International Labor Defense. Martin, Charles H. (review article). 1932-37. *591*

Georgia (Savannah). Discrimination. Elites. Negroes. New Deal. Works Progress Administration. ca 1930-39. *374*

Georgia (Warm Springs). Henderson, F. P. Marines. Roosevelt, Franklin D. 1937. *188*

German Americans. Elections (presidential). Iowa. Roosevelt, Franklin D. 1936-40. *234*

—. Nazism. 1924-41. *578*

German-American Bund. Coughlin, Charles. Countersubversives. Fascism (review article). Nazism, American (review article). 1924-41. *701*

Germany. Anti-Semitism. Nazism. *New York Times*. Reporters and Reporting. 1932-33. *749*

—. Boxing. Louis, Joe. Nazism. Negroes. Schmeling, Max. 1936-38. *784*

—. Boycotts. Olympic Games. 1932-36. *825*

—. Disasters. *Hindenburg* (dirigible). New Jersey (Lakehurst). 1937. *555*

—. Economic Policy (similarities). Nazism. New Deal. ca 1933-36. *340*

—. Jews. Refugees. Relief organizations. World War II. 1933-45. *602*

Germany (Berlin). American Olympic Committee. Anti-Semitism. Boycotts, proposed. Brundage, Avery. "Fair Play for American Athletes" (pamphlet). Olympic Games. 1935-36. *851*

—. Boycotts, proposed. Olympic Games. Racism, issue of. 1933-36. *843*

Giannini, Amadeo P. Bank of America. California. Elections (gubernatorial). Merriam, Frank. Roosevelt, Franklin D. Sinclair, Upton. ca 1923-34. *138*

Gillespie, Dizzy. Bop (term). Music. 1928-40's. *926*

Gillette, Guy M. Democratic Party. House of Representatives. Iowa. Political Campaigns. Roosevelt, Franklin D. 1932-48. *185*

"Gimme a Pigfoot" (song). Language. Music. Smith, Bessie. 1920's. *925*

Gingrich, Arnold. *Esquire* (periodical). Hughes, Langston. Negroes. Public Opinion. Publishers and Publishing. 1934. *572*

Ginther, Ronald Debs. Artists. Labor unrest. Skid row. ca 1920-69. *937*

Glabermann, Martin. Communist Party. Keeran, Roger. Labor Unions and Organizations. Meier, August. Negroes. Rudwick, Elliot. United Automobile Workers of America (review article). 1930's-40's. *651*

Glacier National Park. Civilian Conservation Corps. Montana. 1933-42. *425*

Glass, Carter. Byrd, Harry F. Democratic Party. Roosevelt, Franklin D. Senate. Virginia. 1938. *183*

—. Collectivism (objections to). Liberals. National Recovery Administration. New Deal. 1933-35. *378*

—. Political Campaigns (presidential, senatorial). Virginia. 1936. *197*

G-Men (film). Attorney General. Cummings, Homer Stillé. Federal Bureau of Investigation. Films. Hoover, J. Edgar. 1933-35. *898*

Gold Diggers of 1933 (film). Films (review article). Hove, Arthur. Kawin, Bruce F. Screenplays. *To Have and Have Not* (film). 1930's-44. *911*

Gold, Mike. Communism. Folsom, Michael. Literature. Radical literary movement. 1914-37. *941*

Gone With The Wind (film). Films (as history). *Grapes of Wrath* (film). 1929-39. *890*

Good Neighbor League Colored Committee. Democratic Party (Colored Voters Division). Negroes. Political Campaigns (presidential). Roosevelt, Franklin D. 1936. *251*

Gordon, Caroline. Authors (southern). Letters. New York (Rochester). Tennessee (Benfolly). Wood, Sally. 1930-31. *818*

Gordon, Max (account). American Labor Party. Communist Party. Politics. Popular Front. ca 1930-39. *758*

Government. Capitalism. Marxism. New Deal. Political Theory. 1933-39. 1980. *103*

—. Europe. 1930's. *65*

—. Farmers. Great Plains. Letters. New Deal. 1930-40. *8*

—. Hoover, Herbert C. Industry. New York (Buffalo). Public Welfare. Unemployment. 1929-33. *64*

—. Long, Huey P. Louisiana. Peyton, Rupert (reminiscences). 1917-35. *696*

Government intervention. Baltimore *Sun*, *Evening Sun* (newspapers). Letters-to-the-editor. Maryland. Roosevelt, Franklin D. 1929-33. *384*

Government regulation. Neoconservatism. New Deal. Political Leadership. Republican Party. Social security. 1936-40. *209*

Government, Resistance to. American Liberty League. Business. Civil rights. Federal Regulation. New Deal. 1934-36. *698*

Governors. Aiken, George D. Flood control. Political Campaigns (presidential). Republican Party. Vermont. 1937-39. *235*

—. California. Public Welfare. Ralph, James, Jr. 1931-34. *16*

—. Fiscal Policy. Kump, Herman Guy. State Government. West Virginia. 1933. *169*

—. Horton, Henry. Political Corruption. Tennessee. 1930-31. *201*

Graham, Barney. Coal Mines and Mining. Davidson-Wilder Strike of 1932. Strikes. Tennessee, eastern. United Mine Workers of America. 1932-33. *527*

Graham, Ernest. Florida. Hialeah Charter Bill. Poll tax. 1931-38. *195*

Grain. Livestock. McGregor Land and Livestock Company. Prices. Washington (Columbia Plateau). 1930's-82. *73*

Grapes of Wrath (film). Dust Bowl. Films. Ford, John. 1940. *920*

—. Films (as history). *Gone With The Wind* (film). 1929-39. *890*

Graves, John Temple, II. Liberalism. New Deal. Palm Beach *Times* (newspaper). South. 1933-40. *275*

Gray Goose (aircraft). Colorado (Denver). Design. *Flivver* (aircraft). Lewis-American Aircraft Co. McMahon, Bill. Mooney brothers. 1930-33. *794*

Gray, Harold. Cartoonists. *Little Orphan Annie* (comic strip). Social conservatism. World War II. 1930's-40's. *955*

—. Comic Strips. Conservatism. *Little Orphan Annie* (comic strip). New Deal. World War II. 1920's-40's. *844*

Great Britain. Attitudes. Law. Poor. Vagrancy. 14c-1939. *20*

—. Chaplin, Charlie. Dickens, Charles *(Hard Times).* Films. *Modern Times* (film). 1854. 1936. *923*

—. Economic Policy. New Deal. 1930's. 1980's. *516*

—. Foreign Policy. International trade. 1932-38. *385*

Great Contraction. Bank deposits. Economic Conditions. Money (demand). 1929-33. *34*

Great Plains. Agricultural Policy. Dust Bowl. Federal Government. Unemployment. ca 1930-80. *408*

—. Agricultural Policy. Roosevelt, Franklin D. Shelterbelts. Trees. 1934-44. *486*

—. Agriculture. Dust storms. Ecology. 1930's. *133*

—. All-Party Agricultural Committee. Farmers. North Central States. Political Campaigns (presidential). Roosevelt, Franklin D. 1936. *254*

—. Climatological analysis. Droughts. Western States. 1931-40. *102*

—. Country Life. Documents. Federal Emergency Relief Administration. Hickok, Lorena A. Hopkins, Harry. Iowa. Minnesota. 1933. *284*

—. Droughts. Federal government. Land-use planning. 1930's. *349*

—. Dust storms. 1930's. *46*

—. Editorials. Internationalism. Isolationism. Newspapers. North Central States. 1918-35. *643*

—. Farm Security Administration. Photography. Stryker, Roy Emerson. 1937-39. *322*

—. Farmers. Government. Letters. New Deal. 1930-40. *8*

—. Radicals and Radicalism. State Politics. 1930-36. *190*

Great Plains (southern). Bonnifield, Paul. Dust Bowl (review article). Worster, Donald. ca 1900-39. 1979. *59*

Great Plains states. Liberalism, rural. New Deal. Senators. 1930's. *162*

Great Sitdown (film). General Motors Corporation. Historiography. Strikes. United Automobile Workers of America. *With Babies and Banners* (film). 1937. 1976-79. *855*

Green Mountain Parkway. Ecological decision-making. Vermont. Voting and Voting Behavior. 1935-36. *306*

Greenbelt Towns. New Deal. Ohio (Cincinnati, Greenhills). Tugwell, Rexford G. 1935-39. *333*

—. Poor, rural. Resettlement Administration. Tugwell, Rexford G. 1935-36. *421*

Gumbo Ya-Ya (publication). Dillard University. Federal Writers' Project. Folklore. Louisiana. Negroes. Saxon, Lyle. 1930's. *318*

Guthrie, Woody. Bonneville Power Administration. Films. Folk Songs. 1939-49. *872*

—. California. Migration, Internal. 1937-67. *952*

—. Folk Songs. Oklahoma (Okemah). 1912-29. *871*

Gyroscope: A Literary Magazine. Literature. Periodicals. Winters, Yvor. 1929-30. *767*

H

Haber, William. Michigan. National Youth Administration. Public Welfare. Works Progress Administration. 1930's. *410*

Hague, Frank. Democratic Party. New Deal. New Jersey. Roosevelt, Franklin D. 1932-40. *155*

Hammett, Dashiell. California (San Francisco). Novels, detective. Sam Spade (fictional character). 1920-30's. *866*

—. Literature. Marxism. Novels (detective). Sam Spade (fictional character). 1930's. *862*

Hard, Herbert. Amlie, Thomas R. Farmer-labor movement. New Deal. Ohio Farmer-Labor Progressive Federation. Third Parties. 1930-40. *204*

Harding, Edwin Forrest. *Infantry Journal* (periodical). 1934-38. *764*

Harrison, Byron Patton (Pat). Barkley, Alben W. Democratic Party. Newspapers. Senate (majority leader). 1937. *174*

—. Federal aid to education. Legislation. Mississippi. 1936-41. *493*

—. Mississippi. Political friendship. Roosevelt, Franklin D. 1920-41. *259*

—. Senate. Social Security Act (US, 1935). 1934-35. *492*

Hart, Brooke (murder). California (San Jose; St. James Park). Holmes, John. Kidnapping. Lynching. Thurmond, Thomas. 1933. *665*

Harvard University. "Big Three" relationship. Football. Ivy League. Princeton University. 1926-39. *924*

—. Communist Party. Schlatter, Richard (account). 1930's. *714*

Harvard University, Houghton Library. Manuscripts. Novels. Wolfe, Thomas. 1938. 1975. *845*

Hatch Act (1939). Federal officials. Hatch, Carl. 1939. *439*

Hatch, Carl. Federal officials. Hatch Act (1939). 1939. *439*

Hauptmann, Bruno. Criminal investigations. Kidnapping. Lindbergh, Charles A. New Jersey. 1932-36. *638*
—. Kidnapping. Lindbergh case. Trials. 1935. *573*
Hawaii. Foreign policy. Preparedness. Roosevelt, Franklin D. Works Progress Administration. 1935-40. *446*
Hawley-Smoot Tariff Act (1930). Executive leadership. Hoover, Herbert C. 1922-32. *106*
Hearst, James (reminiscences). Droughts. Farms. Iowa (Black Hawk County). 1934-41. *44*
Hearst, William Randolph. Foreign policy. Isolationism. Newspapers. 1936-41. *556*
—. New Deal. Progressivism. 1930-35. *311*
Heinhold, Fred W. Courter, Claude V. Education, Finance. Ohio (Cincinnati). 1937-59. *22*
Hemingway, Ernest *(For Whom the Bell Tolls)*. Civil War. Fiction. Propaganda. Reporters and Reporting. Spain. 1936-40. *853*
Henderson, Caroline Agnes Boa. Daily Life. Dust Bowl. Farmers. New Deal. Oklahoma, western. 1935. *90*
Henderson, F. P. Georgia (Warm Springs). Marines. Roosevelt, Franklin D. 1937. *188*
Hernández, Federico. Arizona. Ballads. Capital Punishment. "Corrido de los Hermanos" (ballad). Hernández, Manuel. 1934. *724*
Hernández, Manuel. Arizona. Ballads. Capital Punishment. "Corrido de los Hermanos" (ballad). Hernández, Federico. 1934. *724*
Herndon, Angelo. Communist Party. Georgia (Atlanta). International Labor Defense. Negroes. 1932-37. *658*
Herndon v. *Lowry* (US, 1937). Communism. Demonstrations. Georgia Insurrection Law. International Labor Defense. Martin, Charles H. (review article). 1932-37. *591*
Hevener, John W. Coal Mines and Mining. Kentucky (Harlan County). Labor Unions and Organizations. 1930's. *609*
Hialeah Charter Bill. Florida. Graham, Ernest. Poll tax. 1931-38. *195*
Hickok, Lorena A. Country Life. Documents. Federal Emergency Relief Administration. Great Plains. Hopkins, Harry. Iowa. Minnesota. 1933. *284*
—. Federal Emergency Relief Administration. Hopkins, Harry. Kentucky, eastern. Poverty. 1933. *19*
—. Hopkins, Harry. New Deal. Ohio. Roosevelt, Franklin D. Unemployment. 1934-36. *489*
—. New Deal. Pennsylvania, eastern. 1933. *7*
—. Public Welfare. Reporters and Reporting. Roosevelt, Franklin D. (administration). 1913-68. *283*
Hicks, Mary. Economic Reform. Five-Day Plan. Hicks, Mildred. 1931-40. *720*
Hicks, Mildred. Economic Reform. Five-Day Plan. Hicks, Mary. 1931-40. *720*
Higgins, Andrew J. Democratic Party. Political Campaigns (presidential). Roosevelt, Franklin D. 1944. *212*
High Sierra (film). Bogart, Humphrey. Films, gangster. Roy Earle, fictional character. 1930's-41. *762*
Hindenburg (dirigible). Disasters. Germany. New Jersey (Lakehurst). 1937. *555*
Hispanic Americans. California (Hollywood). Films. Spanish language. 1930-39. *896*
Historians. Beard, Charles A. Intellectuals. Isolationism. Liberalism. New Deal. Roosevelt, Franklin D. 1932-48. *296*
Historical accuracy. Cumberland Mountains. Films (documentary). *People of the Cumberland* (film). Tennessee. 1930's. *834*

Historical Records Survey. Evans, Luther H. Iowa. Public records. Works Progress Administration. 1936-42. *334*
Historical sources. Ex-slaves, interviews with. Rawick, George P. (review essay). Slavery. 19c. 1930's. *515*
—. Music (blues). Negroes. Oral History. Recordings. Social Conditions. 1924-41. *888*
Historicity. Intellectual development. Literature. Modernism, nature of. Tate, Allen. Western life. 1929-30. *780*
Historiography. Alabama (Scottsboro). Myths and Symbols. Racism. Trials. 1931-80. *742*
—. Allen, Frederick Lewis *(Only Yesterday)*. Journalism. Liberalism. Puritanism. 1931. *858*
—. Braeman, John (review article). New Deal. Reform. State government. 1930's-40's. *382*
—. Commerce Department (Business Advisory Council). Corporate liberalism (concept). National Recovery Administration (Industrial Advisory Board). New Deal. 1933-35. 1970's. *411*
—. Foreign policy. Isolationism. 1919-39. *541*
—. General Motors Corporation. *Great Sitdown* (film). Strikes. United Automobile Workers of America. *With Babies and Banners* (film). 1937. 1976-79. *855*
—. Hoover, Herbert C. (review article). 1929-33. 1974-75. *36*
—. Hughes, Charles Evans. New Deal. Supreme Court. 1930's. 1950's-60's. *223*
—. Isolationism. World War II. 1930's-40's. *583*
—. New Deal. 1936-39. *480*
—. Socialist Party. Warren, Frank (review article). 1930-40. *700*
Historiography (revisionist). Liberalism. Reform. Roosevelt, Franklin D. Truman, Harry S. 1932-53. 1960-75. *227*
History. Farrell, James T. *(Studs Lonigan)*. Institutions. Social Organization. 1933-35. *796*
—. Fiction. Long, Huey P. Warren, Robert Penn *(All The King's Men)*. World War II (antecedents). 1930's-46. *839*
History classes, economics in. 1929-33. 1974. *117*
History Teaching. Films. North Carolina. 1930's-74. *806*
—. *First-Person America: Voices from the Thirties* (program). Personal narratives. 1930's. 1980. *768*
Hollins, Jess. International Labor Defense. NAACP. Oklahoma. Race Relations. Rape. Trials. 1931-36. *659*
Hollywood. Authors. Dardis, Tom. Films. Scriptwriting. 1936-45. 1976. *919*
—. Dramatists. Films. Phillips, A. H. (reminiscences). 1930's. *894*
Holmes, John. California (San Jose; St. James Park). Hart, Brooke (murder). Kidnapping. Lynching. Thurmond, Thomas. 1933. *665*
Holt, Rush Dew (papers). New Deal. Senate. West Virginia. 1920-55. *171*
Homesteading and Homesteaders. Clapp, Elsie Ripley. Education, community. New Deal. Roosevelt, Eleanor. West Virginia (Arthurdale). 1933-44. *285*
—. Daily Life. Montana (Plentywood). Vindex, Charles (reminiscences). 1929-34. *123*
Homesteading and Homesteaders (failure of). Federal Government. Montana. Ranchers. 1900-30. *32*
Hook, Sidney. Letters. Santayana, George. Totalitarianism. 1929-38. *832*
Hook, Sidney (review article). Marxism. Philosophy. Pragmatism. 1930's. *593*

Hoover administration. Mexicans. Repatriation. 1930's. *57*
Hoover Dam. Boulder Canyon project. Colorado River. Industrial Workers of the World. Nevada. Strikes. 1931. *702*
—. Boulder Canyon Project. Industrial Workers of the World. Nevada. Six Companies, Inc. Strikes. 1931. *703*
Hoover, Herbert C. Agricultural Policy. Corporatism, concept of. Politics. Roosevelt, Franklin D. 1929-33. *27*
—. Banking. Federal government. Nevada. Reconstruction Finance Corporation. 1932-33. *83*
—. Democratic Party. Elections, congressional. Garner, John Nance. House of Representatives. Republican Party. 1930-31. *258*
—. Dix, I. F. Local politics. Self-help. Unemployed Citizens' League. Washington (Seattle). 1931-32. *75*
—. Droughts. 1930. *42*
—. Economic conditions. Elections (presidential). Political Parties. Roosevelt, Franklin D. South Dakota. 1932. *176*
—. Elections (presidential). Missouri. Roosevelt, Franklin D. 1932. *177*
—. Elections (presidential). Progressivism. Republican Party. Senate. 1930-32. *161*
—. Executive leadership. Hawley-Smoot Tariff Act (1930). 1922-32. *106*
—. Food relief. Red Cross. Wheat, surplus. 1932-33. *61*
—. Government. Industry. New York (Buffalo). Public Welfare. Unemployment. 1929-33. *64*
—. Inventions. Public Policy (recommendations). Roosevelt, Franklin D. (administration). Technology assessment. 1930's-77. *369*
—. Landon, Alfred M. Political Leadership. Republican Party (conference, proposed). 1937-38. *140*
—. New Deal. Political Commentary. Republican Party. 1933-35. *141*
Hoover, Herbert C. (administration). Air mail service. Black, Hugo. Contracts. Farley, James A. Legislative Investigations. 1933-34. *487*
—. Negroes. Republican Party. 1928-32. *168*
Hoover, Herbert C. (party politics). Republican Party. 1920-32. *219*
Hoover, Herbert C. (review article). Historiography. 1929-33. 1974-75. *36*
Hoover, J. Edgar. American Civil Liberties Union. Demonstrations. Federal Bureau of Investigation. Political surveillance. Trade Union Education League. 1924-36. *750*
—. Attorney General. Cummings, Homer Stillé. Federal Bureau of Investigation. Films. *G-Men* (film). 1933-35. *898*
Hoovervilles. Missouri (St. Louis). Philanthropy. 1930-36. *120*
Hopkins, Harry. Arkansas. Federal Aid to Education. Federal Emergency Relief Administration. Public schools. 1933-36. *451*
—. Coan, George W., Jr. North Carolina. Patronage. Works Progress Administration. 1935. *404*
—. Country Life. Documents. Federal Emergency Relief Administration. Great Plains. Hickok, Lorena A. Iowa. Minnesota. 1933. *284*
—. Federal Emergency Relief Administration. Hickok, Lorena A. Kentucky, eastern. Poverty. 1933. *19*
—. Federal Emergency Relief Administration. Letters. Public Welfare. Rhode Island. 1934. *431*
—. Federal Policy. New Deal. Poverty. Roosevelt, Franklin D. Unemployment. 1910's-38. *403*

—. Federal Theatre Project. Flanagan, Hallie. Politics. Theater. Works Progress Administration. 1935-39. *303*
—. Hickok, Lorena A. New Deal. Ohio. Roosevelt, Franklin D. Unemployment. 1934-36. *489*
—. New Deal. Politics. 1912-40. *444*
Hormel, George A., and Co. Labor Unions and Organizations. Minnesota (Austin). Olson, Floyd B. Strikes. 1933. *592*
Horse trading. Dehart, Grant. Federal Writers' Project. Folklore. Nebraska. ca 1938-43. *511*
Horton, Henry. Governors. Political Corruption. Tennessee. 1930-31. *201*
House of Representatives. Chandler, Walter. Crump, Edward. Democratic Party. Tennessee. 1933-40. *149*
—. Democratic Party. Elections, congressional. Garner, John Nance. Republican Party. Hoover, Herbert C. 1930-31. *258*
—. Democratic Party. Gillette, Guy M. Iowa. Political Campaigns. Roosevelt, Franklin D. 1932-48. *185*
—. Executive Power (restrictions). Logan-Walter Bill (vetoed, 1939). Rayburn, Sam. Sumners, Hatton. Texas. 1939. *438*
—. New Deal. Political agenda. Political Parties (realignment). 1925-38. *241*
House of Representatives (speaker of). Rainey, Henry T. 1932-33. *262*
Housing. Architecture. City planning. Europe. Modernism. New Deal. 1932-60. *897*
—. Cumberland Homesteads. Fairfield Glade. New Deal. Resettlement. Tennessee. 1934-80. *482*
—. Negroes. New Deal. Pennsylvania (Philadelphia). 1930's. *281*
Hove, Arthur. Films (review article). *Gold Diggers of 1933* (film). Kawin, Bruce F. Screenplays. *To Have and Have Not* (film). 1930's-44. *911*
Hudson, Hosea. Alabama (Birmingham). Communist Party. Negroes. South. 1920's-70's. *691*
Hughes, Charles Evans. Historiography. New Deal. Supreme Court. 1930's. 1950's-60's. *223*
Hughes, Langston. *Esquire* (periodical). Gingrich, Arnold. Negroes. Public Opinion. Publishers and Publishing. 1934. *572*
Humor. Allen, Fred. Bureaucracies. Commercialism. Criticism. Radio. 1932-49. *824*
—. *Amos 'n Andy* (program). Radio. Social Problems. 1929-30's. *945*
—. Capra, Frank. Films. McCarey, Leo. 1930's. *813*
—. Long, Huey P. Louisiana. 1931. *676*
Hurston, Zora Neale. Federal Writers' Project. Florida. Folklore. Negroes. 1901-60. *826*

I

Ickes, Harold. Bureau of Indian Affairs. Collier, John. Interior Department. Presidential appointments. Roosevelt, Franklin D. 1933. *376*
—. Congress. Federal Regulation. Oil Industry and Trade. Roosevelt, Franklin D. 1933. *388*
—. Construction. Employment. Negroes. Public Works Administration. Quotas. 1933-40. *383*
—. Douglas, Lewis. Public Administration. Public Works Administration. 1933. *448*
Idaho. Democratic Party. New Deal. Pocatello Central Labor Union. Rosqvist, August. 1930-36. *494*

Idaho (Boise). Banking. Reconstruction Finance Corporation. 1932. *80*

Idaho (Moscow). Correspondence courses. Psychiana (religion). Robinson, Frank Bruce. 1929-48. *695*

Idaho (Pocatello). Business. New Deal. 1930's. *495*

Idaho, University of, Southern Branch. Radicals and Radicalism. Roosevelt, Franklin D. Student protest. 1930's. *731*

Ideology. Agar, Herbert. Collins, Seward. Conservatism. Decentralization. Intellectuals. Tate, Allen. 1933-50. *913*

—. Documentaries, historical. Films. Rhetoric. 1930's. *906*

Illinois. American Federation of Labor. Chicago Newspaper Guild. Labor Unions and Organizations (white-collar). 1933-40. *642*

—. Chicago, University of. Communist sympathizers, alleged. Newspapers. Walgreen, Charles R. 1930's. *663*

—. Congress. Keller, Kent. Liberalism. New Deal. 1930-42. *263*

—. Democratic Party. Lucas, Scott W. Senate (majority leader). 1938-50. *237*

Illinois Central Railroad. Blizzards. Iowa. 1936. *622*

Illinois (Chicago). Acculturation. Bellow, Saul. Immigrants. ca 1937-74. *533*

—. City of Progress. Construction. Economic development. 1933-34. *14*

—. Civil rights activity. Negroes. School integration. 1936. *624*

—. Communist Party. Intellectuals. Negroes. Wright, Richard *(American Hunger)*. ca 1930-44. *879*

—. Communist Party. Negroes. Wright, Richard (personal account). 1930's. *954*

—. Kelly, Edward J. New Deal. Political machines. Roosevelt, Franklin D. 1932-40. *193*

—. Radio. 1930-40. *943*

Illinois (Lake Forest). Lake Forest College. "Oral and Community History", course. 1930-40. *799*

Illinois (Pekin). American Distillery Company. American Federation of Labor. General strikes. 1934-36. *550*

Immigrants. Acculturation. Bellow, Saul. Illinois (Chicago). ca 1937-74. *533*

—. Adamic, Louis (writings). Unity in diversity (theme). 1935-45. *782*

—. Deportation. Labor Unions and Organizations. Mexican Americans. New Deal. 1930's. *579*

—. International Brotherhood of Pulp, Sulphite, and Paper Mill Workers. Negroes. Pacific Northwest. South. Women. 1909-40. *754*

Immigration. Economic conditions. Exclusion policy. Filipinos. Split labor market theory. 1927-34. *18*

Import restrictions. Foreign policy. International Steel Cartel. Labor. Steel Workers Organizing Committee. US Steel Corporation. 1937. *646*

Import-Export Bank. Economic Policy. International trade. New Deal. 1934-74. *409*

Inaugural addresses. Democracy. Political Speeches. Roosevelt, Franklin D. Values. 1901-77. *164*

—. Moley, Raymond. Rhetoric. Roosevelt, Franklin D. 1933. *233*

Income. Civilian Conservation Corps. 1937-81. *471*

—. Currie, Lauchlin. Fiscal policy. Keynesianism. New Deal. 1920's-30's. *522*

Income (redistribution). LaFollette, Philip F. National Progressives of America. Politics. Wisconsin. 1930-38. *214*

Indian policy. Cherokee Indians. New Deal. North Carolina, western. 1930's. *508*

Indian Reorganization Act (1934). Assimilation (opposition to). Collier, John. Federal Policy. 1933-45. *377*

Indiana. Automobile Industry and Trade. Labor parties. New Deal. Ohio. United Automobile Workers of America. 1935-40. *652*

—. Federal Writers' Project. Local history. 1936-43. *428*

Indiana (East Chicago). Mexican Americans. Repatriation. 1919-33. *100*

Indiana (Gary). Discrimination. Mexican Americans. Nativism. Repatriation. 1920's-30's. *537*

Indiana (Kokomo). Automobile industry and Trade. Patterson, Robert *(Gas Buggy)*. 1933. *820*

Indiana (Muncie). Dale, George R. Elites. Local Politics. Lynd, Helen Merrell. Lynd, Robert S. 1930-40. *166*

Indians. American Indian Federation. Bureau of Indian Affairs. Collier, John. Jamison, Alice Lee. New Deal. Political activism. 1930's-50's. *351*

—. Anthropology. Bureau of Indian Affairs. Collier, John. Federal Programs. New Deal. 1930's. *375*

—. Art. Iroquois School of Art. New Deal. New York (Akron). Parker, Arthur C. Seneca Arts project. Tonawanda Indian Reservation. 1935-41. *352*

—. Collier, John. Federal Government. Liberalism. Roosevelt, Franklin D. (administration). Truman, Harry S. (administration). 1933-53. *380*

Indians (government relations). Bureau of Indian Affairs. Collier, John. New Deal. 1933-45. *498*

Indians (reservations). Civilian Conservation Corps (Indian Division). Sioux Indians. South Dakota. 1933-42. *300*

Indians (review articles). Federal Policy. New Deal. Parman, Donald L. Philp, Kenneth R. Taylor, Graham D. 1934-74. *612*

Indian-White Relations. Agriculture and Government. New Deal. New Mexico. Pueblo Indians. 1938-48. *503*

Industrial design. Automobiles. Geddes, Norman Bel. Streamlining. 1930-39. *870*

Industrial Rayon Corporation. Strikes. Textile Workers Organizing Committee. Virginia (Covington). 1937-38. *599*

Industrial Relations. Blankenhorn, Heber. LaFollette Committee. Legislative Investigations. Strikes, sit-down. 1935-40. *600*

Industrial Workers of the World. Agricultural Labor. Farmers. Labor Disputes. Ranchers. Washington (Yakima Valley). 1910-36. *685*

—. Boulder Canyon project. Colorado River. Hoover Dam. Nevada. Strikes. 1931. *702*

—. Boulder Canyon Project. Hoover Dam. Nevada. Six Companies, Inc. Strikes. 1931. *703*

—. Farmers. North Dakota. O'Connor, Hugh (interview). Women. 1900's-30's. *113*

—. Labor Unions and Organizations. Strikes. Washington (Yakima Valley). 1933. *570*

Industrialization. Agrarianism. Alienation. Tate, Allen. 1930's. *835*

—. Authors. Social Conditions. South. Urbanization. 1930's. *908*

Industry. Architecture. Design (review article). Meikle, Jeffrey L. 1925-39. 1979. *823*

—. Government. Hoover, Herbert C. New York (Buffalo). Public Welfare. Unemployment. 1929-33. *64*

Infantry Journal (periodical). Harding, Edwin Forrest. 1934-38. *764*

Institutions. Farrell, James T. *(Studs Lonigan).*
History. Social Organization. 1933-35. *796*
Intellectual development. Historicity. Literature.
Modernism, nature of. Tate, Allen. Western life.
1929-30. *780*
Intellectual trends. Culture, concept of. Economic
theory. Relativism. Theology. 1930's. *883*
Intellectuals. Agar, Herbert. Collins, Seward.
Conservatism. Decentralization. Ideology.
Tate, Allen. 1933-50. *913*
—. Alienation. Jews. Leftism. New Deal.
Roosevelt, Franklin D. 1930's. *757*
—. Beard, Charles A. Historians. Isolationism.
Liberalism. New Deal. Roosevelt, Franklin D.
1932-48. *296*
—. Communism. Jews. Menorah Group. 1930's.
744
—. Communist Party. Culture. Negroes. New
York City (Harlem). Popular Front. 1935-39.
678
—. Communist Party. Illinois (Chicago). Negroes.
Wright, Richard *(American Hunger).* ca
1930-44. *879*
—. Communist Party. Literature. Popular Front
Against Fascism. 1929-39. *613*
—. Cowley, Malcolm. Literature. Marxism. New
York City. 1932-40. *763*
—. Ethnicity. National Characteristics. Public
Opinion. 1930's. *747*
—. New Deal. Progressivism. 1930's. *272*
Interior decorating. Art deco. Deskey, Donald.
Genauer, Emily (account). New York City.
Radio City Music Hall. 1929-37. *815*
Interior Department. Bureau of Indian Affairs.
Collier, John. Ickes, Harold. Presidential
appointments. Roosevelt, Franklin D. 1933.
376
—. Fortas, Abe. Lawyers. Letters. Peres, Hardwig.
Roosevelt, Franklin D. 1930-44. *373*
International Brotherhood of Pulp, Sulphite, and
Paper Mill Workers. American Federation of
Labor. Labor Unions and Organizations.
Militancy. Paper industry. 1933-35. *753*
—. Immigrants. Negroes. Pacific Northwest.
South. Women. 1909-40. *754*
International cooperation. Foreign Policy.
Isolationism. League of Nations Association.
Peace. 1934-38. *525*
International Labor Defense. Communism.
Demonstrations. Georgia Insurrection Law.
Herndon v. *Lowry* (US, 1937). Martin, Charles
H. (review article). 1932-37. *591*
—. Communist Party. Georgia (Atlanta). Herndon,
Angelo. Negroes. 1932-37. *658*
—. Hollins, Jess. NAACP. Oklahoma. Race
Relations. Rape. Trials. 1931-36. *659*
International Labor Organization. Foreign Policy.
Isolationism. New Deal. Perkins, Frances.
Roosevelt, Franklin D. 1921-34. *429*
International Ladies' Garment Workers' Union.
American Federation of Labor. Jews. Labor
Unions and Organizations. 1930's. *528*
—. California (Los Angeles). Mexican Americans.
Women. Working Conditions. 1933-39. *673*
International Longshoremen's and Warehousemen's
Union. Far Western States. Labor Unions and
Organizations. 1934-37. *542*
International Steel Cartel. Foreign policy. Import
restrictions. Labor. Steel Workers Organizing
Committee. US Steel Corporation. 1937.
646
International Trade. Adams, Frederick C. (review
article). Credit. Export-Import Bank. Foreign
policy. 1934-39. 1976. *52*
—. China. Congress. Lobbying. Roosevelt,
Franklin D. (administration). Silver Purchase
Act (1934). 1934. *341*

—. China. Pittman, Key. Senate. Silver Purchase
Act (1934). 1933-40. *472*
—. Economic Policy. Import-Export Bank. New
Deal. 1934-74. *409*
—. Foreign Policy. Great Britain. 1932-38. *385*
Internationalism. Democratic Party. Domestic
Policy. New Deal. Political Campaigns.
Roosevelt, Franklin D. 1938-40. *160*
—. Editorials. Great Plains. Isolationism.
Newspapers. North Central States. 1918-35.
643
Interstate relations. Bridges (toll, free). Oklahoma
National Guard. Red River Bridge Company.
Texas Rangers. 1931. *30*
Intervention. Bibliographies. Leadership. Political
Attitudes. 1929-41. *580*
Interviews. Biography. Family history. Louisiana
State University. Students. Works Progress
Administration. 1930's. 1978. *321*
—. Family. Slavery. South. Works Progress
Administration. 1850's-60's. 1930's. *387*
—. Federal Writers' Project. Finnish Americans.
Minnesota. 1930's. *381*
—. Federal Writers' Project. Genovese, Eugene D.
Methodology. Rawick, George P. Slavery.
1930's. 1970's. *484*
Invasions. Black nationalism. Ethiopia. Italy.
Negroes. Pan-Africanism. 1934-36. *716*
Inventions. Hoover, Herbert C. Public Policy
(recommendations). Roosevelt, Franklin D.
(administration). Technology assessment.
1930's-77. *369*
Iowa. Blizzards. Illinois Central Railroad. 1936.
622
—. Country Life. Documents. Federal Emergency
Relief Administration. Great Plains. Hickok,
Lorena A. Hopkins, Harry. Minnesota. 1933.
284
—. Democratic Party. Elections (presidential).
Roosevelt, Franklin D. 1932. *172*
—. Democratic Party. Gillette, Guy M. House of
Representatives. Political Campaigns. Roosevelt,
Franklin D. 1932-48. *185*
—. Elections (presidential). German Americans.
Roosevelt, Franklin D. 1936-40. *234*
—. Evans, Luther H. Historical Records Survey.
Public records. Works Progress Administration.
1936-42. *334*
—. Murals. New Deal. 1934-42. *880*
Iowa (Black Hawk County). Droughts. Farms.
Hearst, James (reminiscences). 1934-41. *44*
Iowa (Boone County). Agricultural Adjustment
Administration. Agriculture and Government.
"Corn-hog" program. Farmers. Powers, Elmer
G. (diary). 1934. *345*
—. Farmers. Powers, Elmer G. (diary). 1936.
37
Iowa (Cedar Rapids). Theatricals, amateur.
Universal Production Company. Women.
1926-30's. *800*
Iowa (Granger). Federal Subsistence Homesteads
Corporation. Ligutti, Luigi. New Deal. Social
experiments. 1934-51. *469*
Ireland (Dublin). Airplane flights, transatlantic.
Corrigan, Douglas. New York City. 1938-50.
950
Ironwork. Dawson, Oliver B. (reminiscences).
Oregon. Timberline Lodge. Works Progress
Administration. 1935-37. *326*
Iroquois School of Art. Art. Indians. New Deal.
New York (Akron). Parker, Arthur C. Seneca
Arts project. Tonawanda Indian Reservation.
1935-41. *352*
Irrigation. Agricultural Production. Kansas.
1930's-70's. *47*
Isolationism. Armaments. Embargoes. Neutrality
Act (US, 1935). 1935. *756*

—. Beard, Charles A. Historians. Intellectuals. Liberalism. New Deal. Roosevelt, Franklin D. 1932-48. *296*
—. Business. Conservatism. New Deal. Sears, Roebuck and Company. Wood, Robert E. 1928-50's. *581*
—. Editorials. Great Plains. Internationalism. Newspapers. North Central States. 1918-35. *643*
—. Foreign policy. Hearst, William Randolph. Newspapers. 1936-41. *556*
—. Foreign policy. Historiography. 1919-39. *541*
—. Foreign Policy. International cooperation. League of Nations Association. Peace. 1934-38. *525*
—. Foreign Policy. International Labor Organization. New Deal. Perkins, Frances. Roosevelt, Franklin D. 1921-34. *429*
—. Foreign policy. Johnson, Hiram. Nye Committee. Roosevelt, Franklin D. (administration). ca 1933-34. *576*
—. Foreign policy. Political Leadership. Roosevelt, Franklin D. Senate. World Court. 1935. *194*
—. Historiography. World War II. 1930's-40's. *583*
Isolationism (review article). Politics. 1935-52. *582*
Isotopes. Biochemistry. Research. Schoenheimer, Rudolf. 1934-41. *640*
Italian Americans. Fascism. Michigan (Detroit). Sociopolitical integration. 1933-35. *554*
Italy. Black nationalism. Ethiopia. Invasions. Negroes. Pan-Africanism. 1934-36. *716*
—. Fascism. Monetary policy. Mussolini, Benito. New Deal. Roosevelt, Franklin D. 1922-36. *433*
Ivy League. "Big Three" relationship. Football. Harvard University. Princeton University. 1926-39. *924*

J

Jackson, Robert H. Education. Presidency. Roosevelt, Franklin D. 1933-45. *271*
James, Arthur H. Elections (gubernatorial). Pennsylvania. 1938. *215*
Jamison, Alice Lee. American Indian Federation. Bureau of Indian Affairs. Collier, John. Indians. New Deal. Political activism. 1930's-50's. *351*
Japan. Berry pickers. California (El Monte). Foreign Relations. Mexico. Strikes. 1933. *619*
Japanese Americans. Arizona (Salt River Valley). Farmers. Race Relations. 1934-35. *529*
Jazz. Music. Swing (term). 1908-30's. *927*
Jeffries, John W. Andersen, Kristi. Blumberg, Barbara. Fine, Sidney. New Deal (review article). Roosevelt, Franklin D. Swain, Martha H. 1933-39. *143*
Jewish Community Council. Anti-Semitism. Boxerman, William I. Coughlin, Charles. Michigan (Detroit). Radio. 1939. *725*
Jews. Alienation. Intellectuals. Leftism. New Deal. Roosevelt, Franklin D. 1930's. *757*
—. American Federation of Labor. International Ladies' Garment Workers' Union. Labor Unions and Organizations. 1930's. *528*
—. Communism. Intellectuals. Menorah Group. 1930's. *744*
—. Garment industry. Labor movement. 1920's-30's. *546*
—. Germany. Refugees. Relief organizations. World War II. 1933-45. *602*

John Reed Clubs. Communist Party. Literature, proletarian. Proletcult. 1929-35. *623*
Johnson, Hiram. Foreign policy. Isolationism. Nye Committee. Roosevelt, Franklin D. (administration). ca 1933-34. *576*
—. New Deal. Roosevelt, Franklin D. 1920's-41. *180*
Johnson, Hugh S. (career). Authors. Military officers. National Recovery Administration. ca 1903-42. *426*
Johnson, Lyndon B. Kennedy, John F. New Deal. Truman, Harry S. 1933-68. *394*
Johnston, Oscar Goodbar. Cotton industry. Delta & Pine Land Company. Economic Regulations. Federal Government. Subsidies. 1933-37. *424*
Jones, Marvin. Agricultural Policy. Legislation. New Deal. Political Leadership. 1916-40. *406*
Journalism. Agee, James. Literature. Steinbeck, John. 1935-39. *899*
—. Allen, Frederick Lewis *(Only Yesterday)*. Historiography. Liberalism. Puritanism. 1931. *858*
—. Antidemocratism. Cynicism. Mencken, H. L. Satire. 1920's-56. *914*
—. Chisum, Melvin J. Negroes. Roosevelt, Franklin D. (election). *Tribune* (newspaper). ca 1932. *892*
Joyce, James *(Ulysses)*. Censorship. Cerf, Bennett. Ernst, Morris. *United States* v. *One Book Called "Ulysses"* (US, 1932). 1922-32. *840*
Judges. Autobiography. Douglas, William O. (review article). Roosevelt, Franklin D. (administration). 1933-39. 1974. *337*
Juma, Charlie (interview). North Dakota (Ross). Syrian Americans. 1900's-30's. *111*
Justice Department. Antitrust. Appellate Courts. Arnold, Thurman W. Roosevelt, Franklin D. (administration). 1935-43. *415*
—. Crime and Criminals. Federal Bureau of Investigation. Law enforcement. 1933-34. *614*

K

Kael, Pauline (review article). California (Hollywood). *Citizen Kane* (film). Films. 1930-39. *859*
Kansas. Agricultural Production. Irrigation. 1930's-70's. *47*
—. Agricultural programs. Droughts. New Deal. Political Campaigns (presidential). 1936. *464*
—. Conservatism. Constitutional law. New Deal. Newspapers. Supreme Court. 1934-35. *329*
—. Disaster Relief. Droughts. Farmers. Federal Government. New Deal. 1934. *465*
—. Elections (senatorial). McGill, George S. 1938. *210*
—. State Politics. Woodring, Harry Hines. 1905-33. *211*
Kansas (Decatur County). Country Life. Family. Webb, Bernice Larson (reminiscences). 1930's. *125*
Kansas (Sherman County). Country life. Droughts. Shaver, James H. (reminiscences). 1923-35. *99*
Kautsky, Karl. Factionalism. Lee, Algernon. Letters. Socialist Party. 1930-35. *589*
Kawin, Bruce F. Films (review article). *Gold Diggers of 1933* (film). Hove, Arthur. Screenplays. *To Have and Have Not* (film). 1930's-44. *911*
Keep America Out of War Congress. Antiwar Sentiment. Socialist Party. Thomas, Norman. Villard, Oswald Garrison. World War II (antecedents). 1938-41. *584*

Keeran, Roger. Automobile Industry and Trade. Communist Party (review article). Labor Unions and Organizations. 1930-39. 1980. *645*
—. Communist Party. Glabermann, Martin. Labor Unions and Organizations. Meier, August. Negroes. Rudwick, Elliot. United Automobile Workers of America (review article). 1930's-40's. *651*
Keller, Kent. Congress. Illinois. Liberalism. New Deal. 1930-42. *263*
Kelly, Edward J. Illinois (Chicago). New Deal. Political machines. Roosevelt, Franklin D. 1932-40. *193*
Kendrick, John B. Legislation. North Platte River. Water Supply. Western States. 1917-33. *314*
Kennedy, John F. Johnson, Lyndon B. New Deal. Truman, Harry S. 1933-68. *394*
Kennedy, Susan Estabrook (review article). Banking crisis. 1933. 1973. *17*
Kentucky. Alabama. Labor Unions and Organizations (development). United Mine Workers of America. 1932-33. *634*
—. Automobile, advent of. Peddlers, disappearance of. 1930's. *727*
—. Chandler, A. B. ("Happy"). Elections (gubernatorial). Federal Emergency Relief Administration. Works Progress Administration. 1935. *202*
—. Lincoln Institute. Negroes. Tydings, J. Mansir. Young, Whitney M. 1935-37. *134*
Kentucky (Bell County, London). American Civil Liberties Union. Civil rights. Miners. Trials. 1932-38. *733*
Kentucky, eastern. Federal Emergency Relief Administration. Hickok, Lorena A. Hopkins, Harry. Poverty. 1933. *19*
Kentucky (Harlan County). Coal Mines and Mining. Editors and Editing. Evans, Herndon J. Pineville *Sun* (newspaper). Strikes. 1929-32. *730*
—. Coal Mines and Mining. Hevener, John W. Labor Unions and Organizations. 1930's. *609*
Kentucky (Louisville). Callahan, Patrick Henry. Catholic Church. Democratic Party. 1866-1940. *158*
—. Democratic Party. National Democratic Issues Convention. New Deal policies. 1975. *332*
Keynes, John Maynard. Attitudes. Chicago, University of. Economic Theory. Simons, Henry. 1930's. *85*
—. Economic Theory. New Deal. 1920's-30's. *63*
—. Frankfurter, Felix. New Deal. Public works. 1932-35. *280*
Keynesian Economics. Economic Policy. Fiscal policy. Public administration. 1930's. *12*
Keynesianism. Commerce Department (Business Advisory Council). Committee for Economic Development. New Deal. Roosevelt, Franklin D. (administration). Scholars. 1933-42. *319*
—. Currie, Lauchlin. Fiscal policy. Income. New Deal. 1920's-30's. *522*
—. Federal Reserve Board. Monetary policy. New Deal. Private sector. 1929-79. *6*
Kidnapping. California (San Jose; St. James Park). Hart, Brooke (murder). Holmes, John. Lynching. Thurmond, Thomas. 1933. *665*
—. Criminal investigations. Hauptmann, Bruno. Lindbergh, Charles A. New Jersey. 1932-36. *638*
—. Hauptmann, Bruno. Lindbergh case. Trials. 1935. *573*
Kindleberger, Charles P. Depressions (review article). Economic policy. VanderWee, Herman. 1930's. *26*
Kollmorgen, Walter M. Agriculture Department. Geography. 1936-45. *379*

Kreher, Ernest. Federal loan. Florida (Tampa). Public Works Administration. Tampa Shipbuilding and Engineering Company. 1932-37. *401*
Kump, Herman Guy. Fiscal Policy. Governors. State Government. West Virginia. 1933. *169*
Kuusinen, Aino (pseud. A. Morton). Comintern. Communist Party. Finnish Workers' Federation. 1930-33. *641*

L

La Guardia, Fiorello Henry. City Government (relations with state government). Emergency Economy Bill (New York, 1934). New York City. 1934. *144*
Labor. Attitudes. Blitzstein, Marc *(Cradle Will Rock)*. Censorship. Federal Theatre Project. New York City. Works Progress Administration. 1937. *502*
—. California. Public welfare administration. ca 1930-45. *390*
—. Congress of Industrial Organizations. New Hampshire (Berlin). Nonpartisan League. Political Parties. 1932-36. *574*
—. Discrimination, Employment. Georgia (Atlanta). Racism. Women. 1930's. *539*
—. Economic Conditions. New Deal. Texas. 1929-39. *430*
—. Ethnic Groups. Georgia (Atlanta). Louisiana (New Orleans). Texas (San Antonio). Women. 1930-40. *540*
—. Foreign policy. Import restrictions. International Steel Cartel. Steel Workers Organizing Committee. US Steel Corporation. 1937. *646*
—. Liberalism. Psychology. Society for the Psychological Study of Social Issues. 1930's. *596*
—. Middle Classes. Values. Women. 1930's. *11*
Labor Department. Negroes. New Deal. Perkins, Frances. 1933-45. *347*
Labor Disputes. Agricultural Labor. Farmers. Industrial Workers of the World. Ranchers. Washington (Yakima Valley). 1910-36. *685*
—. Communism. Films. Propaganda. Workers' Film and Photo League. 1930-38. *808*
—. Congress of Industrial Organizations. New Deal. Newspapers. South. 1930-39. *518*
Labor force. Segregation, sexual. Women. 1930's. *671*
Labor law. Agricultural Labor Relations Act (1975). California. Emergency Farm Labor Supply Program. New Deal. ca 1930-79. *338*
Labor markets. California (San Francisco). Longshoremen. Strikes. 1934-39. *635*
—. Economic structure. Sex roles. Women. 1930's. *626*
Labor movement. Garment industry. Jews. 1920's-30's. *546*
Labor Non-Partisan League. Congress of Industrial Organizations. Elections (presidential). Pennsylvania. Roosevelt, Franklin D. 1936. *252*
—. Legislation. Political representation. Working conditions. 1936-38. *741*
Labor organizations. Michigan (Detroit). Radicals and Radicalism. 1920's-30's. *656*
Labor parties. Automobile Industry and Trade. Indiana. New Deal. Ohio. United Automobile Workers of America. 1935-40. *652*
Labor policy. New Deal. Radicals and Radicalism. Working class. 1930's. *627*

Labor reform. Coal Mines and Mining. Colorado. Roche, Josephine. Roosevelt, Franklin D. (administration). Social work. 1886-1976. *365*

—. Minimum Wage. New York. *Tipaldo* v. *Morehead* (New York, 1934). 1933-37. *367*

Labor union journals. Constitutional issues. Editorials. New Deal. Supreme Court. 1935-37. *588*

Labor Unions and Organizations *See also* names of labor unions and organizations, e.g. American Federation of Labor, United Automobile Workers, etc.

—. Agricultural Adjustment Administration. Sharecroppers. Southern Tenant Farmers' Union. ca 1930's. *736*

—. Agricultural Labor. California. National Industrial Recovery Act (1933). 1933-34. *323*

—. Agricultural laborers. California. Migration, Internal. "Okies". 1930's. *115*

—. American Federation of Labor. Communist Party. Radicals and Radicalism. Trade Union Unity League. 1933-35. *569*

—. American Federation of Labor. International Brotherhood of Pulp, Sulphite, and Paper Mill Workers. Militancy. Paper industry. 1933-35. *753*

—. American Federation of Labor. International Ladies' Garment Workers' Union. Jews. 1930's. *528*

—. Automobile Industry and Trade. Communist Party (review article). Keeran, Roger. 1930-39. 1980. *645*

—. Automobile Workers Union. Communist Party. Michigan (Detroit). 1920's-1935. *699*

—. Bell Telephone System. Company unions. 1919-37. *713*

—. Brookwood Labor College. New York. 1926-36. *644*

—. Bulosan, Carlos (autobiography). California. Filipino Americans. Leftism. 1934-38. *552*

—. Business. New Deal. Taft-Hartley Act (US, 1947). Wagner Act (US, 1935). World War II. 1935-47. *543*

—. Coal Mines and Mining. Hevener, John W. Kentucky (Harlan County). 1930's. *609*

—. Communist Party. Glabermann, Martin. Keeran, Roger. Meier, August. Negroes. Rudwick, Elliot. United Automobile Workers of America (review article). 1930's-40's. *651*

—. Communist Party. Mexico. 1935-39. *648*

—. Communist Party. Ohio (Youngstown). Steel Workers Organizing Committee. Steuben, John. 1936. *608*

—. Deportation. Immigrants. Mexican Americans. New Deal. 1930's. *579*

—. Far Western States. International Longshoremen's and Warehousemen's Union. 1934-37. *542*

—. Hormel, George A., and Co. Minnesota (Austin). Olson, Floyd B. Strikes. 1933. *592*

—. Industrial Workers of the World. Strikes. Washington (Yakima Valley). 1933. *570*

—. Leadership. New Deal. 1933-40. *650*

—. Lewis, John L. Reorganized United Mine Workers of America. 1920-36. *559*

—. New Deal. Radicals and Radicalism. 1930-39. *653*

—. Unemployment. Working Class. 1930-40's. *674*

—. United Electrical and Radio Workers of America. 1933-37. *594*

Labor Unions and Organizations (development). Alabama. Kentucky. United Mine Workers of America. 1932-33. *634*

Labor Unions and Organizations (membership). Collective bargaining. New Deal. Public policy. 1933-45. *289*

Labor Unions and Organizations (white-collar). American Federation of Labor. Chicago Newspaper Guild. Illinois. 1933-40. *642*

Labor unrest. Artists. Ginther, Ronald Debs. Skid row. ca 1920-69. *937*

LaFollette Committee. Blankenhorn, Heber. Industrial Relations. Legislative Investigations. Strikes, sit-down. 1935-40. *600*

LaFollette, Philip F. Income (redistribution). National Progressives of America. Politics. Wisconsin. 1930-38. *214*

—. New Deal. Progressivism. Roosevelt, Franklin D. Wisconsin Works Bill. 1935. *414*

Lake Forest College. Illinois (Lake Forest). "Oral and Community History", course. 1930-40. *799*

Land. Agriculture and Government. Langer, William. Mortgage moratoria. North Dakota. 1930's. *3*

Land reform. Negroes. New Deal. Public Policy. Resettlement. 1930's-60's. *458*

Land utilization movement. Agricultural production, limited. Farm leaders. 1920's. *41*

Landis, James M. Brandeis, Louis D. Dawson, Nelson L. Frankfurter, Felix. Law. New Deal (review article). Ritchie, Donald A. 1930's. *512*

Landon, Alfred M. Hoover, Herbert C. Political Leadership. Republican Party (conference, proposed). 1937-38. *140*

Land-use planning. Droughts. Federal government. Great Plains. 1930's. *349*

Langer, William. Agriculture and Government. Land. Mortgage moratoria. North Dakota. 1930's. *3*

Language. Agee, James. Literature. Social criticism. 1930-40. *850*

—. Agee, James *(Let Us Now Praise Famous Men)*. Literary criticism. Richards, Ivor Armstrong. 1930-40. *833*

—. "Gimme a Pigfoot" (song). Music. Smith, Bessie. 1933. *925*

Law. Attitudes. Great Britain. Poor. Vagrancy. 14c-1939. *20*

—. Brandeis, Louis D. Dawson, Nelson L. Frankfurter, Felix. Landis, James M. New Deal (review article). Ritchie, Donald A. 1930's. *512*

—. Brandeis, Louis D. Freund, Paul A. (reminiscences). Supreme Court. 1932-33. *167*

Law enforcement. Bootlegging. Florida (Hernando County). Liquor. Prohibition. 1929-33. *562*

—. Crime and Criminals. Federal Bureau of Investigation. Justice Department. 1933-34. *614*

—. Diplomacy. Drug Abuse. Mexico. Salazar Viniegra, Leopold. 1936-40. *745*

Lawsuits. Breach of contract. Miller, Zack. Mix, Tom. Sells-Floto Circus. Verbal agreements. 101 Ranch Real Wild West Show. 1929-34. *819*

Lawyers. Career patterns. New Deal. 1918-41. *4*

—. Fortas, Abe. Interior Department. Letters. Peres, Hardwig. Roosevelt, Franklin D. 1930-44. *373*

—. Frank, Jerome (papers). 1916-57. *517*

Lazarsfeld, Paul F. Adorno, Theodor W. Culture. Music. Princeton Radio Research Project. Social organization. 1930's. *875*

Leadership. Bibliographies. Intervention. Political Attitudes. 1929-41. *580*

—. Labor Unions and Organizations. New Deal. 1933-40. *650*

League of American Writers. American Writers'
Congress. Capitalism. Comintern. 1935.
567
League of Nations Association. Foreign Policy.
International cooperation. Isolationism. Peace.
1934-38. *525*
Lee, Algernon. Factionalism. Kautsky, Karl.
Letters. Socialist Party. 1930-35. *589*
Lee, Russell. Attitudes. Daily Life. Photographs.
1932-40. *827*
Leftism. Alienation. Intellectuals. Jews. New Deal.
Roosevelt, Franklin D. 1930's. *757*
—. Andersen, Kristi (review article). Democratic
Party. 1928-36. 1979. *182*
—. Antiwar sentiment. Colleges and Universities.
Political Protest. 1920-36. *547*
—. Appalachia. Mountaineers. Music.
Resettlement Administration (music program).
Seeger, Charles. Social Organization. 1935-37.
506
—. Bulosan, Carlos (autobiography). California.
Filipino Americans. Labor Unions and
Organizations. 1934-38. *552*
—. Composers Collective. Folk Songs. New York
City. 1931-36. *798*
—. New Deal. Roosevelt, Franklin D. 1933-79.
535
Legal education. Douglas, William O. (memoirs).
Yale University Law School. 1928-34. *585*
Legal order, equalitarian. Civil Rights.
Constitutional History. 1930-50. *611*
Legislation. Agricultural Policy. Jones, Marvin.
New Deal. Political Leadership. 1916-40.
406
—. Ehringhaus, J. C. B. North Carolina. Social
Security Act (US, 1935). Unemployment
insurance. 1935-37. *420*
—. Epstein, Abraham. Old age security. Pension
systems. Voluntary associations. 1920-35.
647
—. Farmers. New Deal. North Dakota (Landa).
Taralseth, Rueben P. (interview). 1900's-30's.
114
—. Federal aid to education. Harrison, Byron
Patton (Pat). Mississippi. 1936-41. *493*
—. Kendrick, John B. North Platte River. Water
Supply. Western States. 1917-33. *314*
—. Labor Non-Partisan League. Political
representation. Working conditions. 1936-38.
741
—. Political Parties (realignment). Public Welfare.
1933-54. *479*
Legislation (proposed). Bonus Army. District of
Columbia. Patman, Wright. Veterans'
certificates. 1932. *666*
Legislative Investigations. Air mail service. Black,
Hugo. Contracts. Farley, James A. Hoover,
Herbert C. (administration). 1933-34. *487*
—. Blankenhorn, Heber. Industrial Relations.
LaFollette Committee. Strikes, sit-down.
1935-40. *600*
Lemon, J. Stanley. Chafe, William H. Politics.
Women's movement (review article). 1920-70.
610
Lenin, V. I. *(Imperialism: The Highest Stage of
Capitalism)*. Film industry. Finance capitalism
(concept). Monopolies. 1916-39. *817*
Leonidov, Ivan. Architecture. Melnikov,
Konstantin. 1929-31. *848*
Letters. Agriculture. Mississippi. Roosevelt,
Franklin D. 1932-33. *95*
—. Amyotrophic lateral sclerosis. Baseball.
Character. Gehrig, Lou. New York Yankees
(team). 1939. *777*
—. Atlanta *Georgian* (newspaper). Economic
Conditions. Georgia. Seydell, Mildred. 1930's.
10

—. Authors (southern). Gordon, Caroline. New
York (Rochester). Tennessee (Benfolly). Wood,
Sally. 1930-31. *818*
—. Cowen, Wilson. Dust Bowl. Farm Security
Administration. Migration, Internal. Texas
(Amarillo). 1940. *48*
—. Factionalism. Kautsky, Karl. Lee, Algernon.
Socialist Party. 1930-35. *589*
—. Farmers. Government. Great Plains. New
Deal. 1930-40. *8*
—. Federal Emergency Relief Administration.
Hopkins, Harry. Public Welfare. Rhode Island.
1934. *431*
—. Fortas, Abe. Interior Department. Lawyers.
Peres, Hardwig. Roosevelt, Franklin D.
1930-44. *373*
—. Hook, Sidney. Santayana, George.
Totalitarianism. 1929-38. *832*
—. Migrant Labor. Sletten, Myron. Travel
(accounts). Western States. 1930-32. *104*
Letters-to-the-editor. Baltimore *Sun*, *Evening Sun*
(newspapers). Government intervention.
Maryland. Roosevelt, Franklin D. 1929-33.
384
Lewis, John L. Domestic Policy. Elections
(presidential). Foreign policy. Roosevelt,
Franklin D. 1936-40. *230*
—. General Motors Corporation. Strikes, sit-down.
1936-37. *595*
—. Labor Unions and Organizations. Reorganized
United Mine Workers of America. 1920-33.
559
Lewis, Sinclair. Dreiser, Theodore. Literature.
Nobel Prizes. Public Opinion. Sweden.
1920's-30. *857*
Lewis-American Aircraft Co. Colorado (Denver).
Design. *Flivver* (aircraft). *Gray Goose*
(aircraft). McMahon, Bill. Mooney brothers.
1930-33. *794*
Libel. Anti-Semitism. Edmondson, Robert Edward.
Trials. 1934-44. *597*
Liberalism. Allen, Frederick Lewis *(Only
Yesterday)*. Historiography. Journalism.
Puritanism. 1931. *858*
—. Beard, Charles A. Historians. Intellectuals.
Isolationism. New Deal. Roosevelt, Franklin D.
1932-48. *296*
—. Carbone, Peter F., Jr. (review article). Public
Schools. Reform. Rugg, Harold. 1930's.
689
—. Collier, John. Federal Government. Indians.
Roosevelt, Franklin D. (administration).
Truman, Harry S. (administration). 1933-53.
380
—. Congress. Illinois. Keller, Kent. New Deal.
1930-42. *263*
—. Editors and Editing. Milton, George Fort.
New Deal. Tennessee. 1930's. *362*
—. Graves, John Temple, II. New Deal. Palm
Beach *Times* (newspaper). South. 1933-40.
275
—. Historiography (revisionist). Reform. Roosevelt,
Franklin D. Truman, Harry S. 1932-53.
1960-75. *227*
—. Labor. Psychology. Society for the
Psychological Study of Social Issues. 1930's.
596
—. New Deal. Political activism. Socialist Party.
Unemployment. 1929-36. *707*
Liberalism, rural. Great Plains states. New Deal.
Senators. 1930's. *162*
Liberals. Amlie, Thomas R. Economic programs.
New Deal. Politics. Wisconsin. 1931-39.
264
—. Collectivism (objections to). Glass, Carter.
National Recovery Administration. New Deal.
1933-35. *378*

—. Democracy. Niebuhr, Reinhold. Religion. 1930-45. *598*
Libraries (public). New Deal. 1933-39. *295*
Lieutenant governors. Allen, DeLacey. Elections (state). Georgia. Pope, J. Ellis. Proposition 2. Scott, W. Fred. 1936. *156*
Ligutti, Luigi. Federal Subsistence Homesteads Corporation. Iowa (Granger). New Deal. Social experiments. 1934-51. *469*
Lilly, Octave, Jr. (obituary). Negroes. Poetry. South. 1930-60. *793*
Lincoln Institute. Kentucky. Negroes. Tydings, J. Mansir. Young, Whitney M. 1935-37. *134*
Lind, Leo (reminiscences). Daily life. Economic conditions. Markham and Callow Railroad. Oregon. 1929-38. *67*
Lindbergh case. Hauptmann, Bruno. Kidnapping. Trials. 1935. *573*
Lindbergh, Charles A. Criminal investigations. Hauptmann, Bruno. Kidnapping. New Jersey. 1932-36. *638*
Lindbergh, Charles A. (tribute). Brecht, Bertolt. Music. Radio broadcasts. Weill, Kurt. 1929-31. *849*
Lippmann, Walter. Frankfurter, Felix. New Deal. Roosevelt, Franklin D. World War II. 1932-45. *432*
Lipset, Seymour Martin. Colleges and Universities. Feuer, Lewis. Politics. Student activism. 1930's-40's. *715*
Liquor. Bootlegging. Florida (Hernando County). Law enforcement. Prohibition. 1929-33. *562*
Literary criticism. Agee, James *(Let Us Now Praise Famous Men)*. Language. Richards, Ivor Armstrong. 1930-40. *833*
—. Marxism. Political Participation. Wilson, Edmund. 1930's. *940*
Literature. Agee, James. Eyster, Warren. Films. Personal narratives. 1935-41. *802*
—. Agee, James. Journalism. Steinbeck, John. 1935-39. *899*
—. Agee, James. Language. Social criticism. 1930-40. *850*
—. Agee, James *(Let Us Now Praise Famous Men)*. Daily Life. Realism. 1930-41. *846*
—. Art. 1930's. *891*
—. Bibliographies. 1930's. *776*
—. Bibliographies. Negroes. 1930's. *878*
—. California (San Francisco). Dreiser, Theodore (interview). Social Conditions. 1939. *904*
—. *Challenge* (periodical). McKay, Claude. Negroes. 1930's. *838*
—. Communism. Folsom, Michael. Gold, Mike. Radical literary movement. 1914-37. *941*
—. Communist Party. Intellectuals. Popular Front Against Fascism. 1929-39. *613*
—. Cowley, Malcolm. Intellectuals. Marxism. New York City. 1932-40. *763*
—. Dreiser, Theodore. Lewis, Sinclair. Nobel Prizes. Public Opinion. Sweden. 1920's-30. *857*
—. Federal Writers' Project. New Deal. Penkower, Monty Noam (review article). 1930's. 1977. *454*
—. Ford, Ford Madox. Louisiana (Baton Rouge). South. Writers' Conference on Literature and Reading in the South and Southwest. 1935. *942*
—. *Gyroscope: A Literary Magazine*. Periodicals. Winters, Yvor. 1929-30. *767*
—. Hammett, Dashiell. Marxism. Novels (detective). Sam Spade (fictional character). 1930's. *862*
—. Historicity. Intellectual development. Modernism, nature of. Tate, Allen. Western life. 1929-30. *780*
—. Myths and Symbols. Roth, Henry *(Call It Sleep)*. Symbolism. 1934. *901*

—. *Partisan Review* (periodical). Politics. Radicals and Radicalism. 1930's. *895*
—. Sandoz, Mari. Violence. 1935-37. *947*
—. *Scribner's Magazine* (periodical). Wolfe, Thomas. 1929-40. *830*
Literature (novels, memoirs). 1932-42. *788*
Literature, proletarian. Communist Party. John Reed Clubs. Proletcult. 1929-35. *623*
Literature (review article). Bergonzi, Bernard. Salzman, Jack. Spender, Stephen. Zanderer, Leo. ca 1930-39. 1978-79. *775*
Little Orphan Annie (comic strip). Cartoonists. Gray, Harold. Social conservatism. World War II. 1930's-40's. *955*
—. Comic Strips. Conservatism. Gray, Harold. New Deal. World War II. 1920's-40's. *844*
Livestock. Grain. McGregor Land and Livestock Company. Prices. Washington (Columbia Plateau). 1930's-82. *73*
Llano del Rio colony. Communes. New Mexico (Gila). 1932-35. *675*
Lobbying. China. Congress. International Trade. Roosevelt, Franklin D. (administration). Silver Purchase Act (1934). 1934. *341*
Local government. Benefactor-aversion hypothesis. Nixon, Richard M. (administration). Roosevelt, Franklin D. (administration). State Government. 1933-45. 1969-74. *392*
Local history. Federal Writers' Project. Indiana. 1936-43. *428*
Local Politics. Dale, George R. Elites. Indiana (Muncie). Lynd, Helen Merrell. Lynd, Robert S. 1930-40. *166*
—. Dix, I. F. Hoover, Herbert C. Self-help. Unemployed Citizens' League. Washington (Seattle). 1931-32. *75*
Logan-Walter Bill (vetoed, 1939). Executive Power (restrictions). House of Representatives. Rayburn, Sam. Sumners, Hatton. Texas. 1939. *438*
Lone Ranger (program). Michigan (Detroit). Radio. WXYZ (station). 1933-34. *887*
Long, Huey P. Basso, Hamilton. Demagoguery, concept of. Louisiana. Novels. 1920-76. *726*
—. Conservatism. Louisiana. Share Our Wealth movement. Smith, Gerald L. K. Speeches and addresses. 1929-35. *632*
—. Cotton Acreage Control Law (Texas, 1931). Crop limitation. New Deal. South. 1931-33. *127*
—. Cotton production. Louisiana. South. Texas. 1931. *108*
—. Economic Reform. Share Our Wealth movement. 1932-35. *548*
—. Elections (presidential). Roosevelt, Franklin D. Share Our Wealth movement. 1932-36. *245*
—. Fiction. History. Warren, Robert Penn *(All The King's Men)*. World War II (antecedents). 1930's-46. *839*
—. Fundamentalism. North Central States. Populism. Progressivism. Smith, Gerald L. K. 1934-48. *633*
—. Government. Louisiana. Peyton, Rupert (reminiscences). 1917-35. *696*
—. Humor. Louisiana. 1931. *676*
—. Louisiana. Politics. Share Our Wealth movement. Smith, Gerald L. K. 1930's. *631*
—. New Deal (criticism of). Reform. 1933-35. *315*
—. Political Leadership. Share Our Wealth movement. 1928-35. *630*
Long Island Sound. Connecticut. New York. Ships. 1930-35. *587*
Longshoremen. California (San Francisco). Labor markets. Strikes. 1934-39. *635*
—. Christianity. Oxford Group movement. Strikes. Washington (Seattle). 1921-34. *738*

Lorentz, Pare. Environment. Films. New Deal. Roosevelt, Franklin D. (administration). Westward movement. 1936-40. *905*

Louis, Joe. Anti-Nazi sentiments. Boxing. Racism. Schmeling, Max. 1930's. *801*

—. Boxing. Germany. Nazism. Negroes. Schmeling, Max. 1936-38. *784*

Louisiana. Basso, Hamilton. Demagoguery, concept of. Long, Huey P. Novels. 1920-76. *726*

—. Civil Works Administration. 1932-34. *416*

—. Conservatism. Long, Huey P. Share Our Wealth movement. Smith, Gerald L. K. Speeches and addresses. 1929-35. *632*

—. Cotton production. Long, Huey P. South. Texas. 1931. *108*

—. Dillard University. Federal Writers' Project. Folklore. *Gumbo Ya-Ya* (publication). Negroes. Saxon, Lyle. 1930's. *318*

—. Government. Long, Huey P. Peyton, Rupert (reminiscences). 1917-35. *696*

—. Humor. Long, Huey P. 1931. *676*

—. Long, Huey P. Politics. Share Our Wealth movement. Smith, Gerald L. K. 1930's. *631*

—. Novels. Plantation life. Regionalism. Saxon, Lyle *(Children of Strangers)*. 1920's-40's. *932*

Louisiana (Baton Rouge). Ford, Ford Madox. Literature. South. Writers' Conference on Literature and Reading in the South and Southwest. 1935. *942*

Louisiana Emergency Relief Administration. Relief, federal. Sources. 1933-35. *368*

Louisiana (New Orleans). Ethnic Groups. Georgia (Atlanta). Labor. Texas (San Antonio). Women. 1930-40. *540*

—. Public opinion. Street, Electric Railway and Motor Coach Employees of America. Strikes. 1929-30. *557*

Louisiana State University. Biography. Family history. Interviews. Students. Works Progress Administration. 1930's. 1978. *321*

Lovecraft, H. P. Science fiction. Vermont (Windham County). 1931. *946*

Lowry, Tom (interview). Coal Mines and Mining. Folk songs. Tennessee. 1932. *765*

Lubin, Isador. Bureau of Labor Statistics. New Deal. Perkins, Frances. Statistics. Unemployment. 1920-49. *342*

Lucas, Scott W. Democratic Party. Illinois. Senate (majority leader). 1938-50. *237*

Lumber and Lumbering. National Recovery Administration. 1933-35. *453*

Lumber code. National Recovery Administration. Southern Pine Association. 1933-35. *335*

Lynching. Ames, Jessie Daniel. Association of Southern Women for the Prevention of Lynching. South. Women. 1928-42. *672*

—. Association of Southern Women for the Prevention of Lynching. Negroes. South. Women. 1930-42. *530*

—. California (San Jose; St. James Park). Hart, Brooke (murder). Holmes, John. Kidnapping. Thurmond, Thomas. 1933. *665*

—. Florida (Greenwood). Neal, Claude. Negroes. 1930-40. *668*

Lynd, Helen Merrell. Dale, George R. Elites. Indiana (Muncie). Local Politics. Lynd, Robert S. 1930-40. *166*

Lynd, Robert S. Consumerism. Research. Sociology. 1930's. *105*

—. Dale, George R. Elites. Indiana (Muncie). Local Politics. Lynd, Helen Merrell. 1930-40. *166*

M

Maine (Auburn, Lewiston). Shoe industry. Strikes. United Shoe Workers of America. 1937. *563*

Mangione, Jerre. Federal funding. Folklore (review article). McDonald, William F. 1935-43. *331*

Mangione, Jerre (review article). Federal Writers' Project. New Deal. 1935-43. *509*

Manuscript dating. Fiction. Steinbeck, John. 1934. *953*

Manuscripts. Harvard University, Houghton Library. Novels. Wolfe, Thomas. 1938. 1975. *845*

March of Time (series). Films (documentary). Political Attitudes. *The World Today* (series). 1930's. *761*

—. News, dramatization of. Radio. Smith, Fred. 1928-45. *856*

Marihuana Tax Act (US, 1937). Bureau of Narcotics. 1937. *601*

Marine Workers' Industrial Union. Federal Programs. Maryland (Baltimore). Unemployment. 1933-37. *274*

Marines. Georgia (Warm Springs). Henderson, F. P. Roosevelt, Franklin D. 1937. *188*

—. Military service. Verduci, Joseph P. 1934-38. *682*

Markham and Callow Railroad. Daily life. Economic conditions. Lind, Leo (reminiscences). Oregon. 1929-38. *67*

Marsh, Reginald. Artists. City life. New York City. 1930's. *958*

Martin, Charles H. (review article). Communism. Demonstrations. Georgia Insurrection Law. *Herndon* v. *Lowry* (US, 1937). International Labor Defense. 1932-37. *591*

Martin, Homer. Communists. Factionalism. Michigan. United Automobile Workers of America. 1937-39. *636*

Marxism. Capitalism. Government. New Deal. Political Theory. 1933-39. 1980. *103*

—. Capitalism. Niebuhr, Reinhold. *Radical Religion* (periodical). Roosevelt, Franklin D. (administration). 1930-43. *532*

—. Cowley, Malcolm. Intellectuals. Literature. New York City. 1932-40. *763*

—. Hammett, Dashiell. Literature. Novels (detective). Sam Spade (fictional character). 1930's. *862*

—. Hook, Sidney (review article). Philosophy. Pragmatism. 1930's. *593*

—. Literary Criticism. Political Participation. Wilson, Edmund. 1930's. *940*

Marxist opinions. Academic Freedom. Muller, Hermann J. (dismissal). Texas, University of. 1936. *586*

Maryland. Baltimore *Sun, Evening Sun* (newspapers). Government intervention. Letters-to-the-editor. Roosevelt, Franklin D. 1929-33. *384*

Maryland (Baltimore). Congress of Industrial Organizations. Negroes. 1930-41. *711*

—. Federal assistance (opposition to). Ritchie, Albert C. State Government. 1929-33. *56*

—. Federal Programs. Marine Workers' Industrial Union. Unemployment. 1933-37. *274*

Maryland (Carroll County). Charities. Children's Aid Society. Rural areas. 1928-35. *66*

Mass Media. Professionalism. Women. 1930's. *723*

Massachusetts. Clergy. New Deal. Roosevelt, Franklin D. Social problems. 1933-36. *291*

—. Democratic Party. Elections (presidential). Roosevelt, Franklin D. Smith, Al. 1928-32. *178*

—. Oral history. Sullivan, Anna (interview). Textile Workers Union of America. Women. 1918-76. *688*

Massachusetts (Boston). City Politics. New Deal. Roosevelt, Franklin D. (administration). Trout, Charles H. (review article). 1929-39. 1977. *157*

—. Methodology. New Deal. Trout, Charles H. (views). Urban history. 1930's. 1977-79. *122*

McAdoo, William G. Branion-Williams case (California). California. Federal Civil Works Administration. Patronage. Social workers. 1933-34. *468*

McCarey, Leo. Capra, Frank. Films. Humor. 1930's. *813*

McCloud, Emma Gudger (reminiscences). Sharecroppers. South. Whites. 1916-79. *70*

McDonald, William F. Federal funding. Folklore (review article). Mangione, Jerre. 1935-43. *331*

McGill, George S. Elections (senatorial). Kansas. 1938. *210*

McGregor Land and Livestock Company. Grain. Livestock. Prices. Washington (Columbia Plateau). 1930's-82. *73*

McKay, Claude. *Challenge* (periodical). Literature. Negroes. 1930's. *838*

McKinney, Fred (reminiscences). Chicago, University of (Psychology Department). Functionalism. Psychology. 1929-31. *669*

McKinzie, Richard D. (review article). Arts, visual. New Deal. Subsidies. 1933-40. *328*

McMahon, Bill. Colorado (Denver). Design. *Flivver* (aircraft). *Gray Goose* (aircraft). Lewis-American Aircraft Co. Mooney brothers. 1930-33. *794*

Meat preservation. Farmers. North Dakota (Kidder County). Oil Industry and Trade. Schools, rural. Wick family (interview). 1900's-30's. *112*

Mecklenburg, George H. Minnesota (Minneapolis). Organized Unemployed, Inc. Poor. Self-help. 1932-35. *740*

Medical Care (costs). American Medical Association (Committee on the Cost of Medical Care). Attitudes. *Medical Care for the American People* (report). 1926-31. *124*

Medical Care for the American People (report). American Medical Association (Committee on the Cost of Medical Care). Attitudes. Medical Care (costs). 1926-31. *124*

Meier, August. Communist Party. Glabermann, Martin. Keeran, Roger. Labor Unions and Organizations. Negroes. Rudwick, Elliot. United Automobile Workers of America (review article). 1930's-40's. *651*

Meikle, Jeffrey L. Architecture. Design (review article). Industry. 1925-39. 1979. *823*

Melnikov, Konstantin. Architecture. Leonidov, Ivan. 1929-31. *848*

Mencken, H. L. *American Mercury* (periodical). 1920's-30's. *910*

—. *American Mercury* (periodical). Conroy, Jack. Publishers and Publishing. 1930-33. *910*

—. Antidemocratism. Cynicism. Journalism. Satire. 1920's-56. *914*

—. Anti-Semitism. Elites. Freedom of speech. Public opinion. 1917-41. *769*

Mencken, H. L. (letters). Authors. End Poverty in California program. Sinclair, Upton (letters). Social Reform. ca 1918-51. *902*

Mennonites. Country Life. Farm Security Administration. Photographs. Western States. 1930's. *929*

Menorah Group. Communism. Intellectuals. Jews. 1930's. *744*

Merchant Marine. Air Mail Service. Contracts. Ocean mail service. Roosevelt, Franklin D. 1933-37. *488*

Merriam, Frank. Bank of America. California. Elections (gubernatorial). Giannini, Amadeo P. Roosevelt, Franklin D. Sinclair, Upton. ca 1923-34. *138*

Methodology. Federal Writers' Project. Genovese, Eugene D. Interviews. Rawick, George P. Slavery. 1930's. 1970's. *484*

—. Massachusetts (Boston). New Deal. Trout, Charles H. (views). Urban history. 1930's. 1977-79. *122*

—. Oral history. Terkel, Studs (review article). 1930-72. *809*

—. Unemployment estimates. 1934-41. *23*

Mexican Americans. California (Los Angeles). International Ladies' Garment Workers' Union. Women. Working Conditions. 1933-39. *673*

—. Deportation. Immigrants. Labor Unions and Organizations. New Deal. 1930's. *579*

—. Discrimination. Indiana (Gary). Nativism. Repatriation. 1920's-30's. *537*

—. Indiana (East Chicago). Repatriation. 1919-33. *100*

Mexican Labor in the United States (study). Field research interviews. National Endowment for the Humanities. Taylor, Paul S. 1927-30. *621*

Mexicans. Arizona (Superior). Brodie, J. C. (correspondence). Bureau of Immigration. Deportation. 1930-34. *620*

—. California (Los Angeles County). Davis, James J. Deportation. Unemployment. 1931. *363*

—. Hoover administration. Repatriation. 1930's. *57*

Mexico. Art. Murals. New York school. 1930's. *760*

—. Berry pickers. California (El Monte). Foreign Relations. Japan. Strikes. 1933. *619*

—. Communist Party. Labor Unions and Organizations. 1935-39. *648*

—. Diplomacy. Drug Abuse. Law enforcement. Salazar Viniegra, Leopold. 1936-40. *745*

Michigan. Automobile Industry and Trade. Dillon, Francis. Motor Products Corporation. Strikes. United Automobile Workers of America. 1933-39. *545*

—. Banking crisis. Reconstruction Finance Corporation. 1933. *54*

—. Brucker, Wilber M. Murphy, Frank. Unemployment. 1929-33. *84*

—. Brucker, Wilber M. Politics. Tax reform. 1929-33. *222*

—. Communists. Factionalism. Martin, Homer. United Automobile Workers of America. 1937-39. *636*

—. Farmer-Labor Party. New Deal. State Politics. 1933-37. *203*

—. Haber, William. National Youth Administration. Public Welfare. Works Progress Administration. 1930's. *410*

Michigan (Detroit). Anti-Semitism. Boxerman, William I. Coughlin, Charles. Jewish Community Council. Radio. 1939. *725*

—. Automobile Workers Union. Communist Party. Labor Unions and Organizations. 1920's-1935. *699*

—. City Government. Fine, Sidney (review article). Murphy, Frank. 1930-33. 1975. *150*

—. Fascism. Italian Americans. Sociopolitical integration. 1933-35. *554*

—. Friedlander, Peter (review article). United Automobile Workers of America. Working Class. 1936-39. 1975. *549*

—. Labor organizations. Radicals and Radicalism. 1920's-30's. *656*

—. *Lone Ranger* (program). Radio. WXYZ (station). 1933-34. *887*

Michigan (Flint). Films (documentary). Strikes. United Automobile Workers of America. *With Babies and Banners* (film). Women. 1937. *903*

—. General Motors Corporation. Strikes. United Automobile Workers of America. 1936-37. *718*

Middle Classes. Labor. Values. Women. 1930's. *11*

Migrant Labor. Dust Bowl. Farmers, truck. Migration, Internal. Oklahoma. 1930's. *43*

—. Letters. Sletten, Myron. Travel (accounts). Western States. 1930-32. *104*

Migration, Internal. Agricultural laborers. California. Labor Unions and Organizations. "Okies". 1930's. *115*

—. California. Guthrie, Woody. 1937-67. *952*

—. Cowen, Wilson. Dust Bowl. Farm Security Administration. Letters. Texas (Amarillo). 1940. *48*

—. Dust Bowl. Farmers, truck. Migrant Labor. Oklahoma. 1930's. *43*

—. Dust Bowl. Oklahoma. Route 66. Southwest. 1930's. *88*

—. Social Problems. Transients. 1930-36. *130*

Migration, Internal (necessity). Dust Bowl. Farmers. Oklahoma. Soil depletion. 1921-30's. *72*

Milburn, George. Fiction. Folklore. Oklahoma. Ozark Mountains. 1930's. *797*

Militancy. American Federation of Labor. International Brotherhood of Pulp, Sulphite, and Paper Mill Workers. Labor Unions and Organizations. Paper industry. 1933-35. *753*

—. Factionalism. United Automobile Workers of America. 1937-41. *544*

Military. Advertising. Carter, Boake. News. Political Commentary. Radio. 1931-38. *803*

Military officers. Authors. Johnson, Hugh S. (career). National Recovery Administration. ca 1903-42. *426*

Military Organization. Army. Civilian Conservation Corps. Negroes. 1933-42. *370*

Military Recruitment. Volunteer Armies. 1930-40. *40*

Military service. Marines. Verduci, Joseph P. 1934-38. *682*

Miller, Zack. Breach of contract. Lawsuits. Mix, Tom. Sells-Floto Circus. Verbal agreements. 101 Ranch Real Wild West Show. 1929-34. *819*

Milles, Carl *(God of Peace)*. Minnesota (St. Paul). Myths and Symbols. Public Opinion. Sculpture. War memorials. 1932-80. *811*

Milton, George Fort. Editors and Editing. Liberalism. New Deal. Tennessee. 1930's. *362*

Miners. American Civil Liberties Union. Civil rights. Kentucky (Bell County, London). Trials. 1932-38. *733*

Miners (resettlement of). National Industrial Recovery Act (1933). New Deal. Roosevelt, Eleanor. Subsistence Homesteads Program. West Virginia (Arthurdale). 1930-46. *320*

Minimum Wage. Labor Reform. New York. *Tipaldo* v. *Morehead* (New York, 1934). 1933-37. *367*

Minnesota. Anti-Semitism. Benson, Elmer A. Political Campaigns (gubernatorial). 1930's. *536*

—. Country Life. Documents. Federal Emergency Relief Administration. Great Plains. Hickok, Lorena A. Hopkins, Harry. Iowa. 1933. *284*

—. Democratic Party. Oleson, Anna Dickie. Politics. Women. 1905-71. *371*

—. Federal Writers' Project. Finnish Americans. Interviews. 1930's. *381*

Minnesota (Austin). Hormel, George A., and Co. Labor Unions and Organizations. Olson, Floyd B. Strikes. 1933. *592*

Minnesota (Minneapolis). Mecklenburg, George H. Organized Unemployed, Inc. Poor. Self-help. 1932-35. *740*

Minnesota (St. Paul). Milles, Carl *(God of Peace)*. Myths and Symbols. Public Opinion. Sculpture. War memorials. 1932-80. *811*

Minorities in Politics. Employment. Negroes. New Deal. Roosevelt, Franklin D. 1930-42. *470*

Miracle Woman (film). Capra, Frank. Values. 1930's. *934*

Mississippi. Agricultural Industry. Economic Regulations. Federal government. Prices. Texas. Voluntarism. 1925-40. *71*

—. Agriculture. Letters. Roosevelt, Franklin D. 1932-33. *95*

—. Congress. Political Leadership. 1931-37. *179*

—. Cotton holiday movement. Prices. 1931. *107*

—. Farm tenancy. Protestant Churches. Theologians, neoorthodox. 1936-40. *629*

—. Federal aid to education. Harrison, Byron Patton (Pat). Legislation. 1936-41. *493*

—. Harrison, Byron Patton (Pat). Political friendship. Roosevelt, Franklin D. 1920-41. *259*

—. Negroes (interviews). 1929-34. 1970's. *607*

Mississippi (Jackson). Daily Life. Fiction. Welty, Eudora ("Death of a Traveling Salesman"). 1936-79. *944*

Mississippi (Oxford). Accidents. Daily Life. Faulkner, Jim. Faulkner, William. Personal narratives. Youth. 1930-39. *804*

Mississippi River (lower). Army Corps of Engineers. Flood control. Politics. 1927-41. *449*

Missouri. Advertising. Censorship. Newspapers. Pulitzer, Joseph, II. St. Louis *Post Dispatch*. 1929-39. *893*

—. Clark, Bennett Champ. Committee of One. Democratic Party. Political Campaigns (presidential). 1936. *250*

—. Democratic Party. Elections (senatorial). New Deal. Primaries. Truman, Harry S. 1934. *175*

—. Democratic Party. Pendergast, Thomas J. Political Conventions. Roosevelt, Franklin D. State Politics. 1932. *238*

—. Democratic Party. Political coalitions. Republican Party. Roosevelt, Franklin D. 1936-52. *246*

—. Elections (presidential). Hoover, Herbert C. Roosevelt, Franklin D. 1932. *177*

Missouri River. Army Corps of Engineers. Employment. Fort Peck Dam. Montana. 1932-61. *457*

—. Causeways. Civilian Conservation Corps (co. 796). South Dakota (Farm Island). 1934. *521*

Missouri (St. Louis). Garment industry. Personal narratives. Photographic essays. Strikes. Women. ca 1930-39. *565*

—. Hoovervilles. Philanthropy. 1930-36. *120*

Mr. Deeds Goes to Town (film). Capitalism. Capra, Frank. Films. Social Organization. 1936. *861*

Mr. Smith Goes To Washington (film). Capra, Frank. Films. Politics. Populism. 1939. *881*

Mitchell, Ewing Young. Commerce Department. Pendergast, Thomas J. Political machines. Progressivism. Roosevelt, Franklin D. 1933-36. *239*

Mitchell, Margaret. Scarlett O'Hara (character). Sex roles. Women. 1936-39. *877*

Mix, Tom. Breach of contract. Lawsuits. Miller, Zack. Sells-Floto Circus. Verbal agreements. 101 Ranch Real Wild West Show. 1929-34. *819*

Models. Depressions (causes). Economic History. Monetary Systems. Temin, Peter (review article). 1920's. 1976. *118*

Modern Monthly (periodical). Communism. Wilson, Edmund. 1934-35. *603*

Modern Times (film). Chaplin, Charlie. Dickens, Charles *(Hard Times)*. Films. Great Britain. 1854. 1936. *923*

Modernism. Architecture. City planning. Europe. Housing. New Deal. 1932-60. *897*

Modernism, nature of. Historicity. Intellectual development. Literature. Tate, Allen. Western life. 1929-30. *780*

Modernization. Oregon (Neahkahnie Mountain). Public Finance. Roads. West. 1850-1977. *496*

Moley, Raymond. Inaugural Addresses. Rhetoric. Roosevelt, Franklin D. 1933. *233*

Monetary Act (US, 1939). Pittman, Key. Senate. Silver. 1939. *440*

Monetary policy *See also* Fiscal policy.
—. Banking. New Deal. Roosevelt, Franklin D. (administration). Warburg, James P. 1932-41. *413*
—. Fascism. Italy. Mussolini, Benito. New Deal. Roosevelt, Franklin D. 1922-36. *433*
—. Federal Reserve Board. Keynesianism. New Deal. Private sector. 1929-70. *6*

Monetary Systems. Depressions (causes). Economic History. Models. Temin, Peter (review article). 1920's. 1976. *118*
—. Federal Reserve System. 1924-33. *121*
—. Temin, Peter. 1929-39. 1976. *2*

Money. Banking. Panic of 1930. 1920-30. *132*

Money (demand). Bank deposits. Economic Conditions. Great Contraction. 1929-33. *34*
—. Economic Policy. Federal Reserve System. 1929-76. *33*

Monopolies. Film industry. Finance capitalism (concept). Lenin, V. I. *(Imperialism: The Highest Stage of Capitalism)*. 1916-39. *817*

Montana. Army Corps of Engineers. Employment. Fort Peck Dam. Missouri River. 1932-61. *457*
—. Civilian Conservation Corps. Glacier National Park. 1933-42. *425*
—. Democratic Party. Erickson, John E. State Politics. Walsh, Thomas J. 1932-33. *208*
—. Federal Government. Homesteading and Homesteaders (failure of). Ranchers. 1900-30. *32*
—. Political Attitudes. Roosevelt, Franklin D. Senate. Wheeler, Burton K. 1904-46. *232*

Montana (Plentywood). Daily Life. Homesteading and Homesteaders. Vindex, Charles (reminiscences). 1929-34. *123*

Mooney brothers. Colorado (Denver). Design. *Flivver* (aircraft). *Gray Goose* (aircraft). Lewis-American Aircraft Co. McMahon, Bill. 1930-33. *794*

Moore, Alfred. Buildings. Cincinnati Union Terminal. Ohio. Railroads. 1933-73. *933*

Morality. Attitudes. Sex. 1918-55. *662*

Morro Castle (vessel). Fire. 1934. *590*

Mortgage moratoria. Agriculture and Government. Land. Langer, William. North Dakota. 1930's. *3*

Motor Carrier Act (US, 1935). Moving industry. Trucks and Trucking. 1930-35. *359*

Motor Products Corporation. Automobile Industry and Trade. Dillon, Francis. Michigan. Strikes. United Automobile Workers of America. 1933-39. *545*

Motors. Agriculture. Alcohol. Business. Fuel. Prices. Surpluses. 1930's. *604*

Mountaineers. Appalachia. Leftism. Music. Resettlement Administration (music program). Seeger, Charles. Social Organization. 1935-37. *506*

Moving industry. Motor Carrier Act (US, 1935). Trucks and Trucking. 1930-35. *359*

Muller, Hermann J. (dismissal). Academic Freedom. Marxist opinions. Texas, University of. 1936. *586*

Murals. Art. Mexico. New York school. 1930's. *760*
—. Buildings, public. California. National Self-image. New Deal. 1933-46. *814*
—. Iowa. New Deal. 1934-42. *880*

Murphy, Frank. Brucker, Wilber M. Michigan. Unemployment. 1929-33. *84*
—. City Government. Fine, Sidney (review article). Michigan (Detroit). 1930-33. 1975. *150*
—. Fine, Sidney (review article). New Deal. 1936-42. *151*

Music. Adorno, Theodor W. Culture. Lazarsfeld, Paul F. Princeton Radio Research Project. Social organization. 1930's. *875*
—. Appalachia. Leftism. Mountaineers. Resettlement Administration (music program). Seeger, Charles. Social Organization. 1935-37. *506*
—. Arts. Berger, Arthur. Criticism. Personal narratives. Works Progress Administration. 1930-80. *786*
—. Bands. Swing Era. 1934-45. *921*
—. Bop (term). Gillespie, Dizzy. 1928-40's. *926*
—. Brecht, Bertolt. Lindbergh, Charles A. (tribute). Radio broadcasts. Weill, Kurt. 1929-31. *849*
—. "Gimme a Pigfoot" (song). Language. Smith, Bessie. 1933. *925*
—. Jazz. Swing (term). 1908-30's. *927*

Music (blues). Historical sources. Negroes. Oral History. Recordings. Social Conditions. 1924-41. *888*

Music, country. Rodgers, Jimmie. 1927-33. *770*

Music (jazz). Austin, Gene. Waller, Fats. 1929-39. *860*

Mussolini, Benito. Fascism. Italy. Monetary policy. New Deal. Roosevelt, Franklin D. 1922-36. *433*

Muste, Abraham J. Radicals and Radicalism. Unemployed Leagues. 1932-36. *706*

Myths and Symbols. Alabama (Scottsboro). Historiography. Racism. Trials. 1931-80. *742*
—. Literature. Roth, Henry *(Call It Sleep)*. Symbolism. 1934. *901*
—. Milles, Carl *(God of Peace)*. Minnesota (St. Paul). Public Opinion. Sculpture. War memorials. 1932-80. *811*

N

NAACP. Alabama. Norris, Clarence. Pardon request. Scottsboro Case. 1931-76. *657*
—. Attica State Prison. Negroes. New York. Prison conditions. 1932. *751*
—. Class consciousness. Negroes. Pennsylvania (Philadelphia). Race. 1930's. *684*
—. Democratic Party. Negro Suffrage. Primaries. *Smith* v. *Allwright* (US, 1944). South. Supreme Court. 1890's-1944. *617*
—. Hollins, Jess. International Labor Defense. Oklahoma. Race Relations. Rape. Trials. 1931-36. *659*
—. North Carolina. Parker, John J. Supreme Court (nominations). White, Walter F. 1930. *618*

Nancy Drew books. Fiction, formula. New Deal. Stereotypes. 1930's. 1960's-70's. *841*

National Association of Manufacturers. Business. New Deal. Public relations. 1930's. *734*

National Characteristics. Ethnicity. Intellectuals. Public Opinion. 1930's. *747*

National Cooperative Council. Agricultural Policy. New Deal. Trade associations. 1929-42. *346*

National Democratic Issues Convention. Democratic Party. Kentucky (Louisville). New Deal policies. 1975. *332*

National Emergency Council (report). Economic conditions. Foreman, Clark Howell. Politics. Roosevelt, Franklin D. South. 1938. *24*

National Endowment for the Humanities. Field research interviews. *Mexican Labor in the United States* (study). Taylor, Paul S. 1927-30. *621*

National Guard. California (San Francisco). General strikes. Waterfronts. 1934. *625*

—. Coal Mines and Mining. Ohio. Strikes. White, George. 1932. *687*

—. Davey, Martin L. Ohio. Steel Industry. Strikes. 1937. *722*

National Industrial Recovery Act (1933). Agricultural Labor. California. Labor Unions and Organizations. 1933-34. *323*

—. American Newspaper Publishers Association. Daily Newspaper Code. Freedom of the press. National Recovery Administration. Politics and Media. 1933-34. *774*

—. Miners (resettlement of). New Deal. Roosevelt, Eleanor. Subsistence Homesteads Program. West Virginia (Arthurdale). 1930-46. *320*

National Miners Union. Carbon County Coal Strike (1933). Strikes. United Mine Workers of America. Utah. 1900-39. *693*

—. Negroes. Pennsylvania, western. United Mine Workers of America. 1925-31. *686*

National Negro Congress. Bunche, Ralph. Negroes. New Deal. Political Attitudes. 1930-39. *639*

National Progressives of America. Income (redistribution). LaFollette, Philip F. Politics. Wisconsin. 1930-38. *214*

National Recovery Administration. Agricultural Adjustment Administration. Federal Government. 1933-39. *481*

—. American Newspaper Publishers Association. Daily Newspaper Code. Freedom of the press. National Industrial Recovery Act (1933). Politics and Media. 1933-34. *774*

—. Authors. Johnson, Hugh S. (career). Military officers. ca 1903-42. *426*

—. Collectivism (objections to). Glass, Carter. Liberals. New Deal. 1933-35. *378*

—. Dust Bowl. New Deal. Oklahoma. Public Welfare. 1932-35. *505*

—. Economic Conditions. New Deal. Supreme Court. Virginia. 1933-35. *353*

—. Georgia. State Government. Strikes. Talmadge, Eugene. Textile industry. 1934. *526*

—. Lumber and Lumbering. 1933-35. *453*

—. Lumber code. Southern Pine Association. 1933-35. *335*

National Recovery Administration (Industrial Advisory Board). Commerce Department (Business Advisory Council). Corporate liberalism (concept). Historiography. New Deal. 1933-35. 1970's. *411*

National Self-image. Buildings, public. California. Murals. New Deal. 1933-46. *814*

National Textile Workers Union. North Carolina (Gastonia). Strikes. Textile Industry. Weisbord, Vera Buch (reminiscences). 1929. *746*

National Women's Party. Equal Rights Amendment (proposed). Florida. Politics. West, Helen Hunt. Women. 1917-52. *667*

National Youth Administration. Bethune, Mary McLeod. Black Cabinet. Negroes. New Deal. 1930-40. *455*

—. Bethune, Mary McLeod. Equal opportunity. Negroes. Public Policy. Youth. 1935-44. *483*

—. Civilian Conservation Corps. North Dakota. 1930-45. *358*

—. Employment, part-time. New Deal. South Dakota. Struble, Anna C. Youth. 1935-43. *355*

—. Haber, William. Michigan. Public Welfare. Works Progress Administration. 1930's. *410*

Nativism. Discrimination. Indiana (Gary). Mexican Americans. Repatriation. 1920's-30's. *537*

Navies. Chief of Naval Operations. Pratt, William Veazie. 1930-33. *732*

Nazism. Anti-Semitism. Germany. *New York Times.* Reporters and Reporting. 1932-33. *749*

—. Boxing. Germany. Louis, Joe. Negroes. Schmeling, Max. 1936-38. *784*

—. Communism. Press. Red Fascism analogy. Totalitarianism. 1930's. 1970's. *654*

—. Economic Policy (similarities). Germany. New Deal. ca 1933-36. *340*

—. German Americans. 1924-41. *578*

Nazism, American (review article). Coughlin, Charles. Countersubversives. Fascism (review article). German-American Bund. 1924-41. *701*

Neal, Claude. Florida (Greenwood). Lynching. Negroes. 1930-40. *668*

Near v. Minnesota (US, 1931). Freedom of the Press. Friendly, Fred W. (review article). 1931. *805*

Nebbia v. New York (US, 1934). Brandeis, Louis D. Due process. Economic Regulations. *New State Ice v. Liebmann* (US, 1932). Supreme Court. *West Coast Hotel v. Parrish* (US, 1937). 1897-1937. *476*

Nebraska. Dehart, Grant. Federal Writers' Project. Folklore. Horse trading. ca 1938-43. *511*

—. Farmers. New Deal. Norris, George W. Relief funds. 1933-36. *397*

—. Shelterbelts. Tree Planting. 1939. *400*

Nebraska (Dawson County). New Deal. Voting and Voting Behavior. 1933-40. *478*

Negro Leagues. Baseball. Davis, Lorenzo Piper (interview). 1930's-40's. *907*

Negro Suffrage. Democratic Party. NAACP. Primaries. *Smith v. Allwright* (US, 1944). South. Supreme Court. 1890's-1944. *617*

Negroes. Africa, West. Basketmaking. Works Progress Administration. 1935-78. *935*

—. Alabama (Birmingham). Communist Party. Hudson, Hosea. South. 1920's-70's. *691*

—. Allison, Hughes. Drama. Federal Theatre Project. Ward, Theodore. Wilson, Frank. 1930's. *874*

—. American Order of Fascisti. Employment. Georgia. White supremacy. 1930-33. *660*

—. *Amos 'n Andy* (program). Boycotts. Comic strips. Radio. Stereotypes. 1930's. *719*

—. Army. Civilian Conservation Corps. Military Organization. 1933-42. *370*

—. Art and Society. New York City. Painting. Stage Setting and Scenery. Stettheimer, Florine. 1929-44. *882*

—. Association of Southern Women for the Prevention of Lynching. Lynching. South. Women. 1930-42. *530*

—. Attica State Prison. NAACP. New York. Prison conditions. 1932. *751*

—. Baseball, semiprofessional. North Dakota (Dickinson). Otto, Solomon (reminiscences). Race Relations. 1929-31. *889*

—. Bethune, Mary McLeod. Black Cabinet. National Youth Administration. New Deal. 1930-40. *455*
—. Bethune, Mary McLeod. Equal opportunity. National Youth Administration. Public Policy. Youth. 1935-44. *483*
—. Bibliographies. Literature. 1930's. *878*
—. Black nationalism. Ethiopia. Invasions. Italy. Pan-Africanism. 1934-36. *716*
—. Boxing. Germany. Louis, Joe. Nazism. Schmeling, Max. 1936-38. *784*
—. Bunche, Ralph. National Negro Congress. New Deal. Political Attitudes. 1930-39. *639*
—. Capital Punishment. Newspapers. Rape. Reporters and Reporting. Scottsboro Case. Trials. 1931-32. *697*
—. *Challenge* (periodical). Literature. McKay, Claude. 1930's. *838*
—. Chisum, Melvin J. Journalism. Roosevelt, Franklin D. (election). *Tribune* (newspaper). ca 1932. *892*
—. Civil rights activity. Illinois (Chicago). School integration. 1936. *624*
—. Civilian Conservation Corps. Discrimination, employment. New York. 1933-42. *441*
—. Civilian Conservation Corps. Equal opportunity (failure). New Deal. 1933-42. *344*
—. Class consciousness. NAACP. Pennsylvania (Philadelphia). Race. 1930's. *684*
—. Communist Party. Culture. Intellectuals. New York City (Harlem). Popular Front. 1935-39. *678*
—. Communist Party. Georgia (Atlanta). Herndon, Angelo. International Labor Defense. 1932-37. *658*
—. Communist Party. Glabermann, Martin. Keeran, Roger. Labor Unions and Organizations. Meier, August. Rudwick, Elliot. United Automobile Workers of America (review article). 1930's-40's. *651*
—. Communist Party. Illinois (Chicago). Intellectuals. Wright, Richard *(American Hunger)*. ca 1930-44. *879*
—. Communist Party. Illinois (Chicago). Wright, Richard (personal account). 1930's. *954*
—. Communist Party. New York City (Harlem). 1928-36. *679*
—. Congress of Industrial Organizations. Maryland (Baltimore). 1930-41. *711*
—. Construction. Employment. Ickes, Harold. Public Works Administration. Quotas. 1933-40. *383*
—. Cooperatives (proposed). DuBois, W. E. B. Economic Theory. 1940. *575*
—. Dance. Entertainers. Robinson, Bill "Bojangles". 1930's-49. *868*
—. Democratic Party (Colored Voters Division). Good Neighbor League Colored Committee. Political Campaigns (presidential). Roosevelt, Franklin D. 1936. *251*
—. Dillard University. Federal Writers' Project. Folklore. *Gumbo Ya-Ya* (publication). Louisiana. Saxon, Lyle. 1930's. *318*
—. Discrimination. Elites. Georgia (Savannah). New Deal. Works Progress Administration. ca 1930-39. *374*
—. Economic conditions. South. Woodson, Carter G. 1930. *39*
—. Elites. 1930-40. *664*
—. Emigration. Ethiopia (Addis Ababa). Ford, Arnold. 1930-35. *717*
—. Employment. Minorities in Politics. New Deal. Roosevelt, Franklin D. 1930-42. *470*
—. *Esquire* (periodical). Gingrich, Arnold. Hughes, Langston. Public Opinion. Publishers and Publishing. 1934. *572*
—. Federal Theatre Project. Public Records. Theater, black. 1930's-70's. *304*

—. Federal Theatre Project. Theater. 1935-39. *456*
—. Federal Writers' Project. Florida. Folklore. Hurston, Zora Neale. 1901-60. *826*
—. Federal Writers' Project. Slavery, memories of. Tennessee. 1930's. *350*
—. Florida (Greenwood). Lynching. Neal, Claude. 1930-40. *668*
—. Historical sources. Music (blues). Oral History. Recordings. Social Conditions. 1924-41. *888*
—. Hoover, Herbert C. (administration). Republican Party. 1928-32. *168*
—. Housing. New Deal. Pennsylvania (Philadelphia). 1930's. *281*
—. Immigrants. International Brotherhood of Pulp, Sulphite, and Paper Mill Workers. Pacific Northwest. South. Women. 1909-40. *754*
—. Kentucky. Lincoln Institute. Tydings, J. Mansir. Young, Whitney M. 1935-37. *134*
—. Labor Department. New Deal. Perkins, Frances. 1933-45. *347*
—. Land reform. New Deal. Public Policy. Resettlement. 1930's-60's. *458*
—. Lilly, Octave, Jr. (obituary). Poetry. South. 1930-60. *793*
—. National Miners Union. Pennsylvania, western. United Mine Workers of America. 1925-31. *686*
—. Ohio. Republican Party, fission in the. 1920-32. *170*
—. Progressive education. South. 1930-45. *605*
Negroes (interviews). Mississippi. 1929-34. 1970's. *607*
Neoconservatism. Government regulation. New Deal. Political Leadership. Republican Party. Social security. 1936-40. *209*
Neutrality Act (US, 1935). Armaments. Embargoes. Isolationism. 1935. *756*
Neutrality Act, 1939 (proposed). Austin, Warren R. Foreign Policy. Roosevelt, Franklin D. Senate. 1935-39. *759*
Nevada. Banking. Federal government. Hoover, Herbert C. Reconstruction Finance Corporation. 1932-33. *83*
—. Boulder Canyon project. Colorado River. Hoover Dam. Industrial Workers of the World. Strikes. 1931. *702*
—. Boulder Canyon Project. Hoover Dam. Industrial Workers of the World. Six Companies, Inc. Strikes. 1931. *703*
—. Creel, Cecil. Democratic Party. New Deal. Pittman, Key. Political Factions. Public Welfare. 1933-34. *244*
Nevada (Las Vegas). New Deal. Public works. 1933-40. *417*
Nevada (Tobar). Daily life. 1930's. *89*
New Deal. Agar, Herbert. *Free America* (periodical). 1937-47. *649*
—. Agricultural Adjustment Administration. Agricultural policy. Attitudes. 1920-33. *336*
—. Agricultural Adjustment Administration. Farmers. Federal Policy. New York, western. 1934. *308*
—. Agricultural Adjustment Administration. North Carolina. Senate. Virginia. 1933-39. *366*
—. Agricultural Adjustment Administration. Soil Conservation Service. 1933-41. *459*
—. Agricultural experiment stations. Arizona. New Mexico. Oklahoma. Texas. 1926-39. *407*
—. Agricultural Labor Relations Act (1975). California. Emergency Farm Labor Supply Program. Labor law. ca 1930-79. *338*
—. Agricultural Policy. Association of Southern Commissioners of Agriculture. Cotton. South. Tennessee (Memphis). 1936-37. *423*
—. Agricultural Policy. Dust Bowl. Texas Panhandle. 1930's. *76*

—. Agricultural Policy. Jones, Marvin. Legislation. Political Leadership. 1916-40. *406*

—. Agricultural Policy. National Cooperative Council. Trade associations. 1929-42. *346*

—. Agricultural programs. Droughts. Kansas. Political Campaigns (presidential). 1936. *464*

—. Agricultural Reform. Catholic Church. Roosevelt, Franklin D. (administration). Social Theory. 1933-39. *473*

—. Agriculture and Government. Constitutional issues. Farm journals. 1935-36. *330*

—. Agriculture and Government. Indian-White Relations. New Mexico. Pueblo Indians. 1938-48. *503*

—. Alabama. Clergy. Roosevelt, Franklin D. 1935-36. *290*

—. Alienation. Intellectuals. Jews. Leftism. Roosevelt, Franklin D. 1930's. *757*

—. American Federation of Labor. Carmody, John. Civil Works Administration. Work relief. 1933-34. *467*

—. American Federation of Labor. Third parties (suggested). 1920's-30's. *205*

—. American Indian Federation. Bureau of Indian Affairs. Collier, John. Indians. Jamison, Alice Lee. Political activism. 1930's-50's. *351*

—. American Liberty League. Business. Civil rights. Federal Regulation. Government, Resistance to. 1934-36. *698*

—. Amlie, Thomas R. Economic programs. Liberals. Politics. Wisconsin. 1931-39. *264*

—. Amlie, Thomas R. Farmer-labor movement. Hard, Herbert. Ohio Farmer-Labor Progressive Federation. Third Parties. 1930-40. *204*

—. Amlie, Thomas R. Farmer-Labor Party. Wisconsin. 1930-38. *206*

—. Amlie, Thomas R. (political career). Radicals and Radicalism. Roosevelt, Franklin D. Wisconsin. 1930-39. *704*

—. Anthropology. Bureau of Indian Affairs. Collier, John. Federal Programs. Indians. 1930's. *375*

—. Appalachia. Congressmen. 1933-39. *173*

—. Architecture. City planning. Europe. Housing. Modernism. 1932-60. *897*

—. Archives, National. Conservation of natural resources. 1930's. 1976. *435*

—. Armies. Civilian Conservation Corps. 1933-42. *443*

—. Armstrong Cork Company. Business. Pennsylvania (Lancaster). Prentis, Henning Webb, Jr. 1934-40. *514*

—. Art. Indians. Iroquois School of Art. New York (Akron). Parker, Arthur C. Seneca Arts project. Tonawanda Indian Reservation. 1935-41. *352*

—. Art and State. New Jersey. Public Works of Art Project. 1932-40. *519*

—. Artists. 1930's. *928*

—. Artists. 1933-41. *501*

—. Artists. Buildings, public. Federal Programs. 1930's. *436*

—. Arts. Cultural democracy. 1933-42. *405*

—. Arts, visual. McKinzie, Richard D. (review article). Subsidies. 1933-40. *328*

—. Attitudes. Federal Policy. Technology. 1927-40. *442*

—. Attitudes. Films. 1930-40. *778*

—. Attitudes. Roper, Elmo. Socialism, failure of. Working class. 1939. *743*

—. Automobile Industry and Trade. Indiana. Labor parties. Ohio. United Automobile Workers of America. 1935-40. *652*

—. Banking. Monetary policy. Roosevelt, Franklin D. (administration). Warburg, James P. 1932-41. *413*

—. Beard, Charles A. Historians. Intellectuals. Isolationism. Liberalism. Roosevelt, Franklin D. 1932-48. *296*

—. Bethune, Mary McLeod. Black Cabinet. National Youth Administration. Negroes. 1930-40. *455*

—. Biography. Couch, W. T. Federal Writers' Project. South. 1938-39. *499*

—. Bonneville Power Administration. Electric utilities. Pacific Northwest. Public Utilities. 1937-42. *339*

—. Braeman, John (review article). Historiography. Reform. State government. 1930's-40's. *382*

—. Brandeis, Louis D. Frankfurter, Felix. Politics. Roosevelt, Franklin D. World War I. 1917-33. *154*

—. Budgets (state allocations). Democratic Party. Political Campaigns. 1932-40. *270*

—. Buildings, public. California. Murals. National Self-image. 1933-46. *814*

—. Bunche, Ralph. National Negro Congress. Negroes. Political Attitudes. 1930-39. *639*

—. Bureau of Indian Affairs. Collier, John. Indians (government relations). 1933-45. *498*

—. Bureau of Indian Affairs. Collier, John. Public Administration. Social sciences principles. 1933-45. *497*

—. Bureau of Labor Statistics. Lubin, Isador. Perkins, Frances. Statistics. Unemployment. 1920-49. *342*

—. Business. Conservatism. Isolationism. Sears, Roebuck and Company. Wood, Robert E. 1928-50's. *581*

—. Business. Idaho (Pocatello). 1930's. *495*

—. Business. Labor Unions and Organizations. Taft-Hartley Act (US, 1947). Wagner Act (US, 1935). World War II. 1935-47. *543*

—. Business. National Association of Manufacturers. Public relations. 1930's. *734*

—. Capitalism. Government. Marxism. Political Theory. 1933-39. 1980. *103*

—. Career patterns. Lawyers. 1918-41. *4*

—. Carter, Boake. News commentator. Political criticism. Radio. Roosevelt, Franklin D. 1935-38. *790*

—. Catholic Church. Farm programs. Rural life movement. 1930's. *721*

—. Cherokee Indians. Indian policy. North Carolina, western. 1930's. *508*

—. City Politics. Massachusetts (Boston). Roosevelt, Franklin D. (administration). Trout, Charles H. (review article). 1929-39. 1977. *157*

—. Civil Works Administration. Work relief. 1933-39. *298*

—. Civilian Conservation Corps. Economic Conditions. Vermont. 1933-42. *900*

—. Civilian Conservation Corps. Equal opportunity (failure). Negroes. 1933-42. *344*

—. Civilian Conservation Corps. Pennsylvania. 1933-40. *356*

—. Clapp, Elsie Ripley. Education, community. Homesteading and Homesteaders. Roosevelt, Eleanor. West Virginia (Arthurdale). 1933-44. *285*

—. Clergy. Massachusetts. Roosevelt, Franklin D. Social problems. 1933-36. *291*

—. Coal industry. Congress. Supreme Court. 1932-40. *395*

—. Cohen, Benjamin V. Corcoran, Thomas Gardiner. Democratic Party. District of Columbia. 1933-37. *396*

—. Collective bargaining. Labor Unions and Organizations (membership). Public policy. 1933-45. *289*

—. Collectivism (objections to). Glass, Carter. Liberals. National Recovery Administration. 1933-35. *378*

—. Comic Strips. Conservatism. Gray, Harold. *Little Orphan Annie* (comic strip). World War II. 1920's-40's. *844*

—. Comintern (7th Congress). Communist Party. Socialist Party. 1935-39. *655*

—. Commerce Department (Business Advisory Council). Committee for Economic Development. Keynesianism. Roosevelt, Franklin D. (administration). Scholars. 1933-42. *319*

—. Commerce Department (Business Advisory Council). Corporate liberalism (concept). Historiography. National Recovery Administration (Industrial Advisory Board). 1933-35. 1970's. *411*

—. Congress. Illinois. Keller, Kent. Liberalism. 1930-42. *263*

—. Congress. Political attitudes. Roosevelt, Franklin D. Tennessee. 1933-40. *148*

—. Congress. Roosevelt, Franklin D. Social Security Act (US, 1935). Unemployment insurance. 1934-35. *277*

—. Congress. Roosevelt, Franklin D. South Dakota. 1933. *312*

—. Congress of Industrial Organizations. Labor Disputes. Newspapers. South. 1930-39. *518*

—. Congressmen. Politics. Roosevelt, Franklin D. Virginia. Woodrum, Clifton A. 1922-45. *236*

—. Conservation of Natural Resources. Cooke, Morris L. Rural Electrification Administration. 1933-51. *316*

—. Conservatism. Constitutional law. Kansas. Newspapers. Supreme Court. 1934-35. *329*

—. Conservatism. Creel, George. Progressivism. Works Progress Administration. 1900-53. *273*

—. Conservatism. Economy Act (US, 1933). Fiscal Policy. Roosevelt, Franklin D. 1932-36. *462*

—. Conservatism. New York. Republican Party. Snell, Bertrand H. 1933-39. *139*

—. Constitutional issues. Editorials. Labor union journals. Supreme Court. 1935-37. *588*

—. Corporate structure. General Electric Co. 1933-40. *670*

—. Cotton Acreage Control Law (Texas, 1931). Crop limitation. Long, Huey P. South. 1931-33. *127*

—. Country life. Delano, Jack. Farm Security Administration. Photography. South Carolina (Santee-Cooper). 1941. *327*

—. Creel, Cecil. Democratic Party. Nevada. Pittman, Key. Political Factions. Public Welfare. 1933-34. *244*

—. Crime and Criminals. Working class. 1929-39. *98*

—. Culture. Federal Art Project. Wyoming. 1933-41. *795*

—. Cumberland Homesteads. Fairfield Glade. Housing. Resettlement. Tennessee. 1934-80. *482*

—. Currie, Lauchlin. Economic Policy. 1935-46. *51*

—. Currie, Lauchlin. Fiscal policy. Income. Keynesianism. 1920's-30's. *522*

—. Daily Life. Dust Bowl. Farmers. Henderson, Caroline Agnes Boa. Oklahoma, western. 1935. *90*

—. Democratic Party. Domestic Policy. Internationalism. Political Campaigns. Roosevelt, Franklin D. 1938-40. *160*

—. Democratic Party. Elections (senatorial). Missouri. Primaries. Truman, Harry S. 1934. *175*

—. Democratic Party. Georgia. Roosevelt, Franklin D. Talmadge, Eugene. 1926-38. *146*

—. Democratic Party. Hague, Frank. New Jersey. Roosevelt, Franklin D. 1932-40. *155*

—. Democratic Party. Idaho. Pocatello Central Labor Union. Rosqvist, August. 1930-36. *494*

—. Democratic Party. Ohio. Political Campaigns (presidential). 1936. *249*

—. Democratic Party. Pennsylvania (Pittsburgh). Political Theory. Quantitative Methods. Voting and Voting Behavior. Wisconsin. 1912-40. *228*

—. Democratic Party. Primaries (senatorial). Russell, Richard B. Talmadge, Eugene. 1936. *213*

—. Deportation. Immigrants. Labor Unions and Organizations. Mexican Americans. 1930's. *579*

—. Disaster Relief. Droughts. Farmers. Federal Government. Kansas. 1934. *465*

—. Discrimination. Elites. Georgia (Savannah). Negroes. Works Progress Administration. ca 1930-39. *374*

—. Documentary expression (review article). Federal Writers' Project. Works Progress Administration. 1930's. *886*

—. Douglas, Lewis. Economic Policy. Roosevelt, Franklin D. 1933-34. *461*

—. Drama. Federal Theatre Project. South. 1930's. *884*

—. Dust Bowl. National Recovery Administration. Oklahoma. Public Welfare. 1932-35. *505*

—. Economic Conditions. 1933-38. *389*

—. Economic Conditions. Labor. Texas. 1929-39. *430*

—. Economic Conditions. National Recovery Administration. Supreme Court. Virginia. 1933-35. *353*

—. Economic planning. Public policy. 1932-41. *393*

—. Economic policy. Foreign Policy. Public works programs, global. Roosevelt, Franklin D. 1933. *419*

—. Economic policy. Freidel, Frank (review article). Political leadership. Roosevelt, Franklin D. 1930's. *147*

—. Economic Policy. Great Britain. 1930's. 1980's. *516*

—. Economic Policy. Import-Export Bank. International trade. 1934-74. *409*

—. Economic Policy (similarities). Germany. Nazism. ca 1933-36. *340*

—. Economic Regulations. Securities Exchange Act of 1934. Stock market. 1934. *287*

—. Economic Theory. Keynes, John Maynard. 1920's-30's. *63*

—. Editors and Editing. Liberalism. Milton, George Fort. Tennessee. 1930's. *362*

—. Elections, congressional. Republican Party. Roosevelt, Franklin D. 1937-38. *226*

—. Employment. Minorities in Politics. Negroes. Roosevelt, Franklin D. 1930-42. *470*

—. Employment, part-time. National Youth Administration. South Dakota. Struble, Anna C. Youth. 1935-43. *355*

—. Environment. Films. Lorentz, Pare. Roosevelt, Franklin D. (administration). Westward movement. 1936-40. *905*

—. Escott, Paul D. (review article). Federal Writers' Project. Slave narratives. 1935-39. 1979. *828*

—. Farmer-Labor Party. Michigan. State Politics. 1933-37. *203*

—. Farmers. Government. Great Plains. Letters. 1930-40. *8*

—. Farmers. Legislation. North Dakota (Landa). Taralseth, Rueben P. (interview). 1900's-30's. *114*

—. Farmers. Nebraska. Norris, George W. Relief funds. 1933-36. *397*
—. Fascism. Italy. Monetary policy. Mussolini, Benito. Roosevelt, Franklin D. 1922-36. *433*
—. Federal expenditures. States. 1933-39. *447*
—. Federal government. Press. Progressivism. Reform. 1890's-1930's. *294*
—. Federal government. Public health. 1933-39. *402*
—. Federal Policy. Hopkins, Harry. Poverty. Roosevelt, Franklin D. Unemployment. 1910's-38. *403*
—. Federal Policy. Indians (review articles). Parman, Donald L. Philp, Kenneth R. Taylor, Graham D. 1934-74. *612*
—. Federal Reserve Board. Keynesianism. Monetary policy. Private sector. 1929-79. *6*
—. Federal Subsistence Homesteads Corporation. Iowa (Granger). Ligutti, Luigi. Social experiments. 1934-51. *469*
—. Federal Writers' Project. Literature. Penkower, Monty Noam (review article). 1930's. 1977. *454*
—. Federal Writers' Project. Mangione, Jerre (review article). 1935-43. *509*
—. Feinman, Ronald L. (review article). Progressivism. Republican Party. Senate. Western States. 1929-41. *199*
—. Fiction, formula. Nancy Drew books. Stereotypes. 1930's. 1960's-70's. *841*
—. Fine, Sidney (review article). Murphy, Frank. 1936-42. *151*
—. Foreign Policy. International Labor Organization. Isolationism. Perkins, Frances. Roosevelt, Franklin D. 1921-34. *429*
—. Frankfurter, Felix. Keynes, John Maynard. Public works. 1932-35. *280*
—. Frankfurter, Felix. Lippmann, Walter. Roosevelt, Franklin D. World War II. 1932-45. *432*
—. Government regulation. Neoconservatism. Political Leadership. Republican Party. Social security. 1936-40. *209*
—. Graves, John Temple, II. Liberalism. Palm Beach *Times* (newspaper). South. 1933-40. *275*
—. Great Plains states. Liberalism, rural. Senators. 1930's. *162*
—. Greenbelt Towns. Ohio (Cincinnati, Greenhills). Tugwell, Rexford G. 1935-39. *333*
—. Hearst, William Randolph. Progressivism. 1930-35. *311*
—. Hickok, Lorena A. Hopkins, Harry. Ohio. Roosevelt, Franklin D. Unemployment. 1934-36. *489*
—. Hickok, Lorena A. Pennsylvania, eastern. 1933. *7*
—. Historiography. 1936-39. *480*
—. Historiography. Hughes, Charles Evans. Supreme Court. 1930's. 1950's-60's. *223*
—. Holt, Rush Dew (papers). Senate. West Virginia. 1920-55. *171*
—. Hoover, Herbert C. Political Commentary. Republican Party. 1933-35. *141*
—. Hopkins, Harry. Politics. 1912-40. *444*
—. House of Representatives. Political agenda. Political Parties (realignment). 1925-38. *241*
—. Housing. Negroes. Pennsylvania (Philadelphia). 1930's. *281*
—. Illinois (Chicago). Kelly, Edward J. Political machines. Roosevelt, Franklin D. 1932-40. *193*
—. Intellectuals. Progressivism. 1930's. *272*
—. Iowa. Murals. 1934-42. *880*
—. Johnson, Hiram. Roosevelt, Franklin D. 1920's-41. *180*
—. Johnson, Lyndon B. Kennedy, John F. Truman, Harry S. 1933-68. *394*
—. Labor Department. Negroes. Perkins, Frances. 1933-45. *347*
—. Labor policy. Radicals and Radicalism. Working class. 1930's. *627*
—. Labor Unions and Organizations. Leadership. 1933-40. *650*
—. Labor Unions and Organizations. Radicals and Radicalism. 1930-39. *653*
—. LaFollette, Philip F. Progressivism. Roosevelt, Franklin D. Wisconsin Works Bill. 1935. *414*
—. Land reform. Negroes. Public Policy. Resettlement. 1930's-60's. *458*
—. Leftism. Roosevelt, Franklin D. 1933-79. *535*
—. Liberalism. Political activism. Socialist Party. Unemployment. 1929-36. *707*
—. Libraries (public). 1933-39. *295*
—. Massachusetts (Boston). Methodology. Trout, Charles H. (views). Urban history. 1930's. 1977-79. *122*
—. Miners (resettlement of). National Industrial Recovery Act (1933). Roosevelt, Eleanor. Subsistence Homesteads Program. West Virginia (Arthurdale). 1930-46. *320*
—. Nebraska (Dawson County). Voting and Voting Behavior. 1933-40. *478*
—. Nevada (Las Vegas). Public works. 1933-40. *417*
—. New Hampshire. Political Campaigns (presidential). Roosevelt, Franklin D. 1936. *253*
—. Pennsylvania (Avondale). Political Commentary. Roosevelt, Franklin D. Sullivan, Mark. 1924-52. *305*
—. Political Attitudes. Public Welfare. South Dakota. 1930's-70's. *276*
—. Political Systems. Voting and Voting Behavior. 1894-1975. *257*
—. Progressive insurgents. Roosevelt, Franklin D. Senate. 1935-36. *217*
—. Progressives. Senate. 1933-34. *218*
—. Public Welfare. Roosevelt, Franklin D. State capitalism. 1929-52. *293*
—. Reform. Roosevelt, Franklin D. 1900-33. *299*
—. Resettlement Administration. Rural Development. Texas (Ropesville). 1933-43. *372*
—. Science Advisory Board. 1933-35. *491*
New Deal (criticism of). Long, Huey P. Reform. 1933-35. *315*
—. Philips, Waite (letters). Political philosophy. 1940. *434*
New Deal (opposition to). American Liberty League. Davis, John W. Political Campaigns. 1932-36. *191*
New Deal policies. Democratic Party. Kentucky (Louisville). National Democratic Issues Convention. 1975. *332*
—. Garner, John Nance. Roosevelt, Franklin D. 1933-38. *225*
New Deal (policies, programs). Braeman, John (review article). Politics. Roosevelt, Franklin D. 1930's. *399*
New Deal (review article). Andersen, Kristi. Blumberg, Barbara. Fine, Sidney. Jeffries, John W. Roosevelt, Franklin D. Swain, Martha H. 1933-39. *143*
—. Brandeis, Louis D. Dawson, Nelson L. Frankfurter, Felix. Landis, James M. Law. Ritchie, Donald A. 1930's. *512*
New Hampshire. New Deal. Political Campaigns (presidential). Roosevelt, Franklin D. 1936. *253*

New Hampshire (Berlin). Congress of Industrial Organizations. Labor. Nonpartisan League. Political Parties. 1932-36. *574*
New Jersey. Art and State. New Deal. Public Works of Art Project. 1932-40. *519*
—. Criminal investigations. Hauptmann, Bruno. Kidnapping. Lindbergh, Charles A. 1932-36. *638*
—. Democratic Party. Hague, Frank. New Deal. Roosevelt, Franklin D. 1932-40. *155*
New Jersey (Lakehurst). Disasters. Germany. *Hindenburg* (dirigible). 1937. *555*
New Jersey (Paterson). City government. Fiscal Policy. Public Welfare. Textile industry. 1920-32. *77*
New Jersey (Union Township). Schools. Taxpayers Association. 1929-38. *15*
New Mexico. Agricultural experiment stations. Arizona. New Deal. Oklahoma. Texas. 1926-39. *407*
—. Agriculture and Government. Indian-White Relations. New Deal. Pueblo Indians. 1938-48. *503*
—. *American Mercury* (periodical). Anderson, Maxwell *(Night Over Taos)*. 18c-19c. 1932. *885*
—. Cutting, Bronson M. Democratic Party. Political Campaigns. Roosevelt, Franklin D. Senate. 1934. *269*
—. Pound, Ezra ("Pithy Promulgations"). Santa Fe *New Mexican* (newspaper). 1935. *783*
New Mexico (Gallup). American Federation of Labor. Coal Mines and Mining. Strikes. 1933. *708*
New Mexico (Gila). Communes. Llano del Rio colony. 1932-35. *675*
New State Ice v. *Liebmann* (US, 1932). Brandeis, Louis D. Due process. Economic Regulations. *Nebbia* v. *New York* (US, 1934). Supreme Court. *West Coast Hotel* v. *Parrish* (US, 1937). 1897-1937. *476*
New York. Albok, John. Photographs. 1933-45. *948*
—. Attica State Prison. NAACP. Negroes. Prison conditions. 1932. *751*
—. Brookwood Labor College. Labor Unions and Organizations. 1926-36. *644*
—. Civilian Conservation Corps. Discrimination, employment. Negroes. 1933-42. *441*
—. Connecticut. Long Island Sound. Ships. 1930-35. *587*
—. Conservatism. New Deal. Republican Party. Snell, Bertrand H. 1933-39. *139*
—. Labor Reform. Minimum Wage. *Tipaldo* v. *Morehead* (New York, 1934). 1933-37. *367*
—. Pell, Herbert. Political Campaigns (presidential). Roosevelt, Franklin D. Upper Classes. 1936. *142*
New York (Akron). Art. Indians. Iroquois School of Art. New Deal. Parker, Arthur C. Seneca Arts project. Tonawanda Indian Reservation. 1935-41. *352*
New York (Buffalo). Government. Hoover, Herbert C. Industry. Public Welfare. Unemployment. 1929-33. *64*
New York City. Airplane flights, transatlantic. Corrigan, Douglas. Ireland (Dublin). 1938-50. *950*
—. Art and Society. Negroes. Painting. Stage Setting and Scenery. Stettheimer, Florine. 1929-44. *882*
—. Art deco. Deskey, Donald. Genauer, Emily (account). Interior decorating. Radio City Music Hall. 1929-37. *815*
—. Artists. City life. Marsh, Reginald. 1930's. *958*

—. Attitudes. Blitzstein, Marc *(Cradle Will Rock)*. Censorship. Federal Theatre Project. Labor. Works Progress Administration. 1937. *502*
—. City Government (relations with state government). Emergency Economy Bill (New York, 1934). La Guardia, Fiorello Henry. 1934. *144*
—. City Life. Personal Narratives. Pessen, Edward. 1929-39. *87*
—. Composers Collective. Folk Songs. Leftism. 1931-36. *798*
—. Cowley, Malcolm. Intellectuals. Literature. Marxism. 1932-40. *763*
—. Painting. Rivera, Diego. Rockefeller Center. 1933. *912*
—. Stock Exchange. 1929. *91*
New York City (Harlem). Black nationalism. Communism. Garvey, Marcus. 1931-39. *681*
—. Communist Party. Culture. Intellectuals. Negroes. Popular Front. 1935-39. *678*
—. Communist Party. Negroes. 1928-36. *679*
New York (Rochester). Authors (southern). Gordon, Caroline. Letters. Tennessee (Benfolly). Wood, Sally. 1930-31. *818*
New York school. Art. Mexico. Murals. 1930's. *760*
New York Times. Anti-Semitism. Germany. Nazism. Reporters and Reporting. 1932-33. *749*
—. Finance. Newspaper columns. Stock Exchange. 1929. *13*
New York, western. Agricultural Adjustment Administration. Farmers. Federal Policy. New Deal. 1934. *308*
New York Yankees (team). Amyotrophic lateral sclerosis. Baseball. Character. Gehrig, Lou. Letters. 1939. *777*
New York (43rd Congressional District). Elections. Townsend Movement. 1936. *551*
News. Advertising. Carter, Boake. Military. Political Commentary. Radio. 1931-38. *803*
News commentator. Carter, Boake. New Deal. Political criticism. Radio. Roosevelt, Franklin D. 1935-38. *790*
—. Radio. Social history. Swing, Raymond Gram. 1930's. *791*
News, dramatization of. *March of Time* (series). Radio. Smith, Fred. 1928-45. *856*
Newspaper columns. Finance. *New York Times*. Stock Exchange. 1929. *13*
Newspapers. Advertising. Censorship. Missouri. Pulitzer, Joseph, II. St. Louis *Post Dispatch*. 1929-39. *893*
—. Barkley, Alben W. Democratic Party. Harrison, Byron Patton (Pat). Senate (majority leader). 1937. *174*
—. Capital Punishment. Negroes. Rape. Reporters and Reporting. Scottsboro Case. Trials. 1931-32. *697*
—. Chicago, University of. Communist sympathizers, alleged. Illinois. Walgreen, Charles R. 1930's. *663*
—. Congress of Industrial Organizations. Labor Disputes. New Deal. South. 1930-39. *518*
—. Conservatism. Constitutional law. Kansas. New Deal. Supreme Court. 1934-35. *329*
—. Editorials. Great Plains. Internationalism. Isolationism. North Central States. 1918-35. *643*
—. Editorials. Radio. *War of the Worlds* (broadcast). Welles, Orson. 1938. *951*
—. Foreign policy. Hearst, William Randolph. Isolationism. 1936-41. *556*
Niebuhr, Reinhold. Capitalism. Marxism. *Radical Religion* (periodical). Roosevelt, Franklin D. (administration). 1930-43. *532*
—. Democracy. Liberals. Religion. 1930-45. *598*

Nixon, Richard M. (administration). Benefactor-aversion hypothesis. Local government. Roosevelt, Franklin D. (administration). State Government. 1933-45. 1969-74. *392*

Nobel Prizes. Dreiser, Theodore. Lewis, Sinclair. Literature. Public Opinion. Sweden. 1920's-30. *857*

Noble, Robert. Advertising. Allen, Laurence. Allen, Willis. California Life Payments Plan. Economic structure. Pensions. Referendum. 1937-39. *755*

Nonpartisan League. Congress of Industrial Organizations. Labor. New Hampshire (Berlin). Political Parties. 1932-36. *574*

Norris, Clarence. Alabama. NAACP. Pardon request. Scottsboro Case. 1931-76. *657*

Norris, George W. Congress. Roosevelt, Franklin D. Supreme Court (issue). 1937. *207*

—. Farmers. Nebraska. New Deal. Relief funds. 1933-36. *397*

North Carolina. Agricultural Adjustment Administration. New Deal. Senate. Virginia. 1933-39. *366*

—. American Legion. Bonus Army. District of Columbia. Political Protest. Stevens, Henry L., Jr. Veterans (benefits). 1932. *694*

—. Branson, Eugene C. Electric Power. Poe, Clarence H. Rural Electrification Administration. State Government. 1917-36. *302*

—. Coan, George W., Jr. Hopkins, Harry. Patronage. Works Progress Administration. 1935. *404*

—. Ehringhaus, J. C. B. Legislation. Social Security Act (US, 1935). Unemployment insurance. 1935-37. *420*

—. Films. History Teaching. 1930's-74. *806*

—. NAACP. Parker, John J. Supreme Court (nominations). White, Walter F. 1930. *618*

North Carolina (Gastonia). National Textile Workers Union. Strikes. Textile Industry. Weisbord, Vera Buch (reminiscences). 1929. *746*

North Carolina, University of (Southern Historical Collection). Federal Writers' Project. Oral History. 1935-80. *523*

North Carolina, western. Cherokee Indians. Indian policy. New Deal. 1930's. *508*

North Central States. All-Party Agricultural Committee. Farmers. Great Plains. Political Campaigns (presidential). Roosevelt, Franklin D. 1936. *254*

—. Editorials. Great Plains. Internationalism. Isolationism. Newspapers. 1918-35. *643*

—. Fundamentalism. Long, Huey P. Populism. Progressivism. Smith, Gerald L. K. 1934-48. *633*

North Dakota. Agriculture and Government. Land. Langer, William. Mortgage moratoria. 1930's. *3*

—. Civilian Conservation Corps. National Youth Administration. 1930-45. *358*

—. Farm Security Administration (Resettlement Administration). Orvedal, O. Leonard (interview). 1930's. *313*

—. Farmers. Industrial Workers of the World. O'Connor, Hugh (interview). Women. 1900's-30's. *113*

—. Farmers. Prices. Strikes. 1932. *92*

North Dakota (Dickinson). Baseball, semiprofessional. Negroes. Otto, Solomon (reminiscences). Race Relations. 1929-31. *889*

North Dakota (Kidder County). Farmers. Meat preservation. Oil Industry and Trade. Schools, rural. Wick family (interview). 1900's-30's. *112*

North Dakota (Landa). Farmers. Legislation. New Deal. Taralseth, Rueben P. (interview). 1900's-30's. *114*

North Dakota (Ross). Juma, Charlie (interview). Syrian Americans. 1900's-30's. *111*

North Dakota (Williston). Butchering. Soup kitchen. Vohs, Al J. (interview). 1900's-30's. *110*

North Platte River. Kendrick, John B. Legislation. Water Supply. Western States. 1917-33. *314*

Novels. Autobiography. Wolfe, Thomas. 1924-38. *873*

—. Basso, Hamilton. Demagoguery, concept of. Long, Huey P. Louisiana. 1920-76. *726*

—. Cain, James M. California (Los Angeles). 1925-45. *807*

—. Documentarism. Film industry. Steinbeck, John *(The Grapes of Wrath)*. 1939-40. *779*

—. Harvard University, Houghton Library. Manuscripts. Wolfe, Thomas. 1938. 1975. *845*

—. Louisiana. Plantation life. Regionalism. Saxon, Lyle *(Children of Strangers)*. 1920's-40's. *932*

—. Social consciousness. Zugsmith, Leane. 1930's. *842*

Novels, detective. California (San Francisco). Hammett, Dashiell. Sam Spade (fictional character). 1920-30's. *866*

—. Hammett, Dashiell. Literature. Marxism. Sam Spade (fictional character). 1930's. *862*

Novels (pulp). Bedford-Jones, H. Gardner, Erle Stanley. 1920's-30's. *810*

Nye Committee. Foreign policy. Isolationism. Johnson, Hiram. Roosevelt, Franklin D. (administration). ca 1933-34. *576*

O

Ocean mail service. Air Mail Service. Contracts. Merchant Marine. Roosevelt, Franklin D. 1933-37. *488*

O'Connor, Hugh (interview). Farmers. Industrial Workers of the World. North Dakota. Women. 1900's-30's. *113*

Ohio. Automobile Industry and Trade. Indiana. Labor parties. New Deal. United Automobile Workers of America. 1935-40. *652*

—. Buildings. Cincinnati Union Terminal. Moore, Alfred. Railroads. 1933-73. *933*

—. Bulkley, Robert J. Elections. Prohibition. Senate. 1918-30. *256*

—. Cleveland Public Library. Federal Writers' Project. Works Progress Administration. 1933-39. *450*

—. Coal Mines and Mining. National Guard. Strikes. White, George. 1932. *687*

—. Company towns. Social Classes. Steel Industry. Strikes. 1937. *531*

—. Davey, Martin L. National Guard. Steel Industry. Strikes. 1937. *722*

—. Democratic Party. New Deal. Political Campaigns (presidential). 1936. *249*

—. First ladies (state). State Government. White, George. White, Mary (reminiscences). 1931-35. *265*

—. Hickok, Lorena A. Hopkins, Harry. New Deal. Roosevelt, Franklin D. Unemployment. 1934-36. *489*

—. Negroes. Republican Party, fission in the. 1920-32. *170*

Ohio (Akron). Rubber industry. Strikes, sit-down. 1934-38. *683*

Ohio (Cincinnati). Actors, employment of. Drama. Federal Theatre Project. Works Progress Administration. 1935-39. *865*

—. Courter, Claude V. Education, Finance. Heinhold, Fred W. 1937-59. *22*

Ohio (Cincinnati, Greenhills). Greenbelt Towns. New Deal. Tugwell, Rexford G. 1935-39. *333*

Ohio Farmer-Labor Progressive Federation. Amlie, Thomas R. Farmer-labor movement. Hard, Herbert. New Deal. Third Parties. 1930-40. *204*

Ohio (Toledo). Public Welfare. 1933-37. *485*

Ohio (Youngstown). Communist Party. Labor Unions and Organizations. Steel Workers Organizing Committee. Steuben, John. 1936. *608*

Oil Industry and Trade. Boomtowns. Texas (Conroe). 1929-33. *82*

—. Congress. Federal Regulation. Ickes, Harold. Roosevelt, Franklin D. 1933. *388*

—. Farmers. Meat preservation. North Dakota (Kidder County). Schools, rural. Wick family (interview). 1900's-30's. *112*

"Okies". Agricultural laborers. California. Labor Unions and Organizations. Migration, Internal. 1930's. *115*

Oklahoma. Aeronautics. Circumnavigation (solo). Post, Wiley. 1920's-35. *560*

—. Agricultural experiment stations. Arizona. New Deal. New Mexico. Texas. 1926-39. *407*

—. Balloons. Carter, "Red". First Balloon Squadron. Fort Sill. 1930's. *561*

—. Cultural identity. State Government. 1930's. *31*

—. Dust Bowl. Farmers. Migration, Internal (necessity). Soil depletion. 1921-30's. *72*

—. Dust Bowl. Farmers, truck. Migrant Labor. Migration, Internal. 1930's. *43*

—. Dust Bowl. Migration, Internal. Route 66. Southwest. 1930's. *88*

—. Dust Bowl. National Recovery Administration. New Deal. Public Welfare. 1932-35. *505*

—. Fiction. Folklore. Milburn, George. Ozark Mountains. 1930's. *797*

—. Hollins, Jess. International Labor Defense. NAACP. Race Relations. Rape. Trials. 1931-36. *659*

Oklahoma (Bartlesville). Agrarianism. Broadacre City. City Planning. Decentralization. Wright, Frank Lloyd. 1935. *864*

Oklahoma, eastern. Agriculture. Cotton. Sharecroppers. 1920-40. *38*

Oklahoma National Guard. Bridges (toll, free). Interstate relations. Red River Bridge Company. Texas Rangers. 1931. *30*

Oklahoma (Okemah). Folk Songs. Guthrie, Woody. 1912-29. *871*

Oklahoma (Tulsa, Oklahoma City). Civilian Conservation Corps. Segregation. Urban programs. 1930's. *364*

Oklahoma, western. Daily Life. Dust Bowl. Farmers. Henderson, Caroline Agnes Boa. New Deal. 1935. *90*

Old age security. Epstein, Abraham. Legislation. Pension systems. Voluntary associations. 1920-35. *647*

Oleson, Anna Dickie. Democratic Party. Minnesota. Politics. Women. 1905-71. *371*

Olson, Floyd B. Hormel, George A., and Co. Labor Unions and Organizations. Minnesota (Austin). Strikes. 1933. *592*

Olympic Games. American Olympic Committee. Anti-Semitism. Boycotts, proposed. Brundage, Avery. "Fair Play for American Athletes" (pamphlet). Germany (Berlin). 1935-36. *851*

—. Boycotts. Brundage, Avery. 1936. *863*

—. Boycotts. Germany. 1932-36. *825*

—. Boycotts, proposed. Germany (Berlin). Racism, issue of. 1933-36. *843*

—. California (Los Angeles). 1932. *956*

O'Mahoney, Joseph C. Democratic Party. Patronage. Postal Service. Roosevelt, Franklin D. Senate. Wyoming. 1916-45. *220*

O'Neill, Eugene *(The Iceman Cometh)*. Drama. Political communities. 1939. *949*

Opportunity (periodical). Censorship. *Crisis* (periodical). District of Columbia. Public schools. School Boards. 1936. *571*

"Oral and Community History", course. Illinois (Lake Forest). Lake Forest College. 1930-40. *799*

Oral history. Autobiography. Federal Writers' Project. South. 1930-39. *361*

—. Federal Writers' Project. North Carolina, University of (Southern Historical Collection). 1935-80. *523*

—. Historical sources. Music (blues). Negroes. Recordings. Social Conditions. 1924-41. *888*

—. Massachusetts. Sullivan, Anna (interview). Textile Workers Union of America. Women. 1918-76. *688*

—. Methodology. Terkel, Studs (review article). 1930-72. *809*

Oregon. Daily life. Economic conditions. Lind, Leo (reminiscences). Markham and Callow Railroad. 1929-38. *67*

—. Dawson, Oliver B. (reminiscences). Ironwork. Timberline Lodge. Works Progress Administration. 1935-37. *326*

Oregon (Neahkahnie Mountain). Modernization. Public Finance. Roads. West. 1850-1977. *496*

Organizations. Artists. Radicals and Radicalism. 1930's. *938*

Organized Unemployed, Inc. Mecklenburg, George H. Minnesota (Minneapolis). Poor. Self-help. 1932-35. *740*

Orvedal, O. Leonard (interview). Farm Security Administration (Resettlement Administration). North Dakota. 1930's. *313*

Otto, Solomon (reminiscences). Baseball, semiprofessional. Negroes. North Dakota (Dickinson). Race Relations. 1929-31. *889*

Oxford Group movement. Christianity. Longshoremen. Strikes. Washington (Seattle). 1921-34. *738*

Ozark Mountains. Fiction. Folklore. Milburn, George. Oklahoma. 1930's. *797*

P

Pacific Area. Anti-Imperialism. Foreign Policy (critics). Roosevelt, Franklin D. World War II (antecedents). 1930's. *692*

Pacific Northwest. Bonneville Power Administration. Electric utilities. New Deal. Public Utilities. 1937-42. *339*

—. Immigrants. International Brotherhood of Pulp, Sulphite, and Paper Mill Workers. Negroes. South. Women. 1909-40. *754*

Pacifism. Films. War. World War I. 1930-39. *836*

Painting. Art and Society. Negroes. New York City. Stage Setting and Scenery. Stettheimer, Florine. 1929-44. *882*

—. New York City. Rivera, Diego. Rockefeller Center. 1933. *912*

Palm Beach *Times* (newspaper). Graves, John Temple, II. Liberalism. New Deal. South. 1933-40. *275*

Pamphlets. Communist Party. Rhetoric. 1929-39. *553*

Pan-Africanism. Black nationalism. Ethiopia. Invasions. Italy. Negroes. 1934-36. *716*

Panic of 1930. Banking. Money. 1920-30. *132*

Paper industry. American Federation of Labor. International Brotherhood of Pulp, Sulphite, and Paper Mill Workers. Labor Unions and Organizations. Militancy. 1933-35. *753*

Pardon request. Alabama. NAACP. Norris, Clarence. Scottsboro Case. 1931-76. *657*

Parker, Arthur C. Art. Indians. Iroquois School of Art. New Deal. New York (Akron). Seneca Arts project. Tonawanda Indian Reservation. 1935-41. *352*

Parker, Bonnie. Barrow, Clyde. Ford automobile. Gangster myth. Rich, Carroll Y. Warren, Jesse. 1934-67. *957*

Parker, John J. NAACP. North Carolina. Supreme Court (nominations). White, Walter F. 1930. *618*

Parman, Donald L. Federal Policy. Indians (review articles). New Deal. Philp, Kenneth R. Taylor, Graham D. 1934-74. *612*

Partisan Review (periodical). Editors and Editing. Socialism. Stalinism. 1930's. *564*

—. Literature. Politics. Radicals and Radicalism. 1930's. *895*

Partisanship. Andersen, Kristi. Democratic Party. Republican Party. Voting and Voting Behavior. 1920-32. *229*

—. Political Theory. Voting and Voting Behavior. Washington. 1889-1950. *136*

Patman, Wright. Bonus Army. District of Columbia. Legislation (proposed). Veterans' certificates. 1932. *666*

Patronage. Branion-Williams case (California). California. Federal Civil Works Administration. McAdoo, William G. Social workers. 1933-34. *468*

—. Byrd, Harry F. Democratic Party. Senate. Virginia. 1935-39. *196*

—. Coan, George W., Jr. Hopkins, Harry. North Carolina. Works Progress Administration. 1935. *404*

—. Democratic Party. O'Mahoney, Joseph C. Postal Service. Roosevelt, Franklin D. Senate. Wyoming. 1916-45. *220*

Patterson, Robert *(Gas Buggy)*. Automobile industry and Trade. Indiana (Kokomo). 1933. *820*

Peace. Foreign Policy. International cooperation. Isolationism. League of Nations Association. 1934-38. *525*

Pecora, Ferdinand. Public Opinion. Senate Banking and Currency Committee. Stock Exchange (manipulation). 1933. *452*

Peddlers, disappearance of. Automobile, advent of. Kentucky. 1930's. *727*

Pell, Herbert. New York. Political Campaigns (presidential). Roosevelt, Franklin D. Upper Classes. 1936. *142*

Pendergast, Thomas J. Commerce Department. Mitchell, Ewing Young. Political machines. Progressivism. Roosevelt, Franklin D. 1933-36. *239*

—. Democratic Party. Missouri. Political Conventions. Roosevelt, Franklin D. State Politics. 1932. *238*

Penkower, Monty Noam (review article). Federal Writers' Project. Literature. New Deal. 1930's. 1977. *454*

Pennsylvania. Civilian Conservation Corps. New Deal. 1933-40. *356*

—. Congress of Industrial Organizations. Elections (presidential). Labor Non-Partisan League. Roosevelt, Franklin D. 1936. *252*

—. Elections (gubernatorial). James, Arthur H. 1938. *215*

Pennsylvania (Avondale). New Deal. Political Commentary. Roosevelt, Franklin D. Sullivan, Mark. 1924-52. *305*

Pennsylvania, eastern. Hickok, Lorena A. New Deal. 1933. *7*

Pennsylvania (Lancaster). Armstrong Cork Company. Business. New Deal. Prentis, Henning Webb, Jr. 1934-40. *514*

Pennsylvania (Lancaster County). Agriculture. 1928-36. 1970's. *28*

Pennsylvania (Philadelphia). Bureaucrats. Public housing. 1929-41. *282*

—. Class consciousness. NAACP. Negroes. Race. 1930's. *684*

—. Democratic Party. Elections (critical, concept). Ethnic groups. 1924-36. *240*

—. Democratic Party (reformist). Elections (city). 1933. *181*

—. Housing. Negroes. New Deal. 1930's. *281*

Pennsylvania (Pittsburgh). Democratic Party. New Deal. Political Theory. Quantitative Methods. Voting and Voting Behavior. Wisconsin. 1912-40. *228*

Pennsylvania, western. National Miners Union. Negroes. United Mine Workers of America. 1925-31. *686*

Pension systems. Epstein, Abraham. Legislation. Old age security. Voluntary associations. 1920-35. *647*

Pensions. Advertising. Allen, Laurence. Allen, Willis. California Life Payments Plan. Economic structure. Noble, Robert. Referendum. 1937-39. *525*

People of the Cumberland (film). Cumberland Mountains. Films (documentary). Historical accuracy. Tennessee. 1930's. *834*

Peres, Hardwig. Fortas, Abe. Interior Department. Lawyers. Letters. Roosevelt, Franklin D. 1930-44. *373*

Periodicals. *Gyroscope: A Literary Magazine.* Literature. Winters, Yvor. 1929-30. *767*

Perkins, Frances. Bureau of Labor Statistics. Lubin, Isador. New Deal. Statistics. Unemployment. 1920-49. *342*

—. Foreign Policy. International Labor Organization. Isolationism. New Deal. Roosevelt, Franklin D. 1921-34. *429*

—. Labor Department. Negroes. New Deal. 1933-45. *347*

Personal narratives. Accidents. Daily Life. Faulkner, Jim. Faulkner, William. Mississippi (Oxford). Youth. 1930-39. *804*

—. Agee, James. Eyster, Warren. Films. Literature. 1935-41. *802*

—. Arts. Berger, Arthur. Criticism. Music. Works Progress Administration. 1930-80. *786*

—. Chicago, University of. Educators. Shils, Edward. Sociology. 1932-36. *915*

—. City Life. New York City. Pessen, Edward. 1929-39. *87*

—. *First-Person America: Voices from the Thirties* (program). History Teaching. 1930's. 1980. *768*

—. Garment industry. Missouri (St. Louis). Photographic essays. Strikes. Women. ca 1930-39. *565*

Pessen, Edward. City Life. New York City. Personal Narratives. 1929-39. *87*

Peyton, Rupert (reminiscences). Government. Long, Huey P. Louisiana. 1917-35. *696*

Pharmacy. Federal Aid to Education. George-Barden Act (US, 1946). George-Deen Act (US, 1936). Vocational education. Wisconsin Plan. 1936-49. *307*

Philanthropy. California (Santa Barbara). Fleischmann, Max. Relief work. Unemployment. 1930-32. *78*

—. Hoovervilles. Missouri (St. Louis). 1930-36. *120*

Philips, Waite (letters). New Deal (criticism of). Political philosophy. 1940. *434*

Phillips, A. H. (reminiscences). Dramatists. Films. Hollywood. 1930's. *894*

Philosophy. Hook, Sidney (review article). Marxism. Pragmatism. 1930's. *593*

Philp, Kenneth R. Federal Policy. Indians (review articles). New Deal. Parman, Donald L. Taylor, Graham D. 1934-74. *612*

Photographic essays. Garment industry. Missouri (St. Louis). Personal narratives. Strikes. Women. ca 1930-39. *565*

Photographs. Airplanes. Douglas, Donald. 1932-38. *752*

—. Albok, John. New York. 1933-45. *948*

—. Attitudes. Daily Life. Lee, Russell. 1932-40. *827*

—. Country Life. Farm Security Administration. Mennonites. Western States. 1930's. *929*

—. Short, John D., Jr. (reminiscences). Steinbeck, John. 1930's. *916*

Photography. California (Hollywood). Films. Popular Culture. Publicity. 1930's. *847*

—. Country life. Delano, Jack. Farm Security Administration. New Deal. South Carolina (Santee-Cooper). 1941. *327*

—. Farm Security Administration. Great Plains. Stryker, Roy Emerson. 1937-39. *322*

—. Public Relations. Roosevelt, Franklin D. 1933-37. *267*

Photography, documentary. Agee, James *(Let Us Now Praise Famous Men)*. Daily Life. Evans, Walker. Sharecroppers. South. 1930-1941. *792*

Pilots. Airplane Industry and Trade. Public Relations. Safety. Women. 1927-40. *566*

—. Doolittle, Jimmy. Gee Bee (aircraft). 1930-32. *900*

Pineville *Sun* (newspaper). Coal Mines and Mining. Editors and Editing. Evans, Herndon J. Kentucky (Harlan County). Strikes. 1929-32. *730*

Pittman, Key. China. International Trade. Senate. Silver Purchase Act (1934). 1933-40. *472*

—. Creel, Cecil. Democratic Party. Nevada. New Deal. Political Factions. Public Welfare. 1933-34. *244*

—. Monetary Act (US, 1939). Senate. Silver. 1939. *440*

Plantation life. Louisiana. Novels. Regionalism. Saxon, Lyle *(Children of Strangers)*. 1920's-40's. *932*

Pocatello Central Labor Union. Democratic Party. Idaho. New Deal. Rosqvist, August. 1930-36. *494*

Poe, Clarence H. Branson, Eugene C. Electric Power. North Carolina. Rural Electrification Administration. State Government. 1917-36. *302*

Poetry. Lilly, Octave, Jr. (obituary). Negroes. South. 1930-60. *793*

Policymaking. Communist Party. Roosevelt, Franklin D. (administration). 1933-45. *534*

Political Activism. Actors and Actresses. Douglas, Melvyn. 1936-42. *766*

—. American Indian Federation. Bureau of Indian Affairs. Collier, John. Indians. Jamison, Alice Lee. New Deal. 1930's-50's. *351*

—. Liberalism. New Deal. Socialist Party. Unemployment. 1929-36. *707*

Political activities, dissident. Federal Bureau of Investigation. Presidential directives. 1936-53. *500*

Political agenda. House of Representatives. New Deal. Political Parties (realignment). 1925-38. *241*

Political Attitudes. Bibliographies. Intervention. Leadership. 1929-41. *580*

—. Bunche, Ralph. National Negro Congress. Negroes. New Deal. 1930-39. *639*

—. Capitalism. Radicals and Radicalism. Texas. 1929-33. *128*

—. Congress. New Deal. Roosevelt, Franklin D. Tennessee. 1933-40. *148*

—. Films (documentary). *March of Time* (series). *The World Today* (series). 1930's. *761*

—. Montana. Roosevelt, Franklin D. Senate. Wheeler, Burton K. 1904-46. *232*

—. New Deal. Public Welfare. South Dakota. 1930's-70's. *276*

Political Campaigns. American Liberty League. Davis, John W. New Deal (opposition to). 1932-36. *191*

—. Budgets (state allocations). Democratic Party. New Deal. 1932-40. *270*

—. Byrd, Harry F. Democratic Party (convention). Presidential nomination. Roosevelt, Franklin D. 1932. *187*

—. Cutting, Bronson M. Democratic Party. New Mexico. Roosevelt, Franklin D. Senate. 1934. *269*

—. Democratic Party. Domestic Policy. Internationalism. New Deal. Roosevelt, Franklin D. 1938-40. *160*

—. Democratic Party. Gillette, Guy M. House of Representatives. Iowa. Roosevelt, Franklin D. 1932-48. *185*

Political Campaigns (gubernatorial). Aiken, George D. Republican Party. Vermont. 1933-36. *184*

—. Anti-Semitism. Benson, Elmer A. Minnesota. 1930's. *536*

—. California. Democratic Party. End Poverty In California program. Sinclair, Upton. ca 1933-34. *242*

Political Campaigns (presidential). Agricultural programs. Droughts. Kansas. New Deal. 1936. *464*

—. Aiken, George D. Flood control. Governors. Republican Party. Vermont. 1937-39. *235*

—. All-Party Agricultural Committee. Farmers. Great Plains. North Central States. Roosevelt, Franklin D. 1936. *254*

—. Clark, Bennett Champ. Committee of One. Democratic Party. Missouri. 1936. *250*

—. Democratic Party. Higgins, Andrew J. Roosevelt, Franklin D. 1944. *212*

—. Democratic Party. New Deal. Ohio. 1936. *249*

—. Democratic Party. Republican Party. 1936. *248*

—. Democratic Party (Colored Voters Division). Good Neighbor League Colored Committee. Negroes. Roosevelt, Franklin D. 1936. *251*

—. New Deal. New Hampshire. Roosevelt, Franklin D. 1936. *253*

—. New York. Pell, Herbert. Roosevelt, Franklin D. Upper Classes. 1936. *142*

Political Campaigns (presidential, senatorial). Glass, Carter. Virginia. 1936. *197*

Political Change. Congressmen, conservative. Democratic Party. George, Walter F. Roosevelt, Franklin D. 1938. *145*

Political coalitions. Democratic Party. Missouri. Republican Party. Roosevelt, Franklin D. 1936-52. *146*

Political Commentary. Advertising. Carter, Boake. Military. News. Radio. 1931-38. *803*

—. Hoover, Herbert C. New Deal. Republican Party. 1933-35. *141*

—. New Deal. Pennsylvania (Avondale). Roosevelt, Franklin D. Sullivan, Mark. 1924-52. *305*

Political communities. Drama. O'Neill, Eugene *(The Iceman Cometh)*. 1939. *949*

Political Conventions. Democratic Party. Missouri. Pendergast, Thomas J. Roosevelt, Franklin D. State Politics. 1932. *238*
Political Corruption. Berry, Harry S. Tennessee (Nashville). Works Progress Administration. 1935-43. *309*
—. City Government. Flogging case. Florida (Tampa). Vigilantism. 1935-38. *628*
—. Governors. Horton, Henry. Tennessee. 1930-31. *201*
Political criticism. Carter, Boake. New Deal. News commentator. Radio. Roosevelt, Franklin D. 1935-38. *790*
Political Factions. Creel, Cecil. Democratic Party. Nevada. New Deal. Pittman, Key. Public Welfare. 1933-34. *244*
Political friendship. Harrison, Byron Patton (Pat). Mississippi. Roosevelt, Franklin D. 1920-41. *259*
Political history. Probability theory. Quantitative methods. Roosevelt, Franklin D. Supreme Court. 1937. 1970's. *216*
Political Leadership. 1929-76. *119*
—. Agricultural Policy. Jones, Marvin. Legislation. New Deal. 1916-40. *406*
—. Congress. Mississippi. 1931-37. *179*
—. Economic policy. Freidel, Frank (review article). New Deal. Roosevelt, Franklin D. 1930's. *147*
—. Foreign policy. Isolationism. Roosevelt, Franklin D. Senate. World Court. 1935. *194*
—. Government regulation. Neoconservatism. New Deal. Republican Party. Social security. 1936-40. *209*
—. Hoover, Herbert C. Landon, Alfred M. Republican Party (conference, proposed). 1937-38. *140*
—. Long, Huey P. Share Our Wealth movement. 1928-35. *630*
Political machines. Browning, Gordon. Elections (gubernatorial). Tennessee. 1936. *135*
—. Commerce Department. Mitchell, Ewing Young. Pendergast, Thomas J. Progressivism. Roosevelt, Franklin D. 1933-36. *239*
—. Illinois (Chicago). Kelly, Edward J. New Deal. Roosevelt, Franklin D. 1932-40. *193*
Political Participation. Literary Criticism. Marxism. Wilson, Edmund. 1930's. *940*
Political Parties *See also* names of political parties, e.g. Democratic party, etc.
—. Congress of Industrial Organizations. Labor. New Hampshire (Berlin). Nonpartisan League. 1932-36. *574*
—. Economic conditions. Elections (presidential). Hoover, Herbert C. Roosevelt, Franklin D. South Dakota. 1932. *176*
Political Parties (realignment). House of Representatives. New Deal. Political agenda. 1925-38. *241*
—. Legislation. Public Welfare. 1933-54. *479*
Political philosophy. New Deal (criticism of). Philips, Waite (letters). 1940. *434*
Political Protest. American Legion. Bonus Army. District of Columbia. North Carolina. Stevens, Henry L., Jr. Veterans (benefits). 1932. *694*
—. Antiwar sentiment. Colleges and Universities. Leftism. 1920-36. *547*
Political representation. Labor Non-Partisan League. Legislation. Working conditions. 1936-38. *741*
Political Speeches. Democracy. Inaugural addresses. Roosevelt, Franklin D. Values. 1901-77. *164*
Political surveillance. American Civil Liberties Union. Demonstrations. Federal Bureau of Investigation. Hoover, J. Edgar. Trade Union Education League. 1924-36. *750*

Political Systems. New Deal. Voting and Voting Behavior. 1894-1975. *257*
Political Theory. Capitalism. Government. Marxism. New Deal. 1933-39. 1980. *103*
—. Democratic Party. New Deal. Pennsylvania (Pittsburgh). Quantitative Methods. Voting and Voting Behavior. Wisconsin. 1912-40. *228*
—. Partisanship. Voting and Voting Behavior. Washington. 1889-1950. *136*
Politics. Agricultural Policy. Corporatism, concept of. Hoover, Herbert C. Roosevelt, Franklin D. 1929-33. *27*
—. Agriculture. Reno, Milo. Wallace, Henry A. 1932-33. *466*
—. Airplane flights. Alaska (Fairbanks). Army Air Corps. B-10 (aircraft). District of Columbia. 1934. *821*
—. Alien Property Custodian. Banking. Crowley, Leo T. Federal Deposit Insurance Corporation. Roosevelt, Franklin D. (administration). 1934-45. *510*
—. American Labor Party. Communist Party. Gordon, Max (account). Popular Front. ca 1930-39. *758*
—. Amlie, Thomas R. Economic programs. Liberals. New Deal. Wisconsin. 1931-39. *264*
—. Army Corps of Engineers. Flood control. Mississippi River (lower). 1927-41. *449*
—. Braeman, John (review article). New Deal (policies, programs). Roosevelt, Franklin D. 1930's. *399*
—. Brandeis, Louis D. Frankfurter, Felix. New Deal. Roosevelt, Franklin D. World War I. 1917-33. *154*
—. Brucker, Wilber M. Michigan. Tax reform. 1929-33. *222*
—. Capra, Frank. Films. *Mr. Smith Goes To Washington* (film). Populism. 1939. *881*
—. Capra, Frank. Films. Yankee (character). 1936-41. *812*
—. Chafe, William H. Lemon, J. Stanley. Women's movement (review article). 1920-70. *610*
—. Colleges and Universities. Feuer, Lewis. Lipset, Seymour Martin. Student activism. 1930's-40's. *715*
—. Congressmen. New Deal. Roosevelt, Franklin D. Virginia. Woodrum, Clifton A. 1922-45. *236*
—. Crump, Edward. Democratic Party. Elections (gubernatorial). Tennessee (Shelby County). 1932. *200*
—. Democratic Party. Minnesota. Oleson, Anna Dickie. Women. 1905-71. *371*
—. Economic conditions. Foreman, Clark Howell. National Emergency Council (report). Roosevelt, Franklin D. South. 1938. *24*
—. Equal Rights Amendment (proposed). Florida. National Women's Party. West, Helen Hunt. Women. 1917-52. *667*
—. Federal Theatre Project. Flanagan, Hallie. Hopkins, Harry. Theater. Works Progress Administration. 1935-39. *303*
—. Hopkins, Harry. New Deal. 1912-40. *444*
—. Income (redistribution). LaFollette, Philip F. National Progressives of America. Wisconsin. 1930-38. *214*
—. Isolationism (review article). 1935-52. *582*
—. Literature. *Partisan Review* (periodical). Radicals and Radicalism. 1930's. *895*
—. Long, Huey P. Louisiana. Share Our Wealth movement. Smith, Gerald L. K. 1930's. *631*
—. Public opinion. Roosevelt, Franklin D. 1930's-40's. *255*
—. Roosevelt, Franklin D. Supreme Court. 1937. *261*

Politics and Media. American Newspaper Publishers Association. Daily Newspaper Code. Freedom of the press. National Industrial Recovery Act (1933). National Recovery Administration. 1933-34. *774*

Poll tax. Florida. Graham, Ernest. Hialeah Charter Bill. 1931-38. *195*

Poor. Attitudes. Great Britain. Law. Vagrancy. 14c-1939. *20*

—. Mecklenburg, George H. Minnesota (Minneapolis). Organized Unemployed, Inc. Self-help. 1932-35. *740*

Poor, rural. Greenbelt towns. Resettlement Administration. Tugwell, Rexford G. 1935-36. *421*

Pope, J. Ellis. Allen, DeLacey. Elections (state). Georgia. Lieutenant governors. Proposition 2. Scott, W. Fred. 1936. *156*

Popular Culture. Astaire, Fred. Films. Rogers, Ginger. 1930-39. *930*

—. California (Hollywood). Films. Photography. Publicity. 1930-39. *847*

Popular Front. American Labor Party. Communist Party. Gordon, Max (account). Politics. ca 1930-39. *758*

—. Communist Party. Culture. Intellectuals. Negroes. New York City (Harlem). 1935-39. *678*

Popular Front Against Fascism. Communist Party. Intellectuals. Literature. 1929-39. *613*

Populism. Capra, Frank. Films. *Mr. Smith Goes To Washington* (film). Politics. 1939. *881*

—. Fundamentalism. Long, Huey P. North Central States. Progressivism. Smith, Gerald L. K. 1934-48. *633*

Post, Wiley. Aeronautics. Circumnavigation (solo). Oklahoma. 1920's-35. *560*

Postal savings system. 1930's. *79*

Postal service. Air mail service. Army Air Corps. Foulois, Benjamin D. 1933-34. *348*

—. Democratic Party. O'Mahoney, Joseph C. Patronage. Roosevelt, Franklin D. Senate. Wyoming. 1916-45. *220*

Pound, Ezra ("Pithy Promulgations"). New Mexico. Santa Fe *New Mexican* (newspaper). 1935. *783*

Poverty. Federal Emergency Relief Administration. Hickok, Lorena A. Hopkins, Harry. Kentucky, eastern. 1933. *19*

—. Federal Policy. Hopkins, Harry. New Deal. Roosevelt, Franklin D. Unemployment. 1910's-38. *403*

—. Reconstruction Finance Corporation. West Virginia. 1932-33. *81*

Powers, Elmer G. (diary). Agricultural Adjustment Administration. Agriculture and Government. "Corn-hog" program. Farmers. Iowa (Boone County). 1934. *345*

—. Farmers. Iowa (Boone County). 1936. *37*

Pragmatism. Hook, Sidney (review article). Marxism. Philosophy. 1930's. *593*

Pratt, William Veazie. Chief of Naval Operations. Navies. 1930-33. *732*

Prentis, Henning Webb, Jr. Armstrong Cork Company. Business. New Deal. Pennsylvania (Lancaster). 1934-40. *514*

Preparedness. Foreign policy. Hawaii. Roosevelt, Franklin D. Works Progress Administration. 1935-40. *446*

Presidency. Education. Jackson, Robert H. Roosevelt, Franklin D. 1933-45. *271*

Presidential appointments. Bureau of Indian Affairs. Collier, John. Ickes, Harold. Interior Department. Roosevelt, Franklin D. 1933. *376*

Presidential directives. Federal Bureau of Investigation. Political activities, dissident. 1936-53. *500*

Presidential nomination. Byrd, Harry F. Democratic Party (convention). Political Campaigns. Roosevelt, Franklin D. 1932. *187*

Press. Communism. Nazism. Red Fascism analogy. Totalitarianism. 1930's. 1970's. *654*

—. Federal government. New Deal. Progressivism. Reform. 1890's-1930's. *294*

Press Conference Association. Roosevelt, Eleanor. Women. 1932-45. *266*

Press conferences. Public Opinion. Roosevelt, Franklin D. 1933-37. *268*

Prices. Agricultural Industry. Economic Regulations. Federal government. Mississippi. Texas. Voluntarism. 1925-40. *71*

—. Agriculture. Alcohol. Business. Fuel. Motors. Surpluses. 1930's. *604*

—. Cotton holiday movement. Mississippi. 1931. *107*

—. Farmers. North Dakota. Strikes. 1932. *92*

—. Grain. Livestock. McGregor Land and Livestock Company. Washington (Columbia Plateau). 1890's-82. *73*

Primaries. Democratic Party. Elections (senatorial). Missouri. New Deal. Truman, Harry S. 1934. *175*

—. Democratic Party. NAACP. Negro Suffrage. *Smith* v. *Allwright* (US, 1944). South. Supreme Court. 1890's-1944. *617*

Primaries (senatorial). Democratic Party. New Deal. Russell, Richard B. Talmadge, Eugene. 1936. *213*

Princeton Radio Research Project. Adorno, Theodor W. Culture. Lazarsfeld, Paul F. Music. Social organization. 1930's. *875*

Princeton University. "Big Three" relationship. Football. Harvard University. Ivy League. 1926-39. *924*

Prison conditions. Attica State Prison. NAACP. Negroes. New York. 1932. *751*

Private sector. Federal Reserve Board. Keynesianism. Monetary policy. New Deal. 1929-79. *6*

Probability theory. Political history. Quantitative methods. Roosevelt, Franklin D. Supreme Court. 1937. 1970's. *216*

—. Quantitative Methods. Roosevelt, Franklin D. Supreme Court. 1937. 1970's. *165*

Professionalism. Mass Media. Women. 1930's. *723*

Professions. Unemployment. 1929-35. *97*

Progressive education. California. ca 1930-40. *615*

—. Ethnicity. Race. 1929-45. *606*

—. Negroes. South. 1930-45. *605*

Progressive insurgents. New Deal. Roosevelt, Franklin D. Senate. 1935-36. *217*

Progressives. New Deal. Senate. 1933-34. *218*

Progressivism. Commerce Department. Mitchell, Ewing Young. Pendergast, Thomas J. Political machines. Roosevelt, Franklin D. 1933-36. *239*

—. Conservatism. Creel, George. New Deal. Works Progress Administration. 1900-53. *273*

—. Elections (presidential). Hoover, Herbert C. Republican Party. Senate. 1930-32. *161*

—. Federal government. New Deal. Press. Reform. 1890's-1930's. *294*

—. Feinman, Ronald L. (review article). New Deal. Republican Party. Senate. Western States. 1929-41. *199*

—. Fundamentalism. Long, Huey P. North Central States. Populism. Smith, Gerald L. K. 1934-48. *633*

—. Hearst, William Randolph. New Deal. 1930-35. *311*

—. Intellectuals. New Deal. 1930's. *272*

—. LaFollette, Philip F. New Deal. Roosevelt, Franklin D. Wisconsin Works Bill. 1935. *414*

Prohibition. Bootlegging. Florida (Hernando County). Law enforcement. Liquor. 1929-33. *562*

—. Bulkley, Robert J. Elections. Ohio. Senate. 1918-30. *256*

Prohibition repeal. Constitutional Amendments (18th and 21st). Democratic Party (convention). Raskob, John J. Roosevelt, Franklin D. 1928-33. *198*

Proletcult. Communist Party. John Reed Clubs. Literature, proletarian. 1929-35. *623*

Propaganda. Civil War. Fiction. Hemingway, Ernest *(For Whom the Bell Tolls)*. Reporters and Reporting. Spain. 1936-40. *853*

—. Communism. Films. Labor Disputes. Workers' Film and Photo League. 1930-38. *808*

Proposition 2. Allen, DeLacey. Elections (state). Georgia. Lieutenant governors. Pope, J. Ellis. Scott, W. Fred. 1936. *156*

Protestant Churches. Farm tenancy. Mississippi. Theologians, neoorthodox. 1936-40. *629*

Psychiana (religion). Correspondence courses. Idaho (Moscow). Robinson, Frank Bruce. 1929-48. *695*

Psychology. Chicago, University of (Psychology Department). Functionalism. McKinney, Fred (reminiscences). 1929-31. *669*

—. Labor. Liberalism. Society for the Psychological Study of Social Issues. 1930's. *596*

Public Administration. Bureau of Indian Affairs. Collier, John. New Deal. Social sciences principles. 1933-45. *497*

—. Douglas, Lewis. Ickes, Harold. Public Works Administration. 1933. *448*

—. Economic Policy. Fiscal policy. Keynesian Economics. 1930's. *12*

Public Finance. Modernization. Oregon (Neahkahnie Mountain). Roads. West. 1850-1977. *496*

Public health. Federal government. New Deal. 1933-39. *402*

Public housing. Bauer, Catherine. Federal Policy. Reform. Wagner-Steagall Act (US, 1937). Wood, Edith Elmer. 1890's-1940's. *292*

—. Bureaucrats. Pennsylvania (Philadelphia). 1929-41. *282*

Public opinion. Anti-Semitism. Elites. Freedom of speech. Mencken, H. L. 1917-41. *769*

—. Dreiser, Theodore. Lewis, Sinclair. Literature. Nobel Prizes. Sweden. 1920's-30. *857*

—. *Esquire* (periodical). Gingrich, Arnold. Hughes, Langston. Negroes. Publishers and Publishing. 1934. *572*

—. Ethnicity. Intellectuals. National Characteristics. 1930's. *747*

—. Louisiana (New Orleans). Street, Electric Railway and Motor Coach Employees of America. Strikes. 1929-30. *557*

—. Milles, Carl *(God of Peace)*. Minnesota (St. Paul). Myths and Symbols. Sculpture. War memorials. 1932-80. *811*

—. Pecora, Ferdinand. Senate Banking and Currency Committee. Stock Exchange (manipulation). 1933. *452*

—. Politics. Roosevelt, Franklin D. 1930's-40's. *255*

—. Press conferences. Roosevelt, Franklin D. 1933-37. *268*

Public Policy. Bethune, Mary McLeod. Equal opportunity. National Youth Administration. Negroes. Youth. 1935-44. *483*

—. Collective bargaining. Labor Unions and Organizations (membership). New Deal. 1933-45. *289*

—. Economic planning. New Deal. 1932-41. *393*

—. General Education Board. Rockefeller, John D. Secondary education. Social change. 1930's. *538*

—. Land reform. Negroes. New Deal. Resettlement. 1930's-60's. *458*

—. Public service organizations. Works Progress Administration. 1930's-70's. *463*

Public Policy (recommendations). Hoover, Herbert C. Inventions. Roosevelt, Franklin D. (administration). Technology assessment. 1930's-77. *369*

Public records. Evans, Luther H. Historical Records Survey. Iowa. Works Progress Administration. 1936-42. *334*

—. Federal Theatre Project. Negroes. Theater, black. 1930's-70's. *304*

Public Relations. Airplane Industry and Trade. Pilots. Safety. Women. 1927-40. *566*

—. Business. National Association of Manufacturers. New Deal. 1930's. *734*

—. Photography. Roosevelt, Franklin D. 1933-37. *267*

Public schools. Arkansas. Federal Aid to Education. Federal Emergency Relief Administration. Hopkins, Harry. 1933-36. *451*

—. Carbone, Peter F., Jr. (review article). Liberalism. Reform. Rugg, Harold. 1930's. *689*

—. Censorship. *Crisis* (periodical). District of Columbia. *Opportunity* (periodical). School Boards. 1936. *571*

—. Economic policy. Federal Government. Roosevelt, Franklin D. Youth. 1918-45. *279*

Public service organizations. Public policy. Works Progress Administration. 1930's-70's. *463*

Public Utilities. Alabama (Muscle Shoals). Electric Power. Tennessee (Memphis). Tennessee Valley Authority. 1880-1940. *513*

—. Bonneville Power Administration. Electric utilities. New Deal. Pacific Northwest. 1937-42. *339*

Public Welfare. California. Governors. Ralph, James, Jr. 1931-34. *16*

—. City government. Fiscal Policy. New Jersey (Paterson). Textile industry. 1920-32. *77*

—. Creel, Cecil. Democratic Party. Nevada. New Deal. Pittman, Key. Political Factions. 1933-34. *244*

—. Dust Bowl. National Recovery Administration. New Deal. Oklahoma. 1932-35. *505*

—. Federal Emergency Relief Administration. Hopkins, Harry. Letters. Rhode Island. 1934. *431*

—. Government. Hoover, Herbert C. Industry. New York (Buffalo). Unemployment. 1929-33. *64*

—. Haber, William. Michigan. National Youth Administration. Works Progress Administration. 1930's. *410*

—. Hickok, Lorena A. Reporters and Reporting. Roosevelt, Franklin D. (administration). 1913-68. *283*

—. Legislation. Political Parties (realignment). 1933-54. *479*

—. New Deal. Political Attitudes. South Dakota. 1930's-70's. *276*

—. New Deal. Roosevelt, Franklin D. State capitalism. 1929-52. *293*

—. Ohio (Toledo). 1933-37. *485*

Public welfare administration. California. Labor. ca 1930-45. *390*

Public works. Frankfurter, Felix. Keynes, John
Maynard. New Deal. 1932-35. *280*
—. Nevada (Las Vegas). New Deal. 1933-40.
417
Public Works Administration. Construction.
Employment. Ickes, Harold. Negroes. Quotas.
1933-40. *383*
—. Douglas, Lewis. Ickes, Harold.
Public Administration. 1933.
448
—. Economic Development. Employment. Texas.
1933-34. *507*
—. Federal loan. Florida (Tampa). Kreher, Ernest.
Tampa Shipbuilding and Engineering Company.
1932-37. *401*
Public Works of Art Project. Art and State. New
Deal. New Jersey. 1932-40. *519*
Public works programs, global. Economic policy.
Foreign Policy. New Deal. Roosevelt, Franklin
D. 1933. *419*
Publicity. California (Hollywood). Films.
Photography. Popular Culture. 1930-39. *847*
Publishers and Publishing. *American Mercury*
(periodical). Conroy, Jack. Mencken, H. L.
1930-33. *910*
—. *Esquire* (periodical). Gingrich, Arnold.
Hughes, Langston. Negroes. Public Opinion.
1934. *572*
Pueblo Indians. Agriculture and Government.
Indian-White Relations. New Deal. New
Mexico. 1938-48. *503*
Pulitzer, Joseph, II. Advertising. Censorship.
Missouri. Newspapers. St. Louis *Post Dispatch.*
1929-39. *893*
Puritanism. Allen, Frederick Lewis *(Only
Yesterday).* Historiography. Journalism.
Liberalism. 1931. *858*

Q

Quantitative Methods. Democratic Party. New
Deal. Pennsylvania (Pittsburgh). Political
Theory. Voting and Voting Behavior.
Wisconsin. 1912-40. *228*
—. Political history. Probability theory. Roosevelt,
Franklin D. Supreme Court. 1937. 1970's.
216
—. Probability Theory. Roosevelt, Franklin D.
Supreme Court. 1937. 1970's. *165*
Quotas. Construction. Employment. Ickes, Harold.
Negroes. Public Works Adminstration. 1933-40.
383

R

Race. Class consciousness. NAACP. Negroes.
Pennsylvania (Philadelphia). 1930's. *684*
—. Ethnicity. Progressive education. 1929-45.
606
Race Relations. Alabama. Rape, alleged.
Scottsboro case. Trials. 1931-49. *729*
—. Arizona (Salt River Valley). Farmers. Japanese
Americans. 1934-35. *529*
—. Baseball, semiprofessional. Negroes. North
Dakota (Dickinson). Otto, Solomon
(reminiscences). 1929-31. *889*
—. Hollins, Jess. International Labor Defense.
NAACP. Oklahoma. Rape. Trials. 1931-36.
659
Racism. Alabama (Scottsboro). Historiography.
Myths and Symbols. Trials. 1931-80. *742*
—. Anti-Nazi sentiments. Boxing. Louis, Joe.
Schmeling, Max. 1930's. *801*
—. California (Watsonville). Filipino Americans.
Riots. Violence. 1926-30. *577*

—. Discrimination, Employment. Georgia (Atlanta).
Labor. Women. 1930's. *539*
Racism, issue of. Boycotts, proposed. Germany
(Berlin). Olympic Games. 1933-36. *843*
Radical literary movement. Communism. Folsom,
Michael. Gold, Mike. Literature. 1914-37.
941
Radical Religion (periodical). Capitalism. Marxism.
Niebuhr, Reinhold. Roosevelt, Franklin D.
(administration). 1930-43. *532*
Radicals and Radicalism. American Federation of
Labor. Communist Party. Labor Unions and
Organizations. Trade Union Unity League.
1933-35. *569*
—. Amlie, Thomas R. (political career). New Deal.
Roosevelt, Franklin D. Wisconsin. 1930-39.
704
—. Artists. Organizations. 1930's. *938*
—. Capitalism. Political Attitudes. Texas. 1929-33.
128
—. Colleges and Universities. Education,
Experimental Methods (review article). 1930's.
735
—. Great Plains. State Politics. 1930-36. *190*
—. Idaho, University of, Southern Branch.
Roosevelt, Franklin D. Student protest. 1930's.
731
—. Labor organizations. Michigan (Detroit).
1920's-30's. *656*
—. Labor policy. New Deal. Working class.
1930's. *627*
—. Labor Unions and Organizations. New Deal.
1930-39. *653*
—. Literature. *Partisan Review* (periodical).
Politics. 1930's. *895*
—. Muste, Abraham J. Unemployed Leagues.
1932-36. *706*
—. Unemployed councils. 1929-33. *705*
Radio. Advertising. Carter, Boake. Military.
News. Political Commentary. 1931-38. *803*
—. Allen, Fred. Bureaucracies. Commercialism.
Criticism. Humor. 1932-49. *824*
—. *Amos 'n Andy* (program). Boycotts. Comic
strips. Negroes. Stereotypes. 1930's. *719*
—. *Amos 'n Andy* (program). Humor. Social
Problems. 1929-30's. *945*
—. Anti-Semitism. Boxerman, William I. Coughlin,
Charles. Jewish Community Council. Michigan
(Detroit). 1939. *725*
—. Behavior. Welles, Orson. Wells, H. G. *(War of
the Worlds).* 1938. *876*
—. Carter, Boake. New Deal. News commentator.
Political criticism. Roosevelt, Franklin D.
1935-38. *790*
—. Editorials. Newspapers. *War of the Worlds*
(broadcast). Welles, Orson. 1938. *951*
—. Family. Folklore. Values. *Vic and Sade*
(program). Women. 1932-46. *96*
—. Federal Communications Commission. Federal
Radio Commission. Sykes, Eugene O. 1927-39.
412
—. Illinois (Chicago). 1930-40. *943*
—. *Lone Ranger* (program). Michigan (Detroit).
WXYZ (station). 1933-34. *887*
—. *March of Time* (series). News, dramatization of.
Smith, Fred. 1928-45. *856*
—. News commentator. Social history. Swing,
Raymond Gram. 1930's. *791*
Radio broadcasts. Brecht, Bertolt. Lindbergh,
Charles A. (tribute). Music. Weill, Kurt.
1929-31. *849*
Radio City Music Hall. Art deco. Deskey, Donald.
Genauer, Emily (account). Interior decorating.
New York City. 1929-37. *815*
Radio equipment. Aeronautics. Circumnavigation,
attempted. Earhart, Amelia. 1937. *819*
Railroads. Buildings. Cincinnati Union Terminal.
Moore, Alfred. Ohio. 1933-73. *933*

Rainey, Henry T. House of Representatives (speaker of). 1932-33. *262*

Ralph, James, Jr. California. Governors. Public Welfare. 1931-34. *16*

Ranchers. Agricultural Labor. Farmers. Industrial Workers of the World. Labor Disputes. Washington (Yakima Valley). 1910-36. *685*

—. Federal Government. Homesteading and Homesteaders (failure of). Montana. 1900-30. *32*

Rape. Capital Punishment. Negroes. Newspapers. Reporters and Reporting. Scottsboro Case. Trials. 1931-32. *697*

—. Hollins, Jess. International Labor Defense. NAACP. Oklahoma. Race Relations. Trials. 1931-36. *659*

Rape, alleged. Alabama. Race Relations. Scottsboro case. Trials. 1931-49. *729*

Raskob, John J. Constitutional Amendments (18th and 21st). Democratic Party (convention). Prohibition repeal. Roosevelt, Franklin D. 1928-33. *198*

Rawick, George P. Federal Writers' Project. Genovese, Eugene D. Interviews. Methodology. Slavery. 1930's. 1970's. *484*

Rawick, George P. (review essay). Ex-slaves, interviews with. Historical sources. Slavery. 19c. 1930's. *515*

Rayburn, Sam. Democratic Party (convention). Garner, John Nance. Roosevelt, Franklin D. 1932. *224*

—. Executive Power (restrictions). House of Representatives. Logan-Walter Bill (vetoed, 1939). Sumners, Hatton. Texas. 1939. *438*

Realism. Agee, James *(Let Us Now Praise Famous Men)*. Daily Life. Literature. 1930-41. *846*

Recall. California (Los Angeles). City Government. Clinton, Clifford. Shaw, Frank. 1938. *189*

Recessions. Currie, Lauchlin. Economic Theory. 1932-38. *21*

Reclamation of Land. Drainage districts. Wyoming. 1888-1939. *25*

Reconstruction Finance Corporation. Banking. Federal government. Hoover, Herbert C. Nevada. 1932-33. *83*

—. Banking. Idaho (Boise). 1932. *80*

—. Banking crisis. Michigan. 1933. *54*

—. Couch, Harvey C. 1932-34. *427*

—. Poverty. West Virginia. 1932-33. *81*

Recordings. Historical sources. Music (blues). Negroes. Oral History. Social Conditions. 1924-41. *888*

Red Cross. Food relief. Hoover, Herbert C. Wheat, surplus. 1932-33. *61*

Red Fascism analogy. Communism. Nazism. Press. Totalitarianism. 1930's. 1970's. *654*

Red River Bridge Company. Bridges (toll, free). Interstate relations. Oklahoma National Guard. Texas Rangers. 1931. *30*

Referendum. Advertising. Allen, Laurence. Allen, Willis. California Life Payments Plan. Economic structure. Noble, Robert. Pensions. 1937-39. *755*

Reform. Bauer, Catherine. Federal Policy. Public housing. Wagner-Steagall Act (US, 1937). Wood, Edith Elmer. 1890's-1940's. *292*

—. Braeman, John (review article). Historiography. New Deal. State government. 1930's-40's. *382*

—. Carbone, Peter F., Jr. (review article). Liberalism. Public Schools. Rugg, Harold. 1930's. *689*

—. Federal government. New Deal. Press. Progressivism. 1890's-1930's. *294*

—. Historiography (revisionist). Liberalism. Roosevelt, Franklin D. Truman, Harry S. 1932-53. 1960-75. *227*

—. Long, Huey P. New Deal (criticism of). 1933-35. *315*

—. New Deal. Roosevelt, Franklin D. 1900-33. *299*

Refugees. Germany. Jews. Relief organizations. World War II. 1933-45. *602*

Regionalism. Louisiana. Novels. Plantation life. Saxon, Lyle *(Children of Strangers)*. 1920's-40's. *932*

Relativism. Culture, concept of. Economic theory. Intellectual trends. Theology. 1930's. *883*

Relief, federal. Louisiana Emergency Relief Administration. Sources. 1933-35. 1973. *368*

Relief funds. Farmers. Nebraska. New Deal. Norris, George W. 1933-36. *397*

Relief organizations. Germany. Jews. Refugees. World War II. 1933-45. *602*

Relief work. California (Santa Barbara). Fleischmann, Max. Philanthropy. Unemployment. 1930-32. *78*

Religion. Democracy. Liberals. Niebuhr, Reinhold. 1930-45. *598*

—. Elections (presidential). Ethnic groups. Roosevelt, Franklin D. Social Classes. 1940. *192*

Reno, Milo. Agriculture. Politics. Wallace, Henry A. 1932-33. *466*

Reorganized United Mine Workers of America. Labor Unions and Organizations. Lewis, John L. 1920-33. *559*

Repatriation. Discrimination. Indiana (Gary). Mexican Americans. Nativism. 1920's-30's. *537*

—. Hoover administration. Mexicans. 1930's. *57*

—. Indiana (East Chicago). Mexican Americans. 1919-33. *100*

Reporters and Reporting. Anti-Semitism. Germany. Nazism. *New York Times.* 1932-33. *749*

—. Capital Punishment. Negroes. Newspapers. Rape. Scottsboro Case. Trials. 1931-32. *697*

—. Civil War. Fiction. Hemingway, Ernest *(For Whom the Bell Tolls)*. Propaganda. Spain. 1936-40. *853*

—. Hickok, Lorena A. Public Welfare. Roosevelt, Franklin D. (administration). 1913-68. *283*

Republican Party. Aiken, George D. Flood control. Governors. Political Campaigns (presidential). Vermont. 1937-39. *235*

—. Aiken, George D. Political Campaigns (gubernatorial). Vermont. 1933-36. *184*

—. Andersen, Kristi. Democratic Party. Partisanship. Voting and Voting Behavior. 1920-32. *229*

—. Conservatism. New Deal. New York. Snell, Bertrand H. 1933-39. *139*

—. Democratic Party. Elections, congressional. Garner, John Nance. Hoover, Herbert C. House of Representatives. 1930-31. *258*

—. Democratic Party. Missouri. Political coalitions. Roosevelt, Franklin D. 1936-52. *246*

—. Democratic Party. Political Campaigns (presidential). 1936. *248*

—. Elections, congressional. New Deal. Roosevelt, Franklin D. 1937-38. *226*

—. Elections (presidential). Hoover, Herbert C. Progressivism. 1930-32. *161*

—. Feinman, Ronald L. (review article). New Deal. Progressivism. Senate. Western States. 1929-41. *199*

—. Government regulation. Neoconservatism. New Deal. Political Leadership. Social security. 1936-40. *209*

—. Hoover, Herbert C. New Deal. Political Commentary. 1933-35. *141*

—. Hoover, Herbert C. (administration). Negroes. 1928-32. *168*
—. Hoover, Herbert C. (party politics). 1920-32. *219*
Republican Party (conference, proposed). Hoover, Herbert C. Landon, Alfred M. Political Leadership. 1937-38. *140*
Republican Party, fission in the. Negroes. Ohio. 1920-32. *170*
Research. Biochemistry. Isotopes. Schoenheimer, Rudolf. 1934-41. *640*
—. Consumerism. Lynd, Robert S. Sociology. 1930's. *105*
Resettlement. Cumberland Homesteads. Fairfield Glade. Housing. New Deal. Tennessee. 1934-80. *482*
—. Land reform. Negroes. New Deal. Public Policy. 1930's-60's. *458*
Resettlement Administration. Greenbelt towns. Poor, rural. Tugwell, Rexford G. 1935-36. *421*
—. New Deal. Rural Development. Texas (Ropesville). 1933-43. *372*
Resettlement Administration (music program). Appalachia. Leftism. Mountaineers. Music. Seeger, Charles. Social Organization. 1935-37. *506*
Resettlement projects. Agricultural Reform. Clawson, Marion (report). Economic conditions. Farm Security Administration. 1935-43. *317*
Reuther, Victor G. (review article). Reuther, Walter P. United Automobile Workers of America. 1930's. 1976. *637*
Reuther, Walter P. Reuther, Victor G. (review article). United Automobile Workers of America. 1930's. 1976. *637*
Rhetoric. Communist Party. Pamphlets. 1929-39. *553*
—. Documentaries, historical. Films. Ideology. 1930's. *906*
—. Inaugural Addresses. Moley, Raymond. Roosevelt, Franklin D. 1933. *233*
Rhode Island. Federal Emergency Relief Administration. Hopkins, Harry. Letters. Public Welfare. 1934. *431*
Rich, Carroll Y. Barrow, Clyde. Ford automobile. Gangster myth. Parker, Bonnie. Warren, Jesse. 1934-67. *957*
Richards, Ivor Armstrong. Agee, James *(Let Us Now Praise Famous Men)*. Language. Literary criticism. 1930-40. *833*
Rider, Keith. Aeronautics. R-6 (aircraft). 1936-37. *852*
Rider R-3 (aircraft). Air races. Bradley Air Museum. Connecticut. 1930's-70's. *922*
Riots. California (Watsonville). Filipino Americans. Racism. Violence. 1926-30. *577*
Ritchie, Albert C. Federal assistance (opposition to). Maryland (Baltimore). State Government. 1929-33. *56*
Ritchie, Donald A. Brandeis, Louis D. Dawson, Nelson L. Frankfurter, Felix. Landis, James M. Law. New Deal (review article). 1930's. *512*
Rivera, Diego. New York City. Painting. Rockefeller Center. 1933. *912*
Roads. Modernization. Oregon (Neahkahnie Mountain). Public Finance. West. 1850-1977. *496*
Robinson, Bill "Bojangles". Dance. Entertainers. Negroes. 1930's-49. *868*
Robinson, Frank Bruce. Correspondence courses. Idaho (Moscow). Psychiana (religion). 1929-48. *695*
Roche, Josephine. Coal Mines and Mining. Colorado. Labor reform. Roosevelt, Franklin D. (administration). Social work. 1886-1976. *365*

Rockefeller Center. New York City. Painting. Rivera, Diego. 1933. *912*
Rockefeller, John D. General Education Board. Public policy. Secondary education. Social change. 1930's. *538*
Rodgers, Jimmie. Music, country. 1927-33. *770*
Rogers, Ginger. Astaire, Fred. Films. Popular Culture. 1930-39. *930*
Roosevelt, Eleanor. Clapp, Elsie Ripley. Education, community. Homesteading and Homesteaders. New Deal. West Virginia (Arthurdale). 1933-44. *285*
—. Miners (resettlement of). National Industrial Recovery Act (1933). New Deal. Subsistence Homesteads Program. West Virginia (Arthurdale). 1930-46. *320*
—. Press Conference Association. Women. 1932-45. *266*
Roosevelt, Franklin D. 1882-1945. *137*
—. Agricultural Policy. Corporatism, concept of. Hoover, Herbert C. Politics. 1929-33. *27*
—. Agricultural Policy. Great Plains. Shelterbelts. Trees. 1934-44. *486*
—. Agriculture. Letters. Mississippi. 1932-33. *95*
—. Air Mail Service. Contracts. Merchant Marine. Ocean mail service. 1933-37. *488*
—. Alabama. Clergy. New Deal. 1935-36. *290*
—. Alienation. Intellectuals. Jews. Leftism. New Deal. 1930's. *757*
—. All-Party Agricultural Committee. Farmers. Great Plains. North Central States. Political Campaigns (presidential). 1936. *254*
—. Amlie, Thomas R. (political career). New Deal. Radicals and Radicalism. Wisconsin. 1930-39. *704*
—. Andersen, Kristi. Blumberg, Barbara. Fine, Sidney. Jeffries, John W. New Deal (review article). Swain, Martha H. 1933-39. *143*
—. Anti-Imperialism. Foreign Policy (critics). Pacific Area. World War II (antecedents). 1930's. *692*
—. Arkansas. Bank holiday. Business. 1933. *126*
—. Assassination. Cermak, Anton. Florida (Miami). Zangara, Giuseppi. 1933. *152*
—. Assassination, attempted. Florida (Miami). Zangara, Giuseppi. 1933. *231*
—. Austin, Warren R. Foreign Policy. Neutrality Act, 1939 (proposed). Senate. 1935-39. *759*
—. Baltimore *Sun*, *Evening Sun* (newspapers). Government intervention. Letters-to-the-editor. Maryland. 1929-33. *384*
—. Bank of America. California. Elections (gubernatorial). Giannini, Amadeo P. Merriam, Frank. Sinclair, Upton. ca 1923-34. *138*
—. Barkley, Alben W. Democratic Party. Senate (majority leader). Supreme Court (issue). 1937. *153*
—. Beard, Charles A. Historians. Intellectuals. Isolationism. Liberalism. New Deal. 1932-48. *296*
—. Braeman, John (review article). New Deal (policies, programs). Politics. 1930's. *399*
—. Brandeis, Louis D. Frankfurter, Felix. New Deal. Politics. World War I. 1917-33. *154*
—. Bureau of Indian Affairs. Collier, John. Ickes, Harold. Interior Department. Presidential appointments. 1933. *376*
—. Byrd, Harry F. Democratic Party. Elections (presidential). State Politics. Virginia. 1932. *260*
—. Byrd, Harry F. Democratic Party. Glass, Carter. Senate. Virginia. 1938. *183*
—. Byrd, Harry F. Democratic Party (convention). Political Campaigns. Presidential nomination. 1932. *187*

—. Carter, Boake. New Deal. News commentator. Political criticism. Radio. 1935-38. *790*

—. Civil Rights. Federal Bureau of Investigation. 1936-80. *288*

—. Clergy. Massachusetts. New Deal. Social problems. 1933-36. *291*

—. Commerce Department. Mitchell, Ewing Young. Pendergast, Thomas J. Political machines. Progressivism. 1933-36. *239*

—. Congress. Federal Regulation. Ickes, Harold. Oil Industry and Trade. 1933. *388*

—. Congress. New Deal. Political attitudes. Tennessee. 1933-40. *148*

—. Congress. New Deal. Social Security Act (US, 1935). Unemployment insurance. 1934-35. *277*

—. Congress. New Deal. South Dakota. 1933. *312*

—. Congress. Norris, George W. Supreme Court (issue). 1937. *207*

—. Congress of Industrial Organizations. Elections (presidential). Labor Non-Partisan League. Pennsylvania. 1936. *252*

—. Congressmen. New Deal. Politics. Virginia. Woodrum, Clifton A. 1922-45. *236*

—. Congressmen, conservative. Democratic Party. George, Walter F. Political Change. 1938. *145*

—. Conservatism. Economy Act (US, 1933). Fiscal Policy. New Deal. 1932-36. *462*

—. Constitutional Amendments (18th and 21st). Democratic Party (convention). Prohibition repeal. Raskob, John J. 1928-33. *198*

—. Cutting, Bronson M. Democratic Party. New Mexico. Political Campaigns. Senate. 1934. *269*

—. Democracy. Inaugural addresses. Political Speeches. Values. 1901-77. *164*

—. Democratic Party. Domestic Policy. Internationalism. New Deal. Political Campaigns. 1938-40. *160*

—. Democratic Party. Elections (presidential). Iowa. 1932. *172*

—. Democratic Party. Elections (presidential). Massachusetts. Smith, Al. 1928-32. *178*

—. Democratic Party. Georgia. New Deal. Talmadge, Eugene. 1926-38. *146*

—. Democratic Party. Gillette, Guy M. House of Representatives. Iowa. Political Campaigns. 1932-48. *185*

—. Democratic Party. Hague, Frank. New Deal. New Jersey. 1932-40. *155*

—. Democratic Party. Higgins, Andrew J. Political Campaigns (presidential). 1944. *212*

—. Democratic Party. Missouri. Pendergast, Thomas J. Political Conventions. State Politics. 1932. *238*

—. Democratic Party. Missouri. Political coalitions. Republican Party. 1936-52. *246*

—. Democratic Party. O'Mahoney, Joseph C. Patronage. Postal Service. Senate. Wyoming. 1916-45. *220*

—. Democratic Party (Colored Voters Division). Good Neighbor League Colored Committee. Negroes. Political Campaigns (presidential). 1936. *251*

—. Democratic Party (convention). Garner, John Nance. Rayburn, Sam. 1932. *224*

—. Domestic Policy. Elections (presidential). Foreign policy. Lewis, John L. 1936-40. *230*

—. Domestic Policy. Foreign Policy. 1920-79. *247*

—. Domestic Policy. Foreign policy. 1933-36. *460*

—. Douglas, Lewis. Economic Policy. New Deal. 1933-34. *461*

—. Economic conditions. Elections (presidential). Hoover, Herbert C. Political Parties. South Dakota. 1932. *176*

—. Economic conditions. Foreman, Clark Howell. National Emergency Council (report). Politics. South. 1938. *24*

—. Economic policy. Federal Government. Public Schools. Youth. 1918-45. *279*

—. Economic policy. Foreign Policy. New Deal. Public works programs, global. 1933. *419*

—. Economic policy. Freidel, Frank (review article). New Deal. Political leadership. 1930's. *147*

—. Economic Reform. Fisher, Irving. 1930's. *1*

—. Education. Jackson, Robert H. Presidency. 1933-45. *271*

—. Elections, congressional. New Deal. Republican Party. 1937-38. *226*

—. Elections (presidential). Ethnic groups. Religion. Social Classes. 1940. *192*

—. Elections (presidential). German Americans. Iowa. 1936-40. *234*

—. Elections (presidential). Hoover, Herbert C. Missouri. 1932. *177*

—. Elections (presidential). Long, Huey P. Share Our Wealth movement. 1932-36. *245*

—. Employment. Minorities in Politics. Negroes. New Deal. 1930-42. *470*

—. Executive Power (expansion). 1933-45. *243*

—. Fascism. Italy. Monetary policy. Mussolini, Benito. New Deal. 1922-36. *433*

—. Federal Policy. Hopkins, Harry. New Deal. Poverty. Unemployment. 1910's-38. *403*

—. Federal programs. State Legislatures. 1933-70's. *391*

—. Foreign policy. Hawaii. Preparedness. Works Progress Administration. 1935-40. *446*

—. Foreign Policy. International Labor Organization. Isolationism. New Deal. Perkins, Frances. 1921-34. *429*

—. Foreign policy. Isolationism. Political Leadership. Senate. World Court. 1935. *194*

—. Fortas, Abe. Interior Department. Lawyers. Letters. Peres, Hardwig. 1930-44. *373*

—. Frankfurter, Felix. Lippmann, Walter. New Deal. World War II. 1932-45. *432*

—. Garner, John Nance. New Deal policies. 1933-38. *225*

—. Georgia (Warm Springs). Henderson, F. P. Marines. 1937. *188*

—. Harrison, Byron Patton (Pat). Mississippi. Political friendship. 1920-41. *259*

—. Hickok, Lorena A. Hopkins, Harry. New Deal. Ohio. Unemployment. 1934-36. *489*

—. Historiography (revisionist). Liberalism. Reform. Truman, Harry S. 1932-53. 1960-75. *227*

—. Idaho, University of, Southern Branch. Radicals and Radicalism. Student protest. 1930's. *731*

—. Illinois (Chicago). Kelly, Edward J. New Deal. Political machines. 1932-40. *193*

—. Inaugural Addresses. Moley, Raymond. Rhetoric. 1933. *233*

—. Johnson, Hiram. New Deal. 1920's-41. *180*

—. LaFollette, Philip F. New Deal. Progressivism. Wisconsin Works Bill. 1935. *414*

—. Leftism. New Deal. 1933-79. *535*

—. Montana. Political Attitudes. Senate. Wheeler, Burton K. 1904-46. *232*

—. New Deal. New Hampshire. Political Campaigns (presidential). 1936. *253*

—. New Deal. Pennsylvania (Avondale). Political Commentary. Sullivan, Mark. 1924-52. *305*

—. New Deal. Progressive insurgents. Senate. 1935-36. *217*

—. New Deal. Public Welfare. State capitalism. 1929-52. *293*

—. New Deal. Reform. 1900-33. *299*

—. New York. Pell, Herbert. Political Campaigns (presidential). Upper Classes. 1936. *142*

—. Photography. Public Relations. 1933-37. *267*

—. Political history. Probability theory. Quantitative methods. Supreme Court. 1937. 1970's. *216*

—. Politics. Public opinion. 1930's-40's. *255*

—. Politics. Supreme Court. 1937. *261*

—. Press conferences. Public Opinion. 1933-37. *268*

—. Probability Theory. Quantitative Methods. Supreme Court. 1937. 1970's. *165*

Roosevelt, Franklin D. (administration). Agricultural Reform. Catholic Church. New Deal. Social Theory. 1933-39. *473*

—. Alien Property Custodian. Banking. Crowley, Leo T. Federal Deposit Insurance Corporation. Politics. 1934-45. *510*

—. Antitrust. Appellate Courts. Arnold, Thurman W. Justice Department. 1935-43. *415*

—. Autobiography. Douglas, William O. (review article). Judges. 1933-39. 1974. *337*

—. Banking. Monetary policy. New Deal. Warburg, James P. 1932-41. *413*

—. Benefactor-aversion hypothesis. Local government. Nixon, Richard M. (administration). State Government. 1969-74. *392*

—. Capitalism. Marxism. Niebuhr, Reinhold. *Radical Religion* (periodical). 1930-43. *532*

—. Carter, Jimmy (administration). Executive reorganization. 1937-38. 1977-78. *437*

—. China. Congress. International Trade. Lobbying. Silver Purchase Act (1934). 1934. *341*

—. City Politics. Massachusetts (Boston). New Deal. Trout, Charles H. (review article). 1929-39. 1977. *157*

—. Coal Mines and Mining. Colorado. Labor reform. Roche, Josephine. Social work. 1886-1976. *365*

—. Collier, John. Federal Government. Indians. Liberalism. Truman, Harry S. (administration). 1933-53. *380*

—. Commerce Department (Business Advisory Council). Committee for Economic Development. Keynesianism. New Deal. Scholars. 1933-42. *319*

—. Communist Party. 1933-39. *728*

—. Communist Party. Policymaking. 1933-45. *534*

—. Economic policy. Foreign Relations. 1933-34. *386*

—. Environment. Films. Lorentz, Pare. New Deal. Westward movement. 1936-40. *905*

—. Foreign policy. Isolationism. Johnson, Hiram. Nye Committee. ca 1933-34. *576*

—. Hickok, Lorena A. Public Welfare. Reporters and Reporting. 1913-68. *283*

—. Hoover, Herbert C. Inventions. Public Policy (recommendations). Technology assessment. 1930's-77. *369*

—. Social Security Act (US, 1935). ca 1933-37. *325*

Roosevelt, Franklin D. (election). Chisum, Melvin J. Journalism. Negroes. *Tribune* (newspaper). ca 1932. *892*

Roosevelt, Franklin D. (programs). Conservatism. Davidson, Donald. South. Tennessee Valley Authority. 1930's. *474*

Roper, Elmo. Attitudes. New Deal. Socialism, failure of. Working class. 1939. *743*

Rosqvist, August. Democratic Party. Idaho. New Deal. Pocatello Central Labor Union. 1930-36. *494*

Roth, Henry (*Call It Sleep*). Literature. Myths and Symbols. Symbolism. 1934. *901*

Route 66. Dust Bowl. Migration, Internal. Oklahoma. Southwest. 1930's. *88*

Roy Earle, fictional character. Bogart, Humphrey. Films, gangster. *High Sierra* (film). 1930's-41. *762*

Rubber industry. Ohio (Akron). Strikes, sit-down. 1934-38. *683*

Rudwick, Elliot. Communist Party. Glabermann, Martin. Keeran, Roger. Labor Unions and Organizations. Meier, August. Negroes. United Automobile Workers of America (review article). 1930's-40's. *651*

Rugg, Harold. Carbone, Peter F., Jr. (review article). Liberalism. Public Schools. Reform. 1930's. *689*

Rural areas. Charities. Children's Aid Society. Maryland (Carroll County). 1928-35. *66*

Rural Development *See also* Agriculture, Farmers.

—. Agriculture. South. 1930-80. *324*

—. New Deal. Resettlement Administration. Texas (Ropesville). 1933-43. *372*

Rural Electrification Administration. Arkansas Light and Power Company. Electrification, rural. 1933-40. *301*

—. Branson, Eugene C. Electric Power. North Carolina. Poe, Clarence H. State Government. 1917-36. *302*

—. Conservation of Natural Resources. Cooke, Morris L. New Deal. 1933-51. *316*

Rural financial crisis. Bank failures. Credit overextension. Economic Conditions. 1920's. *49*

Rural life movement. Catholic Church. Farm programs. New Deal. 1930's. *721*

Rural rehabilitation. Alaska (Palmer). Defense. Works Progress Administration. 1935-40. *445*

Rural-urban issues. Baseball. *Sporting News* (newspaper). 1920's-30's. *789*

Russell, Richard B. Democratic Party. New Deal. Primaries (senatorial). Talmadge, Eugene. 1936. *213*

R-6 (aircraft). Aeronautics. Rider, Keith. 1936-37. *852*

S

Safety. Airplane Industry and Trade. Pilots. Public Relations. Women. 1927-40. *566*

St. Louis *Post Dispatch*. Advertising. Censorship. Missouri. Newspapers. Pulitzer, Joseph, II. 1929-39. *893*

Salazar Viniegra, Leopold. Diplomacy. Drug Abuse. Law enforcement. Mexico. 1936-40. *745*

Salzman, Jack. Bergonzi, Bernard. Literature (review article). Spender, Stephen. Zanderer, Leo. ca 1930-39. 1978-79. *775*

Sam Spade (fictional character). California (San Francisco). Hammett, Dashiell. Novels, detective. 1920-30's. *866*

—. Hammett, Dashiell. Literature. Marxism. Novels (detective). 1930's. *862*

San Francisco *Chronicle* (newspaper). Air Mail Service (private). Contracts. Editorials. 1934. *690*

San Francisco (film). Films (musicals). *Show Boat* (film). 1936. *917*

Sandoz, Mari. Literature. Violence. 1935-37. *947*

Santa Fe *New Mexican* (newspaper). New Mexico. Pound, Ezra ("Pithy Promulgations"). 1935. *783*

Santayana, George. Hook, Sidney. Letters. Totalitarianism. 1929-38. *832*

Satire. Antidemocratism. Cynicism. Journalism. Mencken, H. L. 1920's-56. *914*

Saturday Evening Post (periodical). Fiction. Stereotypes. Women. 1931-36. *831*

Saxon, Lyle. Dillard University. Federal Writers' Project. Folklore. *Gumbo Ya-Ya* (publication). Louisiana. Negroes. 1930's. *318*

Saxon, Lyle *(Children of Strangers)*. Louisiana. Novels. Plantation life. Regionalism. 1920's-40's. *932*

Scarlett O'Hara (character). Mitchell, Margaret. Sex roles. Women. 1936-39. *877*

Scharf, Lois (review article). Employment. Feminism. Women. 1929-39. *709*

Schlatter, Richard (account). Communist Party. Harvard University. 1930's. *714*

Schmeling, Max. Anti-Nazi sentiments. Boxing. Louis, Joe. Racism. 1930's. *801*

—. Boxing. Germany. Louis, Joe. Nazism. Negroes. 1936-38. *784*

Schoenheimer, Rudolf. Biochemistry. Isotopes. Research. 1934-41. *640*

Scholars. Commerce Department (Business Advisory Council). Committee for Economic Development. Keynesianism. New Deal. Roosevelt, Franklin D. (administration). 1933-42. *319*

School Boards. Censorship. *Crisis* (periodical). District of Columbia. *Opportunity* (periodical). Public schools. 1936. *571*

School integration. Civil rights activity. Illinois (Chicago). Negroes. 1936. *624*

Schools. New Jersey (Union Township). Taxpayers Association. 1929-38. *15*

Schools, rural. Farmers. Meat preservation. North Dakota (Kidder County). Oil Industry and Trade. Wick family (interview). 1900's-30's. *112*

Schwartz, Anna. Economic History. Friedman, Milton. Temin, Peter. 1894-1938. 1963-76. *69*

Science Advisory Board. New Deal. 1933-35. *491*

Science fiction. Lovecraft, H. P. Vermont (Windham County). 1931. *946*

Scott, W. Fred. Allen, DeLacey. Elections (state). Georgia. Lieutenant governors. Pope, J. Ellis. Proposition 2. 1936. *156*

Scottsboro Case. Alabama. NAACP. Norris, Clarence. Pardon request. 1931-76. *657*

—. Alabama. Race Relations. Rape, alleged. Trials. 1931-49. *729*

—. Capital Punishment. Negroes. Newspapers. Rape. Reporters and Reporting. Trials. 1931-32. *697*

Screenplays. Films (review article). *Gold Diggers of 1933* (film). Hove, Arthur. Kawin, Bruce F. *To Have and Have Not* (film). 1930's-44. *911*

Scribner's Magazine (periodical). Literature. Wolfe, Thomas. 1929-40. *830*

Scriptwriting. Authors. Dardis, Tom. Films. Hollywood. 1936-45. 1976. *919*

Sculpture. Milles, Carl *(God of Peace)*. Minnesota (St. Paul). Myths and Symbols. Public Opinion. War memorials. 1932-80. *811*

Sears, Roebuck and Company. Business. Conservatism. Isolationism. New Deal. Wood, Robert E. 1928-50's. *581*

Secondary education. General Education Board. Public policy. Rockefeller, John D. Social change. 1930's. *538*

Sectionalism. Agriculture (legislation). Senate farm bloc. 1921-33. *221*

Securities Exchange Act of 1934. Economic Regulations. New Deal. Stock market. 1934. *287*

Seeger, Charles. Appalachia. Leftism. Mountaineers. Music. Resettlement Administration (music program). Social Organization. 1935-37. *506*

Segregation. Civilian Conservation Corps. Oklahoma (Tulsa, Oklahoma City). Urban programs. 1930's. *364*

Segregation, sexual. Labor force. Women. 1930's. *671*

Self-help. Dix, I. F. Hoover, Herbert C. Local politics. Unemployed Citizens' League. Washington (Seattle). 1931-32. *75*

—. Mecklenburg, George H. Minnesota (Minneapolis). Organized Unemployed, Inc. Poor. 1932-35. *740*

Self-perception. Unemployment. Working Class. 1920's-30's. *116*

Sells-Floto Circus. Breach of contract. Lawsuits. Miller, Zack. Mix, Tom. Verbal agreements. 101 Ranch Real Wild West Show. 1929-34. *819*

Senate. Agricultural Adjustment Administration. New Deal. North Carolina. Virginia. 1933-39. *366*

—. Austin, Warren R. Foreign Policy. Neutrality Act, 1939 (proposed). Roosevelt, Franklin D. 1935-39. *759*

—. Bulkley, Robert J. Elections. Ohio. Prohibition. 1918-30. *256*

—. Byrd, Harry F. Democratic Party. Glass, Carter. Roosevelt, Franklin D. Virginia. 1938. *183*

—. Byrd, Harry F. Democratic Party. Patronage. Virginia. 1935-39. *196*

—. China. International Trade. Pittman, Key. Silver Purchase Act (1934). 1933-40. *472*

—. Cutting, Bronson M. Democratic Party. New Mexico. Political Campaigns. Roosevelt, Franklin D. 1934. *269*

—. Democratic Party. O'Mahoney, Joseph C. Patronage. Postal Service. Roosevelt, Franklin D. Wyoming. 1916-45. *220*

—. Elections (presidential). Hoover, Herbert C. Progressivism. Republican Party. 1930-32. *161*

—. Feinman, Ronald L. (review article). New Deal. Progressivism. Republican Party. Western States. 1929-41. *199*

—. Foreign policy. Isolationism. Political Leadership. Roosevelt, Franklin D. World Court. 1935. *194*

—. Harrison, Byron Patton (Pat). Social Security Act (US, 1935). 1934-35. *492*

—. Holt, Rush Dew (papers). New Deal. West Virginia. 1920-55. *171*

—. Monetary Act (US, 1939). Pittman, Key. Silver. 1939. *440*

—. Montana. Political Attitudes. Roosevelt, Franklin D. Wheeler, Burton K. 1904-46. *232*

—. New Deal. Progressive insurgents. Roosevelt, Franklin D. 1935-36. *217*

—. New Deal. Progressives. 1933-34. *218*

—. Truman, Harry S. 1935-44. *163*

Senate Banking and Currency Committee. Pecora, Ferdinand. Public Opinion. Stock Exchange (manipulation). 1933. *452*

Senate farm bloc. Agriculture (legislation). Sectionalism. 1921-33. *221*

Senate (majority leader). Barkley, Alben W. Democratic Party. Harrison, Byron Patton (Pat). Newspapers. 1937. *174*

—. Barkley, Alben W. Democratic Party. Roosevelt, Franklin D. Supreme Court (issue). 1937. *153*

—. Democratic Party. Illinois. Lucas, Scott W. 1938-50. *237*

Senators. Great Plains states. Liberalism, rural. New Deal. 1930's. *162*

Seneca Arts project. Art. Indians. Iroquois School of Art. New Deal. New York (Akron). Parker, Arthur C. Tonawanda Indian Reservation. 1935-41. *352*

Senior, Clarence. Continental Congress of Workers and Farmers. Socialist Party. 1933. *748*

Sex. Attitudes. Morality. 1918-55. *662*

Sex roles. Economic structure. Labor markets. Women. 1930's. *626*

—. Mitchell, Margaret. Scarlett O'Hara (character). Women. 1936-39. *877*

Seydell, Mildred. Atlanta *Georgian* (newspaper). Economic Conditions. Georgia. Letters. 1930's. *10*

Share Our Wealth movement. Conservatism. Long, Huey P. Louisiana. Smith, Gerald L. K. Speeches and addresses. 1929-35. *632*

—. Economic Reform. Long, Huey P. 1932-35. *548*

—. Elections (presidential). Long, Huey P. Roosevelt, Franklin D. 1932-36. *245*

—. Long, Huey P. Louisiana. Politics. Smith, Gerald L. K. 1930's. *631*

—. Long, Huey P. Political Leadership. 1928-35. *630*

Sharecroppers. Agee, James *(Let Us Now Praise Famous Men)*. Daily Life. Evans, Walker. Photography, documentary. South. 1930-1941. *792*

—. Agricultural Adjustment Administration. Labor Unions and Organizations. Southern Tenant Farmers' Union. ca 1930's. *736*

—. Agriculture. Cotton. Oklahoma, eastern. 1920-40. *38*

—. McCloud, Emma Gudger (reminiscences). South. Whites. 1916-79. *70*

Shaver, James H. (reminiscences). Country life. Droughts. Kansas (Sherman County). 1923-35. *99*

Shaw, Frank. California (Los Angeles). City Government. Clinton, Clifford. Recall. 1938. *189*

Shelterbelts. Agricultural Policy. Great Plains. Roosevelt, Franklin D. Trees. 1934-44. *486*

—. Nebraska. Tree Planting. 1939. *400*

Shenandoah National Park. Virginia. 1924-36. *477*

Shils, Edward. Chicago, University of. Educators. Personal Narratives. Sociology. 1932-36. *915*

Ships. Connecticut. Long Island Sound. New York. 1930-35. *587*

Shoe industry. Maine (Auburn, Lewiston). Strikes. United Shoe Workers of America. 1937. *563*

Short, John D., Jr. (reminiscences). Photographs. Steinbeck, John. 1930's. *916*

Show Boat (film). Films (musicals). *San Francisco* (film). 1936. *917*

Silver. Monetary Act (US, 1939). Pittman, Key. Senate. 1939. *440*

Silver Purchase Act (1934). China. Congress. International Trade. Lobbying. Roosevelt, Franklin D. (administration). 1934. *341*

—. China. International Trade. Pittman, Key. Senate. 1933-40. *472*

Simons, Henry. Attitudes. Chicago, University of. Economic Theory. Keynes, John Maynard. 1930's. *85*

Sinclair, Upton. Bank of America. California. Elections (gubernatorial). Giannini, Amadeo P. Merriam, Frank. Roosevelt, Franklin D. ca 1923-34. *138*

—. California. Democratic Party. End Poverty In California program. Political Campaigns (gubernatorial). ca 1933-34. *242*

Sinclair, Upton (letters). Authors. End Poverty in California program. Mencken, H. L. (letters). Social Reform. ca 1918-51. *902*

Sioux Indians. Civilian Conservation Corps (Indian Division). Indians (reservations). South Dakota. 1933-42. *300*

Six Companies, Inc. Boulder Canyon Project. Hoover Dam. Industrial Workers of the World. Nevada. Strikes. 1931. *703*

Skid row. Artists. Ginther, Ronald Debs. Labor unrest. ca 1920-69. *937*

Slave narratives. Escott, Paul D. (review article). Federal Writers' Project. New Deal. 1935-39. 1979. *828*

Slavery. Ex-slaves, interviews with. Historical sources. Rawick, George P. (review essay). 19c. 1930's. *515*

—. Family. Interviews. South. Works Progress Administration. 1850's-60's. 1930's. *387*

—. Federal Writers' Project. Genovese, Eugene D. Interviews. Methodology. Rawick, George P. 1930's. 1970's. *484*

Slavery, memories of. Federal Writers' Project. Negroes. Tennessee. 1930's. *350*

Sletten, Myron. Letters. Migrant Labor. Travel (accounts). Western States. 1930-32. *104*

Smith, Al. Democratic Party. Elections (presidential). Massachusetts. Roosevelt, Franklin D. 1928-32. *178*

Smith, Bessie. "Gimme a Pigfoot" (song). Language. Music. 1933. *925*

Smith, Fred. *March of Time* (series). News, dramatization of. Radio. 1928-45. *856*

Smith, Gerald L. K. Conservatism. Long, Huey P. Louisiana. Share Our Wealth movement. Speeches and addresses. 1929-35. *632*

—. Fundamentalism. Long, Huey P. North Central States. Populism. Progressivism. 1934-48. *633*

—. Long, Huey P. Louisiana. Politics. Share Our Wealth movement. 1930's. *631*

Smith v. *Allwright* (US, 1944). Democratic Party. NAACP. Negro Suffrage. Primaries. South. Supreme Court. 1890's-1944. *617*

Snell, Bertrand H. Conservatism. New Deal. New York. Republican Party. 1933-39. *139*

Social change. General Education Board. Public policy. Rockefeller, John D. Secondary education. 1930's. *538*

Social Classes. Company towns. Ohio. Steel Industry. Strikes. 1937. *531*

—. Elections (presidential). Ethnic groups. Religion. Roosevelt, Franklin D. 1940. *192*

Social Conditions. Authors. Industrialization. South. Urbanization. 1930's. *908*

—. California (San Francisco). Dreiser, Theodore (interview). Literature. 1939. *904*

—. Depressions (causes). Economic Conditions. 1900-33. *5*

—. Historical sources. Music (blues). Negroes. Oral History. Recordings. 1924-41. *888*

Social consciousness. Novels. Zugsmith, Leane. 1930's. *842*

Social conservatism. Cartoonists. Gray, Harold. *Little Orphan Annie* (comic strip). World War II. 1930's-40's. *955*

Social criticism. Agee, James. Language. Literature. 1930-40. *850*

—. *City* (film). City Planning. Steiner, Ralph. VanDyke, Willard. 1932-39. *867*

Social experiments. Federal Subsistence Homesteads Corporation. Iowa (Granger). Ligutti, Luigi. New Deal. 1934-51. *919*

Social history. News commentator. Radio. Swing, Raymond Gram. 1930's. *791*

Social organization. Adorno, Theodor W. Culture. Lazarsfeld, Paul F. Music. Princeton Radio Research Project. 1930's. *875*

—. American Abstract Artists. American Artists' Congress. Artists. Surrealism. 1935-45. *310*
—. Appalachia. Leftism. Mountaineers. Music. Resettlement Administration (music program). Seeger, Charles. 1935-37. *506*
—. Capitalism. Capra, Frank. Films. *Mr. Deeds Goes to Town* (film). 1936. *861*
—. Farrell, James T. *(Studs Lonigan).* History. Institutions. 1933-35. *796*
Social Problems. *Amos 'n Andy* (program). Humor. Radio. 1929-30's. *945*
—. Clergy. Massachusetts. New Deal. Roosevelt, Franklin D. 1933-36. *291*
—. Migration, Internal. Transients. 1930-36. *130*
Social Reform. Authors. End Poverty in California program. Mencken, H. L. (letters). Sinclair, Upton (letters). ca 1918-51. *902*
Social sciences principles. Bureau of Indian Affairs. Collier, John. New Deal. Public Administration. 1933-45. *497*
Social Security. 1935-80. *422*
—. Government regulation. Neoconservatism. New Deal. Political Leadership. Republican Party. 1936-40. *209*
Social Security Act (US, 1935). Congress. New Deal. Roosevelt, Franklin D. Unemployment insurance. 1934-35. *277*
—. Ehringhaus, J. C. B. Legislation. North Carolina. Unemployment insurance. 1935-37. *420*
—. Harrison, Byron Patton (Pat). Senate. 1934-35. *492*
—. Roosevelt, Franklin D. (administration). ca 1933-37. *325*
Social Theory. Agricultural Reform. Catholic Church. New Deal. Roosevelt, Franklin D. (administration). 1933-39. *473*
Social work. Coal Mines and Mining. Colorado. Labor reform. Roche, Josephine. Roosevelt, Franklin D. (administration). 1886-1976. *365*
Social workers. Branion-Williams case (California). California. Federal Civil Works Administration. McAdoo, William G. Patronage. 1933-34. *468*
Socialism. Editors and Editing. *Partisan Review* (periodical). Stalinism. 1930's. *564*
Socialism, failure of. Attitudes. New Deal. Roper, Elmo. Working class. 1939. *743*
Socialist Party. Antiwar Sentiment. Keep America Out of War Congress. Thomas, Norman. Villard, Oswald Garrison. World War II (antecedents). 1938-41. *584*
—. Comintern (7th Congress). Communist Party. New Deal. 1935-39. *655*
—. Continental Congress of Workers and Farmers. Senior, Clarence. 1933. *748*
—. Factionalism. Kautsky, Karl. Lee, Algernon. Letters. 1930-35. *589*
—. Historiography. Warren, Frank (review article). 1930-40. *700*
—. Liberalism. New Deal. Political activism. Unemployment. 1929-36. *707*
Society for the Psychological Study of Social Issues. Labor. Liberalism. Psychology. 1930's. *596*
Sociology. Chicago, University of. Educators. Personal Narratives. Shils, Edward. 1932-36. *915*
—. Consumerism. Lynd, Robert S. Research. 1930's. *105*
Sociopolitical integration. Fascism. Italian Americans. Michigan (Detroit). 1933-35. *554*
Soil Conservation Service. Agricultural Adjustment Administration. New Deal. 1933-41. *459*
Soil depletion. Dust Bowl. Farmers. Migration, Internal (necessity). Oklahoma. 1921-30's. *72*

Soup kitchen. Butchering. North Dakota (Williston). Vohs, Al J. (interview). 1900's-30's. *110*
Sources. Louisiana Emergency Relief Administration. Relief, federal. 1933-35. 1973. *368*
South. Agee, James *(Let Us Now Praise Famous Men).* Daily Life. Evans, Walker. Photography, documentary. Sharecroppers. 1930-1941. *792*
—. Agricultural Policy. Association of Southern Commissioners of Agriculture. Cotton. New Deal. Tennessee (Memphis). 1936-37. *423*
—. Agriculture. Rural Development. 1930-80. *324*
—. Alabama (Birmingham). Communist Party. Hudson, Hosea. Negroes. 1920's-70's. *691*
—. Ames, Jessie Daniel. Association of Southern Women for the Prevention of Lynching. Lynching. Women. 1928-42. *672*
— Association of Southern Women for the Prevention of Lynching. Lynching. Negroes. Women. 1930-42. *530*
—. Authors. Industrialization. Social Conditions. Urbanization. 1930's. *908*
—. Autobiography. Federal Writers' Project. Oral history. 1930-39. *361*
—. Biography. Couch, W. T. Federal Writers' Project. New Deal. 1938-39. *499*
—. Chain stores. Taxes. ca 1925-40. *94*
—. Congress of Industrial Organizations. Labor Disputes. New Deal. Newspapers. 1930-39. *518*
—. Conservation of Natural Resources. Electric power. Tennessee Valley Authority. 1917-70's. *297*
—. Conservatism. Davidson, Donald. Roosevelt, Franklin D. (programs). Tennessee Valley Authority. 1930's. *474*
—. Cotton Acreage Control Law (Texas, 1931). Crop limitation. Long, Huey P. New Deal. 1931-33. *127*
—. Cotton production. Long, Huey P. Louisiana. Texas. 1931. *108*
—. Democratic Party. NAACP. Negro Suffrage. Primaries. *Smith* v. *Allwright* (US, 1944). Supreme Court. 1890's-1944. *617*
—. Drama. Federal Theatre Project. New Deal. 1930's. *884*
—. Economic conditions. Foreman, Clark Howell. National Emergency Council (report). Politics. Roosevelt, Franklin D. 1938. *24*
—. Economic conditions. Negroes. Woodson, Carter G. 1930. *39*
—. Family. Interviews. Slavery. Works Progress Administration. 1850's-60's. 1930's. *387*
—. Ford, Ford Madox. Literature. Louisiana (Baton Rouge). Writers' Conference on Literature and Reading in the South and Southwest. 1935. *942*
—. Graves, John Temple, II. Liberalism. New Deal. Palm Beach *Times* (newspaper). 1933-40. *275*
—. Immigrants. International Brotherhood of Pulp, Sulphite, and Paper Mill Workers. Negroes. Pacific Northwest. Women. 1909-40. *754*
—. Lilly, Octave, Jr. (obituary). Negroes. Poetry. 1930-60. *793*
—. McCloud, Emma Gudger (reminiscences). Sharecroppers. Whites. 1916-79. *70*
—. Negroes. Progressive education. 1930-45. *605*
South Carolina (Santee-Cooper). Country life. Delano, Jack. Farm Security Administration. New Deal. Photography. 1941. *327*
South Dakota. Civilian Conservation Corps. Employment. Environment. 1933-42. *357*

—. Civilian Conservation Corps (Indian Division). Indians (reservations). Sioux Indians. 1933-42. *300*

—. Communism. Farm protest. United Farmers League. 1923-34. *661*

—. Congress. New Deal. Roosevelt, Franklin D. 1933. *312*

—. Economic conditions. Elections (presidential). Hoover, Herbert C. Political Parties. Roosevelt, Franklin D. 1932. *176*

—. Employment, part-time. National Youth Administration. New Deal. Struble, Anna C. Youth. 1935-43. *355*

—. New Deal. Political Attitudes. Public Welfare. 1930's-70's. *276*

South Dakota (Farm Island). Causeways. Civilian Conservation Corps (co. 796). Missouri River. 1934. *521*

Southern Pine Association. Lumber code. National Recovery Administration. 1933-35. *335*

Southern Tenant Farmers' Union. Agricultural Adjustment Administration. Labor Unions and Organizations. Sharecroppers. ca 1930's. *736*

Southwest. Dust Bowl. Migration, Internal. Oklahoma. Route 66. 1930's. *88*

Spain. Civil War. Fiction. Hemingway, Ernest *(For Whom the Bell Tolls)*. Propaganda. Reporters and Reporting. 1936-40. *853*

Spanish language. California (Hollywood). Films. Hispanic Americans. 1930-39. *896*

Speeches and addresses. Conservatism. Long, Huey P. Louisiana. Share Our Wealth movement. Smith, Gerald L. K. 1929-35. *632*

Spender, Stephen. Bergonzi, Bernard. Literature (review article). Salzman, Jack. Zanderer, Leo. ca 1930-39. 1978-79. *775*

Split labor market theory. Economic conditions. Exclusion policy. Filipinos. Immigration. 1927-34. *18*

Sporting News (newspaper). Baseball. Rural-urban issues. 1920's-30's. *789*

Sports. Communist Party. 1920's-40's. *680*

Spring, Agnes Wright. Christensen, Mart. Federal Writers' Project. Works Progress Administration. Wyoming. 1935-41. *354*

Stage Setting and Scenery. Art and Society. Negroes. New York City. Painting. Stettheimer, Florine. 1929-44. *882*

Stalinism. Editors and Editing. *Partisan Review* (periodical). Socialism. 1930's. *564*

State capitalism. New Deal. Public Welfare. Roosevelt, Franklin D. 1929-52. *293*

State Government. Benefactor-aversion hypothesis. Local government. Nixon, Richard M. (administration). Roosevelt, Franklin D. (administration). 1933-45. 1969-74. *392*

—. Braeman, John (review article). Historiography. New Deal. Reform. 1930's-40's. *382*

—. Branson, Eugene C. Electric Power. North Carolina. Poe, Clarence H. Rural Electrification Administration. 1917-36. *302*

—. Cultural identity. Oklahoma. 1930's. *31*

—. Federal assistance (opposition to). Maryland (Baltimore). Ritchie, Albert C. 1929-33. *56*

—. First ladies (state). Ohio. White, George. White, Mary (reminiscences). 1931-35. *265*

—. Fiscal Policy. Governors. Kump, Herman Guy. West Virginia. 1933. *169*

—. Georgia. National Recovery Administration. Strikes. Talmadge, Eugene. Textile industry. 1934. *526*

State Legislatures. Federal programs. Roosevelt, Franklin D. 1933-70's. *391*

State Politics. Byrd, Harry F. Democratic Party. Elections (presidential). Roosevelt, Franklin D. Virginia. 1932. *260*

—. Democratic Party. Erickson, John E. Montana. Walsh, Thomas J. 1932-33. *208*

—. Democratic Party. Missouri. Pendergast, Thomas J. Political Conventions. Roosevelt, Franklin D. 1932. *238*

—. Farmer-Labor Party. Michigan. New Deal. 1933-37. *203*

—. Great Plains. Radicals and Radicalism. 1930-36. *190*

—. Kansas. Woodring, Harry Hines. 1905-33. *211*

States. Federal expenditures. New Deal. 1933-39. *447*

Statistics. Bureau of Labor Statistics. Lubin, Isador. New Deal. Perkins, Frances. Unemployment. 1920-49. *342*

Steel Industry. Company towns. Ohio. Social Classes. Strikes. 1937. *531*

—. Davey, Martin L. National Guard. Ohio. Strikes. 1937. *722*

Steel Workers Organizing Committee. Communist Party. Labor Unions and Organizations. Ohio (Youngstown). Steuben, John. 1936. *608*

—. Foreign policy. Import restrictions. International Steel Cartel. Labor. US Steel Corporation. 1937. *646*

Stein, Gertrude. Fiction (detective). Women. 1933-36. *854*

Steinbeck, John. Agee, James. Journalism. Literature. 1935-39. *899*

—. Fiction. Manuscript dating. 1934. *953*

—. Photographs. Short, John D., Jr. (reminiscences). 1930's. *916*

Steinbeck, John *(In Dubious Battle)*. Agricultural Labor. California, southern. Strikes. 1933. *773*

Steinbeck, John *(The Grapes of Wrath)*. 1930's. *837*

—. Documentarism. Film industry. Novels. 1939-40. *779*

Steiner, Ralph. *City* (film). City Planning. Social criticism. VanDyke, Willard. 1932-39. *867*

Stereotypes. *Amos 'n Andy* (program). Boycotts. Comic strips. Negroes. Radio. 1930's. *719*

—. Ethnic Groups. Films. *Flash Gordon* (film). 1936-38. *771*

—. Fiction. *Saturday Evening Post* (periodical). Women. 1931-36. *831*

—. Fiction, formula. Nancy Drew books. New Deal. 1930's. 1960's-70's. *841*

Stettheimer, Florine. Art and Society. Negroes. New York City. Painting. Stage Setting and Scenery. 1929-44. *882*

Steuben, John. Communist Party. Labor Unions and Organizations. Ohio (Youngstown). Steel Workers Organizing Committee. 1936. *608*

Stevens, Albert W. Anderson, Orvil A. Balloon flights, stratospheric. 1920's-35. *712*

Stevens, Henry L., Jr. American Legion. Bonus Army. District of Columbia. North Carolina. Political Protest. Veterans (benefits). 1932. *694*

Stock Exchange. Finance. *New York Times*. Newspaper columns. 1929. *13*

—. New York City. 1929. *91*

Stock Exchange (manipulation). Pecora, Ferdinand. Public Opinion. Senate Banking and Currency Committee. 1933. *452*

Stock market. Economic Regulations. New Deal. Securities Exchange Act of 1934. 1934. *287*

Stock Market Crash. Attitudes. Texas (western). 1929-33. *131*

Stocks and Bonds (median price-earnings ratio). Economic speculation. 1929. *101*

Streamlining. Automobiles. Geddes, Norman Bel. Industrial design. 1930-39. *870*

Street, Electric Railway and Motor Coach Employees of America. Louisiana (New Orleans). Public opinion. Strikes. 1929-30. *557*

Strikes. Agricultural Labor. California, southern. Steinbeck, John *(In Dubious Battle)*. 1933. *773*

—. American Federation of Labor. Coal Mines and Mining. New Mexico (Gallup). 1933. *708*

—. Automobile Industry and Trade. Dillon, Francis. Michigan. Motor Products Corporation. United Automobile Workers of America. 1933-39. *545*

—. Berry pickers. California (El Monte). Foreign Relations. Japan. Mexico. 1933. *619*

—. Boulder Canyon project. Colorado River. Hoover Dam. Industrial Workers of the World. Nevada. 1931. *702*

—. Boulder Canyon Project. Hoover Dam. Industrial Workers of the World. Nevada. Six Companies, Inc. 1931. *703*

—. California (San Francisco). Labor markets. Longshoremen. 1934-39. *635*

—. Carbon County Coal Strike (1933). National Miners Union. United Mine Workers of America. Utah. 1900-39. *693*

—. Christianity. Longshoremen. Oxford Group movement. Washington (Seattle). 1921-34. *738*

—. Coal Mines and Mining. Davidson-Wilder Strike of 1932. Graham, Barney. Tennessee, eastern. United Mine Workers of America. 1932-33. *527*

—. Coal Mines and Mining. Editors and Editing. Evans, Herndon J. Kentucky (Harlan County). Pineville *Sun* (newspaper). 1929-32. *730*

—. Coal Mines and Mining. National Guard. Ohio. White, George. 1932. *687*

—. Company towns. Ohio. Social Classes. Steel Industry. 1937. *531*

—. Davey, Martin L. National Guard. Ohio. Steel Industry. 1937. *722*

—. Farmers. North Dakota. Prices. 1932. *92*

—. Films (documentary). Michigan (Flint). United Automobile Workers of America. *With Babies and Banners* (film). Women. 1937. *903*

—. Garment industry. Missouri (St. Louis). Personal narratives. Photographic essays. Women. ca 1930-39. *565*

—. General Motors Corporation. Georgia (Atlanta). United Automobile Workers of America. 1936. *616*

—. General Motors Corporation. *Great Sitdown* (film). Historiography. United Automobile Workers of America. *With Babies and Banners* (film). 1937. 1976-79. *855*

—. General Motors Corporation. Michigan (Flint). United Automobile Workers of America. 1936-37. *718*

—. Georgia. National Recovery Administration. State Government. Talmadge, Eugene. Textile industry. 1934. *526*

—. Hormel, George A., and Co. Labor Unions and Organizations. Minnesota (Austin). Olson, Floyd B. 1933. *592*

—. Industrial Rayon Corporation. Textile Workers Organizing Committee. Virginia (Covington). 1937-38. *599*

—. Industrial Workers of the World. Labor Unions and Organizations. Washington (Yakima Valley). 1933. *570*

—. Louisiana (New Orleans). Public opinion. Street, Electric Railway and Motor Coach Employees of America. 1929-30. *557*

—. Maine (Auburn, Lewiston). Shoe industry. United Shoe Workers of America. 1937. *563*

—. National Textile Workers Union. North Carolina (Gastonia). Textile Industry. Weisbord, Vera Buch (reminiscences). 1929. *746*

Strikes, sit-down. Blankenhorn, Heber. Industrial Relations. LaFollette Committee. Legislative Investigations. 1935-40. *600*

—. General Motors Corporation. Lewis, John L. 1936-37. *595*

—. Ohio (Akron). Rubber industry. 1934-38. *683*

Struble, Anna C. Employment, part-time. National Youth Administration. New Deal. South Dakota. Youth. 1935-43. *355*

Stryker, Roy Emerson. Farm Security Administration. Great Plains. Photography. 1937-39. *322*

Student activism. Colleges and Universities. Feuer, Lewis. Lipset, Seymour Martin. Politics. 1930's-40's. *715*

Student protest. Idaho, University of, Southern Branch. Radicals and Radicalism. Roosevelt, Franklin D. 1930's. *731*

Students. Biography. Family history. Interviews. Louisiana State University. Works Progress Administration. 1930's. 1978. *321*

Subsidies. Arts, visual. McKinzie, Richard D. (review article). New Deal. 1933-40. *328*

—. Cotton industry. Delta & Pine Land Company. Economic Regulations. Federal Government. Johnston, Oscar Goodbar. 1933-37. *424*

Subsistence Homesteads Program. Miners (resettlement of). National Industrial Recovery Act (1933). New Deal. Roosevelt, Eleanor. West Virginia (Arthurdale). 1930-46. *320*

Sullivan, Anna (interview). Massachusetts. Oral history. Textile Workers Union of America. Women. 1918-76. *688*

Sullivan, Mark. New Deal. Pennsylvania (Avondale). Political Commentary. Roosevelt, Franklin D. 1924-52. *305*

Sumners, Hatton. Executive Power (restrictions). House of Representatives. Logan-Walter Bill (vetoed, 1939). Rayburn, Sam. Texas. 1939. *438*

Supreme Court. Brandeis, Louis D. Due process. Economic Regulations. *Nebbia* v. *New York* (US, 1934). *New State Ice* v. *Liebmann* (US, 1932). *West Coast Hotel* v. *Parrish* (US, 1937). 1897-1937. *476*

—. Brandeis, Louis D. Freund, Paul A. (reminiscences). Law. 1932-33. *167*

—. Buildings. 1789-1935. *918*

—. Coal industry. Congress. New Deal. 1932-40. *395*

—. Conservatism. Constitutional law. Kansas. New Deal. Newspapers. 1934-35. *329*

—. Constitutional issues. Editorials. Labor union journals. New Deal. 1935-37. *588*

—. Democratic Party. NAACP. Negro Suffrage. Primaries. *Smith* v. *Allwright* (US, 1944). South. 1890's-1944. *617*

—. Economic Conditions. National Recovery Administration. New Deal. Virginia. 1933-35. *353*

—. Historiography. Hughes, Charles Evans. New Deal. 1930's. 1950's-60's. *223*

—. Political history. Probability theory. Quantitative methods. Roosevelt, Franklin D. 1937. 1970's. *216*

—. Politics. Roosevelt, Franklin D. 1937. *261*

—. Probability Theory. Quantitative Methods. Roosevelt, Franklin D. 1937. 1970's. *165*

Supreme Court (issue). Barkley, Alben W. Democratic Party. Roosevelt, Franklin D. Senate (majority leader). 1937. *153*

—. Congress. Norris, George W. Roosevelt, Franklin D. 1937. *207*

Supreme Court (nominations). NAACP. North Carolina. Parker, John J. White, Walter F. 1930. *618*

Surpluses. Agriculture. Alcohol. Business. Fuel. Motors. Prices. 1930's. *604*
Surrealism. American Abstract Artists. American Artists' Congress. Artists. Social Organization. 1935-45. *310*
Swain, Martha H. Andersen, Kristi. Blumberg, Barbara. Fine, Sidney. Jeffries, John W. New Deal (review article). Roosevelt, Franklin D. 1933-39. *143*
Sweden. Dreiser, Theodore. Lewis, Sinclair. Literature. Nobel Prizes. Public Opinion. 1920's-30. *857*
Sweezy, Paul. Baran, Paul. Capitalism (review article). 1930's. 1966. *53*
Swing Era. Bands. Music. 1934-45. *921*
Swing, Raymond Gram. News commentator. Radio. Social history. 1930's. *791*
Swing (term). Jazz. Music. 1908-30's. *927*
Sykes, Eugene O. Federal Communications Commission. Federal Radio Commission. Radio. 1927-39. *412*
Symbolism. Literature. Myths and Symbols. Roth, Henry (*Call It Sleep*). 1934. *901*
Syrian Americans. Juma, Charlie (interview). North Dakota (Ross). 1900's-30's. *111*

T

Taft-Hartley Act (US, 1947). Business. Labor Unions and Organizations. New Deal. Wagner Act (US, 1935). World War II. 1935-47. *543*
Talmadge, Eugene. Democratic Party. Georgia. New Deal. Roosevelt, Franklin D. 1926-38. *146*
—. Democratic Party. New Deal. Primaries (senatorial). Russell, Richard B. 1936. *213*
—. Georgia. National Recovery Administration. State Government. Strikes. Textile industry. 1934. *526*
Tampa Shipbuilding and Engineering Company. Federal loan. Florida (Tampa). Kreher, Ernest. Public Works Administration. 1932-37. *401*
Taralseth, Rueben P. (interview). Farmers. Legislation. New Deal. North Dakota (Landa). 1900's-30's. *114*
Tate, Allen. Agar, Herbert. Collins, Seward. Conservatism. Decentralization. Ideology. Intellectuals. 1933-50. *913*
—. Agrarianism. Alienation. Industrialization. 1930's. *835*
—. Historicity. Intellectual development. Literature. Modernism, nature of. Western life. 1929-30. *780*
Tax reform. Brucker, Wilber M. Michigan. Politics. 1929-33. *222*
Taxes. Chain stores. South. ca 1925-40. *94*
Taxpayers Association. New Jersey (Union Township). Schools. 1929-38. *15*
Taylor, Graham D. Federal Policy. Indians (review articles). New Deal. Parman, Donald L. Philp, Kenneth R. 1934-74. *612*
Taylor, Paul S. Field research interviews. *Mexican Labor in the United States* (study). National Endowment for the Humanities. 1927-30. *621*
Technology. Attitudes. Federal Policy. New Deal. 1927-40. *442*
Technology assessment. Hoover, Herbert C. Inventions. Public Policy (recommendations). Roosevelt, Franklin D. (administration). 1930's-77. *369*
Temin, Peter. Economic History. Friedman, Milton. Schwartz, Anna. 1894-1938. 1963-76. *69*
—. Monetary Systems. 1929-39. 1976. *2*

Temin, Peter (review article). Depressions (causes). Economic History. Models. Monetary Systems. 1920's. 1976. *118*
Temin, Peter (theory). Consumption, decline in. 1930-41. *68*
Tennessee. Browning, Gordon. Elections (gubernatorial). Political machines. 1936. *135*
—. Chandler, Walter. Crump, Edward. Democratic Party. House of Representatives. 1933-40. *149*
—. Coal Mines and Mining. Folk songs. Lowry, Tom (interview). 1932. *765*
—. Congress. New Deal. Political attitudes. Roosevelt, Franklin D. 1933-40. *148*
—. Cumberland Homesteads. Fairfield Glade. Housing. New Deal. Resettlement. 1934-80. *482*
—. Cumberland Mountains. Films (documentary). Historical accuracy. *People of the Cumberland* (film). 1930's. *834*
—. Editors and Editing. Liberalism. Milton, George Fort. New Deal. 1930's. *362*
—. Federal Writers' Project. Negroes. Slavery, memories of. 1930's. *350*
—. Governors. Horton, Henry. Political Corruption. 1930-31. *201*
Tennessee (Benfolly). Authors (southern). Gordon, Caroline. Letters. New York (Rochester). Wood, Sally. 1930-31. *818*
Tennessee, eastern. Coal Mines and Mining. Davidson-Wilder Strike of 1932. Graham, Barney. Strikes. United Mine Workers of America. 1932-33. *527*
Tennessee (Memphis). Agricultural Policy. Association of Southern Commissioners of Agriculture. Cotton. New Deal. South. 1936-37. *423*
—. Alabama (Muscle Shoals). Electric Power. Public Utilities. Tennessee Valley Authority. 1880-1940. *513*
Tennessee (Nashville). Berry, Harry S. Political Corruption. Works Progress Administration. 1935-43. *309*
Tennessee (Shelby County). Crump, Edward. Democratic Party. Elections (gubernatorial). Politics. 1932. *200*
Tennessee Valley Authority. Alabama (Muscle Shoals). Electric Power. Public Utilities. Tennessee (Memphis). 1880-1940. *513*
—. Conservation of Natural Resources. Electric power. South. 1917-70's. *297*
—. Conservatism. Davidson, Donald. Roosevelt, Franklin D. (programs). South. 1930's. *474*
Terkel, Studs (review article). Methodology. Oral history. 1930-72. *809*
Texas. Agricultural experiment stations. Arizona. New Deal. New Mexico. Oklahoma. 1926-39. *407*
—. Agricultural Industry. Economic Regulations. Federal government. Mississippi. Prices. Voluntarism. 1925-40. *129*
—. Attitudes. 1929-33. *129*
—. Capitalism. Political Attitudes. Radicals and Radicalism. 1929-33. *128*
—. Cotton production. Long, Huey P. Louisiana. South. 1931. *108*
—. Economic Conditions. Labor. New Deal. 1929-39. *430*
—. Economic Development. Employment. Public Works Administration. 1933-34. *507*
—. Executive Power (restrictions). House of Representatives. Logan-Walter Bill (vetoed, 1939). Rayburn, Sam. Sumners, Hatton. 1939. *438*
Texas (Amarillo). Cowen, Wilson. Dust Bowl. Farm Security Administration. Letters. Migration, Internal. 1940. *48*

Texas (Conroe). Boomtowns. Oil Industry and Trade. 1929-33. *82*

Texas Panhandle. Agricultural Policy. Dust Bowl. New Deal. 1930's. *76*

Texas Rangers. Bridges (toll, free). Interstate relations. Oklahoma National Guard. Red River Bridge Company. 1931. *30*

Texas (Ropesville). New Deal. Resettlement Administration. Rural Development. 1933-43. *372*

Texas (San Antonio). Ethnic Groups. Georgia (Atlanta). Labor. Louisiana (New Orleans). Women. 1930-40. *540*

Texas, University of. Academic Freedom. Marxist opinions. Muller, Hermann J. (dismissal). 1936. *586*

Texas (western). Attitudes. Stock Market Crash. 1929-33. *131*

Textile industry. City government. Fiscal Policy. New Jersey (Paterson). Public Welfare. 1920-32. *77*

—. Georgia. National Recovery Administration. State Government. Strikes. Talmadge, Eugene. 1934. *526*

—. National Textile Workers Union. North Carolina (Gastonia). Strikes. Weisbord, Vera Buch (reminiscences). 1929. *746*

Textile Workers Organizing Committee. Industrial Rayon Corporation. Strikes. Virginia (Covington). 1937-38. *599*

Textile Workers Union of America. Massachusetts. Oral history. Sullivan, Anna (interview). Women. 1918-76. *688*

Theater. Federal Theatre Project. Flanagan, Hallie. Hopkins, Harry. Politics. Works Progress Administration. 1935-39. *303*

—. Federal Theatre Project. Negroes. 1935-39. *456*

Theater, black. Federal Theatre Project. Negroes. Public Records. 1930's-70's. *304*

Theatricals, amateur. Iowa (Cedar Rapids). Universal Production Company. Women. 1926-30's. *800*

Theologians, neoorthodox. Farm tenancy. Mississippi. Protestant Churches. 1936-40. *629*

Theology. Culture, concept of. Economic theory. Intellectual trends. Relativism. 1930's. *883*

Third Parties. Amlie, Thomas R. Farmer-labor movement. Hard, Herbert. New Deal. Ohio Farmer-Labor Progressive Federation. 1930-40. *204*

Third parties (suggested). American Federation of Labor. New Deal. 1920's-30's. *205*

Thomas, Norman. Antiwar Sentiment. Keep America Out of War Congress. Socialist Party. Villard, Oswald Garrison. World War II (antecedents). 1938-41. *584*

Thurmond, Thomas. California (San Jose; St. James Park). Hart, Brooke (murder). Holmes, John. Kidnapping. Lynching. 1933. *665*

Timberline Lodge. Dawson, Oliver B. (reminiscences). Ironwork. Oregon. Works Progress Administration. 1935-37. *326*

Tipaldo v. Morehead (New York, 1934). Labor Reform. Minimum Wage. New York. 1933-37. *367*

To Have and Have Not (film). Films (review article). *Gold Diggers of 1933* (film). Hove, Arthur. Kawin, Bruce F. Screenplays. 1930's-44. *911*

Tobacco. Federal Writers' Project. 1933-39. *278*

Tonawanda Indian Reservation. Art. Indians. Iroquois School of Art. New Deal. New York (Akron). Parker, Arthur C. Seneca Arts project. 1935-41. *352*

Totalitarianism. Communism. Nazism. Press. Red Fascism analogy. 1930's. 1970's. *654*

—. Hook, Sidney. Letters. Santayana, George. 1929-38. *832*

Townsend Movement. Elections. New York (43rd Congressional District). 1936. *551*

Trade associations. Agricultural Policy. National Cooperative Council. New Deal. 1929-42. *346*

Trade Union Education League. American Civil Liberties Union. Demonstrations. Federal Bureau of Investigation. Hoover, J. Edgar. Political surveillance. 1924-36. *750*

Trade Union Unity League. American Federation of Labor. Communist Party. Labor Unions and Organizations. Radicals and Radicalism. 1933-35. *569*

Transients. Migration, Internal. Social Problems. 1930-36. *130*

Trans-polar flight (nonstop). Aeronautics. California. USSR (Moscow). 1937. *785*

Travel (accounts). Letters. Migrant Labor. Sletten, Myron. Western States. 1930-32. *104*

Tree Planting. Nebraska. Shelterbelts. 1939. *400*

Trees. Agricultural Policy. Great Plains. Roosevelt, Franklin D. Shelterbelts. 1934-44. *486*

Trials. Alabama. Race Relations. Rape, alleged. Scottsboro case. 1931-49. *729*

—. Alabama (Scottsboro). Historiography. Myths and Symbols. Racism. 1931-80. *742*

—. American Civil Liberties Union. Civil rights. Kentucky (Bell County, London). Miners. 1932-38. *733*

—. Anti-Semitism. Edmondson, Robert Edward. Libel. 1934-44. *597*

—. Capital Punishment. Negroes. Newspapers. Rape. Reporters and Reporting. Scottsboro Case. 1931-32. *697*

—. Hauptmann, Bruno. Kidnapping. Lindbergh case. 1935. *573*

—. Hollins, Jess. International Labor Defense. NAACP. Oklahoma. Race Relations. Rape. 1931-36. *659*

Tribune (newspaper). Chisum, Melvin J. Journalism. Negroes. Roosevelt, Franklin D. (election). ca 1932. *892*

Trilling, Lionel. Anti-Semitism. Columbia University. 1930's. *739*

Trotskyism. 1930's-40. *677*

Trout, Charles H. Cities (review article). Democratic Party. Dorsett, Lyle W. Fine, Sidney. 1930-40. *186*

Trout, Charles H. (review article). City Politics. Massachusetts (Boston). New Deal. Roosevelt, Franklin D. (administration). 1929-39. 1977. *157*

Trout, Charles H. (views). Massachusetts (Boston). Methodology. New Deal. Urban history. 1930's. 1977-79. *122*

Trucks and Trucking. Motor Carrier Act (US, 1935). Moving industry. 1930-35. *359*

Truman, Harry S. Democratic Party. Elections (senatorial). Missouri. New Deal. Primaries. 1934. *175*

—. Historiography (revisionist). Liberalism. Reform. Roosevelt, Franklin D. 1932-53. 1960-75. *227*

—. Johnson, Lyndon B. Kennedy, John F. New Deal. 1933-68. *394*

—. Senate. 1935-44. *163*

Truman, Harry S. (administration). Collier, John. Federal Government. Indians. Liberalism. Roosevelt, Franklin D. (administration). 1933-53. *380*

Tugwell, Rexford G. Greenbelt Towns. New Deal. Ohio (Cincinnati, Greenhills). 1935-39. *333*

—. Greenbelt towns. Poor, rural. Resettlement Administration. 1935-36. *421*

Twain, Mark (short story). Book Collecting. 1930-31. *936*
Tydings, J. Mansir. Kentucky. Lincoln Institute. Negroes. Young, Whitney M. 1935-37. *134*

U

Unemployed Citizens' League. Dix, I. F. Hoover, Herbert C. Local politics. Self-help. Washington (Seattle). 1931-32. *75*
Unemployed councils. Radicals and Radicalism. 1929-33. *705*
Unemployed Leagues. Muste, Abraham J. Radicals and Radicalism. 1932-36. *706*
Unemployment *See also* Employment.
—. Agricultural Policy. Dust Bowl. Federal Government. Great Plains. ca 1930-80. *408*
—. Brucker, Wilber M. Michigan. Murphy, Frank. 1929-33. *84*
—. Bureau of Labor Statistics. Lubin, Isador. New Deal. Perkins, Frances. Statistics. 1920-49. *342*
—. California (Los Angeles County). Davis, James J. Deportation. Mexicans. 1931. *363*
—. California (Santa Barbara). Fleischmann, Max. Philanthropy. Relief work. 1930-32. *78*
—. Economic Conditions. 1929. 1974. *93*
—. Europe, western. 1929-41. *35*
—. Federal Policy. Hopkins, Harry. New Deal. Poverty. Roosevelt, Franklin D. 1910's-38. *403*
—. Federal Programs. Marine Workers' Industrial Union. Maryland (Baltimore). 1933-37. *274*
—. Government. Hoover, Herbert C. Industry. New York (Buffalo). Public Welfare. 1929-33. *64*
—. Hickok, Lorena A. Hopkins, Harry. New Deal. Ohio. Roosevelt, Franklin D. 1934-36. *489*
—. Labor Unions and Organizations. Working Class. 1930-40's. *674*
—. Liberalism. New Deal. Political activism. Socialist Party. 1929-36. *707*
—. Professions. 1929-35. *97*
—. Self-perception. Working Class. 1920's-30's. *116*
Unemployment estimates. Methodology. 1934-41. *23*
Unemployment insurance. Congress. New Deal. Roosevelt, Franklin D. Social Security Act (US, 1935). 1934-35. *277*
—. Ehringhaus, J. C. B. Legislation. North Carolina. Social Security Act (US, 1935). 1935-37. *420*
United Automobile Workers of America. Automobile Industry and Trade. Dillon, Francis. Michigan. Motor Products Corporation. Strikes. 1933-39. *545*
—. Automobile Industry and Trade. Indiana. Labor parties. New Deal. Ohio. 1935-40. *652*
—. Communists. Factionalism. Martin, Homer. Michigan. 1937-39. *636*
—. Factionalism. Militancy. 1937-41. *544*
—. Films (documentary). Michigan (Flint). Strikes. *With Babies and Banners* (film). Women. 1937. *903*
—. Friedlander, Peter (review article). Michigan (Detroit). Working Class. 1936-39. 1975. *549*
—. General Motors Corporation. Georgia (Atlanta). Strikes. 1936. *616*
—. General Motors Corporation. *Great Sitdown* (film). Historiography. Strikes. *With Babies and Banners* (film). 1937. 1976-79. *855*
—. General Motors Corporation. Michigan (Flint). Strikes. 1936-37. *718*
—. Reuther, Victor G. (review article). Reuther, Walter P. 1930's. 1976. *637*
United Automobile Workers of America (review article). Communist Party. Glabermann, Martin. Keeran, Roger. Labor Unions and Organizations. Meier, August. Negroes. Rudwick, Elliot. 1930's-40's. *651*
United Electrical and Radio Workers of America. Labor Unions and Organizations. 1933-37. *594*
United Farmers League. Communism. Farm protest. South Dakota. 1923-34. *661*
United Mine Workers of America. Alabama. Kentucky. Labor Unions and Organizations (development). 1932-33. *634*
—. Carbon County Coal Strike (1933). National Miners Union. Strikes. Utah. 1900-39. *693*
—. Coal Mines and Mining. Davidson-Wilder Strike of 1932. Graham, Barney. Strikes. Tennessee, eastern. 1932-33. *527*
—. National Miners Union. Negroes. Pennsylvania, western. 1925-31. *686*
United Shoe Workers of America. Maine (Auburn, Lewiston). Shoe industry. Strikes. 1937. *563*
United States v. *One Book Called "Ulysses"* (US, 1932). Censorship. Cerf, Bennett. Ernst, Morris. Joyce, James *(Ulysses)*. 1922-32. *840*
Unity in diversity (theme). Adamic, Louis (writings). Immigrants. 1935-45. *782*
Universal Production Company. Iowa (Cedar Rapids). Theatricals, amateur. Women. 1926-30's. *800*
Upper Classes. New York. Pell, Herbert. Political Campaigns (presidential). Roosevelt, Franklin D. 1936. *142*
Urban history. Massachusetts (Boston). Methodology. New Deal. Trout, Charles H. (views). 1930's. 1977-79. *122*
Urban programs. Civilian Conservation Corps. Oklahoma (Tulsa, Oklahoma City). Segregation. 1930's. *364*
Urbanization. Authors. Industrialization. Social Conditions. South. 1930's. *908*
US Steel Corporation. Foreign policy. Import restrictions. International Steel Cartel. Labor. Steel Workers Organizing Committee. 1937. *646*
USSR (Moscow). Aeronautics. California. Trans-polar flight (nonstop). 1937. *785*
Utah. Carbon County Coal Strike (1933). National Miners Union. Strikes. United Mine Workers of America. 1900-39. *693*

V

Vagrancy. Attitudes. Great Britain. Law. Poor. 14c-1939. *20*
Values *See also* Attitudes.
—. Capra, Frank. *Miracle Woman* (film). 1930's. *934*
—. Democracy. Inaugural addresses. Political Speeches. Roosevelt, Franklin D. 1901-77. *164*
—. Family. Folklore. Radio. *Vic and Sade* (program). Women. 1932-46. *96*
—. Labor. Middle Classes. Women. 1930's. *11*
VanderWee, Herman. Depressions (review article). Economic policy. Kindleberger, Charles P. 1930's. *26*
VanDyke, Willard. *City* (film). City Planning. Social criticism. Steiner, Ralph. 1932-39. *867*

Verbal agreements. Breach of contract. Lawsuits. Miller, Zack. Mix, Tom. Sells-Floto Circus. 101 Ranch Real Wild West Show. 1929-34. *819*

Verduci, Joseph P. Marines. Military service. 1934-38. *682*

Vermont. Aiken, George D. Flood control. Governors. Political Campaigns (presidential). Republican Party. 1937-39. *235*

—. Aiken, George D. Political Campaigns (gubernatorial). Republican Party. 1933-36. *184*

—. Civilian Conservation Corps. Economic Conditions. New Deal. 1933-42. *490*

—. Ecological decision-making. Green Mountain Parkway. Voting and Voting Behavior. 1935-36. *306*

Vermont (Windham County). Lovecraft, H. P. Science fiction. 1931. *946*

Veterans (benefits). American Legion. Bonus Army. District of Columbia. North Carolina. Political Protest. Stevens, Henry L., Jr. 1932. *694*

Veterans' certificates. Bonus Army. District of Columbia. Legislation (proposed). Patman, Wright. 1932. *666*

Vic and Sade (program). Family. Folklore. Radio. Values. Women. 1932-46. *96*

Vigilantism. City Government. Flogging case. Florida (Tampa). Political Corruption. 1935-38. *628*

Villard, Oswald Garrison. Antiwar Sentiment. Keep America Out of War Congress. Socialist Party. Thomas, Norman. World War II (antecedents). 1938-41. *584*

Vindex, Charles (reminiscences). Daily Life. Homesteading and Homesteaders. Montana (Plentywood). 1929-34. *123*

Violence. California (Watsonville). Filipino Americans. Racism. Riots. 1926-30. *577*

—. Literature. Sandoz, Mari. 1935-37. *947*

Virginia. Agricultural Adjustment Administration. New Deal. North Carolina. Senate. 1933-39. *366*

—. Byrd, Harry F. Democratic Party. Elections (presidential). Roosevelt, Franklin D. State Politics. 1932. *260*

—. Byrd, Harry F. Democratic Party. Glass, Carter. Roosevelt, Franklin D. Senate. 1938. *183*

—. Byrd, Harry F. Democratic Party. Patronage. Senate. 1935-39. *196*

—. Congressmen. New Deal. Politics. Roosevelt, Franklin D. Woodrum, Clifton A. 1922-45. *236*

—. Economic Conditions. National Recovery Administration. New Deal. Supreme Court. 1933-35. *353*

—. Glass, Carter. Political Campaigns (presidential, senatorial). 1936. *197*

—. Shenandoah National Park. 1924-36. *477*

Virginia (Covington). Industrial Rayon Corporation. Strikes. Textile Workers Organizing Committee. 1937-38. *599*

Vocational education. Federal Aid to Education. George-Barden Act (US, 1946). George-Deen Act (US, 1936). Pharmacy. Wisconsin Plan. 1936-49. *307*

Vohs, Al J. (interview). Butchering. North Dakota (Williston). Soup kitchen. 1900's-30's. *110*

Voluntarism. Agricultural Industry. Economic Regulations. Federal government. Mississippi. Prices. Texas. 1925-40. *71*

Voluntary associations. Epstein, Abraham. Legislation. Old age security. Pension systems. 1920-35. *647*

Volunteer Armies. Military Recruitment. 1930-40. *40*

Voting and Voting Behavior. Andersen, Kristi. Democratic Party. Partisanship. Republican Party. 1920-32. *229*

—. Democratic Party. 1928-36. *159*

—. Democratic Party. New Deal. Pennsylvania (Pittsburgh). Political Theory. Quantitative Methods. Wisconsin. 1912-40. *228*

—. Ecological decision-making. Green Mountain Parkway. Vermont. 1935-36. *306*

—. Nebraska (Dawson County). New Deal. 1933-40. *478*

—. New Deal. Political Systems. 1894-1975. *257*

—. Partisanship. Political Theory. Washington. 1889-1950. *136*

W

Wagner Act (US, 1935). Business. Labor Unions and Organizations. New Deal. Taft-Hartley Act (US, 1947). World War II. 1935-47. *543*

Wagner-Steagall Act (US, 1937). Bauer, Catherine. Federal Policy. Public housing. Reform. Wood, Edith Elmer. 1890's-1940's. *292*

Walgreen, Charles R. Chicago, University of. Communist sympathizers, alleged. Illinois. Newspapers. 1930's. *663*

Wallace, Henry A. Agricultural Adjustment Administration (Office of the General Counsel). Dale, Chester. Frank, Jerome. 1935. *398*

—. Agriculture. Politics. Reno, Milo. 1932-33. *466*

Waller, Fats. Austin, Gene. Music (jazz). 1929-39. *860*

Walsh, Thomas J. Democratic Party. Erickson, John E. Montana. State Politics. 1932-33. *208*

War. Films. Pacifism. World War I. 1930-39. *836*

War memorials. Milles, Carl (*God of Peace*). Minnesota (St. Paul). Myths and Symbols. Public Opinion. Sculpture. 1932-80. *811*

War of the Worlds (broadcast). Editorials. Newspapers. Radio. Welles, Orson. 1938. *951*

Warburg, James P. Banking. Monetary policy. New Deal. Roosevelt, Franklin D. (administration). 1932-41. *413*

Ward, Theodore. Allison, Hughes. Drama. Federal Theatre Project. Negroes. Wilson, Frank. 1930's. *874*

War-related debts. 1929. *29*

Warren, Frank (review article). Historiography. Socialist Party. 1930-40. *700*

Warren, Jesse. Barrow, Clyde. Ford automobile. Gangster myth. Parker, Bonnie. Rich, Carroll Y. 1934-67. *957*

Warren, Robert Penn (*All The King's Men*). Fiction. History. Long, Huey P. World War II (antecedents). 1930's-46. *839*

Washington. Partisanship. Political Theory. Voting and Voting Behavior. 1889-1950. *136*

Washington (Columbia Plateau). Grain. Livestock. McGregor Land and Livestock Company. Prices. 1930's-82. *73*

Washington (Seattle). Christianity. Longshoremen. Oxford Group movement. Strikes. 1921-34. *738*

—. Dix, I. F. Hoover, Herbert C. Local politics. Self-help. Unemployed Citizens' League. 1931-32. *75*

Washington (Yakima Valley). Agricultural Labor. Farmers. Industrial Workers of the World. Labor Disputes. Ranchers. 1910-36. *685*

—. Industrial Workers of the World. Labor Unions and Organizations. Strikes. 1933. *570*

Water Supply. Kendrick, John B. Legislation. North Platte River. Western States. 1917-33. *314*

Waterfronts. California (San Francisco). General strikes. National Guard. 1934. *625*

Webb, Bernice Larson (reminiscences). Country Life. Family. Kansas (Decatur County). 1930's. *125*

Weill, Kurt. Brecht, Bertolt. Lindbergh, Charles A. (tribute). Music. Radio broadcasts. 1929-31. *849*

Weisbord, Vera Buch (reminiscences). National Textile Workers Union. North Carolina (Gastonia). Strikes. Textile Industry. 1929. *746*

Welles, Orson. Behavior. Radio. Wells, H. G. *(War of the Worlds)*. 1938. *876*

—. *Citizen Kane* (filmscript). 1940. *781*

—. Editorials. Newspapers. Radio. *War of the Worlds* (broadcast). 1938. *951*

Wells, H. G. *(War of the Worlds)*. Behavior. Radio. Welles, Orson. 1938. *876*

Welty, Eudora ("Death of a Traveling Salesman"). Daily Life. Fiction. Mississippi (Jackson). 1936-79. *944*

West. Modernization. Oregon (Neahkahnie Mountain). Public Finance. Roads. 1850-1977. *496*

West Coast Hotel v. *Parrish* (US, 1937). Brandeis, Louis D. Due process. Economic Regulations. *Nebbia* v. *New York* (US, 1934). *New State Ice* v. *Liebmann* (US, 1932). Supreme Court. 1897-1937. *476*

West, Helen Hunt. Equal Rights Amendment (proposed). Florida. National Women's Party. Politics. Women. 1917-52. *667*

West Virginia. Fiscal Policy. Governors. Kump, Herman Guy. State Government. 1933. *169*

—. Holt, Rush Dew (papers). New Deal. Senate. 1920-55. *171*

—. Poverty. Reconstruction Finance Corporation. 1932-33. *81*

West Virginia (Arthurdale). Clapp, Elsie Ripley. Education, community. Homesteading and Homesteaders. New Deal. Roosevelt, Eleanor. 1933-44. *285*

—. Miners (resettlement of). National Industrial Recovery Act (1933). New Deal. Roosevelt, Eleanor. Subsistence Homesteads Program. 1930-46. *320*

Western life. Historicity. Intellectual development. Literature. Modernism, nature of. Tate, Allen. 1929-30. *780*

Western States. Climatological analysis. Droughts. Great Plains. 1931-40. *102*

—. Country Life. Farm Security Administration. Mennonites. Photographs. 1930's. *929*

—. Feinman, Ronald L. (review article). New Deal. Progressivism. Republican Party. Senate. 1929-41. *199*

—. Kendrick, John B. Legislation. North Platte River. Water Supply. 1917-33. *314*

—. Letters. Migrant Labor. Sletten, Myron. Travel (accounts). 1930-32. *104*

Westward movement. Environment. Films. Lorentz, Pare. New Deal. Roosevelt, Franklin D. (administration). 1936-40. *905*

Wheat, surplus. Food relief. Hoover, Herbert C. Red Cross. 1932-33. *61*

Wheeler, Burton K. Montana. Political Attitudes. Roosevelt, Franklin D. Senate. 1904-46. *232*

White, George. Coal Mines and Mining. National Guard. Ohio. Strikes. 1932. *687*

—. First ladies (state). Ohio. State Government. White, Mary (reminiscences). 1931-35. *265*

White, Mary (reminiscences). First ladies (state). Ohio. State Government. White, George. 1931-35. *265*

White supremacy. American Order of Fascisti. Employment. Georgia. Negroes. 1930-33. *660*

White, Walter F. NAACP. North Carolina. Parker, John J. Supreme Court (nominations). 1930. *618*

Whites. McCloud, Emma Gudger (reminiscences). Sharecroppers. South. 1916-79. *70*

Wick family (interview). Farmers. Meat preservation. North Dakota (Kidder County). Oil Industry and Trade. Schools, rural. 1900's-30's. *112*

Wilson, Edmund. Communism. *Modern Monthly* (periodical). 1934-35. *603*

—. Literary Criticism. Marxism. Political Participation. 1930's. *940*

Wilson, Frank. Allison, Hughes. Drama. Federal Theatre Project. Negroes. Ward, Theodore. 1930's. *874*

Winters, Yvor. *Gyroscope: A Literary Magazine.* Literature. Periodicals. 1929-30. *767*

Wisconsin. Amlie, Thomas R. Economic programs. Liberals. New Deal. Politics. 1931-39. *264*

—. Amlie, Thomas R. Farmer-Labor Party. New Deal. 1930-38. *206*

—. Amlie, Thomas R. (political career). New Deal. Radicals and Radicalism. Roosevelt, Franklin D. 1930-39. *704*

—. Democratic Party. New Deal. Pennsylvania (Pittsburgh). Political Theory. Quantitative Methods. Voting and Voting Behavior. 1912-40. *228*

—. Income (redistribution). LaFollette, Philip F. National Progressives of America. Politics. 1930-38. *214*

Wisconsin (Milwaukee). Beer. Cullen-Harrison Act (US, 1933). Festivals. 1933. *520*

—. Daily Life. Family. 1929-41. *60*

Wisconsin Plan. Federal Aid to Education. George-Barden Act (US, 1946). George-Deen Act (US, 1936). Pharmacy. Vocational education. 1936-49. *307*

Wisconsin Works Bill. LaFollette, Philip F. New Deal. Progressivism. Roosevelt, Franklin D. 1935. *414*

With Babies and Banners (film). Films (documentary). Michigan (Flint). Strikes. United Automobile Workers of America. Women. 1937. *903*

—. General Motors Corporation. *Great Sitdown* (film). Historiography. Strikes. United Automobile Workers of America. 1937. 1976-79. *855*

Wolfe, Thomas. Autobiography. Novels. 1924-38. *873*

—. Harvard University, Houghton Library. Manuscripts. Novels. 1938. 1975. *845*

—. Literature. *Scribner's Magazine* (periodical). 1929-40. *830*

Wolfe, Thomas (death). Desert fungus. 1938. *869*

Women. Airplane Industry and Trade. Pilots. Public Relations. Safety. 1927-40. *566*

—. Ames, Jessie Daniel. Association of Southern Women for the Prevention of Lynching. South. 1928-42. *672*

—. Association of Southern Women for the Prevention of Lynching. Lynching. Negroes. South. 1930-42. *530*

—. Berkeley Guidance Study. California. Employment. Family. 1930-70. *9*

—. California (Los Angeles). International Ladies' Garment Workers' Union. Mexican Americans. Working Conditions. 1933-39. *673*

—. Democratic Party. Minnesota. Oleson, Anna Dickie. Politics. 1905-71. *371*

—. Discrimination, Employment. Georgia (Atlanta). Labor. Racism. 1930's. *539*

—. Economic structure. Labor markets. Sex roles. 1930's. *626*

—. Employment. Feminism. Scharf, Lois (review article). 1929-39. *709*

—. Equal Rights Amendment (proposed). Florida. National Women's Party. Politics. West, Helen Hunt. 1917-52. *667*

—. Ethnic Groups. Georgia (Atlanta). Labor. Louisiana (New Orleans). Texas (San Antonio). 1930-40. *540*

—. Family. Folklore. Radio. Values. *Vic and Sade* (program). 1932-46. *96*

—. Farmers. Industrial Workers of the World. North Dakota. O'Connor, Hugh (interview). 1900's-30's. *113*

—. Fiction. *Saturday Evening Post* (periodical). Stereotypes. 1931-36. *831*

—. Fiction (detective). Stein, Gertrude. 1933-36. *854*

—. Films (documentary). Michigan (Flint). Strikes. United Automobile Workers of America. *With Babies and Banners* (film). 1937. *903*

—. Garment industry. Missouri (St. Louis). Personal narratives. Photographic essays. Strikes. ca 1930-39. *565*

—. Immigrants. International Brotherhood of Pulp, Sulphite, and Paper Mill Workers. Negroes. Pacific Northwest. South. 1909-40. *754*

—. Iowa (Cedar Rapids). Theatricals, amateur. Universal Production Company. 1926-30's. *800*

—. Labor. Middle Classes. Values. 1930's. *11*

—. Labor force. Segregation, sexual. 1930's. *671*

—. Mass Media. Professionalism. 1930's. *723*

—. Massachusetts. Oral history. Sullivan, Anna (interview). Textile Workers Union of America. 1918-76. *688*

—. Mitchell, Margaret. Scarlett O'Hara (character). Sex roles. 1936-39. *877*

—. Press Conference Association. Roosevelt, Eleanor. 1932-45. *266*

Women's movement (review article). Chafe, William H. Lemon, J. Stanley. Politics. 1920-70. *610*

Wood, Edith Elmer. Bauer, Catherine. Federal Policy. Public housing. Reform. Wagner-Steagall Act (US, 1937). 1890's-1940's. *292*

Wood, Robert E. Business. Conservatism. Isolationism. New Deal. Sears, Roebuck and Company. 1928-50's. *581*

Wood, Sally. Authors (southern). Gordon, Caroline. Letters. New York (Rochester). Tennessee (Benfolly). 1930-31. *818*

Woodring, Harry Hines. Kansas. State Politics. 1905-33. *211*

Woodrum, Clifton A. Congressmen. New Deal. Politics. Roosevelt, Franklin D. Virginia. 1922-45. *236*

Woodson, Carter G. Economic conditions. Negroes. South. 1930. *39*

Work relief. American Federation of Labor. Carmody, John. Civil Works Administration. New Deal. 1933-34. *467*

—. Civil Works Administration. New Deal. 1933-39. *298*

Workers' Film and Photo League. Communism. Films. Labor Disputes. Propaganda. 1930-38. *808*

Working class. Attitudes. New Deal. Roper, Elmo. Socialism, failure of. 1939. *743*

—. Crime and Criminals. New Deal. 1929-39. *98*

—. Friedlander, Peter (review article). Michigan (Detroit). United Automobile Workers of America. 1936-39. 1975. *549*

—. Labor policy. New Deal. Radicals and Radicalism. 1930's. *627*

—. Labor Unions and Organizations. Unemployment. 1930-40's. *674*

—. Self-perception. Unemployment. 1920's-30's. *116*

Working Conditions. California (Los Angeles). International Ladies' Garment Workers' Union. Mexican Americans. Women. 1933-39. *673*

—. Labor Non-Partisan League. Legislation. Political representation. 1936-38. *741*

Works Progress Administration. Actors, employment of. Drama. Federal Theatre Project. Ohio (Cincinnati). 1935-39. *865*

—. Africa, West. Basketmaking. Negroes. 1935-78. *935*

—. Alaska (Palmer). Defense. Rural rehabilitation. 1935-40. *445*

—. Artists. Communist Party. Federal funding. 1930's. *418*

—. Arts. Berger, Arthur. Criticism. Music. Personal narratives. 1930-80. *786*

—. Attitudes. Blitzstein, Marc *(Cradle Will Rock)*. Censorship. Federal Theatre Project. Labor. New York City. 1937. *502*

—. Berry, Harry S. Political Corruption. Tennessee (Nashville). 1935-43. *309*

—. Biography. Family history. Interviews. Louisiana State University. Students. 1930's. 1978. *321*

—. Chandler, A. B. ("Happy"). Elections (gubernatorial). Federal Emergency Relief Administration. Kentucky. 1935. *202*

—. Christensen, Mart. Federal Writers' Project. Spring, Agnes Wright. Wyoming. 1935-41. *354*

—. Cleveland Public Library. Federal Writers' Project. Ohio. 1933-39. *450*

—. Coan, George W., Jr. Hopkins, Harry. North Carolina. Patronage. 1935. *404*

—. Conservatism. Creel, George. New Deal. Progressivism. 1900-53. *273*

—. Dawson, Oliver B. (reminiscences). Ironwork. Oregon. Timberline Lodge. 1935-37. *326*

—. Discrimination. Elites. Georgia (Savannah). Negroes. New Deal. ca 1930-39. *374*

—. Documentary expression (review article). Federal Writers' Project. New Deal. 1930's. *886*

—. Evans, Luther H. Historical Records Survey. Iowa. Public records. 1936-42. *334*

—. Family. Interviews. Slavery. South. 1850's-60's. 1930's. *387*

—. Federal Theatre Project. Flanagan, Hallie. Hopkins, Harry. Politics. Theater. 1935-39. *303*

—. Foreign policy. Hawaii. Preparedness. Roosevelt, Franklin D. 1935-40. *446*

—. Haber, William. Michigan. National Youth Administration. Public Welfare. 1930's. *410*

—. Public policy. Public service organizations. 1930's-70's. *463*

World Court. Foreign policy. Isolationism. Political Leadership. Roosevelt, Franklin D. Senate. 1935. *194*

The World Today (series). Films (documentary). *March of Time* (series). Political Attitudes. 1930's. *761*

World War I. Brandeis, Louis D. Frankfurter, Felix. New Deal. Politics. Roosevelt, Franklin D. 1917-33. *154*

—. Films. Pacifism. War. 1930-39. *836*

World War II. Business. Labor Unions and Organizations. New Deal. Taft-Hartley Act (US, 1947). Wagner Act (US, 1935). 1935-47. *543*

—. Cartoonists. Gray, Harold. *Little Orphan Annie* (comic strip). Social conservatism. 1930's-40's. *955*

—. Comic Strips. Conservatism. Gray, Harold. *Little Orphan Annie* (comic strip). New Deal. 1920's-40's. *844*

—. Frankfurter, Felix. Lippmann, Walter. New Deal. Roosevelt, Franklin D. 1932-45. *432*

—. Germany. Jews. Refugees. Relief organizations. 1933-45. *602*

—. Historiography. Isolationism. 1930's-40's. *583*

World War II (antecedents). Anti-Imperialism. Foreign Policy (critics). Pacific Area. Roosevelt, Franklin D. 1930's. *692*

—. Antiwar Sentiment. Keep America Out of War Congress. Socialist Party. Thomas, Norman. Villard, Oswald Garrison. 1938-41. *584*

—. Fiction. History. Long, Huey P. Warren, Robert Penn *(All The King's Men)*. 1930's-46. *839*

Worster, Donald. Bonnifield, Paul. Dust Bowl (review article). Great Plains (southern). ca 1900-39. 1979. *59*

Wright, Frank Lloyd. Agrarianism. Broadacre City. City Planning. Decentralization. Oklahoma (Bartlesville). 1935. *864*

Wright, Richard *(American Hunger)*. Communist Party. Illinois (Chicago). Intellectuals. Negroes. ca 1930-44. *879*

Wright, Richard (personal account). Communist Party. Illinois (Chicago). Negroes. 1930's. *954*

Writers' Conference on Literature and Reading in the South and Southwest. Ford, Ford Madox. Literature. Louisiana (Baton Rouge). South. 1935. *942*

WXYZ (station). *Lone Ranger* (program). Michigan (Detroit). Radio. 1933-34. *887*

Wyoming. Christensen, Mart. Federal Writers' Project. Spring, Agnes Wright. Works Progress Administration. 1935-41. *354*

—. Culture. Federal Art Project. New Deal. 1933-41. *795*

—. Democratic Party. O'Mahoney, Joseph C.

Patronage. Postal Service. Roosevelt, Franklin D. Senate. 1916-45. *220*

—. Drainage districts. Reclamation of Land. 1888-1939. *25*

Y

Yale University Law School. Douglas, William O. (memoirs). Legal education. 1928-34. *585*

Yankee (character). Capra, Frank. Films. Politics. 1936-41. *812*

Young, Whitney M. Kentucky. Lincoln Institute. Negroes. Tydings, J. Mansir. 1935-37. *134*

Youth. Accidents. Daily Life. Faulkner, Jim. Faulkner, William. Mississippi (Oxford). Personal narratives. 1930-39. *804*

—. Bethune, Mary McLeod. Equal opportunity. National Youth Administration. Negroes. Public Policy. 1935-44. *483*

—. Economic policy. Federal Government. Public Schools. Roosevelt, Franklin D. 1918-45. *279*

—. Employment, part-time. National Youth Administration. New Deal. South Dakota. Struble, Anna C. 1935-43. *355*

Z

Zanderer, Leo. Bergonzi, Bernard. Literature (review article). Salzman, Jack. Spender, Stephen. ca 1930-39. 1978-79. *775*

Zangara, Giuseppi. Assassination. Cermak, Anton. Florida (Miami). Roosevelt, Franklin D. 1933. *152*

—. Assassination, attempted. Florida (Miami). Roosevelt, Franklin D. 1933. *231*

Zugsmith, Leane. Novels. Social consciousness. 1930's. *842*

101 Ranch Real Wild West Show. Breach of contract. Lawsuits. Miller, Zack. Mix, Tom. Sells-Floto Circus. Verbal agreements. 1929-34. *819*

AUTHOR INDEX

A

Abrahams, Edward 524
Accinelli, Robert D. 525
Adams, J. W. 135
Ahlander, Leslie Judd 760
Alexander, William 761
Allen, Howard W. 136
Allen, John E. 526
Allen, William R. 1
Alley, Kenneth D. 762
Alsop, Joseph 137
Alter, Robert 763
Amoruso, Vito 272
Anders, Leslie 764
Anderson, Barry L. 2
Anhalt, Walter C. 3
Annunziata, Frank 273
Ansley, Fran 527 765
Antognini, Richard 138
Argersinger, Jo Ann E. 274
Armbrester, Margaret E. 275
Arthur, Thomas H. 766
Artzi, Pinhas 757
Asher, Robert 528
Auerbach, Jerold S. 4
August, Jack 529
Austin, Erik W. 136
Avery, Inda 276

B

Babu, B. Ramesh 277
Baker, Howard 767
Banks, Ann 278 768
Banks, Dean 769
Barber, Clarence L. 5
Barber, Henry E. 530
Bardach, Eugene 4
Barnard, Harry V. 279
Barone, Louis A. 139
Barra, Allen 770
Barro, Robert J. 6
Barron, Hal Seth 650
Barshay, Robert 771
Baskerville, Stephen W. 280
Bauer, Harry C. 772
Baughman, James L. 531
Bauman, John F. 7 19 281 282
Baylen, Joseph O. 613
Beasley, Maurine 283 284
Becker, William H. 532
Beddow, James B. 8
Beezer, Bruce G. 285
Bell, Brenda 527 765
Bellow, Saul 533
Bellush, Bernard 534
Bellush, Jewel 534 535
Benjamin, Daniel K. 504
Benjamin, Jules R. 286
Bennett, Sheila Kishler 9
Benson, Jackson J. 773
Benson, Thomas W. 867
Benston, George J. 287
Berens, John F. 288
Berman, Hyman 536
Bernstein, Irving 289
Best, Gary Dean 140 141
Best, John H. 279
Betten, Neil 537
Biebel, Charles D. 538
Billington, Monroe 290 291
Birch, Eugenie Ladner 292

Black, Wilfred W. 293
Blackwelder, Julia Kirk 10 539 540
Blanchard, Margaret A. 294 774
Blaynery, Michael S. 295
Blayney, Michael Stewart 142
Bogardus, Ralph F. 775
Bohn, Thomas W. 856
Bolin, Winifred D. Wandersee 11
Bolt, Ernest C., Jr. 541
Bonner, Thomas, Jr. 776
Bonthius, Andrew 542
Borisiuk, V. I. 543
Bornemann, Alfred H. 12
Boryczka, Ray 544 545
Bow, James 13
Brady, Gabriel M. 777
Braeman, John 143 296
Brandes, Joseph 546
Branscome, James 297
Brauer, Ralph A. 778
Brax, Ralph S. 547
Bremer, William W. 298
Brinckmann, Christine 779
Brinkley, Alan 299 548
Brody, David 549
Bromert, Roger 300
Brooks, Cleanth 780
Brown, D. Clayton 301 302
Brown, Lorraine 303 304
Brown, Richard C. 305
Brune, Lester H. 550
Bruno, Kenneth 306
Bryan, Frank M. 306
Buerki, Robert A. 307
Bulkley, Peter B. 308 551
Bulosan, Carlos 552
Burgchardt, Carl R. 553
Burran, James A. 309
Butkiewicz, James L. 2
Byford, Liz 82
Bystryn, Marcia N. 310

C

Cahan, Cathy 14
Cahan, Richard 14
Caliguire, Joseph A., Jr. 15
Cannistraro, Philip V. 554
Capaldo, Charles 555
Carlisle, Rodney P. 311 556
Carlson, Paul H. 312
Carlson, Robert 313
Carpenter, Gerald 557
Carpenter, Joel A. 558
Carringer, Robert L. 781
Carroll, Eugene T. 314
Cary, Lorin Lee 559
Casey, Kareta G. 560
Cassity, Michael J. 315
Chalmers, Leonard 144
Chan, Loren B. 16
Chandler, Lester V. 17
Christian, Henry A. 782
Christiansen, John B. 18
Christie, Jean 316
Christy, Joe 561
Clark, Cal 291
Clark, William Bedford 783
Clawson, Marion 317
Clayton, Ronnie W. 318
Cobb, James C. 145 146
Coburn, Mark D. 784

Cofer, Richard 562
Cole, Martin 785
Collins, Robert M. 319
Condon, Richard H. 563
Conkin, Paul K. 147
Conlin, Joseph R. 685 703
Coode, Thomas H. 7 19 148 149 320
Cooney, Terry A. 564
Coppock, James 786
Corbett, Katharine T. 565
Corn, Joseph J. 566 787
Cowley, Malcolm 567 788
Coy, Harold 568
Coy, Mildred 568
Crepeau, Richard C. 789
Crouse, Joan M. 20
Culbert, David H. 321 790 791
Culley, John J. 322
Currie, Lauchlin 21 522
Curry, Robert P. 22
Curtis, James C. 792

D

Damiani, Alessandro 569
Daniel, Cletus E. 323 570
Daniel, Pete 324
Daniel, Walter C. 571 572
Daniels, Roger 150 151
Darby, Michael R. 23
Davidson, David 573
Davin, Eric Leif 574
Davis, Kenneth S. 152 325
Davis, Polly 153
Davis, Steve 24
Dawson, Nelson L. 154
Dawson, Oliver B. 326
Day, Greg 327
Delano, Jack 327
DelCastillo, Adelaida R. 673
DeLong, Lea Rosson 880
DeMarco, Joseph P. 575
Dennis, James M. 328
Dent, Tom 793
Deutrich, Mabel E. 483 610
deVries, John A. 794
DeWitt, Howard A. 576 577
Diamond, Sander A. 578
Dieterich, Herbert R. 795
Dinwoodie, D. H. 579
Doenecke, Justus D. 580 581 582 583 584
Donahue, Jim 25
Dorsett, Lyle W. 155
Douglas, Ann 796
Douglas, William O. 585
Downs, Alexis 797
Dubay, Robert W. 156
Dugger, Ronnie 586
Dunaway, David King 798
Dunbaugh, Edwin L. 587
Duram, James C. 329 330 588
Duran, James C. 589
Dwyer-Shick, Susan 331

E

Easley, David 79
Ebner, Michael H. 157 799
Eckey, Lorelei F. 800
Edmonds, Anthony O. 801

Edward, C. 590
Ehrenhalt, Alan 332
Eisenberg, Gerson 384
Elder, Glen H., Jr. 9
Elder, Harris J. 905
Ellis, William E. 158
Emerson, Thomas I. 591
Engelmann, Larry D. 592
Engerman, Stanley L. 26
Erikson, Robert S. 159
Errico, Charles J. 160
Eyster, Warren 802

F

Fabbri, Dennis E. 320
Fairbanks, Robert B. 333
Fang, Irving E. 803
Farran, Don 334
Faulkner, Jim 804
Fausold, Martin L. 27
Feinman, Ronald L. 161
Fellman, David 805
Feuer, Lewis S. 593
Fickle, James E. 335
Filene, Peter 806
Filippelli, Ronald L. 594
Fine, David M. 807
Fine, Sidney 595
Finegold, Kenneth 336 481
Finison, Lorenz J. 596
Fink, Gary M. 162 163 526 557
Finkelstein, Leo, Jr. 164
Fisch, Dov 597
Fischhoff, Baruch 165
Fishbein, Leslie 808
Fisher, Gideon L. 28
Fleisig, Heywood 29
Fossey, W. Richard 30 31
Fox, Richard W. 598
Frank, Carrolyle M. 166
Freidel, Frank 337
Freund, Paul A. 167
Frisch, Michael 809
Fry, Joseph A. 599
Fulton, Dan 32
Fulton, Tom 338
Funigiello, Philip J. 339

G

Gall, Gilbert J. 600
Galliher, John F. 601
Gandolfi, Arthur E. 33 34
Garcia, George F. 168
Garcia, Lois B. 810
Garraty, John A. 35 340
Garvey, Timothy J. 811
Gatrell, A. Steven 169
Gehring, Wes D. 812 813
Gelber, Steven M. 814
Genauer, Emily 815
Genizi, Haim 602 603
Ghosh, Partha Sarathy 341
Giebelhaus, August W. 604
Giffin, William 170
Gillette, Howard 816
Glad, Paul W. 36
Goldberg, Joseph P. 342
Gomery, Douglas 817
Goode, Thomas H. 171
Goodenow, Ronald K. 605 606
Gordon, Caroline 818
Gordon, Lawrence 607
Gordon, Max 608 758
Gossard, Wayne H., Jr. 819

Gottlieb, Peter 609
Gower, Calvin W. 343 344
Grannen, Sheila 792
Grant, H. Roger 37 345
Grant, Philip A. 172
Grant, Philip A., Jr. 173 174 175 176 177 178 179
Graves, Gregory R. 38
Gray, Ralph D. 820
Greenbaum, Fred 180
Greenberg, Irwin F. 181
Greene, Lorenzo J. 39
Greene, Murray 821
Greer, Edward 182
Griffis, Ken 959
Griffith, Robert K., Jr. 40
Gustafson, Richard 822
Guth, James L. 346
Guttenberg, Albert Z. 41
Guzda, Henry P. 347

H

Haines, Gerald K. 541
Hall, Alvin L. 183
Hamilton, David E. 42
Hamilton, Virginia Van Der Veer 348
Hand, Samuel B. 184
Hargreaves, Mary W. M. 349 610
Harrington, Jerry 185
Harris, Neil 823
Harrison, Lowell H. 350
Haslam, Gerald 43
Hass, Edward F. 186
Hastie, William H. 611
Hauptman, Laurence M. 351 352 612
Havig, Alan R. 824
Hearst, James 44
Hein, Virginia H. 613
Heinemann, Ronald L. 187 353
Helicher, Karl 271
Hellerstein, Alice 825
Helmer, William J. 614
Hemenway, Robert 826
Henderson, F. P. 188
Hendrick, Irving J. 615
Hendrickson, Gordon O. 354
Hendrickson, Kenneth E. 355
Hendrickson, Kenneth E., Jr. 356 357 358
Henstell, Bruce 189
Herman, Alan 190
Herring, Neill 616
Hewins, Dana C. 359
Hicks, Floyd W. 360
Hightower, Paul 827
Hilty, James W. 163
Hine, Darlene Clark 617 618
Hirsch, Jerrold 361 499 523 828
Hodges, James A. 362
Hodgkinson, Anthony W. 829
Hoffman, Abraham 363 619 620 621
Hofsommer, Donovan L. 622
Holland, Reid 364
Holman, C. Hugh 830
Holmes, Michael S. 45
Homberger, Eric 623
Homel, Michael W. 624
Honey, Maureen 831
Hook, Sidney 832
Hoopes, James 833
Hornbein, Marjorie 365
Howard, Walter T. 668
Hudson, Hosea 691

Hudson, James J. 625
Humphries, Jane 626
Hundley, Patrick D. 834
Hunter, Robert F. 366
Hurd, Rick 627
Hurt, R. Douglas 46 47 48
Hux, Samuel 835

I

Ingalls, Robert P. 367 628
Ingram, Earl 368
Inouye, Arlene 369
Isenberg, Michael T. 836

J

Jacklin, Thomas M. 629
Jakoubek, Robert E. 191
Jayne, Edward 837
Jeansonne, Glen 630 631 632 633
Jensen, Richard 192
Johnson, Abby Arthur 838
Johnson, Charles 370
Johnson, Dolores DeBower 371
Johnson, Glen M. 839
Johnson, H. Thomas 49
Johnson, James P. 50 634
Johnson, Ronald W. 838
Johnson, William R. 372
Jones, Alfred Haworth 840
Jones, Byrd L. 51 522
Jones, Gene Delon 193
Jones, James P. 841
Josephson, Matthew 842

K

Kahn, Gilbert N. 194
Kahn, Lawrence M. 635
Kalin, Berkley 373
Kalmar, Karen L. 374
Kass, D. A. 843
Kaufman, Burton I. 52
Keeran, Roger R. 636 637
Kehl, James A. 844
Keller, Allan 638
Keller, Robert R. 53
Kelly, Lawrence C. 375 376 377
Kennedy, Richard S. 845
Kennedy, Susan Estabrook 54
Kesselman, Jonathan R. 55
Kimberly, Charles M. 56
Kirby, John B. 639
Kiser, George 57
Kleiner, Lydia 688
Klingman, Peter D. 195
Klug, Michael A. 846
Kobal, John 847
Koeniger, A. Cash 196 197 378
Kohler, Robert E., Jr. 640
Kollmorgen, Walter M. 379
Komatsu, Satoshi 58
Koolhaas, Rem 848
Koppes, Clayton R. 59 380
Koprowski-Kraut, Gayle 60
Kostiainen, Auvo 381 641
Kowalke, Kim H. 849
Kramer, Victor A. 850
Kreuter, Gretchen 371
Kritzberg, Barry 642
Krost, Martin 522
Krueger, Thomas A. 382
Kruger, Arnd 851
Kruman, Marie W. 383

Kuehl, Warren F. 643
Kusenda, Mike 852
Kyvig, David E. 198

L

Lal, Malashri 853
Lambert, C. Roger 61 360
Lamoreaux, David 384
Landon, Brooks 854
Láng, Imre 62 63 385 386
Lansky, Lewis 64
Lantz, Herman R. 387
Lanza, Aldo 644
Laslett, John H. M. 645
Lauderbaugh, Richard A. 646
Leab, Daniel J. 855
Lear, Linda J. 199 388
Lee, Bradford A. 389
Lee, David D. 200
Lee, David L. 201
Legueu, F. F. 65
Leiby, James 390
Leiter, William M. 391 392
Leotta, Louis 647
Lepawsky, Albert 393
Leuchtenburg, William E. 394
Leupold, Robert J. 202
Levenstein, Harvey 648
Leverette, William E., Jr. 649
Levering, Patricia W. 66
Levering, Ralph B. 66
Licht, Walter 650
Lichtenstein, Nelson 651
Lichty, Lawrence W. 856
Lind, Leo 67
Little, Monroe H. 664
Loftis, Anne 773
Longin, Thomas C. 395
Lothian, James R. 33
Louchheim, Katie 396
Lovin, Hugh T. 203 204 205 206 652
Lowitt, Richard 207 397 398 399 400
Lowry, Charles B. 401
Lubove, Roy 402
Lundén, Rolf 857
Lynd, Staughton 574 653
Lynn, Kenneth S. 858

M

Macmillan, Robert 859
Maddux, Thomas R. 654
Magnusson, Tor 860
Maland, Charles 861
Mal'kov, V. L. 403 655
Malone, Michael P. 208
Manykin, A. S. 209
Marcello, Ronald E. 404
Marcus, Steven 862
Marquart, Frank 656
Marr, Warren 657
Martin, Charles H. 658 659 660
Marvin, Carolyn 863
Massu, Claude 864
Mathews, Allan 661
Mathews, Jane De Hart 405
Maurer, D. W. 662
Maurer, Joyce C. 865
May, Irvin M., Jr. 406 407
Mayer, Milton 663
Mayer, Thomas 68 69
Mazuzan, George H. 759
McBride, David 664

McCloud, Emma Gudger 70
McCorkle, James L., Jr. 71
McCoy, Donald R. 210
McDean, Harry C. 72 408
McFarland, Keith D. 211
McGinty, Brian 665 866
McGoff, Kevin 666
McGovern, James R. 667 668
McGregor, Alexander C. 73
McGuire, Jack B. 212
McHale, James M. 409
McKinney, Fred 669
McLaughlin, Doris B. 410
McQuaid, Kim 411 670
Mead, Howard N. 213
Medhurst, Martin J. 867
Meehan, James 868 869
Meek, Edwin E. 412
Meikle, Jeffrey L. 870
Menig, Harry 871 872
Michelet, Jean 873
Michelman, Irving S. 413
Milkman, Ruth 671
Miller, Jeanne-Marie A. 874
Miller, John E. 214 414
Miller, Kathleen Atkinson 672
Miscamble, Wilson D. 415
Mishkin, Frederick S. 74
Mitchell, Virgil L. 416
Moehring, Eugene P. 417
Mohl, Raymond A. 537
Monroe, Gerald M. 418
Monroy, Douglas 673
Montgomery, David 674
Moore, James R. 419
Mora, Magdalena 673
Morgan, Alfred L. 215
Morgan, Thomas S., Jr. 420
Morris, James K. 675
Morrison, David E. 875
Morrison, Rodney J. 216
Morson, Gary Saul 876
Morton, Marian J. 877
Mugleston, William F. 676
Mulder, Ronald A. 217 218
Mullins, William H. 75
Myers, Carol Fairbanks 878
Myers, Constance Ashton 677
Myhra, David 421
Myles, John 422

N

Naison, Mark 678 679 680 879
Naison, Mark D. 681
Nall, Garry L. 76
Narber, Gregg R. 880
Nastri, Anthony D. 682
Nelsen, Clair E. 219
Nelson, Daniel 683
Nelson, H. Viscount 684
Nelson, Joyce 881
Nelson, Lawrence J. 423 424
Newbill, James G. 685
Ninneman, Thomas R. 220
Noble, Richard A. 77
Nochlin, Linda 882
Nyden, Linda 686
Nye, Ronald L. 78
Nye, Russel B. 883

O

Ober, Michael J. 425
O'Brien, Larry D. 687
O'Brien, Patrick G. 221

O'Connor, John 884
O'Farrell, M. Brigid 688
O'Hara, Maureen 79
Ohl, John Kennedy 426
Oliver, Donald W. 689
Olson, James S. 80 81 82 83 427
O'Neill, Robert K. 428
Orlin, Lena Cowen 885
O'Rourke, James S. 690
Ortquist, Richard T. 84 222
Orvell, Miles 886
Osgood, Richard 887
Ostrower, Gary B. 429
Otto, John Solomon 888 889
Otto, Solomon 889

P

Painter, Nell 691
Papachristou, Judith 692
Papanikolas, Helen Z. 693
Parker, Robert V. 694
Parrish, E. 223
Patenaude, Lionel V. 224 225 430
Patinkin, Don 85
Patterson, James T. 431
Pauly, Thomas H. 890
Pechatnov, Vladimir O. 432
Peck, David 891
Pellanda, Anna 433
Peppers, Larry C. 86
Perry, Thelma D. 892
Pessen, Edward 87
Petersen, Peter L. 322
Peterson, Keith 695
Pew, Thomas W., Jr. 88
Peyton, Rupert 696
Pfaff, Daniel W. 697 893
Phillips, A. H. 894
Phillips, Waite 434
Phillips, William 895
Pietrusza, David A. 698
Pinkett, Harold T. 435
Pintó, Alfonso 896
Platschek, Hans 436
Plesur, Milton 20 64 139 226 258
Polenberg, Richard 227 437
Pommer, Richard 897
Porter, David 438 439
Porter, David L. 440 759
Porter, Steve 312
Potter, Barrett G. 441
Powell, Charles Stewart 89
Powers, Richard Gid 898
Pratt, Linda Ray 899
Prickett, James R. 699
Prindle, David F. 228
Prouty, L. Fletcher 900
Purcell, L. Edward 37 345
Purdy, Virginia C. 90 483 610
Pursell, Carroll W., Jr. 442
Putnam, Carl M. 443

R

Rader, Frank J. 444 445 446
Radosh, Ronald 700
Rapport, Leonard 523
Reading, Don C. 447
Redding, Mary Edrich 901
Reece, Florence 765
Reed, Merl E. 526 557
Rees, Garonowy 91
Reeves, William D. 448
Reiter, Howard L. 229
Remele, Larry 92

Remley, David A. 902
Reuss, Martin 449
Reverby, Susan 903
Ribuffo, Leo 701
Rich, Carroll Y. 957
Riggio, Thomas P. 904
Riggs, Agnew M. 171
Ring, Daniel F. 450
Rison, David 451
Ritchie, Donald A. 452
Robbins, William G. 453
Roberts, Dick 93
Rocha, Guy Louis 702 703
Rollins, Peter 905
Rollins, Peter C. 906
Roosevelt, James 271
Rosengarten, Theodore 907
Rosenof, Theodore 704
Rosenstone, Robert A. 454
Rosenzweig, Roy 705 706 707
Ross, B. Joyce 455
Ross, Hugh 230
Ross, Irwin 231
Ross, Ronald 456
Rubenstein, Harry R. 708
Rubin, Louis D., Jr. 908
Ruetten, Richard T. 232
Rupp, Leila J. 709
Ryan, Halford Ross 233
Ryan, James Gilbert 710
Ryan, Thomas G. 234
Ryant, Carl G. 94
Ryon, Roderick M. 711

S

Sageser, A. Bower 712
Saindon, Bob 457
Salamon, Lester M. 458
Salo, Mauno 909
Saloutos, Theodore 459
Salzman, Jack 910
Sanford, D. Gregory 184 235
Sargent, James E. 236 460 461
    462
Savin, N. E. 55
Schacht, John N. 713
Schapsmeier, Edward L. 237
Schapsmeier, Frederick H. 237
Schatz, Ronald 674
Scheurer, Timothy E. 911
Schlatter, Richard 714
Schlozman, Kay Lehman 743
Schmidt, William T. 95
Schnell, J. Christopher 238 239
Schnell, R. L. 715
Schön, Donald A. 463
Schroeder, Fred E. H. 96
Schuyler, Michael W. 464 465
    466
Schwartz, Bonnie Fox 467 468
Schwieder, Dorothy 469
Scott, Robert L. 912
Scott, William R. 716 717
Scriabine, Christine Brendel 97
Sears, James M. 470
Sears, Stephen W. 718
Seretan, L. Glen 98
Severson, Robert F., Jr. 471
Sewall, Arthur F. 472
Shankman, Arnold 719 720
Shapiro, Edward S. 473 474 721
    913
Shaver, James H. 99
Sheffer, Martin S. 271
Shepardson, D. E. 914
Shi, Daniel E. 649

Shils, Edward 915
Shiner, John F. 475 722
Sholes, Elizabeth 723
Short, John D., Jr. 916
Shout, John D. 917
Shover, John L. 240
Siegan, Bernard H. 476
Sifuentes, Roberto 724
Silverman, David 57
Simmons, Dennis E. 477
Simmons, Jerold 478
Simms, Adam 725
Simon, Daniel T. 100
Sinclair, Barbara Deckard 241
    479
Singer, Donald L. 242
Sirkin, Gerald 101
Sivachev, N. V. 480
Skaggs, Richard H. 102
Skau, George H. 243
Skefos, Catherine Hetos 918
Skocpol, Theda 103 481
Sletten, Harvey 104
Smathers, Mike 482
Smith, Elaine M. 483
Smith, Glen H. 3
Smith, Harold T. 244
Smith, Mark C. 105
Snyder, J. Richard 106
Snyder, Robert E. 107 108 245
    726
Snyder, Stephen 919
Soapes, Thomas F. 246 484
Sobchack, Vivian C. 920
Sobczak, John N. 485
Soderbergh, Peter A. 921
Sofar, Allan J. 486
Sonnichsen, C. L. 109
Spackman, S. G. F. 247
Spears, James E. 727
Spencer, Thomas T. 248 249 250
    251 252 253 254 487 488
Sprunk, Larry J. 110 111 112 113
    114
Steele, Richard W. 255
Stegh, Leslie J. 256
Stein, Walter J. 115
Stepanek, Robert H. 922
Stephanson, Anders 728
Sternsher, Bernard 116 257 489
Stetson, Frederick W. 490
Stevens, Susan 258
Stewart, Garrett 923
Strogovich, M. S. 729
Strong, Elizabeth 491
Strotzka, Heinz 117
Stuhler, Barbara 371
Sullivan, Bunky 457
Supina, Philip D. 730
Susskind, Charles 369
Swain, Martha H. 259 492 493
Swanson, Joseph A. 118
Swanson, Merwin R. 494 495 731
Swartout, Robert, Jr. 496
Symonds, Craig L. 732
Synott, Marcia G. 924

T

Tamony, Peter 925 926 927
Tarter, Brent 260
Taylor, Graham D. 497 498
Taylor, Joshua C. 928
Taylor, Paul F. 733
Tedin, Kent L. 159
Tedlow, Richard S. 734
Teichroew, Allan 929

Telotte, J. P. 930
Temin, Peter 119
Terrill, Tom E. 361 499 523
Theoharis, Athan G. 500
Thomas, Donald W. 931
Thomas, James W. 932
Thorp, Gregory 933
Thrasher, Sue 616 735 736
Tibbetts, John 934
Tissot, Roland 501
Tomlins, Christopher L. 737
Towey, Martin G. 120
Toy, Eckard, V., Jr. 738
Trafzer, Clifford E. 434
Trescott, Paul B. 121
Trilling, Diana 739
Trout, Charles H. 122
Tselos, George 740
Twining, Mary 935

U

Underhill, Irving S. 936

V

Vacha, J. E. 502
Valerina, A. F. 261 741
VanWest, Carroll 742
Verba, Sidney 743
Vindex, Charles 123
Vitz, Robert C. 938 939
Vlasich, James A. 503

W

Wald, Alan 744 940 941
Walker, Allyn 601
Walker, Forrest A. 124
Walker, J. Samuel 541
Walker, William O., III 745
Waller, Robert A. 262
Wallis, John Joseph 504
Waltzer, Kenneth 758
Ware, James 505
Warren-Findley, Jannelle 506
Watson, Thomas 507
Webb, Bernice Larson 125
Webb, Max 942
Webb, Pamela 126
Weeks, Charles J. 508
Weinrott, Lester A. 943
Weisberger, Bernard A. 509
Weisbord, Vera Buch 746
Weiss, Richard 747
Weiss, Stuart 263 510
Weiss, Stuart L. 264
Welsch, Roger L. 511
Welty, Eudora 944
Wertheim, Arthur Frank 945
Wheelock, Alan S. 946
Whisenhunt, Donald W. 127 128
    129 130 131 748
Whitaker, Rosemary 947
Whitaker, W. Richard 749
White, Mary 265
Whitehead, James L. 948
Wicker, Elmus 132
Wigdor, David 512
Wiles, Timothy J. 949
Wilkinson, Dave 950
Williams, Bobby Joe 513
Williams, David 750
Williams, Lillian S. 751
Williams, R. E. 752

Winfield, Betty Houchin 266 267
    268
Winpenny, Thomas R. 514
Wise, Leah 736
Wolf, T. Phillip 269
Wolfe, G. Joseph 951
Wolfenstein, Judith 952
Wollheim, Peter 957
Woodward, C. Vann 515
Woodward, Robert H. 953
Worster, Donald 133
Wright, Esmond 516
Wright, Gavin 270
Wright, George C. 134
Wright, Richard 954

Wrigley, Linda 517
Wyche, Billy H. 518

Y

York, Hildreth 519
Young, William H. 955

Z

Zeidel, Robert F. 520
Zieger, Robert H. 753 754
Zimmerman, Paul 956
Zimmerman, Tom 755
Zolov, A. V. 756
Zucker, Bat-Ami 757